D1709636

# ENCYCLOPEDIA OF COMPUTER SCIENCE AND TECHNOLOGY

VOLUME 6

# INTERNATIONAL EDITORIAL ADVISORY BOARD

# ENCYCLOPEDIA OF COMPUTER SCIENCE AND TECHNOLOGY

EXECUTIVE EDITORS

*Jack Belzer*    *Albert G. Holzman*    *Allen Kent*

UNIVERSITY OF PITTSBURGH
PITTSBURGH, PENNSYLVANIA

## VOLUME 6

*Computer Selection to Curriculum*

MARCEL DEKKER, INC. • NEW YORK and BASEL

MARCEL DEKKER, INC.
270 Madison Avenue, New York, New York 10016

LIBRARY OF CONGRESS CATALOG CARD NUMBER: 74-29436
ISBN:   08246-2256-6

Current printing (last digit):
10   9   8   7   6   5   4   3   2   1

PRINTED IN THE UNITED STATES OF AMERICA

# CONTENTS OF VOLUME 6

# CONTRIBUTORS TO VOLUME 6

FARID R. AHMED, National Research Council of Canada, Ottawa, Canada: *Crystallography*

WILLIAM F. ATCHISON, Ph.D., Department of Computer Science, University of Maryland, College Park, Maryland: *Curriculum Committee on Computer Science*

WILLIAM E. BILES, Ph.D., Department of Aerospace and Mechanical Engineering, University of Notre Dame, Notre Dame, Indiana: *Courts*

RAYMOND M. BRACH, Ph.D., P.E., Department of Aerospace and Mechanical Engineering, University of Notre Dame, Notre Dame, Indiana: *Courts*

HOWARD CAMPAIGNE, Department of Mathematics, Eastern New Mexico University, Portales, New Mexico: *Cryptanalysis*

JAMES M. DASCHBACH, Ph.D., Department of Aerospace and Mechanical Engineering, University of Notre Dame, Notre Dame, Indiana: *Courts*

MICHAEL A. DUGGAN, Professor of Business Law and Computer Service, Department of General Business, University of Texas, Austin, Texas: *Copyright and Computers*

GERALD L. ENGEL, Ph.D., Virginia Institute of Marine Science, Gloucester Point, Virginia: *Curriculum Committee on Computer Science*

ARNOLD F. GOODMAN, Ph.D., Planning Manager, Administrative Services, Products Division, Atlantic Richfield Company, Los Angeles, California: *Computers and Statistics—Evolution of the Interface*

ARTHUR L. GREENSITE, Design Specialist, Rohr Industries, Inc., San Diego, California: *Control System Optimization*

EUGENE W. HENRY, Ph.D., Department of Electrical Engineering, University of Notre Dame, Notre Dame, Indiana: *Courts*

CAROL E. HICKS, Computer Science Department, Cleveland State University, Cleveland, Ohio: *Content Analysis*

DAVID T. LINK, J.D., Dean of the Law School, University of Notre Dame, Notre Dame, Indiana: *Courts*

SOLOMON KULLBACK, Professor Emeritus of Statistics, Department of Statistics, The George Washington University, Washington, D.C.: *Contingency Table Analysis*

**CONTRIBUTORS TO VOLUME 6**

DON MITTLEMAN, Department of Mathematics, Oberlin College, Oberlin, Ohio: *Computer Selection Criteria*

JOSEPH J. MODER, Ph.D., Professor of Management Science and Industrial Engineering, University of Miami, Coral Gables, Florida: *Critical Path Methods*

DONN B. PARKER, Stanford Research Institute, Menlo Park, California: *Crime*

JAMES E. RUSH, The Ohio College Library Center, Columbus, Ohio: *Content Analysis*

MICHAEL K. SAIN, Ph.D., Department of Electrical Engineering, University of Notre Dame, Notre Dame, Indiana: *Courts*

ABIMBOLA SALAKO, Computer Science Department, University of Pittsburgh, Pittsburgh, Pennsylvania: *Concurrent Processing*

TIMOTHY L. SHAFTEL, College of Business and Public Administration, The University of Arizona, Tucson, Arizona, and School of Business, Queen's University, Kingston, Canada: *Convergence of Algorithms*

SUZANNE M. STRONG, The Ohio College Library Center, Columbus, Ohio: *Content Analysis*

NEIL H. TIMM, School of Education, University of Pittsburgh, Pittsburgh, Pennsylvania: *Correlation and Regression*

JOHN J. UHRAN, JR. Ph.D., Department of Electrical Engineering, University of Notre Dame, Notre Dame, Indiana: *Courts*

# COMPUTER SELECTION CRITERIA

The selection of a computer is a process dependent upon many factors. However the process proceeds, ultimately the monetary factor will govern. It is important to recognize the total costs involved; not only the obvious initial costs of the acquisition of the new hardware and the immediately attendant software and the continuing costs associated with the maintenance of hardware, software, and updating of the facility, but also the personnel costs that must be budgeted to continue the infusion of viable applications. It is from this trunk that the branches grow.[1]

## ESTABLISHING THE NEED

The environment in which the computer is to function should be carefully defined. A research-oriented organization exhibits characteristics quite different from those of a commercial one, and the needs of both are again different from those of an educational institution. It becomes necessary, therefore, for each organization to study its own identity and to prepare a definition of its needs. The more thoroughly and clearly this is done, the easier it will be for the prospective vendors to configure suitable sets of computer components to meet these needs, but more importantly, the easier it will be to evaluate the proposals submitted. By way of example, the following study is illustrative. At a medium size university (6000 undergraduates, 1000 graduate students) the search for identity took the form of a marketing survey. A questionnaire was distributed to all faculty and staff soliciting information on their current usage, which was batch oriented, and on their expected usage for the next 10 years. While 10 years was probably too long a period for which to plan, the time from the initiation of the survey to the installation of the new equipment was estimated to be of the order of 2 years as a minimum. When coupled with the fact that the presence of the newer equipment will undoubtedly generate problems and create demands beyond those originally planned, and this in turn will consume resources at a rate higher than planned, a useful life of about 6 years may be expected. With the current rate of invention and innovation within computing, and the attendant obsolescence, 6 years is not an unreasonable period for which to plan.

The response of the faculty and staff was, as expected, in proportion to their current involvement. In those areas and disciplines currently heavily involved, 100% response was expected and achieved; in those areas and disciplines where computer involvement was sporadic or not realized, the response dropped to about 15%.

The survey should consist of more than a mailing of a questionnaire to

---

[1] The thrust of this article is toward those with computer experience who are contemplating upgrading rather than those who are venturing into the field. The stakes are too high for the neophyte.

individuals identifiable as potential users. A personal follow-up to review the information submitted or the reasons for failure to return the questionnaire is indicated if the full involvement and support of the users are to be obtained. In some instances potential applications had been dismissed either because the long-range significance of the commitment was not appreciated or because the cost had been improperly evaluated. In particular, the potential for sharing of resources across disciplines had to be developed.

From the user's articulated needs, hardware and software parameters can be approximated. Table 1 illustrates one method for organizing the data representing the needs for peripheral equipment. Similar tables should be prepared for storage requirements as well as processing needs. Research areas are designated under R and classroom courses under E; the numbers represent the number of courses or research areas requiring the devices, not the number of devices required.

The table indicates the extent to which the computer has pervaded both the education and research programs; in the fully developed survey it was extended to include administrative needs as well.

The possibilities for sharing devices need still be determined. However, the local geographic and political climate would undoubtedly be of such importance as to be the overriding considerations. Also, to err on the conservative side would not be disastrous; additional peripheral devices can be acquired at incremental costs.

The software requirements are summarized in Table 2 followed by a sample offering an intermediate degree of detail.

E, courses requiring: This heading includes both those courses presently requiring computer solutions for problem solving and those which have a high expectation of computer utilization with the acquisition of the specialized peripheral devices and the possibility for interactive, time-sharing.

R, research area requiring: Only present research needs are included in this category because shifting research interests make forecasting too unreliable.

Area 1, Statistical analysis: This heading encompasses normal, binomial, Student's $t$, $F$ and Poisson distributions, measures of central tendency of dispersion, elements of probability and probability sampling, estimation and hypothesis testing, chi-square analysis, analysis of variance, regression and correlation, time series analysis, index number analysis, and multivariate analysis. Also included are sets, functions, decision making under uncertainty, game theory, queuing theory and Monte Carlo techniques, Markov analysis, and reduction and processing of laboratory and research data.

Area 2, Solution of integral and differential equations: Included under this heading is the numerical integration of higher order differential equations and the finite difference and finite element solution of differential equations. Particular computer usage in the areas of research includes the numerical integration of the matrix equations of motion, a three-dimensional energy density function, and the fifth- and seventh-order nonlinear ordinary differential equations in semi-infinite domains.

**TABLE 1**
Peripheral Equipment Needs

| Equipment | Art | | English | | Philosophy | | Sociology | | Architecture | | Electrical Engineering | | Mechanical Engineering | | Accounting | | Marketing | | Biology | | Geology | | Mathematics | | Chemistry | | Physics | | Computer Science | | Total | |
|---|---|---|---|---|---|---|---|---|---|---|---|---|---|---|---|---|---|---|---|---|---|---|---|---|---|---|---|---|---|---|---|---|
| | R | E | R | E | R | E | R | E | R | E | R | E | R | E | R | E | R | E | R | E | R | E | R | E | R | E | R | E | R | E | R | E |
| **CRT** | | | | | | | | | | | | | | | | | | | | | | | | | | | | | | | | |
| Vector | 0 | 0 | 0 | 2 | 0 | 0 | 0 | 5 | 0 | 0 | 0 | 0 | 0 | 0 | 0 | 0 | 0 | 0 | 3 | 7 | 0 | 0 | 0 | 0 | 1 | 0 | 0 | 1 | 2 | 0 | 6 | 15 |
| Light pen | 0 | 0 | 0 | 0 | 0 | 0 | 0 | 0 | 0 | 2 | 0 | 2 | 3 | 1 | 0 | 0 | 0 | 0 | 0 | 0 | 0 | 0 | 0 | 0 | 0 | 0 | 0 | 0 | 0 | 0 | 3 | 3 |
| Hard copy | 0 | 10 | 0 | 0 | 2 | 0 | 0 | 4 | 0 | 2 | 4 | 3 | 0 | 2 | 0 | 0 | 0 | 0 | 0 | 0 | 0 | 0 | 0 | 0 | 0 | 0 | 0 | 0 | 0 | 0 | 6 | 21 |
| Rotating perspective | 0 | 5 | 0 | 0 | 0 | 0 | 0 | 0 | 0 | 11 | 0 | 0 | 0 | 0 | 0 | 0 | 0 | 0 | 0 | 0 | 0 | 0 | 0 | 0 | 5 | 10 | 2 | 8 | 4 | 7 | 11 | 41 |
| Color | 1 | 4 | 0 | 0 | 0 | 0 | 0 | 0 | 0 | 2 | 1 | 4 | 1 | 3 | 1 | 2 | 2 | 1 | 0 | 0 | 1 | 0 | 0 | 0 | 0 | 0 | 0 | 0 | 1 | 0 | 2 | 6 |
| Alphanumeric | 6 | 0 | 0 | 2 | 0 | 0 | 0 | 4 | 0 | 8 | 2 | 8 | 3 | 4 | 1 | 5 | 1 | 8 | 0 | 0 | 0 | 0 | 0 | 0 | 0 | 0 | 0 | 0 | 3 | 0 | 15 | 12 |
| Remote conversational terminal | 0 | 6 | 0 | 5 | 0 | 0 | 0 | 3 | 0 | 8 | 2 | 6 | 2 | 7 | 1 | 5 | 1 | 2 | 4 | 10 | 0 | 7 | 3 | 2 | 4 | 12 | 2 | 9 | 6 | 16 | 7 | 48 |
| Paper tape (cassette) I/O | 0 | 3 | 3 | 3 | 1 | 4 | 0 | 5 | 0 | 14 | 7 | 10 | 6 | 5 | 0 | 0 | 0 | 0 | 0 | 0 | 3 | 2 | 0 | 0 | 2 | 5 | 1 | 1 | 1 | 0 | 29 | 103 |
| Remote card I/O | 0 | 5 | 3 | 3 | 2 | 3 | 0 | 6 | 0 | 12 | 7 | 10 | 6 | 6 | 0 | 0 | 0 | 0 | 0 | 0 | 0 | 0 | 0 | 0 | 1 | 1 | 1 | 0 | 3 | 2 | 22 | 49 |
| Remote printer | 0 | 5 | 3 | 3 | 1 | 4 | 0 | 7 | 0 | 14 | 0 | 1 | 0 | 1 | 0 | 0 | 0 | 0 | 2 | 0 | 0 | 0 | 0 | 0 | 1 | 0 | 1 | 0 | 0 | 0 | 21 | 51 |
| Optical character reader | 0 | 9 | 3 | 4 | 1 | 2 | 0 | 2 | 0 | 2 | 1 | 2 | 2 | 3 | 0 | 0 | 0 | 0 | 2 | 0 | 0 | 0 | 0 | 0 | 2 | 5 | 2 | 5 | 0 | 0 | 8 | 26 |
| Card or tape output | 0 | 0 | 1 | 0 | 0 | 0 | 0 | 0 | 0 | 1 | 0 | 4 | 0 | 0 | 0 | 0 | 0 | 0 | 1 | 2 | 0 | 1 | 0 | 0 | 0 | 0 | 2 | 5 | 0 | 0 | 8 | 18 |
| Scanning digitizer | 1 | 2 | 0 | 0 | 0 | 0 | 0 | 0 | 0 | 8 | 0 | 0 | 0 | 0 | 0 | 0 | 0 | 0 | 0 | 0 | 0 | 0 | 0 | 0 | 3 | 4 | 3 | 4 | 0 | 1 | 2 | 13 |
| Real time on-line monitored experiments | 0 | 0 | 0 | 0 | 0 | 0 | 0 | 0 | 2 | 2 | 1 | 3 | 1 | 1 | 0 | 0 | 0 | 0 | 1 | 2 | 0 | 3 | 0 | 0 | 0 | 0 | 3 | 4 | 0 | 1 | 6 | 15 |
| Two-dimensional plotting | 0 | 0 | 0 | 0 | 0 | 0 | 0 | 3 | 2 | 2 | 1 | 3 | 2 | 1 | 0 | 0 | 0 | 0 | 1 | 2 | 0 | 0 | 0 | 0 | 3 | 0 | 3 | 0 | 2 | 0 | 13 | 14 |
| Movie making | 0 | 1 | 0 | 0 | 0 | 0 | 0 | 1 | 1 | 0 | 0 | 0 | 2 | 1 | 0 | 0 | 0 | 0 | 0 | 0 | 0 | 0 | 0 | 0 | 0 | 0 | 1 | 0 | 1 | 0 | 5 | 3 |

Department

TABLE 2
Software Requirements

| Areas in which software is needed | E, courses requiring | R, research areas requiring |
|---|---|---|
| 1. Statistical analysis | 115 | 102 |
| 2. Solution of integral and differential equations | 49 | 34 |
| 3. Information storage and retrieval | 48 | 24 |
| 4. Linear, nonlinear, static and dynamic programming | 26 | 5 |
| 5. Matrix manipulation | 41 | 6 |
| 6. Mathematical modeling (simulation) | 83 | 39 |
| 7. Contour and graphical plotting | 13 | 12 |
| 8. Simplified language | 123 | 25 |
| 9. Structural analysis | 10 | 4 |
| 10. Financial analysis | 13 | — |
| 11. PERT and CPM analysis | 5 | — |
| 12. Numerical taxonomy—Numerical classification procedures | 6 | 1 |
| 13. Theoretical curve fitting | 2 | 9 |
| 14. Linguistic stylistic analysis | 4 | 1 |
| 15. Fourier series analysis | 8 | — |
| 16. Numerical iteration techniques | 4 | 1 |
| 17. Solution of boundary-value problems | 4 | 3 |
| 18. General program for quantum chemistry | 6 | 2 |
| 19. Spectroscopy program | 4 | 10 |
| 20. Miscellaneous | 29 | 21 |

Computing center records of past utilization of the computer by individuals, separately reported by course load and research interest, show the consumption of the current facility. These figures may be used to form a base for each user upon which to estimate his future needs. While such estimates may not be precise, they do offer the best information available at the time. Table 3 illustrates a method for collecting and exhibiting these present and future research needs; Table 4 extends the search for projected needs to the classroom. The administrative needs would be exhibited in another table.

## THE REQUEST FOR PROPOSAL (RFP)

As soon as it becomes apparent that there is a reasonable expectation of acquiring a new computer, it is prudent to notify computer vendors of this expectation. From this time forward, the informal dissemination of the needs to the vendors and their active participation in helping to organize the requirements has the twofold advantage of getting independent and competing reviews of

**TABLE 3**
Computing Resources (hours:minutes of CPU time)

Department: Physics          Chairperson: A. B. Carter

| Researcher | Actual | | | | | | | | | Projected | | |
|---|---|---|---|---|---|---|---|---|---|---|---|---|
| | 1972–73 | | | 1973–74 | | | 1974–75 | | | 1983–84 | | |
| | Fall | Spring | Summer | Fall | Spring | Summer | Fall | Spring | Summer | Fall | Spring | Summer |
| T. H. Remm | 1:28 | 3:15 | 3:45 | 2:59 | :32 | 2:25 | 2:15 | 1:45 | 2:30 | 10:00 | 10:00 | 10:00 |
| K. L. Gelowe | 7:37 | 7:04 | 7:09 | 18:51 | 16:22 | 17:22 | 20:00 | 20:00 | 20:00 | 30:00 | 30:00 | 30:00 |
| S. F. Bleer | 2:14 | :43 | 2:19 | 2:12 | 1:57 | 2:39 | 1:45 | 2:00 | 1:45 | 10:00 | 10:00 | 5:00 |
| W. L. Grasdon | 1:10 | :00 | :01 | 1:50 | :38 | 1:24 | 1:30 | :30 | 1:00 | 6:00 | 8:00 | 5:00 |
| H. J. Dolivier | :32 | 2:25 | :54 | 2:01 | 1:27 | 1:48 | 1:00 | 3:00 | 2:00 | 6:00 | 6:00 | 6:00 |
| Total | 13:01 | 13:27 | 14:08 | 27:53 | 20:56 | 25:38 | 8:30 | 9:15 | 27:15 | 62:00 | 64:00 | 56:00 |

# COMPUTER SELECTION CRITERIA

## TABLE 4

| Course Number | Actual | | | | | | Projected | | | | | |
|---|---|---|---|---|---|---|---|---|---|---|---|---|
| | 1972–73 | | | 1973–74 | | | 1974–75 | | | 1983–84 | | |
| | Fall | Spring | Summer | Fall | Spring | Summer | Fall | Spring | Summer | Fall | Spring | Summer |
| 11 | 0:07 | — | — | 0:12 | — | — | 0:10 | — | — | 0:50 | — | — |
| 67 | 1:15 | 7:21 | 2:41 | 12:35 | — | 0:26 | 2:30 | 5:00 | 2:30 | 5:00 | 10:00 | 5:00 |
| 123 | — | 4:15 | — | — | 5:47 | — | — | 5:00 | — | — | 7:00 | — |
| 127 | — | — | 6:32 | 9:50 | — | — | — | — | 5:30 | — | — | 10:00 |
| 129 | 4:29 | — | — | 2:46 | — | 3:46 | 5:00 | — | 2:00 | — | 10:00 | — |
| 216 | :26 | :16 | 1:53 | 2:07 | — | 2:05 | 3:00 | 2:00 | — | 5:00 | 5:00 | — |
| 247 | 2:47 | 1:44 | — | 5:01 | 4:12 | — | 5:00 | 1:00 | — | 8:00 | 2:00 | — |
| 298 | 2:49 | 2:01 | — | 2:33 | 2:47 | — | 5:00 | 1:00 | — | 8:00 | 2:00 | — |
| 302 | 3:05 | 3:22 | — | 1:55 | 3:49 | — | 5:00 | 1:00 | — | 8:00 | 2:00 | — |
| 317 | 4:35 | 2:45 | 5:52 | 6:12 | 2:33 | 4:47 | 8:00 | 6:00 | 8:00 | 20:00 | 10:00 | 20:00 |
| 398 | 1:45 | 2:16 | — | — | 2:49 | 1:01 | 2:00 | 3:00 | 1:00 | 4:00 | 5:00 | 2:00 |
| 501 | 2:38 | 2:01 | 4:29 | 2:57 | 2:45 | 12:07 | 3:00 | 3:00 | 6:00 | 8:00 | 8:00 | 30:00 |
| Total | 23:56 | 26:01 | 21:27 | 46:08 | 24:42 | 24:12 | 38:40 | 27:00 | 25:00 | 66:50 | 61:50 | 67:00 |

substantive data being collected as well as giving each of them (the vendors) as much time as possible to organize the proposal that will be offered. The more deeply enmeshed a vendor becomes in this preliminary work, the greater his initial financial commitment, the more anxious he will be to protect this investment. Also, realistically, it may not be possible to write an RFP which is totally unambiguous; giving the vendors access to the persons having input to the RFP tends to improve their understanding.

The formal RFP represents the distillation of the thoughts of many persons. As such, to insure that no need has been overlooked, it should be made available for comment to all members of the organization who may wish to examine it. As indicated, not only will this insure accuracy, but, since in every organization there are competing needs for resources, spokesmen for these competing needs will have had the opportunity to evaluate their own expenditure requirements vis-à-vis this proposed acquisition. While unanimity of opinion may be desirable, it is not necessary; adequate organizational commitment is.

In addition to submitting the formal RFP to the various vendors, it is desirable to follow this with a formal, technical review session to which all vendors are invited. The purposes of this technical review session are many. A senior officer of the organization can welcome them, stress the significance of the new facility to the organization, and indicate the commitment toward its acquisition. This will reinforce in the vendors' minds that the probability for acquisition is indeed high.

The presence of staff members to respond to questions raised by the vendors, as well as to insure that proper stress is placed on specific sections of the RFP , enhances the image of commitment to this project.

Assuming that no covert commitment had been made, either consciously or otherwise, the openness of this forum tends to insure a best effort on the part of each vendor. While some reticence is apparent, at least as may be sensed from the questions asked and inferred from those unasked, the effect is salutary.

**Introduction to the RFP**

The material to be presented in the RFP should, as a minimum, include the current usage and projected needs as ascertained, and details on the current hardware configuration and the available software. The philosophy of the current mode of operation and the change that is expected with the new equipment should be indicated.

**Expected Mode and Level of Operation (Hardware Needs)**

Following these introductory remarks, details of the expected mode and level of operation, as complete as possible, should be presented. For example, if the computer is to be used interactively, in a time-sharing mode, with remote terminals, the minimum number of ports to be available on installation should be specified. Expansion capabilities, and the time frame, should be indicated. The distribution between hardwired and dial-up terminals should be given as well as the data transmission rates that are expected. Questions concerning the capability of the communications components of the equipment to recognize terminal speed and the character set used and to perform automatic translation are typical of those to be asked. If there is no compunction toward acquiring some of these components, i.e., the terminals, cabling, etc., from other sources, this should also be indicated.

For central site job entry, the desired operation characteristics of the I/O devices, i.e., card and tape readers, punches, and printers, should be specified. As for all items for which information is requested by indicating the operational need, permit the vendor to suggest alternatives which may improve the price/performance ratio.

If remote job entry is either an immediate need or has reasonable future expectation, indicate this. Ask for equipment description and prices for future expansion in this area, including, for example, the possibilities of multiplexing.

The possibility that much of the future requirements may be met by attaching the acquired computer to either a regional or national network should not be overlooked. It is not unreasonable to request that any additional equipment necessary to do so be indicated and its cost given.

Planning for enhancement of the facility during the time frame under consideration cannot be overlooked. Choices of equipment for initial installation may significantly affect the price of growth. Require adequate information from the vendor about the availability of devices and their prices to support your expected growth pattern. While a computer installation may not have the expected useful life of other capital equipment, its expected useful life may be substantially increased if initial planning allows for expansion.

## Software Support

After covering the details of needs as may be met by hardware, another area in which information is needed is software support: (1) operating systems, (2) programming languages, and (3) applications packages. Also, there will probably be one or more specialized areas which will need software support. For example, the more specialized requirements associated with a data-based management system may assume significant importance. Adherence to the specifications and recommendations of industry-wide study groups may be weighed in evaluating the proposal. Again, details on the expected use should be given; it will behoove the vendor to be specific in his reply.

## Conversion

Of the programs either operational or under development on the current equipment, some or all will have to be made operational on the new equipment. This conversion effort is generally never trivial and can be quite horrendous. Determine from the vendor the support he will offer to accomplish this conversion and weigh this response carefully with other alternatives such as doing the work internally with current staff, hiring additional staff for this purpose, or contracting with a service bureau. The current usage data that had been accumulated will serve as the basis for the reply. Acceptable minima must be specified.

It is at this time that an enhancement to the current operation may be obtained at moderate cost. Programs in related areas may have accumulated over the past years and too little attention given to subsume these separate programs into an integrated one which could have such desirable characteristics as reduced running time, be easier for operations, and be less subject to external errors. The conversion of existing programs one-to-one may not be significantly less than converting a group into an integrated system. The comparative costs should be determined.

Emulation of the present computer may not be desirable but possibly can be tolerated. The justification for such acceptance would undoubtedly vary from one organization to the next, but should be articulated.

## Special Projects

Attention must be called to those special projects currently operational which had required special hardware or software for their development. For example, analog-to-digital and digital-to-analog conversions at very high rates in real time may pose seemingly unrealistic requirements for some vendors. The vendor must be required to indicate how these special projects will be supported on the system he intends to propose.

## Maintenance

### Software

The request for proposal should inquire into the availability of software maintenance in the areas of operating systems, languages, and applications programming. The specific terms for the maintenance, including such factors as cost, times of availability, and location of dispatch points, as well as other factors deemed desirable for proper support, should be stated.

### Hardware

The proposal should specify the costs for various levels of maintenance, including plans for hours covered, provisions for calls out of covered hours, and provision for on-site maintenance.

### Internal Maintenance

The possibility exists that some installations may wish to consider supporting either software, hardware, or both internally. To do this, personnel will need to be trained; additional needs could include detailed documentation for software, wiring diagrams, special test programs and equipment, spare parts, price lists for components, and sources of supply. Advice on training programs and support, as well as associated costs, should be included.

### Third Party Support

While it may not be appropriate for inclusion in the RFP, it is not unreasonable to ask of a vendor if any other installations using his equipment is also maintaining it or using third party maintenance. Comparative costs should be developed.

### General Considerations

Request information on those specifics of the installation which could have a material affect, i.e., special air conditioning and humidity requirements, water lines, power and voltage regulation requirements, special circuit breakers, etc. By offering detailed information on the proposed site for the installation of the equipment, misunderstandings resulting in last minute delays and overruns can be avoided.

### Expected Performance

The history of the past utilization of the computing facility has been available. By coupling the statements concerning the expected mode and level of operation with the expected performance characteristics, a picture should emerge indicating the overall expected performance. Perhaps an illustration would suffice. A current computer facility consists of two machines, one dedicated to batch processing and the other supporting interactive time-sharing via remote terminals. The machine dedicated to batch processing runs under two distinct operating systems, one suitable for processing scientific and engineering-type problems, the other suitable for processing business-oriented-type problems. The overall requirements for the new machine are to process both business and scientific/engineering-type problems in batch mode when appropriate while concurrently supporting the interactive, time-sharing terminals. Whereas presently programs submitted for batch processing are run consecutively according to an algorithm prescribing priority, it is expected that (for definitiveness for this illustration) three batch streams would be available in the new computer, again with an algorithm assigning programs to each of the streams and allocating priorities for sharing such resources as the central processor(s).

If a mix of problems running on the present equipment was to be presented, such factors as throughput time minus I/O time could be measured and used as one of several criteria to specify the efficiency of the current facility. It could be required that the proposed computer process the same job mix similarly (single stream) and that the resulting timings be no more than some fraction (i.e., $\frac{1}{2}$) of the present ones. Since, however, single stream operation is not the desired mode, this same mix of jobs could be run in the three stream mode and at the same time the time-sharing terminals would be active. Data on the resulting processing time for each job in the mix and for the entire mix could be recorded; the degradation, if any, in the response times at the terminals could be measured. From these data it would be possible to measure the expected performance of the new system; alternatively, expected performance criteria could be thusly specified.

Whether the procedure outlined above or another is used, it is important that the vendor clearly understands how the performance of his installed equipment will be measured. He should be in a position to *guarantee* this performance. The details of the text, carefully thought through, carefully documented, and carefully presented, should be at the apex of all criteria.

### Growth

Times of rapidly fluctuating monetary conditions, coupled with uncertainties in the expected rate of growth in the utilization of the system, make long-range planning difficult. In order to minimize these uncertainties, commitments from the vendor fixing such items as long-term rental rates, interest, and maintenance rates are desirable. Provision for delivery of equipment several years hence, at current prices, protects growth plans. The additional stipulation allowing cancellation prior to shipment offers protection against obsolescence as well as an overoptimistic estimate of growth.

At this point the RFP is reasonably complete. The present situation has been detailed; the future expectations have been expressed; channels for communication have been established to eliminate ambiguities. Two subsequent events are anticipated: (1) receiving the proposals and evaluating these, and (2) entering into the contract negotiations. At this point a digression is appropriate.

At the time of contract negotiations the following posture may be expected on the part of the vendor. First, there will be a general disclaimer of the information presented in the proposal. This generally takes the form of a statement which indicates that the vendor will honor only the commitments specified in the contract and that the language of the contract supersedes all other statements, either written or oral, made by his representative. Thus, those sections of the proposal which are critical must be incorporated into and made a part of the contract.

A computer vendor would like to take the position that he will deliver and connect the various components, demonstrate that from an electrical and mechanical point of view these function, and demonstrate an operating system. At this point he would like to be paid.

As the purchaser (or lessor) of the equipment, it is necessary to insure that all of the promises made in the proposal have indeed been kept. A reasonably safe way to insure this is to indicate in the RFP the conditions for acceptance and to insist in the contract that these conditions be met. Typically, the acceptance criteria which must be met by the hardware and software delivered and installed on site should include: (1) satisfactory physical performance of the equipment; (2) satisfactory performance of the vendor-supplied software, i.e., operating systems, languages, specialized programs, etc.; (3) completion of the conversion; (4) demonstration that the special projects are operable; and (5) successful completion of the benchmark test.

Additional language of the following sort places the burden of compliance with all terms of the contract upon the vendor: ''Upon delivery and installation of the physical equipment and software, no part may be removed by the vendor if he has successfully completed all phases of the acceptance testing unless the purchaser (lessor) defaults in payment as agreed upon.'' The thrust of this statement is to insure that a vendor who has had to bring in additional equipment in order to meet the acceptance criteria may not subsequently remove it. Such excess equipment should, as a minimum, be made available to the customer at no additional cost.

Another stipulation that may be added provides for uninterrupted service, even in the case of failure of the equipment to meet all acceptance criteria. ''In the case that the physical equipment or the software fails to meet the acceptance tests, the equipment and software shall remain on site unitl that time that replacement of equipment or software from another vendor is completed. The original vendor shall be liable for all expenses, direct and indirect, that the purchaser (lessor) may incur if acquisition from a subsequent vendor becomes necessary.''[2]

## THE EVALUATION OF THE PROPOSALS

There will be general areas in each of which specific questions will need to be asked and answers obtained and evaluated. On the technical side, the two broad categories are software and hardware; on the management side, there is the question of commitment of the vendor to remain a viable force in the marketplace.

One format for presenting the factors which will enter into the evaluation is as follows: At the top of a page, succinctly state the factor to be evaluated; for example: ''Memory Access Speed.'' A brief description indicative of the characteristics sought and the reasons for these should be given; for example: ''Access times to memory influence processing times and consequently throughput. Generally low access times imply short processing times and increased

[2] (a) EUDCOM has compiled and published a list of special contractual terms that have been negotiated by colleges and universities: *Contracting for Computing: A Checklist of Terms and Clauses for Use in Contracting with Vendors for Computing Resources*, EDUCOM, Interuniversity Communications Council, Inc., P.O. Box 364, Princeton, New Jersey, July 1973. (b) The General Services Administration of the U.S. Government annually negotiates contracts with vendors. The government is in ''a most favored customer'' position and as such has been able to specify contractual terms suited to its operation.

throughput.'' Then, for each of the vendors submitting a proposal, listing a succinct comment evaluating his equipment on this point is appropriate.

It is not the intent at this level to evaluate competing computing systems but rather to indicate significant factors, remembering that these may vary depending on the particular environment in which the computer is to function. The following presents such a list.

## Software Pricing Policies

In 1970 IBM announced its unbundling policy stating that it would no longer provide free programming packages with its equipment but would charge separately for these. Also unbundled were support services such as the generation of new software systems and the correction of errors in some software. The reactions of other computer vendors to IBM's lead have been varied.

Questions to be asked relating to current pricing policies:

1. Is systems software and support, including the control program (operating system) and other basic components needed to make the hardware operable, a cost item?
2. Is actual implementation of the system a cost item?
3. What are the costs for providing and supporting programming languages, such as BASIC, FORTRAN, and COBOL?
4. What are the costs for providing and supporting utilities needed to maintain user files?
5. What are the costs for providing and supporting the software needed to implement a data-based management information system?
6. What are the costs for providing and supporting programming packages used for simulation, report writer, etc.?
7. What are the costs for documentation of the above?
8. What are the costs for education of staff and other personnel in the installation and use of the software?

## Control Program Characteristics

The control program (operating system, executive, monitor) is the most important single software item of the computing system. It is also, in almost any computing system one would wish to study, far too complex to evaluate on other than certain specific points. It is the combination of the control program and the hardware which provides the power, security, reliability, and ease of use of the entire computing system. An organization which is concerned with providing services to users would be well advised to consider the salutary following control program characteristics.

COMPUTER SELECTION CRITERIA

*Ease of Use*

Ease of use is a judgment based on the anticipated needs of three distinct types of computer user:

*Novice:* Someone using a computer in the performance of an unrelated task such as a clerk entering data via a terminal or a student responding to a list of questions.

*General:* Those persons engaged in tasks such as learning to program, statistically analyzing data via a terminal, or conducting research in some specialized area. It is assumed that some experience exists at this level.

*Staff:* The Computing Center staff who would require sophisticated tools to configure the system to the needs of the organization and to aid other users.

In order to satisfy these requirements, certain features are needed. Relevant questions follow:

1. Is there automatic initiation of a given program for a given account number or terminal (for example, for the clerk function)?
2. Is there common file format across all languages and applications?
3. Is there file security and back-up; how is it handled?
4. Do batch and time-sharing programs require control language changes between modes?
5. Does there exist a simple job control language with a subset for beginners, but with the power necessary for the professional?
6. Is there a job control library?

*Ease of Operation*

Normally one would hope to minimize the degree of sophistication required of the operator and his interaction with the equipment. Ideally, the system should run itself, notifying the operator only of physical needs such as paper changes, tape and disk mounts, or equipment failures. Furthermore, the power of the operator over the system should be limited so as to avoid mismanagement of a system balancing multiple tasks and to preclude circumventing normal security provisions. Based upon a scale of difficulty, there should be questions concerning the complexity of the operation.

1. What is the extent of training required for an operator, experienced on other equipment?
2. What is the extent of training required for an operator with no prior experience?
3. Can an operator bypass security and run privileged jobs?
4. If yes to (3), can this be restricted?

*Failure Recovery*

Failure recovery is the ability of the system to detect an error and perform the necessary readjustment to continue. Continuance could range from switching to alternative hardware or procedures and continuing uninterrupted to shutting down, notifying, and requesting help from the operator. Among the specific questions that could be significant in a given installation are:

1. In the case of power failure, is there the recovery of all tasks, each to its respective status prior to failure, upon the return of power?
2. In the case of hardware failure, can the control program automatically detect and circumvent the problem area?
3. In the case of hardware failure which cannot be circumvented, is there notification pinpointing the problem?
4. Can the control program detect and correct system errors as well as notify the operator of these?

*File Security*

Emphasis is placed on file compatability as an important asset so as to avoid the need to convert a file for use with another program or language. Unfortunately, if files are compatible, the possibility for unauthorized users to inadvertently or deliberately browse through sensitive files increases.

Security may affect authorized file access also since the ability to easily back-out transactions or recover from programming errors may be significantly important in on-line systems.

1. How many different levels of account numbers, codes, passwords, etc., are available in the system?
2. Is there notification of excessive abortive attempts within short periods of time to gain access to a given file?

*System Reliability*

The control program must be able to perform for extended periods without requiring a restart due to a failure. System failures are of three types: deadlocks or logic errors, lack of protection from user or operator errors, and hardware failures. As hardware errors are discussed elsewhere, only the first and second errors are addressed here.

There is only one test of the control program: its ability to operate and provide the appropriate action for any possible situation it may encounter. If a deadlock occurs or a program can cause failure, then the control program is inadequate. As perfection is unattainable, a degree of reliability on the order not to exceed a single restart of the system per day is desired. This goal should be adequate to allow relatively unattended operation during nights, holidays, and weekends.

Specific questions to be considered are:

1. What is the mean time to failure as reported by the company?
2. What is the mean time to failure as reported by users?

## Programming Languages

In evaluating programming languages, emphasis is placed on the productivity of the individual. Debugging aids, interactive prompters, clarity of error messages, and ease of conversion of imported programs are all factors affecting productivity. Of importance also is multilanguage linkage and file compatability, eliminating the need to write programs to convert a file for use by another language or program. While the relative speeds cannot be measured without comprehensive tests, it is known that machine resources can be minimized through the use of reentry compilers, run-time packages, and code. Since some manufacturers provide separate compilers for batch and interactive use, the question of compatability must be raised. Any program should run without change regardless of its origin (terminal, batch, remote batch) or destination given only the media considered.

Specific languages and characteristics may be factors peculiar to a particular institution. While there are general characteristics which should be ascertained for each language, such as core requirements and whether the compiler, run-time package, and code produced are reentrant, there may be special characteristics which are of significance. Only a few of the better known languages are discussed; the totality of languages and their dialects number in the thousands. (J. Sammet, *Programming Languages: History and Fundamentals*, Prentice-Hall, Englewood Cliffs, New Jersey, 1969.)

## *ALGOL*

ALGOL is an algorithmic language suited for computer science instruction, written communication, and scientific programming.

Specific questions that may be raised should include:

1. Is the implementation oriented to ease of use, i.e., are good diagnostic and debugging aids provided?
2. Can the language be used for general programming with file compatability and multilanguage linkage?

## *BASIC*

BASIC is used heavily in computer science instruction as well as for elementary scientific programming; it is similar to FORTRAN and is used often as the first language of students. It should be easy to learn, to use, and should be sufficiently powerful so that knowledge of an additional language for research need not be necessary.

Specific questions to be asked should include:

1. Is the language oriented to the beginner with good diagnostic and debugging aids?
2. Is there file compatability?
3. Is immediate mode (ability to simulate a desk calculator) provided?

## COBOL

COBOL is the most heavily used language for business applications. Its Englishlike structure is an aid toward writing self-documenting programs; long efforts at standardization have produced a reasonable level of compatability across the industry. Terminal entry and data base inquiry capabilities may be considerations.

Specific questions that might be asked in this category include:

1. Does the language provide good diagnostic and debugging aids?
2. Are the files compatible and is there multilanguage linkage?
3. Does it support the CODASYL DBLTG report as its standard data base access methods?
4. Can present programs currently written in COBOL be run without modification (will the conversion effort be minimal)?

## FORTRAN

FORTRAN is the principal language used for scientific programming. Since many operational programs are written in FORTRAN, minimum reeducation and conversion will be essential. Exchange of programs with other institutions may be important.

Specific questions that might be asked:

1. Is the language oriented to both beginning and experienced programmers, i.e., are there good diagnostic and debugging aids?
2. Are files compatible and is there multilanguage linkage?
3. Can present programs be run without modification?

Some programmers have a tendency to mix FORTRAN and assembly language statements within a program. Under these circumstances, conversion will present an additional problem. In this case, as well as in any other which may arise, it would be well to identify those programs which would require extensive modification before they can be successfully converted and run.

## *RPG*

RPG (Report Program Generator) may still be used in existing production facilities which have a history of growth from electromechanical equipment utilizing wired boards. As with other older languages, a decision must be made as to whether to retain and continue to run these older programs or to convert, for example, to a data-based management inquiry, report writer system. The response of the vendor must be clear as to the options available and their costs.

1. Does the vendor support RPG?
2. Is conversion to COBOL (or to a data base) recommended?
3. What would the cost for conversion be?

## *Other Languages and Packages*

Most vendors supply a host of languages and packages for special purposes. In any given institution, it would be necessary to evaluate the need for these special languages and packages and to paraphrase the questions asked above relative to these. A short list of such is appended: APL, CAI (Computer-Aided Instruction), graphics, linear programming, LISP (list processing), PL/I, simulation, SNOBOL4, SPSS (Statistical Package for the Social Sciences), text editor.

## Conversion Policies

For a painless transition to a new computing system, it is essential that existing programs and data files be converted and in working order by the time the new computer is accepted. Ideally, there should be a time during which the two computer systems will overlap operationally; otherwise, specific arrangements must be made so that no time lag occurs during which essential current programs cannot be run, i.e., one cannot afford to miss a payroll.

Specific questions that should be asked:

1. Will the conversion be part of the contract for the acquisition of the equipment or will it be a separate agreement? If it is to be a separate agreement, but with the vendor supplying the hardware, contractually tie the completion dates for the conversion and acceptance of the converted programs to the acceptance of the hardware.
2. What is the schedule for completion?
3. What is the charge for conversion?
4. Will the conversion be one-to-one, or are there possibilities for the amalgamation of many, simple programs into a single large but more efficient one?

## Data-Base Systems

The need to integrate data bases into one highly organized and flexible system may be of critical importance. Data management systems eliminate conversion of files from one system to another by allowing data to be accessed for a variety of different purposes; on the other hand, there must also be appropriate security against unauthorized access. Also important are the report writing and inquiry packages which make the one-time report a task measured in hours, not days. If these tools are sufficiently refined, some of the programming as well as the file maintenance may be substantially reduced.

Specific questions should include:

1. To maintain compatability for exchange within industry-wide associations, does the data management system meet current CODASYL specifications?
2. Does the data management system have inquiry and report writer utilities?
3. Would a data-base administrator have control over both the makeup of the data base as well as the security of the individual records?
4. Are there design and optimization tools available to run the data management system?
5. What types of logical structures are permitted?
6. What types of access methods are allowed?
7. What is the relationship between programs such as Bill of Materials Processor and the data-base management system?
8. Does the data management system operate in both batch and interactive mode?
9. Is the data-base management system reentrant?
10. Can it interface to other than COBOL?

## Hardware—General

The capability of the hardware to support the totality of varied uses to which the system is to be put is paramount. Capability for performance of different tasks (computation, data retrieval, communications, etc.) will vary with the design as do the technical details (word length, number of registers, memory module size, etc.). Error detection and correction capability bear heavily on the overall reliability.

Computer hardware may be treated as a black box and examined through the masks of diagnostic software, the control program, or other specialized programs. If one wants to do more, to compare design criteria and techniques as these vary from one vendor to another or to the state-of-the-art, other questions must be asked. Ultimately, of course, no matter how sophisticated the overall design or how advanced the design of components, for the user the decisive factors will have to be those that deal with reliability, support, and capacity.

While hardware failures may be expected to be less common than software failures, the failure of the hardware generally results in a shut down of the facility measured in hours as a minimum. However, failure of certain components of the hardware may result only in impaired operations. Thus peripheral units relating to user and system files can fail (but not, for example, the disk controller) without halting processing. Some types of memory failures may only reduce the available memory. However, failure of the central processor or the input-output processor in those systems which have only one will be fatal. A reasonable precaution would be to locate available back-up sites and to verify that support may be expected in case of emergency.

In the event that a multiprocessing system is under consideration, it would be desirable to confirm that the several processors are all under the control of one operating system. Also, in the event that one of the processors became inoperable, would there be automatic scheduling of programs, so that the processing would continue on the other CPU's?

## Hardware Service and Support

### Remedial Maintenance

Accepting as axiomatic that hardware failures will occur, it is reasonable to ascertain the responsiveness of the vendor so as to minimize down time.

The following questions are based upon the assumption that neither in-house nor third party maintenance is being considered:

1. Where will service personnel be located during the service contract shift?
2. Is out-of-contract hours service guaranteed?
3. What are the costs for the various types of service contracts?
4. Where are back-up service personnel stationed?
5. Under what conditions are back-up service personnel brought in?

### Preventive Maintenance

Hopefully, hardware failures may be anticipated and prevented during preventive maintenance. Scheduling, and assuring that the schedule, once agreed upon, will be maintained may present problems.

A clearer understanding of the preventive maintenance that is being offered can sometimes be got from answers to questions of the sort:

1. How many personnel will be assigned to this installation for preventive maintenance?
2. Assuming that there are similar installations in your geographic area, how many times during the past year has preventive maintenance at an installation been either postponed or cancelled?

If third party or in-house maintenance is being considered, it is reasonably clear how these concerns may be rephrased so as to be applicable to those situations. Detailed criteria for the comparative evaluation of the quality of service offered by different maintenance vendors may have to include the evaluation of the technical competence of specific individuals assigned to the installation; this degree of refinement is beyond the scope of this article.

## Disks

The disk subsystem is critical in a time-sharing environment since there is insufficient main memory for all tasks. Swapping of programs to disk allows sharing of memory; however, swapping need be restricted so as not to become too great a factor in the total processing time. Disks are used also to store data and programs, with time sharing requiring a large amount of disk space in lieu of card storage.

The following factors are relevant in evaluating proposed disk systems:

For the swapping system:

1. Are the heads fixed or movable?
2. Is there rotation sensing?
3. Is there single or multiple channel access?
4. Are there separate I/O paths to memory?
5. What are minimum, average, and maximum access times?
6. What is the transfer rate?

For the mass storage system:

1. Are disks mountable (i.e., replaceable)?
2. Is there rotation sensing?
3. Is there single or multiple channel access?
4. What are minimum, average, and maximum access times?
5. What is the transfer rate?

## Digital-to-Analog and Analog-to-Digital

Special projects may have requirements for digital-to-analog and analog-to-digital equipment. The specifics of the application will dictate the specifics of the conversion rates. Detailed questions would depend, of course, on the applications; general questions that may be asked normally include:

1. Is a-to-d and d-to-a a normal hardware function?
2. Is a-to-d and d-to-a a normal software function?
3. What methods do you propose to provide a-to-d and d-to-a conversion?

## Communications Subsystems

The degree of dependency on communications subsystems will be a function of the need as it currently exists and as perceived by the organization for the future. Among the characteristics to be considered are the capability and reliability of the communications equipment for day-to-day performance. In an environment in which it is anticipated that these needs will be rapidly changing, any initial commitment to hardware should be such as to provide the maximum capability for enhancement as new needs may arise. Within this general context the following questions seem reasonable:

1. Is there automatic speed translation and character translation?
2. Is the communications subsystem sufficiently independent of the main system so that it would have the ability to notify users and maintain the network if the central system becomes unavailable?
3. In the event of the failure of the I/O equipment at the central site, does the communications subsystem have sufficient capability so that some special terminal may act in its place and thus maintain the operability of the entire system?

## Growth within Product Line

As careful as the planning may have been, the growth of demand on the new computing system may not have been adequately calculated. Unexpected developments may antiquate the system prior to the expected time. Upgrading of the equipment may prove to be a much less costly procedure than acquiring a new computing system. Thus it is significant to note if and how the proposed new computing configuration may be enlarged. The following questions are reasonable:

1. What is the maximum memory that can be put on the system?
2. If, for example, a single processor is being considered, what is the maximum number of processors that can be interconnected?
3. What is the maximum number of I/O processors that can be connected?

The computer being considered may be one in a product line. As such, it would be reasonable to know just wherein that product line the proposed computer configuration lies. Following this, it should be ascertained if a field engineering change is all that may be required to upgrade the configuration. Alternatively, if this is not the case, just what is the extent of disruption that may be expected, as well as the cost, if upgrading becomes necessary.

## General Hardware Characteristics

### Memory Transfer Speeds

An index frequently used to measure the efficiency of the computer is the memory transfer speeds. While fast memory transfers can often be subverted by inefficient operating systems or inappropriate architecture in other parts of the design of the computer, they do offer some indication of the absolute maximum speed that can be obtained in any specific computation. As such, some creditability is attached to fast memory speeds. Specific numbers can be obtained upon request from the vendor.

## Memory Module Size

Generally the main memory is assembled from memory modules. Thus a 128$K$ memory might be composed of two 64$K$ modules or eight 16$K$ modules. Tailoring the memory to your specific requirements would seem to be easier, as well as less costly, if the memory modules size were small.

A further advantage to small size memory modules can be realized if there is a larger number of channels to memory. Storage of programs or data which may be logically connected need not be contiguous. As a consequence, the storage and retrieval may be faster if there are multiple small memory modules coupled with numerous channels to memory.

## Maximum Memory Size

The initial memory size to be ordered will undoubtedly be less than the maximum memory possible for the computer. However, if there is any anticipation for future growth in this direction, it would be well to inquire as to the maximum size of the memory.

## Mixed Main Memory

Initially it may be desirable to have all main memory at the same speed. However, with the growth of the system over the years and the possibility of adding memory from another vendor, it would be reasonable to inquire if the proposed system, hardware and software, can support memories of different speeds.

## Program Size

Are there any hardware limitations on the program size, taking into account virtual addressing if available?

## Memory Fault Correction

Describe the technique used to correct or circumvent memory fault.

## Memory Mapping Techniques

Describe the techniques used to map memory.

COMPUTER SELECTION CRITERIA

## CPU– I/O Processor Relationships

What are these relationships?

### Peripheral Hardware Characteristics

#### Card Readers

*Speed.* The method of operation may dictate a large volume of card handling and consequently the number of cards per minute that can be read may be significant.

*Jams.* Card readers are notorious for their ability to mutilate cards and jam on these torn and ripped cards. If a large volume of cards to be read is anticipated, the ease with which the operator can restore the card reader to its functional status after jamming may be important. An indication of the performance of the card reader may be had both from the manufacturer and from inquiries to user installations. A reasonable measure would be mean number of cards between failures.

#### Printers

*Train vs Drum.* A difference in the quality of print depending upon the type of printer may be expected. Generally, though not always, train printers produce better quality printout than do drum printers. The value of good print quality to the organization should be made know to the vendor.

*Speed.* The number of lines per second for a given character set should be specified. Determine what the change in the number of lines per minute will be for different character sets.

*Character Sets.* If printing of different characters (i.e., upper and lower case) is needed, it will be necessary, using the same printer, to change character sets. Determine beforehand whether or not this will be possible with the printer suggested to you.

*Print Positions.* Determine the number of print positions per line that are available.

#### Card Punch

For those operations which require a large volume of card punching, the characteristics of the card punch should be carefully noted. Such factors as speed and mean time to failure can be significant.

*Disk Capacity and Access*

Inquiry should be made as to the maximum disk capacity capable of being supported by the system. It is assumed that the original proposal includes disk capacity adequate for the initial installation.

If disk requirements are large, disk channel contention can become a problem; multiple channels may become necessary. The feasibility to field upgrade to multiple channels as well as the costs to do so should be considered.

*Communication Lines*

Undoubtedly there will be an initial requirement for a number of communication lines; the circumstances under which this number will grow may not be known at that time. However, inquiry can be made as to the maximum number of lines that can be supported.

Not all communication lines will be at the same speed. It is desirable to know the number of different speeds and the number of different terminals at these speeds that can be simultaneously supported.

*Terminal Distance*

While it is certainly possible to locate terminals at any distance from the central site, the added cost for doing so may make it impractical. Under certain circumstances terminals may be located in an adjacent room or on an adjacent floor of the building housing the central computer. The maximum distance at which such a terminal can be located from the central site will be of importance if one wishes to minimize the cost inherent in the installation of modems and associated telephone charges.

**Other Software Considerations**

While to some extent the following has been discussed under other headings elsewhere, its importance is so great that it bears repeating. During the normal course of operation of the computer, part of the main memory will be constantly occupied. For example, segments of the operating system will be resident as will segments of the various compilers and, if there should be a data-based management system, such additional programs as report writer and inquiry language. The resident components of all these programs, while they are occupying the main memory, can leave only a remainder available as working space for program development and execution. It is significant to determine the amount of main memory that will be occupied by these resident programs and thus the amount of main memory that will then be available to the users for their specific programs. Certainly an estimate of minimum main memory size can be ascertained from these figures.

## Benchmarks

Having indicated in the request for proposal that the computing system will be evaluated according to the preceding characteristics and will be benchmarked, it now becomes necessary to specify the benchmark. As has been stressed so often, each installation must decide for itself the characteristics of its current operation and how it intends to function when the new computer is installed. Based upon this definition, a benchmark must be prepared which will be used to test the proposed configurations, assuming, of course, that each vendor will be able to supply a configuration identical or at least very similar to the one proposed. Notwithstanding all of the responses that had been tabulated on previous questions, the evaluation of the benchmark should be the most critical test. For example, the computer configuration recommended by one vendor was rated superior when the benchmark consisted of 50 programs being submitted simultaneously via remote terminals in a timesharing mode when the program sizes were of the order of 2000 to 5000 statements each. However, when the program sizes were cut to between 50 and 100 statements each, the computer configuration proposed by a different vendor turned out to be superior. The factors considered in this particular comparison were: (1) response time to input statements, (2) compile time, and (3) execute time. The benchmark component of the evaluation can dramatically demonstrate significant differences between computers when these are subjected to different program mixes.

## THE EVALUATION MODEL

For each of the factors that was considered in previous sections, i.e., factors that were deemed significant in evaluating the proposals submitted by the vendors, assign a numerical weight which is your opinion concerning the relative significance of that factor in relation to all other factors considered.

The numerical weight to be assigned to a specific factor should correlate directly with your estimate of the significance of that factor to your needs. Choose a convenient scale, say 0 to 100, with 100 assigned to the most important factors and smaller numbers assigned to less significant ones. For example, if the initial configuration actually requires 40 time-sharing teletype terminals, the weight attached to this factor might be 100. While an interactive COBOL compiler may be desirable, your opinion concerning its significance to your operation may cause you to weight it only at 25. Then, for each of the factors, rank each vendor on a 0 to 1 scale insofar as that specific factor is concerned. Finally, multiply the rank by the weight and sum over all of the factors considered. That vendor which scores highest should be the desired choice.

Another measure of acceptability of a proposal is measured by the distance that the given proposal differs from an ideal. In this model, a weight is also attached to each factor. For each factor, a number which is used as a reference coordinate is arbitrarily chosen; it may as well be zero. Then, for the given factor and a given computer, a numerical estimate can be given which would indicate how far away from zero (the ideal value) you feel the component lies. Square this number and multiply it by the weight of the factor; finally, sum over all factors. This model is a quadratic one and, in a sense, measures the distance that a given computer configuration lies from the origin, or ideal. The configuration for which the distance from the ideal is smallest should be the choice.

It would be difficult at this time to try to justify either this particular linear model or the quadratic one. It would be equally difficult to try to justify any other mathematical model. Their only defense would be their ease of use and the ability to test the sensitivity of the models to different weighting factors.

The sensitivity testing in itself can be significant. If a small change in the numerical values of the weights does not produce a change in the relative ordering of the vendors, it would then be reasonable to assume that the ordering that was produced by the original model is stable and probably reflects the best choice for the installation. However, if small variations in the weights produce different ordering of the vendors, then clearly the model is not very stable. In that case, one would have to go back and examine those components which are producing this shifting in relative values; further study would be needed in order to ascribe any degree of confidence in these.

If both models are sensitive to the weighting parameters, to the extent that small variations produce changes in the ordering of the vendors, then it would be reasonable to conclude that, for the factors considered, there is no really discernible difference between the proposals. The decision would then have to be based on additional factors still to be introduced, factors which could undoubtedly seem capricious. In this situation, however, nothing is really lost in that if no discernible difference can be measured, then any of the choices is acceptable.


## THE CONTRACT

After having made the decision to acquire a specific computer, it becomes necessary to enter into the detailed contract negotiations with the vendor. At this point, one must be prepared to accept variations from the original proposal that the vendor made and to evaluate these variations in light of your own needs. On the other hand, by this time you will have had contact with other users of this particular vendor's equipment. From them you should be able to determine any special consideration that the vendor had given to them and decide if these special considerations are significant to you. If these are, you have every reason to ask for and expect to receive similar considerations although they may not have been part of your original request for proposal. Information is available from other user installations concerning those concessions that had been made to them; avail yourself of it.[3]

---

[3] Each vendor works with, and in some cases may provide support to, a user group. Attending one or more meetings of these groups and becoming acquainted with the individuals who participate can lead to revealing discussions.

It is difficult, if not impossible, to describe how one goes about negotiating with vendors over prices and conditions. Initially, of course, ask for everything you might conceivably want; some vendor may offer concessions in one area, another vendor in another area. Inquire as to the precise reasons why certain conditions cannot be offered; require that the vendor's sales force go to his management in an effort to secure the terms you need. Arrangements can be arrived at in face-to-face negotiations with senior company representatives, arrangements that sales force personnel would not consider possible. These negotiations demand a sense of timing and reasonableness; they are dependent on the vendor's particular marketing strategy at the time. For example, a vendor may not be particularly interested in a sale at the time, he may be more interested in establishing a broader leasing base. Also, there are instances when it is impossible to get any concession from a vendor for circumstances which may be beyond his control, i.e., perhaps a court order prevents deviation from the standard contract.

Certain factors, however, are reasonably standard and should be mentioned. These include delivery dates, installation procedures, and responsibility for certification that the equipment is as agreed to. It is this last factor which is exceedingly important.

Under the assumption that the benchmark has been run at the vendor's installation, you can insist in the contract that the same benchmark be run on the equipment installed at your site. The purpose for doing so is to insure that the equipment upon which the benchmark was tested is not different from the equipment that you had contracted for and expect to be delivered. It is recommended that no equipment be accepted and paid for until the benchmark agreed to by both parties has actually been demonstrated to your satisfaction to have been run on your equipment. The contract should contain the stipulation that the benchmark, when run on the equipment delivered to you, performs as agreed upon or as had been demonstrated previously by the vendor; in the event that the performance falls short, the vendor will supply at no additional cost such additional hardware and/or software as may be necessary to insure compliance with this performance criterion.

As a final note, renting versus purchase should have been considered as well as the alternative of leasing from a third party. With the rapid growth of networks imminent, it is reasonable to evaluate your needs in light of the possibility of attaching to a network. The total cost for service may be less than the acquisition of the new computer and the support of personnel needed to keep it running.

## BIBLIOGRAPHY

Primarily a source to relevant materials.

Bucci, R. A., Avoiding hassles with vendors, *Datamation* **20**(4), 68–72 (July 1974).
*Computer Characteristics: Infosystems* **21**(5), 39–47, 52–59 (May 1974), Hitchcock, Wheaton, Illinois.

*Computer Characteristics Quarterly*, Adams Associates, Inc., 128 The Great Road, Bedford, Massachusetts 01730.

*Computers, Control & Information Theory*, National Technical Information Service, Weekly Government Abstracts: 5285 Port Royal Road, Springfield, Virginia 22151. See, for example, D. W. Fife, K. Rankin, E. Fong, J. C. Walker, and B. A. Marron, *A technical index of interactive information systems*, WGA-62-74-25 134 (June 24, 1974).

DATAPRO Research Corp., *DATAPRO 70*, 1805 Underwood Blvd., Delran, New Jersey 08075.

Federal Information Processing Standards Publication Series, National Bureau of Standards, U.S. Department of Commerce, Washington, D.C. 20234. For example: FIPS PUB 21: (C13.52:21) *Common Business Oriented Language*(COBOL) (*Software Standard, Programming Language*).

More on synthetic benchmarks, in *EDP Performance Rev.* 2(5), 1–6 (May 1974), Applied Computer Research, 8808 North Central Avenue, Phoenix, Arizona 85020.

Timmreck, E. M., Computer selection methodology, *ACM Comput. Surv.* 5(4), 199–222 (December 1973).

*Don Mittleman*

# COMPUTERS AND STATISTICS— EVOLUTION OF THE INTERFACE

## INTRODUCTION

Today's world is characterized by an increasing dependence upon data for planning, operating, and monitoring, as well as for research. Expensive resources are used in data collection, and significant decisions await data analysis. This situation poses the challenge of effectively extracting information from a growing volume of data in order to make important decisions.

Computers store, retrieve, and process data, while statistics converts data into information to aid decisions. Wallis and Roberts [33] portray statistics as a collection of techniques for implementing the scientific method. Similarly, computer science and technology involve application of computers to the scientific method—and *vice versa*.

Computers and statistics have, therefore, become fundamental to both management and technical progress. The area of interaction—or interface—of computers and statistics may well become more essential than the interface of computers and any other discipline, except electrical engineering for its contribution to computer hardware and mathematics for its contribution to computer software.

There is considerable documentation on either computers or statistics separately, yet there is limited documentation on computers and statistics jointly—such as that in Refs. 11, 19, 20, 29, and 47. An introduction to the interface is presented under *American Statistical Association* in Volume 1 of this encyclopedia. What follows is a summary of the evolution of the interface with an historical survey and a recent status report.

The historical survey is divided into time periods which extend from an ancient Chinese abacus to Leibniz' calculating machine, from *Ars Conjectandi* of Bernoulli to the difference engine of Babbage, and from *Laws of Thought* by Boole to Univac I at the U.S. Bureau of the Census. It traces an interweaving of foundations for computer hardware and software with foundations for probability and statistics. Since many famous mathematicians have contributed to both computers and statistics, the interweaving has greater breadth and depth than one might expect.

Composition of the interface is described in terms of structural components. A discussion of interface activity is then followed by overviews of interface coverage by professional meetings and technical publications.


## ABACUS TO CALCULATING MACHINE

An initial connection between computers and statistics occurred in ancient China, where computers as well as probability have their roots. Around the sixth century B.C., the Chinese invented the bamboo rod abacus, primitive ancestor of the computer [37, Vol. 1]. The ancient Chinese also were probably the first to realize that a number's most natural representation is the binary abbreviation for its polynomial expansion in powers of two [24, Vol. 1]. Sun-Tze, who might have lived as early as the third century B.C., is credited with the first discussion of a problem involving probability [32]. This problem concerned the likelihood of an expected child being male.

Two connections between the theory of equations and probability happened in Renaissance Italy. In 1494, Pacioli published his *Summa de Arithmetica,* which summarized algebra as it then existed and signaled a general attack upon the cubic equation [32, 40]. Pacioli also composed a volume on double-entry bookkeeping [26] and introduced into mathematical literature the first probabilistic problem on gambling: how to divide stakes fairly between two players of unequal skill in a game interrupted before its logical conclusion [32]. Cardano published *Ars Magna*, a 1545 masterpiece on the theory of equations, as well as composing a handbook for gamblers called *De Ludo Aleae* [32].

During 1642, Pascal invented the first adding machine having toothed-wheel counters which carried numbers to the next column [45]. The 1645 correspondence between Pascal and another renowned French mathematician, Fermat, treated probability questions posed to Pascal by a prominent gambler named de Mere [32]. Among the questions posed was the problem of Pacioli [32]. In their correspondence, Pascal and Fermat "generalized the problem more and more, until at its close, that which had first appeared as a mere source of perplexity to a gambler had been elevated to a mathematical concept of great import" [32]. Fermat founded the theory of numbers as well as making great contributions to analytic geometry and calculus [4]. In addition, brief references to probability were made by Kepler and Galileo, two seventeenth century astronomers credited with substantial contributions to computational mathematics [28,32].

The well-known Dutch mathematician, Huygens, followed the Pascal-Fermat correspondence with *De Ratiociniis in Ludo Aleae* [32]. This small tract not only published the first probabilistic treatment for games of chance, but also stimulated Jacques Bernoulli and De Moivre in their subsequent work on probability [32]. *Horologium Oscillatorium,* Huygen's 1673 book on pendulum clocks, represents the most advanced state of calculus prior to Leibniz and Newton [28].

An impressive connection between computers and statistics is due to the eminent German mathematician, Leibniz. During 1671, he invented a calculating machine which added, substracted, multiplied, divided, and extracted roots [4, 24 (Vol. 1)]. Independent of Newton, Leibniz also developed his own version of the calculus, an accomplishment of great magnitude [4]. The combinatorial analysis contained in his *De Arte Combinatoria* was a link between primitive beginnings by Pascal and Fermat and the greatly refined versions termed laws of thought by Boole and symbolic logic by Whitehead and Russell.

## *ARS CONJECTANDI* TO DIFFERENCE ENGINE

Jacques Bernoulli was among the first to develop calculus significantly beyond Leibniz and Newton, as well as producing superb work on analytic geometry and the calculus of variations [4]. That so famous and well-rounded a mathematician wrote *Ars Conjectandi,* the first book devoted entirely to probability, testified to an importance already attained by the subject [32]. In addition, he anticipated the concept of inverse probability that is so essential to statistics [32]. Bernoulli and Leibniz, as did Pascal and Fermat before them, exchanged ideas through an extensive correspondence on both combinatorial analysis and calculus [28, 32].

Most of those discussed here are known primarily for their development of mathematics in general, and only secondarily for their development of probability or statistics. Although De Moivre made contributions to infinite series and trigonometry, he is valued for his contributions to probability [32]. De Moivre's *Doctrine of Chances* is essentially a gambler's manual, but his *Approximatio Summam Terminorum Binomii* $\overline{a + b}^n$ *in Seriem Expansi* of 1733 reveals him as the formulator for a law of errors and the discoverer of the normal distribution [32]. La Grange first suggested a sample survey around 1790, as well as being a major force behind analytical mechanics and the calculus of variations [18].

Emergence of probability from being merely a basis for analyzing games of chance to becoming a foundation for collecting and analyzing data had to await the related contributions of Legendre, Gauss, and Laplace [32]. Legendre initially published the method of least squares in 1806, yet Gauss had formulated it in an unpublished manuscript sent to Olbers in 1802 [4]. Through numerous works on astronomy and science, Gauss established a firm footing for the theory of errors in measurement, from which statistics has decended [32]. Laplace, with his *Theorie Analytique des Probabilities* of 1812 and *Essai Philosophique sur les Probabilities* of 1814, made a great advancement in probability [32]. He also made considerable progress in calculus and mathematical astronomy, which he called celestial mechanics [32]. Although Gauss was Legendre's superior in mathematical breadth and depth, they both made significant contributions to calculus, computation of tables, and the theory of numbers [28].

Babbage cofounded the Statistical Society of London, which later became the Royal Statistical Society, as well as conceiving difference and analytical engines during the 1820s and 1830s [22, 23]. Famous mathematicians who wrote important papers on probability and the theory of errors prior to 1850 include Bessel, Cauchy, DeMorgan, Fourier, Poisson, and Chebyshev [32]. In addition, probability was applied to computation of mortality tables and annuities by other well-known mathematicians such as Daniel Bernoulli, d'Alembert, Euler, and Halley [32].

## *LAWS OF THOUGHT* TO UNIVAC I

An increase in the collection of statistical data had occurred in parallel with the construction of a probabilistic basis for data analysis [32]. From these emerged two matched cornerstones of statistics: an empirical need for collecting and analyzing data, with a mathematical theory for treating randomness in data [32].

*Laws of Thought,* published by Boole in 1854, provided a mathematical basis for symbol logic, probability, and statistics [5].

Tabulation equipment has performed a statistical function since its invention by Hollerith in the 1880s. As a statistician and engineer, he was motivated by the U.S. Bureau of the Census to develop a mechanical means for processing 1890 census data [17]. His census machine utilized punched cards and is credited with saving the bureau $5,000,000 as well as with making census results available reasonably soon [37 (Vol. 4), 41]. Prior to 1890, the Baltimore Department of Health had used the first electrical tabulation equipment employing punched cards to handle vital statistics [17].

Hollerith himself constructed an electrical sorting machine and electrical keypunch machine before 1900, both perfected later by IBM [17, 37 (Vol. 4)]. Mechanical and electrical calculators evolved during the early twentieth century, with Pearson and Snedecor being representative of the many statisticians who utilized such equipment [32, 46]. As a matter of fact, Snedecor and Wallace— who later became a U.S. Vice President under Roosevelt—published the initial booklet on *Correlation and Machine Calculation* in 1925 [46].

Iowa State University, long a center of applied statistics, is now credited with being home to the first electronic digital computer [10]. Atanasoff not only invented the modern computer at Iowa State in 1939 [10], but also co-authored a 1936 paper on the use of statistical computing techniques to calculate complex spectra [2]. In addition, the University's Agricultural Experiment Station provided partial support for development of Atanasoff's computer, plus consistent support for the Statistical Laboratory headed by Snedecor [3].

The most eminent twentieth century mathematician making substantial contributions to both computers and statistics was von Neumann. In 1944 he and Morgenstern published the *Theory of Games and Economic Behavior,* which greatly influenced both social science and statistics [21]. A modern computer not only stores and processes data, but also stores and implements the software which defines this processing. Von Neumann was one of the pioneers in computer hardware and software, too, with such papers as "The General and Logical Theory of Automata" [24, Vol. 4].

In 1951, Remington Rand delivered the first commercial electronic digital computer, Univac I, to the Bureau of the Census [27]. The era of modern computers was also launched by a statistical application, creating the current interface of computers and statistics.

## COMPOSITION OF THE INTERFACE

The interface becomes more specific when viewed in terms of three structural components: computers for statistical purposes, statistics in computer functions, and computers and statistics within today's world. Measurement of computer systems yields a particularly relevant application area for statistics in computer functions. A summary is now given for the more detailed coverage of these components in Volume 1.

Utilization of computers for statistical purposes includes statistical analysis, table generation, and training. The first use of a modern computer for statistics was when the Bureau of the Census acquired Univac I during 1951. Since then, more and more data have been processed better and better, as well as faster and faster.

That significant dividends might result from applying statistics to computer functions is, however, a recent concept. Artificial intelligence, computer management, simulation, and text processing form a sampling of these applications. The growing requirement for management of computer systems generates a need for measurement of computer systems. Measurement provides not only a bridge between design promises and operational performance, but also needed guidance to computer management—an art in search of science.

The current significance of computers and statistics is described by the Introduction. As an illustration of this significance, a recent list of professional societies interested in data processing [36] includes:

American Institute of Certified Public Accountants, Association for Systems Management, and Society for Management Information Systems.

American Institute of Aeronautics and Astronautics, Biomedical Computing Society, and Institute of Electrical and Electronic Engineers.
Geoscience Information Society, Society for Data Educators, and Special Libraries Association.

They characterize the contribution, as well as the potential, of computers and statistics in today's world.


## ACTIVITY ON THE INTERFACE

Although computers were employed for statistical purposes in the 1950s, organization and characterization of that employment began in the 1960s. Activity revolved around the documentation and evaluation of statistical computer programs. Biomedical (BMD) Computer Programs [7] are the most used and influential package of such programs. Started in 1959, they were documented in 1961 [15] and have evolved into a virtual international standard.

A Statistics Subcommittee was initiated within the SHARE association of IBM computer users during 1960, becoming the Statistics Project in 1962, and the Statistical Methodology and Systems Project around 1963 [44, Vols. XVIII and XXI]. Serving as a center for cooperation in statistical computer programming, the project was the first organization on the interface.

A second organization concerned solely with the interface was the Statistical Program Evaluation Committee (SPEC), founded in Los Angeles during 1961. Its goals included documentation and evaluation of statistical programs, and it produced a bibliography of program abstracts [30] as well as a survey of problem solutions [25]. In addition, SPEC acquired affiliates around Buffalo during 1964 and around Seattle during 1965.

A British Working Party on Statistical Computing was organized following a 1966 meeting [6]. During 1968, the American Statistical Association (ASA) appointed a Committee on Computers in Statistics, which evolved into a Statistical Computing Section in 1971, as well as affiliating with the American Federation of Information Processing Societies (AFIPS).

Formed in 1964, the SHARE Hardware Evaluation Committee became the Computer Measurement and Evaluation Project in 1970 [44, Vol. XXXV], with some of its contributions being described by Hall [14]. Special Interest Groups on Measurement and Evaluation—called SIGMETRICS—were founded during 1971 by the Los Angeles Chapter of the Association for Computing Machinery (ACM), and then by ACM itself [12]. Across the Atlantic, the British Computer Society also organized a Performance Measurement Specialist Group in 1971 [12].


## PROFESSIONAL MEETINGS

The breadth of the interface is indicated by this composition and activity. On the other hand, papers presented at professional meetings and contained within technical publications characterize its depth in considerable detail. An overview of interface treatment at meetings is followed by one for publications.

ASA meetings from 1960 to 1972 and Computer Science and Statistics: Annual Symposia on the Interface from 1967 to 1972 are covered. This is complemented by a limited survey of 1960–1970 papers on statistics in computer functions from the Spring and Fall Joint Computer Conferences (SJCC and FJCC), as well as from selected ACM National Conferences and Conferences on Applications of Simulation (CAS). In addition, 1971 and 1972 meetings concerned with measurement of computer systems are summarized.

Among the pioneer sessions at ASA meetings were 1960 ones on computers in statistical research and statistical training for data processing [34, Vol. 14]. At the 1961 Meeting, there were groups of papers involving computer usage in social statistics, computer applications, and computers in statistical training [34, Vol. 15]. These were followed by the employment of computers for clinical research and programmed statistical instruction in 1962 [34, Vol. 16]. New data reduction processes, information storage and retrieval, plus computer uses in engineering and medicine were scheduled during 1963 [34, Vol. 17]. In 1964 there was an ASA session concerning problems of information systems [34, Vol. 18]. Computer uses in introductory statistics, simulation in marketing research, and computer techniques in biometry received treatment during 1965 [34, Vol. 19]. The 1966 Meeting included sessions about data retrieval metrics, design of statistical data banks, programmed instruction for statistics, and statistics in planning computer centers [34, Vol. 20]. That same year produced a paper on Markov models for computer systems at the SJCC [42, Vol. 28], as well as papers on a Markov data transmission system, decision functions for character recognition, and multinominal acceptance sampling at the ACM Conference [43, Vol. 21].

The Southern California Chapter of ASA, the Los Angeles Chapter of ACM, SPEC, and the University of California at Los Angeles joined to inaugurate an Annual Symposium on the Interface during 1967 [11]. The First Symposium had sessions covering artifical intelligence, computational linguistics, computer simulation, and interface applications [11]. Computer aids to statistical education, computer techniques, system analysis, applications on the interface, as well as jurimetrics—measurement and law—were included in the second one [11]. During 1969 the symposium involved biomathematics, computer science and technology, national information systems, problem-oriented languages, random number generation, simulation, and social applications [11].

There were sessions about the design of simulation experiments and computerized statistical systems at the 1967 ASA Meeting [34, Vol. 21]. The bridge between computers and statistics was a topic not only for ASA in 1967 and 1968, but also for ACM in 1969 [34 (Vols. 21 and 22), 43 (Vol. 24)]. Process control, a systems approach to marketing research, computers in statistics, plus the computer for teaching statistics were 1968 ASA subjects, too [34, Vol. 22]. In 1969 came computers and social science data analysis, graphical methods, computer-assisted simulation, and statistical computing [34, Vol. 23]. Joint Computer Conferences for 1967 and 1968 included failure detection probability and system reliability, statistical validation of software, statistics of JOSS performance, as well as analysis of experimental data on batch-processing versus time-sharing [42, Vols. 30–32]. ACM and CAS had 1969 papers involving reliability modeling of computer systems and statistical improvement of simulation efficiency [41 (Vol. 3), 43 (Vol. 24)].

The Fourth Interface Symposium scheduled workshops on biomedical statistics and computation, computer languages for statistics, computer science and statistics in secondary education, and statistics for measurement of computer systems—which led directly to formation of the Los Angeles ACM SIGMETRICS [11]. These were followed by decision sciences, extractive industries, higher education, measurement of computer systems, and time series at the 1971 Symposium [20]. Graphics, large-scale computer-aided statistics, management science, medical information storage and retrieval, numerical analysis, as well as consultation and education were covered during the Sixth Symposium [29].

Within 1970, ASA topics included algorithms for statistical computing, biomedical computation, computers in teaching statistics, data handling, and large-scale statistical information systems [34, Vol. 24]. The 1971 Meeting had sessions on communication between statisticians and computer personnel, exploitation of data-rich environments, information needs for financial analysis, interactive computing in statistics, and national criminal data systems [34, Vol. 25]. Analysis of variance programs, interactive graphics in statistics, national information banks, statistics for large data bases, plus new techniques of Monte Carlo simulation were scheduled in 1972 [34, Vol. 26].

A paper on statistical estimation of software running time was presented to the 1970 FJCC [42, Vol. 37]. There were sessions involving system evaluation and diagnostics at the 1971 SJCC [42, Vol. 38], operating system models and measures at the 1971 FJCC [43, Vol. 39], and system performance measurement and evaluation at the 1972 SJCC [42, Vol. 40], as well as a 2-day meeting on measurement of computer systems at the 1972 FJCC [12, 42 (Vol. 41)]. ACM sponsored a 1971 Workshop on System Performance Evaluation [9], a 1972 Conference on Proving Assertions about Programs [1], and a 1972 Symposium on Computer Program Test Methods [16]. Finally, 1971 and 1972 witnessed a Conference on Statistical Methods of Evaluation of Computer Systems [8], a Symposium on Effective versus Efficient Computing [13], plus two Princeton Conferences on Information Sciences and Systems with sessions about computer system models [31, Vols. 5 and 6].

## TECHNICAL PUBLICATIONS

An overview of relevant papers in ASA and ACM publications completes characterization of the interface. *The American Statistician* (AMSTAT) and *Journal of the American Statistical Association* (JASA) are covered from 1960 to 1972. In addition, a limited survey of 1960–1970 papers concerning statistics in computer functions was conducted in *Communications of the ACM* (CACM) and *Journal of the Association for Computing Machinery* (JACM).

AMSTAT contained an article about card tabulation by adding machine during 1960, as well as articles about statistics in post office automation and organizational plans for a university computing service during 1961 [34, Vols. 14 and 15]. There was a bibliography of simulation, gaming, artificial intelligence, and related topics within the 1960 JASA [38, Vol. 55]. In 1960 and 1962, JACM had papers involving probabilistic indexing and information retrieval, and combinatorial properties of searching and sorting [39, Vols. 7 and 9].

Computational forms of chi-square and roundoff error for regression analysis appeared within the 1964 AMSTAT, while using a computer as an instructional tool for statistics appeared within the 1965 AMSTAT [34, Vols. 18 and 19]. In 1966, JASA published papers dealing with computer editing of survey data and a computer method to calculate Kendall's tau [38, Vol. 61]. CACM presented least squares analysis on small computers, probabilistic models for roundoff errors, design of simulation experiments, plus statistics in time-sharing systems during 1965 and 1966 [35, Vols. 8 and 9]. *A priori* probabilities for character recognition, statistical pattern recognition, statistical complexity in algorithms, and a queuing model of sequential computers were treated by JACM for 1964–1966 [39, Vols. 11–13].

AMSTAT provided coverage of design for a federal statistical data center, privacy for a national data center, and programmed instruction for statistics within 1967; the computer and economic analysis, a British Working Party on Statistical Computing, an historical perspective on the interface, computers and social science statisticians, statistical analysis on time-shared computers, and statistical research on time-sharing computers within 1968; and computerized data generation for teaching statistics within 1969 [34, Vols. 21–23]. This coverage was complemented by JASA which dealt with automatic data editing, an autoregressive Monte Carlo study, least squares computer programs, experimental design in computer simulation, and computer simulation of the textile industry during 1967; time-shared computers in a statistics curriculum and optimal linkage for records during 1968; and computerized error inspection plans and inspection of correction error for data processing during 1969 [38, Vols. 62–64].

There were four articles on experimental comparison of time-sharing versus batch-processing systems, two articles on statistical analysis of simulation experiments, and articles on both hardware and software behavior in CACM during 1967, 1968, and 1969 [35, Vols. 10–12]. Five papers concerning probability in software and system models, and two papers concerning statistical estimation of software characteristics appeared in the 1967, 1968, and 1969 JACM [39, Vols. 14–16].

AMSTAT produced articles on design and appraisal of statistical information systems and principles of processing statistical data in 1970, as well as an article on time-shared computer systems as a teaching tool in 1972 [34, Vols. 24 and 26]. There were JASA papers treating the accuracy of least squares computer programs within 1970; random normal number generation, roundoff error in least squares regression plus Monte Carlo investigation of robustness within 1971; and Monte Carlo study for analysis of variance and competing rank tests, a simple algorithm to generate binomial random variables for large $n$, simulating the small sample properties of econometric estimators, plus test data for least squares and analysis of variance algorithms within 1972 [38, Vols. 65–67]. CACM published 1970 articles involving application of sequential sampling to simulation and probability distributions for computer communication models [35, Vol. 13]. Finishing the publication survey, there were three papers about queuing theory for computer systems and one about statistical properties of the buddy system in JACM for 1970 [39, Vol. 17].

## ACKNOWLEDGMENTS

Gratefully acknowledged are the critical review of this article by Theodore Bancroft, Herman Chernoff, Joseph Daly, Wilfrid Dixon, William Kennedy, Louis Robinson, and John Tauchi; the assistance of John Lehman, Edgar Bisgyer, and the American Statistical Association staff in obtaining information on ASA meetings and publications; as well as the personal research by Theodore Bancroft on Atanasoff at Iowa State University.

## REFERENCES

1.  Adams, J. M., J. B. Johnston, and R. H. Stark (eds.), *Proceedings of the ACM Conference on Proving Assertions about Programs*, ACM Special Interest Groups on Programming Languages and on Automata and Computability Theory, New York, 1972.
2.  Atanasoff, J. V., and A. E. Brandt, Application of punched card equipment to the analysis of complex spectra, *J. Opt. Soc. Am.* **26**(2), 83–88 (1936).
3.  Bancroft, T. A., Personal correspondence with Arnold F. Goodman, March 6, April 1, and May 7, 1974.
4.  Bell, E. T., *Men of Mathematics*, Simon and Schuster, New York, 1937.
5.  Boole, G., *Laws of Thought*, Dover, New York (American printing of 1854 edition).
6.  Chambers, J. M., A British Working Party on Statistical Computing, *Am. Stat.* **22**(2), 19–20 (1968)
7.  Dixon, W. J. (ed.), *BMD: Biomedical Computer Programs*, 3rd ed., University of California Press, Los Angeles, 1973.
8.  Freiberger, W. F. (ed.), *Statistical Computer Performance Evaluation*, Academic, New York, 1972.
9.  Gagliardi, U. O. (ed.), *Workshop on System Performance Evaluation*, ACM Special Interest Group on Operating Systems, New York, 1971.
10. Gardner, W. D., Will the inventor of the first digital computer please stand up, *Datamation* **20**(2), 84–90 (1974).
11. Goodman, A. F. (ed.), *Computer Science and Statistics: 4th Annual Symposium on the Interface—An Interpretative Summary*, Western Periodicals, North Hollywood, California, 1971.
12. Goodman, A. F., Measurement of computer systems—An introduction, in *Proceedings of the 1972 Fall Joint Computer Conference*, pp. 669–680.

13. Gruenberger, F. (ed.), *Effective versus Efficient Computing,* Prentice-Hall, Englewood Cliffs, New Jersey, 1973.
14. Hall, G. (ed.), *Computer Measurement and Evaluation: Selected Papers from the SHARE Project,* SHARE, New York, 1972.
15. Hayward, L. C. (ed.), *BIMD Computer Programs Manual,* School of Medicine, University of California, Los Angeles, 1961.
16. Hetzel, W. C. (ed.), *Program Testing Methods,* Prentice-Hall, Englewood Cliffs, New Jersey, 1972.
17. Horn, J., Ready-read card, *Datamation* **11**(5). 59 (1965).
18. Kendall, M. G., Measurement in the study of society, in *Man and the Social Sciences* (W. A. Robson, ed.), Allen and Unwin, London, 1972, pp. 133–147.
19. Kennedy, W. J. (ed.), *Proceedings of Computer Science and Statistics: 7th Annual Symposium on the Interface,* Iowa State University, Ames, 1974.
20. Locks, M. O. (ed.), *Proceedings of Computer Science and Statistics: 5th Annual Symposium on the Interface,* Western Periodicals, North Hollywood, California, 1972.
21. Luce, R. D., and H. Raiffa, *Games and Decisions,* Wiley, New York, 1958.
22. Morrison, P., and E. Morrison, The strange life of Charles Babbage, *Sci. Am.* **186**(4), 66–73 (1952).
23. Mullett, C. F., Charles Babbage: A scientific gadfly, *Sci. Mon.* **67**(11), 361–371 (1948).
24. Newman, J. R. (ed.), *The World of Mathematics,* Simon and Schuster, New York, 1956.
25. Robison, D. E. (ed.), *Bibliography of Statistical Problems,* Statistical Program Evaluation Committee, Los Angeles, 1966.
26. Sage, D. M., Information systems: A brief look into history, *Datamation* **14**(11), 63–69 (1968).
27. Schussel, G., IBM versus REMRAND, *Datamation* **11**(5 and 6), 54–57 and 58–66 (1965).
28. Struik, D. J., *A Concise History of Mathematics,* Dover, New York, 1948.
29. Tarter, M. E. (ed.), *Proceedings of Computer Science and Statistics: 6th Annual Symposium on the Interface,* Western Periodicals, North Hollywood, California, 1973.
30. Tauchi, H. J. (ed.), *Abstracts of Statistical Computer Programs,* Statistical Program Evaluation Committee, Los Angeles, 1965.
31. Van Valkenburg, M. E., et al. (eds.), *Proceedings of the Princeton Conference on Information Sciences and Systems,* Vols. 5 and 6, Princeton University, Princeton, New Jersey, 1971 and 1972.
32. Walker, H. M., *Studies in the History of Statistical Method,* Williams and Wilkins, Baltimore, 1929.
33. Wallis, W. A., and H. V. Roberts, *Statistics: A New Approach,* Free Press, Glencoe, Illinois, 1957.
34. *American Statistician* **41–26**(1960–1972).
35. *Communications of the ACM* **3–13**(1960–1970).
36. *Computerworld* **8**(6), 27 (1974).
37. *Encyclopaedia Britannica,* Encyclopaedia Britannica, Chicago, 1961.
38. *Journal of the American Statistical Association* **55–67** (1960–1972).
39. *Journal of the Association for Computing Machinery* **7–17** (1960–1970).
40. *Mathematics (Life Science Library),* Time, Inc., New York, 1963.

41. *Proceedings of the Conference on Applications of Simulation,* Vol. 3, ACM et al., 1969.
42. *Proceedings of the Joint Computer Conference,* Vols. 28–41, AFIPS Conference Proceedings, 1966–1972.
43. *Proceedings of the National Conference,* Vols. 21–24, ACM, 1966–1969.
44. *Proceedings of SHARE Meetings,* Vols. XVIII–XXXV, SHARE, New York, 1962–1970.
45. *The Quiet Revolution: Computers Come of Age,* AFIPS, New York, 1965.
46. Cox, G. M., and P. G. Homeyer, Professional and personal glimpses of George W. Snedecor, *Biometrics* **31**(2), 265–301 (1975).
47. Frane, J. W. (ed.), *Proceedings of Computer Science and Statistics: 8th Annual Symposium on the Interface,* University of California, Los Angeles, 1975.

*Arnold F. Goodman*

# COMPUTING REVIEWS

*See* Association for Computing Machinery

# CONCURRENT PROCESSING

## INTRODUCTION

Developments and growth in computer technology have resulted largely in response to the insatiable demand for faster speed of processing, efficiency of system operation, cheaper cost of computation, and increased system reliability.

While progress has been made in various facets of the technology, the most perceptible developments have been realized in terms of faster speed of processing and decreasing component size. Thus, while the first generation systems with vacuum tube technology, electrostatic tubes, and delay line memory operated in the speed range of milliseconds, their second generation offsprings with transistor technology and magnetic drum and core memory operated in the microsecond range, thereby yielding a speed gain of a factor of 1000. On the other hand, the third generation systems which use integrated circuit technology and semiconductor memory have an appreciable speed gain of a factor of 10 to 100 over their second generation counterparts. The current (late third generation or early fourth) generation systems, using the more advanced large scale integration (LSI) technology have a speed and size advantage over the third generation systems but the factor of difference is not quite as impressive as the difference between the earlier generations. The growth trend (in speed and size) from the first to the current generation is thus observed to mimic an exponential decay, indicating that achievable speed is approaching its maximum limit.

At the same time that we are approaching this limit, the demand for increased computational power mounts, coupled with demands for improved system efficiency, reliability, and cheaper cost of computation. With realizable increases in unit speed being very limited, increased computational power can only be attained through concurrency (parallelism) of operations at both the hardware and software levels. This realization has resulted in the plotting of a new course in the computer growth trend which is reflected in the current generation system's incorporation of myriads of innovations in their organization and the engineering of their supporting software systems in order to achieve a high degree of concurrency and thereby achieve increased computational power. This is evidenced in the rich diversity inherent in their architecture which boasts such features as multiprocessing, parallel processing, pipe lining, and computer networks with operating systems which are capable of supporting different modes of multiprogramming and providing facilities for interprocess communication, dynamic resource sharing, and mutual exclusion of concurrent processes in order to ensure the determinacy of their computational results.

Third generation computer architecture reflects a strong trend toward concurrency (parallelism) of operations, i.e., the simultaneous execution of several computations or processes. Common characteristics of this processing style include: (1) concurrent activity among the central processor and the supporting pseudoprocessors (channels and controllers) and peripheral devices; (2) dynamic resource specification, allocation, and sharing among concurrent processes; (3) communication among concurrent processes that may be cooperating toward the completion of a common task; and (4) the operating system acting as a control program for the coordination of these parallel activities.

**The Process Concept**

Since the process concept is essential to the following discussion, it is necessary to clarify this concept. In order to lend a flexible and yet concrete handle for the understanding of system functions and the formalization of the coordination activities of the operating system, the process concept has been advanced as an abstraction of a processor's activity. Since the operations within a computing system consist of several computations which progress almost independently (e.g., activities by I/O devices, channels, controllers, and processors), the process concept is a formalization of these independent computations

CONCURRENT PROCESSING

viewed as activities generated by independent (sometimes potentially dependent) program units. Several related definitions have been given in the literature. For example, Saltzer defined process as, "program in execution on a pseudo-processor"; Dennis and Van Horn, "Locus of control within an instruction sequence"; Horning and Randell, "sequence of program states." To lend a flavor incorporating the process execution environment, Tsichritzis offers the following definition; "processes are independent computations which execute concurrently and at varying speeds." For the purpose of the ensueing discussion, the simple definition, "a program in execution," will suffice.

Through this definition, we can differentiate between a program as a static sequence of instruction codes as distinct from a process which is the product of the execution of these static codes, giving rise to the activation of certain activities or the occurrence of certain events within the computational environment. Based on this definition then, we can view a process as an active and dynamic entity capable of being in one of several states at any instant of time, with state transitions being effected by certain events. Following the creation of a process and prior to its termination, a process can be in one of three possible states. A process is said to be in the active or running state when it has control of the (or a) processor and the corresponding code is being executed. A process is in the blocked state if it is waiting for the occurrence of some event in order to become active. A process is in the ready state if it is neither logically blocked nor running. For each process, a state vector or process control block, which is a description of its state (at any instant of time), is defined.

**Concurrent Processes**

Within a system we can see several processes in different states at any given time. Thus one process in a uniprocessor environment may be active while another one is waiting for the completion of an I/O request, and yet another may be in the ready state waiting for its turn at the processor. While several processes can be in the ready and blocked state at the same instant of time, only one can be in the active state in a uniprocessor environment. However, in a multiprocessor environment it is possible to have as many tasks as there are processors in the active state at the same time. All these processes that exist at the same time within the system are called concurrent processes. More formally, a set of concurrent processes is defined as two or more processes, all of which are simultaneously in some state of execution; i.e., each member process has been created and its execution has not yet been terminated (Graham), or their execution overlap in time (Hansen). With this definition it must be noted that the ability to have a set of concurrent processes does not require multiprocessing, only multiprogramming. Furthermore, each process operates at an unknown and unpredictable rate. This is an important property of concurrent processes that will be discussed in the later sections.

The set of concurrent processes can be divided into two groups: those that are logically independent or disjoint and those that cooperate toward the completion of common tasks. Disjoint processes interact indirectly by competing for system resources, and therefore the operating system must be responsible for the coordination and control of their concurrency. On the other hand, in addition to competing for system resources, nondisjoint concurrent processes interact directly by sharing common information (variables, data bases, and buffers) and by passing messages. Since this form of direct interaction can be conducted between processes independent of the operating system, the control of concurrency must be explicitly expressed in the process implementation.

## COORDINATION OF CONCURRENT PROCESSES

### Determinacy

A critical requirement of computations in a concurrent environment is that of determinacy, i.e., ensuring the uniqueness of the result of a computation despite variations in task execution rates and the order of task executions (Coffman and Denning). Madnick and Donovan use the term "race condition" to describe the same problem—"A race condition occurs when the scheduling of two or more processes is so critical that the various orders of scheduling them result in different computations." In other words, since processes are asynchronous in nature, the same process must yield exactly the same results no matter how fast or slow it executes and no matter how the order of scheduling its execution is varied in relationship to other processes in the system. This implies that we can make no assumption about the speed at which concurrent processes are executed as the execution of their subtasks can be interleaved and overlapped in an unspecified order. A task system satisfying the determinacy requirement is said to be determinate. A nondeterminate task system can be made determinate by introducing the necessary precedence constraints between the tasks. Coffman and Denning have shown that task systems consisting of mutually disjoint tasks are determinate and, further, that disjointness is a sufficient condition for determinacy.

### Control Problems

Four different but not mutually exclusive problems in the control of concurrent processes can be identified, namely: synchronization, mutual exclusion, coordination of explicit communication between cooperating processes, and the deadlock problem. Most authors in the literature treat the synchronization problem synonymously with the general problem of coordinating concurrent processes. However, Coffman and Denning treat the synchronization problem as that of timing and sequencing. They define synchronization as "the implementation of the requirement that certain task executions be ordered in time." The mutual exclusion problem arises when processes share access to common data or variables. In this respect we can define a critical section as "a set of instructions in which the result of execution may vary unpredictably if variables referenced in the section and available to other concurrent processes are changed during its execution'' (Freeman). Thus the mutual exclusion of processes with respect to a critical section is the requirement that no more than one process can be in its critical section at any given time. Communication problems involve the control of exchange of messages through message buffers common to two or more processes. Deadlock is ''the situation in which one or more processes within a system are blocked forever due to requirements which can never be met'' (Holt). The term deadlock has also been commonly referred to as deadly embrace (Madnick and Donovan, Dijkstra).

From the above definitions it is seen that problems of synchronization are common to deadlock and communications, and to mutual exclusion to a lesser degree. In order to prevent deadlock, it is necessary that some precedence constraints be imposed among the common set of resources. While access to critical sections by mutually excluded processes must be ordered in time, the precise ordering need not, however, be specified. In unit-size message buffer systems, precedence relation is mandated in that a message must be sent into the buffer before it can be received. Therefore, ordering of buffer access must follow the strict sequence: sender, receiver, sender, receiver. . . . However, in an $n$-size ($n > 1$) buffer system, this precedence requirement can be relaxed. In the following discussion we shall treat synchronization commonly with mutual exclusion, communication, and deadlock, in that order.

## The Mutual Exclusion Problem

As stated above, the mutual exclusion problem arises when two or more processes must access the same data base, set of instructions, or variables. We have defined such a common set of codes as a critical section. Two simple examples will demonstrate this problem.

**Example 1.** Consider an airline reservation system in which salesclerks operating from different terminal consoles (possibly distributed over a wide geographical area) must access a common data base in order to sell tickets and confirm flight reservations. The following sequence of events may take place:

1. Salesclerk A interrogates the data base and discovers that there is only one seat remaining on a flight with total capacity of $n$ seats.
2. Salesclerk B also interrogates the data base and finds that $n - 1$ reservations have been made.
3. Salesclerk A confirms a reservation for his customer, changing the total number of confirmed reservations to $n$.
4. Salesclerk B also confirms a reservation for his customer and changes the total number of confirmed reservations to $n$.

Meanwhile, the system indicates $n$ reservations made but, actually, $n + 1$ tickets have been sold. This errant behavior is obviously due to unrestricted concurrent access to the same data base by more than one process. All that needs be done to solve this problem is to restrict access to the data base so that only one salesclerk can access it at any given time.

**Example 2.** A situation similar to the above arises when two different processes execute the following code sequence:

LOAD $X$
ADD 1
STORE $X$

It is possible for the first process to load the current value of $X$ into a register and to be interrupted (placed in the ready state) as a result of the occurrence of a hardware interrupt. This would result in the current value of $X$, contained in a register, being placed in the process' control block. Meanwhile, the second process gains control and executes the three instructions, thereby storing a value of $X + 1$ as the new value of location $X$. When the first process gains control again, his registers are restored and he proceeds to execute the second and third instructions, using the old value of $X$. Thus the final value at location $X$ remains $X + 1$ instead of $X + 2$. The generalization of this problem to $n$ processes in a $n$-parallel processor environment will yield a new value of $X$ ranging between $X + 1$ to $X + n$. Thus the result of the computation is indeterminate. Again, the solution is to treat the sequence of codes as a critical section and to restrict access to one process at a time.

This problem was first observed by Dijkstra, and the first solution was proposed by Dijkstra and Knuth. In the following discussion, we shall follow the logical development presented by Dijkstra in order to develop the necessary control structures for ensuring mutual exclusion to critical sections. The following conditions and assumptions will hold true throughout the ensuing discussion:

1. No assumptions can be made about the relative speed of the processes.
2. Apart from the moments of explicit intercommunication (entrance into critical sections), the individual processes are to be regarded as completely independent of each other.
3. Setting the value of a memory location or reading a value out is an indivisible operation. This implies that if two processes try to store into the same memory location, the accessing mechanism will ensure that the operations are completed one at a time so that the final result will be the value stored by one of the processes rather than a mixture of both values. Similarly, when one process inspects the value of a variable simultaneously with an assignment to the variable by another process, then the former process will find either the old or the new value, but never a mixture.

The analysis is based on the operation of two cyclic processes, say Proc1 and Proc2. In each cycle, a critical section occurs so that at any moment only one of the two processes is allowed to be engaged in its critical section where they have access to a number of common variables. The examples are expressed in ALGOL 60 with extended constructs to allow the description of parallelism of execution (ALGOL 60 symbols are capitalized). The extended constructs are ALGOL-block oriented and of the form:

PARBEGIN $S1$; $S2$; . . . ; $SN$; PAREND

where $S1, S2, . . . , SN$ are ALGOL statements and the above parallel compound implies that $S1, S2, . . . , SN$ are to be executed in parallel and only when they are all finished will the execution of the next statement commence. For example, the extended ALGOL 60 compound statement:

BEGIN $S1$; PARBEGIN $S2$; $S3$; $S4$; PAREND; $S5$; END

corresponds to the execution sequence of Fig. 1, which means that after the completion of $S1$, the statements $S2$, $S3$, and $S4$ are to be executed in parallel and when they have all been finished then statement $S5$ can be executed.

**Proposed First Solution**

```
BEGIN INTEGER turn;
   turn := 1;
   PARBEGIN
   Proc1:      BEGIN   L1:      IF turn = 2 THEN GOTO L1;
                                critical section 1;
                                turn := 2;
                                remainder of cycle 1;
                                GOTO L1;
               END;
   Proc. 2:    BEGIN   L2:      IF turn = 1 THEN GOTO L2;
                                critical section 2;
                                turn := 1;
                                remainder of cycle 2;
                                GOTO L2;
               END;
   PAREND;
END;
```

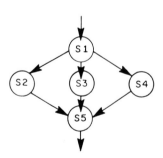

**Fig. 1.** Execution sequence.

A close examination of this solution will reveal that the processes communicate through the common variable "turn," the value of which indicates which of the two processes is next to enter (or is in) its critical section. After the first assignment of 1 to "turn," the only possible sequence of values is 1, 2, 1, 2, corresponding to the alternating sequence Proc1, Proc2, Proc1, Proc2, of access to the respective critical sections. This synchronized sequence violates the process independence condition because it is now possible for one process to hold up the other indefinitely if the former is held up well outside its critical section. In order to avoid this undesirable situation, we must impose the following condition:

4. If one of the processes is stopped well outside its critical section, this must not lead to the potential blocking of the other process. The following solution adheres to this condition:

**Second Solution**

```
BEGIN INTERGER C1, C2;
   C1 := 1;  C2 := 1;
   PARBEGIN
   Proc1:      BEGIN   L1:    IF C2 = 0 THEN GOTO L1;
                              C1 := 0;
                              critical section 1;
                              C1 := 1;
                              remainder of cycle 1;
                              GOTO L1;

               END;
   Proc2:      BEGIN   L2:    IF C1 = 0 THEN GOTO L2;
                              C2 := 0;
                              critical section 2;
                              C2 := 1;
                              remainder of cycle 2;
                              GOTO L2;

               END;
   PAREND:
END:
```

This solution uses two common variables $C1$ and $C2$ to indicate the state of the processes (value 0 indicating that the corresponding process is in its critical section, while value 1 indicates a process is outside its critical section). With this solution, a process outside its critical section can no longer hold up the second process waiting to enter its critical section. But now, this solution raises a new problem: Suppose Proc1 performs the test, "$C2 = 0$," and finds $C2 \neq 0$ at the same time that Proc2 performs the test "$C1 = 0$," finding $C1 \neq 0$, then it is possible for both processes to enter their critical sections at the same time. This solution is definitely unacceptable! Let us consider the following alternative solution:

**Third Solution**

```
BEGIN INTEGER C1, C2;
   C1 := 1;  C2 := 1;
   PARBEGIN
   Proc1:      BEGIN   A1:    C1 := 0;
                       L1:    IF C2 = 0 THEN GOTO L1;
                              critical section 1;
                              C1 := 1;
                              remainder of cycle 1;
                              GOTO A1;
               END:
   Proc2:      BEGIN:  A2:    C2 ;= 0;
                       L2:    IF C1 = 0 THEN GOTO L2;
                              critical section 2;
                              C2 := 1;
                              remainder of cycle 2;
                              GOTO A2;
               END;
   PAREND;
END;
```

Without any doubt, this solution does guarantee mutual exclusion but it raises the possibility of both processes blocking each other indefinitely. This situation can arise if Proc1 sets $C1 := 0$ at the same time Proc2 sets $C2 := 0$. Then at statement $L1$, Proc1 finds that $C2 = 0$, implying that Proc2 is already in its critical section; while Proc2 at $L2$ similarly reaches the conclusion that Proc1 is already in its critical section. Consequently, both processes end up waiting for each other and neither of them ever gets to its critical section. This problem is remedied in the following solution:

**Fourth Solution**

```
BEGIN INTEGER C1, C2;
   C1 := 1;  C2 := 1;
   PARBEGIN
   Proc1:      BEGIN   L1:    C1 := 0;
                              IF C2 = 0 THEN
                                 BEGIN C1 := 1; GOTO L1; END;
                              critical section 1;
                              C1 := 1;
                              remainder of cycle 1;
                              GOTO L1;
               END;
```

Proc2:    BEGIN   *L*2:    $C2 := 0$;
IF $C1 = 0$ THEN
   BEGIN $C2 := 1$; GOTO *L*2; END;
critical section 2;
$C2 := 1$;
remainder of cycle 2:
GOTO *L*2;

    END;

PAREND;

END;

This solution appears to be safe, but on closer study we detect that it has the potential to lead to a deadlock (blocking indefinitely) if both processes happen to proceed uniformly. Remember, we are not allowed to make any assumptions about the speed of execution of the processes. Therefore, if the processes proceed in a uniform manner, the solution will lead to an "after-you," "after you," . . . type of situation. The following correct solution is credited to the Dutch mathematician, Th. J. Dekker. The solution is similar to the above solution but adds the "turn" variable of the first solution. The reader should prove that this solution is indeed correct.

**Fifth Solution**

BEGIN INTEGER $C1$, $C2$, turn;
  $C1 := 1$;  $C2 := 1$;  turn := 1;
  PARBEGIN
  Proc1:    BEGIN   *A*1:    $C1 := 0$;
                     *L*1:    IF $C2 = 0$ THEN
                         BEGIN    IF turn $= 1$ THEN GOTO *L*1;
                                     $C1 := 1$;
                     *B*1:    IF turn $= 2$ THEN GOTO *B*1;
                         GOTO *A*1;
                       END:
                  critical section 1;
                  turn := 2; $C1 := 1$;
                  remainder of cycle 1;
                  GOTO *A*1;
        END;
  Proc2:    BEGIN   *A*2:    $C2 := 0$;
                     *L*2:    IF $C1 = 0$ THEN
                         BEGIN    IF turn $= 2$ THEN GOTO *L*2;
                                     $C2 := 1$;
                     *B*2:    IF turn $= 1$ THEN GOTO *B*2;
                       GOTO *A*2;
                     END:

```
                              critical section 2;
                              turn := 1;   C2 := 1;
                              remainder of cycle 2;
                              GOTO A2;
            END;
    PAREND;
END;
```

## The Generalized Mutual Exclusion Problem

The above problem and its solution can be generalized to the case of $n$ cyclic processes, each with its own critical section. Maintaining the preconditions specified above, the following solution will handle the case of $n$ processes:

```
BEGIN INTEGER ARRAY b, c[0:n];
    INTEGER turn;
    FOR turn := 0 STEP 1 UNTIL n DO
      BEGIN b[turn] := 1; c[turn] := 1; END;
    turn := 0;
    PARBEGIN
    Proc1:BEGIN . . . END;
    Proc2: BEGIN . . . END;
       ⋮
    Procn: BEGIN . . . END;
    PAREND;
END;
```

The $n$ processes are similar and the structure of the $i$th process is as follows:

```
Proci:      BEGIN INTEGER j;
        Ai:      b[i] := 0;
        Li:      IF turn = i THEN
                 BEGIN C[i] := 1;
                    IF b[turn] = 1 THEN turn := i;
                    GOTO Li;
                 END;
                 C[i] := 0;
                 FOR j := 1 STEP 1 UNTIL n DO
                    BEGIN IF j = i AND c[j] = 0 THEN GOTO Li,
                    END;
                 critical section i;
                 turn := 0; c[i] := 1; b[i] := 1;
                 remainder of cycle i
                 GOTO Ai;
            END;
```

The reader should show:

1. That at any moment, at most one of the processes is engaged in its critical section.
2. That the decision as to which of the processes is the first to enter its critical section cannot be postponed indefinitely.
3. That stopping a process outside of its critical section has no effect upon the other processes.

## The Synchronizing Primitives

Though the above solution gets the job done, it gets it done in the most tedious and inefficient way. First, the code for the coordination of the parallel processes is too complex. Second, each process waiting to enter its critical section must continually check to see whether certain variables have some desired values. In other words, while they are waiting, they remain busy using the processor without yielding any productive computation. This is called a "busy form of waiting." What is required is a control mechanism (or mechanisms) that will put a waiting process to sleep if it cannot enter its critical section and wake up a sleeping process the moment an active process exits from its critical section.

The control mechanisms proposed by Dijkstra consist of the following:

1. Special-purpose nonnegative integers called semaphores.
2. Two new primitives, called the $P$-operation and the $V$-operation, which operate on semaphores and represents the only way in which the processes may access the semaphores.

The $P$-operation is an operation with one argument which must be a semaphore. Thus if $S$ is a semaphore, then $P(S)$ is a $P$-operation on $S$. The effect of $P$ is to decrease the value of $S$ by 1 as soon as the resulting value would be nonnegative, i.e.,

$P(S)$:    if $S > 0$,    then $S := S - 1$
           if $S = 0$,    then wait for completion of operation

The checking and the eventual decrementation of $S$ is considered to be an indivisible operation so that once initiated, the operation cannot be interrupted until concluded.

The $V$-operation is also an operation with one argument which must be a semaphore. The effect of $V$ is to increment its operand by 1; this incrementation operation being regarded as an indivisible operation,

$$V(S): S := S + 1$$

The $P$-operation represents the potential delay—when a process initiates a $P$-operation on a semaphore that has a value 0, the $P$-operation cannot be completed until some other process has completed a *V*-operation on the same semaphore, thereby giving it the value 1. At that moment, more than one process may have initiated a *P*-operation on the semaphore. The indivisibility requirement of the operation implies that only one of the initiated *P*-operations will be allowed to be completed. Which one remains unspecified.

The following is a solution of the generalized *n*-process mutual exclusion problem. The solution uses a semaphore "free" in which,

free = 1 means:   none of the processes is engaged in its critical section
free = 0 means:   one of the processes is engaged in its critical section

```
BEGIN INTEGER free;
   free := 1;
   PARBEGIN
   Proc1:        BEGIN . . . END;
   Proc2:        BEGIN . . . END;
     ⋮
   Procn:        BEGIN . . . END;
   PAREND;
END
```

```
Proci:           BEGIN
            Li:     P (free);
                    critical section i;
                    V(free);
                    remainder of cycle i;
                    GOTO Li;
                 END;
```

## The General Semaphore

The semaphores used as operands in the above synchronizing primitives are called binary semaphores in that they can only assume 0, 1 values and are never negative. We can define general semaphores which are capable of having a wider range of values (both positive and negative values). These semaphores are very useful in the general problem of resource allocation. In this context, we can define the *P* and *V* operations as follows:

$P(s)$:   $S := S - 1$;   if $S < 0$, then put the process executing $P$ to sleep in the queue associated with $S$ (say $QS$)

$V(s)$:   $S := S + 1$;   if $S > 0$, then wake up some process from $\bar{Q}S$ and activate it

An important property of these primitives is that a positive value of the semaphore indicates how many units of the resource is available while a negative value indicates how many processes are on the waiting list requesting usage of the resource. Consequently, in this context, the semaphores are referred to as counting semaphores which count the number of requests for the resource it is protecting. As an illustration of the usage of the general semaphores, let us look at the producer–consumer problem.

The producer–consumer problem can be illustrated by the interaction between two processes or two classes of processes. The first class of processes generate records of information to be processed and printed by the second class of processes. To ensure correct operation, we must prevent a producer process from trying to deposit a record at the same time that a consumer process is trying to remove a record. It is assumed that both processes communicate through a common buffer which at any time contains the records that have been produced but not yet processed. The operations of a producer process and a consumer process can be described as follows:

Producer:
$Pi$:        BEGIN
                preduce record;
                deposit record;
                go to $Pi$;
            END

Consumer:
$Ci$:        BEGIN
                remove record;
                process record;
                go to $Ci$;
            END;

The following points in the operation of the processes must be carefully noted:

1. Simultaneous access to the buffer by both the producer (at statement, "deposit record") and the consumer (statement, "remove record") must not be allowed. This implies that the statement "deposit record" can only be executed in a critical section associated with the producer process. Similarly, the statement "remove record" must belong in a critical section associated with the consumer process.
2. When the record buffer is empty, it must be impossible for a consumer process to remove a nonexistent record. Therefore, when access to an empty buffer is attempted by a consumer process, the process must be put to sleep to be awakened at a later time when a producer process deposits a record.
3. We assume a buffer of infinite size so that it is always possible for the producer process to deposit a record in the buffer once it gains access to the buffer.

We shall use the binary semaphore "buffer" to insure mutual exclusion of access to the buffer and the general semaphore "count" to indicate the count of records in the buffer. Thus the producer cycle follows the sequence: produce record, gain access to buffer (critical section), add record to buffer, free the buffer ($V$(buffer)), and increment the record count ($V$(count)). The consumer cycle involves: first checking that the count is positive ($P$(count)), gain access to buffer ($P$(buffer)), remove a record, release the buffer ($V$(buffer)), and then proceed to process the record. The solution of the producer–consumer problem is as follows (we shall show only the cycle for the $i$th producer and consumer):

```
BEGIN INTEGER count, buffer;
    count := 0;
    buffer := 1;
    PARBEGIN
      Producer:
        Pi:           BEGIN
                        produce next record;
                        P(buffer);
                        deposit record;
                        V(buffer);
                        V(count);
                        GOTO Pi;
                      END;

      Consumer:
        Ci:           BEGIN
                        P(count);
                        P(buffer);
                        remove a record;
                        V(buffer);
                        process record;
                        GOTO Ci;
                      END;
    PAREND;
END;
```

The use of the general semaphore is very convenient, otherwise it is superfluous and any control operation that can be implemented using a general semaphore can also be implemented using a binary semaphore. The following solution uses only binary semaphores by introducing the integer variables: number (count of the number of records in the buffer), oldnumber (a local variable within the consume cycle); and the binary semaphore, delay which prevents the consumer from accessing a nonavailable record when the buffer is empty. The solution using only binary semaphores follows (again, we show only the $i$th producer and consumer):

```
BEGIN INTEGER number, buffer, delay;
    number := 0;
    buffer := 1;   delay := 0;
```

```
PARBEGIN
  Producer:
    Pi:          BEGIN
                   produce next record;
                   P(buffer);
                   deposit record;
                   number := number + 1;
                   if number ≥ 1 THEN V(delay);
                   V(buffer);
                   GOTO Pi;
                 END;


  Consumer:
    BEGIN        INTEGER oldnumber;
    Ci:          P(delay);
    Li:          P(buffer);
                 remove a record;
                 number := number − 1;
                 oldnumber := number;
                 V(buffer);
                 process record;
                 if oldnumber = 0 THEN GOTO Ci
                                 ELSE GOTO Li;
    END;
  PAREND;
END;
```

The use of binary semaphores in specifying precedence constraints among a system of processes has been demonstrated by Denning. If process $P_i$ must precede process $P_j$; then define a semaphore $S_{ij}$ with initial value 0, suffix $V(S_{ij})$ to $P_i$ and prefix $P(S_{ij})$ to $P_j$. Using this procedure, the system of processes represented in the precedence graph in Fig. 2 can be implemented as shown

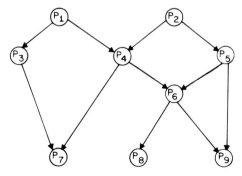

**Fig. 2.** Precedence graph for a system of processes.

below ($S_i$ represents the statements within process $P_i$):

```
PARBEGIN
    P₁:  BEGIN S₁; V(S₁₃); V(S₁₄); END;
    P₂:  BEGIN S₂; V(S₂₄); V(S₂₅); END;
    P₃:  BEGIN P(S₁₃); S₃; V(S₃₇); END;
    P₄:  BEGIN P(S₁₄); P(S₂₅; S₄; V(S₄₇); V(S₄₆); END;
    P₅:  BEGIN P(S₂₅); S₅; V(S₅₆); END;
    P₆:  BEGIN P(S₄₆); P(S₅₆); S₆; V(S₆₈); V(S₆₉); END;
    P₇:  BEGIN P(S₃₇); P(S₄₇); S₇; END;
    P₈:  BEGIN P(S₆₈); S₈; END;
    P₉:  BEGIN P(S₆₉); P(S₅₉); S₉; END;
PAREND;
```

## Other Synchronization Primitives

Several other synchronization primitives which are variations of the $P$ and $V$ primitives have been introduced in the literature. The common ones among them are discussed below.

*The* LOCK *and* UNLOCK *Primitives.* These primitives were proposed by Saltzer (in relation to the implementation of the MULTICS System) to make available the mutual exclusion property of the hardware as a lockout mechanism for critical sections of code. The LOCK and UNLOCK primitives operate on a one-bit lock variable and their operation involves the busy form of waiting and can be described as follows ($w$ is a 1-bit lock variable):

```
         LOCK w:   L:              IF w = 1 THEN GOTO L
                                   ELSE w = 1;
                                   critical section;
         UNLOCK w:   w: = 0;
```

*The* WAIT *and* SIGNAL *Primitives.* The WAIT and SIGNAL primitives are the same as the general semaphores of Dijkstra with WAIT(S) equivalent to $P(S)$, and SIGNAL(S) equivalent to $V(S)$, where $S$ is a semaphore.

*The* BLOCK *and* WAKEUP *Primitives.* These are rather rudimentary primitives that operate on processes to block the target process or place the process in a ready state. The BLOCK and WAKEUP operations can be performed by one process on another, thus requiring a direct form of communication between the processes. Furthermore, the process that is doing the blocking must be completely aware of its execution environment and must also have access to the data structures of the process being operated on. When a process is blocked, it is necessary that the awakening process keep track of the conditions that will enable the blocked process to be awakened. Thus the operation of the primitives imposes a lot of responsibility on the processes involved and may pose a big problem to the implementation of efficient protection mechanisms. The primitives can be defined as follows:

WAKEUP(*P*):   If process *P* is logically blocked, change its execution state to logically ready. Otherwise, set the WWS (wakeup waiting switch) to TRUE.

BLOCK(*P*):   If WWS of process *P* is TRUE, then set WWS to FALSE. Otherwise, change the execution state of *P* to logically blocked.

WWS is a Boolean variable associated with the target process. If the target process is already awake when subjected to a WAKEUP operation, the WWS enables him to remember this wakeup signal, thus allowing him to ignore a subsequent BLOCK command. Thus the WWS provides a unit-memory capability for a process.

*The ENQ and DEQ Primitives.*   These are primitives provided in the form of macroinstructions and used for synchronization involving request of resource usage. The operand of the primitives is an 8-character alphanumeric string identifying the target resource. Each resource has an associated list containing processes currently ENQed on it (both using the resource and blocked waiting to use the resource). ENQ allows the requesting process to specify whether the request is for a shared use or for an exclusive use of the resource. It also allows two kinds of requests: conditional and unconditional. For conditional request, if the resource is available, the requesting process is granted the resource and placed on the ENQ list in the logically ready state. Otherwise the process is notified that the request is ungrantable. If an unconditional request is grantable, it is treated the same way as a grantable conditional request; otherwise, the requesting process is placed on the ENQ list in the logically blocked state. A restriction of the ENQ-DEQ primitives is that they must be paired so that an ENQ must be followed by a DEQ before the occurrence of the next ENQ. This limits the number of units of a resource that can be requested at any given time to one.

*The* POST *and* WAIT *Primitives.*   These macroinstructions (also by IBM) are essentially similar to the ENQ-DEQ macroinstructions except that they operate on event control blocks (ECB). WAIT places the process invoking it in the logically blocked state unless the ECB has previously been posted. On the other hand, POST awakens a process if one is waiting on the ECB. If no process is waiting, a flag is set indicating that the event is already POSTed. WAIT and POST are more or less restricted to direct communication between two processes in which one signals the completion of some activity to a second process since it is impossible to post more than one event at a time. This is a result of the restriction that any flag set must be cleared before an ECB can be used again.

## Synchronization and Interprocess Communication

The synchronization primitives discussed thus far are considered low-level primitives in that they are provided in the underlying control system (the operating system, supervisor, master control program) for the coordination of the concurrent activities in their processing domain. High-level synchronization primitives, on the other hand, are provided for the direct use of the processes so that the processes can directly specify, control, and coordinate communications among themsleves while cooperating toward the completion of a common task or set of tasks. This form of coordination is implemented in the form of messages sent between processes through prespecified message buffers associated with the processes. The function of the primitives, in this respect, is to coordinate the exchange of messages to ensure that messages are delivered to the intended recipients, that recipients are not made to retrieve nonexistent messages from empty buffers, and to maintain proper synchronization between a send operation and the corresponding receive action.

A rather basic set of communication primitives consists of the pair:

$$\text{SEND}(P_r, M) \qquad \text{and} \qquad \text{RECEIVE}(P_s, M)$$

where $P_r$ and $P_s$ are processes and $M$ is a message. The SEND primitive sends a message $M$ to the process $P_r$ while the RECEIVE primitive receives or waits for the message $M$ from process $P_s$. In the usage of these primitives, the underlying system is responsible for the allocation and management of the message buffers so that a full buffer with a SEND operation directed to it would necessitate the blocking of the sender process. Similarly, a RECEIVE request directed at an empty buffer would necessitate the blocking of the message receiver.

More advanced communication primitives built on low-level primitives and developed for the MULTICS System have been described by Spier. The primitives are of the form:

$$\text{NOTIFY}(M,S) \qquad \text{and} \qquad S = \text{WAIT}(M)$$

where $M$ is a mailbox associated with a process. NOTIFY causes message $S$ to be appended to the mailbox $M$ and causes a WAKEUP (a synchronizing primitive already described) to be signaled to the process associated with $M$. On the other hand, the assignment $S = \text{WAIT}(M)$ assigns to $S$ the value of the topmost message which was removed from the mailbox $M$.

A mailbox is a shared data structure associated with a single recipient and has the following attributes or components:

$M.L$: a lock variable operated on by the functions LOCK/UNLOCK.
$M.I$: a binary indicator representing states: empty or NOT empty. The Boolean function TEST($M.I$) returns the value TRUE if $M.I$ is empty.
$M.m$: a single message.
$M.p$: contains a process' identification.

A similarly advanced set of primitives has been described by Brinch Hansen in relation to the design of a multiprogramming system for the RC 4000 computer. These primitives are used both for transmitting I/O records and for higher level interprocess communication. Each process has its own message queue and the system maintains a common pool of buffers for message transmission. The primitives consist of the following:

$$\text{SENDMESSAGE}(P_r, M, B)$$
$$\text{WAITMESSAGE}(P_s, M, B)$$
$$\text{SENDANSWER}(T, A, B)$$
$$\text{WAITANSWER}(T, A, B)$$

where the parameters are defined as follows:

$P_r$:    Identification of the process which is the intended receiver of message.
$M$:    Contents of the message.
$B$:    Buffer to hold the message.
$P_s$:    Identification of the process sending the message.
$A$:    Answer or response to a message.
$T$:    Type of response (real or dummy).
$P$:    Identification of the process invoking a primitive.

The SENDMESSAGE primitive obtains a buffer $B$ from the buffer pool; copies $M$, $P$, and $P_r$ into $B$; ENQ's $B$ on the message queue of $P_r$; and then activate $P_r$ if it is blocked waiting for a message. The WAITMESSAGE primitive blocks $P$ if $P$'s message queue is empty; otherwise, a queue element $B$ is removed from the queue and the message is returned in $M$ and the sender's identity in $P_s$. The SENDANSWER primitive copies $T$, $A$, and $P$ into the buffer $B$; ENQ's $B$ in the message queue of the original sender of the message $P_s$; and activates $P_s$ if it is blocked waiting for an answer. Finally, the WAITANSWER primitive blocks $P$ (the process invoking the primitive) until a message arrives in $B$. When the answer arrives, it is put in $A$ with its type in $T$ and the buffer is then returned to the buffer pool.

A message exchange normally requires the use of all the primitives. A message sender would normally invoke SENDMESSAGE followed later by a WAITANSWER while a message receiver would at some point invoke WAITMES-SAGE followed by a SENDANSWER after the message has been perused. In the event that the receiver of a message no longer exists or never existed, the system would generate a dummy answer and send it to the message sender. Also, since the system must ensure correct matching of messages and receivers, the encoding of the sender's and receiver's identity in the message buffer is an important factor in guaranteeing correct matching which also enables the processes to ignore fake or errant messages.

The synchronization primitives discussed thus far have been involved with the coordination of processes in which there exists the potential of explicit blocking resulting from the direct mode of interaction between the processes. This logical blocking can occur either through the sharing of common variables, programs, or data base in which mutual exclusion must be maintained during each access; or through direct process to process communication in which a process must wait for a signal or message from another process in order to continue its execution. In the next section we deal with coordination problems in which potential (implicit) blocking can occur as a result of implicit (or indirect) interaction among concurrent processes in their competition for the acquisition and usage of the system's resources.

## Dynamic Resource Sharing and Deadlock

A common feature of contemporary multiprogramming systems is the dynamic sharing of system resources among its concurrent processes as a means of increasing resource utilization and effecting better system response. However, in such systems, unless special precautions are taken to prevent it, there always exists the danger of system deadlock. That is, a situation in which two or more processes in the system are blocked forever (so that their progress is permanently inhibited) due to requirements that can never be met, though such requirements are within the system's capacity unless some special action is taken by an external force such as a systems operator.

The collection of resources within a computer system can be grouped into two classes. The first class consists of the serially reusable resources characterized by the following properties:

1. The number of units of the resource is constant.
2. Each unit of the resource is either available or allocated to one process at any given time, so that the same unit cannot be simultaneously shared by two processes.
3. A process may release a unit that has previously been allocated to it.

Resources include the processor, main memory, and storage media; components such as tape drives, disk drives, access mechanisms, and peripherals; and software such as programs, data files, and tables. The second class of resources consists of the consumable resources with the following properties:

1. The number of available units of a consumable resource is potentially unbounded and varies as elements are produced and consumed by processes.
2. A producer process increases the number of available units by releasing one or more units.
3. A consumer process decreases the number of available units by first requesting the units and then consuming the units once they are allocated to the process.

Resources of this type consists of signals such as I/O or timer interrupts, process synchronization signals, messages between processes, and messages for requesting system services and the corresponding answers. Most of the following discussion deals with serially reusable resources unless otherwise specified. A detailed discussion of consumable resources is given by Holt.

Let us briefly consider the allocation of some of the reusable resources considered above. Allocation of the processor is the simplest case since the processor dispatching algorithm ensures that the processor is allocated to a process at a time, and that the switching of the processor from process to process involves context switching and the simultaneous logical blocking of one process while another process is activated and placed in the running state.

In the allocation of main memory and storage space, the deadlock problem is slightly more apparent than the processor case, though not real. Since the storage space is limited in capacity, it is possible to have a situation in which a process holds $x < N$ ($N$ is the memory capacity in pages) pages of memory and needs $x'$ more pages to be able to complete its execution. A second process may hold $y < N$ pages (with $y + x = N$) and require $y'$ more pages to complete its execution. In this case, one of the two processes must be blocked and swapped out to make space for the other process to run to completion, after which the former can be brought back into core to run to completion. While the problem appears rather trivial with two processes, it could lead to the thrashing situation sometimes encountered in a paged system in which the system is burdened with paging programs in and out of core and does little productive work.

The solution to the storage problem is to preempt the storage allocated to one process in favor of another process. Such a solution could prove rather expensive where devices are involved. Consider a system with a card reader and a line printer in which the card reader is allocated to a process and the line printer to a second process. While the first process is holding the card reader, it requires the use of the line printer in order to complete its execution. On the other hand, the second process holding the line printer cannot release it until it has been allocated the card reader. We thus have a real case of deadlock because there is no way either of the two processes can proceed. Furthermore, the two processes will continue to wait on each other until the operator detects the deadlock condition.

Deadlock problems arising from the sharing of common files is similar to the above. It is evident that simultaneous access to common data base must be prevented except for read access. Therefore, for write accesses, only one process must be granted access at any given time. Imagine two processes $P_1$, $P_2$ and common data bases $D_1$ and $D_2$. $P_1$ is in $D_1$ and needs access into $D_2$ at the same time that $P_2$ is in $D_2$ and requires access into $D_1$. Again, the two processes are deadlocked and the deadlock condition must be resolved by an external force.

## Characterization of Deadlock

From the above discussion we can see that the deadlock problem is a logical one that can arise in any situation in which there is contention for limited resources while holders of resources are allowed their exclusive use. This problem can be shown by Fig. 3 in which we have two processes $P_1$ and $P_2$ executing concurrently on the same system and requiring resources $R_1$ and $R_2$ at certain phases of their execution. The $x$-axis of the two-dimensional diagram represents the progress of process $P_1$ while the $y$-axis represents the progress of $P_2$ (concept due to Dijkstra). In this context we use the number of instructions executed subsequent to some selected initial time as the progress of the tasks. Thus the joint progress of $P_1$ and $P_2$ is represented by a point in the progress space, and discrete increments can be noticed only in one coordinate for a uniprocessor system while increases in both coordinates are possible for a multiprocessor system. The intervals in which resources $R_1$ and $R_2$ are required are shown by solid lines in Fig. 3.

Since progress can only be made in the positive direction, then it is not possible to have a decrease in any of the coordinates indicating process progress. Furthermore, since processes are allowed exclusive control of their allocated resource (until released), a progress entering into the blocked area would mean immediate deadlock. If the joint progress enters the area $U$ (the Unsafe region), then deadlock is inevitable since progress would eventually lead to the blocked region. The deadlock situation arising can be attributed to the joint presence of the following conditions:

1. Mutual exclusion: A resource can only be acquired by one process at a time, i.e., exclusive control of the resource.
2. Nonpreemptive condition: Once resources are allocated, they cannot be removed until used to completion and willfully released.
3. Partial allocation: A process can acquire its needed resources piecemeal and as such it can hold resources already allocated while waiting for additional resources.

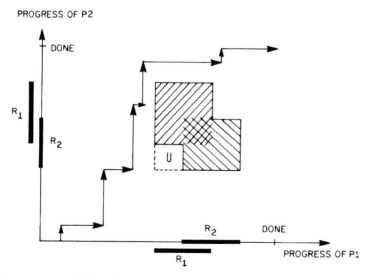

**Fig. 3.** Progress map of $P1$ and $P2$.

NTRINSIC  SEMICONDUCTOR

$$\underline{\qquad n_0 \cdots \qquad} E_v$$

$$n_0 = p_0 = n_i \quad (\text{INTRINSIC})$$

$$\underline{\qquad p_0 \cdots \qquad} E_c$$

$g_i$ = generation rate of electron-hole pairs (i=intrinsic)
= recombination rate of EHP.

$$g_i = g_i(T) \quad \nearrow \text{ with } T$$
$$n_i = n_i(T) \quad \nearrow \text{ with } T$$

ANY $T$, $R_i \propto n_0 p_0$ or

$$\boxed{ n_i = \alpha_R n_0 p_0 = \alpha_R n_i^2 = g_i } \quad \underline{\underline{\text{INTRINSIC}}}$$

NG

CREATE CARRIERS BY ADDING IMPURITIES
TO THE CRYSTAL.

OPED SEMICONDUCTOR IS CALLED EXTRINSIC

4. Circular wait condition: A circular chain of processes exists such that each process holds one or more resources that are being requested by the next in the chain.

## Deadlock Strategies

Since the potential for deadlock exists in any concurrent programming system, procedures must be provided for handling their occurrences. Three strategies have been described, namely: prevention strategies, detection strategies, and recovery strategies. The prevention strategies involve the design of deadlock-secure systems, i.e., systems in which deadlock is not possible. The detection strategies allow deadlocks to occur but they are detected when they do occur. These strategies provide means of examining a system state to determine the sequence of allocations that would prevent (or cause) deadlock from the current state. Through this detection procedure it is then possible to avoid deadlock. For nondeadlock-secure systems without detection procedures, strategies for recovery can be provided through operator intervention.

As stated above, a deadlock -secure system must preclude the four conditions specified above. The following prevention strategies by Havender are effective in preventing deadlock

1. Preallocate of all shared resources: User declares his resource requirements and is not activated until the resources are available. Once allocated, he can keep the resources until completion of his execution. While this strategy works, it is the least efficient and has lots of disadvantages. First, the user may not know all his resource requirements until execution time. Second, one must wait for a resource irrespective of when it is needed. Therefore, when a resource is needed toward the end of processing, one must still wait for it at the beginning. Third, it is wasteful of resources in that a resource kept for the duration of a job's processing may be used for a very short time. Last, a resource allocated to a job may never be used during the execution.

2. Controlled allocation: The user is required to declare his resource requirements as above but the job can get started even when not all resources are immediately available. However, if the request for certain resources is denied, the process must release any resources it is holding and if necessary request them again in addition to the new requests. The major criticism of this strategy is that it is too conservative as resources taken away may not be needed by other processes. Furthermore, the prespecification of needs is still unsatisfactory.

3. Linear allocation pattern: Resource types are ordered by increasing priority. Request for resources must also be ordered so that a process-holding resource of order $n$ can only request resources of order $n + 1, n + 2, \ldots$ in their ordering. If resources of order $i < n$ are to be requested, then all resources of order $i, i + 1, i + 2, \ldots, n$ must be released (and, if necessary, requested later) before the request can be granted. This strategy is the best and most efficient of the three.

The detection problem is the most difficult aspect of deadlock handling and has generally been tackled by developing formal models of system states defined in terms of processes, their resource holdings and requirements, and the system's total resource capacity. Coffman et al. use vectors and matrices to represent the system states; Holt provides extensive analysis and algorithms (using graph models) for examining system states to determine whether they contain deadlock. In addition, Holt's analysis provides necessary and sufficient conditions for deadlock. Haberman also developed algorithms for deciding the safeness of a state. The interested reader is directed to these works for further details.

Given a deadlock situation, the simplest recovery method would be to abort each of the deadlocked jobs or tasks; or in the case where they hold preemptible resources, to preempt the resources. Shoshani and Coffman provide a recovery procedure that assigns a fixed cost to the forced removal of a resource from a deadlocked task that is being aborted. They also provide an algorithm for finding a subset of resources that would incur the minimum cost.

We shall conclude this section with an analysis of the banker's algorithm. Using the semaphore primitives that were introduced earlier, we shall develop a solution to the banker's algorithm. We have earlier showed that the semaphore primitives are very versatile in solving synchronization problems; in the following we show that they are equally versatile in resource allocation problems where they may be used as counting semaphores.

## The Banker's Algorithm

The banker's algorithm is a resource-sharing problem first described and solved by Dijkstra, and the following description of the problem and its solution follows Dijkstra's analysis. The problem is described as follows:

A banker has a fixed capital (expressed in dollars) which he wants to make available as loans to his customers under the following conditions:

1. The customer makes the loan for a transaction that can be completed in a finite period of time.
2. The customer must specify his maximum needs ahead of time.
3. The customer can increase or decrease his loan as long as his total loan does not exceed the initially specified maximum.
4. The customer is guaranteed that a loan request (within his specified maximum) which cannot be granted at the current time will be granted at some time in the future. This guarantee is based on the bankers algorithm which ensures that a loan, once granted, will enable a customer to proceed toward the completion of his transaction, thus ensuring that the loan will be paid back promptly upon completion of the transaction.

The problem is to design the banker's algorithm so that we can know under what conditions he can entertain new customers and under what conditions he can grant the next loan without getting into a deadlock situation.

*Solution:* It is obvious that any new customer whose stated demand does not exceed the banker's capital should be accepted as a customer. In order to solve the second part of the problem, we introduce the following variables:

let:  capital    represent the banker's total capital.
      need[i]    represent the maximum need for customer $i$.
      loan[i]    represent the current loan held by customer $i$; initially loan[i] = 0 for all $i$.
      claim[i]   represent the maximum claim that can be further made by customer $i$.
      cash       represent the current cash holdings of the banker.

Then the following relationships hold:

$$\text{need}[i] \leq \text{capital}, \quad \text{for all } i$$
$$0 \leq \text{loan}[i] \leq \text{need}[i], \quad \text{for all } i$$
$$\text{claim}[i] = \text{need}[i] - \text{loan}[i], \quad \text{for all } i$$
$$\text{cash} = \text{capital} - \sum_{i=1}^{\text{no of customers}} \text{loans}[i]$$
$$0 \leq \text{cash} \leq \text{capital}$$

In order to decide if a requested dollar can be granted, the banker has to consider if loaning the dollar will lead him into a safe or an unsafe situation. A safe situation is such that starting from that situation, all customers' transactions can be guaranteed to run to completion. This situation can be checked by checking to see if there is at least one customer that can complete his transaction given the current cash holdings. If this is true, then the algorithm proceeds by assuming the customer loans are returned and checking to see if there is at least another customer that can complete his transactions. If there is, we again return all his loans and continue with the test until all customers have been shown to be able to complete their transactions. If the customers are numbered 1 through $n$, the following ALGOL routine will inspect a state for safeness or unsafeness:

```
INTEGER freemoney, i; BOOLEAN safe;
BOOLEAN ARRAY doubtful[1:n];
freemoney := cash;
FOR i := 1 STEP 1 UNTIL n DO doubtful[i] := TRUE;
L: FOR i := 1 STEP 1 UNTIL n DO
BEGIN IF doubtful[i] AND claim[i] ≤ freemoney THEN
   BEGIN doubtful[i] := FALSE;
     freemoney := freemoney + loan[i];
     GOTO L;
   END;
END;
IF freemoney = capital THEN safe := TRUE ELSE
     safe := FALSE;
```

In the routine, a TRUE value of the Boolean element doubtful[i] indicates that it is doubtful the $i$th customer can complete his transactions and the variable freemoney indicates how many dollars are available at the current point in the test procedure. In testing for each customer completion, we collect as many payable loans as we can until we can ensure the completion of the customer's transaction. When all customers can be guaranteed completion of their transaction, then freemoney should be equal to the capital.

The banker's algorithm is a general resource allocation problem and, in the concurrent processing context, we can view the banker as the resource allocator and the customers as processes vying for resources which are represented by the dollars. In this context, each dollar will represent a particular resource or a unit of a specific resource; so we need to be able to identify each dollar uniquely by its number.

Let the dollars be numbered 1 through $m$. Let the customers be numbered 1 through $n$ as above. Each customer has a variable "dollano" containing the number of the dollar (resource) the customer has just been granted. Similarly, we will associate a variable "custno" with each dollar, indicating which customer the dollar was just granted to.

Each customer has a state variable "cusvar," indicating whether the customer wants to loan a dollar (cusvar = 1) or not (cusvar = 0); and a semaphore "cussem." Similarly, each dollar has a state variable "dolvar," indicating whether the dollar is available to be loaned (dolvar = 1, i.e., the dollar is in "cash"), or not available (dolvar = 0); and a semaphore "dolsem."

The solution below assumes that a borrowed dollar may not be returned immediately. Furthermore, a returned dollar may not be instantaneously available for subsequent loaning. Thus the loan of the dollar is considered ended only after the dollar has returned to "cash" at which point the dollar signals its return via its borrowing customer semaphore, "returned." Therefore, a $P$-operation on this semaphore prior to every loan request will guard the customer against an overdraft. The initial value of "returned" is "need." The value of the Boolean procedure "trytogiveto" indicates whether an outstanding request for a dollar has been granted. It is assumed that the constants $n$, $m$, and the constant integer array "need" are defined in a globally encompassing block in which the following program is embedded:

```
BEGIN INTEGER ARRAY loan, claim, cussem, cusvar, dollano,
    returned[1:n];
    dolsem, dolvar, custno[1:m];
  INTEGER mutex, cash, k;
  BOOLEAN PROCEDURE trytogiveto(j);
  VALUE j; INTEGER j;
  BEGIN IF cusvar[j] = 1 THEN
      BEGIN INTEGER i, freemoney;
        BOOLEAN ARRAY doubtful[1:n];
        freemoney := cash − 1;
        claim[j] := claim[j] − 1;
        loan[j] := loan[j] + 1;
        FOR i := 1 STEP 1 UNTIL n DO doubtful := TRUE;
```

```
L0: FOR i := 1 STEP 1 UNTIL n DO
        BEGIN IF doubtful[i] and claim[i] ≤ freemoney THEN
            BEGIN IF i ≠ j THEN
                BEGIN doubtful[i] := false;
                    freemoney := freemoney + loan[i];
                    GOTO L0;
                END;
                        ELSE
                BEGIN i := 0;
                L1: i := i + 1;
                    IF dolvar[i] = 0 THEN GOTO L1;
                    dollano[j] := i;
                    custno[i] := j;
                    cusvar[j] := 0;
                    dolvar[i] := 0;
                    cash := cash − 1;
                    trytogiveto := TRUE;
                    V(cussem[j]);
                    V(dolsem[i]); GOTO L2;
                END;
            END:
        END:
        claim[j] := claim[j] + 1; loan[j] := loan[j] − 1;
    END:
    trytogiveto := FALSE;
  L2: END;
    mutex := 1; cash := m;
    for k := 1 STEP 1 UNTIL n DO
    BEGIN loan[k] := 0; cussem[k] := 0; cusvar[k] := 0;
        claim[k] := need[k]; returned[k] := need[k];
    END;
    FOR k := 1 STEP 1 UNTIL m DO
    BEGIN dolsem[k] := 0; dolvar[k] := 1; END;
    PARBEGIN
customer 1:     BEGIN . . . END:
                  ⋮
customer n:     BEGIN . . . END;
dollar L:       BEGIN . . . END;
                  ⋮
dollar m:       BEGIN . . . END;
      PAREND;
END;
```

The request for a new dollar by customer 1 consists of the following statements:

```
                P(returned[1]);
                P(mutex);
                cusvar[1] := 1; trytogiveto(1);
                V(mutex);
                P(cussem[1]);
```

Upon completion of the last statement, dollano[1] contains the identity of the dollar just borrowed. The structure of the dollar $m$ is as follows (custno[$m$] represents the number of the customer who has borrowed the dollar):

```
dollar m:
BEGIN INTEGER h;
start: P(dolsem[m]);
    COMMENT: dollar returns itself to cash as follows:;
      P(mutex);
      claim[custno[m]] := claim[custno[m]] + 1;
      loan[custno[m]] := loan[custno[m]] - 1;
      dolvar[m] := 1;
      cash := cash + 1;
      V(returned[custno[m]]);
      FOR h := 1 STEP UNTIL n DO
          BEGIN IF trytogiveto(h) THEN GOTO leave; END;
    leave: V(mutex);
      GOTO start;
END;
```

The reader should convince himself that this solution does solve the banker's problem. From the customer sequence it is seen that possibility of overdraft is prevented by the semaphore "returned" while "mutex" ensures that loan and return operations are handled in critical sections, thus ensuring correctness of the operations. It should also be noted that the dollar return operation is not complete (i.e., the dollar becomes available for subsequent loaning) until the V(returned[custno[$m$]]) operation has been completed.


## SUMMARY AND FUTURE DIRECTIONS

In our discussion we have identified four principal problems that are encountered in the control of concurrent processing in contemporary computer systems:

1. Determinacy. The requirement that the results of a computation be unique irrespective of variations in task execution rate or order of execution in relationship to other concurrent tasks.
2. Mutual exclusion. The requirement that no more than one process can be in its critical section containing program codes and data that are shared with other concurrent processes.
3. Communication. The synchronization of data, signal, and message passing among cooperating concurrent processes.
4. Deadlock. The problem of indefinite blocking of processes for events that can never occur.

The common solution to all these problems is that of process synchronization or the ordering in time of certain task executions. Several synchronizing primitives were introduced among which are the elegant $P$ and $V$ semaphore primitives developed by Dijkstra. We have demonstrated the versatility of these primitives by employing them in the solution of several synchronization problems.

The concepts introduced above have found widespread usage in the design of third generation computer systems and have given rise to the concept of structured design in operating systems construction. The first operating system based on this design philosophy is the THE operating system (McKeag and Dijkstra) which incorporates hierarchical structuring in a semaphore-based system. Following this system, several other systems have been built on the principle of hierarchical structuring, the nucleus, or kernel approach; all of which view the operating system as the coordinator of concurrent processes which may interact directly or indirectly through the protocols provided in the form of synchronizing primitives within the operating system. The list of such systems is long, but a representative list includes, MULTICS (Saltzer, Spier, Organic, etc), RC-4000 operating system (Brinch Hansen), Project SUE (Atwood, Graham), and TENEX (Bobrow). Based on the degree of success that has been attained in producing well structured operating systems, coupled with research in the design and engineering of reliable software, the day may not be too far into the future when it will be possible to produce operating systems that are and can be proven correct. This is the goal of every systems designer because a correct system is a secure system and a secure system offers the ultimate in integrity and reliability.

## BIBLIOGRAPHY

Anderson, J. P., Program structures for parallel processing, *Commun. ACM* **8**(12), 786–788 (1965).

Aschenbrenner, R. A., M. J. Flynn, and G. A. Robinson, Intrinsic multiprocessing, in *Proceedings of AFIPS, SJCC,* Vol. 32, 1967, pp. 81–86.

Atwood, J. W., et al., Project SUE Status Report, Computer Systems Research Group, Technical Report CSRG-11, University of Toronto, Ontario, Canada, April 1972.

Baer, J. L., Theoretical aspects of multiprocessing, *Comput. Surv.* **5**(1), 31–80 (March 1973).

Balzer, R. M., PORTS-A method for dynamic interprogram communication and job control, in *Proceedings of AFIPS, SICC,* Vol. 38, 1971, pp. 485–489.

Bell, C. G., and A. Newell, *Computer Structures: Readings and Examples,* McGraw-Hill, New York, 1971.

Belpair, G., and J. P. Wilmott, Semantic aspects of concurrent processes, *SIGPLAN Notices* **8,** 42–54 (1973).

Bernstein, A. J., Analysis of programs for parallel processing, *IEEE Trans. Electron. Comput.* **EC-15**(5), 757–763 (October 1966).

Bernstein, A. J., G. D. Detlefsen, and R. H. Kerr, Process control and communication, in *Proceedings of the Second SIGOPS Symposium on Operating Systems Principles,* Association for Computing Machinery, New York, 1969, pp. 60–66.

**CONCURRENT PROCESSING**

Betrourne, C., et al., Process management and resource sharing in the multi-access system ESCOPE, *Commun. ACM* **13**, 727–733 (1970).

Bobrow, D. G., et al., TENEX, a paged time sharing system for the PDP-10, *Commun. ACM* **15**, 135–143 (1972).

Bredt, T. H., *A Survey of Models for Parallel Computing*, Technical Report #8, Stanford Electronic Laboratories, Stanford University, Stanford, California, August 1970.

Bredt, T. H., and E. J. McCluskey, Analysis and synthesis of control mechanisms for parallel processes, in *Parallel Processor Systems, Technologies and Applications* (L. C. Hobbs et al., eds.), Spartan, New York, 1970.

Brinch Hansen, P., The nucleus of a multiprogramming system, *Commun. ACM* **13**, 238–241 (April 1970).

Brinch Hansen, P., A comparison of two synchronizing concepts, *Acta Inf.* **1**(3), 190–199 (1972).

Brinch Hansen, P., Structured multiprogramming, *Commun. ACM* **15**, 574–578 (1972).

Brinch Hansen, P., Concurrent programming concepts, *Comput. Surv.* **5**(4), 223–245 (December 1973).

Brinch Hansen, P., *Operating System Principles*, Prentice-Hall, Englewood Cliffs, New Jersey, 1973.

Carr, S. C., et al., HOST-HOST communication protocol in the ARPA network, in *Proceedings of AFIPS, SJCC*, Vol. 36, 1970, pp. 589–597.

Cerf, V. S., Multiprocessors, Semaphores and a Graph Model of Computations, Ph.D. Thesis, Computer Science Department, University of California, Los Angeles, California, 1972.

Chamberlin, D. D., The "single-assignment" approach to parallel processing, in *Proceedings of AFIPS, FJCC*, Vol. 39, 1971, pp. 263–268.

Chambers, J. M., A user controlled synchronization method, *SIGOPS Oper. Syst. Rev.* **7**(2), 16–25 (April 1973).

Cleary, J. G., Process handling on Burroughs B6500, in *Proceedings of the Fourth Australian Computer Conference, Adelaide, South Australia, 1969*, Griffin Press, Netley, South Australia, 1969, pp. 231–239.

Coffman, E. G., Jr., and P. J. Denning, *Operating Systems Theory*, Prentice-Hall, Englewood Cliffs, New Jersey, 1973.

Coffman, E. G., Jr., M. Elplick, and A. Shoshani, System deadlocks *Comput. Surv.* **3**(2), 67–78 (June 1971).

Cohen, D., A parallel process definition and control system, in *Proceedings of AFIPS, FJCC*, Vol. 33, Part II, 1968, pp. 1043–1050.

Colher, W. W., *System Deadlocks*, IBM Technical Report TR-00-1256, System Development Division, Poughkepsie, New York, 1968.

Constantine, L. L., Control of sequence and parallelism in modular programs, in *Proceedings of AFIPS, SJCC*, Vol. 32, 1968, pp. 409–414.

Conway, M. E., A multiprocessor system design, in *Proceedings of AFIPS, FJCC*, Vol. 24, 1963, pp. 139–146.

Corbato, F. J., and J. H. Saltzer, Multics—The first seven years, in *Proceedings of AFIPS, SJCC*, Vol. 40, 1972, pp. 571–583.

Corbato, F. J., and V. A. Vyssotsky, Introduction and overview of the multics system, in *Proceedings of AFIPS, FJCC*, Vol. 27, Part 1, 1965, pp. 185–196.

Courtois, P. J., F. Haymans, and D. L. Parnas, Comments on "A comparison of two synchronizing concepts" by P. B. Hansen, *Acta Inf.* **1**(4), 375–376 (1972).

Courtois, P. J., F. Haymans, and D. L. Parnas, Concurrent control with "readers" and "writers," *Commun. ACM* **14**(10), 667–668 (1972).

Dahl, O. J., and K. Nygaard, SIMULA—An ALGOL-based simulation language, *Commun. ACM* **9**(9), 671–678 (1966).

Dahm, D. M., F. H. Gerbstadt, and M. M. Pacelli, A system organization for resource allocation, *Commun. ACM* **10**(12), 772–779 (1967).

de Bruijn, N. G., Additional comments on a problem in concurrent programming control, *Commun. ACM* **10**(3), 137–138 (1967).

Denning, P. J., Third generation computer systems, *Comput. Surv.* **3**(4), 175–216 (December 1971).

Dennis, J. B., Programming generality, parallelism, and computer architecture, in *Proceedings of IFIP Congress 1968,* North-Holland, Amsterdam, 1969, pp. 484–492.

Dennis, J. B., and E. C. Van Horn, Programming semantics for multiprogrammed computations, *Commun. ACM* **9**(3), 143–155 (1966).

Dijkstra, E. W., Solution of a problem in concurrent programming control, *Commun. ACM* **8**(9), 569 (1965).

Dijkstra, E. W., The Structure of "THE" multiprogramming system, *Commun. ACM* **11**(5), 341–346 (1968).

Dijkstra, E. W., Cooperating sequential processes, in *Programming Languages* (F. Genuys, ed.), Academic, New York, 1968, pp. 43–112.

Dijkstra, E. W., A class of allocation strategies inducing bounded delays only, in *Proceedings of AFIPS, SJCC,* Vol. 40, 1972, pp. 933–936.

Dingwall, T. J., *Communications within Structured Operating Systems,* Cornell University Technical Report TR 73–167, May 1973.

Easton, W. B., Process synchronization without long-term interlock, *SIGOPS Oper. Syst. Rev.* **6**(1), 95–100 (June 1972).

Eisenberg, M. A., and M. R. McGuire, Further comments on Dijkstra's concurrent programming control problem, *Commun. ACM* **15**(11), 999 (1972).

Enslow, P. H., Jr. (ed.), *Multiprocessors and Parallel Processing, by the Comtre Corporation,* Wiley, New York, 1974.

Ershov, A. P., *Parallel Programming,* Computer Science Department Technical Report CS-224, Stanford University, July 1971.

Fontao, R. O., A concurrent algorithm for avoiding deadlocks in multiprocess multiple resource systems, *SIGOPS Oper. Syst. Rev.* **6**(1), 72–79 (June 1972).

Frailey, D. J., A practical approach to managing resources and avoiding deadlocks, *Commun. ACM* **16**(5), 323–329 (1973).

Freeman, P., *Software Systems Principles: A Survey,* S.R.A. Inc., Chicago, Illinois, 1975.

Gaines, R. S., An operating system based on the concept of a supervisory computer, *Commun. ACM* **15**(3), 150–156 (1972).

Gilberb, P., and J. W. Chandler, Interference between communicating parallel processes, *Commun. ACM* **15**(6), 427–437 (1972).

Gill, S., Parallel programming, *Comput. J.* **1**, 2–10 (April 1958).

Gonzales, M. J., and C. V. Ramamoorthy, A survey of techniques for recognizing parallel processable streams in computer programs, in *Proceedings of AFIPS, FJCC,* Vol. 35, 1969, pp. 1–16.

Goos, G., Some basic principles on structuring operating systems, in *Operating Systems Techniques* (C. S. R. Hoare and R. N. Perrott, eds.), Academic, London, 1972.

Gosden, J. A., Explicit parallel processing description and control in programs for multi- and uniprocessor computers, in *Proceedings of AFIPS, FJCC,* Vol. 29, 1966, pp. 651–660.

Gostelow, K., V. G. Cerf, and G. Estrin, Proper termination of flow-of-control in programs involving concurrent processes, in *Proceedings of the ACM 25th National Conference*, Vol. 2, 1972, pp. 742–754.

Graham, G. S., Protection Structures in Operating Systems, M.S. Thesis, University of Toronto, Ontario, Canada, August 1972.

Graham, G. S., and P. J. Denning, Pretection—Principles and practice, in *Proceedings of AFIPS, SJCC*, Vol. 40, 1972, pp. 417–429.

Gray, J., Locking, in *Proceedings of Project MAC Conference on Concurrent Systems and Parallel Computation, June 1970*, Association for Computing Machinery, New York, 1970, pp. 169–176.

Habermann, N. A., On the Harmonious Cooperation of Abstract Machines, Ph.D. Thesis, Technical University, Eindhoven, The Netherlands, 1967.

Habermann, N. A., Prevention of system deadlocks, *Commun. ACM* 12(7), 373–378 (July 1969).

Habermann, N. A., Synchronization of communicating processes, *Commun. ACM* 15(3), 171–176 (March 1972).

Havender, J. W., Avoiding deadlock in multi-tasking systems, *IBM Syst. J.* 7(2), 74–84 (1968).

Hebalkar, P. G., Deadlock-Free Sharing of Resources in Asynchronous Systems, Sc.D. Thesis, M.I.T. Project MAC Report MAC-TR-75, 1970.

Hill, J. C., Synchronizing processors with memory-content-generated interrupts, *Commun. ACM* 16(6), 350–351 (1973).

Hoare, C. A. R., Towards a theory of parallel programming, in *Operating Systems Techniques* (C. A. R. Hoare and R. N. Perrott, eds.), Academic, London, 1972.

Hoare, C. A. R., A structured paging system, Comput. J. 16(3), 209–214 (August 1973).

Holt, A. W., and F. Commoner, Events and conditions, in *Proceedings of Project MAC Conference on Concurrent Systems and Parallel Computation, June 1970*, Association for Computing Machinery, New York, 1970, pp. 3–52.

Holt, R. C., Comments on prevention of system deadlocks, *Commun. ACM* 14(1), 36–38 (1971).

Holt, R. C., On Deadlock in Computer Systems, Ph.D. Thesis, Technical Report TR-71-91, Computer Science Department, Cornell University, Ithaca, New York, January 1971.

Holt, R. C., Some deadlock properties of computer systems, *Comput. Surv.* 4(3), 179–196 (September 1972).

Holt, R. C., and M. S. Grushcow, A short discussion of interprocess communication in the SUE/360/370 operating system, *SIGPLAN Notices* 8(9), 74–78 (1973).

Hornbuckle, G. D., A multiprogramming monitor for small machines, *Commun. ACM* 10(5), 273–278 (1967).

Horning, J. J., and B. Randell, Process structuring, *Comput. Surv.* 5(1), 5–30 (March 1973).

Howard, J. H., Jr., Mixed solution for the deadlock problem, *Commun. ACM* 16(7), 427–430 (1973).

Howry, S., A multiprogramming system for process control, *SIGOPS Oper. Syst. Rev.* 6(1), 24–30 (June 1972).

Jensen, P., The grok project: Data structures and process communication, *SIGPLAN Notices* 8(9), 82–85 (1973).

Karp, R. M., and R. E. Miller, Parallel program schemata, *J. Comput. Syst. Sci.* 3(2), 147–195 (May 1969).

Knott, G. D., A proposal for certain process management and intercommunication primitives, Part I, *SIGOPS Oper. Syst. Rev.* 8(4), 7–44 (October 1974).

Knuth, D. E., Additional comments on a problem in concurrent programming control, *Commun. ACM* **9**(5), 321–322 (1966).

Kosaraju, S. R., Limitations of Dijkstra's semaphore primitives and petri nets, *SIGOPS Oper. Syst. Rev.* **7**(4), 122–126 (October 1973).

Lampson, B. W., A scheduling philosophy for multiprocessing systems, *Commun. ACM* **11**(5), 347–360 (1968).

Lampson, B. W., Dynamic protection structures, in *Proceedings of AFIPS, FICC,* Vol. 35, 1969, pp. 27–38.

Lorin, H., *Parallelism in Hardware and Software,* Prentice-Hall, Englewood Cliffs, New Jersey, 1972.

Luconi, F. L., Asynchronous Computational Structures, Ph.D. Thesis, M.I.T. Project MAC Report MAC-TR-49.

Madnick, S. E., Multi-processor software lockout, in *Proceedings of the 1968 ACM National Conference,* pp. 19–24.

McKeag, R. M., *The Multiprogramming System,* Queen's University, Belfast, Department of Computer Science, Belfast, Northern Ireland, 1972.

Madnick, S. E., and J. J. Donovan, *Operating Systems,* McGraw-Hill, New York, 1974.

Murphy, J. E., Resource allocation with interlock detection in a multi-task system, in *Proceedings of AFIPS, FJCC,* Vol. 33, Part II, 1968, pp. 1169–1176.

Naur, P. (ed.), Revised report on the algorithmic language ALGOL 60, *Commun. ACM* **6**(3), 1 (1963).

Organick, E. I., *The Multics System,* M.I.T. Press, Cambridge, Massachusetts, 1972.

Organick, E. I., *Computer System Organization: The B5700/6700 Series,* Academic, New York, 1973.

Parmelee, R. P., et al., Virtual storage and virtual machine concepts, *IBM Syst. J.* **11**(2), 99–130 (1972).

Parnas, D. L., On facilitating parallel and multiprocessing in ALGOL, *Commun. ACM* **9**(4), 257 (1966).

Parnas, D. L., On simulating networks of parallel processes in which simultaneous events may occur, *Commun. ACM* **12**(9), 519–531 (1969).

Patil, S. S., Coordination of Asynchronous Events, Ph.D. Thesis, M.I.T. Project MAC Report MAC-TR-72, 1970

Ramamoorthy, C. V., and M. J. Gonzalez, Recognition and representation of parallel processable streams in computer programs—II (task/process parallelism), in *Proceedings of the 1969 National ACM Conference,* pp. 387–398.

Rappaport, R. L., Implementing Multiprocessing Primitives in a Multiplexed Computer System, M.S. Thesis, M.I.T. Project MAC Report MAC-TR-55, 1968.

Rodriguez, J. E., A graph model for parallel computations, M.I.T. Project MAC Report MAC-TR-64, September 1969.

Rosen, S., Electronic computers: A historical survey, *Comput. Surv.* **1**(1), 7–36 (March 1969).

Rosin, R. F., Supervisory and monitor systems, *Comput. Surv.* **1**(1), 37–54 (March 1969).

Russell, R. D., A Model of Deadlock-Free Resource Allocation, Ph.D. Thesis, Computer Science Department, Stanford University, July 1971.

Saltzer, J. H., Traffic control in a multiplexed computer system, M.I.T. Project MAC Report MAC-TR-30, 1966.

Saul, H., and W. Riddle, *Communicating Semaphores,* Computer Science Department Report STAN-CS-71-202, Stanford University, 1971.

Shaw, A. C., *The Logical Design of Operating Systems,* Prentice-Hall, Englewood Cliffs, New Jersey, 1974.

Shoshani, A., and A. J. Bernstein, Synchronization in a parallel accessed data-base, *Commun. ACM* **12**(11), 604–607 (1969).

Shoshani, A., and E. G. Coffman, Prevention, detection, and recovery from system deadlocks, in *Proceedings of the Fourth Annual Princeton Conference on Information Sciences and Systems, March 1970,* Department of Electrical Engineering, Princeton University, Princeton, New Jersey, 1970, pp. 355–360.

Slutz, D. R., The Flow Graph Schemata Model of Parallel Processing, Ph.D. Thesis, M.I.T. Project MAC Report MAC-TR-53, 1968.

Sorenson, P. G., Interprocess communications in real time systems, *SIGOPS Oper. Syst. Rev.* **7**(4), 1–7 (October 1973).

Spier, M. J., T. N. Hastings, and D. N. Cutler, An experimental implementation of the kernel/domain architecture, *SIGOPS Oper. Syst. Rev.* **7**(4), 8–21 (October 1973).

Spier, M. J., and E. I. Organic, The MULTICS Interprocess Communication Facility, *in ACM SIGOPS Second Symposium on Operating System Principles, October 1969,* pp. 83–91.

Tesler, L. G., and H. J. Enea, A language design for concurrent processes, in *Proceedings of AFIPS, SJCC,* Vol. 32, 1968, pp. 403–408.

Tsichritzis, D. C., and P. A. Bernstein, *Operating Systems,* Academic, New York, 1974.

Van Horn, E. C., Jr., Computer Design for Asynchronously Reproducible Multiprocessing, Ph.D. Thesis, Project MAC Report MAC-TR-34, November 1966.

Verner, Y., On Process Communication and Process Synchronization, M.S. Thesis, Department of Computer Science, University of Toronto, Ontario, Canada, October 1971.

Walden, D. C., A system for interprocess communication in a resource sharing computer network, *Commun. ACM* **15**(4), 221–230 (1972).

Weiderman, N. H., Synchronization and Simulation in Operating System Construction, Ph.D. Thesis, Cornell University, September 1971.

Wirth, N., Program structures for parallel processing, *Commun. ACM* **9**(5), 320–321 (1966).

Wirth, N., On multiprogramming, machine coding and computer organization, *Commun. ACM* **12**(9), 489–498 (1969).

*Abimbola Salako*

# CONTENT ANALYSIS

"Is there any other point to which you would wish to draw my attention?" Gregory asked.

"To the curious incident of the dog in the nighttime," Holmes replied.

"The dog did nothing in the nighttime," the inspector retorted.

"That," said Sherlock Holmes, "that was the curious incident" [1].

# THE NATURE AND DEFINITION OF CONTENT ANALYSIS

## Introduction

The ability to draw correct conclusions from apparently trivial or unrelated facts or incidents is a characteristic which mankind prizes highly. Although obscured in the wealth of detail which research in content analysis has generated, it is probably still true that the underlying motivation for content analytical studies is the desire to improve one's ability to infer correct conclusions from the wealth of data presented to him. It is precisely this inferential capability embodied in the fictional character Sherlock Holmes which provides the stories written by Conan Doyle the lasting interest and intrigue which so many people have enjoyed.

Content analysis is a field of endeavor devoted to the development of new tools and techniques through whose use one may improve his deductive abilities. The computer has lent considerable impetus to work in content analysis, and it is the use of computers in this area which draws our primary interest. To be sure, the person who reviews a book, abstracts a technical article, or interprets a diplomatic communique is performing content analysis, however ill-defined the procedures employed may be. While these activities are of general interest in content analysis, our attention will be focused more specifically upon techniques employing digital computers as aids in drawing inferences from textual data.

In this article we describe a variety of methods which have been employed in computer-based analysis of the content of English texts. We begin by considering some basic terminological definitions, then proceed to discuss content analysis studies in detail. Examples are employed throughout to illustrate the various methods, and important references are cited as appropriate. A more comprehensive listing of references may be found in the *Annual Review of Information Science and Technology*, Volumes 1–10 [2].

## Basic Definitions

Content analysis may be defined as follows:

> Content analysis is a procedure for identifying those attributes of a message which have the greatest likelihood of leading to an accurate inference of the intention of the message source.

The disadvantage of this definition is that it employs a number of terms which are themselves undefined and whose definitions must thus also be given. In the first place, a message is that commodity transmitted in the communication process. Messages, as the following paragraph suggests, are essentially quantities of energy moved from a source to a receiver.

Communication may be defined as a system for sending and receiving observable signals (messages). The qualification "observable" is used to emphasize the fact that different organisms (or machines) can observe different kinds and degrees of signal. Most animals, for instance, can observe visual, olfactory, auditory, tactile, and gustatory signals, although in varying degrees depending upon the specific animal. Machines, on the other hand, are more likely to observe electrical or magnetic signals.

For communication to take place there must exist at least two entities (animals, machines, etc.) which are physically situated so as to be able to produce outputs (messages) observable by one another and to actually produce such outputs. Communication can be viewed in terms of the model depicted in Fig. 1 which is based upon the Shannon model of communication [3] modified to accommodate reciprocal signaling between the entities. In other words, communication is a system, for without reciprocity no communication can be said to have occurred.

An ensemble of messages forms a language. Thus language is defined within the context of communication, and amounts to the set of signals observable by source and receiver. Language must therefore be a shared ensemble of messages, but no other restrictions need be placed upon it.

Many different languages are known. Languages may be differentiated through examination of the characteristics of the individual elements or messages of which they are composed. These characteristics may relate to the manner of production of the message or to the manner in which it is received.

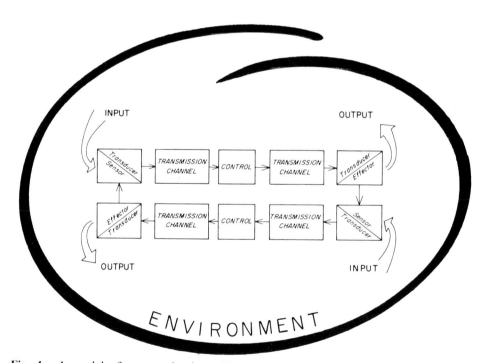

**Fig. 1.** A model of communication which emphasizes reciprocal signaling between source and receiver.

For instance, the gestures and movements that a person makes with his body are referred to as "body language" [4]. This language is used to communicate feelings of nervousness, attitudes of respect or fear, positions of weakness or power [5], and so on.

These examples of language are fairly obvious and the distinction between them is fairly easily made. However, language inferences are generally much more subtle and may be thought of as culturally oriented. A culture is a communication system, and since communication involves language, it is necessary for the components of a communication system to employ a common language if there is to be a reasonable expectation of effective communication.

We see, therefore, that language differentiation is a relatively complex and perhaps hazardous process because languages can be differentiated not only on the basis of elemental or structural characteristics, but on the basis of geography, on the basis of profession, on the basis of ethnic origin, or on religious grounds as well. As a consequence, it is necessary to be careful in content analysis to define the language with which one is dealing.

What we are concerned with in content analysis, therefore, is the study of language or, more properly, tracts of language utterences which we have called messages or which may be called texts, journals, articles, and so on, with the purpose of inferring the intention of the source of the message. In particular we are interested in developing computer aids to manual content analysis or in developing fully automated content analysis systems.


## AREAS OF APPLICATION OF CONTENT ANALYSIS

In its broadest sense, content analysis has almost universal applicability. We shall restrict ourselves to its current manifestations in language processing. Other aspects of content analysis (even though not so categorized) are treated elsewhere in this *Encyclopedia*. We shall first mention several areas of application of content analysis as a means of introducing the reader to the ways in which content analysis can be used. Discussion of these applications will conveniently lead into specific techniques of content analysis.


### Social Sciences

Automated content analysis has proved a useful, although not yet widely used, tool in the social sciences. A variety of techniques has been employed to provide the scientist with data from which inferences about the intention of the message source may be made. Suppose, for example, a political scientist is studying a reporter's articles dealing with a presidential candidate. Can the scientist make supportable statements about the reporter's bias with respect to the candidate? The scientist might attempt to answer this question by employing a group of people to read the article and to state their opinions about the attitude of the reporter. But such opinions or inferences are, like those of the scientist himself, intuitive and subjective in nature. Most people will find it difficult to state precisely why they feel that the attitude of the reporter is biased in one direction or another. What is called for, therefore, is a more objective method of handling content.

Content analysis can be performed objectively by categorizing words or groups of words used to describe the candidate. For example, was the candidate described as stodgy or as down-to-earth? Were his ideas described as creative or radical? In each pair of descriptors (words), one descriptor is inferred to have a positive connotation while the other is considered to have a negative connotation. If words can be so classified, then the totality of these words used in reporting the candidate's actions can serve as a measure of the bias of the report. If a preponderance of words in the report are of the negative sort, the report can be said to be unfavorable to the candidate.

Such an approach as this has, in fact, been employed [6] to infer the bias of news reports dealing with the presidential campaign of 1968 as broadcast by the three major television broadcasting companies in the United States.

This approach is not flawless. There may be disagreements about a particular positive or negative connotation. Or the connotation of a word may depend upon a particular usage or a particular context. For instance, in the following short paragraph from a *National Geographic* article dealing with the Russian-U.S. joint space venture, it seems to us that there is at least a noticeable difference in the manner of reference to the rockets of the respective countries.

> Shrugging free of its shackles, a Vostok rocket lifts Soyuz skyward at the U.S.S.R.'s vast Baykonur Cosmodrome in remote Kazakhstan. In a thunderous echo $7\frac{1}{2}$ hours later, a Saturn rocket hurled Apollo aloft from Kennedy Space Center, Florida, beginning the 44 hours of complex maneuvers that would culminate in the linking [7].

Nevertheless, if categories are clearly formulated, such an approach to content analysis can be useful, and a small amount of error is usually tolerable. The advantage of this rather simplistic approach to content analysis is that inferences may be based upon a set of objective criteria rather than upon intuition. If there is disagreement about the conclusions drawn from the analysis, one may state more precisely why he disagrees [8].

### Political Science

Studies similar to those described above have been performed by political scientists in attempting to assess the attitude of a given country toward the United States. By examining political correspondence, statements in state-controlled news media, and so on, it may be possible to determine whether a country's attitude is aggressive or passive, hostile or friendly toward the United States. Such analyses are typically performed by classifying words in a manner similar to that described in the preceding paragraph, and then observing the occurrence of these words in the correspondence or diplomatic communiques under examination [9, 10].

## Psychology

Psychologists frequently use automated content analysis procedures to aid in the determination of the attitudes of their subjects. For example, the dialog between the psychologist and his subject will be tape recorded to be subsequently transcribed for analysis. The transcription of the subject's speech usually includes not only the basic texts but also the length of the pauses between statements and such other utterances as "um," "er," and "ah." Words, pauses, and syntactic structures are then interpreted as indicators of fear, anxiety, aggressiveness, or peace [11, 12].

A well-known attitudinal measure used by psychologists is Osgood's Semantic Differential [13, 14]. This measure requires that subjects rate specific qualities of some entity according to some scale terminated by strong opposites. Osgood's Semantic Differential is a reasonably reliable measure of strongly polarized attitudes. That is, distinction between positive and negative, strong and weak, active and passive, and other conceptually diametric pairs are rather easily distinguished using the Semantic Differential. See, for example, the work of Patton [15].

## Anthropology

It is fairly well accepted that folklore and myth can convey a good deal of information about the deep-seated moral characteristics and social values of a particular culture of which the folklore or myth are a part [16]. Thus one aim of content analysis in anthropological studies is to establish the attitudinal relationship between a culture's folklore and its currently observable characteristics. For instance, it is of interest to determine what the members of a culture believe concerning honor, morality, and religion, or what values they place upon various artifacts or natural phenomena [17, 18].

## Linguistics

Linguists employ content analysis procedures for a variety of purposes, including authorship attribution studies, interpretation of allegory, language translations, abstracting, and indexing. In fact, one might say that content analysis is concerned with the identification, isolation, and interpretation of metaphore. A well-known application of content analysis is in the work of Mosteller and Wallace, whose main purpose was to test Bayes' theorem in a textual discrimination problem, namely determination of the authorship of certain of the *Federalist Papers* [19]. A comparative analysis of certain of the *Papers* with confirmed authorship showed that Madison and Hamilton employed certain prepositions (to, from, by) with significantly different frequencies, and this fact enabled Mosteller and Wallace to establish authorship of other of the *Federalist Papers* with a high degree of confidence.

Stylistics is another area of study which has received considerable attention [20, 21]. Comparison of the styles of different authors, determination of basic characteristics of style, and the perception of theme are among the important aspects of stylistic analysis.

**Information Storage and Retrieval**

Although not usually mentioned in conjunction with discussions of content analysis, information storage and retrieval is basically concerned with ascertaining the content of documents (e.g., books, articles, case law). The creation of abstracts and indexes and the searching of machine-readable files of text data are content analytical processes. In preparing an abstract, it is necessary to identify and isolate the principal message of the author to form the basis of the abstract. Indexing similarly demands the selection of words and phrases that are significant of content. Extensive discussions of both abstracting and indexing may be found in Refs. 22 and 23; brief discussions of document retrieval, classification, question-answering, and inference systems are included in this article.

**Music**

Formal content analytical procedures have found their uses in music, principally in thematic analysis studies. Such studies have been used both in attempts to identify the recurrence of a theme in two or more of a composer's works, or to identify a theme common to the works of two or more composers. Such studies have also been carried out in an attempt to attribute a work of unknown authorship to some particular composer [24, 25].

**Robotics**

Once a science-fiction concept, robotics is now a more prosaic area for scientific research. In addition to problems of locomotion and control [26], robotics is concerned with the way in which commands are interpreted by a robot to carry out the task(s) expressed in the command [27, 28]. For example, the request

Bring me a glass of water.

requires that the robot to which it is addressed correctly interpret "bring," "me," "a glass of water" in addition to knowing where to get a glass and some water, and where "me" is located. This example merely suggests the complexity of the problem and is but an illustration of the general notion of automated language processing.

Additional areas of application of content analysis may be imagined, many of which deal with languages other than the typical printed or spoken languages. Pattern recognition [29, 30] is a good example of such application areas. These are treated elsewhere in this Encyclopedia, usually under the name of the application.

## TECHNIQUES OF CONTENT ANALYSIS

In preceding paragraphs we have mentioned a variety of applications of content analysis as a way of indicating its scope and as a means of suggesting the range of data to which content analysis may be applied. We turn now to the techniques of content analysis.

Content analysis procedures have frequently used manually derived categories of words which are thought to be distinctive of some particular idea or attitude. The value of the result of such content analysis studies depends upon the appropriateness of these categories to the particular application. If categories are not well-chosen and well-formulated, the value of the analysis may be low. Several more-refined techniques have been developed which may be employed in content analysis and which may yield results with greater validity. We discuss several of these techniques in the remainder of this article. For convenience of presentation, these techniques are categorized as pertaining to elemental analysis (e.g., identification of words, word groups, word frequencies) or to structural analysis (i.e., identification of elements and of the relations between them). The use of these terms will become clearer as the techniques are further defined. Applications illustrative of these analysis techniques conclude each section.

### Techniques of Elemental Analysis

Techniques employed in a determination of the content of a tract of text by analysis of the elementary components of that text we call *elemental analysis techniques*. Such techniques include word frequencies and relative frequencies, use of thesauri, concordances, stemming, stoplists, and part-of-speech determinations.

#### *Stoplists*

The most frequently occurring words in most any text are those generally classified as function words. This class of words includes the prepositions, conjunctions, articles, and similar words that serve a syntactic function in the text but which do not serve directly to express content. We may also include other frequently occurring words which are deemed meaningless. It is possible to eliminate these words from consideration in a text through the use of a table of these words. This table, often called a ''stoplist,'' need not be larger than perhaps a few hundred words (see Fig. 2 for example). Each word in the text is then compared with this stoplist and if it matches an entry in the stoplist, it may be ignored in subsequent processing (e.g., frequency counts). This simple technique makes it possible to eliminate function words from consideration and to concentrate attention on words with a higher probability of content expression.

One must, however, be careful not to exceed the bounds of reason in stoplist development. It is difficult to identify words which are meaningless in every context. The word "of" used as a preposition may well be a poor indicator of content, but when used as a noun, it becomes quite important.

## *Stemming*

The correct identification of word frequencies may be confounded by the appearance of morphologically distinct but conceptually related words. For instance, the word "compute" may take many derivational forms such as computer, computing, computed, computes, computation, computerized, and computer-aided. Since all of these words are conceptually related, it would be desirable that they all be accounted for in the frequency of occurrence of the basic root concept. To do so requires the application of what is frequently referred to as a stemming procedure. In general, a stemming procedure is designed to reduce words to a common root, which may then be used in the word-frequency counts. Stemming algorithms have been developed which recognize and eliminate common inflectional suffixes and prefixes [32, 33]. A typical stemming algorithm embodies an iterative procedure for identification and elimination of inflectional affixes (see, for example, Fig. 3). These affixes may be subdivided according to whether they appear preceding the root word or following the root word.

A somewhat more arbitrary approach to the grouping of etymologically related words involves straightforward word truncation [34]. While this technique has been most often used in query formulation in retrieval systems, it can be used

| | |
|---|---|
| A | HOUSE |
| AMERICAN | INDIA |
| AN | INTERNATIONAL |
| BUREAU | NATIONAL |
| CALIFORNIA | NEW YORK |
| COMMITTEE | OF |
| CONFERENCE | ON |
| CONGRESS | SENATE |
| COUNCIL | SYMPOSIUM |
| DEPARTMENT | THE |
| DEPT. | U.N. |
| GT. BRIT. | U.S. |

**Fig. 2.** A brief stoplist (from Ref. 31).

| worth | cis | al |
|-------|-----|----|
| ally  | fer | an |
| ance  | fic | at |
| ceae  | ful | ch |
| diol  | gen | ct |
| less  | ide | ed |
| lide  | ile | en |
| lite  | ine | er |
| ment  | ing | ic |
| metr  | ion | id |
| ness  | ism | ly |
| xide  | ite | a  |
| age   | ity | c  |
| ale   | mic | i  |
| ant   | nol | o  |
| ase   | sis | x  |
| bil   | str | y  |
| ble   | vit | z  |

**Fig. 3.**  Sample suffix list for use in stemming.

with equal success in refining word-frequency counts or in grouping etymologically similar words.

*Vocabulary Control*

> Yonder stands Barazinbar, the Redhorn, cruel Caradhras; and beyond him are Silvertine and Cloudyhead: Celebdil the White, and Fanuidhol the Grey, that we call Zirakzigil and Bundushathur [35].

In order to avoid boring repetiveness in a text, the author will often resort to the use of synonyms or analogs. While this technique may be beneficial to human readers, it is quite devastating to automated content analysis, particularly that involving the recognition of words representing a particular concept. In the case of frequency of occurrence techniques, for example, its use means that either the frequency counts will be unrelated to the frequency of occurrence of the concept or else interpretation based upon the frequencies obtained will be potentially at variance with the fact. In order to overcome such difficulties, it is necessary to utilize a dictionary of synonyms as part of the content analysis procedure. In order to cope with analogs as well, the dictionary is frequently expanded to a thesaurus so that various other relationships between words in addition to synonymy can be established. But even with the use of a thesaurus, some synonyms must be established dynamically. For instance, in a chemical article it is frequently the case that the author, who wishes to avoid repetition of a long chemical name, will employ shorter words or symbols to represent the compound in question. This might be thought of as dynamically established

**TABLE 1**

Definition of Relations Used in the Authority List for POST

| Relation symbol | Definition of relation |
|---|---|
| US | Replace the main term (MT) with the subordinate term (ST) |
| US* | Cross refer MT to ST |
| UF | Approve MT |
| UF* | Cross refer from ST to MT |
| SN | Scope note—the intension of MT |
| BT | MT generic to ST (no action) |
| BT* | Cross refer from ST to MT (upward reference) |
| NT | MT species of ST (no action) |
| NT* | Cross refer from ST to MT (downward reference) |
| RT | MT related to ST (no action) |
| RT* | Cross refer from ST to MT (see also reference) |
| MU | Multiple entry. Generate added index entries |
| TC | Make index entry at MT and ST and connect with "see also" reference. |
| NC | Make index entry at MT and ST and connect with "see also" reference. |
| XX | Cross refer from ST to ST related to MT by US* |

synonomy. In any event, the basic thesaurus must be augmented by such equivalences established within the text being analyzed. This is by no means a simple matter. It has formed the basis for a great deal of linguistic research and no generally useful solution of the problem has so far been found.

The authority list developed at the Chemical Abstracts Service for use in production of the index to *Polymer Science and Technology* (POST) is a good example of vocabulary control employing elemental analysis techniques [36]. A variety of relationships is employed (see Table 1); these relationships control the entries appearing in the POST index relative to the words or phrases which were present in the abstract or article being indexed. A few examples illustrating the results of application of the POST authority list are given in Table 2.

**TABLE 2**

Examples Illustrating the Effect of the Relations Defined in Table 1

| MT from text | Rel | ST | Result |
|---|---|---|---|
| occurrence | US | occurrence | |
| theory of indexing | US* | indexing theory | theory of indexing *see* indexing theory |
| eigenvalue | UF* | proper value | proper value *see* eigenvalue |
| copolymers | SN | excludes blends | copolymers (excludes blends) |
| nylons | BT* | polyamides | polyamides *see* nylons |
| Orlons | RT* | acrylans | acrylans *see also* Orlons |

An extension of thesaurus techniques to provide an interface between a user and the vocabularies of two or more data bases has recently been described [37]. The interface amounts to a function which maps the user's terminology into that of the data base and is intended to obviate the user having to learn several different vocabularies.

### Concordances and Collations

Concordances are essentially word indexes which list and give the specific location of each occurrence of a word within the source document. Concordances may also display the immediate context in which a word appears. Concordances enable scholars to make inferences about the use of words by a specific author or to compare word usage by two authors as an aid in detecting similarities of style [38]. For instance, study of a concordance of the words of St. Thomas Aquinas indicated that he used the word "virtus" to mean "strength" or "driving force" rather than "self-control" [39]. The use of concordances to fill in missing words in a document has also been explored [40].

Collation of a text and its variant (e.g., a manuscript and the published edition) involves the identification of changes or variations between them. Moore [41] is attempting to formalize this aid to scholarly research and to develop efficient algorithms for producing collations.

### Word Frequency Techniques

The frequency of occurrence of words in a text has often been used as a measure of the content of the text [42]. The hypothesis underlying this measure is that the more frequently a word occurs in a text the more likely is the text to be about the concept which the word represents. For example, if the word "computer" occurs frequently in a text, this may indicate that the article is about "computers." The measure is too simplistic to be employed in serious content analytical studies. Nevertheless, as we shall see, various refinements of the basic hypothesis stated above have led to useful word frequency techniques.

Because accurate frequency counts depend upon correct identification of synonyms or morphologically similar words, some of the techniques described above (stemming, vocabulary control) may be usefully employed as precursors to frequency analysis.

An excellent example of word frequency analysis is afforded by the work of Kucera and Francis on present-day American English [43].

### Relative Frequency Techniques

In addition to the use of stoplists, stemming, and so on, the basic frequency criteria can themselves be refined. Instead of dealing with the simple frequency of occurrence of words in a text, one may consider the frequency of occurrence of a word in a text in contrast with its frequency of occurrence in a large body of text. To effect this comparison, a core of text which is considered to be representative in some sense must first be defined and each word's frequency of occurrence in that core must be determined. (The frequency of occurrence of a word in this core of text may be thought of as its frequency of occurrence in general usage.) Now the frequency of occurrence of a word in a specific text may be compared with the word's frequency of occurrence in general usage. For example, suppose a word occurs with a frequency of 20 in 1000 words of a given text, whereas its frequency of occurrence in the general corpus is 10 in 10000 words of text. Such a word would usually be considered a significant indicator of content in the specific text because its frequency of occurrence is 20 times that found in general text.

Several alternative theories of word significance have been propounded [44]. One theory states that the greater is the occurrence frequency of a word in a document the more indicative is the word of the document's content. Occurrence frequency is defined as

$$\frac{F_{wi}}{\sum\limits_{\forall_i} F_{wi}}$$

where $F_{wi}$ is the frequency of occurrence of the $i$th word, $w_i$, in the document ($1 \le i$).

Relative frequency has also been determined using difference, ratio, and conditional probability measures. The frequency difference measure states that a word in a document ($D$) is significant of content if

$$\left(\frac{F_{wi}}{\sum\limits_{\forall_i} F_{wi}}\right)_D - \left(\frac{F_{wi}}{\sum\limits_{\forall_i} F_{wi}}\right)_C > 0$$

[where the subtrahend is the occurrence frequency of word $i$ in a general corpus ($C$) of text]. The frequency ratio measure

$$\frac{\left(\dfrac{F_{wi}}{\sum\limits_{\forall_i} F_{wi}}\right)_D}{\left(\dfrac{F_{wi}}{\sum\limits_{\forall_i} F_{wi}}\right)_C} > \alpha$$

accords significance to a word when the ratio of its occurrence frequency in a document to that in a general corpus exceeds some prescribed threshold, $\alpha$.

The conditional probability frequency is the probability that a given word type will not appear more frequently in a random sample than in a particular document. This can be calculated by using the hypergeometric distribution, the Poisson standard deviate, or the standard deviate [45].

The use of relative frequency of occurrence as a measure of content is usually more successful than the simple frequency-of-occurrence measure. The major difficulty in employing the relative frequency technique is that of establishing a word's frequency in a sample corpus. One other problem associated with the relative frequency technique is that occasioned by the constant change which language undergoes. This means that the frequency of occurrence of a word in general usage would need to be recalculated from time to time in order to keep pace with language changes.

Although the elemental analysis techniques discussed thus far are of considerable interest and have been used extensively, they are of very limited value in content analysis when contrasted with human analytical abilities. Hence a great deal of effort has been expended in the search for more suitable analytical methods. We shall conclude this discussion of elemental analysis by examining a number of techniques of considerably greater complexity and erudition. These techniques are all based upon a view of a text as a collection of words or word-aggregates, such as phrases, sentences, or clauses.[1]

At the word level, the role or function of each word is of interest. In traditional terms we may consider the analysis of text into word-classes to be equivalent to part-of-speech analysis. However, automated analyses usually gives significantly different results because the application of the results usually demands it.

### Defining Grammatical Classes

The words which comprise the vocabulary of a language are traditionally classified into eight parts of speech or grammatical classes. Dionysios Thrax is credited with first proposing eight parts of speech: noun, verb, participle, article, pronoun, preposition, adverb, and conjunction [46]. The interjection is often added to this list. For English, Priestly classified words into the above eight parts of speech in 1761 [47]. Some parts of speech are given definitions based upon their *lexical meaning*. For instance, a noun is defined as the name of a person, place, or thing. On the other hand, an adjective is defined as a word which modifies a noun. Such a definition is based upon *function*.

Gleason [48] has suggested an alternative method of defining grammatical classes. Three criteria are used as a definitional basis. the first criterion consists of a model for each of the four classes: noun, verb, adjective, and pronoun. Each model consists of possible inflectional endings which signal membership in the appropriate class. the second criterion lists words whose membership in one of the four classes is signaled by a change in word form rather than by the addition of inflectional endings (e.g., mouse and mice). The third criterion is the syntax of the sentence in which a word occurs. This criterion, Gleason feels, is a less sure basis for word class identification than the first two.

---

[1] These word-aggregates might be thought of as analogous to functional groups or molecular fragments in chemical terms.

Fries, in contrast with Gleason, has defined the parts of speech in terms of a basic structural frame or pattern [49]. Each position within a structural frame is occupied by a particular word class. Any word which can fit into a given position in the frame belongs to the corresponding word class. For illustration, consider the sample frame sentences:

1. The concert was good (always).
2. The clerk remembered the tax (suddenly).
3. The team went there.

A word which can replace either "concert," "clerk," "tax," or "team" belongs to *Class 1*. Words which can replace "was," "remembered," or "went" are members of *Class 2*. Any word which can replace "good" is placed in *Class 3*, and words which can replace "always," "suddenly," or "there" are placed in *Class 4*.

In addition to the four classes defined above, Fries defined a fifth class of words (*Class 5*) whose elements serve as structural markers within a sentence. These are frequently referred to as *function words*. The members of this class are most readily defined ostensively since there appear to be so few of them (Fries identified just 154). Some of the groups within this class are the auxiliary verbs, conjunctions, prepositions, relative pronouns, and determiners.

There are significant differences between the first four classes and *Class 5*. For the first four classes, lexical meanings are easily separable from structural meanings. For function words (*Class 5*) no clear distinction can be made, perhaps because such words may have no lexical meanings. Furthermore, whereas the first four classes are open ended, *Class 5* appears to be a closed class.

Fries found that function words accounted for almost a third of the total number of word occurrences in text. And in a more recent analysis of more than 1,000,000 words of text, Kucera and Francis have found that these words account for nearly 46% of the total number of words in the text studied [43].

Finally, it is easy to show that in order to understand certain structural signals within English text, *Class 5* words must be known as items. For instance, the two sentences

> The boys and the leaders were invited.
> The boys of the leaders were invited.

are indistinguishable on the basis of class assignment. In fact, the only way in which a structural distinction may be made between the two sentences is to know the words *and* and *of* as items.

The importance of the role which function words play in grammatical class assignment will be seen in the brief discussions to follow of several automated procedures for assignment of words of a text to their respective grammatical classes. In addition, the use of function words to resolve ambiguity in syntactic analysis has been described by Klein and Simmons [50], and Beckmann has shown that function words in English serve the purpose of an error-detecting code [51].

### Procedures for Grammatical Class Assignment

Several procedures for assigning words of a text to their respective grammatical classes are described in the following paragraphs as a means of illustrating the variety of approaches which has been taken to solution of this problem.

*The Economic Parser.* A program called the Economic Parser, which assigns words to grammatical classes, identifies phrase types, and marks clause boundaries, was developed by Clark and Wall [52]. The program first performs a dictionary look-up. The dictionary consists of about 1000 entries. The entries include function words, inflectional endings, and a list of words which are exceptions to regular inflection (i.e., "thing" is not a verb even though it ends in "ing"). Words which are not found in the dictionary are assigned an ambiguous noun/verb category. In a second pass, phrase boundaries are tentatively identified. In the third pass clause boundaries are identified and clauses are tested for well-formedness. If a clause does not contain a verb, noun phrases are examined in a left-to-right manner and the first word which has been assigned to the noun/verb class is identified as a verb. The algorithm was applied to abstracts of technical material and is reported to attain 91% accuracy in the identification of grammatical classes.

*The Computational Grammar Coder.* Klein and Simmons have implemented a Computational Grammar Coder (CGC) which assigns words in English text to the appropriate grammatical class [50]. The CGC is the initial phase of a syntactic analyzer which is part of a question-answering system. The CGC contains two types of dictionaries: (1) a function-word dictionary containing about 400 words, and (2) two dictionaries containing those nouns, verbs, and adjectives which are exceptions in various suffix texts. These dictionaries contained about 1500 words.

The algorithm of the CGC begins by putting each word through a series of independent tests. These tests include a function word test, a capitalization test, a numeral test, and a series of suffix tests. Each test may result in the assignment of a set of codes to the word. If a particular test yields no information about a word, the system assumes that the classes noun, adjective, and verb are possible. A final set of codes is obtained by taking the intersection of the set of codes assigned in each test.

After each word in a sentence has been identified in this manner, the context-frame test is made. This test sequentially processes strings of ambiguously coded words which are bounded by uniquely coded words. Every possible combination of codes of an ambiguously coded string is checked against a context-triad-frame table which contains permissible combinations of codes in such strings.

In tests using scientific text, the CGC correctly assigned approximately 90% of the words.

*The WISSYN System.*   The WISSYN system, designed to make grammatical class assignments to words in English text, was developed by Stolz, Tannenbaum, and Carstensen [53]. WISSYN contains dictionaries which are similar to those used in the CGC. The function-word dictionary contains about 300 words. If a word in a sentence is not found in the dictionary of function words, it is checked against a dictionary of suffixes and exceptions.

A third phase attempts to resolve the ambiguity of certain function words. For example the word "that" may be used in the following ways:

that dog jumped<br>
the dog that jumped

In this phase, a set of frames similar to those implemented by Klein and Simmons is used to resolve residual ambiguity.

A final phase of WISSYN uses the statistical frequencies of structural patterns of English sentences to assign grammatical classes. The operation of this phase can be easily understood by considering an illustration. Given a sentence whose elements have been identified as:

$$T \; D \; N \; X_1 \; P \; D \; N \; P \; X_2 \; X_3 \; T$$

where T is a terminal marker, D is a determiner, N is a noun, P is a pronoun, and $X_i$ is the $i$th unidentified word ($i \geq 1$). When an unidentified word is encountered, the probabilities of the three longest strings consisting of four or fewer words surrounding the unidentified word are considered. Thus the probability of $X_1$ being a noun, verb, adjective, or adverb would be calculated using the statistics of Table 3. The element $X_1$ would be designated as a verb, since this was the most probable case.

In a test of literary, scientific, and newspaper articles, an accuracy as high as 93% was attained.

*MYRA.*   A grammatical class assignment procedure first reported by Marvin, Rush, and Young [54] and subsequently refined by Young [55, 56], called MYRA, is built on the premise that function words together with a set of rules

**TABLE 3**
Conditional Probabilities

| Predictor | Noun | Verb | Adjective | Adverb |
|---|---|---|---|---|
| D N $X_1$ P D | .046 | .819 | .013 | .122 |
| $X_1$ P D N P | .438 | .359 | .068 | .135 |
| N $X_1$ P D N | .017 | .591 | .078 | .314 |
| Joint product | .00034 | .17377 | .00007 | .00517 |

(exemplified below) constitute necessary and sufficient conditions for the unambiguous determination of the grammatical classes of all words present in an English sentence. The principal classes to be determined are NAME and PRIMARY RELATION; SECONDARY RELATIONS are "known" *a priori* through use of a dictionary.[2] The rules constitute a set of context sensitive productions written by means of a simple notation. A simple example will serve to illustrate the rules. The rule:

$$... \text{THR XXX} ... \Rightarrow ... \text{THR VRB} ...$$

means that if the function word subclass THR is immediately followed by an unclassified word (XXX) in a sentence, then the unclassified word is assigned to the class VRB.

MYRA accepts English text as input in a continuous string without any prior formatting or marking. (This fact has two implications. First, MYRA does not "know" that the input is English text, but the text will be processed as though it were. Second, MYRA must break the string up into individual words.)

MYRA operates on the input text in three stages.

In the first stage, the individual words, exclusive of punctuation, are looked up in the dictionary. If a match occurs, the code for the dictionary element is entered into a vector which corresponds with the sequence of words between elements of EOS. For instance, the input string

The mouse ate the cheese.

would have already been partitioned as

The/mouse/ate/the/cheese/.

The vector resulting at the end of stage one will be

DTR XXX XXX DTR XXX EOS

In the second stage, MYRA applies the first 101 rules. Application is signalled by the presence in the vector of an element of FUNCTION WORD or of some other element(s) already classified, so that only rules which can reasonably be expected to produce classifications are applied. In the example, a rule for DTR can first be applied. Its application yields

DTR ADJ NON DTR XXX EOS

Moving to the right in the vector, we see that a second rule for DTR is called for. Its application yields

DTR ADJ NON DTR NON EOS

At the end of stage two, the vector may or may not be complete. It is completed and verified in stage three.

In stage three MYRA first classifies any previously unclassified WORDS. Finally, the vector is checked to see if a PRIMARY RELATION is present. If no PRIMARY RELATION is present, then elements of the vector are reclassified so

---

[2] Two alternative dictionaries were employed, one containing 217 entries and the other 431 entries.

that a PRIMARY RELATION is included. The analysis is thus completed and the results are output. In the example, at the end of stage two the vector contained no PRIMARY RELATION. Application of a final rule yields:

DTR NON VRB DTR NON EOS

MYRA was tested on some 6000 words of text and was reported to achieve an accuracy of 91% using the limited dictionary and 94% using the extended dictionary [56].

Knowledge of the classes to which words belong is essential to any subsequent syntactic analysis of text. In addition to the procedures described above, grammatical class assignments have also been made manually and embodied in dictionaries for use in automated syntactic analysis procedures.

## Procedures for Syntactic Analysis

In the preceding section we described techniques for grammatical class assignment. These techniques may be used in isolation for content analysis, but they are principally used as the basis for syntactic analysis.

Syntactic analysis, which involves the identification and characterization of aggregates of words, is intermediate between elemental analysis and structural analysis.[3] Syntactic analysis procedures of many kinds have been developed, based upon a variety of theories. Several of the more important syntactic analysis procedures are described in the following paragraphs. We include syntactic analysis among elemental analysis techniques because the results they yield do not expose the conceptual structure of text but extend the basis for content determinations provided by word-analysis procedures.

**The Multiple-Path Syntactic Analyzer.** A well-known program for syntactic analysis is the Multiple-Path Syntactic Analyzer developed by Oettinger and Kuno [57]. This system is based on a context-free grammar of 3400 rules and a top-to-bottom (top-down) analytical procedure employing a pushdown store. The dictionary used by this procedure gives a highly refined division of syntactic classes. For example, "are" belongs to three syntactic classes: one when used as an intransitive verb, one when used as a finite copula, and one when used as an auxiliary to another verb. Each possible analysis of the sentence is explored in a left-to-right manner and verified or invalidated by the context-free grammar. The production of multiple analyses is useful for research purposes, but it is a decided disadvantage in practical application. Processing time is not directly dependent upon the length of a sentence but depends primarily on the number of possible surface structures which the sentence can generate.

**Syntactic Analysis for Transformational Grammar.** Zwicky [58] has included syntactic analysis in an attempt to implement a transformational grammar for sentences. The first phase of the program is a phrase-structure grammar which

---

[3] It may be thought of as being analogous to functional-group analysis in chemistry.

handles a subset (32 of a possible 134 rules have been implemented) of English. The initial step in Zwicky's procedure consists of a dictionary look-up of each word in a sentence. The dictionary contains all possible syntactic classes for a word, along with attributes such as tense, transitivity, and number. This lexical entry also represents an entry in terms of more abstract elements, for example, "none" is defined as "neg any." After all possible syntactic classes for a word in a sentence have been retrieved, all possible analyses of a sentence are examined. The sentence

Can the airplane fly?

has 15 possible surface structures. In the next step a context-free grammar is applied to each of these analyses, and some structures are eliminated. Transformational rules are applied next in an effort to eliminate the spurious surface structures. No discussion of the lexicon or of the rules used in either the context-free grammar or the transformational grammar is given. Although the process has been only partially implemented, Zwicky concludes that highly efficient routines are needed to obtain the correct surface structures.

***Syntactic Analysis Based on a Regular Grammar.*** Thorne, Bratley, and Dewar have written a syntactic analyzer as part of a system which assigns the deep structure and surface structure to English sentences [59]. In this syntactic analyzer, five types of sentences, six types of clauses, and several other syntactic categories including gerund subjects, active verbs, modifiers, and indirect objects are identified.

The analyzer employs a dictionary of fewer than 200 words. It contains function words (referred to as closed-class words), verbs, suffixes, and exceptions to these suffixes. The analyzer is based upon a form of transformational grammar [60]. The operation of the system is as follows. First, all of the function words in a sentence are identified. Based on these function words and on the information provided by the grammar as it relates to the sentence, a set of predictions is made. These predictions are tested, and based upon the results of these tests, new predictions are made for successive parts of the sentence. All of the possible predictions are tested, and every prediction which holds produces a distinct analysis for the sentence. See Fig. 4 for example.

In some sentences none of the predictions which are made are satisfied. This happens when the sentence is improperly constructed or because the grammar is not complete. In this case a program produces a message indicating that the analyzer has failed for this sentence.

***The Economic Parser.*** The syntactic analyzer developed by Clark and Wall [52] and mentioned earlier in conjunction with grammatical class assignment, demonstrates that a relatively simple analysis may yield substantial syntactic information. Clark and Wall developed a limited phrase-structure parser for use in mechanized indexing. They adopted a "computational" dictionary similar to the one developed by Klein and Simmons. The grammar they employ identifies only phrases and clauses, and no attempt is made to mark relations between phrases.

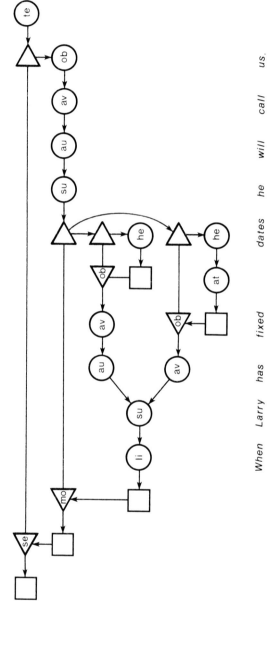

**Fig. 4.** A two-path analysis structure produced by the Thorne, Bratley, and Dewar procedure.

*When Larry has fixed dates he will call us.*

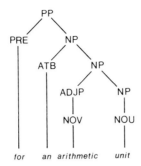

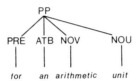

**Fig. 5.** Tree structure representations of a complete phrase-structure analysis (top), and a Clark-Wall modified phrase-structure analysis (bottom).

The difference between a "complete" phrase structure and the Clark and Wall model is illustrated in Fig. 5.

The Clark-Wall algorithm is a set of procedures for assigning an allowable syntactic structure to an input string. The first pass incorporates a dictionary look-up and phrase boundary placement. Pass two establishes clause boundaries and tests well-formedness. Clark and Wall report an average accuracy of 91%. Though encouraged with these results, Clark and Wall are careful to emphasize that the parser is of a limited nature and is "scored" solely on correct identification of phrases.

*A Limited Program for Syntactic Analysis.*   Resnikoff and Dolby have written a program for grammatical class assignment which consists of fewer than 100 COMIT instructions [61]. This program utilizes a dictionary of 200 function words and 200 affixes. At the time their paper was published, Resnikoff and Dolby intended to expand the dictionary to about 1000 words. In preliminary tests on texts which include parts of *Ulysses* by James Joyce and a *New York Times* editorial, the results were reported as being "evidently high."

*PROSE.*   Another theory of grammar is employed by Vigor, Urquhart, and Wilkinson in the parsing algorithm for their Parsing Recognizer Outputting Sentences in English (PROSE) [62]. Their analysis is based upon a dependency grammar analogous to the one described by Hays [63]. Figure 6 contrasts a

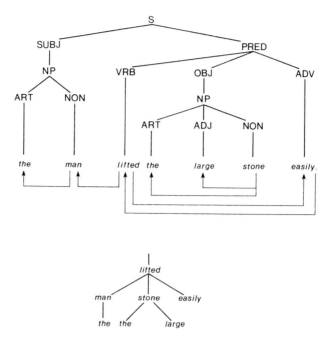

**Fig. 6.** A phrase-structured tree with word-dependency relationships marked (top), and a dependency-analysis tree of the type employed in the PROSE project (bottom).

phrase structure (such as used by Clark and Wall or Thorne, Bratley, and Dewar) with a dependency analysis.

A phrase structure postulates a hierarchy of phrases and subphrases comprising the nodes of a tree. In a dependency grammar, the words of the text are the internal nodes of the tree. Vigor, Urquhart, and Wilkinson have identified two measures of dependencies which they call binding and determinacy. Binding is a function of physical position. Determinacy is a function of possible contexts. The two values for binding are *bound* or *loose*; the two values for determinacy are *determinate* or *recursive*. The relationship of an article and its noun is bound determinate. The relationship of a conjunction to the words it relates is loose recursive.

Vigor, Urquhart, and Wilkinson describe the parsing process as setting up a dependency tree by "plugging in plugs." For example, "the" has a "plug" which can only be satisfied by a noun "outlet." "Sits" has a required "plug" for a singular noun or pronoun and an optional "plug" for a positional preposition.

**Syntactic Analysis Based on String Analysis.** In a project headed by Sager a string analysis grammar [64] is the basis of a syntactic analysis program. In this analysis a sentence is viewed as a set of elementary strings (clauses). Modifiers and prepositional phrases are defined as adjuncts. Thus the sentence

Cars without brakes cause accidents.

is described by the elementary string N t V N (i.e., noun, tensed verb, noun) and an adjunction class P N (preposition, noun). Rules are developed for the analysis of relative clauses and of clauses joined by coordinate conjunctions. In the first step of the program, the possible syntactic classes of each word in the sentence are retrieved from a dictionary. The assignments made during this step are:

$$\begin{array}{ccccc} \text{Cars} & \text{without} & \text{brakes} & \text{cause} & \text{accidents.} \\ \text{N} & \text{P} & \text{N/tV} & \text{N/tV/V} & \text{N} \end{array}$$

In the next phase of the program, the syntactic categories are examined in a left-to-right manner while the grammar rules for elementary strings and adjuncts are matched to the possible analyses of the sentence. If a grammar rule fails to match up correctly with the sentence, the program backs up to the initial word of an adjunct or string and attempts to apply a different rule. Sager estimates that an adequate grammar for English could be accomplished with about 150 rules plus another 150 restrictions. These restrictions analyze elements of the elementary string and check for such things as subject-verb agreement and well-formedness.

***Syntactic Analysis Based on Transition Network Grammars.*** Woods has developed a grammar described in terms of an augmented transition network [65]. A recursive transition network is a directed graph with labeled states and arcs. The labels on the arcs may be state names or terminal symbols. An arc labeled with a state name produces the following action: the state at the end of the arc is stored in a pushdown stack and control passes to the state indicated by the arc label. Control is passed back to the saved state by popping the stack. This network is augmented by adding to each arc of the transition network an arbitrary condition which must be satisfied in order for the arc to be followed and a set of structure-building actions to be executed if the arc is followed. The algorithm accepts as input words of a sentence along with the grammatical class of each word of the sentence. The algorithm produces a labeled bracketing of the phrases of the sentence; an identification of the subject, object, and verb; and an assignment of the sentence type (e.g., interrogative or declarative). The transition network model requires about the same processing time as predicative analyzers [66].

***Syntactic Analysis in the Simulation of Natural Language Processes.*** Winograd has recently published a system designed to explore how humans process language [28]. The system includes procedures for both syntactic and semantic analysis. The syntactic analysis procedures are based on a systemic theory of grammar [67, 68]. Although the theories of this grammar have not been stated in a unified way, the emphasis of this grammar is on the "informational units" [69] of a language. Winograd interprets these "informational units" as amounting to clauses and phrases.

In his procedures for syntactic analysis, Winograd has defined 18 word classes, four group types (noun, verb, adjective, and preposition) and two clause types. The 18 word classes are a finer division of the traditional word classes.

The two types of clauses are denoted as major and secondary. Associated with each of these units is a set of attributes. Every unit belonging to a word class, group, or clause is assigned a subset of these attributes. For example, a verb (e.g., "began") may have the attributes "past," "infinitive"; a preposition group (e.g., "in the kitchen") may have the attribute "locational object"; and a clause may have attributes such as "transitive," "passive," and "causality."

The components of the syntactic analysis process are a dictionary, a context-free grammar, and a pushdown list (PDL). The dictionary contains the vocabulary of the language along with each entry's syntactic class and attributes. The program which implements the context-free grammar contains several functions which give the grammar context-sensitive aspects. As an example, one function checks for agreement between subject and predicate. A bottom-up parser is used to apply the context-free grammar.

**Syntactic Analysis Based on the Notion of Naming in Language.** Young [56] has offered an approach to syntactic analysis based upon the notion that language is a system of things and relations between them, and that its vocabulary consists of *names of things* and *names of relations*. A "thing" is defined as any directly or indirectly observable entity, and a relation is defined as any observable change of state (behavior) of a thing with respect to time. For example, "driving a nail with a hammer" involves two sensible objects, "nail" and "hammer," which are related by "driving." Young refers to things simply as NAMES and to relations between things as RELATIONS.

Many researchers have, in one way or another, treated languages as relational systems. Rothstein has proposed the use of binary relations in representing strings of language [70]. In a model of verbal understanding, Simmons [71] has defined primitive elements of his model to be *concepts* and *relations*; these primitives are essentially equivalent to Young's *thing* and *relation,* and as will be seen subsequently, the views of Montgomery [72], Fillmore [73], Chafe [74], and others are also compatible with this relational view of language.

**The Naming Process in Language.**

> "The name of the song is called '*Haddocks' Eyes*'." "Oh, that's the name of the song, is it?" Alice said, trying to feel interested. "No, you don't understand," the Knight said, looking a little vexed. "That's what the name is *called*. The name really *is* '*The Aged Aged Man.*'" Then I ought to have said 'That's what the *song* is called'?" Alice corrected herself. "No, you oughtn't: that's quite another thing! The *song* is called '*Ways and Means*': but that's only what it's *called,* you know!" "Well, what *is* the song, then?" said Alice, who was by this time completely bewildered. "I was coming to that," the Knight said. "The song really *is* '*A-sitting On a Gate*': and the tune's my own invention" [75].

In Young's conception, NAMES and RELATIONS denote basic elements of a language, but it will usually be found that simple NAMES (single words) may be combined for naming many things or behaviors so that it is unnecessary to assign a unique name to every thing or behavior. In other words, the basic vocabulary of a language will be found usually to be rather quickly extended to practical limits, and that additional linguistic devices are required to continue to name things and behaviors in a practical way. For instance, there are many horses in the world and it would be cumbersome at best to have to assign a unique word as a NAME to each and every one, even though the language might provide the capability of doing so. Instead, languages provide for the modification of basic NAMEs by permitting several NAMEs to be related to one another in special ways. For example, the relation between "brown" and "horse" in the NAME "brown horse" is established, in English, by the juxtaposition of the words, while explicit relational words are often used as in "house of wax," where "of" serves this purpose.

By providing appropriately for combining single NAMEs to form more complex ones, a language becomes more powerful without the burden of a huge vocabulary.

This view of naming forms the basis for a type of phrase-structure syntactic analysis which emphasizes the centrality of RELATIONS. The decomposition of a sentence as a hierarchy of name-relation-name triples is shown in Fig. 7. An extensive treatment of this analysis procedure is given in [56]. Pepinsky has more recently discussed and amplified the name-relation-name concept [76].

*CALAS.* A rather comprehensive system of programs to aid in the analysis of text, called CALAS, has been developed [77, 78]. CALAS is an outgrowth of the earlier work of Young and her colleagues [54–56].

CALAS operates in three stages. In the first stage individual words are identified and are assigned to their respective grammatical classes. A feedback mechanism is provided so that assignment errors may be corrected, although an accuracy of about 95% is usually obtained without human editing.

In the second stage, words of a sentence are grouped into phrases. Again, a feedback mechanism provides for correction of analysis errors.

The third stage of CALAS marks clause boundaries and makes case role [73] assignments (case grammar is discussed later).

CALAS provides a great deal of information which humans can use to more objectively draw inferences about the content of text.

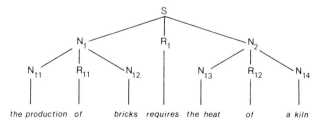

**Fig. 7.** Name-relation-name decomposition of an English sentence.

## Application of Elemental Analysis Techniques

The elemental analysis techniques described in the preceding paragraphs have received application in a variety of processes. Among these are document retrieval, document classification, question answering, indexing, and abstracting. The first three of these areas of application are discussed in the following sections.

### *Document Retrieval*

In document retrieval, elemental analysis techniques are frequently employed to determine the content of the documents of a collection and to construct a query which is to be processed against the document collection in order to identify documents to be retrieved therefrom.

The information storage and retrieval process, of which document retrieval is a part, is illustrated in Fig. 8. Documents are selected for acquisition and are represented in a form appropriate for the retrieval process. When a user has an information need, he formulates a question, or query, represented in a form acceptable to the system, and the document collection is searched to find the documents which satisfy the query specification [79].

The documents of the collection are rarely stored in their entirety in machine-readable form. A document is usually represented by its title, the authors, and the source (i.e., the journal citation or the publisher and place). This representation is occasionally augmented by the use of manually selected terms which

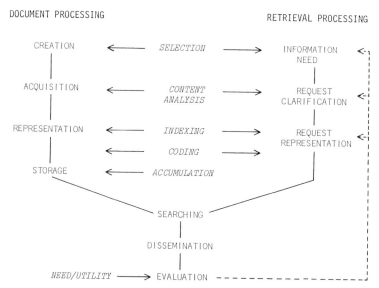

**Fig. 8.** The information storage and retrieval process.

improve the descriptive power of the document representation. Sometimes an abstract of the document is also used to augment the basic document representation. The document representation is usually further processed to produce an index consisting of words or terms derived from the document representation through application of one or more elemental analysis techniques. The semiautomated technique employed by Chemical Abstracts Service for the production of the index to *Polymer Science and Technology* (POST) illustrates such applications (see section entitled Vocabulary Control).

Once such an index has been created it serves as the basis for subsequent retrieval of documents from the collection. A search for desired documents presupposes that a user can identify with some precision the essential elements which characterize the desired documents and which set them apart from the remainder of a document collection. The user must characterize desired documents using terms which are consonant with those employed in the index. The user's document characterization takes the form of a query which is often constructed as a tabular representation as illustrated in Fig. 9. Inspection of Fig. 9 shows that in addition to the terms chosen for document description, the relationship between the terms expressed through the use of Boolean logical operators and the relative value of the terms expressed through the use of weights have also been employed. Further details concerning these refinements of the basic term description can be found in [81]. If a document is to be

Query description: (word description)
Term relationship: $(A + B + C) \cdot (D + \bar{E}) \cdot (F + G + H)$
Threshold weight: 10

| Entry | Logic | Term | Weight |
|-------|-------|------|--------|
| 01 | OR | A | 1 |
| 01 | OR | B | 1 |
| 01 | OR | C | 2 |
| 02 | OR | D | 3 |
| 02 | NOT | E | 2 |
| 03 | OR | F | 3 |
| 03 | OR | G | 4 |
| 03 | OR | H | 4 |

**Fig. 9.** Tabular representation of a query (from Ref. 80).

retrieved according to the specifications shown in Fig. 9, its set of index descriptors must include at least one term from within each entry group (i.e., from within each of the parenthesized terms in the Boolean expression shown in the term relationship). Weighting places further constraints on retrieval, requiring not only that the proper set of terms be identified, but also that the total sum of term weights equal or exceed the query threshold weight specification.

Additional refinements on the document retrieval process described above include the use of stemming or truncation, and the use of a thesaurus to control the term vocabulary employed in the query. These techniques may be applied manually or through computer programs.

## Classification

Rather than indexing a collection of documents by use of words representative of document content, one may instead process the document collection to produce well-defined subsets or classes which are conceptually closely related. These classes may be formed either through a derivative process or through an assignment process.

In derivative classification, the document collection is analyzed and those documents most similar to each other in terms of text characteristics are declared members of the same class. In assignment classification, *a priori* classes are established whose members must satisfy some prescribed criteria. Documents are subsequently analyzed for these criteria.

A good example of derivative classification is the automatic hierarchy generation procedure described by Abraham [82]. It is necessary first to construct a term-document or term-property matrix. The matrix may be of simple binary form where the presence of a term $T_i$ in a document is represented by a 1 in the $k$th cell of document vector $v^i$, otherwise $v_k{}^i = 0$. A weighting function, based perhaps on a frequency measure, may instead be used to give a broader range of values within the matrix.

The terms of the matrix are usually prescribed through a vocabulary-control device or through use of frequency techniques. From the term-document (property) matrix, a term-term similarity (correlation) matrix must be constructed. This matrix, which shows the similarity between terms $T_i$ and $T_j$, may be formed in a variety of ways. For the purpose of hierarchy construction, an asymmetrical measure of similarity is needed because we are interested in generic/specific relationships. Salton [83] gives the measure

$$C_{ij} = \frac{\sum_k \min (v_k^i, v_k^j)}{\sum_k v_k^i}$$

where $C_{ij}$ is the similarity (correlation) between terms $T_i$ and $T_j$. If $T_i = T_j$, $C_{ij} = 1$. If $T_i$ and $T_j$ do not bear any similarity to each other, $C_{ij} = 0$. Of course, a threshold criterion $K$ may be applied to $C$ to arbitrarily differentiate between similar and dissimilar terms. A hierarchy may now be formed by means of the following algorithm [82]:

1. If $C_{ij} < K$ and $C_{ji} < K$, then $T_i$ and $T_j$ are dissimilar.
2. If $C_{ij} > K$ and $C_{ji} > K$, then $T_i \cong T_j$.
3. If $C_{ij} < K$ and $C_{ji} > K$, then $T_i \rightarrow T_j$ in the hierarchy.
4. If $C_{ij} > K$ and $C_{ji} < K$ then $T_i \leftarrow T_j$ in the hierarchy.

In contrast with manually derived hierarchical classification schemes, the hierarchy produced by this method is entirely arbitrary and may not, in fact, be a simple tree (a term may be related to more than one parent term). However, the method has the advantage of being fully automatic, and one can envision a number of refinements which may make the hierarchy more nearly acceptable.

Classification by assignment is a familiar manual process, but its automation has also been achieved with some degree of success. Fried *et al.* [84] proposed an automated technique of assignment classification based on the concept of sequential analysis [85], which has recently been implemented by White *et al.* [86]. The technique requires that a document be assigned to one of $k$ previously established categories, $C_1, \ldots, C_k$. This, in turn, means that the $k$ categories must be established by some means. White *et al.* employed both semiautomated and fully automated procedures for initial category generation and definition. Category definition is extremely important since the definitions serve as discriminators during the assignment of a document to a category. The usual method of category (class) definition is through the use of keywords. As we have already pointed out, words significant of content may be selected in many different ways.

Assume that $n$ keywords are selected to define a category, $w_1, \ldots, w_n$. Next assume that some weight is computed for each word $w_1$ for each category in which it occurs. Let $w_1'$ be a random variable whose value is the weight assigned to keyword $w_1$; generally, let $w_i'$ be a random variable whose value is the weight assigned to keyword $w_i$. Given a document belonging to category $C_j$, the probability $P(w_1 \mid C_j)$ that the document will contain $w_1$ can be estimated by analysis of a sample document collection. More generally, the probability $P_n(w_1', \ldots, w_n' \mid C_j)$ that a *sequence* of keywords $w_1, \ldots, w_n$ will be found in a document belonging to $C_j$ can be estimated. Once keyword selection and probability estimation have been completed for the $k$ categories, documents may be assigned to these categories as follows.

The document is scanned (read) until a keyword (or a sequence of keywords) is found, then one of $k + 2$ decisions must be made: the document is assigned to one of the $k$ categories, the document is considered unclassifiable, or more keywords must be read. At the extreme the entire document would have to be read, but the decision rule (see below) employed is designed to minimize this condition.

The decision rule should be one which permits a document to be assigned to a category as early as possible to avoid unnecessary processing. Each decision will be made with some prescribed limit of error $\alpha$. That is, the decision rule must function so that the probability that a document is misclassified will be less than or equal to $\alpha$. Hence the probability that a document will be correctly classified is $1 - \alpha$. The decision rule suggested by Fried *et al.* follows from a lemma on sequential analysis [86] and has the form

$$\frac{P_n^*(w_1', \ldots, w_n' \mid C_j)}{P_n(w_1', \ldots, w_n' \mid C_j)} \geq \frac{1}{\alpha}$$

where $P_n^*(w_1', \ldots, w_n' \mid C_j)$ is a probability distribution over the sequences $w_1$, $\ldots, w_n$ $(1 < n \leq N)$ of keywords defining a category $C_j$ for each $j$ and each fixed $n$. For each $j$, $P_n^*(w_1', \ldots, w_1' \mid C_j)$ can be taken as an arbitrary but fixed discrete distribution over $N^n$ points. (Several choices for $P_n^*$ are possible, but the choice should result in minimum sample sizes.) $P_n(w_1', \ldots, w_n' \mid C_j)$ is the probability that a document which belongs to category $C_j$ will be observed to contain the sequence of keywords $w_1, \ldots, w_n$. Several alternative methods of estimating $P_n(w_1', \ldots, w_n' \mid C_j)$ have been employed in the studies reported by White *et al.* [86].

The deicision rule is applied iteratively to a document until it is classified or until it is deemed unclassifiable. Figure 10 illustrates the successful assignment of a document to category $C_{j_0}$ after $n_0$ steps.

Document classification employing the above procedures is also somewhat arbitrary, but the results are usually more nearly in accord with manual assignments than are the results of derivative classification procedures.

### Question Answering and Inference Systems

Another important area of application of elemental analysis techniques is that of question answering or inference making. We will briefly describe two of the

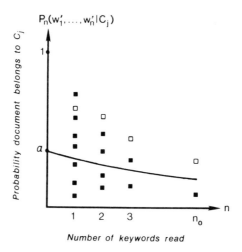

**Fig. 10.** Assignment classification based on sequential analysis.

many examples of these applications. The reader is referred to Borko [87], Simon and Siklóssy [88], and to the references therein for more detail.

*General Operation of a Question Answering System.* The question answering procedure can be conceptually divided into four phases: syntactic analysis, semantic analysis, data retrieval, and data processing, as illustrated schematically in Fig. 11.

The first phase consists of transforming the input sentence into a structure which explicitly represents the grammatical relationships among the words of the sentence. Using this information, the second (semantic analysis) component constructs a representation of the semantic content or meaning of the sentence. When actually implemented, the distinction between these two phases is seldom precise and their interaction is taken into account by the feedback loop shown in Fig. 11.

The third phase is that involving retrieval of relevant data from the data base. Any necessary processing of data is done by the fourth, or data processor, phase. Since data retrieval and deduction are closely linked, the relationship between the "Data Retriever" and the "Data Processor" phases could be compared to that between the "Parser" and the "Interpreter" phases of the system. The output of the "Interpreter" initiates and controls the operations of data retrieval and deduction.

The schematic of Fig. 11 contains a fifth block, called "Answer syntax computer." It may be observed that answer computation takes place in parallel with the four main phases of the question-answerer. The purpose of this block is to put together a syntactically and semantically acceptable natural language string as the answer, or response, to the query. Whatever the processes involved

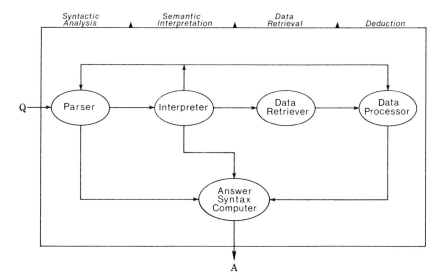

**Fig. 11.** The phases of a question answering system.

within the system may be, it is the output of this block which constitutes a meaningful response to the user and which controls interaction between user and system.

*ELIZA.* ELIZA is a program which makes certain kinds of natural language conversation between man and computer possible [89]. An example dialog is as follows:

>Men are all alike
>IN WHAT WAY?
>They're always bugging us about something or other
>CAN YOU THINK OF A SPECIFIC EXAMPLE?
>Well, my boyfriend made me come here
>YOUR BOYFRIEND MADE YOU COME HERE?
>He says I'm depressed much of the time
>I AM SORRY TO HEAR YOU ARE DEPRESSED.
>⋮

The basic operation of ELIZA is as follows. Text is read and inspected for the presence of a keyword. If a keyword is found, the sentence is transformed according to a rule associated with the keyword; if no keyword is found, a context-free remark is put out or, under certain conditions, an earlier transformation is retrieved. A prepared script provides transformations for ELIZA. The script is a high level program whose statements are not necessarily sequential—the flow of control among command statements in the script is guided by the keywords of the input. Since ELIZA is actually not a question-answerer, no data base is used. Transformational rules and keyword dictionaries form the "brain" of the program. It is relevant to note that a system with such elementary semantic routines has shown promising capabilities in application to a number of computer-aided instruction (CAI) problems and to computer simulation of counseling behavior [90].

*GRANIS.* Coles has described a computer program designed to make inferences about both pictures and natural language [91]. The program, called GRANIS (GRAphical NAtural Inference system), accepts a restricted subset of English together with elementary line drawings (input directly via a graphic display console).

GRANIS is made up of three major components: syntactic, semantic, and pragmatic. The syntactic component consists of clusters of productions for the recognition and translation of well-formed English sentences within the universe of discourse (organic chemistry, plane geometry, electrical circuits).

The semantic component consists of productions which cause the source string (text) to be translated into an expression in a predicate calculus. These expressions amount to interpretations of the input sentences.

A dictionary contains the terminal vocabulary of the source language which is partitioned into referent terminals (nouns, verbs, etc.) and function terminals (conjunctions, prepositions, etc.). The meaning of each lexical item in the set of referent terminals is also provided by the dictionary. The dictionary consists of a collection of Boolean procedures for evaluating predicates corresponding to the referent terminals.

The user of GRANIS draws a picture on a graphics device and then enters sentences (statements) about the picture. GRANIS will indicate whether the sentence is true or false for the given picture.

## *Other Applications*

The use of elemental analysis techniques in automatic abstracting has been fully described elsewhere in this Encyclopedia [22]. More recently, Mathis and Young [92] have described the use of content analysis techniques in procedures for improving the quality of computer-produced abstracts, and Mathis [93] has employed similar techniques in abstract evaluation. Indexing applications have been described by Landry and Rush [23], and uses of elemental analysis techniques in psychology have been described by Pepinsky [76], Patton [15], and Fisher [94]. The reader should consult these sources, as well as the multitude of references cited therein, for details of many applications.

## **Structural Analysis**

> All the innumerable substances which occur on earth—shoes, ships, sealing-wax, cabbages, kings, carpenters, walruses, oysters, everything we can think of—can be analysed into their constituent atoms, either in this or in other ways. It might be thought that a quite incredible number of different kinds of atoms would emerge from the rich variety of substances we find on earth. Actually the number is quite small. The same atoms turn up again and again, and the great variety of substances we find on earth results, not from any great variety of atoms entering into their composition, but from the great variety of ways in which a few types of atoms can be combined. . . [95].

In structural analysis of messages or texts we are interested not just in the component parts (elements) of the message, but also in the relationships between the elements and how these relationships are used to signify content both on the part of the message source and on the part of the message receiver. In other words, structural analysis involves the transformation of texts into structural representations which facilitate the drawing of inferences from the text about the intension of the text source. It must be admitted that the study of structural analysis is not well developed and that many of the techniques and theories to be described are yet in their formative stages. Nevertheless, the work which has been done promises exciting results in the foreseeable future, so that we are moved to suggest applications which have not yet been developed. Consultation of the references cited will enable the reader to form his own conclusions.

*Form and Content*

The content of a message is inextricably linked with its form. Thus, in spite of earlier views, it is now generally accepted that message form is significant in content analysis, but this idea has been long in coming [96]. Viewing messages as linear strings of words seems to have been accepted for as long as language has been studied; this view reached its zenith with the work of Chomsky and his adherents on the notions of deep and surface structures and transformational grammars [60, 97–100]. The hypothesis that the content (meaning) of a message lies "beneath" the text we see (or hear) is a plausible one, but the further hypothesis that the underlying (deep) structures are fewer in number than the corresponding surface structures is not tenable. For instance, the two sentences

> The hiker was attacked by a bear

and

> A bear attacked the hiker

convey essentially the same idea, but do not in all particulars have the same content. There are many subtle aspects of language which the Chomskian view cannot explain. Nevertheless, Chomsky deserves credit for initiating a great resurgence of interest and progress in linguistics and content analysis.

The fact that messages are usually represented as linear strings of sounds or visual signals has, we believe, obscured the real structure (form) of messages and has, until recently, led researchers in the wrong direction.

*Structural Prototypes*

Among the earliest reports of work on the structural approach to content analysis were those by Bernier and Heumann and by Libbey.

*Vocabulary Control.* Bernier and Heumann [101] postulated a "vocabulary ball" consisting of related semantemes. The core of the ball represented the most abstract concept in a document collection. Succeeding layers are composed of terms which are of increasing specificity and of increasing numbers. In general, the structure can be viewed as a collection of ordered relationships among semantemes. A "first-order" relationship is defined as any link between semantemes on adjacent layers, while a "second-order" relationship is defined as any link between semantemes in the same layer. Bernier and Heumann claimed that these relationships constitute a comprehensive classification and that any term could be defined by use of all of its first-order relationships.

Libbey [102] described a somewhat similar approach to term definitions. Each term in a vocabulary is defined by the set of terms from the vocabulary with which the chosen term is most closely related. These strings of terms, called definitors, were designed to improve document retrieval by providing for conceptual linkage between vocabulary elements. The definitor also permits computation of a "pseudometric distance" between queries and documents. Libbey also suggested that the introduction of new terms to a vocabulary and alteration of the bias of descriptor indexes could be facilitated by use of definitors.

*Association Maps.* Sometime later, Doyle [103] proposed the association map, somewhat like a cardiovascular system where the arteries correspond to relationships involving many documents, arterioles fewer, and so forth. Doyle maintained that flexibility in the "capillary" regions was vital and suggested that these regions could be mechanically determined. He thought that the gross organization, however, should be manually determined and fixed. Statistical correlation graphs, called document proxies, were employed to position a document onto the map and to retrieve documents from it. Doyle contended that graphs are easily evaluated at a glance, that differences among documents may be made conspicuous, and that graphs are subject to dynamic control.

*Dependency Theory.* Following the work of Doyle, and independently of it, Hays [63] introduced his dependency theory of language analysis, which was aimed at producing a graph showing directly the interdependencies among words of a sentence, in contrast with a phrase structure in which word dependencies are only implicit. Dependency grammars have been employed in several subsequent studies, some of which are described later in this article.

*Semantic Networks.* Quillian has suggested a view of meaning involving what he called "semantic networks" [104]. Such networks combine the ideas embodied in the definitional notions of Bernier and Heumann and of Libbey with the network concept described by Doyle, but they also allow for predication or modification of a concept within the structure. All factual information is encoded either as a "unit" or a "property." A unit represents some thing, idea, or event, and a property represents any sort of predication. Each unit must contain a link to its superset, and may contain links to properties. Each property must contain links to an attribute and a value and may contain links to other properties. The attribute-value pair may represent the traditional category-value pair (for example, color-white) or any verb-object or preposition-object pair. Figure 12 may help to explain the model.

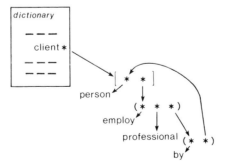

**Fig. 12.** A representation of Quillian's "semantic network" organization for "client" as a "person who employs a professional."

The unit (in brackets) represents the concept "client." It links to its superset "person" and its property whose attribute is "employ" and value is "professional." This property links to another whose attribute is "by" and whose value is "client." Quillian employed this memory model in his Teachable Language Comprehender (TLC). In theory, the TLC can be taught to alter its memory structure with "teacher guidance." Initially, however, it was "spoon-fed" a semantic structure.

Quillian's work, though primarily a semantic model, makes use of certain syntactic relationships (such as predicate-object) within the structural framework. This extension over the name hierarchy proposed by Bernier and by Doyle is an important step toward complete structural representations of texts or messages.

*TOSAR.* A somewhat different approach to structural organization is exhibited in Fugmann's Topological Method for the Representation of Synthetic and Analytical Relations of Concepts [105]. TOSAR is an attempt to expedite literature searches by a predictable indexing scheme. Unlike Bernier, Doyle, and Quillian, Fugmann makes no attempt to structure the document collection. Rather, each document or query is represented as an independent network. Organization is not a concept hierarchy, but rather a type of time line or event sequence. For each document or query, a graph is drawn manually. The graph is then coded and stored (or mechanically matched) with the graphs which represent the document collection.

The relations displayed by the graph are chemical in nature, but Fugmann asserts that "a method of representing relations between concepts precisely and clearly smooths the road to a consistent analytical treatment even of concepts that are not concerned with structural chemistry" [106].

Each process that is carried out is represented by a series of levels. The concepts before the process are arranged on one level and the concepts after the process are displayed at one point on a lower level. For example, the graph in Fig. 13 represents the process described by the sentence: Oligomerization of propylene with the aid of $Al(Alkyl)_3$ to obtain hexene, and separation and purification of the excess propylene by fractional distillation and recycling of the propylene is reported.

*Conceptual Dependency Parser.* Shank and Tesler have described a method of structural representation based on the sentence [107]. Their Conceptual Dependency Parser operates on one word of an input sentence at a time, checking potential links to other words in the sentence with its knowledge of the world and past experience. A linked network is displayed upon the completion of each sentence. A typical network is shown in Fig. 14. The parser employs a five-step process to construct the network: A dictionary look-up, application of realization rules, an idiom check, rewrite procedures, and a semantics check. The dictionary consists of a list of "senses" each composed of a "conceptual category" (such as actor, action, location, etc.) and an "interpretation" (such as: fly—an insect). Guesses as to which sense applies are stacked for testing

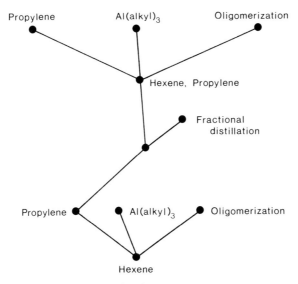

**Fig. 13.** A TOSAR graph for a polymerization process.

against the realization rules and conceptual semantics. The rules define how the word might be connected to previous and future words in the sentence to form the structure. These rules prohibit such constructions as the now famous "ideas sleep" [108] on the basis that such a connection has never been made (in the parser's experience). The semantics check is employed to choose between two feasible interpretations. For example, the parser would attempt to construct

John saw Texas flying to California.

in the same way it handled

John saw the birds flying to California.

until the semantic check disallowed the construction

Texas ⇔ fly

Although Shank and Tesler have stressed that the parser is a conceptual rather

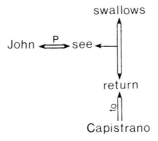

**Fig. 14.** A network produced by Shank and Tesler's "Conceptual Dependency Parser."

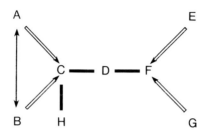

Fig. 15.  Example of the graphical representations described by Rush.

than a syntactic model, the categories they propose align closely (in English) with the traditional grammar classes and with case grammar roles.

*Graphic Representations for Automatic Indexing of Text.*   In 1969, Rush described a method of representing text in structured form [109] which he developed as an outgrowth of work on the use of links and roles [110] to define term/term relationships. An example of Rush's structural representations is shown in Fig. 15. The structures were produced manually and were intended for machine encoding and processing in a manner analogous to that used to process chemical structures [111].

   Young refined the relationships which Rush had used and suggested that the structures could be derived entirely by computer program.

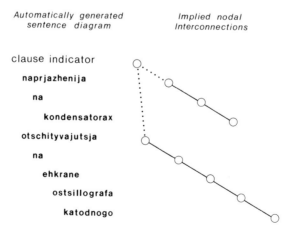

Fig. 16.   A structural representation of a Russian sentence produced by Plath's procedure.

***Graphic Structures for Russian Sentences.*** Plath has described a procedure for constructing diagrams of sentences in Russian [112]. A program embodying the procedure and based upon a projective grammar is used as a means of presenting the output of a predictive syntactic analyzer. The program has also been used to analyze and classify sentences according to their structural properties. An example of Plath's structures is shown in Fig. 16.

***Graphic Structures for French Sentences.*** A program designed to produce structural representations of sentences in French has been implemented by Tesnieré [113], who treats the verb as the central relator of the sentence. The verb appears at the apex of the graph; subject and object substructures appear to the left and right, respectively, and below the verb (see Fig. 17 for illustration).

### Case Grammar

> Polonius: What do you read, my lord?
> Hamlet: Words, words, words.
> Polonius: What is the matter, my lord?
> Hamlet: Between who?
> Polonius: I mean the matter that you read, my lord [114].

Before proceeding further with our discussion of structural analysis, we must digress briefly to consider the notions of case grammar. In contrast with older views of case, which dealt with the role of pronominal forms (e.g., I–me and He–him) and, in some languages, also nominal forms, in the sense usually of subject or object, Fillmore has extended the notion of case in English to cover all nouns (and pronouns) in any syntactic situation.

Fillmore first described his theory of case grammar in 1968 [73]. He defined the sentence to be a modality plus a proposition. The modality constituent embodies the whole sentence and includes such elements as negation, time, and mood. The propositional constituent is a set of noun-verb relationships, called cases. The cases are called agentive, instrument, dative, factitive, locative, and objective, depending upon the role of the noun in the relationship. It is the noun

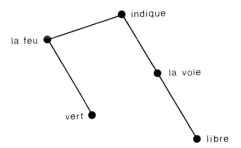

Fig. 17.  A structure produced by the program described by Tesnieré.

which, in the Fillmore analysis, determines the case. Verbs are classified according to the cases which accept them.

A similar model of semantic structure has been proposed by Chafe [74]. A sentence in his analysis consists of one "predicative element" and optionally a set of "nominal elements." Chafe takes the position that "it is the verb which dictates the presence and character of the noun" and not the noun which controls the verb. Chafe then defines four "selectional units": state, process, action, and ambient. Verbs are classified according to these units, and it is these units which "select" the relationship of the noun to the verb. These relationships are the propositional cases Fillmore proposed. Chafe labels them experiencer, agent, benefactive, patient, instrument, locative, and so forth.

Another version of a case grammar was published by Anderson [115]. The labels he adopts for the case roles are different from those of Fillmore and Chafe, but his analysis is similar to theirs. Like Chafe he stresses the centrality of the verb. Anderson's work is important because he has suggested certain syntactic tests for distinguishing between cases.

Young and her colleagues have developed computer programs which implement a case grammar analysis [56, 77] This implementation recognizes the "essential cases" of agent, experiencer, beneficiary, and object and the "peripheral cases" of locative, time, manner, comitative, cause, and purpose. The analysis is a three-phase process. Phase 1 identifies the verb class by dictionary look-up or default. Essential cases are assigned based on the verb class case frame or secondary relators. Phase 2 assigns the time case based on dictionary recognition, and phase 3 assigns the remaining peripheral cases based on prepositions and other syntactic and lexical cues.

The basic verb types usually identified in case grammar analysis are defined in Table 4, after Cook [116]. The case roles assumed by nouns or noun phrases are given in Table 5, after Young [56]. The following examples serve to illustrate the assignment of case roles:

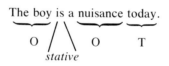

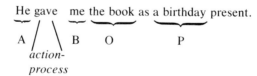

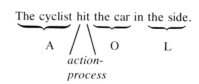

Salton [117], Winograd [28], and Halliday [67] have also suggested or used

**TABLE 4**
Verb Types and the Case Frames They Govern

| Basic verb type | Case frames dictated by each verb type | | | |
|---|---|---|---|---|
| | Simple | Compound | | |
| State | [O] | [E, O] | [B, O] | [O, L] |
| Process | [O] | [E, O] | [B, O] | [O, L] |
| Action | [A] | [A, E] | [A, B] | [A, L] |
| Action-process | [A, O] | [A, E, O] | [A, B, O] | [A, O, L] |

methods of analysis which are essentially case grammar systems, and Montgomery [72] has suggested that Fillmore's case grammar provides a "linguistically-based formalism" for representing content in terms of relationships, although she suggests a lexical rather than computational approach.

The importance of case as described above is that it may well serve to provide

**TABLE 5**
Definition of Essential and Peripheral Case Roles

| Case role | Symbol | No. | Definition of case role |
|---|---|---|---|
| Agent | A | 1 | The source of the action specified by the primary phrase[a] |
| Experiencer | E | 3 | The one who experiences the feeling, sensation, etc., specified by the primary phrase |
| Beneficiary | B | 4 | The possessor (in its broadest sense) of some thing, whether the possession be temporary or permanent, positive or negative |
| Objective | O | 2 | The receiver of the action specified by the primary phrase |
| Locative | L | 5 | The place where the action specified by the primary phrase occurs |
| Time | T | 6 | The time when the action specified by the primary phrase occurs |
| Manner | M | 7 | The way in which the action specified by the primary phrase is performed |
| Comitative | C | 8 | The accompaniment case, a subject accompanying the source of the action specified by the primary phrase |
| Cause | Cs | 9 | The case giving the reason for the action specified by the primary phrase |
| Purpose | P | 10 | The case giving the purpose of the action specified by the primary phrase |

[a] Primary phrase may be thought of as a verb phrase.

the clues needed to identify the concepts contained in a message or text. We have already mentioned that structural analysis involves not only linguistic elements but the relationships between these elements as well. Certain of these relationships may be ascertained through syntactic analysis, but the more important relationships which are susceptible of identification through application of analytical procedures are those defined in the theory of case grammar. It is the answers to questions such as *who, why, where, how, when, what,* and *what for* that case grammar analysis provides, and it is precisely these answers that content analysis has heretofore been unable to deduce. This point may be made clearer by examination of two recent approaches to structural representations of text.

### Derivation of Structures from Text

**Structural Representation of English Sentences.**   Young has proposed a graphic representation of English sentences which builds upon her work in syntactic and case grammar analysis [56]. Each sentence is processed as a set of clauses, and a subgraph is produced for each clause. The nodes of the graph include verbs and nouns (adverbs and adjectives are treated as part of the verb or noun node). The arcs or edges of the graph represent what Young calls secondary relations (prepositions, conjunctions, etc.). Both nodes and edges are labeled, and verb nodes are assigned special symbols (see Table 6). The edge labels are case roles, as given in Table 4. A few examples, presented as Fig. 18, should suffice to illustrate the approach.

Young claims that such representations are susceptible of production by computer program and that they preserve and explicate the NAMES and RELA-

**TABLE 6**

Symbols Used by Young to Represent Case Grammar Classes of Primary Relations

| Primary relation type (case) | Symbology | | |
|---|---|---|---|
| | | Recessive | |
| | Dominant | Participial | Infinitival |
| Stative | —○← | —●← | —⊘← |
| Agentive | —□→ | —■→ | —▨→ |
| Experiencer | —△→ | —▲→ | —◬→ |
| Beneficiary | ←◇← | ←◆← | ←◈→ |
| Reflexive | ←⬡ | ←⬢ | ←⬢ |

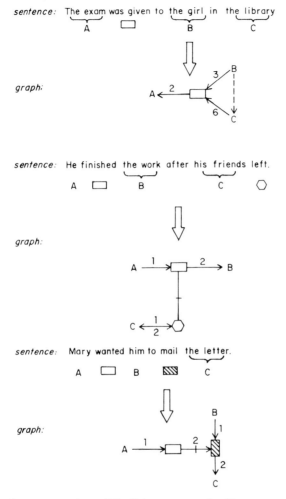

**Fig. 18.** Structural representation of English sentences by Young.

TIONs in a sentence in such a way that index entries of various types may be derived from them in addition to more complex aggregates analogous to structure-based retrieval in chemistry [118, 119].

*AGNES.* The most comprehensive procedure for generation of structural representations of English text so far reported is that described by Strong [120, 121]. She called the procedure an Algorithm for Graphic Notation of English Sentences (AGNES). Each sentence in English is represented by a network comprised of nodes and edges. A sentence is viewed as being composed of one or more clauses, each consisting of a predicate and, optionally, a subject, one or more objects, and/or modifiers. Each of these clause components is, when present in a sentence, represented in the network as a node. Relationships

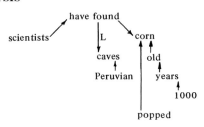

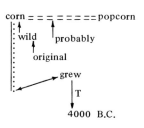

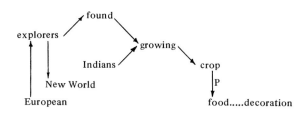

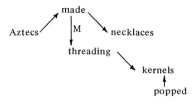

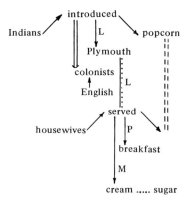

**Fig. 19.** Example of graphs of sentences produced by AGNES.

**TABLE 7**

Directionality of Edges in AGNES Graphs in Relation to Verb Type and Case Frame

| Verb type and case frame | Edge type | | | | |
|---|---|---|---|---|---|
| | Subject-predicate | Predicate-object | Modifier | Conjunctive | Phrase |
| Unspecified | / | \ | ↑ | . . . . | ↓ prep |
| Stative [O] | / | | | | |
| Stative [O, O] | / | ·\ | | | |
| Action [A] | ↗ | | | | |
| Process [O] | ↙ | | | | |
| Action-process [A, O] | ↗ | ↘ | | | |
| Experiencer [E] | ↙ | | | | |
| Stative [E, O] | ↙ | \ | | | |
| Action [A, E] | ↗ | ↘ | | | |
| Process [E, O] | ↙ | ↘ | | | |
| Action-process [A, E, O] | ↗ | ↘ | ↕ | | |
| Stative [B, O] | ↙ | \ | | | |
| Action [A, B] | ↗ | ↘ | | | |
| Process [B, O] | ↙ | ↘ | | | |
| Action-process [A, B, O] | ↗ | ↘ | ⇓ | | |

between nodes are represented as edges of the network. An edge may be labeled with a relational word. Several types of edge are employed; these are defined in Table 7. The basic network is augmented by directionality of the edges which specifies the major case frames extant in the network (see Table 7). Examples of AGNES graphs are given in Fig. 19.

An important extension of the basic AGNES procedures involves explication of intersentence relationships. Strong developed a set of rules which determine how sentences are to be linked. For example, the antecedent of a personal pronoun is linked to the pronoun by a double-dashed edge. Two or more occurrences of the same word in separate sentences will also be linked by a double-dashed edge. The individual sentence graphs of Fig. 19 are shown in Fig. 20 with intersentence relations identified. Although the figures show two-dimensional structures, Strong indicates that at least three dimensions are required for proper graphic representation [120].

### Application of Structural Analysis

This proposal was met with great applause, until an Old Mouse arose and said, "This is all very fine, but who among us is so brave? Who will bell the Cat?" The mice looked at one another in silence and nobody volunteered.

It is easier to suggest a plan than to carry it out [122].

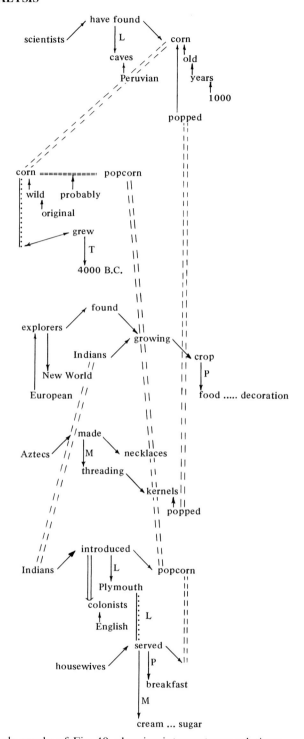

**Fig. 20.** Example graphs of Fig. 19, showing intersentence relations.

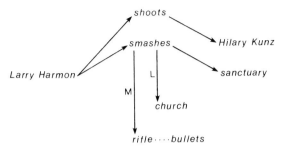

**Fig. 21.** Index display suggested by Strong.

While structural analysis is yet in its formative stages of development, and while many of the proposed techniques of structural analysis have not been reduced to computer programs, it is not unreasonable to suggest one or two applications.

The work of Fugmann and his colleagues on TOSAR [105, 123] has already led to computerized storage and retrieval processes even though the structures are produced manually. The basis for these retrieval techniques is the theory that concepts as expressed in words of a language are properly represented as nonlinear structures and that both the contents of texts and the contents of queries thus represented may be compared node by node and edge by edge to determine correspondence. This approach to retrieval at once overcomes a fundamental weakness of all existing retrieval systems: the inability to specify and/or identify relationships contained in the text or query. The situation is quite analogous to that of structural chemistry, wherein the search for specific structural complexes (structures or substructures) is made vastly simpler and more precise if the relations (bonds) between atoms (elements) as well as the atoms are available for retrieval.

Strong has suggested several applications related to machine indexing [120]. Among these are an index, similar to a Predicasts miniabstract [124], utilizing case roles. A second index proposed by Strong is a graphical one utilizing reduced portions of full structures which are dynamically produced for video display. The display is produced by selecting from the larger graph (with intersentence relations) those nodes with the highest degree (largest number of connections to other nodes) together with the relations directly linking these nodes. Augmentation of the basic graphical index display could then be produced on demand of the user to denote time, place, etc. A sample index display is shown in Fig. 21.

Other applications suggest themselves. We shall leave it to the reader to imagine some of them.

## CONCLUSION

In the world of words, imagination is one of the forces of nature [125].

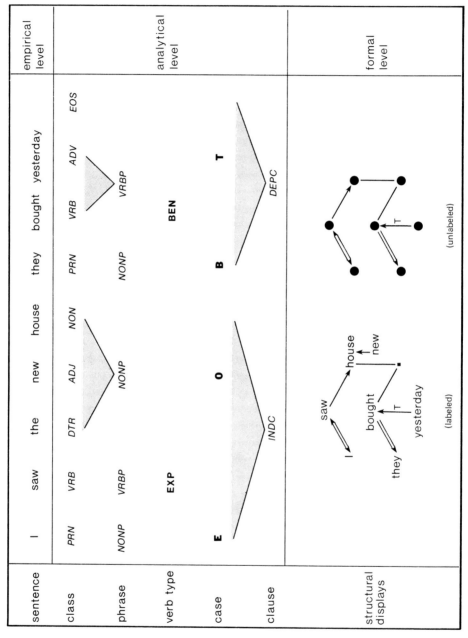

**Fig. 22.** Pepinsky's schemapiric representation of text.

In this article we have attempted to survey the area of study loosely termed content analysis, and we have tried to organize many diverse studies according to whether they concerned elemental or structural analysis. This organization is based upon a chemical metaphor which we believe to be of considerable importance in content analysis because there has been a serious inability to speak in precise terms about the variety of studies described in the literature and to do so in a way which makes evident their basic similarities. Pepinsky, in his "A Metalanguage of Text" [76], emphasizes the need for both analytical and formal levels of analysis in the study of and talk about language or text. His schemapiric representation of text, illustrated in Fig. 22, is a succinct and substantial way of concluding this article.

## ACKNOWLEDGMENTS

The authors wish to thank Harold Pepinsky for the many hours of exciting discussion of many of the topics covered in this article. Thanks are also due Mrs. Corinne Garvey without whose help this article could not have been produced.

## REFERENCES

1. A. C. Doyle, Silver blaze, in W. S. Barring-Gould, *The Annotated Sherlock Holmes*, Vol. 2, Potter, New York, 1967, p. 277.
2. C. A. Cuadra (ed.), *Annual Review of Information Science and Technology*, Wiley, New York (Vols. 1–2), 1966–1967; Encyclopedia Britannica, Chicago (Vols. 3–7), 1968–1972; American Society for Information Science, Washington, D.C. (Vols. 8–10), 1973–1975.
3. C. E. Shannon and W. Weaver, *The Mathematical Theory of Communication*, University of Illinois Press, Urbana, Illinois, 1949, p. 7.
4. J. Fast, *Body Language*, Pocket Books, New York, 1970.
5. M. Korda, *Power! How to Get It, How to Use It*, Random House, New York, 1975.
6. E. Efron, *The News Twisters*, Nash, Los Angeles, California, 1971.
7. T. Y. Canby, Handclasp in space, *National Geographic* 149(2), 184 (1976).
8. P. J. Stone, D. C. Dumphy, M. S. Smith, and D. M. Ogilvie, *The General Inquirer: A Computer Approach to Content Analysis*, M.I.T. Press, Cambridge, Massachusetts, 1966.
9. S. J. Thorson, *Models, Theories, and Political Theory*, Polimetrics Laboratory, The Ohio State University, Columbus, Ohio, 1972.
10. A Bruschi, *Principles and Technique of a Political Metalanguage*, Research Committee 7: Committee on Conceptual and Terminological Analysis (COCTA), presented at the International Political Science Association Meeting, Montreal, 1973.
11. H. Garfinkel and H. Sacks, On formal structures of practical actions, in *Theoretical Sociology: Perspectives and Developments* (J. C. McKinney and E. A. Tiryakian, eds.), Appleton-Century-Crofts, New York, 1970, pp. 337–366.

12. L. C. Hawes, Interpersonal communication: The enactment of routines, in *Exploration in Speech Communication* (J. J. Makay, ed.), Merrill, Columbus, Ohio, 1973, pp. 71–90.

13. C. E. Osgood, G. J. Suci, and P. H. Tannenbaum, *The Measurement of Meaning,* University of Illinois Press, Urbana, Illinois, 1957.

14. J. G. Snider and C. E. Osgood (eds.), *Semantic Differential Techniques,* Aldine, Chicago, 1969.

15. M. J. Patton and A. Fuhriman, *Research on Psychological Counseling Using a Computer-Assisted Metalanguage,* paper presented before the Annual Convention of the American Psychological Association, Chicago, September, 1975.

16. D. Richardson, *Peace Child,* Regal, Glendale, California, 1974.

17. B. N. Colby, G. A. Collier, and S. K. Postal, Comparison of themes in folktales by the General Inquirer system, *J. Am. Folklore* **76**(302), 318–323 (1963).

18. B. N. Colby, Culture grammars, *Science* **187**(4180), 913–919 (1975).

19. E. Mosteller and D. L. Wallace, Inference in an authorship problem, *J. Am. Stat. Assoc.* **58**(302), 275–309 (1963).

20. W. A. Cook, S.J., Stylistics: Measuring style complexity, in *Georgetown University Working Papers on Languages and Linguistics No. 11,* Georgetown University Press, Washington, D.C., 1975.

21. S. Y. Sedelow, *Automated Analysis of Language Style and Structure,* Research Report ONR NR348-005, University of North Carolina, Chapel Hill, North Carolina, September 1970.

22. B. A. Mathis and J. E. Rush, Abstracting, in *Encyclopedia of Computer Science and Technology,* Vol. 1 (J. Belzer, A. G. Holzman, and A. Kent, eds.), Dekker, New York, 1975, pp. 102–142.

23. B. C. Landry and J. E. Rush, Automatic indexing: Progress and prospects, in *Encyclopedia of Computer Science and Technology,* Vol. 2 (J. Belzer, A. G. Holzman, and A. Kent, eds.), Dekker, New York, 1975, pp. 403–447.

24. T. Winograd, Linguistics and the computer analysis of tonal harmony, *J. Music Theory* **12**(1), 2–49 (1968).

25. H. B. Lincoln, Use of the computer in music research: A short report on accomplishments, limitations and future needs, *Computers and the Humanities* **8**(5–6), 285–289 (1974).

26. J. F. Young, *Robotics,* Butterworths, London, 1973.

27. C. Hewitt, PLANNER: A language for proving theorems in robots, in *Proceedings of the International Joint Conferences on Artificial Intelligence,* Mitre Corp., Bedford, Massachusetts, 1969, pp. 295–301.

28. T. Winograd, Understanding natural language, *Cognitive Psychol.* **3**(1), 1–191 (1972).

29. K. S. Fu, *Sequential Methods in Pattern Recognition and Machine Learning,* Academic, New York, 1968.

30. M. S. Watanabe (ed.), *Frontiers of Pattern Recognition,* Academic, New York, 1972.

31. J. D. Smith and J. E. Rush, The relationship between author names and author entries in a large on-line union catalog as retrieved using truncated keys, accepted for publication in the *Journal of the American Society for Information Science,* June 1976.

32. D. S. Colombo, *Automatic Retrieval Systems and Associated Retrieval Languages,* Computer and Information Science Research Center, OSU-CISRC-TR-69-17, The Ohio State University, Columbus, Ohio, 1969.

33.  W. S. Stalcup and A. E. Petrarca, Automatic vocabulary control and its evaluation in computer-produced indexes, in *Proceedings of the American Society for Information Science National Convention*, Boston, 1975.

34.  D. S. Colombo and J. E. Rush, Use of word fragments in computer-based retrieval systems, *J. Chem. Doc.* **9**(1), 47–50 (1969).

35.  J. R. R. Tolkien, *The Lord of the Rings*, Part 1. *The Fellowship of the Ring*, Ballantine, New York, 1965, p. 370.

36.  J. E. Rush, *Work at CAS on Search Guides and Thesauri*, presented at the Chemical Abstracts Service Open Forum, Miami Beach, Florida, April 12, 1967.

37.  R. T. Niehoff, Development of an integrated energy vocabulary and the possibilities for on-line subject switching, *J. Am. Soc. Inf. Sci.* **27**(1), 3–17, (1976).

38.  S. Y. Sedelow and W. A. Sedelow, Jr., Stylistic analysis, in *Automated Language Processing* (H. Borko, ed.), Wiley, New York, 1967, p. 182.

39.  R. Busa, S.J., An inventory of fifteen million words, in *Proceedings of the IBM Literary Data Processing Conference*, September 1964, pp. 171–199.

40.  P. Tasman, *Indexing the Dead Sea Scrolls by Electronic Literary Data Processing Methods*, IBM Brochure, November 1958.

41.  D. J. Moore, Practical algorithms for computer collation of long natural texts for scholarly use, in *Abstracts of Research*, Computer and Information Sciences Research Center, The Ohio State University, Columbus, Ohio, 1975, p. 22.

42.  H. Borko, Indexing and classification, in *Automated Language Processing* (H. Borko, ed.), Wiley, New York, 1967, pp. 99–125.

43.  H. Kucera and W. N. Francis, *Computational Analysis of Present-Day American English*, Brown University, Providence, Rhode Island, 1967.

44.  J. M. Carroll and R. Roeloffs, Computer selection of keywords using word-frequency analysis, *Am. Doc.* **20**(3), 227–233 (1969).

45.  J. W. Sammon, Jr., *Some Mathematics of Information Storage and Retrieval*, Rome Air Development Center, Air Force Systems Command, Griffiss Air Force Base, New York, Technical Report No. RADC-TR-68-178, June 1968.

46.  L. Bloomfield, *Language*, Holt, Rinehart and Winston, New York, 1933, p. 5.

47.  J. Priestly, *Rudiments of English Grammar*, London, 1761, cited in C. C. Fries, *The Structure of English*, Harcourt, Brace and World, New York, 1952.

48.  H. A. Gleason, *An Introduction to Descriptive Linguistics*, Holt, Rinehart and Winston, New York, 1961.

49.  C. C. Fries, *The Structure of English*, Harcourt, Brace and World, New York, 1952, p. 74.

50.  S. Klein and R. Simmons, A computational approach to grammatical coding of English words, *J. Assoc. Comput. Mach.* **10**(3), 334–347 (1963).

51.  P. Beckmann, *The Structure of Language: A New Approach*, Golem, Boulder, Colorado, 1972.

52.  D. C. Clark and R. E. Wall, An economical program for limited parsing of English, *AFIPS Conference Proceedings*, Vol. 27 (Part 1), 1965, pp. 307–316.

53.  W. Stolz, P. Tannenbaum, and P. Carstensen, A stochastic approach to the grammatical coding of English, *Commun. ACM* **8** (6), 399–405 (1965).

54.  S. Marvin, J. Rush, and C. Young, *Grammatical Class Assignment Based on Function Words*, Seventh Annual National Colloquium on Information Retrieval, Philadelphia, Pennsylvania, May 1970.

55.  C. Young, Grammatical Assignment Based on Function Words, M.S. Thesis, The Ohio State University, 1970.

56.  C. Young, *Design and Implementation of Language Analysis Procedures with*

*Application to Automatic Indexing,* Computer and Information Science Research Center, OSU-CISRC-TR-73-2, The Ohio State University, Columbus, Ohio, 1973.

57. A. Oettinger and S. Kuno, Multiple-path syntactic analyzer, in *Proceedings of the International Federation of Information Processing Congress,* North Holland, Amsterdam, 1962, pp. 306–312.

58. A. M. Zwicky, J. Friedman, B. C. Hall, and D. E. Walker, The MITRE syntactic analysis procedure for transformational grammars, *Proceedings of the Fall Joint Computer Conference* Vol. 27(1), 1965, pp. 317–326.

59. J. Thorne, P. Bratley, and H. Dewar, The syntactic analysis of English by machine, in *Machine Intelligence,* Vol. 3 (D. Michie, ed.), American Elsevier, New York, 1968, pp. 281–310.

60. D. T. Langendoen, *The Study of Syntax,* Holt, Rinehart and Winston, New York, 1969.

61. H. L. Resnikoff and J. L. Dolby, Automatic determination of the parts of speech of English words, *Proc. Inst. Electr. and Electron. Eng.* 15(7), 1029 (1963).

62. D. B. Vigor, D. Urquhart, and A. Wilkinson, PROSE—Parsing recognizer outputting sentences in English, in *Machine Intelligence,* Vol. 4 (B. Meltzer and D. Michie, ed.), American Elsevier, New York, 1969, pp. 271–284.

63. D. G. Hays, Dependency theory: A formalism and some observations, *Language* 40(4), 511–525 (1964).

64. N. Sager, Syntactic analysis of natural language, *Adv. Comput.* 8, 153–188 (1967).

65. W. A. Woods, Transition network grammars for natural language analysis, *Commun. ACM* 13(10), 591–606 (1970).

66. R. K. Lindsay, Inferential memory as the basis of machines which understand natural language, in *Computers and Thought* (E. A. Feigenbaum and J. Feldman eds.), McGraw-Hill, New York, 1963, pp. 217–233.

67. M. A. K. Halliday, Notes on transitivity and theme in English; Part 1, *J. Linguistics* 3(1), 37–81 (1967).

68. M. A. K. Halliday, Functional diversity in language as seen from a consideration of modality and mood in English, *Found. Language* 6, 322–361 (1970).

69. M. A. K. Halliday, Notes on transitivity and theme in English, Part 2, *J. Linguistics* 4(2), 179–215 (1968).

70. J. Rothstein, Relational languages, in *Report to the National Science Foundation, Office of Science Information Service,* Computer and Information Science Research Center, The Ohio State University, Columbus, Ohio, 1970, pp. 5.44–5.46.

71. R. Simmons, J. Burger, and R. Schwarcz, A computational model of verbal understanding, *Proceedings of the Fall Joint Computer Conference,* Vol. 33(1), 1968, pp. 411–456.

72. C. A. Montgomery, Linguistics and information science, *J. Am. Soc. Inf. Sci.* 23(3), 195–218 (1972).

73. C. J. Fillmore, The case for case, in *Universals in Linguistic Theory* (E. Bach and R. Harms,eds.), Holt, Rinehart and Winston, New York, 1968, pp. 1–88.

74. W. L. Chafe, *Meaning and the Structure of Language,* University of Chicago Press, Chicago, Illinois, 1970.

75. L. Carroll, Through the looking-glass, and what Alice found there, from *Alice's Adventures in Wonderland and Through the Looking Glass,* Airmont, New York, 1965, p. 228.

76. H. B. Pepinsky, A metalanguage of text, in *Language and Logic in Personality and Society* (H. Fisher and R. Diaz-Guerrero, eds.), Academic, New York, in preparation.

77. J. E. Rush, H. B. Pepinsky, N. M. Meara, S. M. Strong, J. A. Valley, and C. E.

Young, *A Computer-Assisted Language Analysis System,* Computer and Information Science Research Center, OSU-CISRC-TR-74-1, The Ohio State University, Columbus, Ohio, 1974.

78. M. D. Owdom, *Outline of a Computer-Assisted Language Analysis System (CALAS),* Instruction and Research Computer Center, The Ohio State University, Columbus, Ohio, October 1975.

79. K. L. Montgomery, *Document Retrieval Systems: Factors Affecting Search Time,* Dekker, New York, 1975.

80. P. M. Russo, Cellular Networks and Algorithms for Parallel Processing of Non-Numeric Data Encountered in Information Storage and Retrieval, Ph.D. Dissertation, The Ohio State University, 1975.

81. C. H. Davis and J. E. Rush, *Information Storage and Retrieval in Chemistry,* Greenwood, Westport, Connecticut, 1974, Chap. 5.

82. C. T. Abraham, Techniques for thesaurus organization and evaluation, in *Some Problems in Information Science* (M. Kochen, ed.), Scarecrow, New York, 1965, pp. 131–150.

83. G. Salton (ed.), *The SMART Retrieval System: Experiments in Automatic Document Processing,* Prentice-Hall, Englewood Cliffs, New Jersey, 1971, p. 140.

84. J. B. Fried, B. C. Landry, D. M. Liston, Jr., B. P. Price, R. C. Van Buskirk, and D. M. Wachsberger, *Index Simulation Feasibility and Automatic Document Classification,* Computer and Information Science Research Center, OSU-CISRC-TR-68-4, The Ohio State University, Columbus, Ohio, 1968, pp. 11–19.

85. A. Wald, *Sequential Analysis,* Wiley, New York, 1947, Chap. 10.

86. L. J. White, J. D. Smith, G. Kar, D. E. Westbrook, B. J. Brinkman, and R. A. Fisher, *A Sequential Method for Automatic Document Classification,* Computer and Information Science Research Center, OSU-CISRC-TR-75-5, The Ohio State University, Columbus, Ohio, 1975.

87. H. Borko (ed.), *Automated Language Processing,* Wiley, New York, 1967.

88. H. A. Simon and L. Siklóssy (eds.), *Representation and Meaning: Experiments with Information Processing Systems,* Prentice-Hall, Englewood Cliffs, New Jersey, 1972.

89. J. Weizenbaum, ELIZA—A computer program for the study of natural language communication between man and machine, *Commun. ACM* **9**(1), 36–45 (1966).

90. R. F. Simmons, Natural language question-answering systems: 1969, *Commun. ACM* **13**(1), 15–30 (1970).

91. L. S. Coles, Syntax directed interpretation of natural language, in *Representation and Meaning: Experiments with Information Processing Systems* (H. A. Simon and L. Siklóssy, eds.), Prentice-Hall, Englewood Cliffs, New Jersey, 1972, pp. 211–287.

92. B. A. Mathis, J. E. Rush, and C. E. Young, Improvement of automatic abstracts by the use of structural analysis, *J. Am. Soc. Inf. Sci.* **24**(2), 101–109 (1973).

93. B. A. Mathis, *Techniques for the Evaluation and Improvement of Computer-Produced Abstracts,* Computer and Information Science Research Center, OSU-CISRC-TR-72-15, The Ohio State University, Columbus, Ohio, 1972.

94. H. Fisher, An analysis of repression from the point of view of language and logic, *Interam. J. Psychol.* **5**(3–4), 167–181 (1971).

95. J. Jeans, *The Universe Around Us,* 4th ed., The University Press, Cambridge, England, 1945, p. 7.

96. M. Minsky, Form and content in computer science, *J. Assoc. Comput. Mach.* **17**(2), 197–215 (1970).

97. N. Chomsky, *Syntactic Structures,* Moulton, 's-Gravenhage, 1957.

98. N. Chomsky, *Aspects of the Theory of Syntax,* M.I.T. Press, Cambridge, Massachusetts, 1965.

99. R. A. Jacobs and P. S. Rosenbaum, *English Transformational Grammar,* Blaisdell, Waltham, Massachusetts, 1968.

100. E. H. Lenneberg, *Biological Foundations of Language,* Wiley, New York, 1967.

101. C. L. Bernier and K. F. Heumann, Correlative indexes III: Semantic relations among semantemem—The technical thesaurus, *Am. Doc.* **8**(1), 211–220 (1957).

102. M. A. Libbey, The use of second order descriptors for document retrieval, *Am. Doc.* **18**(1), 10–20 (1967).

103. L. B. Doyle, Semantic roadmaps for literature searches, *J. Assoc. Comput. Mach.* **8**(4), 553–578 (1961).

104. M. R. Quillian, The teachable language comprehender: A simulation program and theory of language, *Commun. ACM* **12**(8), 459–476 (1969).

105. R. Fugmann, H. Nickelsen, I. Nickelsen, and J. Winters, TOSAR—A topological method for the representation of synthetic and analytical relations of concepts, *Angew. Chem., Int. Ed. Engl.* **9**(8), 589–595 (1970).

106. Ref. 105, p. 593.

107. R. C. Shank and L. Tesler, *A Conceptual Dependency Parser for Natural Language,* International Conference on Computational Linguistics, Stockholm, Sweden, Preprint No. 2 (1969).

108. V. Mehta, Onward and upward with the arts (linguistics), *New Yorker,* pp. 44–87, May 8, 1971.

109. J. E. Rush, *A New Approach to Indexing,* presented before the Student Chapter of the A.S.I.S., Case-Western Reserve University, Cleveland, Ohio, January 1969.

110. B. A. Montague, Patent indexing by concept coordination using links and roles, *Am. Doc.* **13**(1), 104–111 (1962).

111. H. L. Morgan, The generation of a unique machine description for chemical structures—A technique developed at Chemical Abstracts Service, *J. Chem. Doc.* **5**(2), 107–113 (1965).

112. W. Plath, Automatic sentence diagramming, in *Proceedings of the 1961 International Conference on Machine Translation and Applied Language Analysis,* H.M.S.O., London, 1962, pp. 176–208.

113. L. Tesnieré, *Elements de Syntax Structural,* Klenchsuck, Paris, quoted by R. Pages, Relational aspects of conceptualization in message analysis, in J. M. Perreault (ed.), Proceedings of the international symposium on relational factors in classification, *Inf. Storage Retr.* **3**(4), 177–410 (1967).

114. W. Shakespeare, Hamlet, in *William Shakespeare* (A. S. Downer, ed.), Holt, Rinehart and Winston, New York, 1965, p. 208.

115. J. Anderson, *The Grammar of Case: Towards a Localistic Theory,* Cambridge University Press, Cambridge, England, 1971.

116. W. A. Cook, S. J., A case grammar matrix, in *Georgetown University Working Papers on Languages and Linguistics, No. 6,* Georgetown University Press, Washington, D.C., 1972, pp. 15–48.

117. G. Salton, Manipulation of trees in information retrieval, *Commun. ACM* **5**(2), 105–114 (1962).

118. M. F. Lynch, J. M. Harrison, W. G. Town, and J. E. Ash, *Computer Handling of Chemical Structure Information,* MacDonald, London, 1971.

119. W. T. Wipke, S. R. Heller, R. J. Feldmann, and E. Hyde, *Computer Representation and Manipulation of Chemical Information,* Wiley, New York, 1974.

120. S. M. Strong, *An Algorithm for Generating Structural Surrogates of English Text,*

Computer and Information Science Research Center, OSU-CISRC-TR-73-3, The Ohio State University, Columbus, Ohio, 1973.

121. S. M. Strong, An algorithm for generating structural surrogates of English text, *J. Am. Soc. Inf. Sci.* **25**(1), 10–22 (1974).

122. Aesop's Fables, Belling the cat, in *The Family Treasury of Children's Stories Book II* (P. R. Evans, ed.), Doubleday, Garden City, New York, 1956, p. 6.

123. I. Nickelsen and H. Nickelsen, Mathematische analyse des TOSAR-verfahrens, *Inf. Storage Retr.* **9**(2), 95–119 (1973).

124. R. E. Maizell, J. F. Smith, and T. E. R. Singer, *Abstracting Scientific and Technical Literature*, Wiley-Interscience, New York, 1971, p. 74.

125. W. Stevens, *Opus Posthumous: Poems, Plays, Prose* (S. F. Morse, ed.), Knopf, New York, 1957, p. 170.

*Carol E. Hicks*
*James E. Rush*
*Suzanne M. Strong*

# CONTINGENCY TABLE ANALYSIS

## INTRODUCTION

Data which result from experiments in the physical sciences and engineering are usually outcomes of controlled experiments, and are expressible in quantitative terms. In many other fields, however, the data are seldom the results of controlled experiments. In addition, the observations usually can be expressed only in qualitative or categorical terms, a yes–no, alive–dead, agree–disagree, class A–class B–class C, etc. type of response.

For example, an individual may be classified by sex, by race, by profession, by smoking habit, by age, by incidence of coronary heart disease. If we take observations over a sample of many such individuals, the result will be a multidimensional contingency table with as many dimensions as there are classifications. Contingency tables are cross-classifications of vectors of discrete random variables showing the number of subjects belonging to distinct categories of each of several qualitative or categorical classifications. The number of counts of individuals in a cell of this table represents that portion of the sample having the specific attributes within each of the classifications. A problem of interest, for example, might be to determine the factors that are associated with the presence or absence of coronary heart disease.

## CONTINGENCY TABLE ANALYSIS

Data from many fields are often presented in a cross-tabulated form. Statistical analyses of these types of data have had a long history, as may be seen from the Reference section, but were mainly concerned with the simple kind, the two-way table. Analyses of multidimensional contingency tables have been investigated intensively only during the last decade or so.

Conclusions drawn from contingency tables may be only exploratory in nature. One of the difficulties can be the availability of meaningful and reliable data. The first problem one faces in the analysis of cross-classified data is the decision on the number of classifications to be included and the categories within each classification. Typical among the problems in the analysis is how to segregate the effect on the response of some of the background variables, individually or jointly, from that of the others that are of particular interest. The data analytic attitude is empirical rather than theoretical. A more empirical attitude is natural when detailed theoretical understanding is unavailable. Estimation of parameters in models should be considered less as attempts to discover underlying truths and more as data calibrating devices which make it easier to conceive of noisy data in terms of smooth distributions and relations. With a given data set, a variety of models may be tried on, and one selected on the ground of looks and fit [42].

Consider, for example, an experiment performed to compare the effectiveness of safety release devices for refrigerators in relation to children's safety. Children between 2 to 5 years of age are induced to crawl into refrigerators equipped with six different types of release devices. If a child can open the door of the refrigerator from inside within a certain time period, the response is classified as a success. The background variables studied included age, sex, weight, and socioeconomic status of parents. The experimental variable was one of six devices. (A partial analysis of this data may be found in Ref. 198, p. 581.) Some balancing of the background variables was achieved.

In other instances none of the factors are subject to experimental control, and whatever available data could be collected are reported. The analysis of this type of data, though it may only be seeking preliminary information, can be important in fields of health and safety. The uncontrolled experimental data are sometimes the only realistic data available when these data deal with life, death, health, and safety, and some of these factors and responses are only expressible in qualitative terms in the present state of art.

It is expected that the number of problems calling for the techniques of the analysis of multidimensional contingency tables will increase. Experience at George Washington University with such a growing demand confirms this. The examination and interpretation of data from social phenomena, housing, psychology, education, environmental problems, health, safety, manpower, business, experimental testing of devices, military research and development, etc., are potential source areas.

Critics of methods for contingency table analysis have maintained that most of the procedures used, at least in the past, were only of a global chi-squared test nature. However, for a recent example of this see Patil [9]. Through the use of the principle of minimum discrimination information (m.d.i.) estimation, leading to exponential families or multiplicative models or log-linear models, we shall show, using illustrative examples exhibiting different aspects, that:

1. Estimates of the cell entries under various hypotheses or models can be obtained.
2. The adequacy or fit of the model, or the null hypothesis, can be tested.
3. Main effect and interaction parameters can be estimated.
4. The structure of the table can be studied in detail in terms of the various interrelationships among the classificatory variables.
5. The procedures can be applied to test hypotheses about particular parameters and linear combinations of parameters that are of special interest.
6. The procedures provide indication of outlier cells. These may cause a model not to fit overall, yet fit the other cells excluding the outliers.
7. Since the procedures and concepts are based on a general principle, a unified treatment of multidimensional contingency tables is possible. Sequences of generalizations step by step to higher order dimensional contingency tables are not necessary as has been the case with other *ad hoc* procedures (see, for example, Patil [9] and Sugiura and Otake [10]).
8. The procedure provides estimates based on an observed or sample table which satisfy certain external hypotheses as to underlying probability relations in the population table. These estimates also preserve the inherent properties of the observed data not affected by the hypothesis.
9. In general, the m.d.i. estimates are best asymptotically normal (BAN), and in the many applications of fitting models to a table based on observed sets of marginal values the m.d.i. estimates in particular are maximum-likelihood estimates.
10. The test statistics are m.d.i. statistics which are asymptotically distributed as chi-squared with appropriate degrees of freedom. In the case of fitting models to a table based on observed sets of marginal values, the m.d.i. statistics are log-likelihood ratio statistics. The m.d.i. statistics are additive, as are the associated degrees of freedom, so that the total under an hypothesis can be analyzed into components, each under a subhypothesis. The analysis is analogous to analysis of variance and regression analysis techniques, using a design matrix, a set of regression parameters, and explanatory variables.
11. In models fitting estimates to an observed table based on sets of observed marginal values as explanatory variables, some estimates can be expressed explicitly as products of marginal values. However, this is not generally true, and expected cell frequencies (functions of marginal values) can be computed by an iterative proportional fitting procedure [57], and the use of a computer to perform the iterations becomes necessary. For the foregoing cases, which we shall term internal, and problems involving tests of external hypotheses on underlying populations, a number of iterative computer

programs are available. They provide design matrices, the observed cell entries and the cell estimates as well as their logarithms, parameter estimates, outlier values, m.d.i. statistics and their corresponding significance levels, and covariance matrices of parameter estimates as output to assist in and simplify the numerical aspects of the inference. In this respect it is of interest to cite the following quotation from a book review by Finney [*J. R. Stat. Soc., A (General)* **136**(3), 461 (1973)]: "No mention is made of the extent to which computers have destroyed the need to assess statistical methods in terms of arithmetical simplicity: indeed the emphasis on avoiding lengthy, but easily programmed, iterative calculations is remarkable."

Classical problems in the historical development of the analysis of contingency tables concerned themselves primarily with such questions as the independence or conditional independence of the classificatory variables, or homogeneity or conditional homogeneity of the classificatory variables over time or space, for example, similar to such tests in multivariate analysis as independence, multiple correlation, partial correlation, and canonical correlation. Such classical problems turn out to be special cases of the techniques we shall discuss (see, for example, Kullback *et al.* [197, 198]). These techniques result in analyses which are essentially regression type analyses. As such they enable us to determine the relationship of one or more "dependent" qualitative or categorical variables of interest on a set of "independent" classificatory variables, as well as the relative effects of changes in the "independent" variables on the "dependent variables." The object of the analyses is the study of the interaction between and among the classifications. The term interaction is used here in a general sense to cover both dependence and association (see, for example, Bartlett [303], Simpson [284], Roy and Kastenbaum [254], Ku *et al.* [57]). It may be noted here that in a seminar on a study of the historical development of the concept of interaction in the analysis of multidimensional contingency tables, the following series of papers, among the many that could be selected, was found to be very instructive: Bartlett [303], Lancaster [283], Simpson [284], Roy and Kastenbaum [254], Darroch [192], Lewis [199], Plackett [105, 200], Birch [147, 158, 173], Goodman [47–49, 81, 182], Good [180], Kastenbaum [150], Mantel [142], Berkson [18, 107], Bhapkar and Koch [109, 110], Ku and Kullback [116], Dempster [42], and Ku, Varner, and Kullback [57]. It was pointed out by Darroch [192], "That 'interaction' in contingency tables enjoys only a few of the fortuitously simple properties of interactions in the analysis of variance" (see Kullback [13]).

Following this general introduction, we shall consider further aspects of contingency tables in greater expository detail. We then present an introduction to minimum discrimination information estimation, the log-linear representation, associated design matrices and parameters, without detailed mathematical proofs. This will enable the reader then to study the many illustrative examples that follow and present various aspects of the possible analyses. The mathematical statistical proofs etc. are to be found at the end of the presentation.

# CONTINGENCY TABLES

## Description

There are two ways in which statistical data are collected. In one form, actual measurements are recorded for each individual in the sample; in the other, the individuals are classified as belonging to different categories. On many occasions classifications are used to reduce original data on direct measurements. A well-known example is that of "frequency distributions." Data collected in the form of measurements may later be grouped and presented as a frequency distribution. An important advantage of grouping is that it results in a considerable reduction of data. On the other hand, it is not usually possible to convert grouped or classified data back into the original form.

A contingency table is a form of presentation of grouped data. In the simplest case, a group of $N$ items may be classified into just two groups according to, say, the presence or absence of a certain characteristic. For a fixed (given) characteristic the different groups of classification are called *categories*. For example, a group of $N$ individuals may be classified according to hair color (characteristic), the categories being black, brown, blonde, and "other." The categories may be qualitative, as above, or may be quantitative, as for example in the classification by weight in pounds consisting of five categories: 40–80, 80–120, 120–160, 160–200, 200–240. When there is only one characteristic according to which data are classified, we get a *one-way table*. If there are two ways of classification, say according to rows and columns, the row classification having $r$ categories and the column classification having $c$ categories, the table is called a *two-way table* or a $r \times c$ *table*. The latter notation gives the number of categories in each classification. Carrying this notation further, a $r \times c \times d$ *table* will have three characteristics of classification, the first having $r$ categories, the second having $c$, and the third $d$.

## Examples

**Example 1.** The following is a one-way table with one classification characteristic (geographic area) and four categories. It gives the distribution of students by geographic area.

| East | North | West | South | Total |
|------|-------|------|-------|-------|
| 4,201 | 4,552 | 2,840 | 5,130 | 16,723 |

**Example 2.** Consider the distribution of 20 balls in six cells.

| Cell | 1 | 2 | 3 | 4 | 5 | 6 | Total |
|------|---|---|---|---|---|---|-------|
| Occupancy | 2 | 4 | 4 | 5 | 1 | 4 | 20 |

It may be recalled at this point that in many situations such a distribution of $N$ balls in $k$ cells is adequately described by the multinomial distribution. We may therefore expect that the multinomial distribution will have an important role to play in the analysis of contingency tables.

**Example 3.** The distribution of students by geographic area (as in Example 1) and sex gives rise to a 2 × 4 contingency table (Table 1).

Note that this is called a 2 × 4 table since the row-classification (sex) has 2 categories. If the geographic areas were written in rows and the sex were to correspond to columns, we would get a 4 × 2 table. We will follow this convention throughout.

Observe that for a two-way table there are two sets of marginal totals. In the above table the totals on the right can be looked upon as a one-way table with sex as a characteristic and two categories, male and female. At the bottom of Table 1, we see the one-way table of Example 1. This shows that any two-way table is associated with two one-way tables given by the marginal totals of each characteristic.

**Example 4.** The data below are octane determinations on independent samples of gasoline obtained in two regions of the northeastern United States in the summer of 1953 (Brownlee, *Statistical Theory and Methodology*, Wiley, New York, 1965, p. 306).

```
Region A:    84.0    83.5    84.0    85.0    83.1    83.5    81.7
             85.4    84.1    83.0    85.8    84.0    84.2    82.2
             83.6    84.9
Region D:    80.2    82.9    84.6    84.2    82.8    83.0    82.9
             83.4    83.1    83.5    83.6    86.7    82.6    82.4
             83.4    82.7    82.9    83.7    81.5    81.9    81.7
             82.5
```

The problem of interest was whether the variability in the octane numbers could be regarded as the same for the two regions. Since the number of sample values for Regions A and D are small (16 and 22, respectively), the data can be conveniently analyzed in the given form. For the sake of illustration, suppose that we classify the octane readings into three categories; below 83.5 as "poor," between 83.5 and 84.5 as "normal," and above 84.5 as "better," we will get a 2 × 3 table (Table 2).

This illustrates how to prepare contingency tables from actual measurement data. But the example brings out another important point. The contingency table, in fact, represents *two* frequency distributions, one from Region A and the other for Region D

**TABLE 1**

| Sex | Geographic area | | | | Totals |
|---|---|---|---|---|---|
| | East | North | West | South | |
| Male | 2,201 | 2,350 | 1,400 | 3,100 | 9,051 |
| Female | 2,000 | 2,202 | 1,440 | 2,030 | 7,672 |
| Totals | 4,201 | 4,552 | 2,840 | 5,130 | 16,723 |

**TABLE 2**

| Region | Gasoline quality | | | Totals |
|---|---|---|---|---|
| | Poor | Normal | Better | |
| A | 4 | 8 | 4 | 16 |
| D | 16 | 5 | 1 | 22 |
| Totals | 20 | 13 | 5 | 38 |

*laid side by side*. This table is different from the ones we came across earlier in that we did not start the classification with a total of 38 values, to be classified according to region and quality; rather we had *a priori* a set of 16 values for Region A and 22 values for Region D. (Further, the sampling for the two regions was done independently.) In other words, the set of marginal totals (on the one-way table) for the regions was *fixed* before the experiments. Later on we will have ample opportunities to see the effect of such restrictions on the analyses. At present, it is enough to know that such tables may be regarded as *contingency tables with fixed (restricted) marginal totals*.

**Problems Associated with Contingency Tables**

In the analysis of contingency tables we are usually interested in the relationship between one classification and one or more of the other classifications. Thus in Example 4 on comparison of octane ratings we would like to compare the variability of the values for classifications given by Regions A and D. As another example, consider a three-way $r \times c \times d$ contingency table in which the row classification represents the response of an experiment on animals, the column classification types of treatment, and the depth classification sex. The following hypotheses may be of interest.

1. Response is independent of treatment irrespective of sex.
2. Response is independent of the different combinations of treatment and sex (as against the possibility that a particular treatment is more "effective" in terms of the response for a particular sex).
3. Given sex, response is independent of treatment.

We shall see in subsequent sections how these hypotheses can be formulated mathematically. Of course, not all contingency tables can be interpreted in such a straightforward manner. In some instances, all three classifications can be considered as responses; then we may be interested in the independence or association among these responses. In other cases a classification may be controlled, experimentally or naturally, like three specified levels of fertilizer applied or sex, in which case the classification is termed a factor. For convenience, we shall group all the concepts of association, dependence, etc. under the general term of *interaction*. No interaction between treatment and sex appears to be a more acceptable phrase than independence between treatment and sex, since the term independence is usually reserved to express the relationship between random variables. We may also say that the interaction between response and treatment does not interact with sex, meaning the degree of association between response and treatment is the same for both sexes. This concept gives rise to the idea of second-order interaction. There are a number of different approaches to the mathematical formulation and interpretation of the concept of "no interaction." One such approach, through the concept of "generalized independence," is powerful and general enough to include all hypotheses of "no interaction" (formulated in a specific manner) *and* many other hypotheses about homogeneity, symmetry, etc. that we come across in analyzing contingency tables. Before this concept is introduced, we shall need the necessary symbolism and notation.

**Notation and Preliminaries**

We have seen that the entries in the "cells" of a contingency table are frequencies of occurrence. We will denote these frequencies generically by the letter $x$, with or without subscripts. These frequencies are a result of classification of a fixed number of individuals according to a certain probability distribution. Hence the observed frequencies $x$ can be looked upon as realizations of a random variable $X$.

The cell of a contingency table and the observed frequency in that cell are symbolically associated in the following manner. In Example 1 we have a one-way table representing the distribution of 16,723 students by geographic area. We denote the occurrence in the table by $x(i)$ with the notation

| Characteristic | Index | 1 | 2 | 3 | 4 |
|---|---|---|---|---|---|
| Geographic area | $i$ | East | North | West | South |

Thus $x(3)$, for example, equals 2840. The total 16,723 of all $x(i)$ for $i = 1, 2, 3$, and 4 will be denoted by $x(.)$. That is, $\sum_{i=1}^{4} x(i) = x(.) = 16,723$. For the two-way table of Example 3, we denote the frequencies in the table by $x(ij)$ with the notation given in Table 3. Then $x(2, 3) = 1440$, $x(1, 4) = 3100$, and so on. To denote marginal totals we will use the *dot notation* as before. The *row marginals* are

$$\sum_{j=1}^{4} x(1j) = x(1.) = 9051, \qquad \sum_{j=1}^{4} x(2j) = x(2.) = 7672$$

The *column marginals* are

$$\sum_{i=1}^{2} x((i1) = x(.1) = 4201, \ldots, \qquad \sum_{i=1}^{2} x(i4) = x(.4) = 5130$$

The grand total is denoted by $x(..)$, so that $x(1.) + x(2.) = x(..) = x(.1) + x(.2) + x(.3) + x(.4) = 16723 = N$.

TABLE 3

| Characteristic | Index | 1 | 2 | 3 | 4 |
|---|---|---|---|---|---|
| Sex | $i$ | Male | Female | | |
| Geographic area | $j$ | East | North | West | South |

Now consider the three-way table (Table 4) of the propagation of plum root stocks from root cuttings.

The frequencies in the cells are denoted by $x(ijk)$ with the notation of Table 5. The marginals are as follows:

One-way marginals: 
$$\Sigma_j\Sigma_k \, x(ijk) = x(i..), \, i = 1, 2$$
$$\Sigma_i\Sigma_k \, x(ijk) = x(.j.), \, j = 1, 2$$
$$\Sigma_i\Sigma_j \, x(ijk) = x(..k), \, k = 1, 2$$

Two-way marginals: 
$$\Sigma_i \, x(ijk) = x(.jk), \, j = 1, 2, \quad k = 1, 2$$
$$\Sigma_j \, x(ijk) = x(i.k), \, i = 1, 2, \quad k = 1, 2$$
$$\Sigma_k \, x(ijk) = x(ij.), \, i = 1, 2, \quad j = 1, 2$$

Note that $\Sigma_i \, x(ij.) = x(.j.)$, $\Sigma_j \, x(ij.) = x(i..)$, $\Sigma_i \, x(i..) = x(...)$, etc.

For Table 4, $x(1..) = 378$, $x(2..) = 582$ and $x(...) = 960$. It should be observed that $x(.jk) = 240$ for all the four combinations of $j$ and $k$. This restriction is imposed by the method of experimentation; for each combination of the planting time and cutting length exactly 240 root stocks were used and their mortality observed. This is another case of fixed marginals, similar to the one encountered in Example 4.

The notation for cell frequencies and for marginal totals can be extended in an obvious manner to four-way, five-way, and higher order tables.

Let us now recall that in a contingency table a number of individuals are classified into cells. In other words, for a *given* cell an individual is classified in the cell with a certain probability. In a four-way table, for example, each cell will be denoted by $(i, j, k, l)$ for some values of the indices $i, j, k,$ and $l$. The probability that an individual will be classified in this cell will be denoted by $p(ijkl)$. Just as we defined the marginal totals for the cell frequencies $x(ijkl)$, we

TABLE 4

| Response (mortality) | At once | | Spring | | Totals |
|---|---|---|---|---|---|
| | Long | Short | Long | Short | |
| Alive | 156 | 107 | 84 | 31 | 378 |
| Dead | 84 | 133 | 156 | 209 | 582 |
| Totals | 240 | 240 | 240 | 240 | 960 |

**TABLE 5**

| Characteristic | Index | 1 | 2 |
|---|---|---|---|
| Mortality | $i$ | Alive | Dead |
| Time of planting | $j$ | At once | Spring |
| Length of cutting | $k$ | Long | Short |

may define marginal totals for probabilities. For example,

$$p(i...) = \Sigma_j \Sigma_k \Sigma_l \, p(ijkl)$$
$$p(.j.l) = \Sigma_i \Sigma_k \, p(ijkl)$$
etc.

For a two-way table the cell probabilities will be denoted by $p(ij)$, for a three-way table by $p(ijk)$, and so on. But we would like to develop the theory of *all* contingency tables in a unified manner. For this purpose it is necessary to use a symbol, $\omega$, say, which will generically denote cells like $(ij)$ in a two-way table, $(ijkl)$ in a four-way table, and so on. For example, in a $2 \times 3 \times 5$ table, the symbol $x(\omega)$ will replace $x(ijk)$, being one of the $2 \times 3 \times 5 = 30$ cells. The symbol $\omega$ here corresponds to the triplet $(ijk)$ and takes "values" $(1, 1, 1)$, $(1, 1, 2)$, . . . , $(1, 1, 5)$, $(1, 2, 1)$, . . . , $(2, 3, 5)$.

Let us now go back to some problems associated with the analysis of contingency tables discussed in Example 3 and see how we can formulate them symbolically with the help of the notation developed. We considered a $r \times c \times 2$ table in which the row classification represents response in an experiment on animals, the column classification represents types of treatment, and the depth classification represents sex. The cell probabilities are $p(ijk)$.

1. Response is independent of treatment irrespective of sex.

Since the sex of the animal is immaterial in the statement of the hypothesis, we consider marginal totals of probabilities of the form $p(ij.)$. Now, since the response is postulated to be independent of treatment we further have

$$p(ij.) = p(i..)p(.j.), \qquad i = 1, \ldots, r; j = 1, \ldots, c$$

2. Response is independent of the different combinations of treatment and sex.

The probability corresponding to a particular combination of treatment and sex is given by the (marginal) total $p(.jk)$. The hypothesis is formulated, therefore, as

$$p(ijk) = p(i..)p(.jk), \qquad \begin{aligned} i &= 1, \ldots, r \\ j &= 1, \ldots, c \\ k &= 1, 2 \end{aligned}$$

3. Given sex, response is independent of treatment.

Let the conditional probability of being classified in the cell $(ijk)$, *given* that the individual is classified in the $k$th depth classification (sex), be denoted by $p(ij \mid k)$. Also, the marginal conditional probability of classification in the $i$th category irrespective of the column classification is $p(i.k)/p(..k)$ and a similar marginal probability for the $j$th category of the column classification, given $k$, is $p(.jk)/p(..k)$. The hypothesis then states that

$$p(ij \mid k) = \frac{p(i.k)p(.jk)}{p^2(..k)}, \qquad k = 1, 2; i = 1, \ldots, r; j = 1, \ldots, c$$

But $p(ij \mid k) = p(ijk)/p(..k)$, so that the above relations can be restated as

$$p(ijk) = \frac{p(i.k)p(.jk)}{p(..k)}, \qquad k = 1, 2; j = 1, \ldots, r; j = 1, \ldots, c$$

Observe that $\Sigma_i \Sigma_j \, p(ij \mid k) = 1$, since given that an individual fell into the $k$th category, it must be classified in one of the $(i, j)$ cells corresponding to the fixed $k$. This imposes the restriction that

$$\sum_i \sum_j p(ij \mid k) = 1 = \sum_i \sum_j \frac{p(ijk)}{p(..k)}, \qquad k = 1, 2$$

i.e.,

$$\sum_i \sum_j p(ijk) = p(..k), \qquad k = 1, 2$$

Note that the second hypothesis (of independence) led us to the formulation $p(ijk) = p(i..)p(.jk)$ and the third hypothesis (of conditional independence) led to $p(ijk) = p(i.k)p(.jk)/p(..k)$. The cell probabilities in each case are expressed as products of marginal probabilities. From another point of view, we can say that the trivariate function $p(ijk)$ is expressed as a product of (simpler) univariate and bivariate functions of the form $p(.jk)$ and $p(i..)$, for example. When the cell probabilities are thus expressible as products of functions of a smaller subset of arguments, we say that the probabilities obey *generalized independence*. By generalized independence is meant that the cell probability of a multidimensional contingency table may be expressed as the product of factors which are functions of various marginals [57, 114–116]. The common notions of independence, conditional independence, homogeneity, or conditional homogeneity in contingency tables are all special cases of generalized independence. This is a consequence of the fact that in accordance with the minimum discrimination information theorem, the m.d.i. estimates are formulated as members of an exponential family which may also be expressed as a multiplicative model or a logarithmic linear additive model [57, 114, 115, 229]. Note that we do not assume such a model to start with, as others have, but derive this model by the principle of m.d.i. estimation [81, 91, 126, 142, 173].

## Estimates

We shall denote estimates of the cell entries under various hypotheses or models by $x_\alpha^*(\omega)$, where values of the subscript $\alpha$ will range over the hypotheses or models.

For two-way $2 \times 2$ tables the primary question of interest is whether the row and column variables are independent. An example is shown in Table 6.

To answer this question, one estimates the cell entries under the hypothesis of independence as a product of the marginals, that is, denoting the estimate by $x^*(ij)$, one uses $x^*(ij) = x(i.)x(.j)/n$. Some appropriate measure of the deviation between $x(ij)$ and $x^*(ij)$ is then used to determine whether the differences are "larger" than one would reasonably expect under the hypothesis of independence.

The estimated two-way table under the hypothesis or model of independence is given in Table 7. Note that the estimated table has the same marginals as the observed table $x(ij)$.

A common statistical measure of the association or interaction between the variables of a two-way $2 \times 2$ contingency table is the cross-product ratio, or its logarithm. The cross-product ratio is defined by

$$\frac{x(11)x(22)}{x(12)x(21)}$$

though we shall be more concerned with its logarithm

$$\ln \frac{x(11)x(22)}{x(12)x(21)}$$

We shall use natural logarithms, that is, logarithms to the base $e$, rather than common logarithms to the base 10, because of the nature of the underlying mathematical statistical theory. Note that with the estimate for independence, or no association, the logarithm of the cross-product ratio is zero:

$$\ln \frac{x^*(11)x^*(22)}{x^*(12)x^*(21)} = \ln \frac{\dfrac{x(1.)x(.1)}{n}\dfrac{x(2.)x(.2)}{n}}{\dfrac{x(1.)x(.2)}{n}\dfrac{x(2.)x(.1)}{n}} = \ln 1 = 0$$

### TABLE 6

| | $x(ij)$ | | |
|---|---|---|---|
| | $j = 1$ | $j = 2$ | |
| $i = 1$ | $x(11)$ | $x(12)$ | $x(1.)$ |
| $i = 2$ | $x(21)$ | $x(22)$ | $x(2.)$ |
| | $x(.1)$ | $x(.2)$ | $x(..) = n$ |

TABLE 7
Estimate under Independence

| | $x^*(ij)$ | | |
|---|---|---|---|
| | $j = 1$ | $j = 2$ | |
| $i = 1$ | $x(1.)x(.1)/n$ | $x(1.)x(.2)/n$ | $x(1.)$ |
| $i = 2$ | $x(2.)x(.1)/n$ | $x(2.)x(.2)/n$ | $x(2.)$ |
| | $x(.1)$ | $x(.2)$ | $n$ |

The logarithm of the cross-product ratio is positive if the odds satisfy the inequalities

$$\frac{x(11)}{x(21)} > \frac{x(12)}{x(22)} \quad \text{or} \quad \frac{x(11)}{x(12)} > \frac{x(21)}{x(22)}$$

since then we get for the log-odds

$$\ln \frac{x(11)x(22)}{x(12)x(21)} = \ln \frac{x(11)}{x(21)} - \ln \frac{x(12)}{x(22)} > 0$$

$$= \ln \frac{x(11)}{x(12)} - \ln \frac{x(21)}{x(22)} > 0$$

The logarithm of the cross-product ratio is negative if the odds satisfy the inequalities

$$\frac{x(11)}{x(21)} < \frac{x(12)}{x(22)} \quad \text{or} \quad \frac{x(11)}{x(12)} < \frac{x(21)}{x(22)}$$

since then we get for the log-odds

$$\ln \frac{x(11)x(22)}{x(12)x(21)} = \ln \frac{x(11)}{x(21)} - \ln \frac{x(12)}{x(22)} < 0$$

$$= \ln \frac{x(11)}{x(12)} - \ln \frac{x(21)}{x(22)} < 0$$

The logarithm of the cross-product ratio thus varies from $-\infty$ to $+\infty$. Later we shall consider procedures for assessing the significance of the deviation of the logarithm of the cross-product ratio from zero, the value corresponding to no association or no interaction.

Similar procedures apply to the case of a two-way $r \times c$ contingency table, that is, one with $r$ rows and $c$ columns (Table 8a).

Under a hypothesis or model of independence of row and column categories, $x^*(ij) = x(i.)x(.j)/n$. Even if the row categories, say, are not randomly observed but selected with respect to some characteristic, say time or space, the mathematical procedures are still the same for determining whether the column categories are homogeneous over the row categories, time or space for instance. In the latter case we may consider the two-way table as a set of one-way tables.

**TABLE 8a**
Two-Way $r \times c$ Contingency Table

|  |  | $j$ |  |  |  |
|---|---|---|---|---|---|
| $i$ | 1 | 2 | ... | $c$ |  |
| 1 | $x(11)$ | $x(12)$ | ... | $x(1c)$ | $x(1.)$ |
| 2 | $x(21)$ | $x(22)$ | ... | $x(2c)$ | $x(2.)$ |
| $\vdots$ | ... | ... | ... | ... | ... |
| $r$ | $x(r1)$ | $x(r2)$ | ... | $x(rc)$ | $x(r.)$ |
|  | $x(.1)$ | $x(.2)$ | ... | $x(.c)$ | $n$ |

Terms which cover both the case of independence and homogeneity are "association" or "interaction," that is, we question whether there is association or interaction among the variables.

The estimated two-way $r \times c$ contingency table under the hypothesis or model of independence is given in Table 8b. Note that the estimated table has the same marginals as the observed Table 8a.

A three-way contingency table arises when each observation has three classifications with different possible numbers of categories for each classification. The simplest three-way contingency table is $2 \times 2 \times 2$, that is, with two categories for each classification.

In the general notation we have Table 9.

The two-way marginals are

$$x(11.) = x(111) + x(112)$$
$$x(12.) = x(121) + x(122)$$
$$x(21.) = x(211) + x(212)$$
$$x(22.) = x(221) + x(222)$$
$$x(1.1) = x(111) + x(121)$$
$$x(1.2) = x(112) + x(122)$$
$$x(2.1) = x(211) + x(221)$$
$$x(2.2) = x(212) + x(222)$$
$$x(.11) = x(111) + x(211)$$
$$x(.12) = x(112) + x(212)$$
$$x(.21) = x(121) + x(221)$$
$$x(.22) = x(122) + x(222)$$

The one-way marginals are

$$x(1..) = x(111) + x(112) + x(121) + x(122) = x(11.) + x(12.)$$
$$x(2..) = x(211) + x(212) + x(221) + x(222) = x(21.) + x(22.)$$
$$x(.1.) = x(111) + x(112) + x(211) + x(212) = x(11.) + x(21.)$$
$$x(.2.) = x(121) + x(122) + x(221) + x(222) = x(12.) + x(22.)$$
$$x(..1) = x(111) + x(121) + x(211) + x(221) = x(1.1) + x(2.1)$$
$$x(..2) = x(112) + x(122) + x(212) + x(222) = x(1.2) + x(2.2)$$

The entries $x(ijk)$ in Table 9 may also be considered as three-way marginals.

With more variables there are more possible questions of interest. One may be interested in whether any pair of the variables are independent or show no interaction or association. One may be interested in conditional independence, that is, whether a pair of variables are independent given the third variable. One may be interested in whether the three variables are mutually independent or whether one of the variables is independent of the pair of the other variables. These questions of independence, no interaction, or association are all answered by considering estimates which are explicitly represented in terms of products of various marginals. We list some of these estimates.

| | |
|---|---|
| Mutual independence of $i$, $j$, and $k$ | $x_1^*(ijk) = x(i..)x(.j.)x(..k)/n^2$ |
| Independence of $i$ and $(jk)$ jointly | $x_a^*(ijk) = x(i..)x(.jk)/n$ |
| Conditional independence of $i$ and $j$ given $k$ | $x_b^*(ijk) = x(i.k)x(.jk)/x(..k)$ |

As might be expected, these estimates also apply in the general three-way $r \times s \times t$ contingency table.

We note that the estimate under mutual independence of $i$, $j$, and $k$ has the same one-way marginals as the observed table $x(ijk)$,

$$x_1^*(111) = x(1..)x(.1.)x(..1)/n^2$$
$$x_1^*(112) = x(1..)x(.1.)x(..2)/n^2$$
$$x_1^*(121) = x(1..)x(.2.)x(..1)/n^2$$
$$x_1^*(122) = x(1..)x(.2.)x(..2)/n^2$$
$$x_1^*(211) = x(2..)x(.1.)x(..1)/n^2$$
$$x_1^*(212) = x(2..)x(.1.)x(..2)/n^2$$
$$x_1^*(221) = x(2..)x(.2.)x(..1)/n^2$$
$$x_1^*(222) = x(2..)x(.2.)x(..2)/n^2$$
$$\begin{aligned} x_1^*(1..) &= x_1^*(111) + x_1^*(112) + x_1^*(121) + x_1^*(122) \\ &= x(1..)x(.1.)/n + x(1..)x(.2.)/n \\ &= x(1..) \end{aligned}$$
$$\begin{aligned} x_1^*(2..) &= x_1^*(211) + x_1^*(212) + x_1^*(221) + x_1^*(222) \\ &= x(2..)x(.1.)/n + x(2..)x(.2.)/n \\ &= x(2..) \end{aligned}$$
$$\begin{aligned} x_1^*(.1.) &= x_1^*(111) + x_1^*(112) + x_1^*(211) + x_1^*(212) \\ &= x(1..)x(.1.)/n + x(2..)x(.1.)/n \\ &= x(.1.) \end{aligned}$$
$$\begin{aligned} x_1^*(.2.) &= x_1^*(121) + x_1^*(122) + x_1^*(221) + x_1^*(222) \\ &= x(.2.) \end{aligned}$$
$$\begin{aligned} x_1^*(..1) &= x_1^*(111) + x_1^*(121) + x_1^*(211) + x_1^*(221) \\ &= x(..1) \end{aligned}$$
$$\begin{aligned} x_1^*(..2) &= x_1^*(112) + x_1^*(122) + x_1^*(212) + x_1^*(222) \\ &= x(..2) \end{aligned}$$

However, the two-way marginals of the estimate under mutual independence of $i$, $j$, and $k$ differ from the two-way marginals of the observed table $x(ijk)$. Thus,

**TABLE 8b**
Estimate under Independence: $x^*(ij)$

| $i$ | 1 | 2 | ... | $c$ | |
|---|---|---|---|---|---|
| 1 | $x(1.)x(.1)/n$ | $x(1.)x(.2)/n$ | ... | $x(1.)x(.c)/n$ | $x(1.)$ |
| 2 | $x(2.)x(.1)/n$ | $x(2.)x(.2)/n$ | ... | $x(2.)x(.c)/n$ | $x(2.)$ |
| ⋮ | ... | ... | ... | ... | ... |
| $r$ | $x(r.)x(.1)/n$ | $x(r.)x(.2)/n$ | ... | $x(r.)x(.c)/n$ | $x(r.)$ |
| | $x(.1)$ | $x(.2)$ | ... | $x(.c)$ | $n$ |

for example,

$$\begin{aligned}
x_1^*(11.) &= x_1^*(111) + x_1^*(112) \\
&= x(1..)x(.1.)x(..1)/n^2 + x(1..)x(.1.)x(..2)/n^2 \\
&= x(1..)x(.1.)/n
\end{aligned}$$

and the latter value is not necessarily equal to $x(11.)$.

The estimate under the hypothesis or model of independence of $i$ and $(jk)$ jointly has the same one-way marginals and the same two-way $jk$-marginal as the observed table $x(ijk)$,

$$\begin{aligned}
x_a^*(111) &= x(1..)x(.11)/n \\
x_a^*(112) &= x(1..)x(.12)/n \\
x_a^*(121) &= x(1..)x(.21)/n \\
x_a^*(122) &= x(1..)x(.22)/n \\
x_a^*(211) &= x(2..)x(.11)/n \\
x_a^*(212) &= x(2..)x(.12)/n \\
x_a^*(221) &= x(2..)x(.21)/n \\
x_a^*(222) &= x(2..)x(.22)/n \\
x_a^*(1..) &= x_a^*(111) + x_a^*(112) + x_a^*(121) + x_a^*(122) \\
&= x(1..)x(.11)/n + x(1..)x(.12)/n + x(1..)x(.21)/n + x(1..)x(.22)/n \\
&= x(1..)[x(.11) + x(.12) + x(.21) + x(.22)]/n \\
&= x(1..)
\end{aligned}$$

**TABLE 9**

| | $i = 1$ | | $i = 2$ | | |
|---|---|---|---|---|---|
| | $j = 1$ | $j = 2$ | $j = 1$ | $j = 2$ | |
| $k = 1$ | $x(111)$ | $x(121)$ | $x(211)$ | $x(221)$ | $x(..1)$ |
| $k = 2$ | $x(112)$ | $x(122)$ | $x(212)$ | $x(222)$ | $x(..2)$ |
| | $x(11.)$ | $x(12.)$ | $x(21.)$ | $x(22.)$ | $n$ |

Similar results follow for the other one-way marginals.

$$
\begin{aligned}
x_a{}^*(.11) &= x_a{}^*(111) + x_a{}^*(211) \\
&= x(1..)x(.11)/n + x(2..)x(.11)/n \\
&= x(.11) \\
x_a{}^*(.12) &= x_a{}^*(112) + x_a{}^*(212) \\
&= x(1..)x(.12)/n + x(2..)x(.12)/n \\
&= x(.12) \\
x_a{}^*(.21) &= x_a{}^*(121) + x_a{}^*(221) \\
&= x(1..)x(.21)/n + x(2..)x(.21)/n \\
&= x(.21) \\
x_a{}^*(.22) &= x_a{}^*(122) + x_a{}^*(222) \\
&= x(1..)x(.22)/n + x(2..)x(.22)/n \\
&= x(.22)
\end{aligned}
$$

However, for the other two-way marginals, for example,

$$
\begin{aligned}
x_a{}^*(11.) &= x_a{}^*(111) + x_a{}^*(112) \\
&= x(1..)x(.11)/n + x(1..)x(.12)/n \\
&= x(1..)[x(.11) + x(.12)]/n \\
&= x(1..)x(.1.)/n
\end{aligned}
$$

and the latter value is not necessarily equal to $x(11.)$

$$
\begin{aligned}
x_a{}^*(1.1) &= x_a{}^*(111) + x_a{}^*(121) \\
&= x(1..)x(.11)/n + x(1..)x(.21)/n \\
&= x(1..)[x(.11) + x(.21)]/n \\
&= x(1..)x(..1)/n
\end{aligned}
$$

and the latter value is not necessarily equal to $x(1.1)$.

The estimate under the hypothesis or model of conditional independence of $i$ and $j$ given $k$ has the same one-way marginals and the same two-way $ik$- and $jk$-marginals as the observed table $x(ijk)$,

$$
\begin{aligned}
x_b{}^*(111) &= x(1.1)x(.11)/x(..1) \\
x_b{}^*(112) &= x(1.2)x(.12)/x(..2) \\
x_b{}^*(121) &= x(1.1)x(.21)/x(..1) \\
x_b{}^*(122) &= x(1.2)x(.22)/x(..2) \\
x_b{}^*(211) &= x(2.1)x(.11)/x(..1) \\
x_b{}^*(212) &= x(2.2)x(.12)/x(..2) \\
x_b{}^*(221) &= x(2.1)x(.21)/x(..1) \\
x_b{}^*(222) &= x(2.2)x(.22)/x(..2) \\
x_b{}^*(1..) &= x_b{}^*(111) + x_b{}^*(112) + x_b{}^*(121) + x_b{}^*(122) \\
&= x(1.1)x(.11)/x(..1) + x(1.2)x(.12)/x(..2) \\
&\quad + x(1.1)x(.21)/x(..1) + x(1.2)x(.22)/x(..2) \\
&= x(1.1) + x(1.2) \\
&= x(1..)
\end{aligned}
$$

Similar results follow for the other one-way marginals.

$$\begin{aligned}
x_b{}^*(1.1) &= x_b{}^*(111) + x_b{}^*(121) \\
&= x(1.1)x(.11)/x(..1) + x(1.1)x(.21)/x(..1) \\
&= x(1.1) \\
x_b{}^*(1.2) &= x_b{}^*(112) + x_b{}^*(122) \\
&= x(1.2)x(.12)/x(..2) + x(1.2)x(.22)/x(..2) \\
&= x(1.2)
\end{aligned}$$

and in a similar manner we have

$$\begin{aligned}
x_b{}^*(2.1) &= x(2.1), \qquad x_b{}^*(2.2) = x(2.2) \\
x_b{}^*(.11) &= x_b{}^*(111) + x_b{}^*(211) \\
&= x(1.1)x(.11)/x(..1) + x(2.1)x(.11)/x(..1) \\
&= x(.11) \\
x_b{}^*(.12) &= x_b{}^*(112) + x_b{}^*(212) \\
&= x(1.2)x(.12)/x(..2) + x(2.2)x(.12)/x(..2) \\
&= x(.12)
\end{aligned}$$

and in a similar manner we have

$$x_b{}^*(.21) = x(.21), \qquad x_b{}^*(.22) = x(.22)$$

However, for the other two-way marginals

$$\begin{aligned}
x_b{}^*(11.) &= x_b{}^*(111) + x_b{}^*(112) \\
&= x(1.1)x(.11)/x(..1) + x(1.2)x(.12)/x(..2)
\end{aligned}$$

and the latter value is not necessarily equal to $x(11.)$.

We remark that one of the constraints in the determination of the estimates was that they have certain marginals the same as the observed table.

For the three-way $2 \times 2 \times 2$ contingency table in addition to the classic types of independence, interaction, or association, there arises an additional one, important historically and practically. This is known as no three-factor or no second-order interaction. No three-factor or no second-order interaction implies that the logarithm of the association measured by the cross-product ratio for any two of the variables is the same for all the values of the third variable, that is, there is no second-order interaction if

$$\begin{aligned}
\ln \frac{x(111)x(221)}{x(121)x(211)} &= \ln \frac{x(112)x(222)}{x(122)x(212)}, \qquad i, j \\
\ln \frac{x(111)x(212)}{x(112)x(211)} &= \ln \frac{x(121)x(222)}{x(122)x(221)}, \qquad i, k \qquad (1) \\
\ln \frac{x(111)x(122)}{x(112)x(121)} &= \ln \frac{x(211)x(222)}{x(212)x(221)}, \qquad j, k
\end{aligned}$$

One is concerned with the possible hypothesis or model of no second-order interaction when none of the other types of independence are found. However, in this case the corresponding estimate cannot be expressed explicitly in terms of observed marginals although the estimate is constrained to have the same two-way marginals as the observed table. Straightforward iterative procedures exist to determine the estimate under the hypothesis or model of no second-order interaction. For the general three-way $r \times s \times t$ contingency table there are, of course, many more relations among the log cross-product ratios like (1) which must be satisfied, but the iterative procedures to determine the estimate extend to the general case with no difficulty.

We may be concerned with a set of two-way tables for which it is of interest to determine whether they are homogeneous with respect to a third factor, say space or time. Such problems may also be treated as three-way contingency tables using the space or time factor as the third classification [229].

For four-way and higher order contingency tables the problem of presentation of the data increases, as do the variety and number of questions about relationships of possible interest and varieties of interaction. The basic ideas, concepts, notation, and terminology we have discussed for the two- and three-way contingency tables extend to the more general cases as we consider the methodology [57].


## LOG-LINEAR REPRESENTATION

### Minimum Discrimination Information Estimation

To make the presentation more specific, and with no essential restriction on the generality, we discuss it in terms of the analysis of four-way contingency tables. Let us consider the collection of four-way contingency tables $R \times S \times T \times U$ of dimension $r \times s \times t \times u$. For convenience let us denote the aggregate of all cell identifications, as well as their number, by $\Omega$ with individual cells identified by $\omega$, so that the generic variable is $\omega = (i, j, k, l), i = 1, \ldots, r, j = 1, \ldots, s, k = 1, \ldots, t, l = 1, \ldots, u$. In this case we also identify $\Omega$ as $rstu$. Suppose there are two probability distributions or contingency tables (we shall use these terms interchangeably) defined over the aggregate or space $\Omega$, say $p(\omega), \pi(\omega), \Sigma_\Omega p(\omega) = 1, \Sigma_\Omega \pi(\omega) = 1$. The discrimination information is defined by

$$I(p:\pi) = \sum_\Omega p(\omega) \ln \frac{p(\omega)}{\pi(\omega)}$$

For the various applications we shall consider the $\pi$-distribution, $\pi(\omega)$, according to the problem of interest, may either be specified, may be an estimated distribution, or may be an observed distribution. The $p$-distribution, $p(\omega)$, ranges over or is a member of a family $\mathscr{P}$ of distributions of interest satisfying certain restraints.

Of the various properties of $I(p:\pi)$ we mention in particular the fact that $I(p:\pi) > 0$ and $= 0$ if, and only if, $p(\omega) = \pi(\omega)$ [229].

Many problems in the analysis of contingency tables may be characterized as estimating a distribution or contingency table subject to certain restraints and then comparing the estimated table with an observed table to determine whether the observed table satisfies a null hypothesis or model implied by the restraints. In accordance with the principle of m.d.i. estimation, we determine that member of the collection or family $\mathscr{P}$ of distributions which minimizes the discrimination information $I(p:\pi)$. We denote the m.d.i. estimate by $p^*(\omega)$ so that

$$I(p^*:\pi) = \sum p^*(\omega) \ln \frac{p^*(\omega)}{\pi(\omega)} = \min I(p:\pi),\, p,\, p^* \in \mathscr{P}$$

Unless otherwise stated, the summation is over $\Omega$ which will be omitted.

It may be shown that if $p(\omega)$ is any member of the family $\mathscr{P}$ of distributions, then

$$I(p:\pi) = I(p^*:\pi) + I(p:p^*) \tag{2}$$

The Pythagorean-type property (2) plays an important role in the analysis of information tables.

In a wide class of problems which can be characterized as "smoothing," or fitting a model to an observed contingency table, the restraints specify that the estimated distribution or contingency table have some set of marginals, or more generally, linear functions of observed cell entries, equal to those values for the observed contingency table. In such cases $\pi(\omega)$ is taken to be either the uniform distribution $\pi(ijkl) = 1/rstu$, or a distribution already estimated subject to restraints contained in and implied by the restraints under examination. The latter case includes the classical hypotheses of independence, conditional independence, homogeneity, conditional homogeneity, and interaction, all of which can be considered as instances of generalized independence.

To test whether an observed contingency table is consistent with the null hypothesis, or model, as represented by the minimum discrimination information estimate, we compute a measure of the deviation between the observed distribution and the appropriate estimate by the m.d.i. statistic. For notational and computational convenience, let us denote the estimated contingency table in terms of occurrences by $x^*(\omega) = np^*(\omega)$ where $n$ is the total number of occurrences. For the "smoothing" or fitting class of problems, that is, with the restraints implied by a set of observed marginals (those of a generalized independence hypothesis), or more generally, linear functions of observed cell entries, the m.d.i. statistic is

$$2I(x:x^*) = 2 \sum x(\omega) \ln \frac{x(\omega)}{x^*(\omega)} \tag{3}$$

which is asymptotically distributed as a chi-squared variate with appropriate degrees of freedom under the null hypothesis.

The statistic in (3) is also minus twice the logarithm of the classic likelihood ratio statistic but this is not necessarily true for other kinds of applications of the general theory [18].

## Computational Procedures

An "experiment" has been designed and observations made resulting in a multidimensional contingency table with the desired classifications and categories. All the information the analyst hopes to obtain from the "experiment" is contained in the contingency table. In the process of analysis the aim is to fit the observed table with a minimal or parsimonious number of parameters depending on some of the observed marginals, and/or some general linear combinations of observed cell entries, that is, essentially, to find out how much of this total information is contained in a summary consisting of sets of marginals and/or some linear combinations of observed cell entries.

Indeed, the relationship between the concept of independence or association and interaction in contingency tables and the role the marginals play is evidenced in the historical developments in the extensive literature on the analysis of contingency tables.

Let us denote by $\mathbf{x}$ the $\Omega \times 1$ matrix of entries $x(\omega)$ of the observed contingency table arranged in lexicographic order, and denote by $\mathbf{T}$ an $\Omega \times (m + 1)$ design matrix of rank $m + 1 \leqq \Omega$. We denote the columns of $\mathbf{T}$ by $T_i(\omega)$, $1 \leqq \omega \leqq \Omega$, $0 \leqq i \leqq m$. The condition that the estimate $x^*(\omega)$ have some set of marginals and/or some general linear combination of cell entries equal to the corresponding values of the observed contingency table is written in matrix notation as

$$\mathbf{T}'\mathbf{x}^* = \mathbf{T}'\mathbf{x} \tag{4}$$

Those columns of $\mathbf{T}$ which imply a marginal restraint are the indicator functions of the marginals, that is, the corresponding $T_i(\omega)$ will be one or zero for any cell $\omega$, according as the cell $\omega$ does or does not enter into the marginal in question. We usually take $T_0(\omega) = 1$, for all $\omega$, so that $\Sigma \, x^*(\omega) = \Sigma \, x(\omega) = n$. In accordance with the minimum discrimination information theorem [229], the m.d.i. estimate is the exponential family

$$x^*(\omega) = \exp \, (\tau_0 T_0(\omega) + \tau_1 T_1(\omega) + \cdots + \tau_m T_m(\omega)) n \pi(\omega) \tag{5}$$

If we denote the $\Omega \times 1$ matrix whose entries are $\ln \, (x^*(\omega)/n\pi(\omega))$ in lexicographic order on $\omega$ by $\ln \, (x^*/n\pi)$, then we have from (5) the log-linear regression [6, 27, 46]

$$\ln \, (x^*/n\pi) = \mathbf{T}\tau \tag{6}$$

where $\tau$ is the $(m + 1) \times 1$ matrix of the parameters $\tau_0, \tau_1, \tau_2, \ldots, \tau_m$. We set the normalizing parameter $\tau_0 = L$, and $\tau_1, \ldots, \tau_m$ are main effects and interactions. The parameters in (5) are to be determined so that $x^*(\omega)$ satisfies the condition (4). There are convergent iterative computer algorithms of proportional fitting (among others) which yield the estimate $x^*(\omega)$ satisfying (4), and then the parameters are determined from (6). The iteration may be described as successively cycling through adjustments of the marginals of interest starting with the $\pi(\omega)$ distribution until a desired accuracy of agreement between the set of observed marginals of interest and the computed marginals has been attained

[57]. Note that although $n\pi(\omega)$ is here a constant and could be absorbed into $\tau_0$ or $L$, we prefer to express it explicitly because there are cases in which $n\pi(\omega)$ is not a constant and the expression in (5) or (6) still applies [22, 46, 114, 115].

**Analysis of Information**

The analysis of information is based on the fundamental relation (2) for the m.d.i. statistics. Specifically, if $np_a{}^*(\omega) = x_a{}^*(\omega)$ is the m.d.i. estimate corresponding to a set $H_a$ of given marginals, and $x_b{}^*(\omega)$ is the m.d.i. estimate corresponding to a set $H_b$ of given marginals, where $H_a$ is explicitly or implicitly contained in $H_b$, then the basic relations are

$$
\begin{aligned}
2I(x:n\pi) &= 2I(x_a{}^*:n\pi) + 2I(x:x_a{}^*) \\
2I(x:n\pi) &= 2I(x_b{}^*:n\pi) + 2I(x:x_b{}^*) \\
2I(x_b{}^*:n\pi) &= 2I(x_a{}^*:n\pi) + 2I(x_b{}^*:x_a{}^*) \\
2I(x:x_a{}^*) &= 2I(x_b{}^*:x_a{}^*) + 2I(x:x_b{}^*)
\end{aligned}
\tag{7}
$$

with a corresponding additive relation for the associated degrees of freedom.

In terms of the representation in (5) or (6), as an exponential family, the two extreme cases are the uniform distribution for which all $\tau$'s except $L$ are zero, and the observed contingency table or distribution, the complete model, for which all $\Omega - 1 = rstu - 1$, $\tau$'s in addition to $L$ are needed.

Measures of the form $2I(x:x_a{}^*)$, that is, the comparison of an observed contingency table with an estimated contingency table, are called measures of interaction or goodness-of-fit. Measures of the form $2I(x_b{}^*:x_a{}^*)$, comparing two estimated contingency tables, are called measures of effect, that is, the effect of the marginals in the set $H_b$ but not in the set $H_a$, or the $\tau$'s in $x_b{}^*$ but not in $x_a{}^*$. We note that $2I(x:x_a{}^*)$ tests a null hypothesis that the values of the $\tau$ parameters in the representation of the observed contingency table $x(\omega)$ but not in the representation of the estimated table $x_a{}^*(\omega)$ are zero and the number of these $\tau$'s is the number of degrees of freedom. Similarly $2I(x_b{}^*:x_a{}^*)$ tests a null hypothesis that the values of the set of $\tau$ parameters in the representation of the estimated table $x_b{}^*(\omega)$ but not in the representation of the estimated table $x_a{}^*(\omega)$ are zero, and the number of these $\tau$'s is the number of degrees of freedom. See the section entitled The $2 \times 2 \times 2 \times 2$ Table below.

We summarize the additive relationships of the m.d.i. statistics and the associated degrees of freedom in the analysis of information Table 10.

**TABLE 10**
Analysis of Information Table

| Component due to | | Information | D.F. |
|---|---|---|---|
| $H_a$: | Interaction | $2I(x:x_a{}^*)$ | $N_a$ |
| $H_b$: | Effect | $2I(x_b{}^*:x_a{}^*)$ | $N_a - N_b$ |
| | Interaction | $2I(x:x_b{}^*)$ | $N_b$ |

Since measures of the form $2I(x:x_a{}^*)$ may also be interpreted as measures of the "variation unexplained" by the estimate $x_a{}^*$, the additive relationship leads to the interpretation of the ratio

$$\frac{2I(x:x_a{}^*) - 2I(x:x_b{}^*)}{2I(x:x_a{}^*)} = \frac{2I(x_b{}^*:x_a{}^*)}{2I(x:x_a{}^*)} \qquad (8)$$

as the percentage of the unexplained variation due to $x_a{}^*$ accounted for by the additional constraints defining $x_b{}^*$. The ratio (8) is thus similar to the squared correlation coefficients associated with normal distributions [81].

We remark that the marginals, explicit and implicit, of the estimated table $x_a{}^*(\omega)$, which form the set of restraints $H_a$ used to generate $x_a{}^*(\omega)$, are the same as the corresponding marginals of the observed $x(\omega)$ table and all lower order implied marginals. It may be shown that $2I(x:x_a{}^*)$ is approximately a quadratic in the differences between the remaining marginals of the $x(\omega)$ table and the corresponding ones as calculated from $x_a{}^*(\omega)$.

Similarly, $2I(x_b{}^*:x_a{}^*)$ is also approximately a quadratic in the differences between those additional marginal restraints in $H_b$ but not in $H_a$ and the corresponding marginal values as computed from the $x_a{}^*(\omega)$ table.

The $\tau$'s are determined from the log-linear regression equations (6) as sums and differences of values of $\ln x^*(\omega)$ or as linear combinations thereof. A variety of statistics have been presented in the literature for the analysis of contingency tables, which are quadratics in differences of marginal values or quadratics in the $\tau$'s or the linear combinations of logarithms of the observed or estimated values. The principle of minimum discrimination information estimation and its procedures thus provides a unifying relationship since such statistics may be seen as quadratic approximations of the minimum discrimination information statistic. We remark that the corresponding approximate $\chi^2$'s are not generally additive [18].

We mention the approximations in terms of quadratic forms in the marginals, or the $\tau$'s, as a possible bridge to relate the familiar procedures of classical regression analysis and the procedures proposed here. This may assist in understanding and interpreting the analysis of information tables [229]. The covariance matrix of the $T(\omega)$ functions or the $\tau$'s can be obtained for either the observed table or any of the estimated tables, as well as the inverse matrices, as part of the output of the general computer program.

## The 2 × 2 Table

It may be useful to reexamine the 2 × 2 table from the point of view of the preceding discussion. The algebraic details are simple in this case and exhibit the unification of the information theoretic development.

Suppose we have the observed 2 × 2 table in Table 11. If we obtain the m.d.i. estimate fitting the one-way marginals, the generalized independence hypothesis is the classical independence hypothesis and the m.d.i. estimate is the usual $x^*(ij) = x(i.)x(.j)/n$. By the iterative scaling fitting procedure, we begin with

## TABLE 11

| | | |
|---|---|---|
| $x(11)$ | $x(12)$ | $x(1.)$ |
| $x(21)$ | $x(22)$ | $x(2.)$ |
| $x(.1)$ | $x(.2)$ | $n$ |

$x^{(0)}(ij) = n/4$ in each cell and adjust the $x^{(0)}(ij)$ values by the ratios of the observed row marginals to those of $x^{(0)}(ij)$, that is,

$$x^{(1)}(ij) = x^{(0)}(ij)\frac{x(i.)}{n/2} = x(i.)/2$$

Then we adjust $x^{(1)}(ij)$ by the ratio of observed column marginals to the marginals of $x^{(1)}(ij)$,

$$x^{(2)}(ij) = x^{(1)}(ij)\frac{x(.j)}{n/2} = \frac{x(i.)}{2}\cdot\frac{x(.j)}{n/2}$$
$$= x(i.)x(.j)/n = x^*(ij)$$

Since the row and column marginals of $x^*(ij)$ are now the same as the observed values, no further iterative adjustment is necessary. For fitting a $2 \times 2$ table to externally specified marginals see Ref. 115.

The representation of the log-linear regression for the complete model is given in Table 12. The entries in the columns $\tau_1, \tau_2, \tau_3$ are, respectively, the values of the functions $T_1(ij), T_2(ij), T_3(ij)$ associated with the marginals $x(1.), x(.1), x(11)$, and the column headed $L$ corresponds to the normalizing factor.

We note the interpretation of Table 12 as the log-linear relations

$$\ln\frac{x(11)}{n\pi} = L + \tau_1 + \tau_2 + \tau_3$$
$$\ln\frac{x(12)}{n\pi} = L + \tau_1 \tag{9}$$
$$\ln\frac{x(21)}{n\pi} = L + \tau_2$$
$$\ln\frac{x(22)}{n\pi} = L$$

## TABLE 12

| $i$ | $j$ | $L$ | $\tau_1$ | $\tau_2$ | $\tau_3$ |
|---|---|---|---|---|---|
| 1 | 1 | 1 | 1 | 1 | 1 |
| 1 | 2 | 1 | 1 | | |
| 2 | 1 | 1 | | 1 | |
| 2 | 2 | 1 | | | |

From (9) we find

$$\begin{cases} L = \ln \left( x(22)/n/4 \right) \\ \tau_1 = \ln \left( x(12)/x(22) \right) \\ \tau_2 = \ln \left( x(21)/x(22) \right) \\ \tau_3 = \ln \left( x(11)x(22)/x(12)x(21) \right) \end{cases}$$

or

$$\begin{array}{l} \tau_1 = \ln x(12) - \ln x(22) \\ \tau_2 = \ln x(21) - \ln x(22) \\ \tau_3 = \ln x(11) + \ln x(22) - \ln x(12) - \ln x(21) \end{array} \tag{10}$$

The design matrix $\mathbf{T}$ is the matrix of Table 12, that is,

$$\mathbf{T} = \begin{pmatrix} 1 & 1 & 1 & 1 \\ 1 & 1 & 0 & 0 \\ 1 & 0 & 1 & 0 \\ 1 & 0 & 0 & 0 \end{pmatrix}$$

Define the diagonal matrix $\mathbf{D}$ with main diagonal the elements $x(ij)$, in lexicographic order, that is,

$$\mathbf{D} = \begin{pmatrix} x(11) & 0 & 0 & 0 \\ 0 & x(12) & 0 & 0 \\ 0 & 0 & x(21) & 0 \\ 0 & 0 & 0 & x(22) \end{pmatrix}$$

then the estimate of the covariance matrix of $x(1.), x(.1), x(11)$ for the observed contingency table is $\mathbf{S}_{22.1}$, where

$$\mathbf{S} = \begin{pmatrix} \mathbf{S}_{11} & \mathbf{S}_{12} \\ \mathbf{S}_{21} & \mathbf{S}_{22} \end{pmatrix} = \mathbf{T}'\mathbf{DT}$$

$$\mathbf{S}_{22.1} = \mathbf{S}_{22} - \mathbf{S}_{21}\mathbf{S}_{11}^{-1}\mathbf{S}_{12}$$

and $\mathbf{S}_{11}$ is $1 \times 1$, $\mathbf{S}_{22}$ is $3 \times 3$, $\mathbf{S}_{21}' = \mathbf{S}_{12}$ is $1 \times 3$. It is found that

$$\mathbf{S}_{22.1} = \begin{pmatrix} \dfrac{x(1.)x(2.)}{n} & x(11) - \dfrac{x(1.)x(.1)}{n} & \dfrac{x(11)x(2.)}{n} \\[2ex] x(11) - \dfrac{x(1.)x(.1)}{n} & \dfrac{x(.1)x(.2)}{n} & \dfrac{x(11)x(.2)}{n} \\[2ex] \dfrac{x(11)x(2.)}{n} & \dfrac{x(11)x(.2)}{n} & x(11) - \dfrac{x^2(11)}{n} \end{pmatrix}$$

and the inverse matrix is

$$\mathbf{S}_{22.1}^{-1} = \begin{pmatrix} \dfrac{1}{x(12)} + \dfrac{1}{x(22)} & \dfrac{1}{x(22)} & -\dfrac{1}{x(12)} - \dfrac{1}{x(22)} \\[2ex] \dfrac{1}{x(22)} & \dfrac{1}{x(21)} + \dfrac{1}{x(22)} & -\dfrac{1}{x(21)} - \dfrac{1}{x(22)} \\[2ex] -\dfrac{1}{x(12)} - \dfrac{1}{x(22)} & -\dfrac{1}{x(21)} - \dfrac{1}{x(22)} & \dfrac{1}{x(11)} + \dfrac{1}{x(12)} + \dfrac{1}{x(21)} + \dfrac{1}{x(22)} \end{pmatrix}$$

The matrix $S_{22.1}^{-1}$ is the covariance matrix of the $\tau$'s in (10). Similar results hold in general and for estimated tables [229].

Note that the value of the logarithm of the cross-product ratio, a measure of association or interaction, appears in the course of the analysis as the value of $\tau_3$ for the observed values $x(ij)$. For $x^*(ij)$, the estimate under the hypothesis of independence, the representation as in Table 12 does not involve the last column, since $x^*(ij)$ is obtained by fitting the one-way marginals, and $\tau_3 = 0$.

The log-linear relations for the estimate $x^*(ij)$ are

$$\ln \frac{x^*(11)}{n\pi} = L + \tau_1 + \tau_2$$

$$\ln \frac{x^*(12)}{n\pi} = L + \tau_1 \qquad (11)$$

$$\ln \frac{x^*(21)}{n\pi} = L + \tau_2$$

$$\ln \frac{x^*(22)}{n\pi} = L$$

where the numerical values of $L$, $\tau_1$, $\tau_2$ in (11) must, of course, depend on $x^*$ and differ from the values in (9).

The m.d.i. statistic to test the null hypothesis or model of independence is $2I(x:x^*)$ with one degree of freedom. In this case the quadratic approximation is

$$2I(x:x^*) = \left(x(11) - \frac{x(1.)x(.1)}{n}\right)^2 \left(\frac{1}{x^*(11)} + \frac{1}{x^*(12)} + \frac{1}{x^*(21)} + \frac{1}{x^*(22)}\right) \quad (12)$$

Remembering that $x^*(ij) = x(i.)x(.j)/n$, the right-hand side of (12) may also be shown to be

$$\chi^2 = \sum (x(ij) - x(i.)x(.j)/n)^2 \bigg/ \frac{x(i.)x(.j)}{n} \quad (13)$$

the classical $\chi^2$-test for independence with one degree of freedom. Another test which has been proposed for the null hypothesis of no association or no interaction in the $2 \times 2$ table is

$$(\ln x(11) + \ln x(22) - \ln x(12) - \ln x(21))^2 \left(\frac{1}{x(11)} + \frac{1}{x(12)} + \frac{1}{x(21)} + \frac{1}{x(22)}\right)^{-1}$$

which may be shown to be a quadratic approximation for $2I(x:x^*)$ in terms of $\tau_3$ with the covariance matrix estimated using the observed values and not the estimated values. We remark that if the observed values are used to estimate the covariance matrix then instead of the classical $\chi^2$-test in (13), there is derived the Neyman modified chi-square

$$\chi_1^2 = \sum (x(ij) - x(i.)x(.j)/n)^2/x(ij)$$

## The $2 \times 2 \times 2 \times 2$ Table

A useful graphic representation of the log-linear regression (6) is given in Table 13 for a $2 \times 2 \times 2 \times 2$ contingency table. This is the analog of the design matrix in normal regression theory. The blank spaces in Table 13 represent zero values. The $(ijkl)$ columns are the cell identifications in the same lexicographic order as the cell entries for the estimates in the computer output. Column 1 corresponds to $L$ which is the normalizing factor. Each of the columns 2 to 16 represents the corresponding values of the $T(\omega)$ functions, columns 2 to 5 those for the one-way marginals, columns 6 to 11 those for the two-way marginals, columns 12 to 15 those for the three-way marginals, and column 16 that for the four-way marginal. The $\tau$ parameter associated with the $T(\omega)$ function is given at the head of the column. The superscripts are useful identifications. The complete representation with all the columns of Table 13 generates the observed values. Thus the rows represent

$$\ln \frac{x(ijkl)}{n\pi(ijkl)} = L + \tau_1^i T_1^i(ijkl) + \cdots + \tau_{11}^{ij} T_{11}^{ij}(ijkl)$$

$$+ \cdots + \tau_{111}^{ijk} T_{111}^{ijk}(ijkl) + \cdots + \tau_{1111}^{ijkl} T_{1111}^{ijkl}(ijkl)$$

### TABLE 13
Graphic Representation

| $i$ | $j$ | $k$ | $l$ | 1 $L$ | 2 $\tau_1^i$ | 3 $\tau_1^j$ | 4 $\tau_1^k$ | 5 $\tau_1^l$ | 6 $\tau_{11}^{ij}$ | 7 $\tau_{11}^{ik}$ | 8 $\tau_{11}^{il}$ | 9 $\tau_{11}^{jk}$ | 10 $\tau_{11}^{jl}$ | 11 $\tau_{11}^{kl}$ | 12 $\tau_{111}^{ijk}$ | 13 $\tau_{111}^{ijl}$ | 14 $\tau_{111}^{ikl}$ | 15 $\tau_{111}^{jkl}$ | 16 $\tau_{1111}^{ijkl}$ |
|---|---|---|---|---|---|---|---|---|---|---|---|---|---|---|---|---|---|---|---|
| 1 | 1 | 1 | 1 | 1 | 1 | 1 | 1 | 1 | 1 | 1 | 1 | 1 | 1 | 1 | 1 | 1 | 1 | 1 | 1 |
| 1 | 1 | 1 | 2 | 1 | 1 | 1 | 1 |   | 1 | 1 |   | 1 |   |   | 1 |   |   |   |   |
| 1 | 1 | 2 | 1 | 1 | 1 | 1 |   | 1 | 1 |   | 1 |   | 1 |   |   | 1 |   |   |   |
| 1 | 1 | 2 | 2 | 1 | 1 | 1 |   |   | 1 |   |   |   |   |   |   |   |   |   |   |
| 1 | 2 | 1 | 1 | 1 | 1 |   | 1 | 1 |   | 1 | 1 |   |   | 1 |   |   | 1 |   |   |
| 1 | 2 | 1 | 2 | 1 | 1 |   | 1 |   |   | 1 |   |   |   |   |   |   |   |   |   |
| 1 | 2 | 2 | 1 | 1 | 1 |   |   | 1 |   |   | 1 |   |   |   |   |   |   |   |   |
| 1 | 2 | 2 | 2 | 1 | 1 |   |   |   |   |   |   |   |   |   |   |   |   |   |   |
| 2 | 1 | 1 | 1 | 1 |   | 1 | 1 | 1 |   |   |   | 1 | 1 | 1 |   |   |   | 1 |   |
| 2 | 1 | 1 | 2 | 1 |   | 1 | 1 |   |   |   |   | 1 |   |   |   |   |   |   |   |
| 2 | 1 | 2 | 1 | 1 |   | 1 |   | 1 |   |   |   |   | 1 |   |   |   |   |   |   |
| 2 | 1 | 2 | 2 | 1 |   | 1 |   |   |   |   |   |   |   |   |   |   |   |   |   |
| 2 | 2 | 1 | 1 | 1 |   |   | 1 | 1 |   |   |   |   |   | 1 |   |   |   |   |   |
| 2 | 2 | 1 | 2 | 1 |   |   | 1 |   |   |   |   |   |   |   |   |   |   |   |   |
| 2 | 2 | 2 | 1 | 1 |   |   |   | 1 |   |   |   |   |   |   |   |   |   |   |   |
| 2 | 2 | 2 | 2 | 1 |   |   |   |   |   |   |   |   |   |   |   |   |   |   |   |

where $\pi(ijkl)$ in the $2 \times 2 \times 2 \times 2$ case is $1/2 \times 2 \times 2 \times 2$ and the numerical values of $L$ and the $\tau$'s depend on the observed values $x(ijkl)$. The design matrix corresponding to an estimate uses only those columns associated with the marginals explicit and implied in the fitting process. This is a reflection of the fact that higher order marginals imply certain lower order marginals, for example, the two-way marginal $x(ij..)$ implies, by summation over $i$ and $j$, the one-way marginals $x(.j..)$, $x(i...)$, and the total $n = x(....)$. The representation for the uniform distribution corresponds to column 1 only. The estimate $x_1^*(ijkl)$ based on fitting the one-way marginals will use only columns 1 to 5. The values of $L$ and the $\tau$'s for this estimate will be different from those for $x(ijkl)$ and depend on the estimate $x_1^*(ijkl)$. The representation in Table 13 implies for $x_1^*(ijkl)$

$$\ln \frac{x_1^*(1111)}{n\pi} = L + \tau_1{}^i + \tau_1{}^j + \tau_1{}^k + \tau_1{}^l$$

$$\ln \frac{x_1^*(1112)}{n\pi} = L + \tau_1{}^i + \tau_1{}^j + \tau_1{}^k$$

$$\vdots \qquad \vdots \qquad \vdots$$

$$\ln \frac{x_1^*(2222)}{n\pi} = L$$

The estimate $x_2^*(ijkl)$ based on fitting the two-way marginals will use columns 1 to 11 since the two-way marginals also imply the one-way marginals. The values of $L$ and the $\tau$'s for this estimate will be different from those for the observed values or other estimates and depend on the values of the estimate $x_2^*(ijkl)$. For the estimate fitting the two-way marginals the representation in Table 13 implies

$$\ln \frac{x_2^*(1111)}{n\pi} = L + \tau_1{}^i + \tau_1{}^j + \tau_1{}^k + \tau_1{}^l + \tau_{11}^{ij} + \tau_{11}^{ik}$$
$$+ \tau_{11}^{il} + \tau_{11}^{jk} + \tau_{11}^{jl} + \tau_{11}^{kl}$$

$$\ln \frac{x_2^*(1112)}{n\pi} = L + \tau_1{}^i + \tau_1{}^j + \tau_1{}^k + \tau_{11}^{ij} + \tau_{11}^{ik} + \tau_{11}^{jk}$$

$$\vdots \qquad \vdots \qquad \vdots$$

$$\ln \frac{x_2^*(2222)}{n\pi} = L$$

The estimate $x_3^*(ijkl)$ based on fitting the three-way marginals will use columns 1 to 15 since the three-way marginals also imply the two-way and one-way marginals.

Note that in the graphic representation in Table 13 we set all $\tau$'s with subscript $i = 2$ and/or $j = 2$ and/or $k = 2$ and/or $l = 2$ equal to zero, by convention, to insure linear independence.

The analysis of information table corresponding to the hierarchical fitting of $x_1^*(ijkl)$, $x_2^*(ijkl)$, $x_3^*(ijkl)$ is shown in Table 14. $2I(x:x_1^*)$ tests the null hypothesis that the 11 $\tau$'s of columns 6 to 16 are equal to zero. $2I(x_2^*:x_1^*)$ tests the null hypothesis that the 6 $\tau$'s of columns 6 to 11 are equal to zero. $2I(x:x_2^*)$ tests the null hypothesis that the 5 $\tau$'s of columns 12 to 16 are equal to zero. $2I(x_3^*:x_2^*)$ tests the

**TABLE 14**
Analysis of Information

| Component due to | Information | D.F. |
|---|---|---|
| All one-way marginals | $2I(x:x_1{}^*)$ | 11 |
| All two-way marginals | $2I(x_2{}^*:x_1{}^*)$ | 6 |
| | $2I(x:x_2{}^*)$ | 5 |
| All three-way marginals | $2I(x_3{}^*:x_2{}^*)$ | 4 |
| | $2I(x:x_3{}^*)$ | 1 |

null hypothesis that the 4 $\tau$'s of columns 12 to 15 are zero. $2I(x:x_3{}^*)$ tests the null hypothesis that the $\tau$ of column 16 is zero.

In the examples we shall see other tests on the interaction parameters.


**Algorithms to Calculate Quadratic Approximations**


We now present algorithms to calculate quadratic approximations to $2I(x:x_a{}^*)$, $2I(x_b{}^*:x_a{}^*)$, $2I(x^*:x)$.

1. $2I(x:x_a{}^*)$.
   a. Compute $x_a{}^*$.
   b. Using the **T** design matrix corresponding to $x$ (including the $L$ column), compute the matrix $\mathbf{S} = \mathbf{T'D}_a{}^*\mathbf{T}$, where $\mathbf{D}_a{}^*$ is a diagonal matrix whose entries are the values of $x_a{}^*$ in the same order as for the rows of the **T** matrix.
   c. Let $\mathbf{S} = \begin{pmatrix} \mathbf{S}_{11} & \mathbf{S}_{12} \\ \mathbf{S}_{21} & \mathbf{S}_{22} \end{pmatrix}$, where $\mathbf{S}_{11}$ is a $1 \times 1$ matrix, then

$$\mathbf{S}_{22.1} = \mathbf{S}_{22} - \mathbf{S}_{21}\mathbf{S}_{11}^{-1}\mathbf{S}_{12}$$

   d. Compute $\mathbf{S}_{22.1}^{-1}$.
   e. Consider the marginals which *do not* enter into the specification of $x_a{}^*$, and let $\mathbf{d}'$ be a one-row matrix whose entries are the differences between the set of marginals just considered in the $x$ and $x_a{}^*$ tables.
   f. Let **B** be that submatrix of $\mathbf{S}_{22.1}^{-1}$ whose rows and columns correspond to the $\tau$ columns of the design matrix associated with the set of marginals in step e.
   g. Compute $\mathbf{d'Bd}$. This is the "marginals" approximation to $2I(x:x_a{}^*)$.
   h. Compute the set of $\tau$'s associated with the marginals considered in step e for the $x$ distribution, and call the one-row matrix of these $\tau$'s $\tau'$. Compute $\tau'\mathbf{B}^{-1}\tau$, where $\mathbf{B}^{-1}$ is the inverse of the matrix **B** in step f. $\tau'\mathbf{B}^{-1}\tau$ is the "tau" approximation to $2I(x:x_a{}^*)$.

    i.  The "marginals" approximation is also equal to

$$\sum \frac{(x - x_a^*)^2}{x_a^*}$$

2.  $2I(x_b^* : x_a^*)$.

    a.  Compute $x_b^*$, $x_a^*$.

    b.  Using the **T** design matrix corresponding to $x_b^*$ (including the **L** column), compute the matrix $\mathbf{S} = \mathbf{T}'\mathbf{D}_a^*\mathbf{T}$, where $\mathbf{D}_a^*$ is a diagonal matrix whose entries are the values of $x_a^*$ in the same order as for the rows of the **T** matrix.

    c.  Let $\mathbf{S} = \begin{pmatrix} \mathbf{S}_{11} & \mathbf{S}_{12} \\ \mathbf{S}_{21} & \mathbf{S}_{22} \end{pmatrix}$, where $\mathbf{S}_{11}$ is a $1 \times 1$ matrix, then

$$\mathbf{S}_{22.1} = \mathbf{S}_{22} - \mathbf{S}_{21}\mathbf{S}_{11}^{-1}\mathbf{S}_{12}$$

    d.  Compute $\mathbf{S}_{22.1}^{-1}$.

    e.  Consider the marginals which enter into the specification of $x_b^*$ but *not* in $x_a^*$, and let $\mathbf{d}'$ be a one-row matrix whose entries are the differences between the set of marginals just considered in the $x_b^*$ and $x_a^*$ tables.

    f.  Let **B** be that submatrix of $\mathbf{S}_{22.1}^{-1}$ whose rows and columns correspond to the $\tau$ columns of the design matrix associated with the set of marginals in step e.

    g.  Compute $\mathbf{d}'\mathbf{B}\mathbf{d}$. This is the "marginals" approximation to $2I(x_b^* : x_a^*)$.

    h.  Compute the set of $\tau$'s associated with the marginals considered in step e for the $x_b^*$ distribution and call the one-row matrix of these $\tau$'s $\tau'$. Compute $\tau'\mathbf{B}^{-1}\tau$, where $\mathbf{B}^{-1}$ is the inverse of the matrix **B** in step f. $\tau'\mathbf{B}^{-1}\tau$ is the "tau" approximation to $2I(x_b^* : x_a^*)$.

    i.  The "marginals" approximation is also equal to

$$\sum \frac{(x_b^* - x_a^*)^2}{x_a^*}$$

3.  $2I(x^* : x)$.

    a.  Using the **T** design matrix corresponding to $x^*$ (including the **L** column), compute the matrix $\mathbf{S} = \mathbf{T}'\mathbf{D}_x\mathbf{T}$, where $\mathbf{D}_x$ is a diagonal matrix whose entries are the values of $x$ in the same order as for the rows of the **T** matrix.

    b.  Let $\mathbf{S} = \begin{pmatrix} \mathbf{S}_{11} & \mathbf{S}_{12} \\ \mathbf{S}_{21} & \mathbf{S}_{22} \end{pmatrix}$, where $\mathbf{S}_{11}$ is a $1 \times 1$ matrix, then

$$\mathbf{S}_{22.1} = \mathbf{S}_{22} - \mathbf{S}_{21}\mathbf{S}_{11}^{-1}\mathbf{S}_{12}$$

    c.  Compute $\mathbf{S}_{22.1}^{-1}$.

    d.  Let $\mathbf{d}'$ be a one-row matrix whose entries are the differences between the $\sum_\omega T(\omega)x^*(\omega)$ and $\sum_\omega T(\omega)x(\omega)$. In the case when $x^*(\omega)$ is specified by conditions external to the observed values, the value of $\sum_\omega T(\omega)x^*(\omega)$ is specified without having to compute $x^*(\omega)$.

    e.  Compute $\mathbf{d}'\mathbf{S}_{22.1}^{-1}\mathbf{d}$. This is the approximation to $2I(x^* : x)$. Note that this can be obtained *without* computing $x^*$.

f.  The approximation

$$\sum \frac{(x^* - x)^2}{x}$$

requires the prior computation of $x^*$.

We now consider a number of examples to illustrate more specifically various aspects of the analysis.

## APPLICATIONS

In this section we consider eight examples illustrating various aspects of the model fitting methodology by the analysis of real data.

### Example 1. Classification of Multivariate Dichotomous Populations

This example illustrates the analysis of a five-way $2 \times 2 \times 2 \times 2 \times 2$ contingency table. It introduces the use of log-odds or logit representation, and the multiplicative version of the odds as a product of factors. It also illustrates the interpretation of the parameters and the effect of interaction on the numerical value of the association between classifications. It considers several models with respect to the marginals fitted, the design matrices, and the detailed hierarchical analysis of information.

#### *Introduction*

Multiway contingency tables, or cross-classifications of vectors of discrete random variables, provide a useful approach to the analysis of multivariate discrete data. In the particular application we consider, the individual variates are dichotomous or binary. Note, however, that the procedures and analysis are not restricted to dichotomous or binary data but are also applicable to polychotomous variates.

For background on the study and problem leading to the data we consider, see Solomon [222]. In Ku *et al.* [101] m.d.i. procedures were applied to problems of multivariate binary data in information systems, such as communication, pattern recognition, and learning systems. In Cox [21] there is a review of methods and models for the analysis of multivariate binary data, and Solomon's data are given as a typical example. Martin and Bradley [34] developed a model based on a set of orthogonal polynomials and applied it to Solomon's data. We remark that our procedure based on the principle of m.d.i. estimation applied to the analysis of multiway contingency tables yields a result practically equivalent to that of Martin and Bradley [34]. Goodman [12] discusses Solomon's data in relation to methods for selecting models for contingency tables.

*Solomon's Data*

A total of 2982 high-school seniors were given an attitude questionnaire to assess their attitude toward science. The students were also classified on the basis of an IQ test into high IQ, the upper half, and low IQ, the lower half. The 16 possible response vectors to each of four agree–disagree responses were tabulated. The problem of interest was to determine whether the response vectors could be used as a basis for classifying the students into one of two classes and evaluate possible classification procedures.

*Contingency Table Analysis*

We shall treat the data given in Table 15 as a five way $2 \times 2 \times 2 \times 2 \times 2$ contingency table, denoting the original observations by $x(hijkl)$ (defined in Table 16).

As a first overview of the data to determine the marginals and their related interaction parameters which may furnish significant values in the log-linear representation of the exponential family of the estimates obtained by iterative scaling fitting, we list in Table 17a a sequential hierarchical study of interaction- and effect-type measures [57, 83, 84].

The first estimate we start with is

$$x_a^*(hijkl) = x(h....)x(.ijkl)/n$$

since the minimum discrimination information statistic (interaction-type measure)

$$2I(x:x_a^*) = 2\sum\sum\sum\sum\sum x(hijkl) \ln \frac{x(hijkl)n}{x(h....)x(.ijkl)}$$

tests a null hypothesis that the IQ groupings are homogeneous over the 16 response vectors Kullback [229, Chap. 8]. This null hypothesis is rejected and the subsequent study of effect- and interaction-type measures is an attempt to find a good fit to the data and account for the total variation as measured by $2I(x:x_a^*)$. Although the association between IQ and the response to the first statement as measured by $2I(x_b^*:x_a^*) = 2.376$, 1 D.F., is not significant, it was decided to examine in detail the estimate $x_e^*(hijkl)$ whose numerical values are given in Table 15. It may be shown that

$$2I(x_b^*:x_a^*) = 2\sum\sum x(hi...) \ln \frac{x(hi...)n}{x(h....)x(.i...)}$$

and tests a null hypothesis that IQ is homogeneous over the response to the first question. The estimate $x_e^*(hijkl)$ was selected because the interaction-type measure, $2I(x:x_e^*) = 16.307$, 11 D.F., represents an acceptable fit, the estimate is symmetric with respect to the four statements, and is comparable to the first-order model estimate of Martin and Bradley [34], whose values are also listed in Table 15.

**TABLE 15**
Solomon's Data Classification Procedures

| ij | kl | Observed low IQ x(1ijkl) | Estimates Martin and Bradley | $x_e^*(1ijkl)$ | $x_v^*(1ijkl)$ | $x_w^*(1ijkl)$ | Observed high IQ x(2ijkl) | Estimates Martin and Bradley | $x_e^*(2ijkl)$ | $x_v^*(2ijkl)$ | $x_w^*(2ijkl)$ |
|----|----|----|----|----|----|----|----|----|----|----|----|
| 22 | 22 | 62 | 74.56 | 74.589 | 76.097 | 70.156 | 122 | 109.45 | 109.414 | 107.904 | 113.844 |
| 22 | 21 | 70 | 67.30 | 67.296 | 66.198 | 71.600 | 68 | 70.71 | 70.703 | 71.802 | 66.400 |
| 22 | 12 | 31 | 31.32 | 31.329 | 31.943 | 29.827 | 33 | 32.68 | 32.671 | 32.057 | 34.173 |
| 22 | 11 | 41 | 37.74 | 37.780 | 37.337 | 39.884 | 25 | 28.26 | 28.219 | 28.662 | 26.115 |
| 21 | 22 | 283 | 266.76 | 266.570 | 271.120 | 275.979 | 329 | 345.24 | 345.429 | 340.879 | 336.020 |
| 21 | 21 | 253 | 259.17 | 259.322 | 254.876 | 250.769 | 247 | 240.83 | 240.679 | 245.125 | 249.232 |
| 21 | 12 | 200 | 193.45 | 193.625 | 196.841 | 200.037 | 172 | 178.55 | 178.376 | 175.160 | 171.963 |
| 21 | 11 | 305 | 314.50 | 314.491 | 310.589 | 306.748 | 217 | 207.50 | 207.508 | 211.411 | 215.252 |
| 12 | 22 | 14 | 12.10 | 12.156 | 10.866 | 9.914 | 20 | 21.90 | 21.844 | 23.135 | 24.085 |
| 12 | 21 | 11 | 9.20 | 9.182 | 9.929 | 10.760 | 10 | 11.80 | 11.818 | 11.071 | 10.240 |
| 12 | 12 | 11 | 9.68 | 9.659 | 8.776 | 8.102 | 11 | 12.32 | 12.341 | 13.224 | 13.898 |
| 12 | 11 | 14 | 12.02 | 12.010 | 12.855 | 12.756 | 9 | 10.98 | 10.990 | 10.144 | 9.244 |
| 11 | 22 | 31 | 33.63 | 33.623 | 30.125 | 30.820 | 56 | 53.37 | 53.375 | 56.874 | 56.179 |
| 11 | 21 | 46 | 47.37 | 47.263 | 50.789 | 50.001 | 55 | 53.63 | 53.737 | 50.211 | 50.999 |
| 11 | 12 | 37 | 47.54 | 47.450 | 43.233 | 44.163 | 64 | 53.46 | 53.550 | 57.767 | 56.837 |
| 11 | 11 | 82 | 74.67 | 74.656 | 79.426 | 78.482 | 53 | 60.33 | 60.346 | 55.574 | 56.517 |
| | | 1491 | | | | | 1491 | | | | |

**TABLE 16**

| Characteristic | Index | 1 | 2 |
|---|---|---|---|
| IQ | $h$ | Low IQ | High IQ |
| Response 1 | $i$ | Disagree | Agree |
| Response 2 | $j$ | Disagree | Agree |
| Response 3 | $k$ | Disagree | Agree |
| Response 4 | $l$ | Disagree | Agree |

From the design matrix or log-linear representation in Table 18, we obtain the parametric representation for the log-odds (low IQ/high IQ)

$$\ln (x_e^*(1ijkl)/x_e^*(2ijkl))$$

over the 16 response vectors as given in Table 19a. Thus, for example,

$$\ln \frac{x_e^*(11111)}{x_e^*(21111)} = \tau_1{}^h + \tau_{11}^{hi} + \tau_{11}^{hj} + \tau_{11}^{hk} + \tau_{11}^{hl}$$

that is, a linear regression of the log-odds in terms of a constant $\tau_1{}^h$ and the main effects of each component of the response vector, namely, $\tau_{11}^{hi}, \tau_{11}^{hj}, \tau_{11}^{hk}, \tau_{11}^{hl}$. The numerical values of the log-odds and the parameters are easily obtained from the entries in the computer output and are also given in Table 19a. It is clear that the odds may be expressed in a multiplicative model. The odds and the odds factors are easier to appreciate. From the log-odds representation above we find

$$\frac{x_e^*(11111)}{x_e^*(21111)} = \exp (\tau_1{}^h) \exp (\tau_{11}^{hi}) \exp (\tau_{11}^{hj}) \exp (\tau_{11}^{hk}) \exp (\tau_{11}^{hl})$$

and from the values in Table 19a have

$$1.237 = (.682)(.816)(1.132)(1.406)(1.396)$$

We note from Table 19a that

$$\ln \frac{x_e^*(1ijk1)}{x_e^*(2ijk1)} - \ln \frac{x_e^*(1ijk2)}{x_e^*(2ijk2)} = \tau_{11}^{hl} = 0.3338$$

that is, a change from disagree to agree on the fourth statement is associated with an increase of 0.3338 in the log-odds (low IQ/high IQ). Note also that $\tau_{11}^{hl}$ represents the association between IQ and response to the fourth statement as measured by the log cross-product ratio (log relative odds)

$$\tau_{11}^{hl} = \ln \frac{x_e^*(1ijk1)x_e^*(2ijk2)}{x_e^*(2ijk1)x_e^*(1ijk2)}$$

and is the same for all eight levels of the responses to statements one, two, and three.

**TABLE 17a**
Analysis of Information

| | Marginals fitted | Information | D.F. |
|---|---|---|---|
| a) | $x(.ijkl)$, $x(h....)$ | $2I(x:x_a{}^*) = 68.369$ | 15 |
| b) | $x(.ijkl)$, $x(hi...)$ | $2I(x_b{}^*:x_a{}^*) = 2.376$ | 1 |
| | | $2I(x:x_b{}^*) = 65.993$ | 14 |
| c) | $x(.ijkl)$, $x(hi...)$, $x(h.j..)$ | $2I(x_c{}^*:x_b{}^*) = 4.265$ | 1 |
| | | $2I(x:x_c{}^*) = 61.728$ | 13 |
| d) | $x(.ijkl)$, $x(hi...)$, $x(h.j..)$, $x(h..k.)$ | $2I(x_d{}^*:x_c{}^*) = 25.230$ | 1 |
| | | $2I(x:x_d{}^*) = 36.498$ | 12 |
| e) | $x(.ijkl)$, $x(hi...)$, $x(h.j..)$, $x(h..k.)$, $x(h...l)$ | $2I(x_e{}^*:x_d{}^*) = 20.191$ | 1 |
| | | $2I(x:x_e{}^*) = 16.307$ | 11 |
| f) | $x(.ijkl)$, $x(h..k.)$, $x(h...l)$, $x(hij..)$ | $2I(x_f{}^*:x_e{}^*) = 3.016$ | 1 |
| | | $2I(x:x_f{}^*) = 13.291$ | 10 |
| g) | $x(.ijkl)$, $x(h...l)$, $x(hij..)$, $x(hi.k.)$ | $2I(x_g{}^*:x_f{}^*) = 0.042$ | 1 |
| | | $2I(x:x_g{}^*) = 13.249$ | 9 |
| m) | $x(.ijkl)$, $x(hij..)$, $x(hi.k.)$, $x(hi..l)$ | $2I(x_m{}^*:x_g{}^*) = 4.316$ | 1 |
| | | $2I(x:x_m{}^*) = 8.933$ | 8 |
| n) | $x(.ijkl)$, $x(hij..)$, $x(hi.k.)$, $x(hi..l)$, $x(h.jk.)$ | $2I(x_n{}^*:x_m{}^*) = 0.983$ | 1 |
| | | $2I(x:x_n{}^*) = 7.950$ | 7 |
| p) | $x(.ijkl)$, $x(hij..)$, $x(hi.k.)$, $x(hi..l)$, $x(h.jk.)$, $x(h.j.l)$ | $2I(x_p{}^*:x_n{}^*) = 3.181$ | 1 |
| | | $2I(x:x_p{}^*) = 4.769$ | 6 |
| q) | $x(.ijkl)$, $x(hij..)$, $x(hi.k.)$, $x(hi..l)$, $x(h.jk.)$, $x(h.j.l)$, $x(h..kl)$ | $2I(x_q{}^*:x_p{}^*) = 0.219$ | 1 |
| | | $2I(x:x_q{}^*) = 4.550$ | 5 |
| r) | $x(.ijkl)$, $x(hi..l)$, $x(h.j.l)$, $x(h..kl)$, $x(hijk.)$ | $2I(x_r{}^*:x_q{}^*) = 0.346$ | 1 |
| | | $2I(x:x_r{}^*) = 4.204$ | 4 |
| s) | $x(.ijkl)$, $x(h..kl)$, $x(hijk.)$, $x(hij.l)$ | $2I(x_s{}^*:x_r{}^*) = 2.303$ | 1 |
| | | $2I(x:x_s{}^*) = 1.901$ | 3 |
| t) | $x(.ijkl)$, $x(hijk.)$, $x(hij.l)$, $x(hi.kl)$ | $2I(x_t{}^*:x_s{}^*) = 1.375$ | 1 |
| | | $2I(x:x_t{}^*) = 0.526$ | 2 |
| u) | $x(.ijkl)$, $x(hijk.)$, $x(hij.l)$, $x(hi.kl)$, $x(h.jkl)$ | $2I(x_u{}^*:x_t{}^*) = 0.361$ | 1 |
| | | $2I(x:x_u{}^*) = 0.165$ | 1 |

**TABLE 17b**
Analysis of Information

| | Marginals fitted | Information | D.F. |
|---|---|---|---|
| e) | $x(.ijkl)$, $x(hi...)$, $x(h.j..)$, $x(h..k.)$, $x(h...l)$ | $2I(x:x_e{}^*) = 16.307$ | 11 |
| v) | $x(.ijkl)$, $x(h.j..)$, $x(h..k.)$, $x(hi..l)$ | $2I(x_v{}^*:x_e{}^*) = 3.735$ | 1 |
| | | $2I(x:x_v{}^*) = 12.572$ | 10 |
| w) | $x(.ijkl)$, $x(h..k.)$, $x(hi..l)$, $x(h.j.l)$ | $2I(x_w{}^*:x_v{}^*) = 3.443$ | 1 |
| | | $2I(x:x_w{}^*) = 9.129$ | 9 |

TABLE 18

| h | i | j | k | l | 1 $L$ | 2 $\frac{h}{1}$ | 3 $\frac{i}{1}$ | 4 $\frac{j}{1}$ | 5 $\frac{k}{1}$ | 6 $\frac{l}{1}$ | 7 $\frac{hi}{11}$ | 8 $\frac{hj}{11}$ | 9 $\frac{hk}{11}$ | 10 $\frac{hl}{11}$ | 11 $\frac{ij}{11}$ | 12 $\frac{ik}{11}$ | 13 $\frac{il}{11}$ | 14 $\frac{jk}{11}$ |
|---|---|---|---|---|---|---|---|---|---|---|---|---|---|---|---|---|---|---|
| 1 | 1 | 1 | 1 | 1 | 1 | 1 | 1 | 1 | 1 | 1 | 1 | 1 | 1 | 1 | 1 | 1 | 1 | 1 |
| 1 | 1 | 1 | 1 | 2 | 1 | 1 | 1 | 1 | 1 |   | 1 | 1 | 1 |   | 1 | 1 |   | 1 |
| 1 | 1 | 1 | 2 | 1 | 1 | 1 | 1 | 1 |   | 1 | 1 | 1 |   | 1 | 1 |   | 1 |   |
| 1 | 1 | 1 | 2 | 2 | 1 | 1 | 1 | 1 |   |   | 1 | 1 |   |   | 1 |   |   |   |
| 1 | 1 | 2 | 1 | 1 | 1 | 1 | 1 |   | 1 | 1 | 1 |   | 1 | 1 |   | 1 | 1 |   |
| 1 | 1 | 2 | 1 | 2 | 1 | 1 | 1 |   | 1 |   | 1 |   | 1 |   |   | 1 |   |   |
| 1 | 1 | 2 | 2 | 1 | 1 | 1 | 1 |   |   | 1 | 1 |   |   | 1 |   |   | 1 |   |
| 1 | 1 | 2 | 2 | 2 | 1 | 1 | 1 |   |   |   | 1 |   |   |   |   |   |   |   |
| 1 | 2 | 1 | 1 | 1 | 1 | 1 |   | 1 | 1 | 1 |   | 1 | 1 | 1 |   |   |   | 1 |
| 1 | 2 | 1 | 1 | 2 | 1 | 1 |   | 1 | 1 |   |   | 1 | 1 |   |   |   |   | 1 |
| 1 | 2 | 1 | 2 | 1 | 1 | 1 |   | 1 |   | 1 |   | 1 |   | 1 |   |   |   |   |
| 1 | 2 | 1 | 2 | 2 | 1 | 1 |   | 1 |   |   |   | 1 |   |   |   |   |   |   |
| 1 | 2 | 2 | 1 | 1 | 1 | 1 |   |   | 1 | 1 |   |   | 1 | 1 |   |   |   |   |
| 1 | 2 | 2 | 1 | 2 | 1 | 1 |   |   | 1 |   |   |   | 1 |   |   |   |   |   |
| 1 | 2 | 2 | 2 | 1 | 1 | 1 |   |   |   | 1 |   |   |   | 1 |   |   |   |   |
| 1 | 2 | 2 | 2 | 2 | 1 | 1 |   |   |   |   |   |   |   |   |   |   |   |   |
| 2 | 1 | 1 | 1 | 1 | 1 |   | 1 | 1 | 1 | 1 |   |   |   |   | 1 | 1 | 1 | 1 |
| 2 | 1 | 1 | 1 | 2 | 1 |   | 1 | 1 | 1 |   |   |   |   |   | 1 | 1 |   | 1 |
| 2 | 1 | 1 | 2 | 1 | 1 |   | 1 | 1 |   | 1 |   |   |   |   | 1 |   | 1 |   |
| 2 | 1 | 1 | 2 | 2 | 1 |   | 1 | 1 |   |   |   |   |   |   | 1 |   |   |   |
| 2 | 1 | 2 | 1 | 1 | 1 |   | 1 |   | 1 | 1 |   |   |   |   |   | 1 | 1 |   |
| 2 | 1 | 2 | 1 | 2 | 1 |   | 1 |   | 1 |   |   |   |   |   |   | 1 |   |   |
| 2 | 1 | 2 | 2 | 1 | 1 |   | 1 |   |   | 1 |   |   |   |   |   |   | 1 |   |
| 2 | 1 | 2 | 2 | 2 | 1 |   | 1 |   |   |   |   |   |   |   |   |   |   |   |
| 2 | 2 | 1 | 1 | 1 | 1 |   |   | 1 | 1 | 1 |   |   |   |   |   |   |   | 1 |
| 2 | 2 | 1 | 1 | 2 | 1 |   |   | 1 | 1 |   |   |   |   |   |   |   |   | 1 |
| 2 | 2 | 1 | 2 | 1 | 1 |   |   | 1 |   | 1 |   |   |   |   |   |   |   |   |
| 2 | 2 | 1 | 2 | 2 | 1 |   |   | 1 |   |   |   |   |   |   |   |   |   |   |
| 2 | 2 | 2 | 1 | 1 | 1 |   |   |   | 1 | 1 |   |   |   |   |   |   |   |   |
| 2 | 2 | 2 | 1 | 2 | 1 |   |   |   | 1 |   |   |   |   |   |   |   |   |   |
| 2 | 2 | 2 | 2 | 1 | 1 |   |   |   |   | 1 |   |   |   |   |   |   |   |   |
| 2 | 2 | 2 | 2 | 2 | 1 |   |   |   |   |   |   |   |   |   |   |   |   |   |
|   |   |   |   | $x$ | ✓ | ✓ | ✓ | ✓ | ✓ | ✓ | ✓ | ✓ | ✓ | ✓ | ✓ | ✓ | ✓ | ✓ |
|   |   |   |   | $x_e^*$ | ✓ | ✓ | ✓ | ✓ | ✓ | ✓ | ✓ | ✓ | ✓ | ✓ | ✓ | ✓ | ✓ | ✓ |
|   |   |   |   | $x_v^*$ | ✓ | ✓ | ✓ | ✓ | ✓ | ✓ | ✓ | ✓ | ✓ | ✓ | ✓ | ✓ | ✓ | ✓ |
|   |   |   |   | $x_w^*$ | ✓ | ✓ | ✓ | ✓ | ✓ | ✓ | ✓ | ✓ | ✓ | ✓ | ✓ | ✓ | ✓ | ✓ |

| 15 | 16 | 17 | 18 | 19 | 20 | 21 | 22 | 23 | 24 | 25 | 26 | 27 | 28 | 29 | 30 | 31 | 32 |
|----|----|----|----|----|----|----|----|----|----|----|----|----|----|----|----|----|----|
| *jl* 11 | *kl* 11 | *hij* 111 | *hik* 111 | *hil* 111 | *hjk* 111 | *hjl* 111 | *hkl* 111 | *ijk* 111 | *ijl* 111 | *ikl* 111 | *jkl* 111 | *h i j k* | *h i j l* | *h i k l* | *h j k l* | *i j k l* | *h i j k l* |
| 1 | 1 | 1 | 1 | 1 | 1 | 1 | 1 | 1 | 1 | 1 | 1 | 1 | 1 | 1 | 1 | 1 | 1 |
|  |  | 1 | 1 |  | 1 |  |  | 1 |  |  |  | 1 |  |  |  |  |  |
| 1 |  | 1 |  | 1 |  | 1 |  |  | 1 |  |  |  | 1 |  |  |  |  |
|  |  | 1 |  |  |  |  |  |  |  |  |  |  |  |  |  |  |  |
|  | 1 |  | 1 | 1 |  |  | 1 |  |  | 1 |  |  |  | 1 |  |  |  |
|  |  |  | 1 |  |  |  |  |  |  |  |  |  |  |  |  |  |  |
|  |  |  |  | 1 |  |  |  |  |  |  |  |  |  |  |  |  |  |
| 1 | 1 |  |  |  | 1 | 1 | 1 |  |  |  | 1 |  |  | 1 |  |  |  |
|  |  |  |  |  | 1 |  |  |  |  |  |  |  |  |  |  |  |  |
| 1 |  |  |  |  |  | 1 |  |  |  |  |  |  |  |  |  |  |  |
|  | 1 |  |  |  |  |  | 1 |  |  |  |  |  |  |  |  |  |  |
| 1 | 1 |  |  |  |  |  |  | 1 | 1 | 1 | 1 |  |  |  |  | 1 |  |
|  |  |  |  |  |  |  |  | 1 |  |  |  |  |  |  |  |  |  |
| 1 |  |  |  |  |  |  |  |  | 1 |  |  |  |  |  |  |  |  |
|  | 1 |  |  |  |  |  |  |  |  | 1 |  |  |  |  |  |  |  |
| 1 | 1 |  |  |  |  |  |  |  |  |  | 1 |  |  |  |  |  |  |
| 1 |  |  |  |  |  |  |  |  |  |  |  |  |  |  |  |  |  |
|  | 1 |  |  |  |  |  |  |  |  |  |  |  |  |  |  |  |  |
| √ | √ | √ | √ | √ | √ | √ | √ | √ | √ | √ | √ | √ | √ | √ | √ | √ | √ |
| √ | √ |  |  |  |  |  |  | √ | √ | √ | √ |  |  |  |  | √ |  |
| √ | √ |  |  | √ |  |  |  | √ | √ | √ | √ |  |  |  |  | √ |  |
| √ | √ |  |  | √ |  | √ |  | √ | √ | √ | √ |  |  |  |  | √ |  |

[165]

**TABLE 19a**

Log-odds $\ln \dfrac{x_e{}^*(1ijkl)}{x_e{}^*(2ijkl)}$

| $ijkl$ | Parametric representation | | | | | Log-odds |
|--------|------|------|------|------|------|----------|
| 1111 | $\tau_1^h$ | $+\ \tau_{11}^{hi}$ | $+\ \tau_{11}^{hj}$ | $+\ \tau_{11}^{hk}$ | $+\ \tau_{11}^{hl}$ | 0.2128 |
| 1112 | $\tau_1^h$ | $+\ \tau_{11}^{hi}$ | $+\ \tau_{11}^{hj}$ | $+\ \tau_{11}^{hk}$ | | $-0.1210$ |
| 1121 | $\tau_1^h$ | $+\ \tau_{11}^{hi}$ | $+\ \tau_{11}^{hj}$ | | $+\ \tau_{11}^{hl}$ | $-0.1284$ |
| 1122 | $\tau_1^h$ | $+\ \tau_{11}^{hi}$ | $+\ \tau_{11}^{hj}$ | | | $-0.4621$ |
| 1211 | $\tau_1^h$ | $+\ \tau_{11}^{hi}$ | | $+\ \tau_{11}^{hk}$ | $+\ \tau_{11}^{hl}$ | 0.0888 |
| 1212 | $\tau_1^h$ | $+\ \tau_{11}^{hi}$ | | $+\ \tau_{11}^{hk}$ | | $-0.2450$ |
| 1221 | $\tau_1^h$ | $+\ \tau_{11}^{hi}$ | | | $+\ \tau_{11}^{hl}$ | $-0.2524$ |
| 1222 | $\tau_1^h$ | $+\ \tau_{11}^{hi}$ | | | | $-0.5861$ |
| 2111 | $\tau_1^h$ | | $+\ \tau_{11}^{hj}$ | $+\ \tau_{11}^{hk}$ | $+\ \tau_{11}^{hl}$ | 0.4158 |
| 2112 | $\tau_1^h$ | | $+\ \tau_{11}^{hj}$ | $+\ \tau_{11}^{hk}$ | | 0.0820 |
| 2121 | $\tau_1^h$ | | $+\ \tau_{11}^{hj}$ | | $+\ \tau_{11}^{hl}$ | 0.0746 |
| 2122 | $\tau_1^h$ | | $+\ \tau_{11}^{hj}$ | | | $-0.2592$ |
| 2211 | $\tau_1^h$ | | | $+\ \tau_{11}^{hk}$ | $+\ \tau_{11}^{hl}$ | 0.2918 |
| 2212 | $\tau_1^h$ | | | $+\ \tau_{11}^{hk}$ | | $-0.0420$ |
| 2221 | $\tau_1^h$ | | | | $+\ \tau_{11}^{hl}$ | $-0.0494$ |
| 2222 | $\tau_1^h$ | | | | | $-0.3831$ |

$$\tau_1^h = -0.3831, \quad \tau_{11}^{hi} = -0.2030,$$
$$\tau_{11}^{hj} = 0.1240, \quad \tau_{11}^{hk} = 0.3411, \quad \tau_{11}^{hl} = 0.3338$$

Similarly, it is found that

$$\ln \frac{x_e{}^*(1ij1l)}{x_e{}^*(2ij1l)} - \ln \frac{x_e{}^*(1ij2l)}{x_e{}^*(2ij2l)} = \tau_{11}^{hk} = 0.3411$$

$$\ln \frac{x_e{}^*(1i1kl)}{x_e{}^*(2i1kl)} - \ln \frac{x_e{}^*(1i2kl)}{x_e{}^*(2i2kl)} = \tau_{11}^{hj} = 0.1240$$

$$\ln \frac{x_e{}^*(11jkl)}{x_e{}^*(21jkl)} - \ln \frac{x_e{}^*(12jkl)}{x_e{}^*(22jkl)} = \tau_{11}^{hi} = -0.2030$$

## *Classification*

Since $x(1....) = x_e{}^*(1....) = 1491$, and $x(2....) = x_e{}^*(2....) = 1491$, we assign a response vector $(ijkl)$ to the region

$E_1$: classify as population $h = 1$ (low IQ), when

$$\ln \frac{x_e{}^*(1ijkl)}{x_e{}^*(2ijkl)} \geqq 0$$

and to the complementary region

$E_2$:  classify as population $h = 2$ (high IQ), when

$$\ln \frac{x_e^*(1ijkl)}{x_e^*(2ijkl)} < 0$$

If we set

$$\mu_1(E_1) = \sum_{(ijkl) \in E_1} \frac{x_e^*(1ijkl)}{1491}, \qquad \mu_2(E_1) = \sum_{(ijkl) \in E_1} \frac{x_e^*(2ijkl)}{1491}$$

then the probability of error of the classification procedure is [229, pp. 4, 69, 80]

$$\text{Prob. Error} = p\mu_2(E_1) + q\mu_1(E_2) = (\mu_2(E_1) + \mu_1(E_2))/2$$

since here $p = x(2....)/2982 = \frac{1}{2}$, $q = x(1....)/2982 = \frac{1}{2}$.

The relevant computations with $x_e^*(hijkl)$ are given in Table 20b and show that the Prob. Error = 0.444. The corresponding computations with the original data $x(hijkl)$ are given in Table 20a and yield Prob. Error = 0.441.

### Other Estimates

In view of the measure of the effect of the marginal $x(hi..l)$ (and the associated interaction parameters) in Table 17a, $2I(x_m^*:x_g^*) = 4.316$, 1 D.F., and the marginal $x(h.j.l)$, $2I(x_p^*:x_n^*) = 3.181$, 1 D.F., the m.d.i. estimate $x_v^*(hijkl)$ fitting

**TABLE 19b**

Log-odds $\ln \dfrac{x_v^*(1ijkl)}{x_v^*(2ijkl)}$

| $ijkl$ | Parametric representation | | | | | | Log-odds |
|--------|---|---|---|---|---|---|---------|
| 1111 | $\tau_1^h$ | $+\ \tau_{11}^{hi}$ | $+\ \tau_{11}^{hj}$ | $+\ \tau_{11}^{hk}$ | $+\ \tau_{11}^{hl}$ | $+\ \tau_{111}^{hil}$ | 0.3571 |
| 1112 | $\tau_1^h$ | $+\ \tau_{11}^{hi}$ | $+\ \tau_{11}^{hj}$ | $+\ \tau_{11}^{hk}$ | | | $-0.2898$ |
| 1121 | $\tau_1^h$ | $+\ \tau_{11}^{hi}$ | $+\ \tau_{11}^{hj}$ | | $+\ \tau_{11}^{hl}$ | $+\ \tau_{111}^{hil}$ | 0.0115 |
| 1122 | $\tau_1^h$ | $+\ \tau_{11}^{hi}$ | $+\ \tau_{11}^{hj}$ | | | | $-0.6355$ |
| 1211 | $\tau_1^h$ | $+\ \tau_{11}^{hi}$ | | $+\ \tau_{11}^{hk}$ | $+\ \tau_{11}^{hl}$ | $+\ \tau_{111}^{hil}$ | 0.2366 |
| 1212 | $\tau_1^h$ | $+\ \tau_{11}^{hi}$ | | $+\ \tau_{11}^{hk}$ | | | $-0.4101$ |
| 1221 | $\tau_1^h$ | $+\ \tau_{11}^{hi}$ | | | $+\ \tau_{11}^{hl}$ | $+\ \tau_{111}^{hil}$ | $-0.1088$ |
| 1222 | $\tau_1^h$ | $+\ \tau_{11}^{hi}$ | | | | | $-0.7557$ |
| 2111 | $\tau_1^h$ | | $+\ \tau_{11}^{hj}$ | $+\ \tau_{11}^{hk}$ | $+\ \tau_{11}^{hl}$ | | 0.3847 |
| 2112 | $\tau_1^h$ | | $+\ \tau_{11}^{hj}$ | $+\ \tau_{11}^{hk}$ | | | 0.1167 |
| 2121 | $\tau_1^h$ | | $+\ \tau_{11}^{hj}$ | | $+\ \tau_{11}^{hl}$ | | 0.0390 |
| 2122 | $\tau_1^h$ | | $+\ \tau_{11}^{hj}$ | | | | $-0.2290$ |
| 2211 | $\tau_1^h$ | | | $+\ \tau_{11}^{hk}$ | $+\ \tau_{11}^{hl}$ | | 0.2644 |
| 2212 | $\tau_1^h$ | | | $+\ \tau_{11}^{hk}$ | | | $-0.0036$ |
| 2221 | $\tau_1^h$ | | | | $+\ \tau_{11}^{hl}$ | | $-0.0813$ |
| 2222 | $\tau_1^h$ | | | | | | $-0.3492$ |

$\tau_1^h = -0.3492$, $\tau_{11}^{hi} = -0.4065$, $\tau_{11}^{hj} = 0.1203$, $\tau_{11}^{hk} = 0.3457$, $\tau_{11}^{hl} = 0.2680$, $\tau_{111}^{hil} = 0.3789$

**TABLE 19c**

Log-odds $\ln \dfrac{x_w{}^*(1ijkl)}{x_w{}^*(2ijkl)}$

| ijkl | Parametric representation | | | | | | | Log-odds |
|---|---|---|---|---|---|---|---|---|
| 1111 | $\tau_1^h$ | $+\tau_{11}^{hi}$ | $+\tau_{11}^{hj}$ | $+\tau_{11}^{hk}$ | $+\tau_{11}^{hl}$ | $+\tau_{111}^{hil}$ | $+\tau_{111}^{hjl}$ | 0.3283 |
| 1112 | $\tau_1^h$ | $+\tau_{11}^{hi}$ | $+\tau_{11}^{hj}$ | $+\tau_{11}^{hk}$ | | | | $-0.2523$ |
| 1121 | $\tau_1^h$ | $+\tau_{11}^{hi}$ | $+\tau_{11}^{hj}$ | | $+\tau_{11}^{hl}$ | $+\tau_{111}^{hil}$ | $+\tau_{111}^{hjl}$ | $-0.0197$ |
| 1122 | $\tau_1^h$ | $+\tau_{11}^{hi}$ | $+\tau_{11}^{hj}$ | | | | | $-0.6004$ |
| 1211 | $\tau_1^h$ | $+\tau_{11}^{hi}$ | | $+\tau_{11}^{hk}$ | $+\tau_{11}^{hl}$ | $+\tau_{111}^{hil}$ | | 0.3976 |
| 1212 | $\tau_1^h$ | $+\tau_{11}^{hi}$ | | $+\tau_{11}^{hk}$ | | | | 0.5396 |
| 1221 | $\tau_1^h$ | $+\tau_{11}^{hi}$ | | | $+\tau_{11}^{hl}$ | $+\tau_{111}^{hil}$ | | 0.0495 |
| 1222 | $\tau_1^h$ | $+\tau_{11}^{hi}$ | | | | | | $-0.8876$ |
| 2111 | $\tau_1^h$ | | $+\tau_{11}^{hj}$ | $+\tau_{11}^{hk}$ | $+\tau_{11}^{hl}$ | | $+\tau_{111}^{hjl}$ | 0.3542 |
| 2112 | $\tau_1^h$ | | $+\tau_{11}^{hj}$ | $+\tau_{11}^{hk}$ | | | | 0.1512 |
| 2121 | $\tau_1^h$ | | $+\tau_{11}^{hj}$ | | $+\tau_{11}^{hl}$ | | $+\tau_{111}^{hjl}$ | 0.0061 |
| 2122 | $\tau_1^h$ | | $+\tau_{11}^{hj}$ | | | | | $-0.1968$ |
| 2211 | $\tau_1^h$ | | | $+\tau_{11}^{hk}$ | $+\tau_{11}^{hl}$ | | | 0.4235 |
| 2212 | $\tau_1^h$ | | | $+\tau_{11}^{hk}$ | | | | $-0.1360$ |
| 2221 | $\tau_1^h$ | | | | $+\tau_{11}^{hl}$ | | | 0.0754 |
| 2222 | $\tau_1^h$ | | | | | | | $-0.4841$ |

$\tau_1^h = -0.4841$, $\tau_{11}^{hi} = -0.4035$, $\tau_{11}^{hj} = 0.2873$, $\tau_{11}^{hk} = 0.3481$,
$\tau_{11}^{hl} = 0.5595$, $\tau_{111}^{hil} = 0.3776$, $\tau_{111}^{hjl} = -0.3565$

the marginals $x(.ijkl)$, $x(h.j..)$, $x(h..k.)$, $x(hi..l)$ and the m.d.i. estimate $x_w{}^*(hijkl)$ fitting the marginals $x(.ijkl)$, $x(h..k.)$, $x(hi..l)$, $x(h.j.l)$ were computed. The estimates are given in Table 15 and the relevant analysis of information given in Table 17b.

The values of the log-odds, parametric representation, and the associated interaction parameters are given in Table 19b for $x_v{}^*(hijkl)$ and in Table 19c for $x_w{}^*(hijkl)$. Note from Table 19b that

$$\ln \frac{x_v{}^*(11jk1)}{x_v{}^*(21jk1)} - \ln \frac{x_v{}^*(11jk2)}{x_v{}^*(21jk2)} = \tau_{11}^{hl} + \tau_{111}^{hil} = 0.6469$$

$$\ln \frac{x_v{}^*(12jk1)}{x_v{}^*(22jk1)} - \ln \frac{x_v{}^*(12jk2)}{x_v{}^*(22jk2)} = \tau_{11}^{hl} = 0.2680$$

$$\ln \frac{x_v{}^*(11jk1)}{x_v{}^*(21jk1)} - \ln \frac{x_v{}^*(12jk1)}{x_v{}^*(22jk1)} = \tau_{11}^{hi} + \tau_{111}^{hil} = -0.0276$$

$$\ln \frac{x_v{}^*(11jk2)}{x_v{}^*(21jk2)} - \ln \frac{x_v{}^*(12jk2)}{x_v{}^*(22jk2)} = \tau_{11}^{hi} = -0.4065$$

reflecting the interaction of the responses to the first and fourth statements.

**TABLE 20a**

$E_1$: {$ijkl$: ln odds $\geqq 0$}

$E_1$: Observations

| $ijkl$ | $x(1ijkl)$ | $x(2ijkl)$ |
|---|---|---|
| 1111 | 82 | 53 |
| 1211 | 14 | 9 |
| 1221 | 11 | 10 |
| 2111 | 305 | 217 |
| 2112 | 200 | 172 |
| 2121 | 253 | 247 |
| 2211 | 41 | 25 |
| 2221 | 70 | 68 |
| | 976 | 801 |

$$\mu_2(E_1) = \frac{801}{1491}$$

$$\mu_1(E_2) = \frac{1491 - 976}{1491}$$

$$\text{Prob. Error} = \frac{1}{2}\frac{801 + 515}{1491}$$

$$= \frac{1316}{2 \times 1491} = 0.441$$

**TABLE 20b**

$E_1$: $x_e{}^*$

| $ijkl$ | $x_e{}^*(1ijkl)$ | $x_e{}^*(2ijkl)$ |
|---|---|---|
| 1111 | 74.656 | 60.346 |
| 1211 | 12.010 | 10.990 |
| 2111 | 314.491 | 207.508 |
| 2112 | 193.625 | 178.376 |
| 2121 | 259.322 | 240.679 |
| 2211 | 37.780 | 28.219 |
| | 891.884 | 726.118 |

$$\mu_2(E_1) = \frac{726.118}{1491}$$

$$\mu_1(E_2) = \frac{1491 - 891.884}{1491}$$

$$\text{Prob. Error} = \frac{1}{2}\frac{726.118 + 599.116}{1491}$$

$$= \frac{1325.234}{2982}$$

$$= 0.444$$

From Table 19c it is found, for example, that

$$\ln \frac{x_w{}^*(111k1)}{x_w{}^*(211k1)} - \ln \frac{x_w{}^*(111k2)}{x_w{}^*(211k2)} = \tau_{11}^{hl} + \tau_{111}^{hil} + \tau_{111}^{hjl} = 0.5806$$

$$\ln \frac{x_w{}^*(121k1)}{x_w{}^*(221k1)} - \ln \frac{x_w{}^*(121k2)}{x_w{}^*(221k2)} = \tau_{11}^{hl} + \tau_{111}^{hjl} = 0.2030$$

$$\ln \frac{x_w{}^*(112k1)}{x_w{}^*(212k1)} - \ln \frac{x_w{}^*(112k2)}{x_w{}^*(212k2)} = \tau_{11}^{hl} + \tau_{111}^{hil} = 0.9371$$

$$\ln \frac{x_w{}^*(122k1)}{x_w{}^*(222k1)} - \ln \frac{x_w{}^*(122k2)}{x_w{}^*(222k2)} = \tau_{11}^{hl} = 0.5595$$

reflecting the interactions of the responses to the first, second, and fourth statements.

The computation of the probability of error using the estimates $x_v{}^*(hijkl)$ and $x_w{}^*(hijkl)$ is shown in Table 20c and 20d, respectively, and yields probabilities of error 0.444 and 0.446.

## Remark

Martin and Bradley [34] examined Solomon's data in terms of an estimate they called a first-order or linear model. These estimated values are given in Table 15. It turns out that although the underlying approaches are different, the Martin

**TABLE 20c**

$E_1$: $x_v{}^*$

| $ijkl$ | $x_v{}^*(1ijkl)$ | $x_v{}^*(2ijkl)$ |
|---|---|---|
| 1111 | 79.426 | 55.574 |
| 1121 | 50.789 | 50.211 |
| 1211 | 12.855 | 10.144 |
| 2111 | 310.589 | 211.411 |
| 2112 | 196.841 | 175.160 |
| 2121 | 254.876 | 245.125 |
| 2211 | 37.337 | 28.662 |
|  | 942.713 | 776.287 |

$$\mu_2(E_1) = \frac{776.287}{1491}$$

$$\mu_1(E_2) = \frac{1491 - 942.713}{1491}$$

$$\text{Prob. Error} = \frac{1}{2} \frac{776.287 + 548.287}{1491}$$

$$= \frac{1324.574}{2982}$$

$$= 0.444$$

TABLE 20d
$E_1$: $x_w{}^*$

| $ijkl$ | $x_w{}^*(1ijkl)$ | $x_w{}^*(2ijkl)$ |
|---|---|---|
| 1111 | 78.482 | 56.517 |
| 1211 | 13.756 | 9.244 |
| 1212 | 8.102 | 13.898 |
| 1221 | 10.760 | 10.240 |
| 2111 | 306.748 | 215.252 |
| 2112 | 200.037 | 171.963 |
| 2121 | 250.769 | 249.232 |
| 2211 | 39.884 | 26.115 |
| 2221 | 71.600 | 66.401 |
| | 980.138 | 818.862 |

$$\mu_2(E_1) = \frac{818.862}{1491}$$

$$\mu_1(E_2) = \frac{1491 - 980.138}{1491}$$

$$\text{Prob. Error} = \frac{1}{2}\frac{818.862 + 510.862}{1491}$$

$$= \frac{1329.724}{2982}$$

$$= 0.446$$

and Bradley parameters, their $a_i$, and estimates are practically the same as those for $x_e{}^*(hijkl)$. From Martin and Bradley [34, pp. 216–217], we note that

$$\ln \frac{x_e{}^*(12222)}{x_e{}^*(22222)} = \tau_1{}^h = \ln \frac{1 + a_0 + a_1 + a_2 + a_3 + a_4}{1 - a_0 - a_1 - a_2 - a_3 - a_4}$$

$$\ln \frac{x_e{}^*(12221)}{x_e{}^*(22221)} = \tau_1{}^h + \tau_{11}^{hl} = \ln \frac{1 + a_0 + a_1 + a_2 + a_3 - a_4}{1 - a_0 - a_1 - a_2 - a_3 + a_4}$$

$$\ln \frac{x_e{}^*(12212)}{x_e{}^*(22212)} = \tau_1{}^h + \tau_{11}^{hk} = \ln \frac{1 + a_0 + a_1 + a_2 - a_3 + a_4}{1 - a_0 - a_1 - a_2 + a_3 - a_4}$$

$$\ln \frac{x_e{}^*(12122)}{x_e{}^*(22122)} = \tau_1{}^h + \tau_{11}^{hj} = \ln \frac{1 + a_0 + a_1 - a_2 + a_3 + a_4}{1 - a_0 - a_1 + a_2 - a_3 - a_4}$$

$$\ln \frac{x_e{}^*(11222)}{x_e{}^*(21222)} = \tau_1{}^h + \tau_{11}^{hi} = \ln \frac{1 + a_0 - a_1 + a_2 + a_3 + a_4}{1 - a_0 + a_1 - a_2 - a_3 - a_4}$$

or to a first approximation of the logarithm

$$\tau_1{}^h = 2a_0 + 2a_1 + 2a_2 + 2a_3 + 2a_4$$
$$\tau_1{}^h + \tau_{11}^{hl} = 2a_0 + 2a_1 + 2a_2 + 2a_3 - 2a_4$$
$$\tau_1{}^h + \tau_{11}^{hk} = 2a_0 + 2a_1 + 2a_2 - 2a_3 + 2a_4$$
$$\tau_1{}^h + \tau_{11}^{hj} = 2a_0 + 2a_1 - 2a_2 + 2a_3 + 2a_4$$
$$\tau_1{}^h + \tau_{11}^{hi} = 2a_0 - 2a_1 + 2a_2 + 2a_3 + 2a_4$$

It is found that

$$\tau^{hl}_{11} = -4a_4$$
$$\tau^{hk}_{11} = -4a_3$$
$$\tau^{hj}_{11} = -4a_2$$
$$\tau^{hi}_{11} = -4a_1$$

The values of the parameters given by Martin and Bradley [34, Table 3, p. 217] are

$$a_0 = -0.042, \quad a_1 = 0.049, \quad a_2 = -0.031,$$
$$a_3 = -0.084, \quad a_4 = -0.082$$

so that

$$\tau^{hl}_{11} = 0.3338 = 0.334, \quad -4a_4 = 0.328$$
$$\tau^{hk}_{11} = 0.3411 = 0.341, \quad -4a_3 = 0.336$$
$$\tau^{hj}_{11} = 0.1240 = 0.124, \quad -4a_2 = 0.124$$
$$\tau^{hi}_{11} = -0.2030 = -0.203, \quad -4a_1 = -0.196$$

The computation for the probability of error using the estimates are shown in Table 20e and yields a probability of error 0.445. (Martin and Bradley give a value of the risk as 0.455.)

### TABLE 20e
### [Martin and Bradley]

| $E_1$ | $\hat{x}(1ijkl)$ | $\hat{x}(2ijkl)$ |
|---|---|---|
| 1111 | 74.67 | 60.33 |
| 1211 | 12.02 | 10.98 |
| 2111 | 314.50 | 207.50 |
| 2112 | 193.45 | 178.55 |
| 2121 | 259.17 | 240.83 |
| 2211 | 37.74 | 28.26 |
| | 891.55 | 726.45 |

$$\mu_2(E_1) = \frac{726.45}{1491}$$

$$\mu_1(E_2) = \frac{1491 - 891.55}{1491}$$

$$\text{Prob. Error} = \frac{1}{2} \frac{726.45 + 599.45}{1491}$$

$$= \frac{1325.90}{2982}$$

$$= 0.445$$

## Example 2. Leukemia Death Observation at ABCC

This example illustrates the analysis of a three-way $5 \times 6 \times 2$ contingency table. It illustrates the estimation procedure for the hypothesis of no second-order interaction. It also illustrates the use of a cell, other than the last one, as the reference cell. Details of the computation of the covariance matrix of a set of estimated parameters of interest is given. Confidence intervals for the parameters are computed using the multiple comparison lemma.

Sugiura and Otake [10] have considered the analysis of $k$ $2 \times c$ contingency tables and have applied their procedures to the data in Table 21. We propose to apply the minimum discrimination information estimation and associated concepts to the analysis of the data in Table 21. We denote the occurrences in the three-way contingency Table 21 by $x(ijk)$ with the notation of Table 22.

We get the minimum discrimination information estimates fitting the sets of marginals

$$a) \; x(ij.), \; x(..k)$$
$$b) \; x(ij.), \; x(i.k)$$
$$c) \; x(ij.), \; x(i.k), \; x(.jk)$$
$$d) \; x(ij.), \; x(.jk)$$

We start with the set of marginals $x(ij.), \; x(..k)$ because $x_a^*(ijk) = x(ij.)x(..k)/n$ is the m.d.i. or maximum-likelihood estimate under the null hypothesis that mortality is homogeneous over the age by dose combinations. We summarize the results in Table 23.

We may draw the following inferences from Table 23.

1. Mortality is not homogeneous over the age by dose combinations ($2I(x:x_a^*)$ = 205.983, 29 D.F.).
2. The effects of age by mortality are not significant ($2I(x_b^*:x_a^*)$ = 2.326, 4 D.F., $2I(x_c^*:x_a^*)$ = 4.634, 4 D.F.).
3. The effects of dose by mortality are highly significant ($2I(x_c^*:x_b^*)$ = 175.810, 5 D.F., $2I(x_d^*:x_a^*)$ = 173.502, 5 D.F.).

Since the value of $2I(x:x_d^*)$ = 32.481, 24 D.F. is not significant at the 10% level, we obtained the complete output for $x_d^*$ and the estimates are shown in Table 24b. However, since four outlier values were indicated for $x_d^*$, and for comparison with the results of Sugiura and Otake, it was decided to perform a more complete analysis with the estimate fitting all the two-way marginals, that is, the estimate corresponding to an hypothesis of no second-order interaction. This estimate is given in Table 24a and we have called it $x_2^*(ijk)$, that is, $x_2^*(ijk) \equiv x_c^*(ijk)$.

Again, for easier comparison with the results of Sugiura and Otake, we selected the cell (512) as the reference cell so that the log-linear representation of

**TABLE 21**
Original Data $x(ijk)$

| Age | $i$ | Not in city $j=1$ Dead $k=1$ | Alive $k=2$ | 0–9 $j=2$ Dead $k=1$ | Alive $k=2$ | 10–49 $j=3$ Dead $k=1$ | Alive $k=2$ | 50–99 $j=4$ Dead $k=1$ | Alive $k=2$ | 100–199 $j=5$ Dead $k=1$ | Alive $k=2$ | 200+ $j=6$ Dead $k=1$ | Alive $k=2$ |
|---|---|---|---|---|---|---|---|---|---|---|---|---|---|
| 0–9 | 1 | 0 | 5,015 | 7 | 10,752 | 3 | 2,989 | 1 | 694 | 4 | 418 | 11 | 387 |
| 10–19 | 2 | 5 | 5,973 | 4 | 11,811 | 6 | 2,620 | 1 | 771 | 3 | 792 | 6 | 820 |
| 20–34 | 3 | 2 | 5,669 | 8 | 10,828 | 3 | 2,798 | 1 | 797 | 3 | 596 | 9 | 624 |
| 35–49 | 4 | 3 | 6,158 | 19 | 12,645 | 4 | 3,566 | 2 | 972 | 1 | 694 | 10 | 608 |
| 50+ | 5 | 3 | 3,695 | 7 | 9,053 | 3 | 2,415 | 2 | 655 | 2 | 393 | 6 | 289 |
| | | 13 | 26,510 | 45 | 55,089 | 19 | 14,388 | 7 | 3,889 | 13 | 2,893 | 42 | 2,728 |

TABLE 22

| Variable | Index | 1 | 2 | 3 | 4 | 5 | 6 |
|---|---|---|---|---|---|---|---|
| Age | $i$ | 0–9 | 10–19 | 20–34 | 35–49 | 50+ | |
| Dose | $j$ | Not in city | 0–9 | 10–49 | 50–99 | 100–199 | 200+ |
| Mortality | $k$ | Dead | Alive | | | | |

$x_2^*(ijk)$ is given by

$$\ln \frac{x_2^*(ijk)}{n(1/60)} = L + \tau_1{}^i T_1{}^i(ijk) + \cdots + \tau_4{}^i T_4{}^i(ijk) + \tau_2{}^j T_2{}^j(ijk) + \cdots + \tau_6{}^j T_6{}^j(ijk)$$
$$+ \tau_1{}^k T_1{}^k(ijk) + \tau_{12}^{ij} T_{12}^{ij}(ijk) + \cdots + \tau_{46}^{ij} T_{46}^{ij}(ijk) + \tau_{11}^{ik} T_{11}^{ik}(ijk) + \cdots + \tau_{41}^{ik} T_{41}^{ik}(ijk)$$
$$+ \tau_{21}^{jk} T_{21}^{jk}(ijk) + \cdots + \tau_{61}^{jk} T_{61}^{jk}(ijk)$$

where $L = 1$, the $\tau$'s are main effect and interaction parameters, and the $T(ijk)$ are the explanatory variables, the indicator functions of the corresponding marginals, e.g., $\Sigma_{ijk} T_{12}^{ij}(ijk)x_2^*(ijk) = x_2^*(12.) = x(12.)$, etc. From the log-linear representation of $x_2^*(ijk)$ we have the log-linear representation of the mortality log-odds or logit as

$$\ln \frac{x_2^*(ij1)}{x_2^*(ij2)} = \tau_1{}^k + \tau_{i1}^{ik} + \tau_{j1}^{jk}$$

where $\tau_{51}^{ik} = 0 = \tau_{11}^{jk}$.

Since the computer output includes logs of the $x_2^*$, we can evaluate the $\tau$

TABLE 23<br>Analysis of Information

| Component due to | Information | D.F. |
|---|---|---|
| a) $x(ij.)$, $x(..k)$ | $2I(x:x_a^*) = 205.983$ | 29 |
| b) $x(ij.)$, $x(i.k)$ | $2I(x_b^*:x_a^*) = 2.326$ | 4 |
| | $2I(x:x_b^*) = 203.657$ | 25 |
| c) $x(ij.)$, $x(i.k)$, $x(.jk)$ | $2I(x_c^*:x_b^*) = 175.810$ | 5 |
| | $2I(x:x_c^*) = 27.847$ | 20 |
| a) $x(ij.)$, $x(..k)$ | $2I(x:x_a^*) = 205.983$ | 29 |
| d) $x(ij.)$, $x(.jk)$ | $2I(x_d^*:x_a^*) = 173.502$ | 5 |
| | $2I(x:x_d^*) = 32.481$ | 24 |
| c) $x(ij.)$, $x(.jk)$, $x(i.k)$ | $2I(x_c^*:x_d^*) = 4.634$ | 4 |
| | $2I(x:x_c^*) = 27.847$ | 20 |

**TABLE 24a**

Estimates. $x_2^*(ijk)$ Fitting Marginals $x(ij.)$, $x(i.k)$, $x(.jk)$

| | $j=1$ | | $j=2$ | | $j=3$ | | $j=4$ | | $j=5$ | | $j=6$ | |
|---|---|---|---|---|---|---|---|---|---|---|---|---|
| $i$ | $k=1$ | $k=2$ | $k=1$ | $k=2$ | $k=1$ | $k=2$ | $k=1$ | $k=2$ | $k=1$ | $k=2$ | $k=1$ | $k=2$ |
| 1 | 2.621 | 5,012.379 | 9.282 | 10,749.719 | 4.115 | 2,987.887 | 1.311 | 693.689 | 2.040 | 419.960 | 6.632 | 391.369 |
| 2 | 2.165 | 5,975.828 | 7.066 | 11,807.930 | 2.504 | 2,623.496 | 1.010 | 770.990 | 2.668 | 792.332 | 9.588 | 816.411 |
| 3 | 2.474 | 5,668.520 | 7.804 | 10,828.191 | 3.216 | 2,797.783 | 1.257 | 796.743 | 2.420 | 596.580 | 8.829 | 624.170 |
| 4 | 3.637 | 6,157.359 | 12.341 | 12,651.648 | 5.546 | 3,564.455 | 2.075 | 971.925 | 3.794 | 691.206 | 11.608 | 606.391 |
| 5 | 2.103 | 3,695.898 | 8.507 | 9,051.488 | 3.619 | 2,414.382 | 1.349 | 655.652 | 2.078 | 392.922 | 5.343 | 289.657 |

**TABLE 24b**

$x_d^*(ijk)$ Fitting Marginals $x(ij.), x(.jk), x_d^*(ijk) = x(ij.)x(.jk)/x(.j.)$

| | $j = 1$ | | $j = 2$ | | $j = 3$ | | $j = 4$ | | $j = 5$ | | $j = 6$ | |
|---|---|---|---|---|---|---|---|---|---|---|---|---|
| $i$ | $k=1$ | $k=2$ | $k=1$ | $k=2$ | $k=1$ | $k=2$ | $k=1$ | $k=2$ | $k=1$ | $k=2$ | $k=1$ | $k=2$ |
| 1 | 2.458 | 5,012.543 | 8.781 | 10,750.215 | 3.946 | 2,988.055 | 1.249 | 693.751 | 1.888 | 420.112 | 6.035 | 391.965 |
| 2 | 2.930 | 5,975.070 | 9.643 | 11,805.352 | 3.463 | 2,622.537 | 1.387 | 770.613 | 3.556 | 791.443 | 12.524 | 813.476 |
| 3 | 2.780 | 5,668.219 | 8.844 | 10,827.152 | 3.694 | 2,797.307 | 1.434 | 796.566 | 2.679 | 596.320 | 9.598 | 623.402 |
| 4 | 3.020 | 6,157.980 | 10.336 | 12,653.660 | 4.708 | 3,565.293 | 1.750 | 972.250 | 3.109 | 691.891 | 9.370 | 608.629 |
| 5 | 1.813 | 3,696.189 | 7.395 | 9,052.602 | 3.189 | 2,414.812 | 1.180 | 655.819 | 1.767 | 393.233 | 4.473 | 290.527 |

**TABLE 24c**

$x_e^*(ijk)$—One Outlier Removed from $x_2^*(ijk)$, that is, $x(111)$, $x(112)$

| | $j = 1$ | | $j = 2$ | | $j = 3$ | | $j = 4$ | | $j = 5$ | | $j = 6$ | |
|---|---|---|---|---|---|---|---|---|---|---|---|---|
| $i$ | $k = 1$ | $k = 2$ | $k = 1$ | $k = 2$ | $k = 1$ | $k = 2$ | $k = 1$ | $k = 2$ | $k = 1$ | $k = 2$ | $k = 1$ | $k = 2$ |
| 1 | 0 | 5,015 | 10.303 | 10,748.695 | 4.561 | 2,987.441 | 1.459 | 693.541 | 2.279 | 419.720 | 7.398 | 390.602 |
| 2 | 2.715 | 5,975.285 | 6.870 | 11,808.125 | 2.431 | 2,623.570 | 0.984 | 771.015 | 2.612 | 792.388 | 9.388 | 816.612 |
| 3 | 3.095 | 5,667.902 | 7.573 | 10,828.422 | 3.117 | 2,797.884 | 1.223 | 796.777 | 2.364 | 596.635 | 8.628 | 624.371 |
| 4 | 4.554 | 6,156.441 | 11.984 | 12,652.012 | 5.378 | 3,564.625 | 2.020 | 971.980 | 3.710 | 691.290 | 11.354 | 606.645 |
| 5 | 2.636 | 3,695.365 | 8.270 | 9,051.727 | 3.514 | 2,414.487 | 1.314 | 655.685 | 2.034 | 392.966 | 5.231 | 289.769 |

parameters, for example, as

$$\ln \frac{x_2{}^*(511)}{x_2{}^*(512)} = \tau_1{}^k$$

$$\ln \frac{x_2{}^*(111)}{x_2{}^*(112)} = \tau_1{}^k + \tau_{11}^{ik}$$

$$\vdots$$

$$\ln \frac{x_2{}^*(411)}{x_2{}^*(412)} = \tau_1{}^k + \tau_{41}^{ik}$$

$$\ln \frac{x_2{}^*(521)}{x_2{}^*(522)} = \tau_1{}^k + \tau_{21}^{jk}$$

$$\vdots$$

$$\ln \frac{x_2{}^*(561)}{x_2{}^*(562)} = \tau_1{}^k + \tau_{61}^{jk}$$

The following are the values obtained:

$$
\begin{array}{ll}
\tau_1{}^k = -7.4714 & \tau_{21}^{jk} = 0.5017 \\
\tau_{11}^{ik} = -0.0849 & \tau_{31}^{jk} = 0.9685 \\
\tau_{21}^{ik} = -0.4515 & \tau_{41}^{jk} = 1.2848 \\
\tau_{31}^{ik} = -0.2655 & \tau_{51}^{jk} = 2.2293 \\
\tau_{41}^{ik} = 0.0371 & \tau_{61}^{jk} = 3.4785
\end{array}
$$

Sugiura and Otake used the representation for the log-odds

$$\log \{p_{ij}/(1 - p_{ij})\} = \mu + \alpha_i + \beta_j$$

where $\Sigma_{i=1}^5 \alpha_i = 0$, $\beta_1 = 0$, and give the estimates

$$
\begin{array}{ll}
\hat{\alpha}_1 = 0.068 & \hat{\beta}_2 = 0.502 \\
\hat{\alpha}_2 = -0.299 & \hat{\beta}_3 = 0.969 \\
\hat{\alpha}_3 = -0.113 & \hat{\beta}_4 = 1.285 \\
\hat{\alpha}_4 = 0.190 & \hat{\beta}_5 = 2.229 \\
\hat{\alpha}_5 = 0.153 & \hat{\beta}_6 = 3.478
\end{array}
$$

We note that $\tau_{21}^{jk} = \hat{\beta}_2, \ldots, \tau_{61}^{jk} = \hat{\beta}_6$ and

$$
\begin{aligned}
\mu + \alpha_5 &= \tau_1{}^k \\
\mu + \alpha_1 &= \tau_1{}^k + \tau_{11}^{ik} \\
\mu + \alpha_2 &= \tau_1{}^k + \tau_{21}^{ik} \\
\mu + \alpha_3 &= \tau_1{}^k + \tau_{31}^{ik} \\
\mu + \alpha_4 &= \tau_1{}^k + \tau_{41}^{ik}
\end{aligned}
$$

that is

$$
\begin{aligned}
\alpha_1 &= \tau_{11}^{ik} - (\tau_{11}^{ik} + \tau_{21}^{ik} + \tau_{31}^{ik} + \tau_{41}^{ik})/5 \\
\alpha_2 &= \tau_{21}^{ik} - (\tau_{11}^{ik} + \tau_{21}^{ik} + \tau_{31}^{ik} + \tau_{41}^{ik})/5 \\
\alpha_3 &= \tau_{31}^{ik} - (\tau_{11}^{ik} + \tau_{21}^{ik} + \tau_{31}^{ik} + \tau_{41}^{ik})/5 \\
\alpha_4 &= \tau_{41}^{ik} - (\tau_{11}^{ik} + \tau_{21}^{ik} + \tau_{31}^{ik} + \tau_{41}^{ik})/5 \\
\alpha_5 &= -(\tau_{11}^{ik} + \tau_{21}^{ik} + \tau_{31}^{ik} + \tau_{41}^{ik})/5
\end{aligned}
$$

yielding $\alpha_1 = 0.0680$, $\alpha_2 = -0.2986$, $\alpha_3 = -0.1126$, $\alpha_4 = 0.1900$, $\alpha_5 = 0.1529$.

We determine the covariance matrix of the $\tau$'s in the logit representation as follows.

Let $\mathbf{T}$ denote the $60 \times 40$ matrix whose columns are

$$L, \overbrace{T_1{}^i(ijk), \ldots, T_4{}^i(ijk)}^{4}, \overbrace{T_2{}^j(ijk), \ldots, T_6{}^j(ijk)}^{5}, \overbrace{T_{12}^{ij}(ijk), \ldots, T_{46}^{ij}(ijk)}^{20}$$

$$T_1{}^k(ijk), \underbrace{T_{11}^{ik}(ijk), \ldots, T_{41}^{ik}(ijk)}_{4}, \underbrace{T_{21}^{jk}(ijk), \ldots, T_{61}^{jk}(ijk)}_{5}$$

and let $\mathbf{D}$ denote a $60 \times 60$ diagonal matrix whose diagonal values are $x_2{}^*(ijk)$ (in the same $ijk$ sequence as the $T(ijk)$ functions).

Compute the $40 \times 40$ matrix $\mathbf{S} = \mathbf{T'DT}$:

$$\mathbf{S} = \begin{pmatrix} \mathbf{S}_{11} & \mathbf{S}_{12} \\ \mathbf{S}_{11} & \mathbf{S}_{22} \end{pmatrix}$$

where $\mathbf{S}_{11}$ is $30 \times 30$ and $\mathbf{S}_{22}$ is $10 \times 10$. The covariance matrix of $\tau_1{}^k, \tau_{11}^{ik}, \ldots, \tau_{41}^{ik}, \tau_{21}^{jk}, \ldots, \tau_{61}^{jk}$ is then given by

$$\mathbf{S}_{22.1}^{-1} = (\mathbf{S}_{22} - \mathbf{S}_{21}\mathbf{S}_{11}^{-1}\mathbf{S}_{12})^{-1}$$

The covariance matrix thus obtained is given in Table 25.

To compute confidence intervals for the $\tau^{jk}$'s, following the procedure suggested by Sugiura and Otake using the multiple comparison lemma, [129, p. 282], we computed $\sqrt{11.070V_{\tau_{j1}^{jk}}}$ using the variances in Table 25 and obtained the following confidence intervals:

| | | |
|---|---|---|
| $\tau_{21}^{jk}$ | $-0.5463$ | $1.5497$ |
| $\tau_{31}^{jk}$ | $-0.2295$ | $2.1665$ |
| $\tau_{41}^{jk}$ | $-0.2762$ | $2.8458$ |
| $\tau_{51}^{jk}$ | $0.9233$ | $3.5353$ |
| $\tau_{61}^{jk}$ | $2.4185$ | $4.5385$ |

The confidence intervals for the $\tau^{ik}$'s were obtained by computing $\sqrt{9.488V_{\tau_{i1}^{ik}}}$ using the variances in Table 25 leading to

| | | |
|---|---|---|
| $\tau_{11}^{ik}$ | $-0.9689$ | $0.7991$ |
| $\tau_{21}^{ik}$ | $-0.4515$ | $0.4455$ |
| $\tau_{31}^{ik}$ | $-1.1525$ | $0.6215$ |
| $\tau_{41}^{ik}$ | $-0.7759$ | $0.8501$ |

To relate with the bounds given by Sugiura and Otake for the $\alpha$'s, since we have seen that

$$\alpha_5 = -(\tau_{11}^{ik} + \tau_{21}^{ik} + \tau_{31}^{ik} + \tau_{41}^{ik})/5$$

we have that

$$\text{Var}(\alpha_5) = \tfrac{1}{25}\{\text{Var}(\tau_{11}^{ik}) + \cdots + \text{Var}(\tau_{41}^{ik}) + 2\sum_{m<n}\text{Cov}(\tau_{n1}^{ik}, \tau_{n1}^{ik})\}$$

and from the entries in Table 25 we finally find $\text{Var}(\alpha_5) = 0.0339$, leading to the

**TABLE 25**

Covariance Matrix $\tau_1^{\ k}$, $\tau_{11}^{ik}$, $\tau_{21}^{ik}$, $\tau_{31}^{ik}$, $\tau_{41}^{ik}$, $\tau_{21}^{jk}$, $\tau_{31}^{jk}$, $\tau_{41}^{jk}$, $\tau_{51}^{jk}$, $\tau_{61}^{jk}$

| | $\tau_1^{\ k}$ | $\tau_{11}^{ik}$ | $\tau_{21}^{ik}$ | $\tau_{31}^{ik}$ | $\tau_{41}^{ik}$ | $\tau_{21}^{jk}$ | $\tau_{31}^{jk}$ | $\tau_{41}^{jk}$ | $\tau_{51}^{jk}$ | $\tau_{61}^{jk}$ |
|---|---|---|---|---|---|---|---|---|---|---|
| $\tau_1^{\ k}$ | 0.1140 | −0.0445 | −0.0438 | −0.0443 | −0.0441 | −0.0782 | −0.0782 | −0.0783 | −0.0769 | −0.0755 |
| $\tau_{11}^{ik}$ | | 0.0824 | 0.0438 | 0.0438 | 0.0438 | 0.0010 | 0.0007 | 0.0019 | 0.0016 | 0.0002 |
| $\tau_{21}^{ik}$ | | | 0.0849 | 0.0444 | 0.0441 | 0.0016 | 0.0027 | 0.0023 | −0.0017 | −0.0041 |
| $\tau_{31}^{ik}$ | | | | 0.0829 | 0.0440 | 0.0019 | 0.0021 | 0.0018 | 0.0000 | −0.0024 |
| $\tau_{41}^{ik}$ | | | | | 0.0697 | 0.0013 | 0.0010 | 0.0009 | −0.0004 | −0.0014 |
| $\tau_{21}^{jk}$ | | | | | | 0.0993 | 0.0770 | 0.0770 | 0.0769 | 0.0769 |
| $\tau_{31}^{jk}$ | | | | | | | 0.1298 | 0.0770 | 0.0769 | 0.0768 |
| $\tau_{41}^{jk}$ | | | | | | | | 0.2202 | 0.0770 | 0.0769 |
| $\tau_{51}^{jk}$ | | | | | | | | | 0.1544 | 0.0771 |
| $\tau_{61}^{jk}$ | | | | | | | | | | 0.1015 |

TABLE 26

Analysis of Information

| Component due to | Information | D.F. |
|---|---|---|
| $x(ij.)$, $x(i.k)$, $x(.jk)$ | $2I(x:x_2{}^*) = 27.847$ | 20 |
| as above but omitting $x(111)$, $x(112)$ | $2I(x_e{}^*:x_2{}^*) = 6.223$ | 1 |
| | $2I(x:x_e{}^*) = 21.614$ | 19 |

interval $\alpha_5$ ($-0.4141$, $0.7199$). We did not trouble to compute the others as it is evident that the results are the same.

In the output corresponding to fitting all the two-way marginals, the entry corresponding to the cell $x(111)$ had a large outlier value (5.239). Accordingly, we fitted an estimate fitting all the two-way marginals but omitting the values $x(111)$, $x(112)$. This estimate is denoted by $x_e{}^*(ijk)$ and its values are given in Table 24c.

The associated analysis of information is given in Table 26.

Removing $x(111)$, $x(112)$ from the estimation gives an improved fit. We did not carry out any extensive analysis with $x_e{}^*(ijk)$ but did note the approximate equality of

$$\tau_{61}^{jk} - \tau_{51}^{jk},\ \tau_{51}^{jk} - \tau_{41}^{jk},\ \tau_{41}^{jk} - \tau_{31}^{jk},\ \tau_{31}^{jk} - \tau_{21}^{jk}$$

when computed for $x_e{}^*$ and $x_2{}^*$, the respective values being those given in Table 27.

## Example 3. Automobile Accident Data

This example illustrates the analysis of a four-way $3 \times 4 \times 3 \times 2$ contingency table. It points out that the model fitted determines the form of the log-odds or logit representation, but the converse is not true. The covariance matrix of the estimated parameters is given.

Data used in this example are taken from a study of the relationship between car size and accident injuries as given in Kihlberg *et al.* [166]. The observed data are given in Table 28 and the observed occurrences are denoted by $x(ijkl)$

TABLE 27

| $x_e{}^*$ | $x_2{}^*$ |
|---|---|
| 1.249 | 1.249 |
| 0.949 | 0.944 |
| 0.320 | 0.316 |
| 0.466 | 0.467 |

**TABLE 28**
Accident Data—Drivers Alone—Observed

| Accident type | Accident severity | Not ejected | | | Ejected | | |
|---|---|---|---|---|---|---|---|
| | | Small | Com-pact | Stand-ard | Small | Com-pact | Stand-ard |
| Collision with vehicle | Not severe | 95 | 166 | 1279 | 8 | 7 | 65 |
| | Moderately severe | 31 | 34 | 506 | 2 | 5 | 51 |
| | Severe | 11 | 17 | 186 | 4 | 5 | 54 |
| Collision with object | Not severe | 34 | 55 | 599 | 5 | 6 | 46 |
| | Moderately severe | 8 | 34 | 241 | 2 | 4 | 26 |
| | Severe | 5 | 10 | 89 | 0 | 1 | 30 |
| Rollover without collision | Not severe | 23 | 18 | 65 | 6 | 5 | 11 |
| | Moderately severe | 22 | 17 | 118 | 18 | 9 | 68 |
| | Severe | 5 | 2 | 23 | 5 | 6 | 33 |
| Other rollover | Not severe | 9 | 10 | 83 | 6 | 2 | 11 |
| | Moderately severe | 23 | 26 | 177 | 13 | 16 | 78 |
| | Severe | 8 | 9 | 86 | 7 | 6 | 86 |
| | | 274 | 398 | 3452 | 76 | 72 | 559 |

(defined in Table 29). A condensed $2 \times 2 \times 2 \times 2$ version of this data was studied by Bhapkar and Koch [109] and Ku *et al.* [117].

Since the question of interest is the possible relation of driver ejection on car weight, accident type, and severity, we start the fitting sequence with the marginals $x(ijk.)$, $x(...l)$. This first estimate, $x_a*(ijkl) = x(ijk.)x(...l)/n$, corresponds to a null hypothesis that driver ejection is homogeneous over the 36

**TABLE 29**

| Characteristic | Index | 1 | 2 | 3 | 4 |
|---|---|---|---|---|---|
| Car weight | $h$ | Small | Compact | Standard | |
| Accident type | $j$ | Collision with vehicle | Collision with object | Rollover without collision | Other rollover |
| Severity | $k$ | Not severe | Moderately severe | Severe | |
| Driver ejection | $l$ | Not ejected | Ejected | | |

combinations of the other characteristics. As may be seen from Table 30, this hypothesis is clearly rejected by the data. It is found that by fitting the model incorporating in addition to $x(ijk.)$ the marginals $x(i..l)$, $x(.j.l)$, $x(..kl)$, that is, the interactions of car weight, accident type, and severity, respectively, with driver ejection, a satisfactory fit to the observed data is obtained. The models fitting in addition three-way marginals $x(ij.l)$, etc., showed no significant effects for the associated interaction parameters. The results are summarized in Table 30.

The fitted values $x_b^*(ijkl)$ are given in Table 31. The log-linear regression representation of $x_b^*(ijkl)$ contains the parameters $L$ (a normalizing constant), $\tau_1^i$, $\tau_2^i$, $\tau_1^j$, $\tau_2^j$, $\tau_3^j$, $\tau_1^k$, $\tau_2^k$, $\tau_1^l$, $\tau_{11}^{ij}$, $\tau_{12}^{ij}$, $\tau_{13}^{ij}$, $\tau_{21}^{ij}$, $\tau_{22}^{ij}$, $\tau_{23}^{ij}$, $\tau_{11}^{ik}$, $\tau_{12}^{ik}$, $\tau_{21}^{ik}$, $\tau_{22}^{ik}$, $\tau_{11}^{il}$, $\tau_{21}^{il}$, $\tau_{11}^{jk}$, $\tau_{12}^{jk}$, $\tau_{21}^{jk}$, $\tau_{22}^{jk}$, $\tau_{31}^{jk}$, $\tau_{32}^{jk}$, $\tau_{11}^{jl}$, $\tau_{21}^{jl}$, $\tau_{31}^{jl}$, $\tau_{11}^{kl}$, $\tau_{21}^{kl}$, $\tau_{111}^{ijk}$, $\tau_{112}^{ijk}$, $\tau_{121}^{ijk}$, $\tau_{122}^{ijk}$, $\tau_{131}^{ijk}$, $\tau_{132}^{ijk}$, $\tau_{211}^{ijk}$, $\tau_{212}^{ijk}$, $\tau_{221}^{ijk}$, $\tau_{222}^{ijk}$, $\tau_{231}^{ijk}$, $\tau_{232}^{ijk}$. The 28 additional parameters which would appear in the complete model for $x(ijkl)$ are hypothesized as zero and represent the 28 degrees of freedom of $2I(x:x_b^*)$. The log-odds or logit representation for the estimate $x_b^*$ is

$$\ln \frac{x_b^*(ijk1)}{x_b^*(ijk2)} = \tau_1^l + \tau_{i1}^{il} + \tau_{j1}^{jl} + \tau_{k1}^{kl}$$

Parameters not involving $l$ are common to numerator and denominator of the odds and drop out. The values of the parameters may be obtained as

$$\tau_1^l = \ln \frac{x_b^*(3431)}{x_b^*(3432)}$$

$$\tau_{11}^{il} = \ln \frac{x_b^*(1431)}{x_b^*(1432)} - \tau_1^l$$

$$\tau_{21}^{il} = \ln \frac{x_b^*(2431)}{x_b^*(2432)} - \tau_1^l$$

etc.

The values of the parameters are (in this case provided as computer output)

$$\tau_1^l = -0.0083 \qquad \tau_{11}^{jl} = 1.3655 \qquad \tau_{11}^{kl} = 1.6085$$
$$\tau_{11}^{il} = -0.2936 \qquad \tau_{21}^{jl} = 1.1139 \qquad \tau_{21}^{kl} = 0.8823$$
$$\tau_{21}^{il} = -0.0788 \qquad \tau_{31}^{jl} = -0.2405$$

TABLE 30
Analysis of Information

| Component due to | Information | D.F. |
|---|---|---|
| a) $x(ijk.)$, $x(...l)$ | $2I(x:x_a^*) = 613.102$ | 35 |
| b) $x(ijk.)$, $x(i..l)$, $x(.j.l)$, $x(..kl)$ | $2I(x_b^*:x_a^*) = 587.584$ | 7 |
| | $2I(x:x_b^*) = 25.518$ | 28 |
| c) $x(ijk.)$, $x(ij.l)$, $x(i.kl)$, $x(.jkl)$ | $2I(x_c^*:x_b^*) = 14.491$ | 16 |
| | $2I(x:x_c^*) = 11.028$ | 12 |

TABLE 31
Accident Data—Drivers Alone—Estimate $x_b^*$

| Accident type | Accident severity | Not ejected | | | Ejected | | |
|---|---|---|---|---|---|---|---|
| | | Small | Com-pact | Standard | Small | Com-pact | Standard |
| Collision with vehicle | Not severe | 96.349 | 163.874 | 1278.209 | 6.651 | 9.126 | 65.790 |
| | Moderately severe | 28.879 | 34.973 | 503.433 | 4.121 | 4.027 | 53.567 |
| | Severe | 11.154 | 17.212 | 190.913 | 3.846 | 4.788 | 49.087 |
| Collision with object | Not severe | 35.817 | 56.919 | 604.917 | 3.183 | 4.081 | 40.082 |
| | Moderately severe | 8.448 | 33.095 | 234.832 | 1.552 | 4.905 | 32.167 |
| | Severe | 3.463 | 8.099 | 89.406 | 1.537 | 2.901 | 29.594 |
| Rollover without collision | Not severe | 21.572 | 18.000 | 60.475 | 7.428 | 5.000 | 15.525 |
| | Moderately severe | 23.367 | 16.516 | 121.512 | 16.633 | 9.484 | 64.488 |
| | Severe | 3.676 | 3.351 | 24.535 | 6.324 | 4.649 | 31.465 |
| Other rollover | Not severe | 11.804 | 9.849 | 78.213 | 3.196 | 2.151 | 15.787 |
| | Moderately severe | 23.082 | 28.936 | 179.924 | 12.918 | 13.064 | 75.076 |
| | Severe | 6.377 | 7.174 | 85.645 | 8.623 | 7.826 | 86.355 |
| | | 273.988 | 397.998 | 3452.014 | 76.012 | 72.002 | 558.983 |

We recall that any parameter with a subscript $i = 3$ and/or $j = 4$ and/or $k = 3$ and/or $l = 2$ is by convention zero.

It is important to note that the estimate $x_2^*(ijkl)$ obtained by fitting the two-way marginals $x(ij..)$, $x(i.k.)$, $x(i..l)$, $x(.jk.)$, $x(.j.l)$, $x(..kl)$ would also have the log-odds or logit representation

$$\ln \frac{x_2^*(ijk1)}{x_2^*(ijk2)} = \tau_1^l + \tau_{i1}^{il} + \tau_{j1}^{jl} + \tau_{k1}^{kl}$$

The values of the parameters would depend, however, on the values of the estimate $x_2^*(ijkl)$.

The model fitted determines the form of the log-odds or logit representation but the converse is not true.

For easier interpretation of the numerical values we use the representation of the estimated odds as the multiplicative model

$$\frac{x_b^*(ijk1)}{x_b^*(ijk2)} = \exp(\tau_1^l)\,\exp(\tau_{i1}^{il})\,\exp(\tau_{j1}^{jl})\,\exp(\tau_{k1}^{kl})$$

The factors which determine the odds of not ejected for any combination of the characteristics are presented in Table 32.

**TABLE 32**
Factors

| Base | Car weight | | Accident type | | Severity | |
|------|-----------|------|--------------|------|---------|------|
| 0.99 | Small | 0.75 | Collision with vehicle | 3.92 | Not severe | 5.00 |
| | Compact | 0.92 | Collision with object | 3.05 | Moderately severe | 2.42 |
| | Standard | 1.00 | Rollover without collision | 0.79 | Severe | 1.00 |
| | | | Other rollover | 1.00 | | |

By selecting the combination of characteristics with the largest factors, it is seen that the best odds for not ejected, 19.40, occur for

Standard, Collision with vehicle, Not severe

By selecting the combination of characteristics with the smallest factors, it is seen that the worst odds for Not ejected, 0.59, occur for

Small, Rollover without collision, Severe

The observed odds for Not ejected from the original data are $4124/707 = 5.83$. The estimated odds for any combination of characteristics is easily obtained from the values of $x_b^*$.

The covariance matrix of the parameters for the estimate $x_b^*$ is given in Table 33.

### Example 4.  Minnesota High School Graduates of June 1938

This example illustrates the analysis of a four-way $2 \times 3 \times 7 \times 4$ contingency table. In particular, the "dependent" classification is not dichotomous as in the previous examples but has four categories. The final model leads to log-odds representations involving main effects and interactions.

**TABLE 33**
Covariance Matrix—Parameters of Estimate $x_b^*$

| $\tau_1^l$ | $\tau_{11}^{il}$ | $\tau_{21}^{il}$ | $\tau_{11}^{jl}$ | $\tau_{21}^{jl}$ | $\tau_{31}^{jl}$ | $\tau_{11}^{kl}$ | $\tau_{21}^{kl}$ |
|-----------|-----------|-----------|-----------|-----------|-----------|-----------|-----------|
| .0017 | .0003 | .0003 | .0005 | .0003 | .0003 | .0005 | .0003 |
| | .0039 | −.0003 | .0000 | −.0001 | .0005 | .0001 | .0001 |
| | | .0027 | .0001 | .0000 | .0001 | .0001 | .0000 |
| | | | .0008 | −.0005 | −.0004 | .0003 | .0000 |
| | | | | .0012 | −.0003 | .0002 | .0000 |
| | | | | | .0036 | −.0001 | .0003 |
| | | | | | | .0008 | −.0006 |
| | | | | | | | .0011 |

The data of this $2 \times 3 \times 7 \times 4$ contingency table represents a four-way cross classification of the April 1939 status of 13,968 Minnesota high school graduates of June 1938. The data were presented by Hoyt *et al.* [227]. They formulated and tested various hypotheses of independence using chi-squared statistics. The same data were also used by Kullback *et al.* [198] to illustrate the use of the minimum discrimination information statistics in the analysis of various hypotheses of independence and homogeneity. Patil [9] condensed the original data into a $4 \times 3 \times 7$ table by summing over the sex classification and tested for no second-order interaction in the three-way table by an asymptotic chi-squared statistic.

We shall examine models fitting certain sets of marginals and analyze the data on the basis of the log-linear representation of a model that fits the data well. The original data are listed in Table 34 where we denote the occurrences in the cells by $x(hijk)$ (defined in Table 35).

The problem is to determine the relationship of post-high-school status on the other variables. Note that here the ''dependent'' variable is polychotomous. We summarize in Table 36 the results of fitting three models to the data, or the sets of marginals,

$$H_a: \quad x(hij.), \ x(...k)$$
$$H_b: \quad x(hij.), \ x(h..k), \ x(.i.k), \ x(..jk)$$
$$H_c: \quad x(hij.), \ x(.i.k), \ x(h.jk)$$

The estimate $x_a{}^*$, corresponding to $H_a$, is to determine whether the occurrences of post-high-school status are homogeneously distributed over the 42 combinations of sex, high-school rank, and father's occupational level. We note that $x_a{}^*(hijk) = x(hij.)x(...k)/n$. Since the data do not support the null hypothesis of homogeneity, we consider the estimate $x_b{}^*$ corresponding to $H_b$. This estimate will provide a log-odds or logit representation in terms of a linear combination of the main effects of sex, high-school rank, and father's occupational level on post-high-school status. Since the fit of the estimate $x_b{}^*$ to the data was not considered satisfactory, the effects of various interactions associated with three-way marginals were examined. The interaction with the largest effect, for the additional degrees of freedom, turned out to be that of sex $\times$ father's occupational level $\times$ post-high-school status, that is, associated with the marginal $x(h.jk)$. It was decided to analyze the data in terms of the estimate $x_c{}^*$ corresponding to $H_c$. The values of $x_c{}^*(hijk)$ are listed in Table 37.

From the log-linear representation of the estimate $x_c{}^*$, we arrive at the following representation for the log-odds:

$$\ln \frac{x_c{}^*(hij1)}{x_c{}^*(hij4)} = \tau_1{}^k + \tau_{h1}^{hk} + \tau_{i1}^{ik} + \tau_{j1}^{jk} + \tau_{hj1}^{hjk}$$

$$\ln \frac{x_c{}^*(hij2)}{x_c{}^*(hij4)} = \tau_2{}^k + \tau_{h2}^{hk} + \tau_{i2}^{ik} + \tau_{j2}^{jk} + \tau_{hj2}^{hjk}$$

$$\ln \frac{x_c{}^*(hij3)}{x_c{}^*(hij4)} = \tau_3{}^k + \tau_{h3}^{hk} + \tau_{i3}^{ik} + \tau_{j3}^{jk} + \tau_{hj3}^{hjk}$$

## CONTINGENCY TABLE ANALYSIS

**TABLE 34**

Frequency for Each Sex × High-School Rank × Father's Occupational Level Combination × Post-High-School Status, $x(hijk)$

| Post-high-school status[a] | | Lowest third | | | | Middle third | | | | Upper third | | | |
|---|---|---|---|---|---|---|---|---|---|---|---|---|---|
| | | 1 | 2 | 3 | 4 | 1 | 2 | 3 | 4 | 1 | 2 | 3 | 4 |
| Sex (1) Male | Father's occupational levels | | | | | | | | | | | | |
| | 1 | 87 | 3 | 17 | 105 | 216 | 4 | 14 | 118 | 256 | 2 | 10 | 53 |
| | 2 | 72 | 6 | 18 | 209 | 159 | 14 | 28 | 227 | 176 | 8 | 22 | 95 |
| | 3 | 52 | 17 | 14 | 541 | 119 | 13 | 44 | 578 | 119 | 10 | 33 | 257 |
| | 4 | 88 | 9 | 14 | 328 | 158 | 15 | 36 | 304 | 144 | 12 | 20 | 115 |
| | 5 | 32 | 1 | 12 | 124 | 43 | 5 | 7 | 119 | 42 | 2 | 7 | 56 |
| | 6 | 14 | 2 | 5 | 148 | 24 | 6 | 15 | 131 | 24 | 2 | 4 | 61 |
| | 7 | 20 | 3 | 4 | 109 | 41 | 5 | 13 | 88 | 32 | 2 | 4 | 41 |
| Sex (2) Female | Father's occupational levels | | | | | | | | | | | | |
| | 1 | 55 | 7 | 13 | 76 | 163 | 30 | 28 | 118 | 309 | 17 | 38 | 89 |
| | 2 | 36 | 16 | 11 | 111 | 116 | 41 | 53 | 214 | 225 | 49 | 68 | 210 |
| | 3 | 52 | 28 | 49 | 521 | 162 | 64 | 129 | 708 | 243 | 79 | 184 | 448 |
| | 4 | 48 | 18 | 29 | 191 | 130 | 47 | 62 | 305 | 237 | 57 | 63 | 219 |
| | 5 | 12 | 5 | 10 | 101 | 35 | 11 | 37 | 152 | 72 | 20 | 21 | 95 |
| | 6 | 9 | 1 | 15 | 130 | 19 | 13 | 22 | 174 | 42 | 10 | 19 | 105 |
| | 7 | 3 | 1 | 6 | 88 | 25 | 9 | 15 | 158 | 36 | 14 | 19 | 93 |

[a] Categories of post-high-school status: (1) enrolled in college; (2) enrolled in noncollegiate school; (3) employed full-time; (4) other.

**TABLE 35**

| Characteristic | Index | 1 | 2 | 3 | 4 | 5 | 6 | 7 |
|---|---|---|---|---|---|---|---|---|
| Sex | $h$ | Male | Female | | | | | |
| High-school rank | $i$ | Lowest third | Middle third | Upper third | | | | |
| Father's occupational level | $j$ | 1 | 2 | 3 | 4 | 5 | 6 | 7 |
| Post-high-school status | $k$ | Enrolled in college | Noncollegiate school | Employed full time | Other | | | |

The values of the parameters in the log-odds representations are:

$$\tau_1^{\ k} = -1.0345 \quad \tau_2^{\ k} = -2.2548 \quad \tau_3^{\ k} = -1.7189$$
$$\tau_{11}^{hk} = 0.9935 \quad \tau_{12}^{hk} = -0.3523 \quad \tau_{13}^{hk} = -0.1111$$
$$\tau_{11}^{ik} = -1.5908 \quad \tau_{12}^{ik} = -1.0060 \quad \tau_{13}^{ik} = -1.0682$$
$$\tau_{21}^{ik} = -0.8912 \quad \tau_{22}^{ik} = -0.4542 \quad \tau_{23}^{ik} = -0.4934$$
$$\tau_{11}^{jk} = 2.2731 \quad \tau_{12}^{jk} = 0.9905 \quad \tau_{13}^{jk} = 0.8593$$
$$\tau_{21}^{jk} = 1.2332 \quad \tau_{22}^{jk} = 0.9822 \quad \tau_{23}^{jk} = 0.6872$$
$$\tau_{31}^{jk} = 0.4009 \quad \tau_{32}^{jk} = 0.3932 \quad \tau_{33}^{jk} = 0.6333$$
$$\tau_{41}^{jk} = 1.1259 \quad \tau_{42}^{jk} = 0.8881 \quad \tau_{43}^{jk} = 0.6099$$
$$\tau_{51}^{jk} = 0.6194 \quad \tau_{52}^{jk} = 0.3995 \quad \tau_{53}^{jk} = 0.5254$$
$$\tau_{61}^{jk} = -0.0321 \quad \tau_{62}^{jk} = -0.1397 \quad \tau_{63}^{jk} = 0.1989$$
$$\tau_{111}^{hjk} = -0.7277 \quad \tau_{112}^{hjk} = -1.3054 \quad \tau_{113}^{hjk} = -0.4037$$
$$\tau_{121}^{hjk} = -0.6340 \quad \tau_{122}^{hjk} = -0.8018 \quad \tau_{123}^{hjk} = -0.3643$$
$$\tau_{131}^{hjk} = -1.0923 \quad \tau_{132}^{hjk} = -0.8080 \quad \tau_{133}^{hjk} = -0.9709$$
$$\tau_{141}^{hjk} = -0.8463 \quad \tau_{142}^{hjk} = -0.7581 \quad \tau_{143}^{hjk} = -0.5573$$
$$\tau_{151}^{hjk} = -0.6402 \quad \tau_{152}^{hjk} = -0.8605 \quad \tau_{153}^{hjk} = -0.5508$$
$$\tau_{161}^{hjk} = -0.7587 \quad \tau_{162}^{hjk} = -0.2334 \quad \tau_{163}^{hjk} = -0.4397$$

All parameters with subscripts $h = 2$ and/or $i = 3$ and/or $j = 7$ and/or $k = 4$ are zero by convention.

**TABLE 36**
Analysis of Information

| Component due to | Information | D.F. |
|---|---|---|
| a) $x(hij.)$, $x(...k)$ | $2I(x:x_a^*) = 2824.434$ | 123 |
| b) $x(hij.)$, $x(h..k)$, $x(.i.k)$, $x(..jk)$ | $2I(x_b^*:x_a^*) = 2672.724$ | 27 |
| | $2I(x:x_b^*) = 151.710$ | 96 |
| c) $x(hij.)$, $x(.i.k)$, $x(h.jk)$ | $2I(x_c^*:x_b^*) = 52.850$ | 18 |
| | $2I(x:x_c^*) = 98.860$ | 78 |

## TABLE 37

Estimated Frequency for Each Sex × High-School Rank × Father's Occupational Level Combination × Post-High-School Status, $x_c*(hijk)$

| Post-high-school status[a] | | Lowest third | | | | Middle third | | | | Upper third | | | |
|---|---|---|---|---|---|---|---|---|---|---|---|---|---|
| | | 1 | 2 | 3 | 4 | 1 | 2 | 3 | 4 | 1 | 2 | 3 | 4 |
| Sex (1) Male Father's occupational levels | 1 | 96.076 | 2.062 | 9.106 | 104.751 | 214.142 | 3.964 | 17.913 | 115.981 | 248.782 | 2.975 | 13.981 | 55.269 |
| | 2 | 74.160 | 6.726 | 15.853 | 208.256 | 160.787 | 12.579 | 30.337 | 224.296 | 172.053 | 8.695 | 21.809 | 98.448 |
| | 3 | 52.918 | 9.622 | 21.244 | 540.216 | 114.549 | 17.964 | 40.588 | 580.899 | 122.534 | 12.414 | 29.169 | 254.885 |
| | 4 | 84.275 | 10.004 | 18.926 | 325.787 | 159.270 | 16.308 | 31.570 | 305.852 | 146.455 | 9.687 | 19.503 | 115.361 |
| | 5 | 25.645 | 2.277 | 7.194 | 133.882 | 44.415 | 3.401 | 10.997 | 115.186 | 46.939 | 2.322 | 7.808 | 49.932 |
| | 6 | 13.027 | 2.727 | 6.363 | 146.881 | 24.402 | 4.406 | 10.520 | 136.671 | 24.571 | 2.866 | 7.117 | 56.447 |
| | 7 | 20.818 | 2.871 | 5.867 | 106.443 | 37.619 | 4.474 | 9.357 | 95.549 | 34.562 | 2.655 | 5.776 | 36.008 |
| Sex (2) Female Father's occupational levels | 1 | 53.675 | 7.884 | 11.104 | 76.337 | 168.174 | 21.306 | 30.708 | 118.813 | 303.151 | 24.810 | 37.188 | 87.850 |
| | 2 | 29.353 | 12.096 | 14.462 | 118.093 | 111.908 | 39.776 | 48.665 | 223.655 | 235.739 | 54.129 | 68.873 | 193.253 |
| | 3 | 54.868 | 28.839 | 58.878 | 507.420 | 151.976 | 68.898 | 143.943 | 698.185 | 250.157 | 73.263 | 159.179 | 471.394 |
| | 4 | 44.660 | 18.647 | 22.674 | 200.023 | 134.884 | 48.576 | 60.442 | 300.100 | 235.456 | 54.778 | 70.884 | 214.878 |
| | 5 | 13.289 | 5.649 | 10.289 | 98.774 | 40.924 | 15.005 | 27.967 | 151.105 | 64.787 | 15.346 | 29.744 | 98.121 |
| | 6 | 9.223 | 4.386 | 9.883 | 131.508 | 24.155 | 9.909 | 22.846 | 171.091 | 36.622 | 9.705 | 23.271 | 106.401 |
| | 7 | 6.054 | 3.206 | 5.149 | 83.592 | 22.830 | 10.430 | 17.139 | 156.602 | 35.117 | 10.364 | 17.712 | 98.806 |

[a] Categories of post-high-school status: (1) enrolled in college; (2) enrolled in noncollegiate school; (3) employed full-time; (4) other.

From the representation for the log-odds it is seen that the association between high-school rank and post-high-school status is independent of the combination of sex and father's occupational level, that is,

$$\ln \frac{x_c^*(h1j1)}{x_c^*(h1j4)} - \ln \frac{x_c^*(h2j1)}{x_c^*(h2j4)} = \ln \frac{x_c^*(h1j1)x_c^*(h2j4)}{x_c^*(h1j4)x_c^*(h2j1)} = \tau_{11}^{ik} - \tau_{21}^{ik} = -0.6996$$

$$\ln \frac{x_c^*(h2j1)x_c^*(h3j4)}{x_c^*(h2j4)x_c^*(h3j1)} = \tau_{21}^{ik} = -0.8912$$

$$\ln \frac{x_c^*(h1j2)x_c^*(h2j4)}{x_c^*(h1j4)x_c^*(h2j2)} = \tau_{12}^{ik} - \tau_{22}^{ik} = -0.5518$$

$$\ln \frac{x_c^*(h2j2)x_c^*(h3j4)}{x_c^*(h2j4)x_c^*(h3j2)} = \tau_{22}^{ik} = -0.4542$$

$$\ln \frac{x_c^*(h1j3)x_c^*(h2j3)}{x_c^*(h1j4)x_c^*(h2j4)} = \tau_{13}^{ik} - \tau_{23}^{ik} = -0.5748$$

$$\ln \frac{x_c^*(h2j3)x_c^*(h3j3)}{x_c^*(h2j4)x_c^*(h3j4)} = \tau_{23}^{ik} = -0.4934$$

The association between sex and post-high-school status is, of course, dependent on father's occupational level, that is,

$$\ln \frac{x_c^*(1ij1)}{x_c^*(1ij4)} - \ln \frac{x_c^*(2ij1)}{x_c^*(2ij4)} = \tau_{11}^{hk} + \tau_{1j1}^{hjk}$$

$$\ln \frac{x_c^*(1ij2)}{x_c^*(1ij4)} - \ln \frac{x_c^*(2ij2)}{x_c^*(2ij4)} = \tau_{12}^{hk} + \tau_{1j2}^{hjk}$$

$$\ln \frac{x_c^*(1ij3)}{x_c^*(1ij4)} - \ln \frac{x_c^*(2ij3)}{x_c^*(2ij4)} = \tau_{13}^{hk} + \tau_{1j3}^{hjk}$$

We summarize the numerical values in Table 38.

We remark that father's occupational level 3 shows a peculiarity as compared to other values in the second column of Table 38. Kullback *et al.* [198, p. 593] noted that there was an unusually larger number of girls than boys for the third category of father's occupation. Apparently there was a tendency for the girls not to enroll in college as compared to the boys. In particular, for example, the

**TABLE 38**

| $j$ | $\tau_{11}^{hk} + \tau_{1j1}^{hjk}$ | $\tau_{12}^{hk} + \tau_{1j2}^{hjk}$ | $\tau_{13}^{hk} + \tau_{1j3}^{hjk}$ |
|---|---|---|---|
| 1 | 0.2658 | −1.6577 | −0.5148 |
| 2 | 0.3595 | −1.1541 | −0.4754 |
| 3 | −0.0988 | −1.1603 | −1.0820 |
| 4 | 0.1472 | −1.1104 | −0.6684 |
| 5 | 0.3533 | −1.2128 | −0.6619 |
| 6 | 0.2348 | −0.5857 | −0.5508 |
| 7 | 0.9935 | −0.3523 | −0.1111 |

association between sex and collegiate or noncollegiate school is

$$\ln \frac{x_c^*(1ij1)}{x_c^*(1ij2)} - \ln \frac{x_c^*(2ij1)}{x_c^*(2ij2)} = \tau_{11}^{hk} + \tau_{1j1}^{hjk} - \tau_{12}^{hk} - \tau_{1j2}^{hjk}$$

From the preceding results we have the values of Table 39.

The association between father's occupational level and post-high-school status is dependent on the sex, that is,

$$\ln \frac{x_c^*(hi11)}{x_c^*(hi14)} - \ln \frac{x_c^*(hi71)}{x_c^*(hi74)} = \tau_{11}^{hk} + \tau_{h11}^{hjk}$$

$$\ln \frac{x_c^*(hi21)}{x_c^*(hi24)} - \ln \frac{x_c^*(hi71)}{x_c^*(hi74)} = \tau_{21}^{jk} + \tau_{h21}^{hjk}$$

etc.

$$\ln \frac{x_c^*(hi12)}{x_c^*(hi14)} - \ln \frac{x_c^*(hi72)}{x_c^*(hi74)} = \tau_{12}^{jk} + \tau_{h12}^{hjk}$$

$$\ln \frac{x_c^*(hi22)}{x_c^*(hi24)} - \ln \frac{x_c^*(hi72)}{x_c^*(hi74)} = \tau_{22}^{jk} + \tau_{h22}^{hjk}$$

etc.

$$\ln \frac{x_c^*(hi13)}{x_c^*(hi14)} - \ln \frac{x_c^*(hi73)}{x_c^*(hi74)} = \tau_{13}^{jk} + \tau_{h13}^{hjk}$$

$$\ln \frac{x_c^*(hi23)}{x_c^*(hi24)} - \ln \frac{x_c^*(hi73)}{x_c^*(hi74)} = \tau_{23}^{jk} + \tau_{h23}^{hjk}$$

etc.

A tabulation of these associations is presented in Table 40.

In particular, the association between father's occupational levels 1 and 2 and post-high-school status of collegiate and noncollegiate school, for boys, is

$$\ln \frac{x_c^*(1i11)}{x_c^*(1i12)} - \ln \frac{x_c^*(1i21)}{x_c^*(1i22)} = \tau_{11}^{jk} + \tau_{111}^{hjk} - \tau_{12}^{jk} - \tau_{112}^{hjk} - \tau_{21}^{jk} - \tau_{121}^{hjk} + \tau_{22}^{jk} + \tau_{122}^{hjk}$$

TABLE 39

| $j$ | $\tau_{11}^{hk} + \tau_{1j1}^{hjk} - \tau_{12}^{hk} - \tau_{1j2}^{hjk}$ |
|---|---|
| 1 | 1.9235 |
| 2 | 1.5136 |
| 3 | 1.0615 |
| 4 | 1.2576 |
| 5 | 1.5661 |
| 6 | 0.8205 |
| 7 | 1.3458 |

**TABLE 40**

| | $h = 1$ | | | $h = 2$ | | |
|---|---|---|---|---|---|---|
| $j$ | $k = 1$ | $k = 2$ | $k = 3$ | $k = 1$ | $k = 2$ | $k = 3$ |
| 1 | 1.5094 | −0.3149 | 0.4556 | 2.2731 | 0.9905 | 0.8593 |
| 2 | 0.5992 | 0.1804 | 0.3229 | 1.2332 | 0.9822 | 0.6872 |
| 3 | −0.6914 | −0.4148 | −0.3376 | 0.4009 | 0.3932 | 0.6333 |
| 4 | 0.2796 | 0.1300 | 0.0526 | 1.1259 | 0.8881 | 0.6099 |
| 5 | −0.0208 | −0.4610 | −0.0254 | 0.6194 | 0.3995 | 0.5254 |
| 6 | −0.7908 | −0.3731 | −0.2408 | −0.0321 | −0.1397 | 0.1989 |

We shall not pursue this matter further. The reader should be able to examine any particular associations of interest.

**Example 5. Coronary Heart Disease Risk**

This example illustrates the analysis of a three-way $2 \times 4 \times 4$ contingency table. It illustrates the test of equality of certain parameters in the model of no second-order interaction, both by computing the estimate implied by the hypothesized relation among some of the parameters and by computing the appropriate quadratic approximation.

We are indebted to Professor S. Greenhouse and J. Cornfield [190] for calling our attention to this set of data.

In this example we analyze data from a 3-way, $R \times S \times T$, table resulting from a coronary heart disease study. We denote the observed values by $f(ijk)$ (see Table 41). We ask the reader's indulgence for not using the notation used elsewhere in this article, that is, $x(ijk)$, $x_a^*(ijk)$, etc.

The complete $2 \times 4 \times 4$ table is given in Table 42. A preliminary analysis is given in Table 43, where the various sets of marginal constraints and the corresponding information values and degrees of freedom are listed. Interaction hypotheses corresponding to sets of marginal constraints in the table are

$$H_a: \quad p(ijk) = p(i..)p(.jk)$$
$$H_b: \quad p(ijk) = \frac{p(ij.)p(.jk)}{p(.j.)}$$
$$H_2: \quad \text{no second-order interaction}$$

**TABLE 41**

| Characteristic | Index | | 1 | 2 | 3 | 4 |
|---|---|---|---|---|---|---|
| Coronary heart disease | $R$ | $i$ | Yes | No | | |
| Serum cholesterol, mg/100 cc | $S$ | $j$ | <200 | 200–219 | 220–259 | 260+ |
| Blood pressure, mm Hg | $T$ | $k$ | <127 | 127–146 | 147–166 | 167+ |

TABLE 42
Coronary Heart Disease Risk

| | | $j$: serum cholesterol, mg/ 100 cc | $k$: blood pressure, mm Hg | | | | |
|---|---|---|---|---|---|---|---|
| | | | 1 <127 | 2 127–146 | 3 147–166 | 4 167+ | Total |
| CHD, | 1 | <200 | 2 | 3 | 3 | 4 | 12 |
| $i = 1$ | 2 | 200–219 | 3 | 2 | 0 | 3 | 8 |
| | 3 | 220–259 | 8 | 11 | 6 | 6 | 31 |
| | 4 | 260+ | 7 | 12 | 11 | 11 | 41 |
| | | $j$ total | 20 | 28 | 20 | 24 | 92 |
| NCHD, | 1 | <200 | 117 | 121 | 47 | 22 | 307 |
| $i = 2$ | 2 | 200–219 | 85 | 98 | 43 | 20 | 246 |
| | 3 | 220–259 | 119 | 209 | 68 | 43 | 439 |
| | 4 | 260+ | 67 | 99 | 46 | 33 | 245 |
| | | $j$ total | 388 | 527 | 204 | 118 | 1237 |
| | | Total | 408 | 555 | 224 | 142 | 1329 |

The effects due to addition of each of the three 2-way marginal tables are shown immediately above these interactions. We note that both the information values and the degrees of freedom are additive.

This analysis indicated that a fit to this set of data could be made adequately using as explanatory variables the marginal cell frequencies of three marginal tables of dimensions 2 × 4, 2 × 4, and 4 × 4. The hypothesis tested was that of no second-order interaction in the sense of Bartlett [304] as discussed by Ku *et al.* [57]. We start with $H_a$ because our first concern is whether the incidence of

TABLE 43
Analysis of Information—Coronary Heart Disease Risk Data

| Component due to | Information | D.F. |
|---|---|---|
| a) $f(i..), f(.jk)$ | | |
| Independence $R \times ST$ | $2I(f:f_a^*) = 58.726$ | 15 |
| b) $f(.jk), f(ij.)$ | | |
| RS effect/ST | $2I(f_b^*:f_a^*) = 31.921$ | 3 |
| Conditional independence $R \times T/S$ | $2I(f:f_b^*) = 26.805$ | 12 |
| 2) $f(.jk), f(ij.), f(i.k)$ | | |
| RT effect/ST, RS | $2I(f_2^*:f_b^*) = 18.730$ | 3 |
| Second-order interaction | $2I(f:f_2^*) = 8.075$ | 9 |

coronary heart disease is homogeneous over the factors serum cholesterol and blood pressure. Thus considering $2I(f:f_a)$ in Table 43 as the total "unexplained variation," we may set up the summary analysis of information as in Table 44.

The interpretation of the no second-order interaction hypothesis is:

1. The association between blood pressure and heart disease is the same for different levels of cholesterol.
2. The association between cholesterol level and heart disease is the same for different levels of blood pressure.
3. The association between cholesterol level and blood pressure is the same for subjects with and without heart disease. For the estimate $f_2^*$ under the model of no second-order interaction the log-odds (logit) of the estimated incidence of coronary heart disease is a linear additive function of an average effect, an effect due to cholesterol and an effect due to blood pressure, i.e.,

$$\ln \frac{f_2^*(1jk)}{f_2^*(2jk)} = \tau_1{}^i + \tau_{1j}^{ij} + \tau_{1k}^{ik}$$

Values of $f_2^*$ are shown in Table 45 and the design matrix in Table 46. We note that there are 22 parameters, in addition to $\tau_0$, to be estimated from the $f_2^*$ values. A complete model would include nine additional parameters which, under the no second-order interaction hypothesis, are equal to zero, i.e.,

$$\tau_{111}^{ijk} = \tau_{112}^{ijk} = \tau_{113}^{ijk} = 0$$
$$\tau_{121}^{ijk} = \tau_{122}^{ijk} = \tau_{123}^{ijk} = 0$$
$$\tau_{131}^{ijk} = \tau_{132}^{ijk} = \tau_{133}^{ijk} = 0$$

We note that the number of parameters in the complete model is $23 + 9 = 32$, that is, the number of cells.

The computation of the $\tau$ parameter estimates is straightforward, e.g.,

$$\tau_1{}^i = \ln \frac{f_2^*(144)}{f_2^*(244)} = -0.9374$$

### TABLE 44
Analysis of Information

| Component due to | | Information | D.F. |
|---|---|---|---|
| $f(i..), f(.jk)$ | Total | $2I(f:f_a^*) = 58.726$ | 15 |
| $f(.jk), f(ij.)$ | Cholesterol effect | $2I(f_b^*:f_a^*) = 31.921$ | 3 |
| $f(.jk), f(ij.), f(i.k)$ | Blood pressure effect given cholesterol | $2I(f_2^*:f_b^*) = 18.730$ | 3 |
| Second-order interaction | (Residual) | $2I(f:f_2^*) = 8.075$ | 9 |

**TABLE 45**
Estimated Cell Frequencies under No Second-Order Interaction Hypothesis, $f_2^*$,
Coronary Heart Disease Risk

| | | *j*: serum cholesterol, mg/ 100 cc | *k*: blood pressure, mm Hg | | | | |
|---|---|---|---|---|---|---|---|
| | | | 1 <127 | 2 127–146 | 3 147–166 | 4 167+ | Total |
| CHD, | 1 | <200 | 3.550 | 3.553 | 2.488 | 2.409 | 12.000 |
| *i* = 1 | 2 | 200–219 | 2.144 | 2.340 | 1.754 | 1.762 | 8.000 |
| | 3 | 220–259 | 6.501 | 10.827 | 6.227 | 7.446 | 31.001 |
| | 4 | 260+ | 7.805 | 11.287 | 9.531 | 12.382 | 40.998 |
| | | *j* total | 20.000 | 28.000 | 20.000 | 23.999 | 91.999 |
| NCHD, | 1 | <200 | 115.450 | 120.447 | 47.512 | 23.591 | 307.000 |
| *i* = 2 | 2 | 200–219 | 85.856 | 97.660 | 41.246 | 21.238 | 246.000 |
| | 3 | 220–259 | 120.499 | 209.173 | 67.773 | 41.554 | 438.999 |
| | 4 | 260+ | 66.196 | 99.720 | 47.469 | 31.617 | 245.002 |
| | | *j* total | 388.001 | 527.000 | 204.000 | 118.000 | 1237.001 |
| | | Total | 408.001 | 555.000 | 224.000 | 141.999 | 1329.000 |

etc. The values of the $\tau$'s are listed in Table 47. For simplicity we use $\tau$ with no further diacritical marking.

When the "dependent" variable or response variable is dichotomous, odds and log-odds have long been used as indices indicative of risk. The estimated log-odds,

$$\ln \frac{f_2^*(1jk)}{f_2^*(2jk)} = \tau_1{}^i + \tau_{1j}^{ij} + \tau_{1k}^{ik}$$

and the estimated odds,

$$\frac{f_2^*(1jk)}{f_2^*(2jk)}$$

are given in Table 48.

From the design matrix or the representation of the log-odds we can compute the difference in log-odds of risk of heart disease for change in blood pressure and constant cholesterol concentration in terms of the $\tau$ parameters, e.g.,

$$\ln \frac{f_2^*(1j2)}{f_2^*(2j2)} - \ln \frac{f_2^*(1j1)}{f_2^*(2j1)} = \ln \frac{f_2^*(112)}{f_2^*(212)} - \ln \frac{f_2^*(111)}{f_2^*(211)}$$
$$= \tau_{12}^{ik} - \tau_{11}^{ik} = -0.0415$$

**TABLE 46**

Design Matrix—Coronary Heart Disease Risk

| i | j | k | $\tau_0$ | 1 $i_1$ | 2 $j_1$ | 3 $j_2$ | 4 $j_3$ | 5 $k_1$ | 6 $k_2$ | 7 $k_3$ | 8 $ij_{11}$ | 9 $ij_{12}$ | 10 $ij_{13}$ | 11 $ik_{11}$ | 12 $ik_{12}$ | 13 $ik_{13}$ | 14 $jk_{11}$ | 15 $jk_{12}$ | 16 $jk_{13}$ | 17 $jk_{21}$ | 18 $jk_{22}$ | 19 $jk_{23}$ | 20 $jk_{31}$ | 21 $jk_{32}$ | 22 $jk_{33}$ |
|---|---|---|---|---|---|---|---|---|---|---|---|---|---|---|---|---|---|---|---|---|---|---|---|---|---|
| 1 | 1 | 1 | 1 | 1 | 1 | | | 1 | | | 1 | | | 1 | | | 1 | | | | | | | | |
| 1 | 1 | 2 | 1 | 1 | 1 | | | | 1 | | 1 | | | | 1 | | | 1 | | | | | | | |
| 1 | 1 | 3 | 1 | 1 | 1 | | | | | 1 | 1 | | | | | 1 | | | 1 | | | | | | |
| 1 | 1 | 4 | 1 | 1 | 1 | | | | | | 1 | | | | | | | | | | | | | | |
| 1 | 2 | 1 | 1 | 1 | | 1 | | 1 | | | | 1 | | 1 | | | | | | 1 | | | | | |
| 1 | 2 | 2 | 1 | 1 | | 1 | | | 1 | | | 1 | | | 1 | | | | | | 1 | | | | |
| 1 | 2 | 3 | 1 | 1 | | 1 | | | | 1 | | 1 | | | | 1 | | | | | | 1 | | | |
| 1 | 2 | 4 | 1 | 1 | | 1 | | | | | | 1 | | | | | | | | | | | | | |
| 1 | 3 | 1 | 1 | 1 | | | 1 | 1 | | | | | 1 | 1 | | | | | | | | | 1 | | |
| 1 | 3 | 2 | 1 | 1 | | | 1 | | 1 | | | | 1 | | 1 | | | | | | | | | 1 | |
| 1 | 3 | 3 | 1 | 1 | | | 1 | | | 1 | | | 1 | | | 1 | | | | | | | | | 1 |
| 1 | 3 | 4 | 1 | 1 | | | 1 | | | | | | 1 | | | | | | | | | | | | |
| 1 | 4 | 1 | 1 | 1 | | | | 1 | | | | | | 1 | | | | | | | | | | | |
| 1 | 4 | 2 | 1 | 1 | | | | | 1 | | | | | | 1 | | | | | | | | | | |
| 1 | 4 | 3 | 1 | 1 | | | | | | 1 | | | | | | 1 | | | | | | | | | |
| 1 | 4 | 4 | 1 | 1 | | | | | | | | | | | | | | | | | | | | | |
| 2 | 1 | 1 | 1 | | 1 | | | 1 | | | | | | | | | 1 | | | | | | | | |
| 2 | 1 | 2 | 1 | | 1 | | | | 1 | | | | | | | | | 1 | | | | | | | |
| 2 | 1 | 3 | 1 | | 1 | | | | | 1 | | | | | | | | | 1 | | | | | | |
| 2 | 1 | 4 | 1 | | 1 | | | | | | | | | | | | | | | | | | | | |
| 2 | 2 | 1 | 1 | | | 1 | | 1 | | | | | | | | | | | | 1 | | | | | |
| 2 | 2 | 2 | 1 | | | 1 | | | 1 | | | | | | | | | | | | 1 | | | | |
| 2 | 2 | 3 | 1 | | | 1 | | | | 1 | | | | | | | | | | | | 1 | | | |
| 2 | 2 | 4 | 1 | | | 1 | | | | | | | | | | | | | | | | | | | |
| 2 | 3 | 1 | 1 | | | | 1 | 1 | | | | | | | | | | | | | | | 1 | | |
| 2 | 3 | 2 | 1 | | | | 1 | | 1 | | | | | | | | | | | | | | | 1 | |
| 2 | 3 | 3 | 1 | | | | 1 | | | 1 | | | | | | | | | | | | | | | 1 |
| 2 | 3 | 4 | 1 | | | | 1 | | | | | | | | | | | | | | | | | | |
| 2 | 4 | 1 | 1 | | | | | 1 | | | | | | | | | | | | | | | | | |
| 2 | 4 | 2 | 1 | | | | | | 1 | | | | | | | | | | | | | | | | |
| 2 | 4 | 3 | 1 | | | | | | | 1 | | | | | | | | | | | | | | | |
| 2 | 4 | 4 | 1 | | | | | | | | | | | | | | | | | | | | | | |

Log-linear representation

| | $\tau_0$ | 1 | 2 | 3 | 4 | 5 | 6 | 7 | 8 | 9 | 10 | 11 | 12 | 13 | 14 | 15 | 16 | 17 | 18 | 19 | 20 | 21 | 22 |
|---|---|---|---|---|---|---|---|---|---|---|---|---|---|---|---|---|---|---|---|---|---|---|---|
| $f_1^*$ | √ | √ | √ | √ | √ | √ | √ | √ | | | | | | | | | | | | | | | |
| $f_a^*$ | √ | √ | √ | √ | √ | √ | √ | √ | | | | | | | √ | √ | √ | √ | √ | √ | √ | √ | √ |
| $f_b^*$ | √ | √ | √ | √ | √ | √ | √ | √ | √ | √ | √ | | | | √ | √ | √ | √ | √ | √ | √ | √ | √ |
| $f_2^*$ | √ | √ | √ | √ | √ | √ | √ | √ | √ | √ | √ | √ | √ | √ | √ | √ | √ | √ | √ | √ | √ | √ | √ |

[197]

**TABLE 47**
Values of Estimates of $\tau$ Parameters[a]

| | | |
|---|---|---|
| $\tau_1^i = -0.9374$ | $\tau_{11}^{ij} = -1.3441$ | $\tau_{11}^{jk} = 0.8491$ |
| $\tau_1^j = -0.2929$ | $\tau_{12}^{ij} = -1.5520$ | $\tau_{12}^{jk} = 0.4817$ |
| $\tau_2^j = -0.3979$ | $\tau_{13}^{ij} = -0.7818$ | $\tau_{13}^{jk} = 0.2938$ |
| $\tau_3^j = 0.2733$ | $\tau_{11}^{ik} = -1.2004$ | $\tau_{21}^{jk} = 0.6580$ |
| $\tau_1^k = 0.7389$ | $\tau_{12}^{ik} = -1.2419$ | $\tau_{22}^{jk} = 0.3770$ |
| $\tau_2^k = 1.1481$ | $\tau_{13}^{ik} = -0.6681$ | $\tau_{23}^{jk} = 0.2574$ |
| $\tau_3^k = 0.4064$ | | $\tau_{31}^{jk} = 0.3527$ |
| | | $\tau_{32}^{jk} = 0.4675$ |
| | | $\tau_{33}^{jk} = 0.0828$ |

[a] Any $\tau$ parameter corresponding to a subscript $i = 2$, and/or $j = 4$, and/or $k = 4$ is zero.

Similarly,

$$\ln \frac{f_2^*(1j3)}{f_2^*(2j3)} - \ln \frac{f_2^*(1j2)}{f_2^*(2j2)} = 0.5738$$

$$\ln \frac{f_2^*(1j4)}{f_2^*(2j4)} - \ln \frac{f_2^*(1j3)}{f_2^*(2j3)} = 0.6681$$

The differences in log-odds for change in cholesterol level and constant blood pressure are:

$$\ln \frac{f_2^*(12k)}{f_2^*(22k)} - \ln \frac{f_2^*(11k)}{f_2^*(21k)} = -0.2079$$

$$\ln \frac{f_2^*(13k)}{f_2^*(23k)} - \ln \frac{f_2^*(12k)}{f_2^*(22k)} = 0.7702$$

$$\ln \frac{f_2^*(14k)}{f_2^*(24k)} - \ln \frac{f_2^*(13k)}{f_2^*(23k)} = 0.7818$$

**TABLE 48**
Log-Odds and Odds[a]

| | $k = 1$ | $k = 2$ | $k = 3$ | $k = 4$ |
|---|---|---|---|---|
| $j = 1$ | -3.482 | -3.523 | -2.950 | -2.281 |
| | .0307 | .0295 | .0523 | .1022 |
| $j = 2$ | -3.690 | -3.731 | -3.158 | -2.489 |
| | .0250 | .0240 | .0245 | .0830 |
| $j = 3$ | -2.920 | -2.961 | -2.387 | -1.719 |
| | .0539 | .0518 | .0919 | .1792 |
| $j = 4$ | -2.138 | -2.179 | -1.605 | -0.937 |
| | .1179 | .1132 | .2009 | .3918 |

[a] Entries are log-odds $\ln \dfrac{f_2^*(1jk)}{f_2^*(2jk)}$ and odds $\dfrac{f_2^*(1jk)}{f_2^*(2jk)}$.

The differences in log-odds for change in cholesterol level and change in blood pressure are

$$\ln \frac{f_2^*(122)}{f_2^*(222)} - \ln \frac{f_2^*(111)}{f_2^*(211)} = -0.2494$$
$$\ln \frac{f_2^*(133)}{f_2^*(233)} - \ln \frac{f_2^*(122)}{f_2^*(222)} = 1.3440$$
$$\ln \frac{f_2^*(144)}{f_2^*(244)} - \ln \frac{f_2^*(133)}{f_2^*(233)} = 1.4499$$

In view of the negative values of the changes in log-odds represented by $\tau_{12}^{ik} - \tau_{11}^{ik}$, $\tau_{12}^{ij} - \tau_{11}^{ij}$, we may wish to check the hypothesis that

$$\tau_{11}^{ij} = \tau_{12}^{ij}, \qquad \tau_{11}^{ik} = \tau_{12}^{ik}$$

which would imply that the risk does not begin to manifest itself significantly until the cholestrol level and blood pressure exceed some minimum level, that is, a threshold effect. Let

$$Z_1 = \tau_{12}^{ij} - \tau_{11}^{ij} = -0.2079$$
$$Z_2 = \tau_{12}^{ik} - \tau_{11}^{ik} = -0.0415$$

The variance-covariance matrix of the $\tau$'s for $f_2^*$ is obtained as follows (a weighted version of Kullback [229, p. 217]): Compute $\mathbf{S} = \mathbf{T'DT}$ where $\mathbf{T}$ is the $32 \times 23$ design matrix for the log-linear representation of $f_2^*$ in Table 46, and $\mathbf{D}$ is a diagonal matrix whose entries are the values of $f_2^*$ in the order of the rows of the design matrix. Partition the matrix $\mathbf{S}$ as

$$\begin{pmatrix} \mathbf{S}_{11} & \mathbf{S}_{12} \\ \mathbf{S}_{21} & \mathbf{S}_{22} \end{pmatrix}$$

where $\mathbf{S}_{11}$ is $1 \times 1$.

Then the variance-covariance matrix of the $\tau$'s is

$$(\mathbf{S}_{22} - \mathbf{S}_{21}\mathbf{S}_{11}^{-1}\mathbf{S}_{12})^{-1} \qquad \text{or} \qquad \mathbf{S}_{22.1}^{-1}$$

The covariance matrix of $Z_1$, $Z_2$ is found to be

$$a_{11} = \sigma^{8,8} + \sigma^{9,9} - 2\sigma^{8,9} = 0.2175$$
$$a_{12} = a_{21} = \sigma^{8,11} - \sigma^{9,11} - \sigma^{8,12} + \sigma^{9,12} = -0.0013$$
$$a_{22} = \sigma^{11,11} + \sigma^{12,12} - 2\sigma^{11,12} = 0.0922$$

We found

$$\mathbf{A}^{-1} = \begin{pmatrix} a_{11} & a_{12} \\ a_{21} & a_{22} \end{pmatrix}^{-1} = \begin{pmatrix} 4.5981 & 0.0648 \\ 0.0648 & 10.8469 \end{pmatrix}$$
$$X^2 = (Z_1, Z_2)\mathbf{A}^{-1}\begin{pmatrix} Z_1 \\ Z_2 \end{pmatrix} = 0.2185$$

does not exceed the upper 5% critical value of a chi-squared variate with 2 degrees of freedom.

For this particular hypothesis, we may alternatively revise the design matrix by combining the columns $\tau_{11}^{ij}$ with $\tau_{12}^{ij}$, and $\tau_{11}^{ik}$ with $\tau_{12}^{ik}$, and use the iterative procedure suggested by Gokhale [27] and Kullback [13] for "unusual marginal totals" to obtain the estimated cell frequencies. The resulting estimates $f_d^*$ are given in Table 49. In Table 50 are listed the log-odds

$$\ln \frac{f_d^*(1jk)}{f_d^*(2jk)}$$

and the odds $f_d^*(1jk)/f_d^*(2jk)$. The associated analysis of information table is shown in Table 51. Note that $2I(f_2^* : f_d^*)$ is a test of the hypothesis that $\tau_{11}^{ij} = \tau_{12}^{ij}$, $\tau_{11}^{ik} = \tau_{12}^{ik}$, and is approximated by the test previously given as a quadratic chi-squared variate.

**Example 6. Hospital Data**

This example illustrates the analysis of a pair of related three-way $2 \times 2 \times 2$ contingency tables. In particular it illustrates the procedure to obtain an estimate satisfying certain observed marginal restraints and having certain of the $\tau$ parameters predetermined, that is, the "inheritance" of certain parameters. It also mentions that the $T$-functions of the two-way marginals are the products of the $T$-functions of the related one-way marginals.

The data used are from the field of hospital administration and relate to the matter of innovation in hospitals. We begin with the assumption that the use of

**TABLE 49**

Estimate under $\tau_{11}^{ij} = \tau_{12}^{ij}$, $\tau_{11}^{ik} = \tau_{12}^{ik}$, $f_d^*$, Coronary Heart Disease Risk

|  |  | \multicolumn{4}{c}{$k$: blood pressure, mm Hg} |  |  |  |
|---|---|---|---|---|---|---|
|  | $j$: serum cholesterol, mg/ 100 cc | 1 <127 | 2 127–146 | 3 147–166 | 4 167+ | Total |
| CHD, | 1 <200 | 3.189 | 3.323 | 2.289 | 2.225 | 11.026 |
| $i = 1$ | 2 200–219 | 2.358 | 2.680 | 1.969 | 1.968 | 8.975 |
|  | 3 220–259 | 6.350 | 11.000 | 6.217 | 7.437 | 31.001 |
|  | 4 260+ | 7.640 | 11.460 | 9.525 | 12.374 | 40.999 |
|  | $j$ total | 19.537 | 28.463 | 20.000 | 24.001 | 92.001 |
| NCHD, | 1 <200 | 115.811 | 120.677 | 47.711 | 23.775 | 307.974 |
| $i = 2$ | 2 200–219 | 85.692 | 97.320 | 41.031 | 21.032 | 245.025 |
|  | 3 220–259 | 120.650 | 209.000 | 67.783 | 41.566 | 438.999 |
|  | 4 260+ | 66.360 | 99.539 | 47.475 | 31.626 | 245.000 |
|  | $j$ total | 388.463 | 526.536 | 204.000 | 117.999 | 1236.998 |
|  | Total | 408.000 | 554.999 | 224.000 | 142.000 | 1328.999 |

TABLE 50
The Long-Odds ln $f_d^*(ljk)/f_d^*(2jk)$, and the Odds $f_d^*(ljk)/f_d^*(2jk)^a$

|  |  | Blood pressure | | | |
|---|---|---|---|---|---|
|  |  | $k = 1$ | 2 | 3 | 4 |
| Serum cholesterol | $j = 1$ | −3.592 | −3.592 | −3.037 | −2.369 |
|  |  | 0.0275 | 0.0275 | 0.0480 | 0.0936 |
|  | $j = 2$ | −3.592 | −3.592 | −3.037 | −2.369 |
|  |  | 0.0275 | 0.0275 | 0.0480 | 0.0936 |
|  | $j = 3$ | −2.944 | −2.944 | −2.389 | −1.721 |
|  |  | 0.0526 | 0.0526 | 0.0917 | 0.1788 |
|  | $j = 4$ | −2.162 | −2.162 | −1.606 | −0.938 |
|  |  | 0.1151 | 0.1151 | 0.2006 | 0.3912 |

$^a$-$\ln f_d^*(1jk)/f_d^*(2jk) = \tau_1^i + \tau_{1j}^{ij} + \tau_{1k}^{ik}$
$\tau_1^i = -0.9384$
$\tau_{11}^{ij} = \tau_{12}^{ij} = -1.4306$     $\tau_{11}^{ik} = \tau_{12}^{ik} = -1.2232$
$\tau_{13}^{ij} = -0.7828$     $\tau_{13}^{ik} = -0.6678$

electronic data processing (EDP) in hospitals in the late 1960s was innovative. This assumption is substantiated by a variety of surveys of the use of EDP in hospitals [32]. On this basis the data in a survey of hospitals using EDP conducted by Herner and Co. were combined with data from the Guide Issue of *Hospitals* for the same period so that a file of records reflecting characteristics of hospitals and levels at which EDP was used by these hospitals was created. The hospitals in this survey were selected by stratified sampling. The stratification (fixed variable) was on the basis of hospital size. All hospitals in the large-size category (200 or more beds) were included in the survey and a 10% sample was taken of those in the small-size category. The data from these files were tabulated and arranged in multiway contingency tables. The analysis of the tables for the large and small hospitals will be described here and interrelated (see Kullback and Reeves [8]).

TABLE 51
Analysis of Information

| Component due to | Information | D.F. |
|---|---|---|
| a) $f(i..)$, $f(.jk)$ | $2I(f:f_a^*) = 58.726$ | 15 |
| d) $f(.jk)$, $f(ij.)$, $j = 3, 4$ | $2I(f_a^*:f_a^*) = 50.429$ | 4 |
| $f(i.k)$, $k = 3, 4$ |  |  |
| $f(i1.) + f(i2.)$; $f(i.1) + f(i.2)$ | $2I(f:f_d^*) = 8.297$ | 11 |
| 2) $f(.jk)$, $f(ij.)$, $f(i.k)$ | $2I(f_2^*:f_d^*) = 0.222$ | 2 |
|  | $2I(f:f_2^*) = 8.075$ | 9 |

**TABLE 52**
Large Hospitals $x(ijk)$

|  | Urban | | Rural | | |
|---|---|---|---|---|---|
|  | Short | Long | Short | Long | |
| User | 376 | 40 | 52 | 15 | 483 |
| Nonuser | 217 | 112 | 54 | 57 | 440 |
|  | 593 | 152 | 106 | 72 | 923 |

On the basis of these analyses we conclude that there is a distinct relation of innovation on location and length of stay with a common factor for large and small hospitals. The association (measured by the logarithm of the cross-product ratio) between use of EDP and length of stay is the same for the large and small hospitals. The log-odds (logit) of use of EDP in descending order of magnitude within the large hospitals and within the small hospitals are parallel in terms of the combinations of the factors location and length of stay. The usage of EDP is generally greater in the large hospitals than in the small hospitals except that the best log-odds for the small hospitals is greater than the poorest log-odds for the large hospitals.

In a study to identify characteristics which distinguish hospitals which use EDP from those which do not, that is, to identify characteristics which are significantly associated with use of EDP, data on 1176 hospitals, 923 large and 253 small, were collected with respect to use, location, and length of stay. The data appear in the two three-way $2 \times 2 \times 2$ contingency Tables 52 and 53. In order to determine the relation among the free variables use, location and length of stay, indexed by size of hospital, and interactions that may exist among these characteristics, it seems intuitively clear that an analysis based only on two-way tables would not suffice.

**TABLE 53**
Small Hospitals $y(ijk)$

|  | Urban | | Rural | | |
|---|---|---|---|---|---|
|  | Short | Long | Short | Long | |
| User | 28 | 2 | 11 | 0 | 41 |
| Nonuser | 80 | 14 | 114 | 4 | 212 |
|  | 108 | 16 | 125 | 4 | 253 |

**TABLE 54**
Large Hospitals $x_2^*(ijk)$

|  | Urban | | Rural | | |
|---|---|---|---|---|---|
|  | Short | Long | Short | Long | |
| User | 374.305 | 41.694 | 53.695 | 13.306 | 483.000 |
| Nonuser | 218.693 | 110.308 | 52.307 | 58.692 | 440.000 |
|  | 592.998 | 152.002 | 106.002 | 71.998 | 923.000 |

We shall denote the occurrences in the observed Tables 52 and 53, respectively, by $x(ijk)$, $y(ijk)$ with

$$i = 1, \text{ user}; \quad i = 2, \text{ nonuser}$$
$$j = 1, \text{ urban}; \quad j = 2, \text{ rural}$$
$$k = 1, \text{ short}; \quad k = 2, \text{ long}$$

The proposed procedure provides estimates for the original data analogous to a regression procedure using sets of observed marginals as explanatory variables, and we shall try to find an estimate which does not differ significantly from the observed data. The set of acceptable estimates will indicate the nature of the significant interactions for which we can compute numerical measures.

As a first step in the analysis we shall find "smoothed" estimates of the original data. We shall do this for the large hospitals also, even though the data for all large hospitals was collected. We examine the m.d.i. estimates obtained by a convergent iterative algorithm starting with a uniform table and successively adjusting for sets of observed marginals. It turns out that the sets of two-way marginals are best and the resultant estimates provide a satisfactory fit. The estimated tables have the same two-way and also the same one-way marginals as the original tables. These estimates, which we denote by $x_2^*(ijk)$, $y_2^*(ijk)$, respectively, for the large and small hospitals are given in Tables 54 and 55 and

**TABLE 55**
Small Hospitals $y_2^*(ijk)$

|  | Urban | | Rural | | |
|---|---|---|---|---|---|
|  | Short | Long | Short | Long | |
| User | 28.137 | 1.863 | 10.863 | 0.137 | 41.000 |
| Nonuser | 79.863 | 14.137 | 114.137 | 3.863 | 212.000 |
|  | 108.000 | 16.000 | 125.000 | 4.000 | 253.000 |

imply no second-order (three-factor) interaction. Note that the estimate for the observed $y(122) = 0$ is $y_2^*(122) = 0.137$.

The estimates are given analytically by the log-linear representation of an exponential family

$$\ln \frac{x_2^*(ijk)}{n\pi(ijk)} = L + \tau_1 T_1(ijk) + \tau_2 T_2(ijk) + \tau_3 T_3(ijk)$$
$$+ \tau_4 T_4(ijk) + \tau_5 T_5(ijk) + \tau_6 T_6(ijk) \quad (14)$$

where $n = \Sigma\Sigma\Sigma x(ijk)$, $\pi(ijk) = 1/2 \times 2 \times 2$, $L$ is a normalizing constant, the $\tau$'s are main-effect and interaction parameters, and the $T(ijk)$ are a set of linearly independent random variables, in this case the indicator functions of the respective marginals. A similar representation holds for $y_2^*(ijk)$. The log-linear representations are shown graphically in Table 56. The values in the various columns of Table 56, zeros or ones, are the values of the respective functions $T(ijk)$. Note that

$$T_4(ijk) = T_1(ijk)T_2(ijk), \quad T_5(ijk) = T_1(ijk)T_3(ijk), \quad T_6(ijk) = T_2(ijk)T_3(ijk)$$

To test the goodness-of-fit of the estimates, we compute the statistics

$$2I(x:x_2^*) = 2\sum\sum\sum x(ijk) \ln (x(ijk)/x_2^*(ijk)) = 0.481, 1 \text{ D.F.}$$
$$2I(y:y_2^*) = 2\sum\sum\sum y(ijk) \ln (y(ijk)/y_2^*(ijk)) = 0.294, 1 \text{ D.F.}$$

Since the statistics are asymptotically distributed as $\chi^2$, we conclude that the "smoothed" values $x_2^*$, $y_2^*$ are good estimates and we shall use them in our subsequent analysis.

From the log-linear representation (14) or the graphical presentation in Table 56, we find that the log-odds or logits of the use of EDP for large hospitals is given by the parametric representation

$$\ln \frac{x_2^*(111)}{x_2^*(211)} = \tau_1 + \tau_4 + \tau_5$$
$$\ln \frac{x_2^*(112)}{x_2^*(212)} = \tau_1 + \tau_4$$
$$\ln \frac{x_2^*(121)}{x_2^*(221)} = \tau_1 \qquad + \tau_5 \qquad (15)$$
$$\ln \frac{x_2^*(122)}{x_2^*(222)} = \tau_1$$

where the values of the parameters for the estimate $x_2^*(ijk)$ are found to be

$$\tau_1 = -1.4842, \qquad \tau_4 = 0.5113, \qquad \tau_5 = 1.5103$$

From (15) we also see that for the large hospitals

$$\tau_4 = \ln \frac{x_2^*(111)x_2^*(221)}{x_2^*(211)x_2^*(121)} = \ln \frac{x_2^*(112)x_2^*(222)}{x_2^*(212)x_2^*(122)} = 0.5113$$

that is, the association between usage and location for either short or long stay.

**TABLE 56**
Log-Linear Representation

| $i$ | $j$ | $k$ | $L$ | $\tau_1$ | $\tau_2$ | $\tau_3$ | $\tau_4$ | $\tau_5$ | $\tau_6$ |
|---|---|---|---|---|---|---|---|---|---|
| 1 | 1 | 1 | 1 | 1 | 1 | 1 | 1 | 1 | 1 |
| 1 | 1 | 2 | 1 | 1 | 1 |   | 1 |   |   |
| 1 | 2 | 1 | 1 | 1 |   |   | 1 |   | 1 |
| 1 | 2 | 2 | 1 | 1 |   |   |   |   |   |
| 2 | 1 | 1 | 1 |   |   | 1 | 1 |   |   | 1 |
| 2 | 1 | 2 | 1 |   |   | 1 |   |   |   |
| 2 | 2 | 1 | 1 |   |   |   | 1 |   |   |
| 2 | 2 | 2 | 1 |   |   |   |   |   |   |

Similarly

$$\tau_5 = \ln \frac{x_2{}^*(111)x_2{}^*(212)}{x_2{}^*(211)x_2{}^*(112)} = \ln \frac{x_2{}^*(121)x_2{}^*(222)}{x_2{}^*(221)x_2{}^*(122)} = 1.5103$$

that is, the association between usage and stay for either urban or rural location.
 For the small hospitals the log-odds or logits are

$$\ln \frac{y_2{}^*(111)}{y_2{}^*(211)} = \tau_1 + \tau_4 + \tau_5$$

$$\ln \frac{y_2{}^*(112)}{y_2{}^*(212)} = \tau_1 + \tau_4$$

$$\ln \frac{y_2{}^*(121)}{y_2{}^*(221)} = \tau_1 \quad\quad + \tau_5$$

$$\ln \frac{y_2{}^*(122)}{y_2{}^*(222)} = \tau_1$$

where the values of the parameters for the estimate $y_2{}^*(ijk)$ are found to be

$$\tau_1 = -3.3357, \quad\quad \tau_4 = 1.3088, \quad\quad \tau_5 = 0.9836$$

 For the small hospitals we also have

$$\tau_4 = \ln \frac{y_2{}^*(111)y_2{}^*(221)}{y_2{}^*(211)y_2{}^*(121)} = \ln \frac{y_2{}^*(112)y_2{}^*(222)}{y_2{}^*(212)y_2{}^*(122)} = 1.3088$$

that is, the association between usage and location for either short or long stay.
Similarly

$$\tau_5 = \ln \frac{y_2{}^*(111)y_2{}^*(212)}{y_2{}^*(211)y_2{}^*(112)} = \ln \frac{y_2{}^*(121)y_2{}^*(222)}{y_2{}^*(221)y_2{}^*(122)} = 0.9836$$

that is, the association between usage and stay for either urban or rural locations.

Since the data for the large hospitals reflect observations over all such hospitals, it will be of interest to determine whether there exists a suitable estimate for the small hospitals, other than $y_2^*(ijk)$, which will have some of its interactions (associations) the same as the corresponding values for the large hospitals. This can be accomplished by using the iterative algorithm fitting various subsets of marginals of $y_2^*(ijk)$ (or the original $y(ijk)$) but starting with a distribution which has the same $\tau$ parameters as $x_2^*(ijk)$. The $\tau$ parameters of $x_2^*(ijk)$ not affected by the iterative fitting procedure will be "inherited" by the resultant estimate. We shall use the table $v(ijk) = (253/923)x_2^*(ijk)$ which has the same $\tau$ parameters as the $x_2^*(ijk)$ table with total adjusted to be the same as the observed total of small hospitals.

We summarize the procedure (Table 57) by starting the iterative fitting algorithm with $v(ijk)$ (recall that $y(ijk)$ and $y_2^*(ijk)$ have the same two-way and one-way marginals). In order to test whether the $u^*$ estimates differ significantly from the $y_2^*$ estimates, that is, whether the interaction parameters in $y_2^*$ differ significantly from the interaction parameters in $u^*$ "inherited" from $x_2^*$ or $v$, we compute the statistic

$$2I(y_2^*:u_m^*) = 2\sum\sum\sum y_2^*(ijk)\ln(y_2^*(ijk)/u_m^*(ijk))$$

which is asymptotically distributed as $\chi^2$ with 1 D.F. for $m = a, b, c$; 2 D.F. for $m = d, e, f$; 3 D.F. for $m = g$.

The only case which yielded a nonsignificant value was $u_b^*(ijk)$ for which

$$2I(y_2^*:u_b^*) = 0.408, \quad 1 \text{ D.F.}$$

The values of $u_b^*(ijk)$ are given in Table 58.

The log-linear representation for $u_b^*(ijk)$ in terms of $v(ijk)$ is

$$\ln\frac{u_b^*(ijk)}{v(ijk)} = L + \tau_1 T_1(ijk) + \tau_2 T_2(ijk) + \tau_3 T_3(ijk) + \tau_4 T_4(ijk) + \tau_6 T_6(ijk) \quad (16)$$

Note that $\tau_5$ does not appear explicitly in (16). By using the log-linear representation for $v(ijk)$ itself, we also get the reparametrization or log-linear

TABLE 57

| Marginals fitted | Estimate | $\tau$ Parameters "inherited" from $v(ijk)$ |
|---|---|---|
| a) $y(i.k)$, $y(.jk)$ | $u_a^*(ijk)$ | $\tau_4$ |
| b) $y(ij.)$, $y(.jk)$ | $u_b^*(ijk)$ | $\tau_5$ |
| c) $y(ij.)$, $y(i.k)$ | $u_c^*(ijk)$ | $\tau_6$ |
| d) $y(.jk)$, $y(i..)$ | $u_d^*(ijk)$ | $\tau_4, \tau_5$ |
| e) $y(i.k)$, $y(.j.)$ | $u_e^*(ijk)$ | $\tau_4, \tau_6$ |
| f) $y(ij.)$, $y(..k)$ | $u_f^*(ijk)$ | $\tau_5, \tau_6$ |
| g) $y(i..)$, $y(.j.)$, $y(..k)$ | $u_g^*(ijk)$ | $\tau_4, \tau_5, \tau_6$ |

TABLE 58
Small Hospitals $u_b^*(ijk)$

| | Urban | | Rural | | |
|---|---|---|---|---|---|
| | Short | Long | Short | Long | |
| User | 28.810 | 1.190 | 10.917 | 0.083 | 41.000 |
| Nonuser | 79.190 | 14.810 | 114.083 | 3.917 | 212.000 |
| | 108.000 | 16.000 | 125.000 | 4.000 | 253.000 |

representation for $u_b^*(ijk)$ in terms of the uniform distribution

$$\ln \frac{u_b^*(ijk)}{n\pi(ijk)} = L + \tau_1 T_1(ijk) + \tau_2 T_2(ijk) + \tau_3 T_3(ijk)$$
$$+ \tau_4 T_4(ijk) + \tau_5 T_5(ijk) + \tau_6 T_6(ijk) \quad (17)$$

We remark that the numerical values of the $\tau$'s in (16) and (17) are not the same.

The log-odds or logits of the use of EDP for small hospitals may now be given by the parametric representation

$$\ln \frac{u_b^*(111)}{u_b^*(211)} = \tau_1 + \tau_4 + \tau_5$$
$$\ln \frac{u_b^*(112)}{u_b^*(212)} = \tau_1 + \tau_4 \qquad\qquad (18)$$
$$\ln \frac{u_b^*(121)}{u_b^*(221)} = \tau_1 \qquad + \tau_5$$
$$\ln \frac{u_b^*(122)}{u_b^*(222)} = \tau_1$$

where the values of the parameters in (18) are

$$\tau_1 = -3.8569, \qquad \tau_4 = 1.3354, \qquad \tau_5 = 1.5103$$

For the small hospitals we now have the associations

$$\tau_4 = \ln \frac{u_b^*(111)u_b^*(221)}{u_b^*(211)u_b^*(121)} = \ln \frac{u_b^*(112)u_b^*(222)}{u_b^*(212)u_b^*(122)} = 1.3354$$

and

$$\tau_5 = \ln \frac{u_b^*(111)u_b^*(212)}{u_b^*(211)u_b^*(112)} = \ln \frac{u_b^*(121)u_b^*(222)}{u_b^*(221)u_b^*(122)} = 1.5103$$

Note that $\tau_4$, the association between usage and location for the small hospitals, is still different from that for the large hospitals, but that the association between usage and stay, $\tau_5$, is now the same for both large and small hospitals.

TABLE 59

| Large hospitals | Factors | Small hospitals |
|---|---|---|
| $\ln \dfrac{x_2{}^*(111)}{x_2{}^*(211)} = 0.5374$ | Urban, short | $\ln \dfrac{u_b{}^*(111)}{u_b{}^*(211)} = -1.0111$ |
| $\ln \dfrac{x_2{}^*(121)}{x_2{}^*(221)} = 0.0262$ | Rural, short | $\ln \dfrac{u_b{}^*(121)}{u_b{}^*(221)} = -2.3466$ |
| $\ln \dfrac{x_2{}^*(112)}{x_2{}^*(212)} = -0.9729$ | Urban, long | $\ln \dfrac{u_b{}^*(112)}{u_b{}^*(212)} = -2.5214$ |
| $\ln \dfrac{x_2{}^*(122)}{x^*(222)} = -1.4841$ | Rural, long | $\ln \dfrac{u_b{}^*(122)}{u_b{}^*(222)} = -3.8569$ |

The results of arranging the log-odds of usage in descending order of magnitude within the large hospitals and within the small hospitals are presented in Table 59.

## Example 7. Partitioning Using OUTLIERS

Outliers are observations in one or more cells of a contingency table which apparently deviate significantly from a fitted model. These outliers may lead one to reject a model which fits the other observations.

In other cases, even though a model seems to fit, the outliers contribute much more than reasonable to the measure of deviation between the data and the fitted values of the model. In other words, the outliers make up a large percentage of the "unexplained variation" $2I(x:x^*)$.

A clue to possible outliers is provided by the output of the computer program. In the computer output for each estimate, five entries are listed for each cell. The fourth of these is titled OUTLIER and its numerical value provides a lower bound for the decrease in the corresponding $2I(x:x^*)$, if that cell were not included in the fitting procedure. Since the reduction in the degrees of freedom is $\leq 1$ for each omitted cell, values of OUTLIER greater than, say, 3.5 are of interest. The basis for the OUTLIER computation and interpretation follows. Let $x_a{}^*$ denote the minimum discrimination information estimate subject to certain marginal restraints. Let $x_b{}^*$ denote the minimum discrimination information estimate subject to the same marginal restraints as $x_a{}^*$ except that the value $x(\omega_1)$, say, is not included, so that $x_b{}^*(\omega_1) = x(\omega_1)$. The basic additivity property of the minimum discrimination information statistics states that

$$2I(x:x_a{}^*) = 2I(x_b{}^*:x_a{}^*) + 2I(x:x_b{}^*)$$

or

$$2I(x:x_a{}^*) - 2I(x:x_b{}^*) = 2I(x_b{}^*:x_a{}^*)$$

TABLE 60
Analysis of Information

| Component due to | Information | D.F. |
|---|---|---|
| $H_a$: | $2I(x:x_a{}^*)$ | $N_a$ |
| $H_b$: Same as $H_a$ but omitting $x(\omega_1)$ | $2I(x_b{}^*:x_a{}^*)$ | 1 |
| | $2I(x:x_b{}^*)$ | $N_b = N_a - 1$ |

These results are summarized in Table 60. But

$$2I(x_b{}^*:x_a{}^*) = 2\left(x_b{}^*(\omega_1)\ln\frac{x_b{}^*(\omega_1)}{x_a{}^*(\omega_1)} + \sum_{\Omega-\omega_1} x_b{}^*(\omega)\ln\frac{x_b{}^*(\omega)}{x_a{}^*(\omega)}\right)$$

$$= 2\left(x(\omega_1)\ln\frac{x(\omega_1)}{x_a{}^*(\omega_1)} + \sum_{\Omega-\omega_1} x_b{}^*(\omega)\ln\frac{x_b{}^*(\omega)}{x_a{}^*(\omega)}\right) \tag{19}$$

and using the convexity property which implies that

$$\sum_{\Omega-\omega_1} x_b{}^*(\omega)\ln\frac{x_b{}^*(\omega)}{x_a{}^*(\omega)} \geqq \left(\sum_{\Omega-\omega_1} x_b{}^*(\omega)\right)\ln\frac{\left(\sum_{\Omega-\omega_1} x_b{}^*(\omega)\right)}{\left(\sum_{\Omega-\omega_1} x_a{}^*(\omega)\right)}$$

$$= (n - x_b{}^*(\omega_1))\ln\frac{n - x_b{}^*(\omega_1)}{n - x_a{}^*(\omega_1)} \tag{20}$$

we get from (19) that

$$2I(x_b{}^*:x_a{}^*) \geqq 2\left(x(\omega_1)\ln\frac{x(\omega_1)}{x_a{}^*(\omega_1)} + \left(\sum_{\Omega-\omega_1} x_b{}^*(\omega)\right)\ln\frac{\left(\sum_{\Omega-\omega_1} x_b{}^*(\omega)\right)}{\left(\sum_{\Omega-\omega_1} x_a{}^*(\omega)\right)}\right)$$

$$= 2\left(x(\omega_1)\ln\frac{x(\omega_1)}{x_a{}^*(\omega_1)} + (n - x(\omega_1))\ln\frac{n - x(\omega_1)}{n - x_a{}^*(\omega_1)}\right) \tag{21}$$

The last value can be computed and is listed as the OUTLIER entry for each cell of the computer output for the estimate $x_a{}^*$.

The ratio

$$\frac{2I(x:x_a{}^*) - 2I(x:x_b{}^*)}{2I(x:x_a{}^*)} = \frac{2I(x_b{}^*:x_a{}^*)}{2I(x:x_a{}^*)}$$

then indicates the percentage of the "unexplained variation" due to the outlier value.

This property is also utilized in the next example. See Ireland [31] and Ireland and Kullback [4] for further discussion and application.

We shall use the OUTLIER feature of the CONTAB program to partition a 2 × 7 table into homogeneous segments.

Table 61a presents data on leukemia cases observed. Denoting the entries in the observed table by $x(ij)$, $i = 1, 2; j = 1, 2, \ldots, 7$, we first test whether the incidence of leukemia is homogeneous over the doses by fitting the marginals $x(i.)$, $x(.j)$. The corresponding output is shown in Table 62. We observe that large OUTLIER values are associated with values of $j = 1, 2, 6, 7$ and that $2I(x:x^*) = 44.65$, 6 D.F.

Since the doses are arranged on a scale, we repeat the process, omitting the cells corresponding to $x(ij)$, $i = 1, 2; j = 6, 7$. The corresponding output is shown in Table 63. We observe that a large OUTLIER value is associated with $j = 3$ and that $2I(x:x^*) = 18.92$, 4 D.F.

We continue the process using the original cells corresponding to $j = 3, 4, 5$. The computer output is given in Table 64. Now there are no large OUTLIER values and $2I(x:x^*) = 0.09$, 2 D.F. For the original cells with $j = 6, 7$ the computer output is given in Table 65, and again there are no large OUTLIERS and $2I(x:x^*) = 0.37$, 1 D.F. For the original cells with $j = 1, 2$ the computer output is given in Table 66, and again there are no large OUTLIERS and $2I(x:x^*) = 0.91$, 1 D.F.

We summarize in Table 67.

We now define an overall estimate by

$$x_e^*(ij) = x_d^*(ij), i = 1, 2; j = 1, 2$$
$$x_e^*(ij) = x_b^*(ij), i = 1, 2; j = 3, 4, 5$$
$$x_e^*(ij) = x_c^*(ij), i = 1, 2; j = 6, 7$$

and we have for the associated m.d.i. statistic

$$2I(x:x_e^*) = 1.364, 4 \text{ D.F.}$$

The values of $x_e^*(ij)$ are given in Table 61b.

The data of Table 61a comes from Sugiura and Otake [16]. We arrived at the same partitioning by a different approach.


## Example 8. Respiratory Data

This example deals with two three-way $9 \times 2 \times 2$ contingency tables which are essentially marginal tables of a higher dimensional table, not available to us, listing data on respiratory symptoms among a group of British coal miners. It illustrates the use of OUTLIER to partition second-order interaction in a three-way contingency table. Also illustrated are multivariate logit analysis and the relations among the parameters implied by logit linearity. The generalized iterative scaling algorithm of Darroch and Ratcliff [22] is used to obtain the m.d.i. estimates under the hypothesis of logit linearity.

The analyses progressively consider more complex hypotheses because of basic differences in certain properties of the two sets of data. Among other features the example illustrates a test of the hypothesis of no second-order interaction in a three-way contingency table, multivariate logit analysis, and the partitioning of second-order interaction in a three-way contingency table.

**TABLE 61a**

Number of Leukemia Cases Observed for the Period October 1, 1950 to September 30, 1966 among Hiroshima Male Survivors for the Extended Life Span Study Sample at ABCC Aged 15–19 at the Time of Atomic Bomb

| | Dose (rad) | | | | | | | |
| --- | --- | --- | --- | --- | --- | --- | --- | --- |
| | <5 | 5 | 20 | 50 | 100 | 200 | 300+ | Total |
| Leukemia | 2 | 0 | 3 | 2 | 2 | 2 | 5 | 16 |
| Not leukemia | 4601 | 1161 | 477 | 271 | 243 | 98 | 149 | 7000 |
| Total | 4603 | 1161 | 480 | 273 | 245 | 100 | 154 | 7016 |

**TABLE 61b**
Values of Estimate $x_e^*(ij)$

| | Dose (rad) | | | | | | | |
|---|---|---|---|---|---|---|---|---|
| | <5 | 5 | 20 | 50 | 100 | 200 | 300+ | Total |
| Leukemia | 1.597 | 0.404 | 3.367 | 1.915 | 1.718 | 2.756 | 4.244 | 16 |
| Not leukemia | 4601.398 | 1160.597 | 476.633 | 271.085 | 243.282 | 97.244 | 149.756 | 6999.995 |
| Total | 4602.995 | 1161.000 | 480.000 | 273.000 | 245.000 | 100.000 | 154.000 | 7015.995 |

**TABLE 62**
Cells 1–7

|   |           | 1 | 2 | 3 | 4 | 5 | 6 | 7 |
|---|-----------|---|---|---|---|---|---|---|
| 1 | Observed  | 2.000000   | 0.000001   | 3.000000   | 2.000000   | 2.000000   | 2.000000   | 5.000000   |
| 1 | Predicted | 10.497149  | 2.647662   | 1.094641   | 0.622577   | 0.558723   | 0.228050   | 0.351197   |
| 1 | Residual  | −8.497149  | −2.647661  | 1.905359   | 1.377422   | 1.441277   | 1.771950   | 4.648803   |
| 1 | OUTLIER   | 10.374859  | 5.284845   | 2.244734   | 1.917824   | 2.217709   | 5.146383   | 17.284038  |
| 1 | Log ratio | −2.683566  | −4.060993  | −4.944243  | −5.508558  | −5.616772  | −6.512859  | −6.081078  |
| 2 | Observed  | 4601.000000| 1161.000000| 477.000000 | 271.000000 | 243.000000 | 98.000000  | 149.000000 |
| 2 | Predicted | 4592.500000| 1158.352051| 478.905273 | 272.377197 | 244.441269 | 99.771927  | 153.648758 |
| 2 | Residual  | 8.500000   | 2.647949   | −1.905273  | −1.377197  | −1.441269  | −1.771927  | −4.648758  |
| 2 | OUTLIER   | 0.038748   | 0.013617   | 0.000460   | 0.005398   | 0.006474   | 0.023613   | 0.140827   |
| 2 | Log ratio | 3.397510   | 2.020083   | 1.136832   | 0.572518   | 0.464305   | −0.431783  | −0.000001  |

Sample size: 7016.000000

| Hypothesis | Nonzero effects | Smooth | Zero | $2I(x{:}x^*)$ | D.F. | Prob | $I^*$ | $IC^*$ |
|---|---|---|---|---|---|---|---|---|
| 1 | Marginals, resid-uals | 0.0000 | 0.000001 | 44.649 | 6 | 0.0000 | 0.00 | 0.00 |

OUTLIERS

| $i$ | $j$ |
|---|---|
| 1 | 1 |
| 1 | 2 |
| 1 | 6 |
| 1 | 7 |

CONTINGENCY TABLE ANALYSIS

**TABLE 63**
Cells 1-5

| | | 1 | 2 | 3 | 4 | 5 |
|---|---|---|---|---|---|---|
| 1 | Observed | 2.000000 | 0.000001 | 3.000000 | 2.000000 | 2.00000 |
| 1 | Predicted | 6.126442 | 1.545253 | 0.638864 | 0.363354 | 0.326087 |
| 1 | Residual | -4.126442 | -1.545252 | 2.361135 | 1.636645 | 1.673913 |
| 1 | OUTLIER | 3.771570 | 3.082119 | 4.561651 | 3.548321 | 3.911049 |
| 1 | Log ratio | -3.687312 | -5.064739 | -5.947989 | -6.512304 | -6.620519 |
| 2 | Observed | 4601.000000 | 1161.000000 | 477.000000 | 271.000000 | 243.000000 |
| 2 | Predicted | 4596.871094 | 1159.454834 | 479.361084 | 272.636475 | 244.673859 |
| 2 | Residual | 4.128906 | 1.545166 | -2.361084 | -1.636475 | -1.673859 |
| 2 | OUTLIER | 0.004099 | 0.005678 | 0.011730 | 0.004946 | 0.008045 |
| 2 | Log ratio | 2.933204 | 1.555779 | 0.672527 | 0.108213 | -0.000000 |

Sample size: 6762.000000

| Hypothesis | Nonzero effects | Smooth | Zero | $2I(x:x^*)$ | D.F. | Prob | $I^*$ | $IC^*$ |
|---|---|---|---|---|---|---|---|---|
| 2 | Marginals, residuals | 0.0000 | 0.000001 | 18.915 | 4 | 0.0008 | 0.00 | 0.00 |

$i$
$j$
OUTLIERS
1 3

**TABLE 64**
Original $j = 3, 4, 5$ Only

| | | | 1 | 2 | 3 |
|---|---|---|---|---|---|
| 1 | Observed | 1 | 3.000000 | 2.000000 | 2.000000 |
| 1 | Predicted | 2 | 3.366735 | 1.914830 | 1.718437 |
| 1 | Residual | 3 | −0.366735 | 0.085170 | 0.281563 |
| 1 | OUTLIER | 4 | 0.040434 | 0.004038 | 0.043937 |
| 1 | Log ratio | 5 | −4.280277 | −4.844592 | −4.952806 |
| 2 | Observed | 6 | 477.000000 | 271.000000 | 243.000000 |
| 2 | Predicted | 7 | 476.633301 | 271.085205 | 243.281601 |
| 2 | Residual | 8 | 0.366699 | −0.085205 | −0.281601 |
| 2 | OUTLIER | 9 | −0.000173 | −0.001247 | 0.000072 |
| 2 | Log ratio | 10 | 0.672526 | 0.108213 | −0.000001 |

Sample size: 998.000000

| Hypothesis | Nonzero effects | Smooth | Zero | $2I(x:x^*)$ | D.F. | Prob | $I^*$ | $IC^*$ |
|---|---|---|---|---|---|---|---|---|
| 3 | Marginals, residuals | 0.0000 | 0.000001 | 0.089 | 2 | 0.9566 | 0.00 | 0.00 |
| | $i$ | | | | | | | |
| | $j$ | | | | | | | |

**TABLE 65**
Original $j = 6, 7$ Only

| | | | 1 | 2 |
|---|---|---|---|---|
| 1 | Observed | 1 | 2.000000 | 5.000000 |
| 1 | Predicted | 2 | 2.755905 | 4.244093 |
| 1 | Residual | 3 | −0.755905 | 0.755907 |
| 1 | OUTLIER | 4 | 0.231305 | 0.129557 |
| 1 | Log ratio | 5 | −3.995261 | −3.563478 |
| 2 | Observed | 6 | 98.000000 | 149.000000 |
| 2 | Predicted | 7 | 97.244080 | 149.755875 |
| 2 | Residual | 8 | 0.755920 | −0.755875 |
| 2 | OUTLIER | 9 | 0.009494 | 0.009243 |
| 2 | Log ratio | 10 | −0.431783 | −0.000001 |

Sample size: 254.000000

| Hypothesis | Nonzero effects | Smooth | Zero | $2I(x:x^*)$ | D.F. | Prob | $I^*$ | $IC^*$ |
|---|---|---|---|---|---|---|---|---|
| 4 | Marginals, residuals | 0.0000 | 0.000001 | 0.366 | 1 | 0.5449 | 0.00 | 0.00 |
| | $i$ | | | | | | | |
| | $j$ | | | | | | | |

CONTINGENCY TABLE ANALYSIS

**TABLE 66**
Original $j = 1, 2$ Only

| | | 1 | 2 |
|---|---|---|---|
| 1 Observed | 1 | 2.000000 | 0.000001 |
| 1 Predicted | 2 | 1.597155 | 0.402845 |
| 1 Residual | 3 | 0.402845 | −0.402844 |
| 1 OUTLIER | 4 | 0.094638 | 0.802505 |
| 1 Log ratio | 5 | −6.588467 | −7.965894 |
| 2 Observed | 6 | 4601.000000 | 1161.000000 |
| 2 Predicted | 7 | 4601.398438 | 1160.596924 |
| 2 Residual | 8 | −0.398438 | 0.403076 |
| 2 OUTLIER | 9 | −0.000765 | 0.000905 |
| 2 Log ratio | 10 | 1.377425 | −0.000001 |

Sample size: 5764.000000

| Hypothesis | Nonzero effects | Smooth | Zero | $2I(x:x^*)$ | D.F. | Prob | $I^*$ | $IC^*$ |
|---|---|---|---|---|---|---|---|---|
| 5 | Marginals, residuals | 0.0000 | 0.000001 | 0.909 | 1 | 0.3405 | 0.00 | 0.00 |
| | $i$ | | | | | | | |
| | $j$ | | | | | | | |

The techniques are based on the principle of m.d.i. estimation, the associated log-linear representation, and analysis of information tables (see Ku *et al.* [57], Kullback [83, 84, 229, pp. 36–54, 155–186]). The computational procedures for this example utilized the Deming-Stephan iterative marginal fitting algorithm and its extension to general linear constraints by Darroch and Ratcliff [22]. Since our m.d.i. estimates are constrained to satisfy certain linear relations based on observed values, they are maximum likelihood estimates and the associated m.d.i. test statistics are log-likelihood ratio statistics. The log-linear model has been discussed in many papers and further references may be found in Dempster [42], Gokhale [46], Ku *et al.* [57], and Plackett [105].

In Grizzle [50] a model developed by Grizzle, Starmer, and Koch [96] is specialized to the case of fitting models to correlated logits. Grizzle [50, p. 1060] says, "Unfortunately a test of the goodness-of-fit of the logit model to the joint response data has not been developed." For its methodological interest, we first consider the problem as presented by Grizzle [50] from the m.d.i. estimation approach. Our results (maximum likelihood) are numerically in close agreement with those of Grizzle (BAN), but also include estimates of the cell entries under the logit model and a test of the goodness-of-fit to the joint response data.

In Table 68 is given a $9 \times 2 \times 2$ contingency table of coal miners classified as smokers without radiological pneumoconiosis, between the ages of 20 and 64 years inclusive at the time of their examination, showing the occurrence of breathlessness and wheeze over nine age groupings. We denote the observed

**TABLE 67**
Analysis of Information

| Component due to | Information | D.F. |
|---|---|---|
| Cells $j = 1, \ldots, 7$ | $2I(x:x^*) = 44.649$ | 6 |
| Omit cells $j = 6, 7$ | $2I(x_a^*:x^*) = 25.734$ | 2 |
| Cells $j = 1, \ldots, 5^a$ | $2I(x:x_a^*) = 18.915$ | 4 |
| Omit cells $j = 1, 2$ | $2I(x_b^*:x_a^*) = 18.826$ | 2 |
| Cells $j = 3, 4, 5^b$ | $2I(x:x_b^*) = 0.089$ | 2 |
| | $2I(x:x^*) = 44.649$ | 6 |
| Omit cells $j = 1, 2, 3, 4, 5$ | $2I(x_c^*:x^*) = 44.283$ | 5 |
| Cells $j = 6, 7^c$ | $2I(x:x_c^*) = 0.366$ | 1 |
| | $2I(x:x^*) = 44.649$ | 6 |
| Omit cells $j = 3, 4, 5, 6, 7$ | $2I(x_d^*:x^*) = 43.740$ | 5 |
| Cell $j = 1, 2^d$ | $2I(x:x_d^*) = 0.909$ | 1 |

$^a$ Note that $x_a^*(ij) = x(i.)x(.j)/n, i = 1, 2; j = 1, 2, \ldots, 5$
   $x_a^*(ij) = x(ij), i = 1, 2; j = 6, 7$
$^b$ Note that $x_b^*(ij) = x(i.)x(.j)/n, i = 1, 2; j = 3, 4, 5$
   $x_b^*(ij) = x(ij), i = 1, 2; j = 1, 2, 6, 7$
$^c$ Note that $x_c^*(ij) = x(i.)x(.j)/n, i = 1, 2; j = 6, 7$
   $x_c^*(ij) = x(ij), i = 1, 2; j = 1, 2, 3, 4, 5$
$^d$ Note that $x_d^*(ij) = x(i.)x(.j)/n, i = 1, 2; j = 1, 2,$
   $x_d^*(ij) = x(ij), i = 1, 2; j = 3, 4, 5, 6, 7$

**TABLE 68**
Number of Subjects Responding for the Two Symptoms in Terms of Age Group
[70]

| | | | $x(ijk)$ | | | | |
|---|---|---|---|---|---|---|---|
| Breathlessness: | | | Yes, $j = 1$ | | No, $j = 2$ | | |
| | Wheeze: | Yes, $k = 1$ | No, $k = 2$ | Yes, $k = 1$ | No, $k = 2$ | Total |
| Age groups | 1 | 20–24 | 9 | 7 | 95 | 1841 | 1952 |
| (years), | 2 | 25–29 | 23 | 9 | 105 | 1654 | 1791 |
| $i =$ | 3 | 30–34 | 54 | 19 | 177 | 1863 | 2113 |
| | 4 | 35–39 | 121 | 48 | 257 | 2357 | 2783 |
| | 5 | 40–44 | 169 | 54 | 273 | 1778 | 2274 |
| | 6 | 45–49 | 269 | 88 | 324 | 1712 | 2393 |
| | 7 | 50–54 | 404 | 117 | 245 | 1324 | 2090 |
| | 8 | 55–59 | 406 | 152 | 225 | 967 | 1750 |
| | 9 | 60–64 | 372 | 106 | 132 | 526 | 1136 |

frequency in any cell by $x(ijk)$ in Table 69. These data are discussed and analyzed from a different point of view by Ashford and Sowden [70] and Mantel and Brown [15].

A log-linear representation of the observed values $x(ijk)$ in Table 68 is given in columns 1–36 of Table 70. The representation in Table 70 is a graphic presentation of the design matrix of the complete log-linear regression

$$\ln \frac{x(ijk)}{n\pi(ijk)} = L + \tau_1^A T_1^A(ijk) + \cdots + \tau_8^A T_8^A(ijk) + \tau_1^B T_1^B(ijk) + \tau_1^W T_1^W(ijk)$$
$$+ \tau_{11}^{AB} T_{11}^{AB}(ijk) + \cdots + \tau_{81}^{AB} T_{81}^{AB}(ijk) + \tau_{11}^{AW} T_{11}^{AW}(ijk) + \cdots + \tau_{81}^{AW} T_{81}^{AW}(ijk)$$
$$+ \tau_{11}^{BW} T_{11}^{BW}(ijk) + \tau_{111}^{ABW} T_{111}^{ABW}(ijk) + \cdots + \tau_{811}^{ABW} T_{811}^{ABW}(ijk) \tag{22}$$

where $\Pi(ijk) = 1/9 \times 2 \times 2$, $n$ is the total number of observations, $L$ is a normalizing factor (the negative of the logarithm of a moment generating function), and the $T(ijk)$ are linearly independent indicator functions (explanatory variables) taking on the values given by the columns of Table 70 and whose mean values are the various marginals.

Since Grizzle [50] is concerned with the marginal logits of breathlessness and wheeze, this means implicitly that one is concerned with the m.d.i. estimate, or log-linear representation, obtained by fitting the marginals $x(ij.)$ and $x(i.k)$. If we denote this estimate by $x_d^*(ijk)$, then its log-linear representation or design matrix is given by columns 1–27 of Table 70. It may be verified that $x_d^*$ has the explicit form $x_d^*(ijk) = x(ij.)x(i.k)/x(i..)$ and consequently we have the marginal logits

$$\ln \frac{x_d^*(i1k)}{x_d^*(i2k)} = \ln \frac{x(i1.)x(i.k)x(i..)}{x(i..)x(i2.)x(i.k)} = \ln \frac{x(i1.)}{x(i2.)} \quad \text{(breathlessness)}$$

$$\ln \frac{x_d^*(ij1)}{x_d^*(ij2)} = \ln \frac{x(ij.)x(i.1)x(i..)}{x(i..)x(ij.)x(i.2)} = \ln \frac{x(i.1)}{x(i.2)} \quad \text{(wheeze)}$$

The values of $\ln (x(i1.)/x(i2.))$ and $\ln (x(i.1)/x(i.2))$ are given in Grizzle [50, p. 1060] and the values of $x_d^*(ijk)$ are given in Table 71.

From Table 70 we have the parametric representation

$$\ln \frac{x_d^*(i1k)}{x_d^*(i2k)} = \tau_1^B + \tau_{i1}^{AB}; \quad \ln \frac{x_d^*(ij1)}{x_d^*(ij2)} = \tau_1^W + \tau_{i1}^{AW}, \quad i = 1, 2, \ldots, 8$$

$$\ln \frac{x_d^*(91k)}{x_d^*(92k)} = \tau_1^B; \quad \ln \frac{x_d^*(9j1)}{x_d^*(9j2)} = \tau_1^W$$

**TABLE 69**

| Variable | | Index | 1 | 2 | 3 | 4 | . . . | 9 |
|---|---|---|---|---|---|---|---|---|
| Age group | A | i | 20–24 | 25–29 | 30–34 | 35–39 | . . . | 60–64 |
| Breathlessness | B | j | Yes | No | | | | |
| Wheeze | W | k | Yes | No | | | | |

The values of the parameters in the parametric representation of the logits are

$$\tau_1^B = -0.3196, \qquad \tau_1^W = -0.2263, \qquad \text{and those of Table 72}$$

In particular, Grizzle's objective was to calculate two lines relating the marginal logits to age, that is, to estimate and test the hypothesis

$$\ln \frac{x_d^*(i1k)}{x_d^*(i2k)} = \alpha_1 + i\beta_1; \qquad \ln \frac{x_d^*(ij1)}{x_d^*(ij2)} = \alpha_2 + i\beta_2, \qquad i = 1, \ldots, 9$$

But this hypothesis implies that the first-order differences in logits across age groups are constant, or, in view of the parametric representation, that the first-order differences in the effect parameters are constant. These chains of equalities permit us to express the parameters $\tau_{i1}^{AB}$, $\tau_{i1}^{AW}$ in terms of $\tau_{11}^{AB}$ and $\tau_{11}^{AW}$ as

$$\tau_{i1}^{AB} = \frac{9-i}{8} \tau_{11}^{AB}, \qquad \tau_{i1}^{AW} = \frac{9-i}{8} \tau_{11}^{AW}, \qquad i = 1, \ldots, 8$$

These relations among the parameters mean that in the log-linear representation the terms

$$\cdots \tau_{11}^{AB} T_{11}^{AB}(ijk) + \tau_{21}^{AB} T_{21}^{AB}(ijk) + \cdots + \tau_{81}^{AB} T_{81}^{AB}(ijk) \cdots$$

reduce to

$$\tau_{11}^{AB}(T_{11}^{AB}(ijk) + \tfrac{7}{8}T_{21}^{AB}(ijk) + \tfrac{6}{8}T_{31}^{AB}(ijk) + \cdots + \tfrac{1}{8}T_{81}^{AB}(ijk))$$

and the terms

$$\cdots \tau_{11}^{AW} T_{11}^{AW}(ijk) + \tau_{21}^{AW} T_{21}^{AW}(ijk) + \cdots + \tau_{81}^{AW} T_{81}^{AW}(ijk) \cdots$$

reduce to

$$\tau_{11}^{AW}(T_{11}^{AW}(ijk) + \tfrac{7}{8}T_{21}^{AW}(ijk) + \tfrac{6}{8}T_{31}^{AW}(ijk) + \cdots + \tfrac{1}{8}T_{81}^{AW}(ijk))$$

If we denote the estimate satisfying logit linearity by $x_m^*$, then its design matrix or log-linear representation is given by columns 1–11, 37, 38 of Table 70, where we use $\tau^{AB}$ and $\tau^{AW}$, respectively, instead of $\tau_{11}^{AB}$ and $\tau_{11}^{AW}$.

The values of $x_m^*$ were determined using the generalized iterative scaling procedure of Darroch and Ratcliff [22] subject to the constraints

$$x_m^*(i..) = x(i..), \qquad x_m^*(.j.) = x(.j.), \qquad x_m^*(..k) = x(..k)$$

$$\sum_{i=1}^{8} \frac{9-i}{8} x_m^*(i1.) = \sum_{i=1}^{8} \frac{9-i}{8} x(i1.), \qquad \sum_{i=1}^{8} \frac{9-i}{8} x_m^*(i.1) = \sum_{i=1}^{8} \frac{9-i}{8} x(i.1)$$

The values of $x_m^*(ijk)$ are given in Table 73. The values of the $\tau$ parameters appearing in the linear model of the logits are

$$\tau_1^B = -0.2098, \qquad \tau^{AB} = -4.0996, \qquad \tau_1^W = -0.1841, \qquad \tau^{AW} = -2.6068$$

The corresponding values of the logit representation in terms of the $\alpha$'s and $\beta$'s

# CONTINGENCY TABLE ANALYSIS

**TABLE 70**

| $i$ | $j$ | $k$ | 1 $L$ | 2 $\tau_1^A$ | 3 $\tau_2^A$ | 4 $\tau_3^A$ | 5 $\tau_4^A$ | 6 $\tau_5^A$ | 7 $\tau_6^A$ | 8 $\tau_7^A$ | 9 $\tau_8^A$ | 10 $\tau_1^B$ | 11 $\tau_1^W$ | 12 $\tau_{11}^{AB}$ | 13 $\tau_{21}^{AB}$ | 14 $\tau_{31}^{AB}$ | 15 $\tau_{41}^{AB}$ | 16 $\tau_{51}^{AB}$ | 17 $\tau_{61}^{AB}$ | 18 $\tau_{71}^{AB}$ |
|---|---|---|---|---|---|---|---|---|---|---|---|---|---|---|---|---|---|---|---|---|
| 1 | 1 | 1 | 1 | 1 |  |  |  |  |  |  |  | 1 | 1 | 1 |  |  |  |  |  |  |
| 1 | 1 | 2 | 1 | 1 |  |  |  |  |  |  |  | 1 |  | 1 |  |  |  |  |  |  |
| 1 | 2 | 1 | 1 | 1 |  |  |  |  |  |  |  |  | 1 |  |  |  |  |  |  |  |
| 1 | 2 | 2 | 1 | 1 |  |  |  |  |  |  |  |  |  |  |  |  |  |  |  |  |
| 2 | 1 | 1 | 1 |  | 1 |  |  |  |  |  |  | 1 | 1 |  | 1 |  |  |  |  |  |
| 2 | 1 | 2 | 1 |  | 1 |  |  |  |  |  |  | 1 |  |  | 1 |  |  |  |  |  |
| 2 | 2 | 1 | 1 |  | 1 |  |  |  |  |  |  |  | 1 |  |  |  |  |  |  |  |
| 2 | 2 | 2 | 1 |  | 1 |  |  |  |  |  |  |  |  |  |  |  |  |  |  |  |
| 3 | 1 | 1 | 1 |  |  | 1 |  |  |  |  |  | 1 | 1 |  |  | 1 |  |  |  |  |
| 3 | 1 | 2 | 1 |  |  | 1 |  |  |  |  |  | 1 |  |  |  | 1 |  |  |  |  |
| 3 | 2 | 1 | 1 |  |  | 1 |  |  |  |  |  |  | 1 |  |  |  |  |  |  |  |
| 3 | 2 | 2 | 1 |  |  | 1 |  |  |  |  |  |  |  |  |  |  |  |  |  |  |
| 4 | 1 | 1 | 1 |  |  |  | 1 |  |  |  |  | 1 | 1 |  |  |  | 1 |  |  |  |
| 4 | 1 | 2 | 1 |  |  |  | 1 |  |  |  |  | 1 |  |  |  |  | 1 |  |  |  |
| 4 | 2 | 1 | 1 |  |  |  | 1 |  |  |  |  |  | 1 |  |  |  |  |  |  |  |
| 4 | 2 | 2 | 1 |  |  |  | 1 |  |  |  |  |  |  |  |  |  |  |  |  |  |
| 5 | 1 | 1 | 1 |  |  |  |  | 1 |  |  |  | 1 | 1 |  |  |  |  | 1 |  |  |
| 5 | 1 | 2 | 1 |  |  |  |  | 1 |  |  |  | 1 |  |  |  |  |  | 1 |  |  |
| 5 | 2 | 1 | 1 |  |  |  |  | 1 |  |  |  |  | 1 |  |  |  |  |  |  |  |
| 5 | 2 | 2 | 1 |  |  |  |  | 1 |  |  |  |  |  |  |  |  |  |  |  |  |
| 6 | 1 | 1 | 1 |  |  |  |  |  | 1 |  |  | 1 | 1 |  |  |  |  |  | 1 |  |
| 6 | 1 | 2 | 1 |  |  |  |  |  | 1 |  |  | 1 |  |  |  |  |  |  | 1 |  |
| 6 | 2 | 1 | 1 |  |  |  |  |  | 1 |  |  |  | 1 |  |  |  |  |  |  |  |
| 6 | 2 | 2 | 1 |  |  |  |  |  | 1 |  |  |  |  |  |  |  |  |  |  |  |
| 7 | 1 | 1 | 1 |  |  |  |  |  |  | 1 |  | 1 | 1 |  |  |  |  |  |  | 1 |
| 7 | 1 | 2 | 1 |  |  |  |  |  |  | 1 |  | 1 |  |  |  |  |  |  |  | 1 |
| 7 | 2 | 1 | 1 |  |  |  |  |  |  | 1 |  |  | 1 |  |  |  |  |  |  |  |
| 7 | 2 | 2 | 1 |  |  |  |  |  |  | 1 |  |  |  |  |  |  |  |  |  |  |
| 8 | 1 | 1 | 1 |  |  |  |  |  |  |  | 1 | 1 | 1 |  |  |  |  |  |  |  |
| 8 | 1 | 2 | 1 |  |  |  |  |  |  |  | 1 | 1 |  |  |  |  |  |  |  |  |
| 8 | 2 | 1 | 1 |  |  |  |  |  |  |  | 1 |  | 1 |  |  |  |  |  |  |  |
| 8 | 2 | 2 | 1 |  |  |  |  |  |  |  | 1 |  |  |  |  |  |  |  |  |  |
| 9 | 1 | 1 | 1 |  |  |  |  |  |  |  |  | 1 | 1 |  |  |  |  |  |  |  |
| 9 | 1 | 2 | 1 |  |  |  |  |  |  |  |  | 1 |  |  |  |  |  |  |  |  |
| 9 | 2 | 1 | 1 |  |  |  |  |  |  |  |  |  | 1 |  |  |  |  |  |  |  |
| 9 | 2 | 2 | 1 |  |  |  |  |  |  |  |  |  |  |  |  |  |  |  |  |  |

Log-Linear Representation

| 19 $\tau^{AB}_{81}$ | 20 $\tau^{AW}_{11}$ | 21 $\tau^{AW}_{21}$ | 22 $\tau^{AW}_{31}$ | 23 $\tau^{AW}_{41}$ | 24 $\tau^{AW}_{51}$ | 25 $\tau^{AW}_{61}$ | 26 $\tau^{AW}_{71}$ | 27 $\tau^{AW}_{81}$ | 28 $\tau^{BW}_{11}$ | 29 $\tau^{ABW}_{111}$ | 30 $\tau^{ABW}_{211}$ | 31 $\tau^{ABW}_{311}$ | 32 $\tau^{ABW}_{411}$ | 33 $\tau^{ABW}_{511}$ | 34 $\tau^{ABW}_{611}$ | 35 $\tau^{ABW}_{711}$ | 36 $\tau^{ABW}_{811}$ | 37 $\tau^{AB}$ | 38 $\tau^{AW}$ | 39 $\tau^{ABW}$ |
|---|---|---|---|---|---|---|---|---|---|---|---|---|---|---|---|---|---|---|---|---|
|  | 1 |  |  |  |  |  |  |  | 1 | 1 |  |  |  |  |  |  |  | 1 | 1 | 1 |
|  | 1 |  |  |  |  |  |  |  |  |  |  |  |  |  |  |  |  | 1 | 1 |  |
|  |  | 1 |  |  |  |  |  |  | 1 |  | 1 |  |  |  |  |  |  | $\frac{7}{8}$ | $\frac{7}{8}$ | 1 |
|  |  | 1 |  |  |  |  |  |  |  |  |  |  |  |  |  |  |  | $\frac{7}{8}$ | $\frac{7}{8}$ |  |
|  |  |  | 1 |  |  |  |  |  | 1 |  |  | 1 |  |  |  |  |  | $\frac{6}{8}$ | $\frac{6}{8}$ | 1 |
|  |  |  | 1 |  |  |  |  |  |  |  |  |  |  |  |  |  |  | $\frac{6}{8}$ | $\frac{6}{8}$ |  |
|  |  |  |  | 1 |  |  |  |  | 1 |  |  |  | 1 |  |  |  |  | $\frac{5}{8}$ | $\frac{5}{8}$ | 1 |
|  |  |  |  | 1 |  |  |  |  |  |  |  |  |  |  |  |  |  | $\frac{5}{8}$ | $\frac{5}{8}$ |  |
|  |  |  |  |  | 1 |  |  |  | 1 |  |  |  |  | 1 |  |  |  | $\frac{4}{8}$ | $\frac{4}{8}$ | 1 |
|  |  |  |  |  | 1 |  |  |  |  |  |  |  |  |  |  |  |  | $\frac{4}{8}$ | $\frac{4}{8}$ |  |
|  |  |  |  |  |  | 1 |  |  | 1 |  |  |  |  |  | 1 |  |  | $\frac{3}{8}$ | $\frac{3}{8}$ | 1 |
|  |  |  |  |  |  | 1 |  |  |  |  |  |  |  |  |  |  |  | $\frac{3}{8}$ | $\frac{3}{8}$ |  |
|  |  |  |  |  |  |  | 1 |  | 1 |  |  |  |  |  |  | 1 |  | $\frac{2}{8}$ | $\frac{2}{8}$ | 1 |
|  |  |  |  |  |  |  | 1 |  |  |  |  |  |  |  |  |  |  | $\frac{2}{8}$ | $\frac{2}{8}$ |  |
| 1 |  |  |  |  |  |  |  | 1 | 1 |  |  |  |  |  |  |  | 1 | $\frac{1}{8}$ | $\frac{1}{8}$ | 1 |
| 1 |  |  |  |  |  |  |  | 1 |  |  |  |  |  |  |  |  |  | $\frac{1}{8}$ | $\frac{1}{8}$ |  |
|  |  |  |  |  |  |  |  |  | 1 |  |  |  |  |  |  |  |  |  |  |  |

## CONTINGENCY TABLE ANALYSIS

### TABLE 71

| | | $x_d{}^*(ijk)$ | | |
| | $j = 1$ | | $j = 2$ | |
| $i$ | $k = 1$ | $k = 2$ | $k = 1$ | $k = 2$ |
|---|---|---|---|---|
| 1 | 0.852 | 15.148 | 103.147 | 1832.851 |
| 2 | 2.287 | 29.713 | 125.713 | 1633.287 |
| 3 | 7.981 | 65.019 | 223.019 | 1816.980 |
| 4 | 22.954 | 146.046 | 355.045 | 2258.954 |
| 5 | 43.345 | 179.655 | 398.655 | 1652.344 |
| 6 | 88.467 | 268.533 | 504.533 | 1531.466 |
| 7 | 161.784 | 359.215 | 487.216 | 1081.784 |
| 8 | 201.199 | 356.801 | 429.801 | 762.198 |
| 9 | 212.070 | 265.929 | 291.929 | 366.070 |

as used by Grizzle [50] are obtained from

$$\begin{cases} \alpha_1 + 9\beta_1 = \tau_1{}^B \\ \alpha_1 + \beta_1 = \tau_1{}^B + \tau^{AB} \end{cases} \qquad \begin{cases} \alpha_2 + 9\beta_2 = \tau_1{}^W \\ \alpha_2 + \beta_2 = \tau_1{}^W + \tau^{AW} \end{cases}$$

or

$$\alpha_1 = -4.8219, \qquad \beta_1 = 0.5125, \qquad \alpha_2 = -3.1167, \qquad \beta_2 = 0.3259$$

We also note that

$$\text{Var}(\alpha_1) = \text{Var}(\tau_1{}^B) + (\tfrac{81}{64})\text{Var}(\tau^{AB}) + (\tfrac{18}{8})\text{Cov}(\tau_1{}^B, \tau^{AB})$$

$$\text{Var}(\beta_1) = (\tfrac{1}{64})\text{Var}(\tau^{AB})$$

$$\text{Var}(\alpha_2) = \text{Var}(\tau_1{}^W) + (\tfrac{81}{64})\text{Var}(\tau^{AW}) + (\tfrac{18}{8})\text{Cov}(\tau_1{}^W, \tau^{AW})$$

$$\text{Var}(\beta_2) = (\tfrac{1}{64})\text{Var}(\tau^{AW})$$

### TABLE 72

| $i$ | $\tau_{i1}^{AB}$ | $\tau_{i1}^{AW}$ |
|---|---|---|
| 1 | −4.4762 | −2.6512 |
| 2 | −3.6872 | −2.3380 |
| 3 | −3.0106 | −1.8714 |
| 4 | −2.4191 | −1.6241 |
| 5 | −1.8993 | −1.1955 |
| 6 | −1.4214 | −0.8840 |
| 7 | −0.7828 | −0.5713 |
| 8 | −0.4394 | −0.3466 |
| 9 | 0 | 0 |

TABLE 73

| | $x_m^*(ijk)$ | | | |
| | $j = 1$ | | $j = 2$ | |
| $i$ | $k = 1$ | $k = 2$ | $k = 1$ | $k = 2$ |
|---|---|---|---|---|
| 1 | 1.497 | 24.391 | 111.365 | 1814.747 |
| 2 | 3.079 | 36.225 | 137.235 | 1614.459 |
| 3 | 8.037 | 68.253 | 214.554 | 1822.152 |
| 4 | 22.967 | 140.816 | 367.283 | 2251.931 |
| 5 | 39.612 | 175.330 | 379.461 | 1679.595 |
| 6 | 84.650 | 270.466 | 485.742 | 1552.140 |
| 7 | 142.437 | 328.542 | 489.605 | 1129.413 |
| 8 | 214.641 | 357.415 | 441.955 | 735.987 |
| 9 | 230.975 | 277.656 | 284.884 | 342.486 |

The variance-covariance matrix of the $\tau$'s for $x_m^*$ is obtained as follows (a weighted version of the procedure used in Kullback [229, p. 217]). Compute $\mathbf{S} = \mathbf{T'DT}$ where $\mathbf{T}$ is the design matrix for the log-linear representation of $x_m^*$ (columns 1–11, 37, 38 of Table 70), and $\mathbf{D}$ is a diagonal matrix whose entries are the values of $x_m^*(ijk)$ in the order of the rows of the design matrix. Partition the matrix $\mathbf{S}$ as

$$\begin{pmatrix} \mathbf{S}_{11} & \mathbf{S}_{12} \\ \mathbf{S}_{21} & \mathbf{S}_{22} \end{pmatrix}$$

where $\mathbf{S}_{11}$ is $1 \times 1$. Then the variance-covariance matrix of the $\tau$'s is $(\mathbf{S}_{22} - \mathbf{S}_{21}\mathbf{S}_{11}^{-1}\mathbf{S}_{12})^{-1}$.

For comparison we list the values as given by Grizzle [50] and as computed from $x_m^*$ in Table 74.

The associated analysis of information Table 75 provides a basis for tests of significance and goodness-of-fit.

We infer from $2I(x:x_m^*)$ and $2I(x:x_d^*)$ that neither $x_m^*$ or $x_d^*$ is a good estimate for the joint response data, that is, $2I(x:x_m^*)(2I(x:x_d^*))$ is a measure of the goodness-of-fit of the linear logit model (marginal logit model) to the joint

TABLE 74

| | Grizzle [50] | $x_m^*$ |
|---|---|---|
| $\alpha_1$: | $-4.8174 \pm 0.0848$ | $-4.8219 \pm 0.0835$ |
| $\beta_1$: | $0.5123 \pm 0.0124$ | $0.5125 \pm 0.0129$ |
| $\alpha_2$: | $-3.1135 \pm 0.0558$ | $-3.1167 \pm 0.0549$ |
| $\beta_2$: | $0.3253 \pm 0.0090$ | $0.3258 \pm 0.0089$ |

**TABLE 75**
Analysis of Information

| Component due to | Information | D.F. |
|---|---|---|
| Interaction (linear logit model) | $2I(x:x_m{}^*) = 3077.154$ | 23 |
| Effect | $2I(x_d{}^*:x_m{}^*) = 25.300$ | 14 |
| Interaction (marginal logits) | $2I(x:x_d{}^*) = 3051.854$ | 9 |

response data. $2I(x_d{}^*:x_m{}^*)$ is a measure of the effect of the relationship among the parameters $\tau_{11}^{AB}, \tau_{21}^{AB}, \ldots, \tau_{81}^{AB}$ and $\tau_{11}^{AW}, \tau_{21}^{AW}, \ldots, \tau_{81}^{AW}$ of $x_d{}^*(ijk)$ implied by the hypothesis of logit linearity. We remark that $x_m{}^*$ and $x_d{}^*$ correspond respectively to model 3 and 8 of Mantel and Brown [15].

We shall return to the question of finding a model providing an acceptable fit to the joint response data of Table 68 after considering data giving the prevalence of persistent cough and persistent phlegm among the same group of miners.

In Table 76 is given a $9 \times 2 \times 2$ cross-classification of the same miners as in Table 68, but showing the combined prevalence of persistent cough and persistent phlegm. We denote the observed frequency in any cell by $x(ijk)$ in Table 77.

Since Table 76 has the same dimensions as Table 68, the design matrix and log-linear representation in Table 70 and the log-linear regression (22) for the

**TABLE 76**
Combined Prevalence of Persistent Cough and Persistent Phlegm in British Coal Miners in Terms of Age—All Smokers without Pneumoconiosis [69]

| | | | $x(ijk)$ | | | |
|---|---|---|---|---|---|---|
| | Cough: | | Yes, $j = 1$ | | No, $j = 2$ | |
| | Phlegm: | | Yes, $k = 1$ | No, $k = 2$ | Yes, $k = 1$ | No, $k = 2$ | Total |
| Age groups | 1 | 20–24 | 77 | 29 | 66 | 1,780 | 1,952 |
| (years), | 2 | 25–29 | 89 | 40 | 64 | 1,598 | 1,791 |
| $i =$ | 3 | 30–34 | 145 | 75 | 80 | 1,813 | 2,113 |
| | 4 | 35–39 | 237 | 101 | 107 | 2,338 | 2,783 |
| | 5 | 40–44 | 282 | 116 | 82 | 1,794 | 2,274 |
| | 6 | 45–49 | 373 | 152 | 99 | 1,769 | 2,393 |
| | 7 | 50–54 | 430 | 158 | 95 | 1,407 | 2,090 |
| | 8 | 55–59 | 445 | 122 | 88 | 1,095 | 1,750 |
| | 9 | 60–64 | 321 | 87 | 61 | 667 | 1,136 |
| | | | 2399 | 880 | 742 | 14,261 | 18,282 |

## TABLE 77

| Variable | | Index | 1 | 2 | 3 | 4 | ... | 9 |
|---|---|---|---|---|---|---|---|---|
| Age group | $A$ | $i$ | 20–24 | 25–29 | 30–34 | 35–39 | ... | 60–64 |
| Cough | $C$ | $j$ | Yes | No | | | | |
| Phlegm | $P$ | $k$ | Yes | No | | | | |

$x(ijk)$ values of Table 68 will be the same for the $x(ijk)$ of Table 76 with the replacement of the superscripts $B$, $W$ by $C$, $P$, respectively.

To determine the significance of effects and whether or not there is second-order interaction, we fit a sequence of nested models based on the marginals

$$H_a: \quad x(i..), \; x(.jk)$$
$$H_b: \quad x(.jk), \; x(ij.)$$
$$H_c: \quad x(.jk), \; x(ij.), \; x(i.k)$$

and denote the corresponding m.d.i. estimates by $x_a^*$, $x_b^*$, $x_c^*$, respectively. We note that $x_a^*$ and $x_b^*$ have the explicit form $x_a^*(ijk) = x(i..)x(.jk)/n$, $x_b^*(ijk) = x(ij.)x(.jk)/x(.j.)$, but $x_c^*$ cannot be explicitly represented as a product of marginals. $H_a$ is the null hypothesis that the incidence of cough and phlegm is homogeneous over the age groups. $H_b$ is the null hypothesis that the incidence of phlegm is homogeneous over the age groups given the incidence of cough. $H_c$ is the null hypothesis of no second-order interaction. The columns of Table 70 implied for the design matrix or log-linear representation of the three models are

$$H_a: \quad 1\text{–}11, \; 28$$
$$H_b: \quad 1\text{–}19, \; 28$$
$$H_c: \quad 1\text{–}28$$

The hypotheses may also be stated as implying that the parameters corresponding to the columns of Table 70 not used in the design matrix or for the representation are zero. Table 77a summarizes the results.

From Table 77a we infer that the 8 interaction parameters corresponding to columns 29–36 of Table 70 may be taken as zero. From Table 70 we see that the parametric representation of the log-odds or logits under the model of no second-

## TABLE 77a
### Analysis of Information

| Component due to | Information | D.F. |
|---|---|---|
| a)  $x(i..), \; x(.jk)$ | $2I(x:x_a^*) = 1259.090$ | 24 |
| b)  $x(.jk), \; x(ij.)$ | $2I(x_b^*:x_a^*) = 1180.385$ | 8 |
| | $2I(x:x_b^*) = 78.705$ | 16 |
| c)  $x(.jk), \; x(ij.), \; x(i.k)$ | $2I(x_c^*:x_b^*) = 72.009$ | 8 |
| | $2I(x:x_c^*) = 6.696$ | 8 |

order interaction are

$$\ln \frac{x_c^*(i11)}{x_c^*(i21)} = \tau_1{}^C + \tau_{i1}^{AC} + \tau_{11}^{CP}$$

$$\ln \frac{x_c^*(i12)}{x_c^*(i22)} = \tau_1{}^C + \tau_{i1}^{AC}$$

$$\ln \frac{x_c^*(i11)}{x_c^*(i12)} = \tau_1{}^P + \tau_{i1}^{AP} + \tau_{11}^{CP}$$

$$\ln \frac{x_c^*(i21)}{x_c^*(i22)} = \tau_1{}^P + \tau_{i1}^{AP}, \qquad i = 1, 2, \ldots, 9$$

The values of $x_c^*$ are given in Table 78.

The values of the parameters in the parametric representation of the logits are

$$\tau_1{}^C = -2.0987, \qquad \tau_1{}^P = -2.4756, \qquad \tau_{11}^{CP} = 3.8500, \qquad \text{and those of Table 79}$$

The covariance matrix of these 19 parameters has been computed, but is not given herein.

We mention, however, that the variance of $\tau_{11}^{CP}$ is 0.003116 so that

$$\chi^2 = (3.85)^2/0.003116 = 4756.90$$

is approximately a chi-squared with one degree of freedom. We see in Table 80 a verification of the fact that the association parameter $\tau_{11}^{CP}$ is very significantly different from zero.

We remark that $H_e$: $x(ij.)$, $x(i.k)$ represents the model that cough and phlegm are not associated given the age grouping. The corresponding estimate may be explicitly represented as

$$x_e^*(ijk) = x(ij.)x(i.k)/x(i..)$$

TABLE 78

| | | | $x_c^*$ | |
| | | j = 1 | | j = 2 |
| i | k = 1 | k = 2 | k = 1 | k = 2 |
|---|---|---|---|---|
| 1 | 69.919 | 36.096 | 73.078 | 1772.902 |
| 2 | 85.750 | 43.272 | 67.248 | 1594.727 |
| 3 | 147.105 | 72.942 | 77.893 | 1815.057 |
| 4 | 233.341 | 104.742 | 110.657 | 2334.258 |
| 5 | 276.957 | 121.121 | 87.043 | 1788.881 |
| 6 | 376.455 | 148.600 | 95.546 | 1772.402 |
| 7 | 437.482 | 150.460 | 87.521 | 1414.543 |
| 8 | 446.480 | 120.414 | 86.522 | 1096.588 |
| 9 | 325.511 | 82.354 | 56.491 | 671.648 |

**TABLE 79**

| $i$ | $\tau_{i1}^{AC}$ | $\tau_{i1}^{AP}$ |
|---|---|---|
| 1 | $-1.7955$ | $-0.7132$ |
| 2 | $-1.5083$ | $-0.6904$ |
| 3 | $-1.1155$ | $-0.6729$ |
| 4 | $-1.0052$ | $-0.5734$ |
| 5 | $-0.5939$ | $-0.5473$ |
| 6 | $-0.3801$ | $-0.4448$ |
| 7 | $-0.1422$ | $-0.3070$ |
| 8 | $-0.1103$ | $-0.0639$ |
| 9 | $0$ | $0$ |

$2I(x_c^* : x_e^*)$ tests the null hypothesis that $\tau_{11}^{CP} = 0$ and the value of $2I(x : x_c^*) = 6.696$, 8 D.F. implies that the association between cough and phlegm has the same value over all the age groupings.

We now examine the hypothesis that the logits of $x_c^*$ vary linearly with age, that is, that successive differences of the logits are constant. As before we can express the parameters $\tau_{i1}^{AC}$, $\tau_{i1}^{AP}$ under this hypothesis in terms of $\tau_{11}^{AC}$ and $\tau_{11}^{AP}$ as

$$H_n: \quad \tau_{i1}^{AC} = \frac{9 - i}{8} \tau_{11}^{AC}, \qquad \tau_{i1}^{AP} = \frac{9 - i}{8} \tau_{11}^{AP}, \qquad i = 1, \ldots, 8$$

If we denote the estimate satisfying logit linearity within the model of no second-order interaction by $x_n^*$, then the design matrix or log-linear representation corresponding to $H_n$ is given by columns 1–11, 28, 37, 38 of Table 70 with, of course, the replacement of the superscripts $B$, $W$ by $C$, $P$, respectively, and the use of $\tau^{AC}$, $\tau^{AP}$ instead of $\tau_{11}^{AC}$, $\tau_{11}^{AP}$, respectively, for convenience.

The values of $x_n^*$ are given in Table 81. The values of the parameters in the logit representation under the logit linearity model,

$$\ln \frac{x_n^*(i11)}{x_n^*(i21)} = \tau_1^C + \frac{9 - i}{8} \tau^{AC} + \tau_{11}^{CP}$$

$$\ln \frac{x_n^*(i12)}{x_n^*(i22)} = \tau_1^C + \frac{9 - i}{8} \tau^{AC}$$

$$\ln \frac{x_n^*(i11)}{x_n^*(i12)} = \tau_1^P + \frac{9 - i}{8} \tau^{AP} + \tau_{11}^{CP}$$

$$\ln \frac{x_n^*(i21)}{x_n^*(i22)} = \tau_1^P + \frac{9 - i}{8} \tau^{AP}$$

are

$$\tau_1^C = -1.8939, \qquad \tau_1^P = -2.5495$$
$$\tau^{AC} = -1.8312, \qquad \tau^{AP} = -0.7646, \qquad \tau_{11}^{CP} = 3.8442$$

**TABLE 80**
Analysis of Information

| Component due to | Information | D.F. |
|---|---|---|
| e) $x(ij.)$, $x(i.k)$ | $2I(x:x_e{}^*) = 6273.746$ | 9 |
| c) $x(ij.)$, $x(i.k)$, $x(.jk)$ | $2I(x_c{}^*:x_e{}^*) = 6267.050$ | 1 |
| | $2I(x:x_c{}^*) = 6.696$ | 8 |

The covariance matrix of these five parameters is given in Table 82. The associated analysis of information is given in Table 83.

The value $2I(x:x_n{}^*)$ is a measure of the goodness-of-fit of the logit linearity model and $2I(x_c{}^*:x_n{}^*)$ is a measure of the effect of replacing the common parameters $\tau^{AC}$, $\tau^{AP}$ by $\tau_{i1}^{AC}$, $\tau_{i1}^{AP}$, $i = 1, \ldots, 8$. It is clear that $x_c{}^*$ provides a better fit to the original data than $x_n{}^*$, using more parameters however, but at the 5% level of significance the logit linearity model provides an acceptable fit with a simpler model.

In our analysis of the incidence of cough and phlegm over the age groups we concluded that the association of these factors was the same over all the age groupings. However, in multidimensional contingency tables in which, for example, time or age is one of the classifications, there may occur an age effect such that an hypothesis of interest may be rejected for the entire table, but an hypothesis taking the possible age effect into account may produce an acceptable partitioning. We now propose to illustrate techniques applicable to the solution of such problems by a further study of the $9 \times 2 \times 2$ contingency Table 68, containing nine age groupings, for which the hypothesis of no second-order

**TABLE 81**

| | $x_n{}^*$ | | | |
|---|---|---|---|---|
| | $j = 1$ | | $j = 2$ | |
| $i$ | $k = 1$ | $k = 2$ | $k = 1$ | $k = 2$ |
| 1 | 72.602 | 42.728 | 64.450 | 1772.220 |
| 2 | 90.057 | 48.170 | 63.589 | 1589.185 |
| 3 | 142.725 | 69.383 | 80.161 | 1820.731 |
| 4 | 250.478 | 110.668 | 111.899 | 2309.956 |
| 5 | 269.945 | 108.401 | 95.926 | 1799.728 |
| 6 | 370.019 | 135.044 | 104.586 | 1783.352 |
| 7 | 414.629 | 137.531 | 93.218 | 1444.623 |
| 8 | 437.604 | 131.922 | 78.255 | 1102.219 |
| 9 | 350.939 | 96.152 | 49.918 | 638.992 |

TABLE 82
Covariance Matrix of $\tau_1^C, \tau_1^P, \tau^{AC}, \tau^{AP}, \tau_{11}^{CP}$ values in $x_n^*$

| $\tau_1^C$ | $\tau_1^P$ | $\tau^{AC}$ | $\tau^{AP}$ | $\tau_{11}^{CP}$ |
|---|---|---|---|---|
| 0.0028 | −0.0011 | −0.0038 | 0.0024 | −0.0011 |
| | 0.0037 | 0.0029 | −0.0046 | −0.0019 |
| | | 0.0091 | −0.0060 | −0.0004 |
| | | | 0.0092 | 0.0010 |
| | | | | 0.0031 |

interaction is rejected. An acceptable partitioning is determined. Within the partitioned model we then consider a subhypothesis of logit linearity [14].

Let us now find the estimate under the classic null hypothesis of no second-order interaction. The minimum discrimination information estimate $x_2^*(ijk)$ under the hypothesis $H_2$ of no second-order interaction is obtained by iteratively fitting the marginals $x(ij.)$, $x(i.k)$, $x(.jk)$ (see Ku et al. [57], for example) and is given in Table 84. The design matrix or log-linear representation of $x_2^*(ijk)$ is given by columns 1–28 in Table 70. Indeed, the no second-order interaction hypothesis is that the values of the last eight parameters in $x(ijk)$ have the hypothetical values

$$\tau_{111}^{ABW} = \tau_{211}^{ABW} = \cdots = \tau_{811}^{ABW} = 0 \qquad (23)$$

Computing the associated minimum discrimination information statistic we find

$$2I(x:x_2^*) = 2 \sum \sum \sum x(ijk) \ln (x(ijk)/x_2^*(ijk)) = 26.673, \text{ 8 D.F.}$$

We recall that this is the same as the log-likelihood ratio chi-squared statistic (see, e.g., Darroch [192]). We reject the null hypothesis of no second-order interaction, that is, the hypothetical values in (23) are not acceptable parameters for $x(ijk)$.

Among other properties the null hypothesis of no second-order interaction implies a common value for the association (measured by the logarithm of the cross-product ratio) between breathlessness and wheeze over all age groups. In terms of the parameters defining $x_2^*(ijk)$ this common value as determined from

TABLE 83
Analysis of Information

| Component due to | Information | D.F. |
|---|---|---|
| $H_n$ | $2I(x:x_n^*) = 28.831$ | 22 |
| $H_c$ | $2I(x_c^*:x_n^*) = 22.135$ | 14 |
| | $2I(x:x_c^*) = 6.696$ | 8 |

## TABLE 84
No Second-Order Interaction Estimate for the Data of Table 68[a]

| | $x_2^*(ijk)$ | | | |
|---|---|---|---|---|
| | $j = 1$ | | $j = 2$ | |
| $i$ | $k = 1$ | $k = 2$ | $k = 1$ | $k = 2$ |
| 1 | 7.547 | 8.454 | 96.448 | 1839.547 |
| 2 | 17.089 | 14.914 | 110.907 | 1648.087 |
| 3 | 45.954 | 27.054 | 185.040 | 1854.947 |
| 4 | 111.407 | 57.611 | 266.585 | 2347.390 |
| 5 | 162.527 | 60.504 | 279.467 | 1771.497 |
| 6 | 271.823 | 85.231 | 321.175 | 1714.769 |
| 7 | 398.159 | 122.871 | 250.848 | 1318.129 |
| 8 | 431.692 | 126.271 | 199.319 | 992.729 |
| 9 | 380.802 | 97.091 | 123.210 | 534.909 |

[a] $\ln \dfrac{x_2^*(i11)x_2^*(i22)}{x_2^*(i12)x_2^*(i21)} = \tau_{11}^{BW} = 2.8348.$

columns 1–28 of Table 70 is

$$\ln \frac{x_2^*(i11)x_2^*(i22)}{x_2^*(i12)x_2^*(i21)} = \tau_{11}^{BW} = 2.8348, \qquad i = 1, 2, \ldots, 9$$

We summarize the results and supplement analysis of information Table 75 by Table 85.

The value of $2I(x_2^*:x_d^*)$ implies a significant (nonzero) association between breathlessness and wheeze, but the value of $2I(x:x_2^*)$ leads one to conclude that there is not a common value of this association over all the age groups. We note that the estimate $x_2^*$ corresponds to model 9 of Mantel and Brown [15].

It seems reasonable to conjecture that the presence of second-order interaction may be related to an age effect. That is, there may be a common value of the association between breathlessness and wheeze over some of the younger age groups and a common but different value of this association over the remaining age groups. We therefore reexamined the computer output for $x_2^*$. Among other items, there was given for each cell a number called OUTLIER,

## TABLE 85
Analysis of Information

| Component due to | Information | D.F. |
|---|---|---|
| d) $x(ij.), x(i.k)$ | $2I(x:x_d^*) = 3051.854$ | 9 |
| $H_2$: $x(ij.), x(i.k), x(.jk)$ | $2I(x_2^*:x_d^*) = 3025.181$ | 1 |
| | $2I(x:x_2^*) = 26.673$ | 8 |

the value of

$$2(x(ijk) \ln (x(ijk)/x_2^*(ijk)) + (n - x(ijk)) \ln (n - x(ijk))/(n - x_2^*(ijk)))$$

Ireland [32] has shown that large values of OUTLIER are effective in recognizing outliers under the estimation procedure in question. In the case at hand the value of OUTLIER for cell 812 was 4.959 with the next largest value 2.722 for cell 212.

Let us therefore consider a partitioning of the second-order interaction for the age groups under 55 and for the age groups 55 and over by computing the minimum discrimination information estimate $x_t^*(ijk)$ subject to the marginal restraints of $x_2^*(ijk)$ and also the restraints

$$\tau_{111}^{ABW} = \tau_{211}^{ABW} = \cdots = \tau_{711}^{ABW}, \tau_{811}^{ABW} = \tau_{911}^{ABW} = 0 \qquad (24)$$

The design matrix or log-linear representation for $x_t^*(ijk)$ is given by columns 1–28, 39 in Table 70, that is, with the eight columns corresponding to $\tau_{111}^{ABW}, \tau_{211}^{ABW}, \ldots, \tau_{811}^{ABW}$ replaced by the one column labeled $\tau^{ABW}$. The values of $x_t^*(ijk)$ are given in Table 86. In terms of the parameters defining $x_t^*(ijk)$, from columns 1–28, 39 in Table 70, it is found that

$$\ln \frac{x_t^*(i11)x_t^*(i22)}{x_t^*(i12)x_t^*(i21)} = \tau_{11}^{BW} + \tau^{ABW} = 3.0007, \qquad i = 1, \ldots, 7$$

$$\ln \frac{x_t^*(i11)x_t^*(i22)}{x_t^*(i12)x_t^*(121)} = \tau_{11}^{BW} \qquad = 2.5212, \qquad i = 8, 9$$

The associated analysis of information Table 87 summarizes the results.

**TABLE 86**
Partitioned Second-Order Interaction Estimate[a]

| | $x_t^*(ijk)$ | | | |
|---|---|---|---|---|
| | $j = 1$ | | $j = 2$ | |
| $i$ | $k = 1$ | $k = 2$ | $k = 1$ | $k = 2$ |
| 1 | 8.182 | 7.819 | 95.816 | 1840.183 |
| 2 | 18.306 | 13.695 | 109.692 | 1649.306 |
| 3 | 48.466 | 24.539 | 182.532 | 1857.463 |
| 4 | 116.719 | 52.292 | 261.279 | 2352.709 |
| 5 | 168.521 | 54.497 | 273.479 | 1777.504 |
| 6 | 280.217 | 76.810 | 312.784 | 1723.192 |
| 7 | 408.590 | 112.349 | 240.417 | 1328.652 |
| 8 | 411.545 | 146.550 | 219.454 | 972.450 |
| 9 | 366.455 | 111.450 | 137.546 | 520.550 |

[a] $\ln \dfrac{x_t^*(i11)x_t^*(i22)}{x_t^*(i12)x_t^*(i21)} = 3.0007, \qquad i = 1, \ldots, 7.$

$\ln \dfrac{x_t^*(i11)x_t^*(i22)}{x_t^*(i12)x_t^*(i21)} = 2.5212, \qquad i = 8, 9.$

**TABLE 87**
Analysis of Information

| Component due to | Information | D.F. |
|---|---|---|
| No second-order interaction | $2I(x:x_2^*) = 26.673$ | 8 |
| Effect | $2I(x_t^*:x_2^*) = 16.700$ | 1 |
| Interaction (partition) | $2I(x:x_t^*) = 9.973$ | 7 |

We note that $2I(x_t^*:x_2^*)$, which measures the effect of the hypothesis in (24), is very significant, and from the value of $2I(x:x_t^*)$ we may accept the inference that there is a common association between breathlessness and wheeze for the age groups under 55 and a different but common value for the age groups 55 and over and that, in fact, $x_t^*(ijk)$ is a good fit to the original data.

We remark that, as a matter of fact, the values of $x_t^*(ijk)$ were computed by iteratively fitting all the two-way marginals of the $7 \times 2 \times 2$ table of the age groups under 55 and separately iteratively fitting all the two-way marginals of the $2 \times 2 \times 2$ table of the age groups 55 and over.

To verify the indication given by OUTLIER we also examined the other possible "break points" with the results of Table 88. These values confirm the inference suggested by OUTLIER.

If we now consider the logits for breathlessness and wheeze, respectively, for the age groups under 55 from the design matrix or log-linear representation for $x_t^*(ijk)$ in Table 70 (columns 1–28, 39), we see that

$$\ln \frac{x_t^*(i11)}{x_t^*(i21)} = \tau_1^B + \tau_{i1}^{AB} + \tau_{11}^{BW} + \tau^{ABW}; \qquad \ln \frac{x_t^*(i12)}{x_t^*(i22)}$$

$$= \tau_1^B + \tau_{i1}^{AB}, \qquad i = 1, \dots, 7$$

$$\ln \frac{x_t^*(i11)}{x_t^*(i12)} = \tau_1^W + \tau_{i1}^{AW} + \tau_{11}^{BW} + \tau^{ABW}; \qquad \ln \frac{x_t^*(i21)}{x_t^*(i22)}$$

$$= \tau_1^W + \tau_{i1}^{AW}, \qquad i = 1, \dots, 7$$

**TABLE 88**

| Partition | $2I(x:x_2^*)$ | D.F. |
|---|---|---|
| Under 35 | 0.612 | 2 |
| Over 35 | 15.990 | 5 |
| Under 40 | 1.856 | 3 |
| Over 40 | 11.541 | 4 |
| Under 45 | 3.311 | 4 |
| Over 45 | 8.373 | 3 |
| Under 50 | 8.420 | 5 |
| Over 50 | 7.861 | 2 |

The corresponding logits for the age groups 55 and over are given by

$$\ln \frac{x_t^*(811)}{x_t^*(821)} = \tau_1^B + \tau_{81}^{AB} + \tau_{11}^{BW}; \qquad \ln \frac{x_t^*(812)}{x_t^*(822)} = \tau_1^B + \tau_{81}^{AB}$$

$$\ln \frac{x_t^*(911)}{x_t^*(921)} = \tau_1^B \qquad\quad + \tau_{11}^{BW}; \qquad \ln \frac{x_t^*(912)}{x_t^*(922)} = \tau_1^B$$

$$\ln \frac{x_t^*(811)}{x_t^*(812)} = \tau_1^W + \tau_{81}^{AW} + \tau_{11}^{BW}; \qquad \ln \frac{x_t^*(821)}{x_t^*(822)} = \tau_1^W + \tau_{81}^{AW}$$

$$\ln \frac{x_t^*(911)}{x_t^*(912)} = \tau_1^W \qquad\quad + \tau_{11}^{BW}; \qquad \ln \frac{x_t^*(921)}{x_t^*(922)} = \tau_1^W$$

The numerical values of these logits are given in Table 89.

We now consider the hypothesis that within the partitioned no second-order hypothesis, that is, within the $x_t^*(ijk)$ model, the logits are linearly related for the age groups under 55, in other words, we consider the fitting of straight lines to the logits for the age groups under 55 by assuming that the differences of logits for successive age groups are constant. Thus we shall consider a null hypothesis that

$$\tau_{71}^{AB} - \tau_{61}^{AB} = \tau_{61}^{AB} - \tau_{51}^{AB} = \tau_{51}^{AB} - \tau_{41}^{AB} = \cdots = \tau_{21}^{AB} - \tau_{11}^{AB}$$

$$\tau_{71}^{AW} - \tau_{61}^{AW} = \tau_{61}^{AW} - \tau_{51}^{AW} = \tau_{51}^{AW} - \tau_{41}^{AW} = \cdots = \tau_{21}^{AW} - \tau_{11}^{AW}$$

If, as a matter of convenience, we consider the design matrix or log-linear representation of $x_t^*(ijk)$ as in Table 90, that is, a reparametrization of the log-linear representation in Table 70, then the chains of equalities yield the relations

**TABLE 89**
Logits

| | $\ln \dfrac{x_t^*(i1k)}{x_t^*(i2k)}$ Breathlessness | | $\ln \dfrac{x_t^*(ij1)}{x_t^*(ij2)}$ Wheeze | |
|---|---|---|---|---|
| $i$ | $k = 1$ | $k = 2$ | $j = 1$ | $j = 2$ |
| 1 | $-2.4605$ | $-5.4611$ | 0.0455 | $-2.9552$ |
| 2 | $-1.7904$ | $-4.7911$ | 0.2902 | $-2.7104$ |
| 3 | $-1.3261$ | $-4.3267$ | 0.6806 | $-2.3200$ |
| 4 | $-0.8058$ | $-3.8065$ | 0.8029 | $-2.1977$ |
| 5 | $-0.4842$ | $-3.4848$ | 1.1289 | $-1.8717$ |
| 6 | $-0.1100$ | $-3.1106$ | 1.2942 | $-1.7064$ |
| 7 | 0.5303 | $-2.4703$ | 1.2911 | $-1.7095$ |
| 8 | 0.6288 | $-1.8925$ | 1.0326 | $-1.4887$ |
| 9 | 0.9799 | $-1.5413$ | 1.1903 | $-1.3309$ |

# CONTINGENCY TABLE ANALYSIS

TABLE 90

| i | j | k | 1 L | 2 $\tau_1^A$ | 3 $\tau_2^A$ | 4 $\tau_3^A$ | 5 $\tau_4^A$ | 6 $\tau_5^A$ | 7 $\tau_6^A$ | 8 $\tau_8^A$ | 9 $\tau_9^A$ | 10 $\tau_1^B$ | 11 $\tau_1^W$ | 12 $\tau_{11}^{AB}$ | 13 $\tau_{21}^{AB}$ | 14 $\tau_{31}^{AB}$ |
|---|---|---|---|---|---|---|---|---|---|---|---|---|---|---|---|---|
| 1 | 1 | 1 | 1 | 1 | | | | | | | | 1 | 1 | 1 | | |
| 1 | 1 | 2 | 1 | 1 | | | | | | | | 1 | | 1 | | |
| 1 | 2 | 1 | 1 | 1 | | | | | | | | | 1 | | | |
| 1 | 2 | 2 | 1 | 1 | | | | | | | | | | | | |
| 2 | 1 | 1 | 1 | | 1 | | | | | | | 1 | 1 | | 1 | |
| 2 | 1 | 2 | 1 | | 1 | | | | | | | 1 | | | 1 | |
| 2 | 2 | 1 | 1 | | 1 | | | | | | | | 1 | | | |
| 2 | 2 | 2 | 1 | | 1 | | | | | | | | | | | |
| 3 | 1 | 1 | 1 | | | 1 | | | | | | 1 | 1 | | | 1 |
| 3 | 1 | 2 | 1 | | | 1 | | | | | | 1 | | | | 1 |
| 3 | 2 | 1 | 1 | | | 1 | | | | | | | 1 | | | |
| 3 | 2 | 2 | 1 | | | 1 | | | | | | | | | | |
| 4 | 1 | 1 | 1 | | | | 1 | | | | | 1 | 1 | | | |
| 4 | 1 | 2 | 1 | | | | 1 | | | | | 1 | | | | |
| 4 | 2 | 1 | 1 | | | | 1 | | | | | | 1 | | | |
| 4 | 2 | 2 | 1 | | | | 1 | | | | | | | | | |
| 5 | 1 | 1 | 1 | | | | | 1 | | | | 1 | 1 | | | |
| 5 | 1 | 2 | 1 | | | | | 1 | | | | 1 | | | | |
| 5 | 2 | 1 | 1 | | | | | 1 | | | | | 1 | | | |
| 5 | 2 | 2 | 1 | | | | | 1 | | | | | | | | |
| 6 | 1 | 1 | 1 | | | | | | 1 | | | 1 | 1 | | | |
| 6 | 1 | 2 | 1 | | | | | | 1 | | | 1 | | | | |
| 6 | 2 | 1 | 1 | | | | | | 1 | | | | 1 | | | |
| 6 | 2 | 2 | 1 | | | | | | 1 | | | | | | | |
| 7 | 1 | 1 | 1 | | | | | | | | | 1 | 1 | | | |
| 7 | 1 | 2 | 1 | | | | | | | | | 1 | | | | |
| 7 | 2 | 1 | 1 | | | | | | | | | | 1 | | | |
| 7 | 2 | 2 | 1 | | | | | | | | | | | | | |
| 8 | 1 | 1 | 1 | | | | | | | 1 | | 1 | 1 | | | |
| 8 | 1 | 2 | 1 | | | | | | | 1 | | 1 | | | | |
| 8 | 2 | 1 | 1 | | | | | | | 1 | | | 1 | | | |
| 8 | 2 | 2 | 1 | | | | | | | 1 | | | | | | |
| 9 | 1 | 1 | 1 | | | | | | | | 1 | 1 | 1 | | | |
| 9 | 1 | 2 | 1 | | | | | | | | 1 | 1 | | | | |
| 9 | 2 | 1 | 1 | | | | | | | | 1 | | 1 | | | |
| 9 | 2 | 2 | 1 | | | | | | | | 1 | | | | | |

## Log-Linear Representation

| 15 $\tau^{AB}_{41}$ | 16 $\tau^{AB}_{51}$ | 17 $\tau^{AB}_{61}$ | 18 $\tau^{AB}_{81}$ | 19 $\tau^{AB}_{91}$ | 20 $\tau^{AW}_{11}$ | 21 $\tau^{AW}_{21}$ | 22 $\tau^{AW}_{31}$ | 23 $\tau^{AW}_{41}$ | 24 $\tau^{AW}_{51}$ | 25 $\tau^{AW}_{61}$ | 26 $\tau^{AW}_{81}$ | 27 $\tau^{AW}_{91}$ | 28 $\tau^{BW}_{11}$ | 29 $\tau^{ABW}$ | 30 $\tau^{AB}$ | 31 $\tau^{AW}$ |
|---|---|---|---|---|---|---|---|---|---|---|---|---|---|---|---|---|
|  |  |  |  |  | 1 |  |  |  |  |  |  |  | 1 |  | 1 | 1 |
|  |  |  |  |  | 1 |  |  |  |  |  |  |  |  |  | 1 | 1 |
|  |  |  |  |  |  | 1 |  |  |  |  |  |  | 1 |  | $\frac{5}{6}$ | $\frac{5}{6}$ |
|  |  |  |  |  |  | 1 |  |  |  |  |  |  |  |  | $\frac{5}{6}$ | $\frac{5}{6}$ |
|  |  |  |  |  |  |  | 1 |  |  |  |  |  | 1 |  | $\frac{4}{6}$ | $\frac{4}{6}$ |
|  |  |  |  |  |  |  | 1 |  |  |  |  |  |  |  | $\frac{4}{6}$ | $\frac{4}{6}$ |
| 1 |  |  |  |  |  |  |  | 1 |  |  |  |  | 1 |  | $\frac{3}{6}$ | $\frac{3}{6}$ |
| 1 |  |  |  |  |  |  |  | 1 |  |  |  |  |  |  | $\frac{3}{6}$ | $\frac{3}{6}$ |
|  | 1 |  |  |  |  |  |  |  | 1 |  |  |  | 1 |  | $\frac{2}{6}$ | $\frac{2}{6}$ |
|  | 1 |  |  |  |  |  |  |  | 1 |  |  |  |  |  | $\frac{2}{6}$ | $\frac{2}{6}$ |
|  |  | 1 |  |  |  |  |  |  |  | 1 |  |  | 1 |  | $\frac{1}{6}$ | $\frac{1}{6}$ |
|  |  | 1 |  |  |  |  |  |  |  | 1 |  |  |  |  | $\frac{1}{6}$ | $\frac{1}{6}$ |
|  |  |  |  |  |  |  |  |  |  |  |  |  | 1 |  |  |  |
|  |  |  | 1 |  |  |  |  |  |  |  | 1 |  | 1 | 1 |  |  |
|  |  |  | 1 |  |  |  |  |  |  |  | 1 |  |  |  |  |  |
|  |  |  |  | 1 |  |  |  |  |  |  |  | 1 | 1 | 1 |  |  |
|  |  |  |  | 1 |  |  |  |  |  |  |  | 1 |  |  |  |  |

among the parameters

$$\tau_{i1}^{AB} = \frac{7-i}{6}\,\tau_{11}^{AB}, \qquad \tau_{i1}^{AW} = \frac{7-i}{6}\,\tau_{11}^{AW}, \qquad i = 1, 2, \ldots, 7$$

The design matrix or log-linear representation for the linear logit model estimate $x_v^*(ijk)$, using $\tau^{AB}$ and $\tau^{AW}$, respectively, instead of $\tau_{11}^{AB}$ and $\tau_{11}^{AW}$, is given in columns 1–11, 28–31 of Table 90. The values in columns 30, 31 arise from the fact that in the log-linear representation as in (22) the terms

$$\tau_{11}^{AB} T_{11}^{AB}(ijk) + \tau_{21}^{AB} T_{21}^{AB}(ijk) + \cdots + \tau_{61}^{AB} T_{61}^{AB}(ijk)$$

and the terms

$$\tau_{11}^{AW} T_{11}^{AW}(ijk) + \tau_{21}^{AW} T_{21}^{AW}(ijk) + \cdots + \tau_{61}^{AW} T_{61}^{AW}(ijk)$$

## TABLE 91[a]

| | 111 | 112 | 121 | 122 | 211 | 212 | 221 | 222 | 311 | 312 | 321 | 322 | 411 | 412 |
|---|---|---|---|---|---|---|---|---|---|---|---|---|---|---|
| | | | | | | | $\tau^{AB}$ | | | | | | | |
| $a_1(ijk)$ | 1 | 1 | | | $\frac{5}{6}$ | $\frac{5}{6}$ | | | $\frac{4}{6}$ | $\frac{4}{6}$ | | | $\frac{3}{6}$ | $\frac{3}{6}$ |
| $a_2(ijk)$ | | | 1 | 1 | | | $\frac{5}{6}$ | $\frac{5}{6}$ | | | $\frac{4}{6}$ | $\frac{4}{6}$ | | |
| $a_3(ijk)$ | | | | | $\frac{1}{6}$ | $\frac{1}{6}$ | $\frac{1}{6}$ | $\frac{1}{6}$ | $\frac{2}{6}$ | $\frac{2}{6}$ | $\frac{2}{6}$ | $\frac{2}{6}$ | $\frac{3}{6}$ | $\frac{3}{6}$ |
| | | | | | | | $\tau^{AW}$ | | | | | | | |
| $b_1(ijk)$ | 1 | | 1 | | $\frac{5}{6}$ | | $\frac{5}{6}$ | | $\frac{4}{6}$ | | $\frac{4}{6}$ | | $\frac{3}{6}$ | |
| $b_2(ijk)$ | | 1 | | 1 | | $\frac{5}{6}$ | | $\frac{5}{6}$ | | $\frac{4}{6}$ | | $\frac{4}{6}$ | | $\frac{3}{6}$ |
| $b_3(ijk)$ | | | | | $\frac{1}{6}$ | $\frac{1}{6}$ | $\frac{1}{6}$ | $\frac{1}{6}$ | $\frac{2}{6}$ | $\frac{2}{6}$ | $\frac{2}{6}$ | $\frac{2}{6}$ | $\frac{3}{6}$ | $\frac{3}{6}$ |

| | 421 | 422 | 511 | 512 | 521 | 522 | 611 | 612 | 621 | 622 | 711 | 712 | 721 | 722 |
|---|---|---|---|---|---|---|---|---|---|---|---|---|---|---|
| | | | | | | | $\tau^{AB}$ | | | | | | | |
| $a_1(ijk)$ | | | $\frac{2}{6}$ | $\frac{2}{6}$ | | | $\frac{1}{6}$ | $\frac{1}{6}$ | | | | | | |
| $a_2(ijk)$ | $\frac{3}{6}$ | $\frac{3}{6}$ | | | $\frac{2}{6}$ | $\frac{2}{6}$ | | | $\frac{1}{6}$ | $\frac{1}{6}$ | | | | |
| $a_3(ijk)$ | $\frac{3}{6}$ | $\frac{3}{6}$ | $\frac{4}{6}$ | $\frac{4}{6}$ | $\frac{4}{6}$ | $\frac{4}{6}$ | $\frac{5}{6}$ | $\frac{5}{6}$ | $\frac{5}{6}$ | $\frac{5}{6}$ | 1 | 1 | 1 | 1 |
| | | | | | | | $\tau^{AW}$ | | | | | | | |
| $b_1(ijk)$ | $\frac{3}{6}$ | | $\frac{2}{6}$ | | $\frac{2}{6}$ | | $\frac{1}{6}$ | | $\frac{1}{6}$ | | | | | |
| $b_2(ijk)$ | | $\frac{3}{6}$ | | $\frac{2}{6}$ | | $\frac{2}{6}$ | | $\frac{1}{6}$ | | $\frac{1}{6}$ | | | | |
| $b_3(ijk)$ | $\frac{3}{6}$ | $\frac{3}{6}$ | $\frac{4}{6}$ | $\frac{4}{6}$ | $\frac{4}{6}$ | $\frac{4}{6}$ | $\frac{5}{6}$ | $\frac{5}{6}$ | $\frac{5}{6}$ | $\frac{5}{6}$ | 1 | 1 | 1 | 1 |

$h_1$: $x(11.) + \frac{5}{6}x(21.) + \frac{4}{6}x(31.) + \frac{3}{6}x(41.) + \frac{2}{6}x(51.) + \frac{1}{6}x(61.)$

$h_2$: $x(12.) + \frac{5}{6}x(22.) + \frac{4}{6}x(32.) + \frac{3}{6}x(42.) + \frac{2}{6}x(52.) + \frac{1}{6}x(62.)$

$h_3$: $\frac{1}{6}x(2..) + \frac{2}{6}x(3..) + \frac{3}{6}x(4..) + \frac{4}{6}x(5..) + \frac{5}{6}x(6..) + x(7..)$

$k_1$: $x(1.1) + \frac{5}{6}x(2.1) + \frac{4}{6}x(3.1) + \frac{3}{6}x(4.1) + \frac{2}{6}x(5.1) + \frac{1}{6}x(6.1)$

$k_2$: $x(1.2) + \frac{5}{6}x(2.2) + \frac{4}{6}x(3.2) + \frac{3}{6}x(4.2) + \frac{2}{6}x(5.2) + \frac{1}{6}x(6.2)$

$k_3$: $\frac{1}{6}x(2..) + \frac{2}{6}x(3..) + \frac{3}{6}x(4..) + \frac{4}{6}x(5..) + \frac{5}{6}x(6..) + x(7..)$

[a] All marginals refer to the $7 \times 2 \times 2$ table for age groups under 55.

because of the relations among the parameters reduce to

$$\tau^{AB}(T_{11}^{AB}(ijk) + (\tfrac{5}{6})T_{21}^{AB}(ijk) + (\tfrac{4}{6})T_{31}^{AB}(ijk) + \cdots + (\tfrac{1}{6})T_{61}^{AB}(ijk))$$

and

$$\tau^{AW}(T_{11}^{AW}(ijk) + (\tfrac{5}{6})T_{21}^{AW}(ijk) + (\tfrac{4}{6})T_{31}^{AW}(ijk) + \cdots + (\tfrac{1}{6})T_{61}^{AW}(ijk)$$

respectively.

The iteration used to compute $x_v^*(ijk)$ is (see Darroch and Ratcliff [22])

$$x^{(5n+1)}(ijk) = \frac{x(i..)}{x^{(5n)}(i..)}\,x^{(5n)}(ijk)$$

$$x^{(5n+2)}(ijk) = \frac{x(.j.)}{x^{(5n+1)}(.j.)}\,x^{(5n+1)}(ijk)$$

$$x^{(5n+3)}(ijk) = \frac{x(..k)}{x^{(5n+2)}(..k)}\,x^{(5n+2)}(ijk)$$

$$x^{(5n+4)}(ijk) = \left(\frac{h_1}{h_1^{(5n+3)}}\right)^{a_1(ijk)}\left(\frac{h_2}{h_2^{(5n+3)}}\right)^{a_2(ijk)}\left(\frac{h_3}{h_3^{(5n+3)}}\right)^{a_3(ijk)} x^{(5n+3)}(ijk)$$

$$x^{(5n+5)}(ijk) = \left(\frac{k_1}{k_1^{(5n+4)}}\right)^{b_1(ijk)}\left(\frac{k_2}{k_2^{(5n+4)}}\right)^{b_2(ijk)}\left(\frac{k_3}{k_3^{(5n+4)}}\right)^{b_3(ijk)} x^{(5n+4)}(ijk)$$

$$x^{(0)}(ijk) = n/28, \qquad n = \sum_{i=1}^{7}\sum_{j=1}^{2}\sum_{k=1}^{2} x(ijk)$$

### TABLE 92
### Linear Logit Estimate Within Partitioned Second-Order
### Interaction Model[a]

| | $x_v^*(ijk)$ | | | |
|---|---|---|---|---|
| | $j = 1$ | | $j = 2$ | |
| $i$ | $k = 1$ | $k = 2$ | $k = 1$ | $k = 2$ |
| 1 | 11.860 | 9.990 | 108.934 | 1821.215 |
| 2 | 20.398 | 13.952 | 120.522 | 1636.127 |
| 3 | 44.705 | 24.830 | 169.946 | 1873.519 |
| 4 | 107.932 | 48.677 | 263.913 | 2362.476 |
| 5 | 158.232 | 57.944 | 248.880 | 1808.943 |
| 6 | 288.909 | 85.919 | 292.375 | 1725.797 |
| 7 | 416.964 | 100.688 | 271.429 | 1300.919 |
| 8 | 411.545 | 146.550 | 219.454 | 972.450 |
| 9 | 366.455 | 111.450 | 137.546 | 520.550 |

[a] $\ln \dfrac{x_v^*(i11)x_v^*(i22)}{x_v^*(i12)x_v^*(i21)} = 2.9881, \quad i = 1, \ldots, 7.$

$\ln \dfrac{x_v^*(i11)x_v^*(i22)}{x_v^*(i12)x_v^*(i21)} = 2.5212, \quad i = 8, 9.$

TABLE 93
Analysis of Information

| Component due to | Information | D.F. |
|---|---|---|
| Interaction (linear logits) | $2I(x:x_v{}^*) = 29.560$ | 17 |
| Effect | $2I(x_t{}^*:x_v{}^*) = 19.587$ | 10 |
| Interaction (partition) | $2I(x:x_t{}^*) = 9.973$ | 7 |

All marginals refer to the $7 \times 2 \times 2$ table and the values of $a_m(ijk)$, $b_m(ijk)$, $m = 1, 2, 3$ and the restraints $h_m$, $k_m$, $m = 1, 2, 3$ are given in Table 91. We remark that since $x_v{}^*(ijk) = x_t{}^*(ijk)$ for $i = 8, 9$, we can perform the iteration by consideration of the $7 \times 2 \times 2$ table only. The values of $x_v{}^*(ijk)$ are given in Table 92.

Results are summarized in Table 93.

Since $2I(x:x_v{}^*)$ and $2I(x_t{}^*:x_v{}^*)$ fall between the 5 and 2% values of the tabulated chi-squared values with the appropriate degrees of freedom, we might accept the null hypothesis of linearity of the logits within the partitioned second-order interaction model, that is, infer from the value of $2I(x_t{}^*:x_v{}^*)$ that the parameters $\tau_{11}^{AB}$, $\tau_{21}^{AB}$, ..., $\tau_{71}^{AB}$ and $\tau_{11}^{AW}$, $\tau_{21}^{AW}$, ..., $\tau_{71}^{AW}$ of $x_t{}^*(ijk)$ satisfy the relations among the parameters implied by the logit linearity and that the estimate $x_v{}^*(ijk)$ under the logit linearity model is an acceptable estimate for the original observations.

## ACKNOWLEDGMENTS

This article has been made possible by the support of the U.S. Army Research Office—Durham, North Carolina for which I express my appreciation. It is also the product of the interaction among many people, including my students, colleagues, collaborators, interested statisticians, referees, and editors. The support of The George Washington University in providing an academic environment in which the teaching and research to develop, expand, and use the results presented herein was made possible, stimulated, and encouraged must be, and is, gratefully acknowledged. In particular, the support and collaboration of Professor Henry Solomon, Professor Herbert Solomon, Associate Professor D. V. Gokhale, Associate Professor C. T. Ireland, Dr. H. H. Ku, Dr. Marian R. Fisher, and Mr. John C. Keegel have contributed greatly to any merits this article possesses; its demerits are my responsibility. The many examples were analyzed on the basis of computations using the facilities of the Computer Center of The George Washington University. The research program which underlies this article began under AFOSR Grant No. 932-65, continued under Grants AFOSR-68-1513, AFOSR-72-2348, and Contract No. N00014-67-A-0214-0015 under the joint sponsorship of the Army, Navy, and Air Force. To

Mrs. Glenda Howell for her typing and all the others who have contributed, my sincere thanks.

# REFERENCES

Publications, reports, etc., primarily dealing with the analysis of contingency tables, are listed by year of publication starting with the most recent. This section depends in large part on compilations prepared by Dr. Marvin A. Kastenbaum and Dr. H. H. Ku. Permission to use their results is gratefully acknowledged. We make no claim that all items that should have been included are contained herein, and we express our regrets to authors of items so omitted. Additional references to related topics may be found in the bibliographies contained in the books by D. R. Cox (1970) and H. O. Lancaster (1969).

*1975*

1. Keegel, J. C., Several Numerical Procedures in Regression and Parameter Estimation in Contingency Tables, Ph.D. Dissertation, The Graduate School of Arts and Sciences, The George Washington University, February 1975.

*1974*

2. Fisher, M. R., *User's Guide to CONTABMOD,* Statistics Department, The George Washington University, Washington, D.C., 1974.
3. Gail, M., Value systems for comparing two independent multinomial trials, *Biometrika* **61**(1), 91–100 (1974).
4. Ireland, C. T., and S. Kullback, *The Information in Contingency Tables—An Application of Information-Theoretic Concepts to the Analysis of Contingency Tables,* Statistics Department, Stanford University, Stanford, California.
5. Kastenbaum, M. A., Analysis of categorical data: Some well-known analogues and some new concepts, *Commun. Stat.* **3**(5), 401–417 (1974).
6. Ku, H. H., and S. Kullback, Loglinear models in contingency table analysis, *Am. Stat.* **28**(4), 115–122 (1974).
7. Kullback, S., and M. Fisher, Multivariate logit analysis, *Biom. Z.* **17**(3), 139–146 (1975).
8. Kullback, S., and P. N. Reeves, Analysis of interactions between categorical variables, *Biom. Z.* **17**(1), 3–12 (1975).
9. Patil, K. D., Interaction test for three-dimensional contingency tables, *J. Am. Stat. Assoc.* **69**(345), 164–168 (1974).
10. Sugiura, N., and M. Otake, An extension of Mantel-Haenszel procedure to $k$ 2 $\times$ $c$ contingency tables and the relation to the logit model, *Commun. Stat.* **3**(9), 829–842 (1974).

*1973*

11. Gokhale, D. V., Approximating discrete distributions with applications, *J. Am. Stat. Assoc.* **68**(344), 1009–1012 (1973).
12. Goodman, L. A., Guided and unguided methods for selecting models for a set of $T$ multidimensional contingency tables, *J. Am. Stat. Assoc.* **68**, 165–175 (1973).
13. Kullback, S., Estimating and testing interaction parameters in the log-linear model, *Biom. Z.* **15**, 371–388 (1973).

14. Kullback, S., and M. Fisher, Partitioning second-order interaction in three-way contingency tables, *J. R. Stat. Soc., Ser. C* **22**, 172–184 (1973).

15. Mantel, N., and C. Brown, A logistic reanalysis of Ashford and Sowden's data on respiratory symptoms in British coal miners, *Biometrics* **29**(4), 649–665 (1973).

16. Sugiura, N., and M. Otake, Approximate distribution of the maximum of $c$-1 $\chi^2$-statistics (2 × 2) derived from 2 × $c$ contingency tables, *Commun. Stat.* **1**(1), 9–16 (1973).

*1972*

17. Adam, J., and H. Enke, Analyse mehrdimensionaler kontingenztafeln mit hilfe des informationsmasses von Kullback, *Biom. Z.* **14**(5), 305–323 (1972).

18. Berkson, J., Minimum discrimination information, the "no interaction" problem, and the logistic function, *Biometrics* **28**(2), 443–468 (1972).

19. Brunden, M. N., The analysis of non-independent 2 × 2 tables from 2 × $c$ tables using rank sums, *Biometrics* **28**(2), 603–606 (1972).

20. Causey, B. D., Sensitivity of raked contingency table totals to changes in problem conditions, *Ann. Math. Stat.* **43**(2), 656–658 (1972).

21. Cox, D. R., The analysis of multivariate binary data, *Appl. Stat.* **21**(2), 113–120 (1972).

22. Darroch, J. N., and D. Ratcliff, Generalized iterative scaling for log-linear models, *Ann. Math. Stat.* **43**(5), 1470–1480 (1972).

23. Fienberg, S. E., The analysis of incomplete multiway contingency tables, *Biometrics* **28**(1), 177–202 (1972).

24. Fisher, M. R., An Application of Minimum Discrimination Information Estimation, Ph.D. Dissertation, The Graduate School of Arts and Sciences, The George Washington University, September 1972.

25. Gail, M. H., Mixed quasi-independence models for categorical data, *Biometrics* **28**(3), 703–712 (1972).

26. Gart, J. J., Interaction tests for 2 × $s$ × $t$ contingency tables, *Biometrika* **59**(2), 309–316 (1972).

27. Gokhale, D. V., Analysis of log-linear models, *J. R. Stat. Soc., Ser. B* **34**(3), 371–376 (1972).

28. Goodman, L. A., and W. H. Kruskal, Measures of association for cross-classifications, IV: Simplification of asymptotic variances. *J. Am. Stat. Assoc.* **67**, 415–421 (1972).

29. Grizzle, J. E., and O. D. Williams, Contingency tables having ordered response categories, *J. Am. Stat. Assoc.* **67**, 55–63 (1972).

30. Grizzle, J. E., and O. D. Williams, Log-linear models and tests of independence for contingency tables, *Biometrics* **28**(1), 137–156 (1972).

31. Ireland, C. T., *Sequential Cell Deletion in Contingency Tables,* Statistics Department, The George Washington University, 1972.

32. Jacobs, S. E., P. N. Reeves, and G. L. Hammon, Your guide to surveys of hospital computer usage, *Hosp. Financial Manage.* **26**(9), 5–13 (1972).

33. Koch, G. G., P. B., Imrey, and D. W. Reinfurt, Linear model analysis of categorical data with incomplete response vectors, *Biometrics* **28**(3), 663–692 (1972).

34. Martin, D. C., and R. A. Bradley, Probability models, estimation, and classification for multivariate dichotomous populations, *Biometrics* **28**, 203–221 (1972).

35. Nathan, G., Asymptotic power of tests for independence in contingency tables from stratified samples, *J. Am. Stat. Assoc.* **67**, 917–920 (1972).

36. Victor, N., Zur klassifizierung mehrdimensionaler Kontingenztafeln, *Biometrics* **28**(2), 427–442 (1972).

*1971*

37. Altham, P. M. E., Exact Bayesian analysis of the intraclass $2 \times 2$ table, *Biometrika* **58**(3), 679–680 (1971).
38. Altham, P. M. E., The analysis of matched proportions, *Biometrika* **58**(3), 561–576 (1971).
39. Belle, G. V., and R. G. Cornell, Strengthening tests of symmetry in contingency tables, *Biometrics* **27**, 1074–1078 (1971).
40. Bishop, Y. M. M., Effects of collapsing multidimensional contingency tables, *Biometrics* **27**, 545–562 (1971).
41. Cohen, J. E., Estimation and interaction in a censored $2 \times 2 \times 2$ contingency table, *Biometrics* **27**, 379–386 (1971).
42. Dempster, A. P., An overview of multivariate data analysis, *J. Multivar. Anal.* **1**, 316–347 (1971).
43. Fryer, J. G., On the homogeneity of the marginal distributions of a multidimensional contingency table, *J. R. Stat. Soc., Ser. A* **134**, 368–371 (1971).
44. Gart, J. J., On the ordering of contingency tables for significance tests, *Technometrics* **13**, 910–911 (1971).
45. Gart, J. J., The comparison of proportions: A review of significance tests, confidence intervals, and adjustments for stratification. *Rev. Inst. Int. Stat.* **29**, 148–169 (1971).
46. Gokhale, D. V., An iterative procedure for analysing log-linear models, *Biometrics* **27**, 681–687 (1971).
47. Goodman, L. A., Partitioning of chi-square, analysis of marginal contingency tables, and estimation of expected frequencies in multidimensional contingency tables, *J. Am. Stat. Assoc.* **66**, 339–344 (1971).
48. Goodman, L. A., Some multiplicative models for the analysis of cross-classified data, in *Proceedings of the 6th Berkeley Symposium,* University of California Press, Berkeley, 1971.
49. Goodman, L. A., The analysis of multidimensional contingency tables: Stepwise procedures and direct estimation methods for building models for multiple classifications, *Technometrics* **13**, 33–61 (1971).
50. Grizzle, J. E., Multivariate logit analysis, *Biometrics* **27**, 1057–1062 (1971).
51. Ireland, C. T., *A Computer Program For Analyzing Contingency Tables* (latest version is CONTAB III), Statistics Department, The George Washington University, Washington, D.C., 1971.
52. Johnson, W. D., and G. G. Koch, A note on the weighted least squares analysis of the Ries-Smith contingency table data, *Technometrics* **13**, 438–447 (1971).
53. Koch, G. G., P. B. Imrey, and D. W. Reinfurt, *Linear Model Analysis of Categorical Data with Incomplete Response Vectors* (Institute of Statistics Mimeo Series No. 790), University of North Carolina, Chapel Hill, North Carolina, 1971.
54. Koch, G. G., W. D. Johnson, and H. D. Tolley, *An Application of Linear Models to Analyze Categorical Data Pertaining to the Relationship between Survival and Extent of Disease* (Institute of Statistics Mimeo Series No. 770), University of North Carolina, Chapel Hill, North Carolina, 1971.
55. Koch, G. G., and D. W. Reinfurt, The analysis of categorical data from mixed models, *Biometrics* **27**, 157–173 (1971).
56. Ku, H. H., Analysis of information—An alternative approach to the detection of a

correlation between the sexes of adjacent sibs in human families, *Biometrics* **27,** 175–182 (1971).

57. Ku, H. H., R. Varner, and S. Kullback, On the analysis of multidimensional contingency tables, *J. Am. Stat. Assoc.* **66,** 55–64 (1971).

58. Kullback, S., Marginal homogeneity of multidimensional contingency tables, *Ann. Math. Stat.* **42,** 594–606 (1971).

59. Kullback, S., The homogeneity of the sex ratio of adjacent sibs in human families, *Biometrics* **27,** 452–457 (1971).

60. Nam, J., On two tests for comparing matched proportions, *Biometrics* **27,** 945–959 (1971).

61. Peacock, P. B., The non-comparability of relative risks from different studies, *Biometrics* **27,** 903–907 (1971).

62. Peritz, E., Estimating the ratio of two marginal probabilities in a contingency table, *Biometrics* **27,** 223–225 (1971).

63. Ratcliff, D., Topics on Independence and Correlation for Bounded Sum Variables, Ph.D. Thesis, School of Mathematical Sciences, The Flinders University of South Australia, June 1971.

64. Simon, G. A., *Information Distances and Exponential Families, with Applications to Contingency Tables* (Technical Report No. 32), Department of Statistics, Stanford University, Stanford, California, November 26, 1971.

65. Thomas, D. G., Exact confidence limits for the odds ratio in a $2 \times 2$ table, *Appl. Stat.* **20,** 105–110 (1971).

66. Yasaimaibodi (Yassaee), H., On Comparison of Various Estimators and Their Associated Statistics in $r \times c$ and $r \times c \times 2$ Contingency Tables, Ph.D. Dissertation, The George Washington University, Washington, D.C., 1971.

67. Zelen, M., The analysis of several $2 \times 2$ contingency tables, *Biometrika* **58,** 129–137 (1971).

*1970*

68. Altham, P. M. E., The measurement of association of rows and columns for an $r \times s$ contingency table, *J. R. Stat. Soc., Ser. B* **32,** 63–73 (1970).

69. Ashford, J. R., D. C. Morgan, S. Rae, and R. R. Sowden, Respiratory symptoms in British coal miners, *Am. Rev. Respir. Dis.* **102,** 370–381 (1970).

70. Ashford, J. R., and R. D. Sowden, Multivariate probit analysis, *Biometrics* **26,** 535–546 (1970).

71. Bhapkar, V. P., Categorical data analysis of some multivariate tests, in *Essays in Probability and Statistics* (R. C. Bose et al., eds.), University of North Carolina Press, Chapel Hill, North Carolina, 1970, pp. 85–110.

72. Campbell, L. L., Equivalence of Gauss's principle and minimum discrimination information estimation of probabilities, *Ann. Math. Stat.* **41,** 1011–1015 (1970).

73. Cox, D. R., *The Analysis of Binary Data,* Methuen, London, 1970.

74. Craddock, J. M., and C. R. Flood, (1970). The distribution of the chi-square statistic in small contingency tables, *Appl. Stat.* **19,** 173–181 (1970).

75. Fienberg, S. E., An iterative procedure for estimation in contingency tables, *Ann. Math. Stat.* **41,** 907–917 (1970).

76. Fienberg, S. E., Quasi-independence and maximum likelihood estimation in incomplete contingency tables, *J. Am. Stat. Assoc.* **65**(332), 1610–1616 (1970).

77. Fienberg, S. E., The analysis of multidimensional contingency tables, *Ecology* **51**(2), 419–433 (1970).

78. Fienberg, S. E., and J. P. Gilbert, Geometry of a two by two contingency table, *J. Am. Stat. Assoc.* **65,** 694–701 (1970).

79. Fienberg, S. E., and P. W. Holland, Methods for eliminating zero counts in contingency tables, in *Random Counts in Scientific Work* (G. P. Patil, ed.), Pennsylvania State University Press, University Park, Pennsylvania, 1970.

80. Good, I. J., T. N. Gover, and G. J. Mitchell, Exact distributions for χ-squared and for the likelihood-ratio statistic for the equiprobable multinomial distribution, *J. Am. Stat. Assoc.* **65,** 267–283 (1970).

81. Goodman, L. A., The multivariate analysis of qualitative data: interaction among multiple classifications, *J. Am. Stat. Assoc.* **65,** 226–256 (1970).

82. Kastenbaum, M. A., A review of contingency tables, in *Essays in Probability and Statistics* (R. C. Bose *et al.*, eds.), University of North Carolina Press, Chapel Hill, North Carolina, 1970, pp. 407–438.

83. Kullback, S., Minimum discrimination information estimation and application, in *Proceedings of the Sixteenth Conference on the Design of Experiments in Army Research, Development and Testing, 21 October 1970,* ARO-D Report 71-3, 1-38 Proceedings of the Conference.

84. Kullback, S., Various applications of minimum discrimination information estimation, particularly to problems of contingency table analysis, in *Proceedings of the Meeting on Information Measures, University of Waterloo, Ontario, Canada, April 10–14, 1970,* Faculty of Mathematics, University of Waterloo, Waterloo, Ontario, Canada, 1970, pp. I-33–I-66.

85. Mantel, N., Incomplete contingency tables, *Biometrics* **26,** 291–304 (1970).

86. Molk, Y., On Estimation of Probabilities in Contingency Tables with Restrictions on Marginals, Ph.D. Dissertation, The George Washington University, February 1970.

87. Odoroff, C. L., Minimum logit chi-square estimation and maximum likelihood estimation in contingency tables, *J. Am. Stat. Assoc.* **65**(332), 1617–1631 (1970).

88. Wagner, S. S., The maximum-likelihood estimate for contingency tables with zero diagonal, *J. Am. Stat. Assoc.* **65**(331), 1362–1383 (1970).

*1969*

89. Altham, P. M. E., Exact Bayesian analysis of a $2 \times 2$ contingency table and Fisher's "exact" significance test, *J. R. Stat. Soc., Ser. B.* **31,** 261–269 (1969).

90. Argentiero, P. D., *χ-Squared Statistic for Goodness of Fit Test, Its Derivation and Tables,* NASA Technical Report, TR-R-313, 1969.

91. Bishop, Y. M. M., Full contingency tables, logits, and split contingency tables, *Biometrics* **25,** 383–400 (1969).

92. Bishop, Y. M. M., and S. E. Fienberg, Incomplete two-dimensional contingency tables, *Biometrics* **25,** 119–128 (1969).

93. Dempster, A. P., *Some Theory Related to Fitting Exponential Models* (Research Report S-4), Department of Statistics, Harvard University, Cambridge, Massachusetts, 1969.

94. Fienberg, S. E., Preliminary graphical analysis and quasi-independence for two-way contingency tables, *Appl. Stat.* **18,** 153–168 (1969).

95. Goodman, L. A., On partition χ-squared and detecting partial association in the three-way contingency tables, *J. R. Stat. Soc., Ser. B* **31,** 486–498 (1969).

96. Grizzle, J. E., C. F. Starmer, and G. G. Koch, Analysis of categorical data by linear models, *Biometrics* **25,** 489–504 (1969).

97. Healy, M. J. R., Exact tests of significance in contingency tables, *Technometrics* **11**, 393–395 (1969).

98. Ireland, C. T., H. H. Ku, and S. Kullback, Symmetry and marginal homogeneity of an $r \times r$ contingency table, *J. Am. Stat. Assoc.* **64**, 1323–1341 (1969).

99. Koch, G. G., The effect of non-sampling errors on measures of association in $2 \times 2$ contingency tables, *J. Am. Stat. Assoc.* **64**, 852–863 (1969).

100. Ku, H. H., and S. Kullback, Analysis of multidimensional contingency tables: An information theoretical approach, in *Contributed Papers, 37th Session of the International Statistical Institute, Bull. Int. Stat. Inst.*, London, England, 1969, pp. 156–158.

101. Ku, H. H., and S. Kullback, Approximating discrete probability distributions, *IEEE Trans. Inf. Theory* **IT-15**, 444–447 (1969).

102. Lancaster, H. O., Contingency tables of higher dimensions, *Bull. Int. Stat. Inst.* **43**(1), 143–151 (1969).

103. Lancaster, H. O., *The Chi-Squared Distribution*, Wiley, New York, 1969.

104. Nagnur, B. N., LAMST and the hypotheses of no three factor interaction in contingency tables, *J. Am. Stat. Assoc.* **64**, 207–215 (1969).

105. Plackett, R. L., Multidimensional contingency tables. A survey of models and methods, *Bull. Int. Stat. Inst.* **43**(1), 133–142 (1969).

*1968*

106. Bennett, B. M., Notes on $\chi$-squared tests for matched samples, *J. R. Stat. Soc., Ser. B* **30**, 368–370 (1968).

107. Berkson, J., Application of minimum logit chi-squared estimate to a problem of Grizzle with a notation on the problem of no interaction, *Biometrics* **24**, 75–96 (1968).

108. Bhapkar, V. P., On the analysis of contingency tables with a quantitative response, *Biometrics* **24**, 329–338 (1968).

109. Bhapkar, V. P., and G. G. Koch, Hypotheses of "no interaction" in multidimensional contingency tables, *Technometrics* **10**, 107–123 (1968).

110. Bhapkar, V. P., and G. G. Koch, On the hypotheses of "no interaction" in contingency tables, *Biometrics* **24**, 567–594 (1968).

111. Fienberg, S. E., The geometry of an $r \times c$ contingency table, *Ann. Math. Stat.* **39**, 1186–1190 (1968).

112. Goodman, L. A., The analysis of cross-classified data: Independence, quasi-independence, and interactions in contingency tables with or without missing entries, *J. Am. Stat. Assoc.* **63**, 1091–1131 (1968).

113. Hamdan, M. A., Optimum choice of classes for contingency tables, *J. Am. Stat. Assoc.* **63**, 291–297 (1968).

114. Ireland, C. T., and S. Kullback, Contingency tables with given marginals, *Biometrika* **55**, 179–188 (1968).

115. Ireland, C. T., and S. Kullback, Minimum discrimination information estimation, *Biometrics* **24**, 707–713 (1968).

116. Ku, H. H., and S. Kullback, Interaction in multidimensional contingency tables: An information theoretic approach, *J. Res. Natl. Bur. Stand., Sect. B* **72**, 159–199 (1968).

117. Ku, H. H., R. Varner, and S. Kullback, Analysis of multidimensional contingency tables, in *Proceedings of the Fourteenth Conference on the Design of Experiments in Army Research, Development and Testing*, ARO-D Report 69-2, 1968.

118. Kullback, S., *Information Theory and Statistics*, Dover, New York, 1968.

119. Kullback, S., Probability densities with given marginals, *Ann. Math. Stat.* **39**, 1236–1243 (1968).

120. Leyton, M. K., Rapid calculation of exact probabilities for $2 \times 3$ contingency tables, *Biometrics* **24**, 714–717 (1968).

121. Mathieu, J.-R., and E. Lambert, Un test de l'identite des marges dun tableau de correlation, *C. R. Acad. Sci. Paris* **267**, 832–834 (1968).

122. Mosteller, F., Association and estimation in contingency tables, *J. Am. Stat. Assoc.* **63**, 1–28 (1968).

123. Slakter, M. J., Accuracy of an approximation to the power of the chi-square goodness of fit test with small but equal expected frequencies, *J. Am. Stat. Assoc.* **63**, 912–924 (1968).

124. Sugiura, N., and M. Otake, Numerical comparison of improvised methods of testing in contingency tables with small frequencies, *Ann. Inst. Stat. Math.* **20**, 507–517 (1968).

*1967*

125. Bennett, B. M., Tests of hypothesis concerning matched samples, *J. R. Stat. Soc., Ser. B* **29**, 468–474 (1967).

126. Bishop, Y. M. M., Multidimensional Contingency Tables: Cell Estimates. Ph.D. Dissertation, Harvard University, 1967.

127. Bloch, D. A., and G. S. Watson, A Bayesian study of the multinomial distribution, *Ann. Math. Stat.* **38**, 1423–1435 (1967).

128. Cox, D. R., and E. Lauh, A note on the graphical analysis of multidimensional contingency tables, *Technometrics* **9**, 481–488 (1967).

129. Ferguson, T. S., *Mathematical Statistics,* Academic, New York, 1967.

130. Good, I. J., A Bayesian significance test for multinomial distributions, *J. R. Stat. Soc., Ser. B* **29**, 339–431 (1967).

131. Snedecor, G. W., and W. G. Cochran, *Statistical Methods,* Iowa State University Press, Ames, Iowa, 1967.

*1966*

132. Armitage, P., The chi-square test for heterogeneity of proportions after adjustment for stratification, *J. R. Stat. Soc., Ser. B* **28**,150–163 (1966).

133. Bhapkar, V. P., A note on the equivalence of two test criteria for hypotheses in categorical data, *J. Am. Stat. Assoc.* **61**, 228–235 (1966).

134. Bhapkar, V. P., *Notes on Analysis of Categorical Data* (Institute of Statistics Mimeo Series No. 477), University of North Carolina, Chapel Hill, North Carolina, 1966.

135. Bhat, B. R., and S. R. Kulkarni, LAMP test of linear and loglinear hypotheses in multinomial experiments, *J. Am. Stat. Assoc.* **61**, 236–245 (1966).

136. Cox, D. R., A simple example of a comparison involving quantal data, *Biometrika* **53**, 215–220 (1966).

137. Craddock, J. M., Testing the significance of a $3 \times 3$ contingency table, *Statistician* **16**, 87–94 (1966).

138. Gabriel, K. R., Simultaneous test procedures for multiple comparison on categorical data, *J. Am. Stat. Assoc.* **61**, 1081–1096 (1966).

139. Gart, J. J., Alternative analyses of contingency tables, *J. R. Stat. Soc., Ser. B* **28**, 164–179 (1966).

140. Good, I. J., How to estimate probabilities, *J. Inst. Math. Appl.* **2**, 364–383 (1966).

141. Kullback, S., and M. A. Khairat, A note on minimum discrimination information, *Ann. Math. Stat.* **37**, 279–280 (1966).
142. Mantel, N., Models for complex contingency tables and polychotomous dosage response curves, *Biometrics* **22**, 83–95 (1966).

*1965*

143. Asano, C., On estimating multinomial probabilities by pooling incomplete samples, *Ann. Inst. Stat. Math.* **17**, 1–14 (1965).
144. Bhapkar, V. P., and G. G. Koch, *Hypothesis of "No Interaction" in Four-Dimensional Contingency Tables* (Institute of Statistics Mimeo Series No. 449), University of North Carolina, Chapel Hill, North Carolina, 1965.
145. Bhapkar, V. P., and G. G. Koch, *On the Hypothesis of "No Interaction" in Three-Dimensional Contingency Tables* (Institute of Statistics Mimeo Series No. 440), University of North Carolina, Chapel Hill, North Carolina, 1965.
146. Bhat, B. R., and B. N. Nagnur, Locally asymptotically most stringent tests and Lagrangian multiplier tests of linear hypotheses, *Biometrika* **52**(3 and 4), 459–468 (1965).
147. Birch, M. W., The detection of partial association II: The general case, *J. R. Stat. Soc., Ser. B* **27**, 111–124 (1965).
148. Caussinus, H., Contribution a l'analyse statistique des tableaux de correlation, *Ann. Fac. Sci. Univ. Toulouse* **29**, 77–182 (1965).
149. Good, I. J., *The Estimation of Probabilities: An Essay on Modern Bayesian Methods* (Research Monograph, 30), M.I.T. Press, Cambridge, Massachusetts, 1965.
150. Kastenbaum, M. A., *Contingency Tables: A Review* (MRC Technical Summary Report No. 596), Mathematical Research Center, The University of Wisconsin, Madison, Wisconsin, 1965.
151. Katti, S. K., and A. N. Sastry, Biological examples of small expected frequencies and the chi-square test, *Biometrics* **21**, 49–54 (1965).
152. Lancaster, H. O., and T. A. I. Brown, Size of $\chi$-squared test in the symmetrical multinomials, *Aust. J. Stat.* **7**, 40 (1965).
153. Lewontin, R. C., and J. Felsenstein, The robustness of homogeneity tests in $2 \times n$ tables, *Biometrics* **21**, 19–33 (1965).
154. Mote, V. L., and R. L. Anderson, An investigation of the effect of misclassification on the properties of chi-squared tests in the analysis of categorical data, *Biometrika* **52**, 95–109 (1965).
155. Radhakrishna, S., Combination of results from several $2 \times 2$ contingency tables, *Biometrics* **21**, 86–98 (1965).

*1964*

156. Allison, H. E., Computational forms for chi-square, *Am. Stat.* **18**(1), 17–18 (1964).
157. Bennett, B. M., and E. Nakamura, Tables for testing significance in a $2 \times 3$ contingency table, *Technometrics* **6**(4), 439–458 (1964).
158. Birch, M. W., The detection of partial association I: The $2 \times 2$ case, *J. R. Stat. Soc., Ser. B* **26**, 313–324 (1964).
159. Bross, I. D. J., Taking a covariable into account, *J. Am. Stat. Assoc.* **59**(307), 725–736 (1964).
160. Chew, V., Application of the negative binomial distribution with probability of misclassification, *Va. J. Sci.* **15**(1), 34–40 (1964).

161. Goodman, L. A., Interactions in multidimensional contingency tables, *Ann. Math. Stat.* **35**(2), 632–646 (1964).

162. Goodman, L. A., Simple methods for analyzing three-factor interaction in contingency tables, *J. R. Stat. Soc.* **59**, 319–352 (1964).

163. Goodman, L. A., Simultaneous confidence intervals for contrasts among multinomial populations, *Ann. Math. Stat.* **35**(2), 716–725 (1964).

164. Goodman, L. A., Simultaneous confidence limits for cross-product ratios in contingency tables, *J. R. Stat. Soc., Ser. B* **26**(1), 86–102 (1964).

165. Harkness, W. L., and L. Katz, Comparison of the power functions for the test of independence in $2 \times 2$ contingency tables, *Ann. Math. Stat.* **35**(3), 1115–1127 (1964).

166. Kihlberg, J. K., E. A. Narragon, and B. J. Campbell, Automobile crash injury in relation to car size, *Cornell Aeronaut. Lab. Rep.* **VJ-1823R11** (1964).

167. Lindley, D. V., The Bayesian analysis of contingency tables, *Ann. Math. Stat.* **35**(4), 1622–1643 (1964).

168. Plackett, R. L., The continuity correction in $2 \times 2$ tables, *Biometrika* **21**(3 and 4), 327–338 (1964).

169. Putter, J., The $\chi^2$ goodness-of-fit test for a class of cases of dependent observations, *Biometrika* **51**, 250–252 (1964).

170. Somers, R. H., Simple measures of association for the triple dichotomy, *J. R. Stat. Soc., Ser. A* **127**(3), 409–415 (1964).

171. Tallis, G. M., The use of models in the analysis of some classes of contingency tables, *Biometrics* **24**(4), 832–839 (1964).

*1963*

172. Bennett, B. M., and E. Nakamura, Tables for testing significance in a $2 \times 3$ contingency table, *Technometrics* **5**(4), 501–511 (1963).

173. Birch, M. W., Maximum likelihood in three-way contingency tables, *J. R. Stat. Soc., Ser. B* **25**(1), 220–233 (1963).

174. Darroch, J. N., and S. D. Silvey, On testing more than one hypothesis, *Ann. Math. Stat.* **34**(2), 555–567 (1963).

175. Diamond, E. L., The limiting power of categorical data chi-square tests analogous to normal analysis of variance, *Ann. Math. Stat.* **34**(4), 1432–1441 (1963).

176. Edwards, A. W. F., The measure of association in a $2 \times 2$ table, *J. R. Stat. Soc., Ser. A* **126**(1), 109–114 (1963).

177. Feldman, S. E., and E. Klinger, Short cut calculation of the Fisher-Yates exact test, *Psychometrika* **28**(3), 289–291 (1963).

178. Finney, D. J., R. Latscha, B. M. Bennett, P. Hsu, and E. S. Pearson, *Tables for Testing Significance in a $2 \times 2$ Contingency Table* (Supplement by B. M. Bennett and C. Horst, i + 28), Cambridge University Press, Cambridge, England, 1963, 103 pp.

179. Gold, R. A., Tests auxiliary to $\chi^2$ tests in a Markov chain, *Ann. Math. Stat.* **34**(1), 56–74 (1963).

180. Good, I. J., Maximum entropy for hypothesis formulation, especially for multidimensional contingency tables, *Ann. Math. Stat.* **34**(3), 911–934 (1963).

181. Goodman, L. A., On methods for comparing contingency tables, *J. R. Stat. Soc., Ser. A* **126**(1), 94–108 (1963).

182. Goodman, L. A., On Plackett's test for contingency table interactions, *J. R. Stat. Soc., Ser. B* **25**(1), 179–188 (1963).

183. Goodman, L. A., and W. H. Kruskal, Measures of association for cross classification III: Approximate sampling theory, *J. Am. Stat. Assoc.* **58,** 310–364 (1963).

184. Ku, H. H., A note on contingency tables involving zero frequencies and the $2I$ test, *Technometrics* **5**(3), 398–400 (1963).

185. Mantel, N., Chi-square tests with one degree of freedom: Extensions of the Mantel-Haenszel procedure, *J. Am. Stat. Assoc.* **58,** 690–700 (1963).

186. Newell, D. J., Misclassification in 2 × 2 tables, *Biometrics* **19**(1), 187–188 (1963).

187. Okamato, M., Chi-square statistic based on the pooled frequencies of several observations, *Biometrika* **50,** 524–528 (1963).

188. Ries, P. N., and H. Smith, The use of chi-square for preference testing in multidimensional problems, *Chem. Eng. Prog., Symp. Ser.* **59**(42), 39–43 (1963).

189. Walsh, J. E., Loss in test efficiency due to misclassification for 2 × 2 tables, *Biometrics* **19**(1), 158–162 (1963).

*1962*

190. Cornfield, J., Joint dependence of risk of coronary heart disease on serum cholesterol and systolic blood pressure: a discriminant function analysis. *Fed. Proc.* **4**(II), (Suppl. No. 11), 58–61 (July-August 1962).

191. Daly, C., A simple test for trends in a contingency table, *Biometrics* **18**(1), 114–119 (1962).

192. Darroch, J. N., Interactions in multi-factor contingency tables, *J. R. Stat. Soc., Ser. B* **24**(1), 251–263 (1962).

193. Fisher, Sir Ronald A., Confidence limits for a cross-product ratio, *Aust. J. Stat.* **4**(1), 41 (1962).

194. Gart, J. J., Approximate confidence limits for relative risks, *J. R. Stat. Soc., Ser. B* **24**(2), 454–463 (1962).

195. Gart, J. J., On the combination of relative risks, *Biometrics* **18**(4), 601–610 (1962).

196. Kincaid, W. M., The combination of 2 × $m$ contingency tables, *Biometrics* **18**(2), 224–228 (1962).

197. Kullback, S., M. Kupperman, and H. H. Ku, An application of information theory to the analysis of contingency tables with a table of $2N \ln N$, $N = 1(1)10,000$, *J. Res. Natl. Bur. Stand., Sect. B* **66,** 217–243 (1962).

198. Kullback, S., M. Kupperman, and H. H. Ku, Tests for contingency tables and Markov chains, *Technometrics* **4**(4), 573–608 (1962).

199. Lewis, B. N., On the analysis of interaction in multi-dimensional contingency tables, *J. R. Stat. Soc., Ser. A* **125**(1), 88–117 (1962).

200. Plackett, R. L., A note on interactions in contingency tables, *J. R. Stat. Soc., Ser. B* **24**(1), 162–166 (1962).

201. Tallis, G. M., The maximum likelihood estimation of correlation from contingency tables, *Biometrics* **18**(3), 342–353 (1962).

*1961*

202. Berger, A., On comparing intensities of association between two binary characteristics in two different populations, *J. Am. Stat. Assoc.* **56,** 889–908 (1961).

203. Bhapkar, V. P., Some tests for categorical data, *Ann. Math. Stat.* **32**(1), 72–83 (1961).

204. Billingsley, P., *Statistical Inference for Markov Processes* (Statistical Research Monographs, 2), University of Chicago Press, Chicago, 1961.

205. Claringbold, P. J., The use of orthogonal polynomials in the partition of chi-square, *Aust. J. Stat.* **3**(2), 48–63 (1961).

206. Friedlander, D., A technique for estimating a contingency table, given the marginal totals and some supplementary data, *J. R. Stat. Soc., Ser. A* **124**(3), 412–420 (1961).

207. Garside, R. F., Tables for ascertaining whether differences between percentages are statistically significant at the 1% level, *Br. Med. J.* **1**, 874–876 (1961).

208. Gregory, G., Contingency tables with a dependent classification, *Aust. J. Stat.* **3**(2), 42–47 (1961).

209. Grizzle, J. E., A new method of testing hypotheses and estimating parameters for the logistic model, *Biometrics* **17**(3), 372–385 (1961).

210. Kendall, M. G., and A. Stuart, *The Advanced Theory of Statistics*, Vol. 2, Griffin, London, 1961.

211. Okamato, M., and G. Ishii, Test of independence in intraclass $2 \times 2$ tables, *Biometrika* **48**, 181–190 (1961).

212. Rogot, E., A note on measurement errors and detecting real differences, *J. Am. Stat. Assoc.* **56**, 314–319 (1961).

213. Schull, W. J., Some problems of analysis of multi-factor tables, *Bull. Inst. Int. Stat.* **28**(3), 259–270 (1961).

214. Yates, F., Marginal percentages in multiway tables of quantal data with disproportionate frequencies, *Biometrics* **17**(1), 1–9 (1961).

*1960*

215. Bennett, B. M., and P. Hsu, On the power function of the exact test for the $2 \times 2$ contingency table, *Biometrika* **47**, 393–398 (1960).

216. Gridgeman, N. T., Card-matching experiments: A conspectus of theory, *J. R. Stat. Soc., Ser. A* **123**(1), 45–49 (1960).

217. Ishii, G., Intraclass contingency tables, *Ann. Inst. Stat. Math.* **12**, 161–207 (1960); corrections, p. 279.

218. Kastenbaum, M. A., A note on the additive partitioning of chi-square in contingency tables, *Biometrics* **16**(3), 416–422 (1960).

219. Kupperman, M., On comparing two observed frequency counts, *Appl. Stat.* **9**(1), 37–42 (1960).

220. Lancaster, H. O., On tests of independence in several dimensions, *J. Aust. Math. Soc.* **1**, 241–254 (1960); Corrigendum, **1**, 496 (1960).

221. Robertson, W. H., Programming Fisher's exact method of comparing two percentages, *Technometrics* **2**(1), 103–107 (1960).

222. Solomon, H., Classification procedures based on dichotomous response vectors (no. 36), in *Contributions to Probability and Statistics, Essays in Honor of Harold Hotelling* (I. Olkin *et al.*, eds.), Stanford University Press, Stanford, California, 1960, pp. 414–423. [Also in *Studies in Item Analysis and Prediction* (H. Solomon, ed.), Stanford University Press, Stanford, California, 1961, pp. 177–186.]

*1959*

223. Anderson, R. L., Use of contingency tables in the analysis of consumer preference studies, *Biometrics* **15**(4), 582–590 (1959).

224. Chakravarti, I. M., and C. R. Rao, Tables for some small sample tests of significance for Poisson distributions and $2 \times 3$ contingency tables, *Sankhya* **21**(3 and 4), 315–326 (1959).

225. Goodman, L. A., and W. H. Kruskal, Measures of association for cross classification II: Further discussion and references, *J. Am. Stat. Assoc.* **54**, 123–163 (1959).

226. Haldane, J. B. S., The analysis of heterogeneity, I. *Sankhya* **21**(3 and 4), 209–216 (1959).
227. Hoyt, C. J., P. R. Krishnaiah, and E. P. Torrance, Analysis of complex contingency data, *J. Exp. Educ.* **27,** 187–194 (1959).
228. Kastenbaum, M. A., and D. E. Lamphiear, Calculation of chi-square to test the no three-factor interaction hypothesis, *Biometrics* **15**(1), 107–115 (1959).
229. Kullback, S., *Information Theory and Statistics,* Wiley, New York, 1959.
230. Kupperman, M., A rapid significance test for contingency tables, *Biometrics* **15**(4), 625–628 (1959).
231. Nass, C. A. G., The $\chi^2$ test for small expectations in contingency tables, with special reference to accidents and absenteeism, *Biometrika* **46,** 365–385 (1959).
232. Silvey, S. D., The Lagrangian multiplier test, *Ann. Math. Stat.* **30**(2), 389–407 (1959).
233. Somers, R. H., The rank analogue of product-moment partial correlation and regression, with application to manifold, ordered contingency tables, *Biometrika* **46,** 241–246 (1959).
234. Steyn, H. S., On $\chi^2$-tests for contingency tables of negative binomial type, *Stat. Neerland.* **13,** 433–444 (1959).
235. Weiner, I. B., A note on the use of Mood's likelihood ratio test for item analyses involving 2 × 2 tables with small samples, *Psychometrika* **24**(4), 371–372 (1959).

*1958*

236. Blalock, H. M., Jr., Probabilistic interpretations for the mean square contingency, *J. Am. Stat. Assoc.* **53,** 102–105 (1958).
237. Garside, R. F., Tables for ascertaining whether differences between percentages are statistically significant, *Br. Med. J.* **1,** 1459–1461 (1958).
238. Kastenbaum, M. A., Estimation of relative frequencies of four sperm types in Drosophila melanogaster, *Biometrics* **14**(2), 223–228 (1958).
239. Mitra, S. K., On the limiting power function of the frequency chi-square test, *Ann. Math. Stat.* **29,** 1221–1233 (1958).
240. Snedecor, G. W., Chi-square of Bartlett, Mood and Lancaster in a $2^3$ contingency table, *Biometrics* **14**(4), 560–562 (1958) (Query).

*1957*

241. Bross, I. D. J., and E. L. Kasten, Rapid analysis of 2 × 2 tables, *J. Am. Stat. Assoc.* **52,** 18–28 (1957).
242. Corsten, L. C. A., Partition of experimental vectors connected with multinomial distributions, *Biometrics* **13**(4), 451–484 (1957).
243. Edwards, J. H., A note on the practical interpretation of 2 × 2 tables, *Br. J. Prev. Soc. Med.* **11,** 73–78 (1957).
244. Lancaster, H. O., Some properties of the bivariate normal distribution considered in the form of a contingency table, *Biometrika* **44,** 289–292 (1957).
245. Mote, V. L., An Investigation of the Effect of Misclassification of the Chi-Square Tests in the Analysis of Categorical Data, Unpublished Ph. D. Dissertation, North Carolina State College, Raleigh, North Carolina, 1957 (also Institute of Statistics Mimeo Series No. 182).
246. Roy, S. N., *Some Aspects of Multivariate Analysis,* Wiley, New York, 1957.
247. Sakoda, J. M., and B. H. Cohen, Exact probabilities for contingency tables using binomial coefficients, *Psychometrika* **22**(1), 83–86 (1957).

248. Woolf, B., The log likelihood ratio test (the *G*-test). Methods and tables for tests of heterogeneity in contingency tables, *Ann. Hum. Genet.* **21,** 397–409 (1957).

*1956*

249. Fishman, J. A., A note on Jenkins' "Improved Method for Tetrachoric *r*," *Psychometrika* **20**(3), 305 (1956).
250. Good, I. J., On the estimation of small frequencies in contingency tables, *J. R. Stat. Soc., Ser. B* **18**(1), 113–124 (1956).
251. Gridgeman, N. T., A tasting experiment, *Appl. Stat.* **5**(2), 106–112 (1956).
252. Leander, E. K., and D. J. Finney, An extension of the use of the $\chi^2$ test, *Appl. Stat.* **5**(2), 132–136 (1956).
253. Mainland, D., L. Herrera, and M. I. Sutcliffe, *Statistical Tables for Use with Binomial Samples—Contingency Tests, Confidence Limits, and Sample Size Estimates,* New York University College of Medicine, New York, 1956.
254. Roy, S. N., and M. A. Kastenbaum, On the hypothesis of no "interaction" in a multiway contingency table, *Ann. Math. Stat.* **27**(3), 749–757 (1956).
255. Roy, S. N., and S. K. Mitra, An introduction to some non-parametric generalizations of analysis of variance and multivariate analysis, *Biometrika* **43**(3 and 4), 361–376 (1956).
256. Watson, G. S., Missing and "mixed-up" frequencies in contingency tables, *Biometrics* **12**(1), 47–50 (1956).

*1955*

257. Armitage, P., Tests for linear trends in proportions and frequencies, *Biometrics* **11**(3), 375–386 (1955).
258. Armsen, P., Tables for significance tests of $2 \times 2$ contingency tables, *Biometrika* **42,** 494–505 (1955).
259. Cochran, W. G., A test of a linear function of the deviations between observed and expected numbers, *J. Am. Stat. Assoc.* **50,** 377–397 (1955).
260. Haldane, J. B. S., A problem in the significance of small numbers, *Biometrika* **42,** 266–267 (1955).
261. Haldane, J. B. S., Substitutes for $\chi^2$, *Biometrika* **42,** 265–266 (1955).
262. Haldane, J. B. S., The rapid calculation of $\chi^2$ as a test of homogeneity from a $2 \times n$ table, *Biometrika* **42,** 519–520 (1955).
263. Jenkins, W. L., An improved method for tetrachoric *r*, *Psychometrika* **20**(3), 253–258 (1955).
264. Kastenbaum, M. A., Analysis of Data in Multiway Contingency Tables, Unpublished doctoral dissertation, North Carolina State College, October 1955.
265. Leslie, P. H., A simple method of calculating the exact probability in $2 \times 2$ contingency tables with small marginal totals, *Biometrika* **42,** 522–523 (1955).
266. Mitra, S. K., *Contributions to the Statistical Analysis of Categorical Data* (North Carolina Institute of Statistics Mimeograph Series No. 142), University of North Carolina, Chapel Hill, North Carolina, 1955.
267. Roy, S. N., and M. A. Kastenbaum, *A Generalization of Analysis of Variance and Multivariate Analysis to Data Based on Frequencies in Qualitative Categorical or Class Intervals* (North Carolina Institute of Statistics Mimeograph Series No. 131), University of North Carolina, Chapel Hill, North Carolina, 1955.
268. Roy, S. N., and S. K. Mitra, *An Introduction to Some Non-Parametric Generalizations of Analysis of Variance and Multivariate Analysis* (North Carolina Institute

of Statistics Mimeograph Series No. 139), University of North Carolina, Chapel Hill, North Carolina, 1955.

269. Sekar, C. C., S. P. Agarivala, and P. N. Chakraborty, On the power function of a test of significance for the difference between two proportions, *Sankhya* **15**(4), 381–390 (1955).

270. Stuart, A., A test of homogeneity of the marginal distributions in a two-way classification, *Biometrika* **42**, 412–416 (1955).

271. Woolf, B., On estimating the relation between blood group and disease, *Ann. Hum. Genet.* **19**, 251–253 (1955).

272. Yates, F., A note on the application of the combination of probabilities test to a set of 2 × 2 tables, *Biometrika* **42**, 401–411 (1955).

273. Yates, F., The use of transformations and maximum likelihood in the analysis of quantal experiments involving two treatments, *Biometrika* **42**, 382–403 (1955).

*1954*

274. Bross, I. D. J., Misclassification in 2 × 2 tables, *Biometrics* **10**(4), 478–486 (1954).

275. Cochran, W. G., Some methods for strengthening the common chi-square tests, *Biometrics* **10**(4), 417–451 (1954).

276. Dawson, R. B., A simplified expression for the variance of the $\chi^2$ function on a contingency table, *Biometrika* **41**, 280 (1954).

277. Goodman, L. A., and W. H. Kruskal, Measures of association for cross classification, *J. Am. Stat. Assoc.* **49**, 732–764 (1954).

278. Kimball, A. W., Short-cut formulas for the exact partition of chi-square in contingency tables, *Biometrics* **10**(4), 452–458 (1954).

279. McGill, W. J., Multivariate information transmission, *Psychometrika* **19**(2), 97–116 (1954).

*1952*

280. Cochran, W. G., The $\chi^2$ test of goodness of fit, *Ann. Math. Stat.* **23**(3), 315–345 (1952).

281. Dyke, G. V., and H. D. Patterson, Analysis of factorial arrangements when the data are proportions, *Biometrics* **8**, 1–12 (1952).

*1951*

282. Freeman, G. H., and J. H. Halton, Note on the exact treatment of contingency, goodness of fit and other problems of significance, *Biometrika* **38**, 141–149 (1951).

283. Lancaster, H. O., Complex contingency tables treated by the partition of chi-square, *J. R. Stat. Soc., Ser. B* **13**, 242–249 (1951).

284. Simpson, C. H., The interpretation of interaction in contingency tables, *J. R. Stat. Soc., Ser. B* **13**, 238–241 (1951).

*1950*

285. Tocher, K. D., Extension of the Neyman-Pearson theory of tests to discontinuous variates, *Biometrika* **37**, 130–144 (1950).

*1949*

286. Hsu, P. L., The limiting distributions of functions of sample means and application to testing hypotheses, in *Proceedings of the Berkeley Symposium on Mathematical Statistics and Probability* (1945, 1946), University of California Press, Berkeley, 1949.

287. Irwin, J. O., A note on the subdivision of chi-square into components, *Biometrika* **36,** 130–134 (1949).

288. Lancaster, H. O., The combination of probabilities arising from data in discrete distributions, *Biometrika* **36,** 370–382 (1949); corrigendum, **37,** 452 (1950).

289. Lancaster, H. O., The derivation and partition of chi-square in certain discrete distributions, *Biometrika* **36,** 117–129 (1949).

*1948*

290. Finney, D. J., The Fisher-Yates test of significance in $2 \times 2$ contingency tables, *Biometrika* **35,** 145–156 (1948).

291. Swineford, F., A table for estimating the significance of the difference between correlated percentages, *Psychometrika* **13,** 23–25 (1948).

292. Yates, F., The analysis of contingency tables with groupings based on quantitative characters, *Biometrika* **35,** 176–181 (1948).

*1947*

293. Barnard, G. A., Significance tests for $2 \times 2$ tables, *Biometrika* **34,** 123–138 (1947).

294. Barnard, G. A., $2 \times 2$ tables. A note on E. S. Pearson's paper, *Biometrika* **34,** 168–169 (1947).

295. Pearson, E. S., The choice of statistical tests illustrated on the interpretation of data classed in a $2 \times 2$ table, *Biometrika* **34,** 139–167 (1947).

*1946*

296. Cramér, H., *Mathematical Methods of Statistics,* Princeton University Press, Princeton, New Jersey, 1946, p. 424.

*1945*

297. Norton, H. W., Calculation of chi-square for complex contingency tables, *J. Am. Stat. Assoc.* **40,** 251–258 (1945).

*1943*

298. Wald, A., Tests of statistical hypotheses concerning several parameters when the number of observations is large, *Trans. Am. Math. Soc.* **54,** 426–482 (1943).

*1939*

299. Haldane, J. B. S., Note on the preceding analysis of Mendelian segregations, *Biometrika* **31,** 67–71 (1939).

300. Roberts, E., W. M. Dawson, and M. Madden, Observed and theoretical ratios in Mendelian inheritance, *Biometrika* **31,** 56–66 (1939.

*1938*

301. Fisher, R. A., and F. Yates, *Statistical Tables for Biological, Agricultural and Medical Research,* Oliver and Boyd, Edinburgh, 1938; 6th ed., 1963, x + 146.

302. Swaroop, S., Tables of the exact values of probabilities for testing the significance of differences between proportions based on pairs of small samples, *Sankhya,* **4,** 73–84 (1938).

*1937*

303. Haldane, J. B. S., The exact value of the moments of the distribution of $\chi^2$ used as a test of goodness of fit, when expectations are small, *Biometrika* **29,** 133–143 (1937).

*1935*

304. Bartlett, M. S., Contingency table interactions, *J. R. Stat. Soc., Suppl.* **2**, 248–252 (1935).
305. Irwin, J. O., Tests of significance for differences between percentages based on small numbers, *Metron* **12**(2), 83–94 (1935).
306. Wilks, S. S., The likelihood test of independence in contingency tables, *Ann. Math. Stat.* **6**, 190–196 (1935).

*1934*

307. Fisher, R. A., *Statistical Methods for Research Workers,* 1934, Oliver and Boyd, Edinburgh, 5th and subsequent editions, Section 21.02.
308. Yates, F., Contingency tables involving small numbers and the $\chi^2$ test, *J. R. Stat. Soc., Suppl.* **1**, 217–235 (1934).

*1924*

309. Fisher, R. A., The conditions under which chi-square measures the discrepancy between observation and hypothesis, *J. R. Stat. Soc.* **87**, 442–450 (1924).

*1922*

310. Fisher, R. A., On the interpretation of chi-square from contingency tables, and the calculation of *P*, *J. R. Stat. Soc.* **85**, 87–94 (1922).

*1916*

311. Pearson, K., On the general theory of multiple contingency with special reference to partial contingency, *Biometrika* **11**, 145–158 (1916).

*1915*

312. Greenwood, M., and G. U. Yule, The statistics of anti-typhoid and anti-cholera inoculations and the interpretation of such statistics in general, *Proc. R. Soc. Med.* **8**, 113–194 (1915).

*1912*

313. Yule, G. U., On the methods of measuring association between two attributes, *J. R. Stat. Soc.* **75**, 579 (1912).

*1904*

314. Pearson, K., Mathematical contributions to the theory of evolution. XIII. On the theory of contingency and its relation to association and normal correlation, *Draper's Company Research Memoirs, Biometric Series 1,* 1904, 35 pp.

*1900*

315. Pearson, K., On the criterion that a given system of deviations from the probable in the case of a correlated system of variables is such that it can be reasonably supposed to have arisen from random sampling, *Philos. Mag.* [5] **50**, 157–172 (1900).

*1898*

316. Sheppard, W. F., On the application of the theory of error to cases of normal distribution and normal correlation, *Philos. Trans. R. Soc. London* **A192**, 101–167 (1898).

*Solomon Kullback*

# CONTROL SYSTEM OPTIMIZATION

The practical need (rather than academic desire) to optimize the performance of control systems became evident in the Space Age of the 1960s due to the extremely stringent requirements imposed on the operation of space hardware. Methods for designing highly sophisticated feedback control systems without a so-called optimization constraint were developed and refined during World War II and the period shortly thereafter. Applications of these ideas to such diverse technologies as aerospace, oil refining, industrial production, and communications were characterized by exceptional accuracy attainable, relative immunity to noise, accommodation of external disturbances, etc. To add the requirement that these tasks be performed in a manner that makes optimal use of available resources (minimum time, fuel, energy, etc.) is to introduce a radically new dimension to the problem. Generous government support for such a project, coupled with the availability of the modern high-speed digital computer, served to stimulate the development of versatile mathematical optimization techniques, together with methods for applying these techniques for purposes of optimizing the performance of control systems.

In the first part of this article the physical and mathematical properties of a very general type of control system are surveyed briefly. Following this, the basic problem of control system optimization is posed in precise mathematical terms. At this point the classical mathematical apparatus for the solution of this problem is introduced. After exhibiting the virtually insurmountable difficulties associated with the classical approach (calculus of variations) insofar as obtaining numerical results is concerned (even with the use of sophisticated computers), the main subject matter is presented; namely, the application of mathematical programming methodologies to the solution of problems of optimal control. The term "mathematical programming" is used here in its broadest sense, encompassing the theories of linear, nonlinear, and dynamic programming, as well as the concepts of steepest descent, Newton-Raphson iteration, etc. All of these disciplines are unashamedly computer oriented and could, with some justification, be viewed as "computer compatible" mathematics.

For ease of exposition, the nomenclature to be used throughout is defined at the outset.

## NOMENCLATURE

$\mathbf{a}$     a constant vector of dimension $\rho$
$\mathbf{A}$     an $n \times n$ weighting matrix
$\mathbf{B}$     an $m \times m$ weighting matrix
$\mathbf{c}$     a constant vector of dimension $m$
$\mathbf{c}_1$     a constant vector of dimension $\lambda$

CONTROL SYSTEM OPTIMIZATION

$\mathbf{c}_2$     a constant vector of dimension $\xi$

$\mathbf{D}$     an $m \times \rho$ constant matrix

$\mathbf{D}_1$     a $\lambda \times \rho$ constant matrix

$\mathbf{D}_2$     a $\xi \times \rho$ constant matrix

$\mathbf{f}$     an $n$ vector defined by Eq. (1)

$\mathbf{F}$     an $n \times n$ system matrix

$\mathbf{G}$     an $n \times m$ control matrix

$H$     the hamiltonian; defined by Eq. (13)

$J$     the "cost" function

$\mathbf{K}$     an $n \times l$ gain matrix

$\mathbf{L}$     an $n \times n$ weighting matrix

$\mathbf{M}$     an $n \times n$ matrix obtained as the solution to a Ricatti equation

$\mathbf{p}$     $n$ dimensional costate vector

$\mathbf{P}$     $n \times n$ variance matrix for state vector

$\mathbf{Q}$     $k \times k$ variance matrix for disturbance vector

$\mathbf{r}$     reference vector

$\mathbf{R}$     $l \times l$ variance matrix for noise vector

$t$     time

$t_0$     initial time

$t_f$     final time

$\mathbf{u}$     control vector of dimension $m$

$\mathbf{v}$     noise vector of dimension $l$

$\mathbf{w}$     disturbance vector of dimension $k$

$\mathbf{x}$     $n$ dimension state vector

$\mathbf{y}$     $\rho$ dimensional vector of parameters

$\mathbf{z}$     $l$ dimensional measurement vector

$\boldsymbol{\alpha}$     an equality constraint vector of dimension $\lambda$

$\boldsymbol{\beta}$     an inequality constraint vector of dimension $\xi$

$\gamma$     cost function integrand; see Eq. (7)

$\delta$     Dirac delta function

$\boldsymbol{\eta}$     error vector

$\boldsymbol{\theta}$     initial value of the state vector

$\boldsymbol{\Lambda}$     a $\rho \times \rho$ weighting matrix

$\boldsymbol{\mu}$     a vector of Lagrange multipliers of dimension $q$

$\boldsymbol{\nu}$     value of state vector at "final" time

$\boldsymbol{\sigma}$     a vector of terminal inequality constraints (dimension $\tau$)

$\varphi$     Portion of cost function attributed to terminal value of state vector

$\boldsymbol{\psi}$     a vector of terminal equality constraints (dimension $q$)


## Miscellaneous

$( \ )_f$     denotes value at time $t_f$

$( \ \dot{} \ )$     denotes derivative with respect to time

$( \ )^T$     denotes matrix transpose

$\| u \|$     denotes norm of vector $\mathbf{u} = (\mathbf{u}^T\mathbf{u})^{\frac{1}{2}}$

$\nabla_x( \ )$     denotes gradient with respect to $\mathbf{x}$

Unless otherwise specified, lowercase **boldface** letters denote vectors, and uppercase **boldface** letters denote matrices.

Furthermore, if $c$ is an $m$ vector, and $\alpha$ is a $\lambda$ vector, then $(\partial c/\partial \alpha)$ is an $m \times \lambda$ matrix whose $ij$th component is $\partial c_i/\partial \alpha_j$.

Also, the notation $\partial c/\partial t$ represents an $m$ vector whose $i$th component is $\partial c_i/\partial t$.

## THE CONTROL SYSTEM

### General Overview

A control system, in the modern engineering sense, is fundamentally a teleological abstraction. In essence, it involves the idea of feedback whereby the output of a dynamic process (be it chemical, electrical, mechanical, or whatever) is compared with a reference input to generate an error signal. The latter, usually of a low amplitude, low power level, is applied to an actuator, the output of which is the primary control input to the dynamic process (called the "plant"). The main ideas are depicted schematically in Fig. 1. To accommodate the possibility that there are multiple inputs and outputs, the input **u** is assumed to be a vector (of dimension $m$), and the output (state) vector, **x**, is presumed to be of dimension $n$. There may also be some external forces acting on the plant; these are denoted by the vector **w**. Usually, **w** is derived from the process environment (e.g., the process may be an airplane in flight, in which case **w** would correspond to an aerodynamic gust). The components of the state vector **x** are generally determined by the nature of the dynamic process (plant). For an aerospace vehicle, the components of **x** might represent the velocity and displacement of the vehicle. For a chemical process, the components of **x** might be the temperature, pressure, salinity, etc. of the end product.

It may or may not be possible to sense the state variables directly by appropriate sensors and instrumentation. Quite often, the latter can measure only some known function of the state vector; thus the parameter **z** in Fig. 1 may

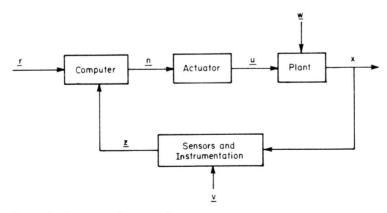

**Fig. 1.** General schematic of a control system.

be viewed as a vector (of dimension $p$) which is a known function of $\mathbf{x}$. Since measurements inevitably contain errors, $\mathbf{z}$ will also be a function of a noise vector, $\mathbf{v}$, which, in some sense, contaminates the measurement.

The function of the computer in Fig. 1 is to compare the reference signal $\mathbf{r}$ with the feedback signal $\mathbf{z}$, and then generate an output $\boldsymbol{\eta}$, which is some function of the error $(\mathbf{r} - \mathbf{x})$. In its simplest form, the "computer" may be a simple differencing device whose output is merely the difference between the inputs. In sophisticated applications the computer in Fig. 1 is indeed a digital computer which, in addition to sensing the difference between the actual and reference state, will perform such functions as signal shaping and stability augmentation. The capabilities of "digital filtering" of data are far superior to those of their analog counterparts. Finally, the error signal $\boldsymbol{\eta}$ operates on the actuator, which is usually some large power device, the latter operating on the plant such that a predetermined task is performed, subject to stipulated constraints in operation.

Most commonly, the performance quality of the control system is judged by such characteristics as stability, accuracy, and sensitivity to noise and disturbances. These topics constitute the usual domain of conventional control theory. The question of control system optimization is, in a general sense, concerned with means of performing a stipulated task in a manner which is the "best possible" theoretically, usually in the sense of making optimal use of available resources. A mathematical formulation of the problem brings it quite naturally into the domain of the calculus of variations.

## MATHEMATICAL STATEMENT OF THE PROBLEM

With reference to the system described in the preceding section, a very general form of the optimization problem may be formulated in mathematical terms as follows. Given the system

$$\dot{\mathbf{x}} = \mathbf{f}(\mathbf{x}, \mathbf{u}, \mathbf{w}, t) \tag{1}$$

A set of path constraints,

$$\boldsymbol{\alpha}(\mathbf{x}, \mathbf{u}) = 0 \tag{2}$$
$$\boldsymbol{\beta}(\mathbf{x}, \mathbf{u}) \lessgtr 0 \tag{3}$$

a set of terminal constraints,

$$\boldsymbol{\sigma}[\mathbf{x}(t_f)] \lessgtr 0 \tag{4}$$
$$\boldsymbol{\psi}[\mathbf{x}(t_f)] = 0 \tag{5}$$

and initial conditions,

$$\mathbf{x}(t_0) = \boldsymbol{\theta} \tag{6}$$

The disturbance vector $\mathbf{w}$ may be deterministic or random, specified either as a known function of time or else characterized by its statistical properties (mean and variance).

It is required to determine $\mathbf{u}(t)$ such that the performance index

$$J = \varphi[\mathbf{x}(t_f), t_f] + \int_{t_0}^{t_f} \gamma[\mathbf{x}(t), \mathbf{u}(t), t] \, dt \tag{7}$$

is a minimum. The performance index $J$ is sufficiently general to accommodate virtually any engineering criterion of interest.

## METHODS OF SOLUTION

There is no simple straightforward solution to the completely general optimization problem formulated in the preceding section. All of the available methods require that one or more of the stipulations be relaxed; e.g.

1. No noise or disturbances
2. No path constraints
3. System equations are linear
4. The system is of low order, etc.

The following optimization subsections outline the currently available techniques, the conditions under which they are applicable, computational features, etc. No one method is recognized as universally superior. In general, the analyst chooses his approach based on the particular problem to be investigated—perhaps influenced to some extent by the nature of the software capabilities of his "home-based" computer installation.

### Calculus of Variations

The optimization problem is formulated in the following way: Given the system

$$\dot{\mathbf{x}} = \mathbf{f}(\mathbf{x}, \mathbf{u}, t) \tag{8}$$

and initial conditions

$$\mathbf{x}(t_0) = \boldsymbol{\theta} \tag{9}$$

There are constraints on the control vector $\mathbf{u}$ expressed formally by

$$\mathbf{u} \in U \tag{10}$$

Typical examples of this are

$$|\mathbf{u}| \lessgtr \mathbf{k}_1 \tag{11}$$
$$\|\mathbf{u}\| \equiv (\mathbf{u}^T\mathbf{u})^{1/2} \lessgtr k_2 \tag{12}$$

A control vector which satisfies (10) is said to be an admissible control.

It is required to determine the admissible control $\mathbf{u}(t)$ such that the cost function $J$, as given by (7), is a minimum.

In this formulation the disturbance **w** and noise **v** are identically zero. To obtain a solution, one first forms the hamiltonian

$$H = \mathbf{p}^T \mathbf{f} + \gamma \tag{13}$$

where **p** is the costate vector derived from

$$\dot{\mathbf{p}}^T = \partial H / \partial \mathbf{x} \tag{14}$$

Note also that in terms of the hamiltonian,

$$\dot{\mathbf{x}}^T = \partial H / \partial \mathbf{p} \tag{15}$$

A determination of the optimal **u**(t) follows from an application of the following theorem (Pontryagin's principle):

A necessary condition for the minimization of the cost function, J, is that **u**(t) be chosen such that the hamiltonian, H, is a minimum.

If there are no constraints on **u,** then the necessary condition for minimizing J is expressed as

$$\partial H / \partial \mathbf{u} = o \tag{16}$$

Taking account of (13), this leads to

$$\left(\frac{\partial \mathbf{f}}{\partial \mathbf{u}}\right)^T \mathbf{p} + \left(\frac{\partial \gamma}{\partial \mathbf{u}}\right)^T = 0 \tag{17}$$

$$\dot{\mathbf{p}} = -\left(\frac{\partial \mathbf{f}}{\partial \mathbf{x}}\right)^T \mathbf{p} - \left(\frac{\partial \gamma}{\partial \mathbf{x}}\right)^T \tag{18}$$

The above equations are, in fact, the matrix form of the Euler-Lagrange equations in the calculus of variations.

It is clear that in order to obtain a numerical solution, one must solve a two-point boundary value problem. The necessary boundary conditions depend on the nature of the terminal conditions, cost function, and whether the terminal time is fixed or free (unspecified). Table 1 summarizes the boundary conditions for the most commonly encountered situations.

In all cases the $n$ initial conditions are given; viz. Eq. (9). Examining case No. 2, for example, we have $(n + q + 1)$ remaining terminal conditions to specify; i.e., the unknown final time $t_f$, the $n$ terminal conditions $\mathbf{p}(t_f)$, and values for the $q$ components of the Lagrange multiplier vector $\mu$. These are obtained from

$$H(t) = H(t_f) = 0 \qquad \text{(one condition)}$$
$$\mathbf{p}(t_f) = (\partial \psi / \partial \mathbf{x})_f^T \mu \qquad \text{($n$ conditions)}$$
$$\psi[\mathbf{x}(t_f)] = 0 \qquad \text{($q$ conditions)}$$

A solution is therefore theoretically obtainable.

**TABLE 1**
Summary of Boundary Conditions

| Case no. | System | Cost $\gamma$ | Cost $\varphi$ | Terminal conditions | $f$ | Boundary conditions[a] |
|---|---|---|---|---|---|---|
| 1 | $\dot{\mathbf{x}} = \mathbf{f}(\mathbf{x}, \mathbf{u})$ | $\gamma(\mathbf{x}, \mathbf{u})$ | 0 | $\mathbf{x}(t_f) = \boldsymbol{\nu}$ | Free | $H(t) = H(t_f) = 0$ |
| 2 | | | 0 | $\boldsymbol{\psi}[\mathbf{x}(t_f)] = 0$ | Free | $H(t) = H(t_f) = 0;\ \mathbf{p}(t_f) = (\partial\boldsymbol{\psi}/\partial\mathbf{x})_f^T \boldsymbol{\mu}$ |
| 3 | | | $\varphi[\mathbf{x}(t_f)]$ | $\mathbf{x}(t_f)$ free | Free | $H(t) = H(t_f) = 0;\ \mathbf{p}(t_f) = (\partial\varphi/\partial\mathbf{x})_f^T$ |
| 4 | | | 0 | $\mathbf{x}(t_f) = \boldsymbol{\nu}$ | Fixed | $H(t) = H(t_f) = \text{constant}$ |
| 5 | | | $\varphi[\mathbf{x}(t_f)]$ | $\boldsymbol{\psi}[\mathbf{x}(t_f)] = 0$ | Fixed | $H(t) = H(t_f) = \text{constant};\ \mathbf{p}(t_f) = (\partial\boldsymbol{\psi}/\partial\mathbf{x})_f^T \boldsymbol{\mu} + (\partial\varphi/\partial\mathbf{x})_f^T$ |
| 6 | $\dot{\mathbf{x}} = \mathbf{f}(\mathbf{x}, \mathbf{u}, t)$ | $\gamma(\mathbf{x}, \mathbf{u}, t)$ | 0 | $\mathbf{x}(t_f) = \boldsymbol{\nu}$ | Free | $H(t_f) = 0$ |
| 7 | | | 0 | $\mathbf{x}(t_f) = \mathbf{h}(t_f)$ | Free | $H(t_f) = [\mathbf{p}^T(d\mathbf{h}/dt)]_f$ |
| 8 | | | $\varphi[\mathbf{x}(t_f), t_f]$ | $\boldsymbol{\psi}[\mathbf{x}(t_f), t_f] = 0$ | Free | $H(t_f) = [\boldsymbol{\mu}^T(\partial\boldsymbol{\psi}/\partial t) - (\partial\varphi/\partial t)]_f;\ \mathbf{p}(t_f) = [(\partial\boldsymbol{\psi}/\partial\mathbf{x})^T \boldsymbol{\mu} - (\partial\varphi/\partial\mathbf{x}^T)]_f$ |
| 9 | | | $\varphi[\mathbf{x}(t_f), t_f]$ | $\mathbf{x}(t_f)$ free | Free | $H(t_f) = -(\partial\varphi/\partial t)_f;\ \mathbf{p}(t_f) = (\partial\varphi/\partial\mathbf{x})_f^T$ |
| 10 | | | 0 | $\mathbf{x}(t_f) = \boldsymbol{\nu}$ | Fixed | — |
| 11 | | | 0 | $\boldsymbol{\psi}[\mathbf{x}(t_f)] = 0$ | Fixed | $\mathbf{p}(t_f) = (\partial\boldsymbol{\psi}/\partial\mathbf{x})_f^T \boldsymbol{\mu}$ |
| 12 | | | $\varphi[\mathbf{x}(t_f), t_f]$ | $\mathbf{x}(t_f)$ free | Fixed | $\mathbf{p}(t_f) = (\partial\varphi/\partial\mathbf{x})_f^T$ |

[a] An $f$ subscript, $(\ )_f$, indicates evaluation at time $t_f$.

CONTROL SYSTEM OPTIMIZATION

## The Two-Point Boundary Value Problem

The results summarized in the foregoing section are deceptive when viewed superficially since they tend to leave the impression that the problem is conceptually solved, and that the trivial (though cumbersome) computational details could be delegated to a digital computer. Except for very simple academic exercises, this is not true. The digital computer is very efficient for the solution of *initial value* problems. However, to obtain a solution to the optimization problem (via the calculus of variations), one must solve a *two-point* boundary value problem. In particular one must find

1. The $n$ state variables $x(t)$
2. The $n$ costate variables $p(t)$
3. *The $m$ control variables $u(t)$*

such that there is simultaneously satisfied

1. The $n$ system differential equations
2. The $n$ adjoint (costate) differential equations
3. The initial and final boundary conditions (involving $x$ and $p$)
4. The $m$ optimality conditions (involving $x$, $p$, and $u$)

The usual approach involves a process of guessing the unknown initial values for the components of the $p$ vector, and then integrating the set of (generally) nonlinear differential equations. If the final values of the variables are not as specified, the guessed initial values are adjusted with the aim of correcting the wrong final values. By proceeding in some systematic fashion, one might expect that each incorrect guess contributes information to permit convergences to the correct final value of the variables.

Experience with this approach has been almost universally frustrating and discouraging. Unsuspected numerical instabilities appear in which minute changes in the initial guessed values lead to violently fluctuating solution curves which defy convergence. An insight into this situation may be obtained by supposing that the system equations are linearized. Then if the system equations are stable (decrease in magnitude with increasing time), the costate equations (which are adjoint to the system equations) are of necessity unstable. Since the number of significant digits that can be carried in a digital computer is limited, regardless of whether fixed point or floating point arithmetic is used, the different growth of $x(t)$ and $p(t)$ contributes greatly to loss in accuracy.

It is precisely this type of difficulty that has motivated the search for alternate approaches to the problem.


## Dynamic Programming

Like many notable concepts, the basic ideas and procedures of dynamic programming appear abstruse to the uninitiated and patently obvious to its practitioners. To facilitate the transition from bewilderment to enlightenment, one must begin with a precise definition of some basic concepts together with what appears initially to be a bizarre nomenclature.

Of fundamental significance are the notions of a multistage decision process, a cost function, and a law of transformation.

The cost function, for present purposes, will be viewed as a discrete version of (7); viz.

$$J_N(\mathbf{x}_N, \mathbf{u}_0, \mathbf{u}_1, \ldots, \mathbf{u}_N) = \sum_{i=0}^{N} g_i(\mathbf{x}_i, \mathbf{u}_i, i) \tag{19}$$

The total time $(t_f - t_0)$ is presumed to be divided into $N$ intervals or stages (in the conventional terminology of dynamic programming). Also, we use the symbol $\mathbf{x}_i$ to mean "the state vector at that point on the trajectory where there are $i$ stages to go," with a similar meaning assigned to the control vector $\mathbf{u}_i$. The cost function $J_N$ is clearly a function of $N$, the number of stages to go, and the sequence of control vectors $\mathbf{u}_0, \mathbf{u}_1, \ldots, \mathbf{u}_N$. Beyond this, it depends only on the *present* state $x_N$ since the subsequent sequence of states is obtained from *the law of transformation*

$$\mathbf{x}_i = \mathbf{f}(\mathbf{x}_{i+1}, \mathbf{u}_{i+1}, i + 1) \tag{20}$$

for a given sequence $\mathbf{u}_i$.

Equation (20) will be recognized as a discrete version of the system equations (8). It states that when in the state $\mathbf{x}_{i+1}$ (with $i + 1$ stages to go), a particular choice for the control vector $\mathbf{u}_{i+1}$ will bring the system to the state $\mathbf{x}_i$ (with $i$ stages to go).

Note that when $i = 0$ there are zero stages to go, which means, in effect, that the system is in the terminal state. Thus we have the equivalence

$$g_0(\mathbf{x}_0, \mathbf{u}_0, 0) = \varphi[x(t_f), t_f] \tag{21}$$

Let us now denote the minimum value of $J_N(\mathbf{x}_N, \mathbf{u}_0, \mathbf{u}_1, \ldots, \mathbf{u}_N)$ by $J_N^*(\mathbf{x}_N)$. Clearly, the minimum value depends only on the present state, $\mathbf{x}_N$ and $N$, the number of stages to go, since the $\mathbf{u}_i$ are chosen to effect this minimization.

In mathematical formalism, this may be expressed as

$$\begin{aligned} J_N^*(\mathbf{x}_N) &= \min_{\mathbf{u}_0,\mathbf{u}_1,\ldots,\mathbf{u}_N} J_N(\mathbf{x}_N, \mathbf{u}_0, \mathbf{u}_1, \ldots, \mathbf{u}_N) \\ &= \min_{\mathbf{u}_0,\mathbf{u}_1,\ldots,\mathbf{u}_N} \{g_N(\mathbf{x}_N, \mathbf{u}_N, N) + \sum_{i=0}^{N-1} g_i(\mathbf{x}_i, \mathbf{u}_i, i)\} \\ &= \min_{\mathbf{u}_N} \{ \min_{\mathbf{u}_0,\mathbf{u}_1,\ldots,\mathbf{u}_N-1} g(\mathbf{x}_N, \mathbf{u}_N, N) + \min_{\mathbf{u}_0,\mathbf{u}_1,\ldots,\mathbf{u}_{N-1}} \sum_{i=0}^{N-1} g(\mathbf{x}_i, \mathbf{u}_i, i)\} \end{aligned} \tag{22}$$

The foregoing symbolic ratiocination is merely a possible scheduling of effort for the determination of the optimal $\mathbf{u}_i$. It remains to show that a productive algorithm will be forthcoming. To do this, it will be noted that (22) reduces to

$$J_N^*(\mathbf{x}_N) = \min_{\mathbf{u}_N}[g_N(\mathbf{x}_N, \mathbf{u}_N, N) + J_{N-1}^*(\mathbf{x}_{N-1})] \tag{23}$$

since $g_N(\mathbf{x}_N, \mathbf{u}_N, N)$ does not depend on $\mathbf{u}_{N-1}, \mathbf{u}_{N-2}, \ldots, \mathbf{u}_0$, and the second term on the right-hand side of (20) is $J_{N-1}^*(\mathbf{x}_{N-1})$ by definition.

Now by virtue of (20) we obtain

$$J_N^*(\mathbf{x}_N) = \min_{\mathbf{u}_N}\{g_N(\mathbf{x}_N, \mathbf{u}_N, N) + J_{N-1}^*[f(\mathbf{x}_N, \mathbf{u}_N, N)]\} \tag{24}$$

This is the basic functional equation of dynamic programming for the problem at hand. In deriving this equation, we have made implicit use of Bellman's principle of optimality.

The initial condition associated with (24) is

$$J_0^*(\mathbf{x}_0) = \varphi[\mathbf{x}(t_f), t_f] \tag{25}$$

The form of the $\varphi$ function is known (given). Therefore, since $\mathbf{x}_0$ and $\mathbf{x}(t_f)$ are alternate notations for the same vector, the function $J_0^*(\mathbf{x}_0)$ may be computed and "stored" for any prescribed range of $\mathbf{x}_0$.

Let us now examine the functional equation (24) with one stage to go; i.e.,

$$J_1^*(\mathbf{x}_1) = \min_{\mathbf{u}_1}\{g_1(\mathbf{x}_1, \mathbf{u}_1, 1) + J_0^*[f(\mathbf{x}_1, \mathbf{u}_1, 1)]\} \tag{26}$$

Select a value for $\mathbf{x}_1$. If, in addition, we select a value for $\mathbf{u}_1$, then the quantity in the braces in (26) acquires a specific numerical value, since $J_0^*$ is now a known function. However, we select not just any value for $\mathbf{u}_1$, but that specific one which minimizes the quantity in the braces in (26). This is strictly a computation/decision operation which is easily programmed into a computer.

Furthermore, in any practical problem the control vector $\mathbf{u}$ is bounded in magnitude. Therefore, after assigning a convenient quantization level to $\mathbf{u}$, only a prescribed finite number of functional evaluations need be performed. Carrying out the indicated operations yields an optimal $\mathbf{u}_1^*$ and $J_1^*$ for a specific $\mathbf{x}_1$. Repeating this for a prescribed range of values for $\mathbf{x}_1$ yields a tabulation

$$\begin{array}{ccc} \mathbf{x}_1 & J_1^*(\mathbf{x}_1) & \mathbf{u}_1^* \\ \vdots & \vdots & \vdots \end{array}$$

The entire procedure is now repeated with the functional equation for two stages to go

$$J_2^*(\mathbf{x}_2) = \min_{\mathbf{u}_2}\{g_2(\mathbf{x}_2, \mathbf{u}_2, 2) + J_1^*[f(\mathbf{x}_2, \mathbf{u}_2, 2)]\} \tag{27}$$

etc.

Ultimately, one obtains a tabulation for $J_N^*(\mathbf{x}_N)$ (with accompanying optimal $\mathbf{u}_N^*$) for a selected range of $\mathbf{x}_N$. Thus one obtains the solution to the problem for a multitude of initial conditions, not just the one specified. This feature is a basic attribute of the dynamic programming approach.

## Critique

Dynamic programming is one of the more powerful tools available for the solution of problems of optimization. For present purposes its most obvious advantage is the conversion of a two-point boundary value problem into an initial value problem. The stipulation of various constraints on the control and/or state vectors, which introduces all sorts of disagreeable complications in the classical approach, actually serves to simplify the dynamic programming solution. Furthermore, insofar as the computational algorithm is concerned, it is a matter of complete indifference whether or not the system equations are linear— or even analytic! When a minimum is obtained it is a global, rather than a local, minimum. In contrast, the use of classical methods generally yields only a local minimum. In addition, the fact that the dynamic programming algorithm automatically generates the solution for a range of initial conditions (rather than just one) provides the analyst with a sensitivity analysis "at no extra cost."

The one serious limitation to the ubiquitous application of the dynamic programming methodology is the problem of dimensionality whereby the demands on computer storage capability become intolerable for even moderately high order systems. For example, if the state vector is three dimensional, and each state variable can have 100 values, then the storage requirements are $(100)^3$ = one million storage cells!

## Mathematical Programming

Mathematical programming is a generic term embracing the concepts of linear, quadratic, or nonlinear programming. The basic problems dealt with are easily stated as follows.

### Linear Programming

Minimize:
$$J = \mathbf{a}^T\mathbf{y} \tag{28}$$

subject to:
$$\mathbf{D}_1\mathbf{y} \geqq \mathbf{c}_1 \tag{29}$$
$$\mathbf{D}_2\mathbf{y} = \mathbf{c}_2$$
$$\mathbf{y} \geqq \mathbf{0}$$

### Quadratic Programming

Minimize:
$$J = \mathbf{a}^T\mathbf{y} + \mathbf{y}^T\mathbf{\Lambda}\mathbf{y} \tag{30}$$

subject to:
$$\mathbf{D}_1\mathbf{y} \geqq \mathbf{c}_1 \tag{31}$$
$$\mathbf{D}_2\mathbf{y} = \mathbf{c}_2 \tag{32}$$
$$\mathbf{y} \geqq \mathbf{0} \tag{33}$$

We note parenthetically that by introducing slack or surplus variables as required, the constraints (31) and (32) may be expressed as an equivalent equality constraint as follows:

$$\mathbf{D}\mathbf{y} = \mathbf{c} \tag{34}$$

This is merely an alternate formulation of the problem.

### Nonlinear Programming

Minimize:

$$J(\mathbf{y}) \tag{35}$$

subject to:

$$\boldsymbol{\alpha}(\mathbf{y}) = \mathbf{0} \tag{36}$$
$$\boldsymbol{\beta}(\mathbf{y}) \geqslant \mathbf{0} \tag{37}$$

There exist at the present time highly refined and efficient techniques for solving the aforementioned optimization problems. Consequently, if it is possible to transform a dynamic control optimization problem to one of the above formats, a significant step may have been taken toward the solution of the problem.

To see how the transformation may be accomplished, we pose the control optimization problem in the following discrete form: Given the system

$$\mathbf{x}(i + 1) = \mathbf{f}[\mathbf{x}(i), \mathbf{u}(i), i] \tag{38}$$

with initial condition

$$\mathbf{x}(0) \equiv \text{given} \tag{39}$$

The notation $\mathbf{x}(i)$ is used to indicate the value of the state vector at time $t_i$. There exist the equality constraints

$$\alpha_j[\mathbf{x}(i), \mathbf{u}(i)] = 0, \qquad j = 1, 2, \ldots, \lambda \tag{40}$$

the inequality constraints

$$\beta_k[\mathbf{x}(i), \mathbf{u}(i)] \geqslant 0, \qquad k = 1, 2, \ldots, \xi \tag{41}$$

and the terminal constraints

$$\sigma_l[\mathbf{x}(N)] \geqslant 0, \qquad l = 1, 2, \ldots, \tau \tag{42}$$

It is required to minimize the performance criterion

$$J = \sum_{i=1}^{N} \gamma[\mathbf{x}(i), \mathbf{u}(i), i] \tag{43}$$

To show that the problem just formulated is one of nonlinear programming, we effect a change of variables as follows:

| | |
|---|---|
| $u_1(0)$ | $y(1)$ |
| $u_2(0)$ | $y(2)$ |
| $\vdots$ | $\vdots$ |
| $u_m(0)$ | $y(m)$ |
| $u_1(1)$ | $y(m + 1)$ |
| $u_2(1)$ | $y(m + 2)$ |
| $\vdots$ | $\vdots$ |
| $u_m(1)$ | $y(2m)$ |
| $\vdots$ | $\vdots$ |
| $u_1(N - 1)$ | $y[(N - 1)m + 1]$ |
| $u_2(N - 1)$ | $y[(N - 1)m + 2]$ |
| $\vdots$ | $\vdots$ |
| $u_m(N - 1)$ | $y(Nm)$ |
| $x_1(1)$ | $y(Nm + 1)$ |
| $x_2(1)$ | $y(Nm + 2)$ |
| $\vdots$ | $\vdots$ |
| $x_n(1)$ | $y(Nm + n)$ |
| $x_1(2)$ | $y(Nm + n + 1)$ |
| $x_2(2)$ | $y(Nm + n + 2)$ |
| $\vdots$ | $\vdots$ |
| $x_n(2)$ | $y(Nm + 2n)$ |
| $\vdots$ | $\vdots$ |
| $x_1(N)$ | $y[Nm + (N - 1)n + 1]$ |
| $x_2(N)$ | $y[Nm + (N - 1)n + 2]$ |
| $\vdots$ | $\vdots$ |
| $x_m(N)$ | $y[N(m + n)]$ |

Substituting in Eq. (43), it becomes evident that the control optimization problem is now in the format of the nonlinear programming problem, Eqs. (35) to (37).

Note also that if $J$, $\alpha$, and $\beta$ are linear in the components of $\mathbf{y}$, we would have a linear programming problem, while if $\alpha$ and $\beta$ are linear and $J$ is quadratic, we would have a quadratic programming problem. In the latter instances it is required that $\mathbf{y} > 0$. However, in a control problem the state variables are not normally restricted to positive values. Therefore, in order to satisfy the nonnegativity requirement for either linear or quadratic programming, it suffices to replace the vector $\mathbf{y}$ by

$$\mathbf{y} = \mathbf{y}^+ - \mathbf{y}^-$$

where $\mathbf{y}^+$ and $\mathbf{y}^-$ are both nonnegative.

**Closed Form Solutions**

In most situations of practical interest it is not possible to derive elegant closed form solutions to the control optimization problem. However, with a certain fortuitous combination of circumstances, a closed form solution can be obtained. As might be anticipated, this situation is the case of a linear system with a quadratic cost function and an unconstrained control vector. Fortunately, this case is of some practical importance since a perturbation analysis (small displacements from a reference steady state) leads to precisely such a situation.

Two possible formulations of the problem will be considered; first, the purely deterministic case, and second, when random noise and disturbances are present.

### Deterministic System

Given the system

$$\dot{\mathbf{x}} = \mathbf{F}(t)\mathbf{x} + \mathbf{G}(t)\mathbf{u}$$

with $\mathbf{x}(t_0)$ known.

It is required that control be exercised such that at time $t_f$,

$$\mathbf{x}(t_f) = 0$$

while, in addition, the quantity

$$J = \tfrac{1}{2}\mathbf{x}^T(t_f)\mathbf{L}\mathbf{x}(t_f) + \tfrac{1}{2}\int_{t_0}^{t_f} [\mathbf{x}^T\mathbf{A}(t)\mathbf{x} + \mathbf{u}^T\mathbf{B}(t)\mathbf{u}]\, dt$$

is a minimum.

The optimal control vector is given by

$$\mathbf{u}(t) = -\mathbf{C}\mathbf{x}(t)$$

where

$$\mathbf{C} = \mathbf{B}^{-1}(t)\mathbf{G}^T(t)\mathbf{M}(t)$$

and $\mathbf{M}(t)$ is obtained as the solution of

$$\dot{\mathbf{M}}(t) = -\mathbf{M}(t)\mathbf{F}(t) - \mathbf{F}^T(t)\mathbf{M}(t) + \mathbf{M}(t)\mathbf{G}(t)\mathbf{B}^{-1}(t)\mathbf{G}^T(t)\mathbf{M}(t) + \mathbf{A}(t)$$

with initial condition

$$\mathbf{M}(t_f) = \mathbf{L}$$

Note that the optimal control $\mathbf{u}(t)$ is a function of the *current* state of the system; i.e., closed loop control. Usually, in most practical instances, the optimal control can be computed only for one specific set of initial conditions; the control is said to be open loop. It will also be observed that $\mathbf{M}(t)$ may be computed *a priori* since it depends only on $t_f$ and known matrices.

### Stochastic System

The system considered here is similar to that in the previous section except for two complicating factors. First is the fact that a random disturbance is present, and second, the measurement of the state vector is corrupted by additive noise.

Specifically, in mathematical form, the system equation is

$$\dot{\mathbf{x}} = \mathbf{F}(t)\mathbf{x} + \mathbf{G}(t)\mathbf{u} + \mathbf{w}$$

while the available measurement is a linear function of the state vector given by

$$\mathbf{z} = \mathbf{H}(t)\mathbf{x} + \mathbf{v}$$

Both $\mathbf{w}$ and $\mathbf{v}$ are Gaussian white noise processes whose statistical characteristics are given by

$$E[\mathbf{w}(t)\mathbf{w}^T(t')] = \mathbf{Q}(t)\delta(t - t')$$
$$E[\mathbf{v}(t)\mathbf{v}^T(t')] = \mathbf{R}(t)\delta(t - t')$$
$$E[\mathbf{w}(t)] = E[\mathbf{v}(t)] = \mathbf{0}$$

In addition, $\mathbf{x}(t_0)$ is a zero mean Gaussian random vector independent of $\mathbf{w}(t)$ and $\mathbf{v}(t)$.

$$E[\mathbf{x}(t_0)] = \mathbf{0}$$
$$E[\mathbf{x}(t_0)\mathbf{v}^T(t)] = \mathbf{0}$$
$$E[\mathbf{x}(t_0)\mathbf{w}^T(t)] = \mathbf{0}$$
$$E[\mathbf{x}(t_0)\mathbf{x}^T(t_0)] = \mathbf{P}_0$$

It is required to choose the control vector $\mathbf{u}(t)$ such that the quantity

$$J = E\left\{ \tfrac{1}{2}\mathbf{x}^T(t_f)\mathbf{L}\mathbf{x}(t_f) + \tfrac{1}{2}\int_{t_0}^{t_f} [\mathbf{x}^T\mathbf{A}(t)\mathbf{x} + \mathbf{u}^T\mathbf{B}(t)\mathbf{u}]\, dt \right\}$$

is a minimum.

It can be shown that the optimal control vector $\mathbf{u}^*(t)$ is given by

$$\mathbf{u}^*(t) = -\mathbf{C}(t)\hat{\mathbf{x}}(t)$$

where $\hat{\mathbf{x}}(t)$ is an optimal estimate obtained from

$$\dot{\hat{\mathbf{x}}}(t) = \mathbf{F}(t)\hat{\mathbf{x}}(t) + \mathbf{G}(t)\mathbf{u}^*(t) + \mathbf{K}(t)[\mathbf{z}(t) - \mathbf{H}(t)\hat{\mathbf{x}}(t)]$$
$$\hat{\mathbf{x}}(t_0) = 0$$

Here,

$$\mathbf{C}(t) = \mathbf{B}^{-1}(t)\mathbf{G}^T(t)\mathbf{M}(t)$$
$$\mathbf{K}(t) = \mathbf{P}(t)\mathbf{H}^T(t)\mathbf{R}^{-1}(t)$$
$$\dot{\mathbf{M}}(t) = -\mathbf{M}(t)\mathbf{F}(t) - \mathbf{F}^T(t)\mathbf{M}(t) + \mathbf{C}^T(t)\mathbf{B}(t)\mathbf{C}(t) - \mathbf{A}(t)$$
$$\mathbf{M}(t_f) = \mathbf{L}$$
$$\dot{\mathbf{P}}(t) = \mathbf{F}(t)\mathbf{P}(t) + \mathbf{P}(t)\mathbf{F}^T(t) - \mathbf{K}(t)\mathbf{R}(t)\mathbf{K}^T(t) + \mathbf{Q}(t)$$
$$\mathbf{P}(t_0) = \mathbf{P}_0$$

There are several noteworthy features of the solution. First, it is noted that the optimal control vector is a linear combination of the *estimated* state variables. The format is the same as for a deterministic system (preceding section). The estimates of the state are optimal in the sense of maximum likelihood or minimum variance. They are obtained from a "model" of the system and a feedback signal that is proportional to the difference between the actual and estimated measurements.

### Discussion

The closed form solutions summarized in the previous two sections are in a sense the cornerstone of modern control theory. The mathematical foundations are rigorous and secure. In practical applications there are problems associated with proper selection of the matrices **A, B,** and **L** insofar as these reflect desired optimality in performance. Furthermore, it is not always a simple matter to obtain good estimates for the variance matrices **Q** and **R**. Consequently, even when closed form solutions are available in a mathematical sense, one cannot formulate simple cookbook procedures that are universally applicable. In this sense, judgment and experience must be combined with theory to achieve viable pragmatic results.

### Gradient Methods

In order to exhibit the basic ideas of the gradient method (of which there are many variants), we consider the system described by Eq. (8) and seek to determine the control vector $\mathbf{u}(t)$ such that the cost function $J$ given by Eq. (7) is a minimum. There may also exist various constraints on the state and control vectors, as well as terminal constraints, whose precise form is (for the moment) not important. The essence of the approach to be described is the selection of a control vector $\mathbf{u}(t)$ for all $t$ in the interval $(t_0, t_f)$ such that all stipulated constraints are satisfied, but which does not necessarily minimize the cost function $J$. In many situations of practical interest it is not too difficult to derive such a control vector. It is crudely analogous to piloting a vehicle to some desired terminal point while keeping clear of visible obstacles.

Having available an admissible control vector $\mathbf{u}(t)$, one may substitute in Eq. (8), obtaining the trajectory $\mathbf{x}(t)$ for all $t$ in the interval $(t_0, t_f)$. This in turn leads to a value for the cost function $J$.

Suppose now that we adopt a new control, $\mathbf{u}(t) + \Delta\mathbf{u}(t)$, which represents a perturbed value of the control vector. It is not too difficult to show that the resultant perturbations in the state vector will have the form

$$\frac{d}{dt}(\Delta\mathbf{x}) = \mathbf{F}(t)\Delta\mathbf{x} + \mathbf{G}(t)\Delta\mathbf{u}$$

With some additional effort it can be shown that the corresponding variation in the cost function is given by

$$\Delta J = \int_{t_0}^{t_f} (\Delta\mathbf{u})^T \mathbf{G}^T(t)\mathbf{p}(t) \, dt$$

where $\mathbf{p}(t)$ is the adjoint to the given system, i.e.,

$$\dot{\mathbf{p}}(t) = -\mathbf{F}(t)\mathbf{p}(t)$$

The essential problem is how to choose $\Delta\mathbf{u}(t)$ such that the resulting change in $\Delta J$ is a maximum.

It will be recalled from the ordinary calculus that in order to choose the $n$ variables, $\Delta x_1, \Delta x_2, \ldots, \Delta x_n$, such that the change in

$$f(x_1, x_2, \ldots, x_n) \equiv f(\mathbf{x})$$

is a maximum, one must select the increment $\Delta\mathbf{x}$ such that

$$\Delta\mathbf{x} = -K\nabla_x f, \qquad K = \text{constant}$$

i.e., the step is taken in the gradient direction.

In analogous fashion, one chooses the control increment as

$$\Delta\mathbf{u}(t) = -K\nabla_\mathbf{u} H$$

which corresponds to the gradient direction in function space. Here $H$ is the hamiltonian defined by

$$H = [\mathbf{F}(t)\Delta\mathbf{x} + \mathbf{G}(t)\Delta\mathbf{u}]^T\mathbf{p}$$

which means that

$$\nabla_\mathbf{u} H = \mathbf{G}^T(t)\mathbf{p}$$

The iterative process is continued until some prespecified convergence criteria are satisfied. Generally, this procedure results in substantial improvements in the cost function for the first few iterations, but convergence characteristics are poor as the optimal solution is approached. At this point, so-called "second-order" gradient methods may be employed if proximity to the theoretical optimum is critical. Second-order gradient methods are characterized by the use of second derivatives of the Hamiltonian, $H$.

## BIBLIOGRAPHY

Athans, M., and P. L. Falb, *Optimal Control,* McGraw-Hill, New York, 1966.

Bryson, A. E., and Y. C. Ho, *Applied Optimal Control,* Blaisdell, New York, 1969.

Bellman, R. E., and S. E. Dreyfus, *Applied Dynamic Programming,* Princeton University Press, Princeton, New Jersey, 1962.

Himmelblau, D. M., *Applied Nonlinear Programming,* McGraw-Hill, New York, 1972.

Tabak, D., and B. C. Kuo, *Optimal Control by Mathematical Programming,* Prentice-Hall, Englewood Cliffs, New Jersey, 1971.

*Arthur L. Greensite*

# CONVERGENCE OF ALGORITHMS

### INTRODUCTION AND DEFINITION

In general, the term convergence implies two basic concepts. First, it implies the *ability* of an algorithm (see *Algorithm,* Vol. 1) to arrive at a desired solution to a particular class of problems. Second, it connotes the *facility* with which the algorithm arrives at the desired solution.

In the above statement, ability refers to a zero–one delineation. Either the algorithm can be shown to arrive at the desired solution sooner or later (perhaps a long time later), or it cannot. If the property that the desired solution is achieved can be shown to be true *all of the time,* we say that the algorithm converges to the desired point. The algorithm, of course, can be said to converge only for the class of problems for which the property has been proved *a priori*.

It is necessary to note here what is meant by the term "desired solution." In many cases the desired solution is the *global optimum* solution; it maximizes or minimizes (i.e., optimizes) some objective function subject to a given set of constraints. In other cases only a *local optimum* solution is desired. A local optimum represents the optimum value of some objective function only in a restricted region around the optimum point. In the latter case we may attempt to locate all of the local optimum solutions and pick the global optimum from among them. In still other cases the desired point may be one which satisfies a predetermined condition or conditions, such as the roots of a quadratic equation. In this case the condition to satisfy would be to find all numbers, $x$, which satisfy the condition that $ax^2 + bx + c = 0$. Objectives of the last type discussed can usually be expressed as an optimization problem. In the example, minimizing the absolute value of $ax^2 + bx + c$ would be appropriate. The term "optimum point" or "optimum solution" will be used throughout the rest of the paper in lieu of the term "desired point."

The word "facility" in the definition of the first paragraph relates to the fact that we are often extremely interested in the fashion in which an algorithm converges. One aspect of this concept was implied earlier when it was stated that sooner or later the algorithm arrives at the optimum solution. If an algorithm can be shown to reach the *exact* optimum solution in a finite number of steps, then it is said to have the property of finite convergence. If, on the other hand, the algorithm will only come arbitrarily close to the optimum solution in a finite number of steps, it is said to be an infinitely converging algorithm. As a simple example, let us say that we wish to find the number with the maximum value which lies between (and including) 2 and 10. One algorithm would be to start with the lowest possible number, 2, and add 1 for each iteration until we exceed the limits of the constraint set. As long as the end points are integers the exact solution, 10, can be found by this finitely converging procedure. An alternate approach would be to start at any point between 2 and 10 and derive a new point half way between the two points. The new point would be used to generate the next, etc. Thus, if we started with the number 6, the sequence of numbers generated would be 6, 8, 9, 9.5, 9.75, 9.875, 9.9375, 9.96875, 9.984375, 9.9921875, . . . . This sequence is infinitely converging. The value 10 cannot be reached in a finite number of steps, but it is the limit point of the sequence which was generated. We can come as close as we like to the optimum value by continuing the sequence far enough. For instance, if we wish to be within 0.001 of the optimum, we can continue the sequence thusly: . . . , 9.99609375, 9.998046875, 9.9990234375.

Also related to the facility of convergence is the speed with which convergence is achieved. In the example above, if we wished to come within 0.001 of the optimum solution, the first algorithm would be superior. The first algorithm would take eight iterations, each iteration being extremely simple. (Note that the number of iterations is dependent on where we start.) For the above problem, the second algorithm would require 12 more complex iterations. Let us now use the two algorithms to solve the following slightly different problem: Within a tolerance of 0.99, find the number with the maximum value which lies between 2,000 and 10,000. We will start both algorithms at 6,000. The first algorithm would require 4,000 iterations to attain the exact optimum. The second algorithm would generate the same sequence as that listed earlier except that each term would be multiplied by $10^3$. Once again the twelfth iteration would provide the desired accuracy with a solution of 9999.0234375. For more accuracy the number of iterations for the first algorithm remains the same while the number of iterations for the second algorithm would increase. From the example we have been discussing, five important aspects of speed of convergence can be deduced:

1. The number of iterations required.
2. The complexity of the calculation at each iteration.
3. The initial solution.
4. How close we desire to be to the optimum solution.
5. The specific problem we are attempting to solve.

A final factor related to the facility with which a particular algorithm converges is its ability to generate good intermediate feasible solutions during the operation of the algorithm. Some algorithms produce many good solutions which satisfy all the requirements of the desired solution but are not optimum. (These are called feasible solutions.) In these cases, if the algorithm must be terminated before completion, then the best solution found before termination is a usable solution. For example, in the first problem given, use the algorithm which starts at an arbitrarily high integer. On each iteration generate a new solution by subtracting 1 from the previous solution. Stop when the feasible region is first reached. This algorithm has the property of finite convergence, but termination before the algorithm is complete will not yield a feasible solution.

CONVERGENCE OF ALGORITHMS

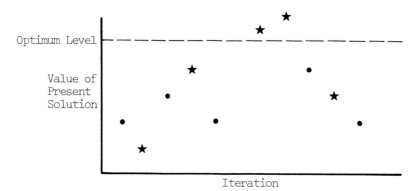

**Fig. 1.** No convergence. • represents a solution which is not the best but which satisfies the constraints (is feasible). ★ represents a solution which is not feasible. This same key is applicable to all the figures.

In summary, the properties which are important to convergence considerations can be described by

1. The ability to converge—yes or no.
2. The facility with which convergence occurs.
    a. Finite versus infinite convergence.
    b. The speed of convergence (five aspects listed above).
    c. Whether or not other feasible but nonoptimal solutions are generated during the operation of the algorithm.

Figures 1 through 6 are included to demonstrate these ideas graphically. Figure 1 demonstrates the case where no convergence takes place. The objective function increases and decreases over time. There is no guarantee that the optimum will be achieved. Figure 2 also shows a case with no convergence. In this example the feasible solutions do approach some upper limit, but it is not

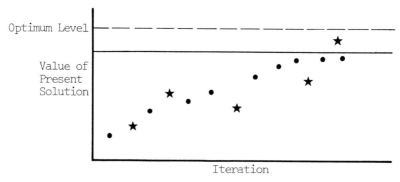

**Fig. 2.** Feasible solutions approach some value but not the best point. No convergence. See Fig. 1 for the key to symbols.

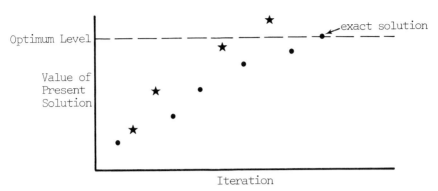

**Fig. 3.** Finite convergence. See Fig. 1 for the key to symbols.

the optimum. In Fig. 3 the feasible solutions increase until the exact optimum is reached; this is finite convergence. Figure 4 represents infinite convergence. The feasible solutions approach the optimum closer and closer but it is never reached. In Fig. 5, although the optimum feasible solution is reached, the interim solutions are not feasible. Finally, Fig. 6 shows the case where several iterations occur before reaching a feasible solution which is an improvement over all the preceding solutions. The blocked circles in the figure represent the converging sequence.

## CONVERGENCE AND ROUNDOFF

An integral part of any discussion of convergence is the accuracy (see *Accuracy*, Vol. 1) of calculations. Any but the simplest of algorithms require sufficient calculations that the number of significant digits available to the calculating mechanism (man or machine) will be overridden. In this case roundoff techniques have to be invoked, making the concept of exact solutions a theoretical one. Under these conditions, converging algorithms can only be

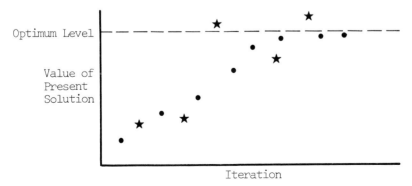

**Fig. 4.** Infinite convergence. See Fig. 1 for the key to symbols.

CONVERGENCE OF ALGORITHMS

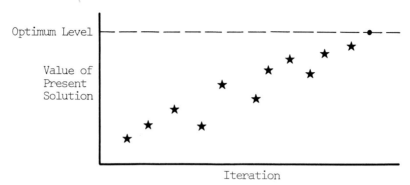

**Fig. 5.** No feasible solution before the best solution is reached. See Fig. 1 for the key to symbols.

expected to, at best, converge to values within the specified number of significant digits. It is possible under these conditions to miss the desired solution for a long time. In the second algorithm presented let us assume that we are only significant to two decimal places. Any digits past the second decimal place are rounded down if it is *less than* 0.005 and rounded up otherwise. The sequence of solutions which would have been generated for the initial problem using this procedure would be 6, 8, 9, 9.5, 9.75, 9.88, 9.94, 9.97, 9.99, 10.0. Note that this sequence converges to the optimum in a finite number of steps. Now let us change the round procedure only slightly so that we round down for values less than *or equal to* 0.005. The sequence would now become 6, 8, 9, 9.5, 9.75, 9.87, 9.93, 9.96, 9.98, 9.99, 9.99, 9.99, . . . , 9.99, . . . . With only this minor change we cannot come closer than 0.01 of the optimum solution. As another example let us assume we are using the first algorithm presented (adding 1 for each iteration) on a machine which uses decimal equivalents for integer

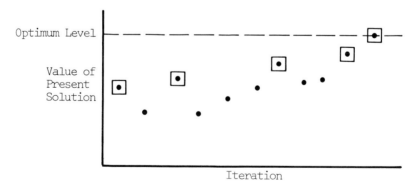

**Fig. 6.** Better solutions appear after several iterations. See Fig. 1 for the key to symbols.

numbers. The number one might be represented as 0.99. The algorithm would then add 0.99 to each iteration and the best feasible solution would be 9.92.

In summation, the ultimate outcome of an algorithm is a complex interaction between the algorithm, the problem solved, the accuracy of the mechanism used to perform the calculations, and the roundoff technique used. Highly accurate computers with many significant digits tend to alleviate the problem in a great number of cases. Exact optimum solutions under these conditions, however, are extremely difficult to assure.


## HEURISTIC SOLUTIONS

No discussion of convergence of algorithms would be complete without including a section on heuristic techniques. Heuristics are techniques which cannot be proved to converge to the optimum solution. It should be stated that algorithms that converge may not be better than heuristic techniques. Many realistic problems can be solved by good heuristic techniques for good solutions in realizable computation time. Converging algorithms applied to the same problem might require so much computation time to solve and so many simplifying assumptions that solutions are costly as well as inadequate. Heuristics also often provide reasonable starting solutions for converging algorithms. The last comment can be misleading; recent literature on solving transportation problems, for instance, has shown that the improved initial solution achieved from more complex starting heuristics requires more time to achieve than is gained. For the first algorithm given earlier, for instance, let us use the starting heuristic that we start at the smallest value of the interval and add 3 to it during each iteration. When the range of the problem is exceeded we go back to the last point and apply the converging algorithm. It is easy to see that the starting heuristic itself will not converge, in general. For the first problem presented, starting at 6, the sequence generated by the algorithm would be 6, 9, and the solution algorithm would then generate the optimum solution in one iteration. With the heuristic the problem requires two iterations to solve. Using the original algorithm by itself would require four iterations. Let us look now at the use of this heuristic with the second algorithm presented. We will use the problem which ranges from 2,000 to 10,000. Starting at the point 6,000, the heuristic yields the sequence 6,000, 6,003, 6,006, 6,009, . . . , 9,992, 9,995, 9,998. The algorithm then yields the point 9,999 which is within the desired accuracy. Note that with the starting heuristic the problem took 2,666 iterations to solve. The solution using only the algorithm required only 12 iterations.

Even heuristics which have been proved successful often leave the user with a great deal of uncertainty, particularly for large problems. Convergence is absolutely necessary if we are to be assured that the results are even close to the optimum (assuming, of course, accurate data and formulation). Reduction of possible error is therefore a prime factor in favor of converging algorithms.

CONVERGENCE OF ALGORITHMS

## PROVING CONVERGENCE

Proofs that a particular algorithm converges follow some variation of the same basic theme:

1. Show that at least one feasible solution exists.
2. Show that some of the solutions found during the iterations of the algorithm are feasible.
3. Show that some guide function always improves.
4. Show that when the guide function no longer improves, some set of conditions which implies optimality is satisfied and that this condition will occur.

In 1. the proof is generally an algorithm itself which finds a starting feasible solution only if one exists. If no starting solution is found, then the algorithm is terminated and the problem has no solution.

Note that the guiding function in 2. is often the objective function itself. In the first two algorithms presented, for instance, we always generate a new point which is feasible, while assuring an increase in the objective function. In many cases the guiding function is essentially a counting device. It makes sure that all possible solutions have been looked at, either explicitly or implicitly, via the operation of the algorithm. When all possible feasible solutions are exhausted, we merely choose the best one and the algorithm is proved.

In 4. the most commonly used set of conditions is called the Kuhn-Tucker problem. For special classes of problems, global or local optimality can be proved by showing that these properties hold for a particular solution. In general, in order to prove convergence we must invoke many special properties of the class of problems with which we are dealing.

As an example of proving convergence, the technique used for proving convergence of a linear optimization problem will be discussed. This example will be a great deal more complex than the earlier problems. However, it represents a much simpler format than most other types of algorithms. Readers not familiar with matrix notation should skip this example. In this example we will not formally prove convergence; we will only point out the necessary aspects of the proof.

The problem can be stated as:

Maximize

$$\theta = cx$$

subject to

$$A'x = b$$
$$x \geq 0$$

where    $c$ = a row $n + m$ vector—the last $m$ elements of this vector are zero
         $x$ = a column $n + m$ vector
         $b$ = a column $m$ vector
         $A'$ = an $m \times n + m$ matrix

We use here only the simplest kind of linear program where the constraints are all less than or equal to the right-hand side. A set of slack variables have already been added to the problem so that $A' = (A : I)$. The initial solution then is to let the basic variables $x^B$ be the $m$ slack variables so that

$$Ix^B = b$$
$$x^B = b$$
$$cx = 0$$

This solution yields an initial starting point and shows that at least one solution exists, thus 1. of the basic scheme is accomplished. Parts 2. and 3. are accomplished by careful selection of each succeeding solution. A column of the old basis is replaced by one of the nonbasic columns to generate a new solution. By appropriate choice of the entering and leaving columns, 2. and 3. can be assured (assuming no degeneracy—this is discussed later). We then use the product form of the inverse to generate $B^{-1}$. We have at this point

$$Bx^B = b$$

so that

$$x^B = B^{-1}b, \qquad x^R = 0$$

and

$$\theta = c^B x^B = c^B B^{-1} b$$

where $c^B$ is the vector made up of the basic elements of $c$, and $x^R$ are nonbasic variables. In hand operations the above procedure is merely the selection of the pivot column and the pivot element. This selection is then followed by the pivot itself which corresponds to the use of the product form of the inverse.

We now have a procedure which starts at a solution to a particular problem and generates new solutions if the entering column is chosen correctly. It can be shown that improvements can always be made (in nondegenerate problems) by allowing column $a_j$ to enter the basis if $c^B B^{-1} a_j - c_j \leq 0$, where $a_j$ is column $j$ of $A$ and $c_j$ is the $j$th element of $c$. For hand calculations the value $c^B B^{-1} a_j - c_j$ is merely the value in the objective function row of the tableau at the particular iteration in question—we can pivot on this column if the indicator is negative. It is now necessary to show item 4. in the general scheme—that when the objective function no longer improves, the optimal solution is achieved. To do this we use the associated Kuhn-Tucker problem of the original linear program [3]. For a particular value of $x$, namely $\bar{x}$, the Kuhn-Tucker problem will be to find an $m$

## CONVERGENCE OF ALGORITHMS

row vector, $u$, such that:

$$uA \geq c \tag{1}$$
$$A\bar{x} \leq b \tag{2}$$
$$u(A\bar{x} - b) = 0 \tag{3}$$
$$u \geq 0 \tag{4}$$

Property (3) is called the Kuhn-Tucker condition; note that the matrix *without* slack variable is used in this statement. In order for a solution $\bar{x}$ to be optimal there must exist a solution $\bar{u}$, to properties (1) through (4) above. Assume that we have arrived at a solution such that $c^B B^{-1} a_j - c_j \geq 0$ for all $j = 1, 2, \ldots, m + n$, i.e., that no more improvement can be made in the objective function. We wish to show that properties (1) through (4) are satisfied. We let $\bar{u} = c^B B^{-1}$. Using this value and the fact that $c^B B^{-1} a_j - c_j \geq 0$ for all $j = 1, 2, \ldots, m + n$, we have $\bar{u}A \geq c$ and $\bar{u} \geq 0$, which satisfies (1) and (4). (2) is satisfied by our pivot selections. Finally, (3) can be shown to be true using the fact that $B^{-1}A\bar{x} = \bar{x}^B = B^{-1}b$ for the basic columns in $A$ since nonbasic variables have the value zero and $c^B = 0$ for the slack variables which are basic. We then have $\bar{u}(A\bar{x} - b) = \bar{u}A\bar{x} - \bar{u}b = c^B B^{-1}A\bar{x} - c^B B^{-1}b = c^B \bar{x}^B - c^B \bar{x}^B = 0$ for basic columns in $A$, and $u = 0$ for basic columns not in $A$ which yields (3).

There is still no guarantee that we will not continue to improve the objective function *ad infinitum* toward a nonoptimal solution (this is the condition shown in Fig. 2). To assure this is not the case, we need two additional comments. First, each basis is associated with a unique objective function value, $\theta$. If we are continuously improving the objective function, we cannot ever go back to a basis already achieved. The number of possible bases, however, is finite so that sooner or later the objective function cannot possibly improve. The second comment refers to the "if" in the last comment. Problems can occur which have at some point a basic variable with a value of 0. This is called a degenerate problem and it is possible that no improvement would occur when the basis is changed. It is necessary in this case to somehow modify the guide function (the objective function) so that it always increases. One technique is to add a small number, $\epsilon$, to the zero right-hand side so that $x_i^B = \epsilon$; we then continue with the possibility that the solution will be incorrect by a small amount. A second excellent technique is called lexiographic ordering [4]. In this technique the basic variables are changed into basic nonzero row vectors the first element of which is $\bar{x}^B$; the other elements make certain that the vector is nonzero. The guide function is now a vector whose first element is $\theta$. The new $\theta$ vector is larger at each succeeding pivot in the sense that the first element of the new $\theta$ vector which is not equal to its corresponding element of the old $\theta$ vector is strictly larger.

One final comment before leaving this example. It should be pointed out that the special structure of this class of problems is significant to proving convergence. The fact that only a basic solution can possibly be the optimum solution is unique to linear problems. Also, the Kuhn-Tucker problem could be used because the linear equations implied a convex feasible region with a concave objective function.

As stated earlier, an approach of complete implicit or explicit enumeration of all possible solutions is quite often used to prove convergence. This technique is similar to that already discussed in that we must be able to locate all the feasible solutions. The guide function for this technique, however, would be a counting device which counts the solutions so that when all possible ones have been enumerated the procedure stops and takes the best one found. Balas' Zero-One L.P. method uses this approach. For instance, assume we have the problem

Maximize

$$\theta = 6x_1 + 4x_2$$

subject to

$$x_1 + x_2 \leq 1$$
$$x_1, x_2 = 0 \text{ or } 1$$

There are four possible solutions. We start by setting $(x_1, x_2) = (0, 0)$. The objective function is 0 and the constraints are satisfied. If we set $x_1 = 1$, we have $\theta$ of at least 6 and $x_1 + x_2 \leq 1 \Rightarrow x_2 \leq 0$. This rules out the solution $(1, 1)$, so we use $(1, 0)$. We also know that for any other solution to have a larger optimum, $6x_1 + 4x_2 \geq 6$. This fact rules out the solution $(0, 1)$. We have explicitly enumerated the solutions $(0, 0)$ and $(1, 0)$, and implicitly enumerated the solutions $(0, 1)$ and $(1, 1)$. Since the entire solution space has been exhausted, we know that $x = (1, 0)$, $\theta = 6$ is the optimum solution.

A third approach to proving convergence is statistical in nature. We attempt to prove that the desired solution is always reached with probability 1. Random selection, albeit time consuming, would eventually select the best possible solution—or show that none existed. Statistical convergence is most often applied to algorithms which deal with stochastic variables. Some information of the statistical nature of the functions being dealt with is necessary for this type of proof. In this type of algorithm we choose a procedure which converges for the deterministic case. In the stochastic case, however, we reduce the amount of change in each succeeding iteration, $n$, by a factor $f_n$ which assumes three things:

1. $f_n$ gets smaller and smaller and approaches 0 in the limit.

2. $\sum_{n=1}^{\infty} f_n = \infty$

3. $\sum_{n=1}^{\infty} (f_n)^2 = 0$

The first condition assures that no error in measurement is weighed too heavily. The second assures that any error term can be eventually eliminated by succeeding iteration. The third condition keeps the error terms from compounding too fast. The harmonic sequence $f_n = 1/n$ is used here since it has all the

CONVERGENCE OF ALGORITHMS

desired properties. Naturally some assumptions must be made concerning the distribution of the error term. In general, we need an unbiased expected value and a finite variance. When these assumptions hold we can prove that the probability of reaching the optimum value is 1 in the limiting case—i.e., as the number of iterations approaches infinity.

For an example of this, let us assume we have an unknown linear function $g(x)$ and we wish to determine its root, i.e., $x$ such that $g(x) = 0$. Our test procedure, however, has an error term so that $\hat{g}(x) = g(x) + \text{error}$. To demonstrate this type of algorithm, use the equation $g(x) = x - 3$. The error term was uniformly distributed at the points $-0.45$, $-0.35$, $-0.25$, $-0.15$, $-0.05$, $0.05$, $0.15$, $0.25$, $0.35$, $0.45$. Start with a step size of 8 and reduce it on each iteration, $n$, by the factor $f_n = 1/n$. If $\hat{g}(x_{n-1})$ is positive, the new test point $x_n$ will be $x_{n-1} - 8/n$. If $\hat{g}(x_{n-1})$ is negative, then $x_n$ will be $x_{n-1} + 8/n$. For this procedure, Table 1 was achieved ($x^*$ is the desired root).

Note that in Table 1 the wrong direction can be chosen due to the error terms (iterations 4 and 18). In these cases, however, the wrong choice is

**TABLE 1**

| $n$ | $8/n$ | $x_n$ | $g(x_n)$ | Error | $\hat{g}(x_n)$ | $\lvert x_n - x^* \rvert$ |
|---|---|---|---|---|---|---|
| 0 | — | 8.000 | 5.000 | −0.45 | 4.550 | 5.000 |
| 1 | 8.000 | 0.000 | −3.000 | 0.25 | −2.750 | 3.000 |
| 2 | 4.000 | 4.000 | 1.000 | −0.15 | 0.850 | 1.000 |
| 3 | 2.667 | 1.333 | −1.667 | −0.45 | −2.117 | 1.667 |
| 4 | 2.000 | 3.333 | 0.333 | −0.45 | −0.117 | 0.333 |
| 5 | 1.600 | 4.933 | 1.933 | 0.45 | 2.383 | 1.933 |
| 6 | 1.333 | 3.600 | 0.600 | 0.05 | 0.650 | 0.600 |
| 7 | 1.143 | 2.457 | −0.543 | −0.05 | −0.593 | 0.543 |
| 8 | 1.000 | 3.457 | 0.457 | −0.25 | 0.207 | 0.457 |
| 9 | 0.889 | 2.568 | −0.432 | 0.35 | −0.082 | 0.432 |
| 10 | 0.800 | 3.368 | 0.368 | 0.05 | 0.418 | 0.368 |
| 11 | 0.727 | 2.641 | −0.359 | 0.25 | −0.109 | 0.359 |
| 12 | 0.667 | 3.308 | 0.308 | 0.15 | 0.458 | 0.308 |
| 13 | 0.615 | 2.693 | −0.307 | −0.45 | −0.757 | 0.307 |
| 14 | 0.571 | 3.264 | 0.264 | 0.35 | 0.614 | 0.264 |
| 15 | 0.533 | 2.731 | −0.269 | −0.05 | −0.319 | 0.269 |
| 16 | 0.500 | 3.231 | 0.231 | 0.25 | 0.481 | 0.231 |
| 17 | 0.470 | 2.761 | −0.239 | −0.15 | −0.389 | 0.239 |
| 18 | 0.444 | 3.205 | 0.205 | −0.45 | −0.245 | 0.205 |
| 19 | 0.421 | 3.626 | 0.626 | −0.45 | 0.176 | 0.626 |
| 20 | 0.400 | 3.226 | 0.226 | 0.45 | 0.676 | 0.226 |
| 21 | 0.381 | 2.845 | −0.155 | 0.05 | −0.105 | 0.155 |
| 22 | 0.364 | 3.209 | 0.209 | −0.05 | 0.159 | 0.209 |
| 23 | 0.348 | 2.861 | −0.139 | −0.25 | −0.389 | 0.139 |
| 24 | 0.333 | 3.194 | 0.194 | 0.35 | 0.544 | 0.194 |
| 25 | 0.320 | 2.874 | −0.126 | 0.05 | −0.076 | 0.126 |

overcome fairly quickly. It can also be seen from the table that $\mid x_n - x^* \mid$ gets smaller *on the average* as the process continues. The algorithm itself is quite slow. This slowness cannot be attributed to the error term as much as to the necessary use of the harmonic sequence. For deterministic algorithms of this type, new solutions are generated by halving the step size on each iteration (Bolzano search) so that the speed of convergence is greatly improved. If this procedure were used with error terms, however, a step chosen in the wrong direction would never be overcome since condition 2. is not satisfied.

As a final remark to proving convergence, it should be noted that an algorithm can be imbedded within another algorithm or a heuristic. At times the resulting algorithm is very much improved by such a procedure. This procedure can also be used to gain convergence of an otherwise nonconverging code.

## CONCLUSIONS

Convergence of algorithms is an extremely complex subject. In this brief discussion the surface of several different facets of the problem have barely been touched. A great deal of research is being done in these areas. Zangwill [6] provides an excellent theoretical discussion of the topic of convergence. For statistical convergence, Refs. 1, 2, and 5 provide good discussions.

## REFERENCES

1.  Blum, J. R., Approximation methods which converge with probability one, *Ann. Math. Stat.* **25,** 382–386 (1954).
2.  Dvoretzky, A., On stochastic approximation, in *Proceedings of the 3rd Berkeley Symposium on Mathematics, Statistics, and Probability* (J. Neyman, ed.), University of California Press, Berkeley, California 1956, pp. 39–55.
3.  Mangasarian, O. L., *Nonlinear Programming,* McGraw-Hill, New York, 1969, Chaps. 6 and 7.
4.  Simonnard, M., *Linear Programming,* Prentice-Hall, Englewood Cliffs, New Jersey, 1966, Chaps. 1, 2, and 5, and Appendixes A and B.
5.  Wilde, D. J., *Optimum Seeking Methods,* Prentice-Hall, Englewood Cliffs, New Jersey, 1964, Chap. 6.
6.  Zangwill, W. I., *Nonlinear Programming,* Prentice-Hall, Englewood Cliffs, New Jersey, 1969, Chaps. 4 and 11.

*Timothy Shaftel*

# COPYRIGHT AND COMPUTERS[1]

## WHAT IS "COPYRIGHT"?

One of the fundamental concepts of Western civilization is the notion of *property,* e.g., certain *rights* over *things* which enabled the *owner* to exclude others from enjoying them. Further, there has been an ever-increasing disposition to recognize, venerate, and worship these rights as quasi-divine, e.g., a *property* was outside the region of positive (court or legislature) law, but instead was an article of natural justice.

This notion contrasts with the idea of special concession or privilege, e.g., if someone walks upon your land or steals your automobile, he is a trespasser or thief. If someone tampers with your concession, he is at best an infringer upon your monopoly (concession). Monopoly is nefarious whereas property is sacred [1].

And thus the battle is joined in defining exactly *what* a copyright is. If one insists, in spite of all historical evidence to the contrary [2], that a book, idea, or computer program is a species of *property,* then it immediately becomes clear that *copyright* is merely a handy catch phrase embodying certain positive legislative procedural enactments which provide the author or programmer with the *means* of protecting his *property.* On the other hand, if one considers the right to copy as a privilege given to certain persons as a means to accomplish socially desirable ends, then one becomes much less concerned with the so-called "natural justice" claims of the author and more concerned with the social effects of this privilege. This article is not intimately concerned with what is the proper philosophical basis for the right to copy; however, one is constrained to note that the "privilege" notion rather than the "property" notion was specified in the Constitution where Congress was given the power:

> To promote the progress of science and useful arts, by securing for limited times to authors and inventors the exclusive right to their respective writings and discoveries [3].

From these few (27) words, one may discern certain limits upon the United States right to copy:

1) The power is permissive, Congress *may* act, but is not required to do so.
2) The primary purpose of copyright is *not* to reward authors and

---

[1] This article is adapted with such additions, changes, and deletions as appeared necessary from an earlier article by the same author which originally appeared in the *Encyclopedia of Library and Information Science,* Volume 6, published by Marcel Dekker, Inc. Copyright © 1972 by Marcel Dekker, Inc.

programmers but rather to achieve certain public benefits, the encouragement of people in devoting themselves to intellectual and artistic creation [4].

Notwithstanding the simple import of the constitutional clause, one is impelled to note there is no adequate legislative history of the constitutional phrase; the courts rarely construe the copyright clause of the Constitution, and the Congress rarely recodifies the positive law surrounding this article.

In his monumental treatise on copyright [5], Nimmer quotes an opinion of the Court of Appeals which begins: "This action for copyright infringement presents us with a picture all too familiar in copyright litigation: a legal problem vexing in its difficulty, a dearth of squarely applicable precedents, a business setting so common that the dearth of precedents seems inexplicable, and an almost complete absence of guidance from the terms of the Copyright Act" [6].

Few observers would quarrel with Nimmer's conclusion that this represents a "generally accurate appraisal of the present status of copyright law," an "area of the law which is almost, if not entirely, unique . . . since copyright represents an application of one of the more striking recent developments of our contemporary culture, the phenomenon of mass communications" [5].

It may be helpful to consider that copyright is an attempt to reconcile three distinct interests in an intangible. First of all, there is the originator, the person who creates the expression; in the constitutional sense, the author: "He to whom anything owes its origin; originator, maker" [7].

The second distinctive interest is that of the publisher. This entity takes that which has been created by the author and transmits it to the recipient. "The role of the publisher in the realm of intellectual property is substantially different than that of the author. . . . The function of the publisher is almost exclusively entrepreneurial: he contracts with an author for the right to issue a book, then contracts with others to have the book printed and bound, and finally contracts with bookstores or bookclubs to have the book sold to the reading public"[8].

The third, but by no means least of the identifiable interests, is that of the users, who buy, read, and make use of the creation; in McLuhan's phrase, "the percussed victims of the new technology" [9].

All three of these interests coalesce in their pursuit and exploitation of that entity which is the object and result of the authorship, publishership, usership, and surely copy-rightship, the so-called "writing" which is the "matter and form of a literary or artistic work" [10].

All four of these copyright terms—author, publisher, user, and writing—are sufficiently imprecise and lacking in epistemological or legal certitude as to be a valid means of communicating the tensions and problems which afflict the computer professional. In the McLuhan sense, he has become the media by which what were four distinct compartments have become an amorphous whole. In an existential sense, he is the author, publisher, user, and, in many instances, the writing as well.

Notwithstanding, it is useful to examine how copyright affects him professionally as well as culturally.

## COPYRIGHTED MATERIAL AS DATA

The computer professional, particularly if he is working in the information retrieval field, is concerned with the materials that he may use in his systems. In a sense he is a lazy creature. If he wishes to use some literary material as a corpus and he finds that such use is prohibited or bordered with barbed-wire restrictions, he may abandon his line of inquiry or utilize some less meaningful source of material. It seems clear that the present and foreseeable technology will not replace the printed text as the primary means of transmitting intelligence in the mass [11], except to a most limited degree [12]. On the other hand, he, and, more importantly, his sponsoring organization, do not wish to expend their limited research funds in quixotic legal battles, particularly when they are placed on notice that the publisher is prepared to battle on ''principle'' [13].

It should be noted that publishers assert that permissions are relatively easy to obtain at the present time [14], however, the mere act of writing to obtain permission, waiting for the return letter, and then being forced to interpret the cautionary language of the publisher's legal representative is sufficient to cool all but the most heated of enthusiasts. However, it may be useful to examine certain areas where the computer professional is already utilizing copyrighted literary data as a corpus for his manipulations.

These areas may be further divided into the relative quantity of the original material utilized in his computer system.

## WHOLE TEXT INPUT

At present there are only a few areas where the computer scientist needs the complete text as input. Some spectacular experiments have been the establishment of authorship of particular essays of the Federalist Papers [15], consistency between the *Iliad* and the *Odyssey,* and single authorship of books of the Bible [16]. Less spectacular but apparently equally useful are the creation of concordances and other bibliographic tools for the humanistic researcher.

As one scholar has noted, ''The computer is taking over jobs which represent dog work for the scholar; the computer can do such tasks more rapidly, more efficiently, and more effectively than can the scholar'' [17].

At the present time, and for the foreseeable future, full text input is costly in preparation and costly in storage availability. While some publishers have made the magnetic or paper tapes, which are used for automatic type setting of text, available for full-text research purposes, these are generally not usable for syntactic or semantic manipulation as is.

Instead, this raw data must be converted into other representations before they can be utilized for information retrieval, and this conversion represents a significant cost. Despite significant advances in memory size and reductions in costs of storage per bit, machine-stored full text is still prohibitively expensive for all but research purposes. Notwithstanding the aforementioned costs, there is a significant body of literature available for experimentation. Here, however, the researchers are taking great pains to publicize the availability of the works in full text so as to avoid unnecessary duplication [18].

Another area of research has been that of the inquirer/questioner. Here a general type of reference work, such as a dictionary or an encyclopedia, is put into the system as a fact base for later inquiry and/or manipulation.

As will be seen, this latter use of complete material has greatly frightened the traditional publisher of technical reference works.

Full-text input has also been of importance in conjunction with research on mechanical translation. While the earlier optimism regarding the possibility of fully automatic translation no longer prevails [19], much effort is continuing in syntactic and semantic analysis. Here again large bodies of complete text are necessary to validate tentative results. The computer scientist here is developing generalized methods of preparing concordances, particularly where the syntactic environment of the word is the center of interest [20].

Still another area that is dependent upon access by computer to the whole text is automatic indexing [21] and possibly abstracting; i.e., "the use of machines to extract or assign index terms [or prepare abstracts of the underlying material] without human intervention once programs or procedural rules have been established" [25].

After an initial surge of interest, it too, like mechanical translation [19], has run into significant difficulties in translating prophecy into practice where theoretical insights are still to be developed.

Other areas of research which utilize full text seem free of copyright considerations since they utilize materials that are clearly in the public domain. Thus full text input of laws and legal cases into an information retrieval system would pose no significant copyright problems [22].

One of the major battles raging about the current efforts to revise the Copyright Laws is the concern as to whether entry into an automated computer system is to be controlled by the author or publisher [32].

At one extreme, the then Registrar of Copyrights has stated:

> It seems clear, for example, that the actual copying of entire works (or substantial portions of them) for "input" or storage in a computer would constitute a "reproduction" under clause (1), whatever form the "copies" take: punchcards, punched or magnetic tape, electronic storage units, etc. Similarly, at the "output" end of the process, the "retrieval" or "print-out" of an entire work (or a substantial part of it) in tangible copies would also come under copyright control [33].

As one proponent of the most restrictive controls over the use of copyrighted works as input observed:

> Kaminstein's [the Registrar of Copyrights quoted earlier] forthright opinion that the mere input of a copyrighted work into a computer system would clearly be an infringement under the new law came as a surprise, not to say a shock, to many people. They could not agree that storage could be

considered as copying, or even as the making of a "derivtive" work. Nor did they understand that the possession of a copy of a work does not give the owner any property rights whatever in the work itself—that the purchaser of a book has indeed bought no more than the right of access to a certain literary or scientific work through the physical form of the particular copy purchased [34].

## PARTIAL TEXT INPUT

Copyright considerations alone may dictate that the computer scientist only utilize portions of text in his retrieval input. Thus many courts which would question the copying of an entire or major portion of a work for input [23], even for scholarly, educational, or research purposes [24], might not look with disfavor upon the use of portions or fractions of books.

Of particular interest is the widespread use of KWIC (Key-Word-in-Context) indices. Here ready acceptance has flowed from the speed with which a complete index to some specific set of reference materials can be produced:

> The KWIC type process is indeed simple and straightforward. The words of the author's title are prepared for input to the computer by keystroking, either to punched cards or to punched paper tape. After being read by the computer, the text of a title is normally processed against a "stop list" to eliminate from further processing the more common words, such as "the," "and," prepositions, and the like, and words so general as to be insignificant for indexing purposes, such as "demonstration," "typical,""steps," and the like. The remaining presumably "significant" or "key" words are then, in effect, taken one at a time to an indexing position or window, where they are sorted in alphabetical order. The result is a listing of each such word together with its surrounding context, out to the limit of the line or lines permitted in a given format. As each keyword is processed, the title itself is moved over so that the next keyword occupies the indexing position, and this process is repeated until the entire title has thus been cyclically permuted.
>
> A number of formats are avilable in which the length of the line, the position of the indexing window, and the extent of "wrap-around" (bringing the end of a title in at the beginning of a line to fill space that would otherwise be left blank) are major variables [20].

Little problem would arise from copyright considerations in copying titles since, "for the most part, copyright may not be claimed in a title" [26]. However, the copying of lists of titles, which lists themselves are properly the subject of copyright, would be a form of full-text input, and would be subject to "fair use" exemptions and restrictions.

In this connection it is noteworthy that due to the economic problems alluded to earlier, some experiments which started off in full text for a data corpus have since gone to already available abstracts and synopses. Thus the LITE system [27], which began with full-text input of federal and state statutes, has confined itself to manual terms selected by human indexers for an important area of decisional law input [28].

At least one authority has indicated that, despite the broad freedom in unauthorized use commonly accorded legal materials [22], copyright restrictions will apply to a meaningful human abstract of the same materials, i.e., even though the full text may be utilized, the headnote or digest may not [29].

## WHOLE TEXT OUTPUT

As has been noted [11], at present there is little commercial incentive to output the complete text of a work of significant length. Even with the highest speed printers, and allowing for a considerable drop in peripheral costs, which seems unlikely, it is doubtful that a computer can replace the printing press, where the entire text has been stored or transferred through the memory. In the absence of significant economic erosion, the courts have been most reluctant to prohibit noncompetitive uses of copyrighted materials, even in full text [30].

The few examples to the contrary may be distinguished on the peculiar fact situations presented [31], or perhaps even by the eminence of counsel representing the plaintiff on appeal [24]. Notwithstanding the present state of the law, which would seem to exempt even the full-text output of copyrighted materials until such time as such becomes the actual rather than the hypothetical threat to the original proprietor, changes may be in store.

## PARTIAL TEXT OUTPUT

Here there is a more difficult area, since it may already be commercially feasible to produce limited output and even destroy an existing market.

Benjamin gives us a vivid example:

> Nor could one usually argue that a computer print-out of a few figures or formulas or small selections of data would contravene the "fair use" doctrine as it has been established by the courts.
>
> Yet the foregoing are exactly the kinds of use that are customarily made of handbooks, data books, and other basic reference works in science and technology.
>
> Let us suppose that a large corporation—say a Monsanto or Du Pont—has established a company-wide (and hence a nationwide) computerized technical information system for use at the touch of dozens of consoles by its hundreds of scientists and engineers. Let us also suppose that the "hardware" camp has prevailed in the copyright argument and that the corporation is free to store the whole of Perry's *Chemical Engineers' Handbook* in its computerized system. Let us finally suppose that the

corporation buys one copy of this handbook, stores its content, and then puts it to the seemingly "fair" uses described above. Obviously, in a situation such as this the one stored copy could take the place of as many as 500 or even 1000 copies of the handbook as it is now used. And if eight or ten other large corporations did likewise, there would be no remaining market sufficient to sustain publication [34]. [N.b.: this is not a hypothetical example! Author.]

Hence it is not entirely impossible that a court could reasonably find that, due to the state of technology—cost of memory for storage, etc.—whole text ouput would not be unreasonable whereas partial output would constitute infringement. The test would be the relative measure of the competing copies. To use Benjamin's example, if it costs $2000 to output the complete Perry's *Chemical Engineers' Handbook* whereas a single copy may be purchased from McGraw-Hill for one-tenth that, a court might well allow such full-text output. However, if a company were to purchase one copy and use it as described to avoid the purchase of additional hard copies, then such use might well be held illicit today.

## NO OUTPUT

Here there seems few problems of copyright significance to the information retrieval scientist. At present there are no restrictions on the use of books from the library shelf as a reference source in solving problems or compiling data.

Similarly, assuming that the copyrighted work can be inputted into the computer system without copyright limitations, the use of the work for analysis or problem solving would seem to be unexceptional. Thus the preparation of a concordance or a word frequency analysis would not cause copyright problems.

At this point it is worth noting that the *tort* problem of *unfair competition* may be relevant. Here, reference is made to the general notion that appropriation of values created by another may be an actionable wrong. However, "the possible situations are infinite and there is no formula, either simple or complex, through which the problems can be adequately poised for judgement. Numerous formulas [for determining when such appropriation is wrongful] have been attempted and most of them work well for a limited number of cases, but inevitably break down when subjected to other situations" [35].

It should be noted that many of the more extreme copyright infringement decisions [36] are in reality recoveries that should have been subsumed under the notion of unfair competition [37].

## CONCLUSIONS

Heretofore the discussion has centered around the types of *textual* material utilized for information retrieval and computer usage. Of necessity, reference was limited to printed matter, generally in book or periodical format. The conclusion reached was that due to the enormous expense presently incurred in converting textual material to machine-readable format, and vice versa, it is unlikely that copyright considerations will interfere with experimental use. To be specific, as of 1977, optical readers are economically able to handle only an unaesthetic upper case-and-numerics-only font [38]. The technology necessary to allow automatic reading of multifont straight textual material can be described as being in an early experiment stage at best. Bluntly put, there have been no significant breakthroughs in the mechanics of putting nonmachine data into a computer and obtaining the results. While memory sizes have increased exponentially, and memory speeds have gone from multiseconds to nanoseconds, and costs of memory have dropped by orders of magnitude per storage bit, the devices which put data in and out have remained relatively static in costs, speeds, and capacities [39].

Based upon these considerations, it is suggested that for the present most copyrighted materials may be introduced into information retrieval and storage systems if the text is converted into machine language. However, if the owner of the copyright or each piece of material used by the system must be contacted prior to input for permission to use the material, then research in this area becomes difficult if not impossible.

While most copyright proprietors seem to be willing to grant permission to use copyrighted material, some may not. However, the necessity for writing to secure permission may be enough to lead researchers, who are not lawyers and may not wish to be put to the trouble of securing permissions well in advance of their experiments, to spend their time in other ways. Avoidance of copyrighted material may have an unfortunate inhibiting effect upon research in the area of automatic information storage and retrieval, and would perhaps completely bias any experimental results.

In another area, many abstracts to be used in information retrieval systems are copyrighted. Writing to secure permission, if such were held necessary, from thousands of individual owners of copyrights on the abstracts as well as on the original material could prove sufficiently burdensome to the designers of the information systems to discourage them from including copyrighted material in their systems. It may be difficult if not impossible, for example, to secure permission to use abstracts of old or out-of-print articles from the author, the publisher, and the abstractor. A different question is raised when the copyrighted material is not converted to machine language for relay *through* a computer. Instead, the computer is used to locate the document and assist in its handling [40]. Here traditional copyright doctrine would apply and the special considerations alluded to above would not be expected to apply.

## THE PROBLEM OF MAKING COPYRIGHT "INPUT" AN INFRINGEMENT [41]

### Arguments in Favor of Making "Input" an Infringement

There are several arguments in favor of making computer input an operation requiring compensation. First, copyrighted material may be fed into a computer and emerge later not in the form of a reproduction, but rather in the form of useful information—such as an answer to a question. When output takes this form it is possible that no compensation might be due at the "output" stage. And, if there is widespread use of the copyrighted material contained within the computer in this way, the sale of the books and journals that the computer contains may decline. For this reason, it is claimed, compensation should be paid, and it must be paid, at the point of input or otherwise it might not be paid at all.

Second, the publishers have argued that unless compensation is exacted at the "input" stage, they may not be able to obtain any compensation for material that is rarely used. For example, at the present time a publisher may sell a copy of a scientific work to each of 10,000 libraries. If these libraries are connected with a computerized information system, however, he may sell only one copy to the system owner. While he will be able to collect royalties whenever the book stored within the computer is called for by a subscribing library (for a reproduction printed on paper or projected on a screen will then be made), it is conceivable that the book may be called for less than 10,000 times a year.

Third, the publishers argue that unless a toll is exacted at the computer input stage, they will have difficulty discovering violations of their copyrights. It is difficult to see why this is so, for, although it may be difficult to keep track of the number of reproductions that the computer makes of a copyrighted work, it is as easy to discover that a computer has made at least one reproduction as it is to discover that a copyrighted work has been fed into the computer in the first place. In fact, one method of showing that work had been put into a system without authorization might be to show that a reproduction had come out of the system. A fee schedule could easily be arranged which simply makes a part of the royalty charge for the first reproduction coming out of the machine that amount that might otherwise be charged as a royalty for input.

Finally, the publishers argue that unless compensation is required at the input stage, they will not be able to make money from selling "machine readable" copies of their books or journals. This argument seems to be another form of the first argument just discussed. Publishers will be able to make money from selling or leasing machine-readable copies of their books or journals. It is true, however, as we have just stated, that a copyright toll will not be charged if the copyrighted material emerges not as a reproduction but in the form of an answer to a question. And, insofar as this type of activity replaces the sale of books or journals, publishers and authors may be injured.

**Arguments Against Making "Input" an Infringement**

Several arguments can be advanced against assessing a copyrighted toll at the "input" stage. First, at the present time almost all copyrighted material fed into a system will emerge in the form of a reproduction. With the possible exception of mathematical tables, certain types of compilations, and similar scientific material, computers by and large do not store and use the full text of copyrighted material to answer questions directly, nor is there reason to believe that they will be able to do so in a significant way in the immediate future. The problems that the situation presents should not be resolved now, but we can wait until we see what actually happens.

Second, insofar as computers can operate directly upon copyrighted material stored within them to solve problems, etc., such operations do not necessarily replace the sales or books of journals. They may stimulate such sales. To impose a copyright toll may discourage the use of such material in computers or retard the development of this type of computer use. There is no reason to pay authors a fee (and at the same time inhibit the use of computers) when no interference with the sale of copyrighted material can be shown.

Third, since almost all copyrighted material now going into computers emerges in the form of a reproduction, and since a toll is thus imposed at the "output" stage, to impose a toll at the input stage is, at the present time, redundant. (Since the *amount* of the toll results from bargaining between users and copyright holders, it should not be affected significantly by the fact that a user is bargaining for the right to reproduce at the output stage rather than for rights to both input and output.)

Fourth, certain users of copyrighted material are exempt from the copyright toll. For example, a new revision of the copyright law partially exempts from royalty payments materials used as part of "face-to-face" teaching. To impose a toll upon computer "input" may seriously erode such exemptions for, although no royalty would have to be paid when material to be used for teaching emerges from the computer, a royalty would be assessed when material was put into the computer. Thus, what is given with one hand would be taken away with the other. It may be that this difficulty cannot be overcome by applying the same exemptions to "input" that are now applicable to "output," for material placed in a computer or an information system may be used in many different ways; probably *some* of those uses should be exempt and others should not be; and it may be impossible to say, at the time the material is placed in the system, to what extent it will be put to exempt uses and to what extent it will be put to nonexempt uses.

Fifth, to charge a toll at the input stage will raise complex and difficult problems when information is transferred from one computer system to another. It may be argued that in such a case there are two inputs, one into the first system and one into the second, but deciding whether such a system is in fact one system composed of many parts or two or more separate systems will also prove difficult. In fact, it is argued, the simplest method of charging a copyright royalty is to charge only for output that takes the form of a reproduction of copyrighted material.

## COPYRIGHT PROTECTION FOR COMPUTER PRODUCTS

### Programs

Considerable difficulty is encountered in attempting to bootstrap a new technology such as data processing into the traditional areas of law. To use one example, there is as yet no satisfactory definition of "program" which appears adequate for legal purposes. In its final report to the President, the Commission on the Patents described a "program" as follows:

> A series of instructions which control or condition the operation of a data processing machine, generally referred to as a "program," shall not be considered patentable regardless of whether the program is claimed as: (a) an article, (b) a process described in terms of the operations performed by a machine pursuant to a program, or (c) one or more machine configurations established by a program [42].

Still another definition proposed is:

> a computer program is basically a plan that controls the activity of the computer, directing the calculations needed to solve a problem and providing for communication of the solution to the outside world [43].

In its notice setting out the criteria for registration of a computer program, the Copyright Office posed the question and answer:

### What Is a Computer Program?

> In general, a computer program is either a set of operating instructions for a computer or a compilation of reference information to be drawn upon by the computer in solving problems. In most cases the preparation of both of these types of programs involves substantial elements of gathering, choosing, rejecting, editing, and arranging material. Some types of programs also embody verbal material which is written by the programmer and could be considered literary expression [44].

In its landmark decision stating that computer programs were not patentable [45], Justice Douglas defined *program* as "a sequence of coded instructions for a digital computer" [46].

Notwithstanding these legal attempts to describe what it is that causes a computer to do its thing [47], the question of how to handle computer programs under the copyright law remains a twofold subject. The question is twofold since the first aspect is whether programs are a proper subject for copyright; and second, if they are, what is the extent of the protection to be accorded to them.

To take the second first, on the one hand we have the statement of the Deputy Register of Copyrights that:

> Lest any misunderstanding arise, it should be emphasized at the outset that the newly announced policy [of the Copyright Office in accepting computer programs for registration on May 19, 1964] will not result in protection to the programmer with respect to the idea or system utilized in preparing the program. Copyrights in the program merely protect him against unauthorized copying of that particular program [48].

This lack of protection flows from a basic Supreme Court decision which stated:

> The copyright of a work on mathematical science cannot give to the author an exclusive right to the methods of operation which he propounds, or to the diagrams which he employs to explain them, so as to prevent an engineer from using them whenever occasion requires [49].

Another author has pointed out that the value of a patent or copyright is most dubious:

> In this rapidly developing science, with programs being quickly and continuously outdated by new developments of all kinds, a program's usefulness will frequently be lost long before a judicial dispute about its ownership can be resolved [50].

On the other hand, some others have looked with a most jaundiced eye at the language in the House Report on Copyright Revision which would clearly and unequivocally set a seal of approval upon the register's doubtful decision to admit computer programs to copyright registration. The EDUCOM Task Force in its statement to the Senate Committee considering the Copyright Review Bill painted a most dismal picture should broad protection be extended to computer programs:

> Inclusion of computer programs as possible subjects of copyright immediately raises the all-important question of proper scope of protection to be accorded programs by virtue of copyright. Is it intended that the copyright monopoly shall extend to the use of the program in combination with the computer to attain the result at which the program is aimed? For example, is it proposed that the plan or scheme of running a steel mill or handling payrolls by computer shall become the property of the person who holds the copyright of the program tapes or punch cards which direct the computer, which in turn directs and monitors the operation?
>
> The Revision Bill does not specifically address itself to this problem, but again we are met with broad statutory language defining the proprietor's exclusive rights. The language could conceivably be read as going the whole length of giving an affirmative answer to the foregoing questions—of giving the copyright proprietor of a program ownership of the process, so to speak, which the program embodies . . . .
>
> On principle, the vice in granting copyright to computer programs in the sense of the process is that it would amount to giving programs a breadth of protection similar to that accorded by patent, but without the safeguards and limitations that rightly surround the grant of a patent. Monopoly of systems, schemes, and the like has been granted by our law in the past only under patent, and only upon proof satisfactory to a governmental agency that there has been real "intervention"—a discovery marking a

material advance over the prior knowledge. Such a monopoly may last only 17 years. Copyright of a computer program, on the other hand, would be available on the basis of "originality," that is, merely an absence of copying without regard to true inventiveness; there would be no serious governmental scrutiny in advance; and the protection would run for a lengthy period of time (the present period is 56 years, and the Revision Bill proposes roughly 75 years). This kind of easy and broad protection for computer programs would threaten to tie up the computer program field and inhibit its progressive development. Had there been such a copyright regime for programs, had programming been constantly carried out under the threat of infringement actions charging plagiarism of existing copyrighted programs, it is doubtful whether the growth of programs and programming techniques of recent years would have been possible. Imagine the condition today if any sizable fraction of the thousands of existing computer programs were held in copyright and copying the processes involved were civilly actionable and even criminally punishable.

The argument has been made in support of, or at least in an apology for, copyright for computer programs covering the processes, that infringement could be avoided simply by changing in some degree the sequence of steps or the problem-solving algorithm of the program. On this view, the presence of a copyright would merely compel an outsider to do some slight work of his own in order to stay out of trouble. The answer to this suggestion is: if copyright of process were accepted, (i) it would make no sense to permit escape from it by trivial variation; (ii) it is very doubtful that courts would take so lighthearted or permissive an attitude toward the infringement question. The tendency of the courts in recent years has been to enlarge rather than to contract the range of actionable plagiarism. Surely it would be most imprudent to assume that courts would be especially gingerly about finding infringement of computer programs, once the basis of protection was established [51].

As the EDUCOM statement points out, even *limited* rights regarding copyright protection for computer programs could prove harmful:

If the process embodied in a computer program ought not to be aggrandized through copyright, it might still seem plausible to allow a narrower copyright of a program—one that would confer upon the copyright proprietor the exclusive right to replicate the instructions themselves, the content of the punch cards, tapes, etc., and the right to bar others from making that replication, thereby compelling those others to buy the punch cards, tapes, etc. from the copyright proprietor. But it becomes evident that this right must be carefully circumscribed. For if the outsider is to be assured full access to the process—full right to practice the art comprised in the computer program—then he must be given the accompanying privilege to replicate the program in order to carry out the process or practice the art. Put another way, were the copyright owner of the program empowered to bar the outsider from replicating the program even for the purpose of practicing the art, he would effectively denied the outsider the ability to practice the art, for the outsider needs to replicate the program or something akin to it in order to instruct his own computer.

On the other hand, the copyright owner of the program might be given the right to prevent others from replicating the content of the punch cards, tapes, etc. simply for the purpose of selling the program on the market or reproducing it in a book on programming. In general, it might not be socially harmful to permit copyright of computer programs limited in scope to replications for purposes other than carrying out the process or practicing the art contained in the programs. Concretely: X prepares a computer program for controlling the production of steel. A copyright of the program by X (obtained on the basis of "originality") should in no event bar Y, an outsider, from producing steel in the same way, and to that end Y, if he chooses, should be at liberty to replicate X's program exactly. (Of course, Y may prefer to buy the punch cards or tapes from X.) On the other hand Y would not be at liberty to replicate X's program simply to sell copies of it to Z; he would not be permitted to enter into a competition with X in any market that may exist for selling the relevant punch cards, tapes, etc. We imagine this sort of limited copyright in X would not be socially hurtful, although we frankly do not know whether it would be necessary or useful [52].

Despite the fears expressed above, a more reasonable approach is to conclude that present copyrights protections, if any, accorded computer programs, do not extend to the ideas embodied in the program, nor to the techniques used in developing or making the program, nor to "its logical sequence of instructions, which constitute the program's greatest value, but only to the program's format" [52]. This follows from the principle enunciated by the Supreme Court in the landmark case of *Baker* v. *Selden* [53].

> The copyright of a work on mathematical science cannot give to the author an exclusive right to the methods of operation which he propounds, or to the diagrams which he employs to explain them, so as to prevent an engineer from using them whenever occasion requires. The very object of publishing a book on science or the useful arts is to communicate to the world the useful knowledge it contains.

This result flows directly from the constitutional provision to "promote the Progress of Science and the useful Arts, by securing for limited Times to Authors and Inventors the exclusive Right to their respective Writings and Discoveries" [3]. This very clear language sets forth the footing for our copyright and patent laws, and may be seen to encompass four basic concepts.

First, the primary purpose of the laws is not to reward authors and inventors no matter how deserving or needy; it is not to benefit publishers, printers, or large corporations. The primary purpose of these laws is to *promote the progress of science and the useful arts*: each and every provision of every law promulgated under Article 1, Section 8, has to be in the broad public interest, as enunciated.

The Supreme Court has made it abundantly clear that the benefit to the author is a "secondary consideration" [54], that the primary purpose of copyright is to obtain "the general benefits derived by the public from the labors of authors" [55]. In *Mazer* v. *Stein*, the Court set forth the Constitutional rationale:

> The economic philosophy behind the clause empowering Congress to grant patents and copyrights is the conviction that encouragement of individual effort by personal gain is the best way to advance public welfare through the talents of authors and inventors in "Science and useful Arts" [56].

Even Nimmer, a notable advocate of expanded copyright protections, concludes:

> Thus the authorization to grant to individual authors the limited monopoly of copyright is predicated upon the dual premises that the public benefits from the creative activities of authors, and that the copyright monopoly is a necessary condition to the full realization of such creative activities. Implicit in this rationale is the assumption that in the absence of such public benefit the grant of a copyright monopoly to individuals would be unjustified. This appears to be consonant with the pervading public policy against according private economic monopolies in the absence of overriding countervailing considerations [philosophical discussion to the contra omitted] [57].

The second basic concept inherent in the constitutional language is that the rights given pursuant to copyright and patent legislation must be *for limited times only* [58]. Thus the patent monopoly only extends for 17 years from the date of grant of the patent. The new copyright term (life of author plus 50 years) seems at best the outermost boundary of the constitutional phrase—*for limited times*. It is certain that the framers of the Constitution, having in mind the many evils under the original English system, while wishing to keep a certain amount of flexibility in a living body of laws, clearly intended to weight the balance *in favor of unrestricted public access at the earliest possible time.*

A landmark case in the field of patent and copyright law is *Pennock* v. *Dialogue* [59]. This case, in discussing the constitutional provision against which any proposed patent or copyright law must be measured, stated that this provision "contemplates, therefore, that this right shall exist *but for a limited period,* and that the period shall be subject to the discretion of Congress" [emphasis added] [60]. At this time the limited period, albeit for a patent, was for 14 years.

In *Pennock* v. *Dialogue* the Supreme Court early recognized the paramount right of the public in early disclosure by correctly setting out the true rationale of the patent and copyright laws:

> While one great object was, by holding out a reasonable reward to inventors, and giving them an exclusive right to their inventions *for a limited period,* to stimulate the efforts of genius; the main object was "to promote the progress of science and useful arts;" and this could be done best, by giving the public at large a right to make, construct, use and vend the thing invented, at as early a period as possible, having a due regard to the rights of the inventor. If an inventor should be permitted to hold back from the knowledge of the public the secrets of his invention; if he should, for a long period of years, retain the monopoly, and make and sell his invention publicly, and thus gather the whole profits of it, relying upon his superior skill and knowledge of the structure; and then only, when the danger of competition should force him to secure the exclusive right, he should be allowed to take out a patent, and thus exclude the public from any further use than what should be derived under it, during his fourteen years; it would materially retard the progress of science and the useful arts, and *give a premium to those who should be least prompt to communicate their discoveries* [emphasis added] [61].

A third concept provided by the Constitution is that the *authors and inventors* are given a limited monopoly. The Constitution gives no direct rights to the employers of *authors and inventors;* it gives no direct rights to the large corporate body; it does not directly provide for the publisher, the printer, the manufacturer, the football league, and others who form a conduit between the *author or inventor* and the *public.* Therefore, one should conclude that if a present or proposed provision of a Copyright or Patent Law does not clearly provide a direct incentive to the author or inventor so that he will continue his innovative efforts, then that provision is of doubtful validity. Similarly, any incentives which do not serve as a goad to him to continue his creative efforts, although they may provide an economic benefit to the author or inventor, should fail. As just one example, there is no persuasive rationale for bringing live unrehearsed athletic contests under the *copyright umbrella.*

The last, but by no means least concept for copyright, is that it must be a "writing" of an "author" [62]. However, Congress and the courts have explicitly expanded the term "writing" far beyond the everyday meaning of actual script, printing, etching, etc., even to nonverbal expressions such as labels, photographs, three-dimensional art forms, and motion pictures; in effect, to all tangible forms of intellectual creation. Banzhaff suggests three prerequisites: "permanence, tangibility, and a form capable of being copies" [63], argues that computer programs meet these physical requirements. The Copyright Office was much more hesitant in deciding whether to accept computer programs for registration:

> The registrability of computer programs involves two basic questions: (1) Whether a program as such is the "writing of an author" and thus

copyrightable, and (2) whether a reproduction of the program in a form actually used to operate or be "read" by a machine is a "copy" that can be accepted for copyright registration.

Both of these are doubtful questions. However, in accordance with its policy of resolving doubtful issues in favor of registration wherever possible, the Copyright Office will consider registration for a computer program if certain requirements have been met . . . .

Registration for a computer will be considered if:

(a) The elements of assembling, selecting, arranging, editing, and literary expression that went into the compilation of the program are sufficient to constitute original authorship.

(b) The program has been published, with the required copyright notice; that is, "copies" (i.e., reproductions of the program in a form perceptible or capable of being made perceptible to the human eye) bearing the notice have been distributed or made available to the public.

(c) The copies deposited for registration consist of or include reproductions in a language intelligible to human beings. If the first publication was in a form (such as machine-readable tape) that cannot be perceived visually or read by humans, something more (such as a print-out of the entire program) must be deposited along with two complete copies of the program as first published . . . [44].

Here it is well to remember that statutory copyright in a published work is obtained by publication with notice of copyright. Registration by the Copyright Office does not create the copyright, but merely records it [64].

Further, it has been held that the Register has a broad, but not unlimited, area of discretion in determining what subject matter, in his opinion, is copyrightable, and thus acceptable for registration [65]. "However, the courts will generally treat with great weight the actual practices of the Copyright Office" [66].

However, despite the traditional weight given the Register of Copyright's determination as to what is registerable, hence copyrightable, most commentators would not attach extreme importance either way to the Copyright Office's consideration of programs for registration, particularly in view of the Register's statement that at best registerability is a doubtful question. Ultimate resolution must await judicial and/or legislative determination.

The physical form of the program presents additional difficulty. As noted above, in its initial announcement the Copyright Office required a printed or visible form such as a machine listing or flowchart "of the complete program."

One commentator in fact concluded:

The other physical forms that a computer program may assume present a more difficult problem. On the basis of existing procedure, a punched deck of cards or tape, a roll of magnetic tape, or similar representations, would probably be denied copyright protection. In and of themselves such forms of information are meaningless to the average reader. Even giving a most sweeping interpretation to *Burrow-Giles Lithographic Co.* v. *Sarony,* which rejected a literary interpretation of the term "writing" in the "copyright clause" of the United Stated Constitution, one would not likely consider a pile of perforated cards, a few yards of sievelike paper tape, or a magnetized tape to be a "writing" of an author [footnotes omitted] [67].

However, once more the ugly facts of life intruded in the first year of registration of computer programs. Of the 16 claims covering programs, 13 consisted of printouts only. In two cases, punched cards with full interpretation at the top were accepted. In one instance, magnetic tape without a complete printout was accepted:

> Since the program on magnetic tape could not be perceived visually or read, it was necessary that a print-out be deposited also. The deposit of magnetic tape presented additional difficulties in view of the size of the particular program; the applicant said that a print-out of the entire program would be approximately 12 feet high. To resolve the problem the reels of tape were deposited along with selected portions of the print-out namely, *the beginning of the work* including the title and copyright notice, *part of the center,* and *the end* [emphasis added] [68].

In conclusion, therefore, it may be said that the copyrightability of computer programs is doubtful; however, deposit for registration with the Register of Copyrights may be had, and the form of the program deposited need not be visible to the unaided human eye.

## COMPUTER PRODUCED OUTPUT

Another area of controversy, as yet unillumed by either statute or court decision, is the protection accorded computer-produced output. Thus annual contests are held for computer-derived drawings and other works of art [69]. As mentioned above, computer-generated concordances, bibliographies, indices, and other literary materials are becoming more and more common. Here, too, the enthusiasm of the dedicated is most contagious:

> Since the electronic computer was invented, its usefulness to society has been limited more by the imagination of man than by the capability of the hardware. The possibility of a computer creating music, art, or literature is perhaps obscure only because our pride forces us to believe these areas are man's exclusive provinces.
>
> At the 1966 Fall Joint Computer Conference, Professor Heinz Von Foerster organized a highly creative, imaginative and enjoyable session on "Computers in Music." The papers presented at the session were received with great enthusiasm; and form the basis of this book. The ideas advanced here may well lead to exciting and publicly accepted music of the future [70].

Roughly speaking, three possible contributions by the computer to music may be expected—and by analogy to other art or literary works: (1) Generation of acoustic tones, (2) melodic and rhythmic composition, and (3) execution of a composition without a human performer/orchestra.

Obviously (1) and (3) are important; witness the hit parade success of the Moog Synthesized version of Bach. However, only (2) need be of concern in considering copyright or literary protection. The Copyright Office has already received works for registration allegedly created by computer: musical compositions, abstract drawings, and compilations of various sorts. Here they feel the test will be the human element involved: "whether the 'work' is basically one of human authorship, with the computer merely being an assisting instrument, or whether the traditional elements of authorship in the work (literary, artistic, or musical expression or elements of selection, arrangement, etc.) were actually conceived and executed not by man but by a machine [71]. It is somewhat paradoxical but accurate to contemplate that the more successful the computer creation is, the less likely it is that the result will be copyrightable [72].

The distinction between the author or producer of stored material and the user of the material in large computer utility operations is already blurred [73]. As noted in our introduction, the user is becoming a part of the writing itself:

> One is reminded of "aleatoric" music in which the line between performer and composer wavers. Professor McLuhan, a professional soothsayer, says broadly that as the imperium in communications passes from books to electronic manifestations, as the "Gutenberg galaxy" decays, not only is the relationship between author and audience radically changed but the author's pretensions to individual ownership and achievement are at a discount: his dependence on the past is better appreciated; he is seen somewhat as a tradition-bearing "singer of tales," as a kind of teacher peculiarly indebted to his teachers before him. (I suppose claims of exempt status for educational uses of copyrighted works dimly reflect such an idea.) [Footnote omitted] [74].

So far, at least, the computer has not invaded the provinces of artistic and literary endeavor to the same extent that it has revolutionized scientific fields. But already the use of computers is impacting the former areas, transforming what was a barrier between technology and creativity into a partnership. As noted above, in music the computer can be a source of sound or a means of compositon. Sound can be converted mathematically into light patterns. The machines can already produce a most vivid prose or poetic work.

In addition, this new tool is bringing the engineer and scientist directly into aesthetic creativity on all fronts. In 1968, an historic exhibition, entitled "cybernetic Serendipity," was held in London and toured the United States in 1969. This exhibition, and its accompanying catalog [75], "surveys the present state of accomplishment in the creation of artistic forms through technological means by experimenters all over the world [76]. It remains to be seen what, if any, legal protections are necessary or will be devised to maintain peace with this new "organic interrelation" and "organic interdependence" where the intake of information fuses with the consumption of the creative enlightenment [77].

Nimmer indicates two requirements that a work must meet to constitute a "writing," i.e., to become eligible for copyright; (1) tangible form and (2) intellectual labor. He further indicates that the "intellectual labor" standard may also be required by the concept of "author" [78].

This would follow from the *Trademark Cases* [79] where the Supreme Court held that a trademark does not constitute a "writing" in the copyright sense; a result consistent with the notion that the value imputed to a trademark is based upon market acceptance for product identification. That is, trademark rights flow from the *use* and only the *use* of the mark—*not* the originality or intellectual creativity involved in selecting the mark [80].

Thus, in trying to ascertain whether a computer result is a "writing" of a [human] "author," one must make a judgment as to whether:

> the intellectual labor expended [by the human] in its creation is so trivial as to be virtually non-existent . . . a very slight degree of [intellectual] labor will be sufficient to qualify the work as a writing in the constitutional sense. Thus, almost any ingenuity [by a human] is selection [possibly from multiple outputs], combination or expression, no matter how crude, humble or obvious, will be sufficient to render the work a "writing" [81].

## "FAIR USE" AS IT AFFECTS THE COMPUTER PROFESSIONAL

One of the most prickly ideas to permeate the field of literary protections is the concept of "fair use."

Briefly stated, "fair use" may be defined as the permissible "use"—copying or performance—of a copyrighted work over the *objection, express or implied,* of the copyright proprietor [82]:

> If there is anything absolute about fair use, it is that it is a concept favoring the user of the copyrighted work and not the owner. It limits the rights of the copyright owner. It has served as a reasonable safety valve to the almost paralytic effect that copyright might have placed on the sensible use and exploitation of published works, if the law had been interpreted as an absolute doctrine. Even the copyright owner recognizes this [83].

In its report on the Copyright Revison Bill [84], the House Judiciary Committee accurately noted that "although the courts have considered and ruled upon the fair use doctrine over and over again, no real definition of the concept has ever emerged. Indeed, since the doctrine is *an equitable rule of reason,* no generally applicable definition is possible, and each case raising the question must be decided on its own facts [85]. Further, the concept "fair use" only comes into play when one is sued for copyright infringement, and raises the affirmative defense that the particular use made is not an infringement but is permitted over the wishes of the copyright proprieter, i.e., it is a fair use.

Nimmer has suggested that the distinction between fair use and infringement may rest upon the question as to whether or not the defendent's use "tends to diminish or prejudice the sale of the plaintiff's work . . . if regardless of medium, the defendent's work . . . performs a different function than that of the plaintiff's, the defense of fair use may be involved," [86].

In its report the House Committee noted four criteria for balancing the equities, and included these criteria in its version of the Copyright Revision Bill for the first statutory recognition of the doctrinc [87]. However, the committee emphasized that its specific language was "intended to restate the present judicial doctrine of fair use, not to change, narrow, or enlarge it in any way" [88]. Thus the committee's definition of "fair use" and the relevant criteria may be considered a basis for establishing workable practices and policies:

> . . . the fair use of copyrighted work . . ., for purposes such as criticism, comment, news reporting, teaching, scholarship, or research, is not an infringement of copyright. In determining whether the use made of a work in any particular case is a fair use, the factors to be considered shall include—
> (1) the purpose and character of the use;
> (2) the nature of the copyrighted work;
> (3) the amount and substantiality of the portion used in relation to the copyrighted work as a whole; and
> (4) the effect of the use upon the potential market for or value of the copyrighted work.

Therefore, one may reasonably conclude that *at present* inclusion of copyrighted material within a computer-based information retrieval system, as described earlier, would constitute fair use, even though changes were made for and profits were realized from the output of the computer system [88]. If the technology and economics develop so that such activities constitute an actual rather than potential threat to traditional copyright uses, then a contrary result may occur, especially if the courts do not find an overwhelming social policy in favor of the new technology [89].

## CONCLUSIONS

Many intriguing and interesting questions are beyond the scope of this discussion other than in a most cursory fashion.

### Antitrust

If computer programs are able to be protected by copyright or patent, then they no longer may be offered on a package basis, but must be offered separately on reasonable terms, i.e., there is a *per se* antitrust rule prohibiting tie-in arrangementments since the latter "serve no useful purpose except to retain competition [90].

Copyright owners may not act together to extend their individual monopolies without running afoul of the antitrust laws [91].

Similarly, it is most doubtful on antitrust grounds whether a dominant computer manufacturer may refuse to sell a copyrighted program [92] or restrict its use to a given central processor in the absence of a strong procompetitive rationale [93].

## Future Prospects

The long-awaited copyright bill, pending since 1966, was enacted in 1976. There appears to be unanimous agreement that the drafters of the copyright revision bill refused to come to grips with "the technological and policy problems caused by computers" [94]. Whether or not the copyright study commission will solve these problems seems problematical in light of the opposition, albeit justified, of certain groups [95]. Since the new copyright legislation is, for the most part, not effective until 1978, early resolution of these dilemmas is unlikely.

Kaplan has pointed a vivid picture of the future of copyright in the new computer-bred technological environment:

> You must imagine, at the eventual heart of things to come, linked or integrated systems or networks of computers capable of storing faithful simulacra of the entire treasure of the accumulated knowledge and artistic production of past ages, and of taking into the store new intelligence of all sorts as produced. The systems will have a prodigious capacity for manipulating the store in useful ways, for selecting portions of it upon call and transmitting them to any distance, where they will be converted as desired to forms directly or indirectly cognizable, whether as printed pages, phonorecords, tapes, transient displays of sights or sounds, or hieroglyphs for further machine uses. Lasers, microwave channels, satellites improving on Comsat's Early Bird, and, no doubt, many devices now unnamable, will operate as ganglions to extend the reach of the systems to the ultimate users as well as to provide a copious array of additional services.
>
> Conceived as conduits or highways for the transmission of signals, the systems will have intense responsibilities of a "public utility" type enforced by law if indeed the systems (or some of them) will not come under direct government ownership and control. Horrors of Orwellian dimensions lurk in far-reaching official regulation of the communications pattern; but to say that is merely to sound a summons to wise public regulation. If the systems will have public duties, so will new intellectual productions once unbosomed and released by the authors—the duties of

submitting themselves to deposit in some form appropriate for archival purposes and to permit any manipulations of indexing, abstracting, and so forth needed to connect them, to key them in, with the existing store. This contribution made by new works need not involve their exposure to full-length use by unwelcome clients. At present, self-interest on the part of authors and publishers has usually resulted in adequate public access to works, and the law has rarely had to become insistent. Probably the law of the future will lose patience rather quickly with the mere idiosyncratic withholding of access. But I should hope there will ever be play for the humane development of the "moral rights" of authors to prevent abuses in the exploitation of their creations. This will indeed be especially important if copyright itself recedes as a significant control.

Copyright is likely to recede, to lose relevance, in respect to most kinds of uses of a great amount of scholarly production which now sees light in a melange of learned journals and in the output of university presses. In the future little of this will ever be published in conventional book or journal form . . . .

. . . For many of the uses available through the machine, exaction of copyright payments will be felt unnecessary to provide incentive or headstart—especially so, when the works owe their origin, as so many will, to one or another kind of public support.

I am suggesting that copyright or the larger part of its controls will appear unneeded, merely obstructive, as applied to certain sectors of production and that here copyright law will lapse into disuse and may disappear. For the rest, copyright will persist to serve its historic purposes. For various early, prime exploitations of particular new works, whether or not accomplished through the electronic systems, there will be individual accountings, with separate financial hazards and successes or failures. The secondary and later exploitations will be largely through the systems . . . .

But what is suggested, on more sober reflection, is methods by which large repertories of works will be made available for a great variety of uses, and charges and remittances figured on a rough-and-ready basis, all with liberal application of some principle of "clearance at the source" to prevent undue bother down the line to the final consumer.

Unless, indeed, the systems are set up by government direct, government will probably intervene to establish fair standards for admission of works into the systems, for giving potential users access to the systems, for figuring rates, for making distributions to copyright owners. But under conditions of extensive government concern with the operations of the systems, which will have become supremely facile and widely encompassing of the transmission of intelligence, it may appear sensible to displace copyright and substitute other, perhaps more direct, encouragements to original production. We may in any case expect legislators of the future to regard copyright as only one among a number of expedients for stimulating creativity [96].

Copyright already is affecting and being affected by the computer revolution. Historically, it developed as "a private concept by a private group." It resulted in a "rigidity" springing from "the application of rules without guiding principles" which in turn resulted from the courts construing "a statute for a particular purpose: to destroy an opprobrious monopoly."

"Copyright [is] not a product of the common law." [The courts did not see it as "a concept used to deal with exceedingly complex issues, issues which require careful distinctions based upon a perceptive awareness of the problems, an understanding of purpose, and appreciation of function."] "It was a product of censorship, guild monopoly, trade regulation statutes, and misunderstanding [97].

In a society where machines compute at the speed of light [98], where man visits the moon on live color television, and where wars are termed "happenings, tragic games" [99], much of the traditional protection of invisible property via copyright seems obsolescent if not obscene. It remains to be seen whether society is well or ill-served by retaining the placebo termed copyright.

## REFERENCES

1.  Birrell, *Seven Lectures on the Law and History of Copyright in Books*, Putnam, New York, 1899; reprinted Kelley, New York, 1971, 228 pp at 11-14.
2.  Ref. 1. See also Kaplan, *An Unhurried View of Copyright*, Columbia University Press, New York, 1967, 142 pp.
3.  U.S. Constitution, art. I, sec. 8, cl 8.
4.  *Goldstein* v. *California*, 412 U.S. 546 (1973).
5.  Nimmer, *Nimmer on Copyright*, Bender, New York, 1974, p. ii(c) citing *Shapiro* v. *Green*, 316 F.2d 304 (CA-2 1963).
6.  *Shapiro, Bernstein & Co., Inc.* v. *H. L. Green Co.*, 316 F.2d 304 (2d Cir. 1963).
7.  *Burrow Giles* v. *Sarony*, 111 U.S. 53 (1884), p. 58.
8.  Hurt and Schuchman, Economic rationale of copyright, *Am. Econ. Rev. Suppl., Papers Proc.* **56,** 426–427 (1966).
9.  McLuhan, *Understudying Media: The Extensions of Man*, Signet, New America Library, New York, 1964, p. 70.
10. McLuhan and Fiore, *The Medium is the Message*, Bantam, London, 1967, p. 122: "The invention of printing did away with anonymity, fostering ideas of literary fame and the habit of considering intellectual effort as private property. Mechanical multiples of the same text created a public—a reading public. The rising consumer-oriented culture became concerned with labels of authenticity and protection against theft and piracy. The idea of copyright—'the exclusive right to reproduce, publish, and sell the matter and form of a literary or artistic work'—was born."
11. Muller, Electronic computers: Storage and retrieval, in *Automated Information Systems and Copyright Law, A Symposium* (Hattery and Bush, eds.), American University, Washington, D.C., 1968, pp. 12–13. [Unabridged reformated edition taken from 114 *Congressional Record*, June 11–14, 1968.]
12. However, one eminent authority has a contrary view based upon what *could* be done with certain existing techniques. See Licklider's testimony in *Hearings on H.*

*R. 8809, A National Science Research Data Processing and Information Retrieval System* before U.S. Congress, House Committee on Education and Labor, 91st Cong., 1st sess., April 29–30, 1969, pp. 240–241.

13. See, e.g., the notice in this book: "Neither this book nor any part may be reproduced or transmitted in any form or by any means, electronic or mechanical, including photocopying, microfilming, and recording, or by any information storage and retrieval system, without permission in writing from the publisher."

14. Lacy, The © quagmire, *Saturday Rev.* pp. 24-28, at 27 (November 27, 1971).

15. Rosenberg, *The Death of Privacy,* Random House, New York, 1969, p. 97.

16. Ref. 15, p. 100.

17. Holland, Futures: A now-summary of the EDUCOM Symposium on the Computer and Humanistic Studies, *Computers and the Humanities* **2,** 57 (1967): "Some scholars use the computer to provide frequency lists of word of other occurrences in bodies of material much too large for mere mortals to manage. Similarly, the computer can scan large amounts of material for accidentals so as to solve attribution problems. It can collate texts with a speed and accuracy far beyond a man's. The making of a concordant—traditional pastime of English vicars—has become common place. John Bartlett took forty years to make his *Concordance to Shakespeare* (producing the *Familiar Quotations* as a kind of by-product); today at Cornell, the job could be done in a month."

18. See the directory of Literary materials in machine-readable form, *Computers and the Humanities* **1,** 75–102 (1967); **2,** 133–144 (1968); **3,** 225–239 (1969).

19. *Language and Machines, Computers in Translation and Linguistics,* National Research Council, Washington, D.C., 1969, p. 19: " 'Machine Translation' presumably means going by algorithm from machine-readable source text to useful target text without recourse to human translation or editing. In this context, there has been no machine translation of general scientific text, and none is in immediate prospect." But see Titus, Nebulous future of machine translation, *Commun. ACM* **10,** 189–191 (March 1967), for some contrary views.

20. Scharfenberg, Smith, and Villani, A concordance generator, *IBM Syst. J.* **3,** 104–111 (1964).

21. Stevens, *Automatic Indexing: A State of the Art Report* (NBS Monograph 91), National Bureau of Standards, Washington, D. C., 1965, p. 3.

22. Lipton, Extent of copyright protection for law books, *Second ASCAP Copyright Law Symposium,* 1946, 11.

23. *College Entrance Book Co.* v. *Ansco Book Co.,* 119 F.2d 874 (2d Cir. 1941).

24. *Wihtol* v. *Crowe,* 309 F.2d 277 (8th Cir. 1962).

25. Ref. 21, p. 41.

26. Ref. 5, §34.

27. *LITE, Legal Information Through Electronics,* hearing before U.S. Congress, House Subcommittee of the Committee on Government Operations, 90th Cong., 1st sess., August 1, 1967. In addition to the testimony of August 1, the Subcommittee reprinted the LITE Issue of the *AF JAG Law Rev.* **8**(6), 1–51 (November 1966), which gives a eulogistic description of the LITE system. See also U.S. Congress, House Committee on Government Operations, *Air Force Project LITE,* 90th Cong., 2d sess., February 29, 1968, H. Rept. 1133. Among the questions *not* raised by the subcommittee were: (a) The legality of the Air Force restrictions upon subsequent use by non-Governmental users of the LITE data base tapes: these appear to use the lease method to obtain copyrightlike benefits for the government despite the explicit prohibition of Sec. 8 of the Copyright Act, 17 U.S.C. Further, they require

the lessee to furnish the government with copies of any results of its research, a practice which would probably be illegal *per se* under the antitrust laws if followed by a private party, cf. Turner, *Antitrust Enforcement Policy,* 29 A.B.A. Antitrust Section Rep. 187, 188, (1969). (b) The propriety of the University of Pittsburgh, the contractor to the Air Force, in allowing private parties to use the Air Force data base in successful litigation against the government; see, e.g., ''Computer search in amicus brief [*C.I.R.* v. *Brown,* 380 U.S. 563 (1965)], *M.U.L.L. [Jurimetrics J.]* 36–38 (March 1966).

28.  Frankel, Legal information retrieval, *Adv. Comput.* **9,** 141 (1969): ''Also project LITE makes extensive use of KWIC indexes, as a form of output of searches, and as a form of dissemination of information. For example, LITE published KWIC indexes of the *total text* of Titles 10, 32, 37, 50, and 50 Appendices of the U.S. Code all of which have particular application to the defense establishment, and of *the scope lines of the decisions* of the Comptroller General of the United States. Also complete cross-indexes of the Internal Revenue Code and of other legal texts were constructed'' [emphasis added and references omitted].

29.  *Opinion of Attorney General of State of New York,* 142 U.S.P.Q. 288 (1964).

30.  Gorman, Copyright protection for the protection and representation of facts, *Harvard Law Rev.* **76,** 1569–1605 (1963), pp. 1603–1604: ''In dealing with fact works, courts feel more competent to exercise judgment on matters of creativity and originality; they deal with fewer problems of aesthetics, with standards less subject to change over time. They have thus occasionally fashioned theories of copyright protection which deny the monopoly right to efforts which seem clearly deserving. The map cases come most quickly to mind. In those hybrid cases of fact works which may embody some element of literary or artistic style, such as common snapshots or representational advertisements, courts again may have been too timorous in admitting works to copyright.

''Although the 'originality' test is a shorthand formula for the features of work that merit copyright, we should not forget that its application is bound up with practical principles of judicial expertise and that its source, the copyright law, is in turn founded upon public and private interests which assume different guises in different cases. With fact works, courts should find 'originality' in the social contribution made by the accurate gathering, verification, and tangible representation of useful information. If the effect of this is to admit to copyright certain classes of works which now go unprotected, the expansion seems a wise one. It will compel courts to resolve the problems of full copyright protection under the rubric of infringement and fair use, rather than of copyrightability. This, in turn, will offer greater flexibility, enabling the courts to label as 'infringement' those works *which interfere unduly with the monopoly of the copyright holder without bringing a commensurate benefit to the public,* and as 'fair use' those works which interfere but slightly with the copyright monopoly while offering much to society'' [emphasis added].

31.  *Macmillan Co.* v. *King,* 223 Fed. 862 (DC Mass 1914).

32.  Ref. 11, pp. 24–27.

33.  Kaminstein, *Copyright Law Revision Part 6, Supplementary Report of the Register of Copyrights on the General Revision of the U. S. Copyright Law: 1965 Revision Bill,* Government Printing Office, Washington, D.C., May 1965, p. 18.

34.  Benjamin, Computers and copyrights, *Science* **152,** 183 (April 8, 1966). Mr. Benjamin is chairman of the board of McGraw-Hill Book Co.

35.  Green, Relational interests, *Illinois Law Rev.* **30,** 1 (1935).

36. Ref. 5, §41, N. 34.

37. *Addison-Wesley Publ. Co.* v. *Brown,* 207 F. Supp. 678 (E.D.N.Y. 1962). See also Ref. 5, §110.3.

38. OCR: A case of minority rules while the user buys blind, *Comput. Decision* **1,** 22 (September 1969): "The crux of the issue is the need, many users believe, for a uniform standard for OCR equipment in this country to protect users from buying equipment that could become obsolete when a standard is chosen.

    "The OCR-B font, adopted by the European Computer Manufacturers Association in 1966, is an alphanumeric upper-and-lower-case character set. OCR-A, adopted by the USA Standards Institute in '66 after six years of development, is a numerical and upper-case set. But a lower-case capability could be developed and added to OCR-A, proponents argue.

    "After simmering controversy, the Institute's X3 Committee on Computers and Information Processing directed its X3.1 subcommittee on optical character recognition to study the matter. The subcommittee concluded that OCR-B was not ready in its present form for adoption as a standard. The study showed that some characters—such as 5 and S, 2 and Z, O and 0—resemble each other too closely. An OCR machine has trouble distinguishing between such conflict pairs, the report said.

    "In an analysis run, 79 characters of the 113-character repertoire—including numeric, upper-case and commonly used punctuation symbols—produced unsatisfactory results, the study showed. Further, it was found that OCR-B could not be read economically in more than a limited number of machine applications."

39. For a description of the tremendous advances in cpu performance, see Knight, Changes in computer performance, *Datamation* **12,** 40 (September 1966).

40. E.g., the NASA RECON System.

41. This section is taken from *The Copyright Law as it Relates to National Informations Systems,* Final Report of the Ad Hoc Task Group on Legal Aspects Involved in National Information Systems, COSATI, Washington, D.C., April 1967, pp. 11–14.

42. *To Promote the Progress of . . . Useful Arts,* Report of the President's Commission on the Patent System, Washington, D.C., 1966, p. 13.

43. Banzhaf, Copyright protection for computer programs, *Columbia Law Rev.* **65,** 1274–1300 (1964), p. 1276.

44. *Computer Programs,* Cir. 31 D, Copyright Office, Library of Congress, Washington, D.C., 1965.

45. *Gottshalk* v. *Benson,* 409 U.S. 63 (1972).

46. Ref. 45 at 65.

47. There are other equally unsatisfactory definitions. The Association for Computing Machinery's 1955 attempt: "Program (1) a plan for the solution of a problem; (2) loosely, a synonym for routine; (3) to prepare a program (IRE)." The 1964 Honeywell version: "Program*, (1) a plan for solving a problem. (4) Loosely, to write a routine. See (routine)." And the 1966 American Standards Association choice: "Program. (1) A plan for solving a problem. (2) Loosely, a routine. (3) To devise a plan for solving a problem. (4) Loosely, to write a routine. (5) See *Computer Program. Object Program Source Program. Target Program.*" It is submitted that when the computing profession itself is unable to define its basic verb, one cannot fault less apt entities for trying.

48. Cary, Copyright registration and computer programs, *Bull. Copyright Soc.* **11,** 362–368 (August 1964), p. 362.

49. *Baker* v. *Selden,* 101 U.S. 99, 103 (1880).

50. Wessel, Legal protection of computer programs, *Harvard Business Rev.* **43,** 97–106 (March–April 1965). However, compare this view with those of Banzhaf in arguing for the advantages of copyright protection over patent protection for computer programs: "By contrast, copyrights are inexpensive, offer immediate protection, are favored by the courts, and *require little showing of creativity. In return, they offer substantial protection and do not require a wide public disclosure*" [emphasis added], *Comm. ACM* **8,** 220 (April 1965).

51. U.S. Congress, Senate, *Copyright Revision Hearings,* 90th Cong., 1st sess., 1967, pp. 571–572. See also *Comm. ACM* **10,** 318 (May 1967).

52. Computer programs and proposed revisions of the patent and copyright laws, *Harvard Law Rev.* **81,** 1541–1557 (1968), p. 1550.

53. Ref. 49; accord, *Mazer* v. *Stein,* 347 U.S. 201, 217 (1954) ("copyright gives no exclusive right to the art disclosed; protection is only given to the expression of the idea—not the idea itself").

    See also the similar language relative to the possible patenting of a program, Ref. 45 at 67: "'A principle, in the abstract, is a fundamental truth; an original cause; a motive; these cannot be patented, as no one can claim in either of them an exclusive right.' *Le Roy* v. *Tatham,* 14 How. (55 U.S.) 156, 175, 14 L. Ed. 367. Phenomena of nature, though just discovered, mental processes, and abstract intellectual concepts are not patentable, as they are the basic tools of scientific and technological work."

54. *U.S.* v. *Paramount Pictures,* 334 U.S. 131, 158 (1948).

55. *Fox Film Corp.* v. *Doyal,* 286 U.S. 123, 127 (1932).

56. 347 U.S. 201, 219 (1954).

57. Ref. 5, §3.1. See also the discussion in Ref. 52, p. 1549: "The rationale seems to be that conferring the limited monopoly which a copyright creates will encourage authors to write and publish by removing fear of plagiarism. A demonstration that copyright will provide incentive to produce and to publish programs while effectively protecting them from copying would thus seem to be the constitutional precondition for the extension of copyright to computer programs. But the courts would probably not declare such an extension of copyright to programs to be unconstitutional just because they disagreed with a congressional declaration of economic need. Although the Supreme Court has declared that legislation passed pursuant to the copyright and patent clause must pertain to objects having a claim to discovery or invention in order to be constitutional, it has refrained from reviewing the policy decisions about whether copyright on a particular work or type of original work would 'promote the Progress of Science and useful Arts.' [Footnote]: U.S. Constitution, art. I, §8; cf. *Cable Vision, Inc.* v. *KUTV, Inc.,* 335 F. 2d 348, 353 (9th Cir. 1964), *cert. denied,* 379 U.S. 989 (1965). Arguments have been made that a program is not a work of authorship or a writing in the constitutional sense and thus not subject to copyright. *E. G., Hearings,* pt. 3, p. 776. See also *Mazer* v. *Stein,* 347 U.S. 201, 219-21 (Douglas, J., dissenting). Also, if the statutory language and history were vague, it could be argued that the courts should decide if programs meet copyright's policy test. But since copyright has come to include objects far removed from literary works and since the bill read together with its congressional history does not seem vague, this Note will assume that the copyrightability of programs is not judicially reviewable."

58. Ref. 5 §5.

59. 27 U.S. 1 (1829).

60. Ref. 59, p. 3.

61. Ref. 59, p. 18.
62. 17 U.S.C. §4.
63. Ref. 43, pp. 1279 and 1280: "Although no clear-cut definition of the word 'writing' emerges from a study of either the statute or case law, three prerequisites have been suggested by cases and commentators; permanence, tangibility, and a form capable of being copied. These standards are clearly met by programs recorded in any of the principal media of printing, punched cards and magnetic tapes. However, two additional criteria—visibility and readability—have been suggested by older cases. Upholding the copyrightability of photographic reproductions, the Supreme Court stated in dictum that the idea in the mind of the author must be given '*visible* expression.' In another context, the Court held that a player piano roll was not an infringing copy of copyrighted sheet music because it did not appeal 'to the eye' and was not 'intended to be read,' unlike the ordinary piece of sheet music which to those skilled in the art 'conveys by reading' definite impressions of the melody. Under these additional requirements, while printed programs could be copyrighted, programs on magnetic tape would not be eligible for protection and programs represented by punched cards would fall into some intermediate category. On the other hand, it should be noted that copyrights have been granted to works (such as microfilms) that are too small to be read by the naked eye. Moreover, the effect of the decision in the player piano case may have been weakened by subsequent amendments to the Copyright Act and technological change with the passage of time. In any case, even if sustained by the courts, visibility and readability are statutory rather than constitutional limitations and subject to revision by Congress.

"The indefiniteness of the statutory category 'writings,' a category defined largely by a process of inclusion and exclusion in individual cases, suggests that the copyrightability of a work may be determined less by abstract analysis than by comparison with similar works that have either been granted or denied protection in the past. A printed program is most clearly analogous to copyrighted works composed of numbers and code words—for instance, a code book, freight tariff table, interest and discount table, and a handwriting chart. Programs on punched cards are also analogous to decks of flash cards for which copyright protection is available. Both types of programs are probably copyrightable. On the other hand, magnetic tapes—because they are recordings of information, invisible to the naked eye, that can be reproduced with the aid of a machine—are technically similar to phonograph records for which copyright registration has been refused. This does not, however, preclude copyrights for magnetic tapes. The denial of protection for records is based upon a particular interpretation of the Copyright Act; the statutory provision for a special, limited protection against infringement of musical compositions by mechanical reproductions has been held to indicate a congressional intent not to grant copyrights to such works. Since computer programs are not musical compositions, the statute does not preclude protection for taped programs simply because of technological similarities to phonograph records. In any case, there would be no constitutional difficulties to legislating protection for magnetic tapes.

"Another analogy to taped programs may be found in videotapes, magnetic tape recordings of television pictures and sound. The two are alike in that neither can be perceived without the aid of an electronic device; they differ in that one is basically a recording of a picture and the other of printed characters. The copyrightability of videotapes has not been tested in the courts, although they have recently been accepted for registration by the Copyright Office" [footnote omitted].
64. Ref. 5, §92.

65. *Public Affairs Associates* v. *Rickover,* 268 F. Supp. 444 (D. D. C. 1967). See also Ref. 5, §95, pp. 357–359.

66. Ref. 5, §95. See also *Annual Report of the Register of Copyrights for the Fiscal Year ending June 30, 1969,* Library of Congress, Washington, D.C., 1969, pp. 12–13: "The growing number of cases that have stressed the weight of the certificate of registration was increased by the holding in *United Merchants and Manufacturers, Inc.* v. *Sarne Co.,* 278 F. Supp. 162 (S.D. N.Y. 1967), that the 'certificate of registration constitutes *prima facie* evidence of the facts stated therein and, in the absence of contradictory evidence, is sufficient proof to establish a valid copyright.'

   "A particularly interesting decision dealing with the evidentiary value of the certificate was *Norton Printing Co.* v. *Augustana Hospital,* 155 U.S.P.Q. 133 (N.D. Ill. 1967), in which Judge Decker, in denying a pretrial motion to dismiss a case involving forms for use in connection with medical laboratory tests, referred to the statement in the *Regulations of the Copyright Office,* 37 C.F.R. §202.1(c), that 'works designed for recording information which do not in themselves convey information' are not copyrightable and cannot be the basis for registration. He concluded that since registration had been made it was '*prima facie* evidence that the Copyright Office considered that these forms convey information.'

   "The effect of a certificate of registration was also an issue in *Gardenia Flowers, Inc.* v. *Joseph Markovits, Inc.,* 280 F. Supp. 776 (S.D. N.Y. 1968), where the court stated that the certificate initially places the burden 'upon the defendant to produce sufficient evidence to overcome this presumption of validity,' but that proof by defendant of facts contrary to the certificate 'shifts the burden of overcoming such evidence to plaintiff . . . even upon issues over which the Register may have exercised his discretion, for such exercise is subject to judicial review.' "

67. Nelson, Copyrightability of computer programs, *Arizona Law Rev.* **7,** 204, 208 (1966).

68. *Annual Report of the Library of Congress 1965,* Government Printing Office, Washington, D.C., 1966, p. 84.

69. *Computers and Automation* **18,** 5 (May 1969), p. 20:

COMPUTER ART AND MUSIC FESTIVAL—CALL FOR CONTRIBUTIONS

The second Annual ACM Computer Art and Music Festival will be held August 26–28, 1969, in San Francisco in conjunction with the ACM 1969 National Conference. Individuals are invited to submit computer-generated art, music, or sculpture for display at the Festival.

70. Davidow, Foreword to *Music by Computers* (Von Forester and Beauchamp, eds.), Wiley, New York, 1969, p. ix. This most interesting book is divided into three broad areas: (1) Programs and systems-crudely put, computer generation of music-like sounds; (2) algorithms in composition; and (3) aesthetics.

71. Ref. 68, p. 85.

72. See Study 3, The meaning of "writings" in the copyright clause of the Constitution, in *34 Studies for the Committee on the Judiciary,* U.S. Congress, Senate, 86th Cong., 1st and 2nd sess., 1960–1961.

73. As noted by Kaplan, *An Unhurried View of Copyright,* Columbia University Press, New York, 1967, p. 118, from *Intrex: Report of a Planning Conference on Information Transfer Experiments* (Overhage and Harman, eds.), M.I.T. Press, Cambridge, Massachusetts, 1965, pp. 34 and 35: "Be that as it may, the members of

the on-line intellectual community work in close partnership with the system—with the computer(s) and the information base(s)—in almost all their work, whether it be formulative thinking, or experimentation involving the control of apparatus, or teaching, or learning, or any of the other things in the list of their activities. Many of the members of the community are skilled in the art of computer programming and fluent in a number of programming languages. These people contribute in an important way to the improvement or extension of the system whenever, in the course of their work, they come to points at which the existing facilities are less than satisfactory—and prepare new procedures to fulfill the required functions or to meet the new circumstances. In that way, they add to the processing capabilities of the system. Other members of the community, not given to programming, may nevertheless add materially to the capability of the system; they do so by introducing new facts, new data, and new documents into the store.

"The system is augmented not only through the contributions of its users, of course, but also through the contributions of full-time organizers, programmers, and maintainers of the system. The contributions of the system professionals were greatest during the early years of the development of the system. During the later years, the fact that the substantively oriented users predominate so greatly in sheer number offsets the greater concentration and, on the whole, greater skill of the professionals. *In many instances, however, it is difficult to distinguish clearly between the contributions of the system professionals,* for the professionals monitor the contributions of the users and often modify substantially, and usually polish, the techniques and programs and the sets of data that are offered to the public files" [emphasis added].

74. Kaplan, Ref. 73, p. 118.
75. Reichart (ed), *Cybernetic Serendipity: The Computer and the Arts,* Praeger, Washington, D.C., 1969.
76. Ref. 75, jacket. See also the Introduction, p. 5: "Cybernetic Serendipity deals with possibilities rather than achievements, and in this sense it is prematurely optimistic. There are no heroic claims to be made because computers have so far neither revolutionized music, nor art, nor poetry, in the same way that they have revolutionized science.

"There are two main points which make this exhibition and this catalogue unusual in the context in which art exhibitions and catalogues are normally seen. The first is that no visitor to the exhibition, unless he reads all the notes relating to all the works, will know whether he is looking at something made by an artist, engineer, mathematician, or architect. Nor is it particularly important to know the background of the makers of the various robots, machines and graphics—it will not alter their impact, although it might make us see them differently.

"The other point is more significant.

"New media, such as plastics, or new systems, such as visual music notation and the parameters of concrete poetry, inevitably alter the shape of art, the characteristics of music, and the content of poetry. New possibilities extend the range of expression of those creative people whom we identify as painters, film makers, composers, and poets. It is very rare, however, that new media and new systems should bring in their wake new people to become involved in creative activity, be it composing music, drawing, constructing or writing.

"This has happened with the advent of computers. The engineers for whom the graphic plotter driven by a computer represented nothing more than a means of solving certain problems visually have occasionally become so interested in the possibilities of this visual output, that they have started to make drawings which bear no practical application, and for which the only real motives are the desire to explore, and the sheer pleasure of seeing a drawing materialize. Thus people who would never have put pencil to paper, or brush to canvas, have started making images, both still and animated, which approximate and often look identical to what we call 'art' and put in public galleries.

"This is the most important single revelation of this exhibit."

77. Ref. 9, p. 306.

78. Ref. 5, §8.3.

79. 100 U.S. 82 (1879).

80. Diggins and LeBlanc, *What the Businessman Should Know About: Patents and Trademarks,* Public Affairs Press, Washington, D.C., 1958, p. 2.

81. Ref. 5, §8.31, citing *Gelles-Widmor Co.* v. *Milton Bradley Co.,* 313 F.2d 143 (CA-7, 1964).

82. Duggan, review of Ref. 83, *Comput. Rev.* **10**(2), 77 (February 1969) [*CR Rev.* **16**, 113].

83. Sophar and Heilprin, *The Determination of Legal Facts and Economic Guideposts with Respect to the Dissemination of Scientific and Educational Information as It is Affected by Copyright—A Status Report,* Committee to Investigate Copyright Problems Affecting Communication in Science and Education, Washington, D.C., 1967.

84. U.S. Congress, House Committee on the Judiciary, *Report No. 2237 on H.R. 4347,* 89th Cong., 2nd sess., October 12, 1966.

85. Ref. 84, p. 58. See also the similar problem regarding unfair appropriation of another's intellectual property, Ref. 35.

86. Ref. 5, §145, pp. 647, n. 190.

87. Ref. 84, p. 61.

88. *Rosemount Enterprises* v. *Random House,* 366 F.2d 303 (2nd Cir. 1966). See also New technology and the law of copyright: Reprography and computers, *U.C.L.A. Law Rev.* **15**:938 (1968).

89. For a sanguinary view of the threat of present technology to traditional publishing, see Gipe, *Nearer to the Dust: Copyright and the Machine,* Williams and Wilkins, Baltimore, 1967; e.g., Fair use is a many-splintered thing, pp. 63–81. The publisher, Williams and Wilkins, lost its suit pending against the United States charging that it is *not* fair use for the federal government to photocopy medical journal articles for requestors on an individual basis; 95 Sup. Ct. 1344 (1975). Basic sources for a discussion of fair use include among many others: (a) Bishop, Fair use of copyrighted books, *Houston Law Rev.* **2**, 206 (1964). (b) Yankwich, What is fair use?, *Univ. Chicago Law Rev.* **22**, 203 (1954); (c) Lipton, Ref. 17; (d) Chaffee, Reflections on the law of copyright, *Columbia Law Rev.* **45**, 503 (1945).

90. Baker, *Antitrust Aspects of the Software Issue,* Antitrust Division, U.S. Department of Justice, Washington, D.C. (March 4, 1969). See also *Fortner Enterprises* v. *United States Steel,* 89 S. Ct. 1252 (1969).

91. *Strauss* v. *American Publishers Association,* 231 U. S. 222 (1913).

92. *U.S.* v. *International Business Machines,* Consent Decree (January 25, 1956) CCH 1946 Trade Cases ¶68,245.

93. As cited by Baker, Ref. 90: "*U.S.* v. *Jerrold Electronics Corp.,* 187 F. Supp. 545 (E. D. Pa. 1960), aff'd per curiam, 365 U.S. 567 (1961) (untried product in infant industry, viz., CATV); *Dehydrating Process Co.* v. *A. O. Smith Corp.,* 292 F.2d 653 (1st Cir. 1961) (extensive record of difficulty when one product used without the

other); and *Susser* v. *Carvel Corporation,* 332 F.2d 505 (2nd Cir. 1964), (high cost of setting controlling standards for tried product). Cf. *Baker* v. *Simmons Company,* 307 F.2d 458, 466–469 (1st Cir. 1962) (upholding requirement that promotional sign using trademark only be displayed in conjunction with trademark owner's product).

94. Ref. 52, p. 1557.
95. Rosenfield, *Major Problems of Copyright Law* . . . , National Education Assoc., Washington, D. C., 1968, pp. 17–19: U.S. Congress, Senate, National Commission on New Technological Uses of Copyrighted Works (90th Cong., 1st sess., S. 216, S. Rept. 640, 1967).
96. Kaplan, Ref. 73, pp. 119–122.
97. Patterson, *Copyright in Historical Perspective,* Vanderbilt University Press, Nashville, Tennessee, 1968, pp. 19 and 229.
98. Current computer speeds are measured in 5 to 10 nsec per operations. One nanosecond, roughly put, is the time it takes an electrical impulse moving at the speed of light to travel 1 ft.
99. Ref. 10, p. 138.

*Michael A. Duggan*

# CORRELATION AND REGRESSION

## HISTORY

Correlation and regression were introduced into statistics by Sir Francis Galton in several papers published during the 1880s to describe and predict hereditary phenomenon involving two variates [64, 96]. However, his ideas on correlation and regression were generally unknown until his book, *Natural Inheritance,* was published in 1889. This work stimulated Pearson [59, 60] to develop a precise mathematical theory of correlation and regression for several variates with the explicit formulation of the normal correlation surface for $p$-variates. Yule [103, 104], a student of Pearson's, brought together Pearson's normal surface theory of correlation and regression with Gauss' theory of least squares [30] for other than normal probability models. However, it was not until Fisher [22, 24] determined the sampling distribution of the correlation coefficient and regression coefficients that the ideas which Galton initiated in the 1880s were finally completed as we apply them today in the physical, social, and biological sciences [41, 80].

## BIVARIATE CORRELATION AND REGRESSION

Galton's discovery of what today is known as the theory of bivariate normal correlation and regression is evident in his 1886 paper where he investigated the relationship between midparent heights $(x)$ and eldest son's heights $(y)$. Initially plotting several randomly selected pairs of height observations $(x_i, y_i)$ in a scatter diagram and then displaying the data in a correlation table, Galton noted that although tall parents tended to have tall offsprings and short parents to have short offsprings, the joint frequency distribution of heights for a particular population was almost identical from generation to generation. With J. D. Hamilton Dickson's assistance, he showed that the data collected on heights approximately followed a bivariate normal distribution, known also as a bivariate normal surface or simply as a normal correlation surface. Looking more carefully at his data, Galton further noted that on the average, children of tall parents are not as tall as their parents, and similarly that the children of short parents are not as short as their parents. That is, there was a tendency for the heights to "regress" toward the mean of the population. This explanation was used by Galton to account for the occurrence of identical distributions over several generations. Galton also found that the mean heights of children followed a straight line for parent heights and called this line the regression line.

Although Galton used correlation tables in his early work, then called tables of stature, it was not until his 1888 paper that the term correlation appeared in statistics.

The scatter diagram in Fig. 1, based upon data collected by Pearson and Lee [66] on the stature of father and sons, illustrates the relationship Galton observed for midparent heights and eldest son's heights. Tall fathers tend to have tall sons and short fathers tend to have short sons.

Superimposing a grid of 1-in. squares over the scatter diagram in Fig. 1, and recording the number of paired observations in each square, a correlation table for Pearson and Lee's data is constructed, Fig. 2. Pairs with values which correspond to grid lines, called class boundaries, are divided equally among adjacent squares. For the observation (70.5, 63.5), where the father's stature is 70.5 in. and the son's stature is 63.5 in., the value .25 is recorded in the class intervals 69.5–70.5 and 70.5–71.5 for the father's height and similarly in the class intervals 62.5–63.5 and 63.5–64.5 for the son's height. In the square identified by the interval 70.5–71.5 for the father's stature and 63.5–64.5 for the son's stature, there was one other observation recorded in the square defined by the boundaries so that the total frequency for the square is given by the value 1.25.

From both the scatter diagram and the correlation table we see that the heights represented in the plane form ellipses. From the frequencies in Fig. 2 we observe that the distribution of heights over the ellipse is bell-shaped, more frequent in the center of the ellipse and less frequent near the edge. Joining the peaks in Fig. 2 with straight lines, a frequency surface for Pearson and Lee's data is constructed, Fig. 3. This surface is very similar to the theoretical normal correlation surface shown in Fig. 4 which indicates that the height data can be described approximately by the bivariate normal distribution.

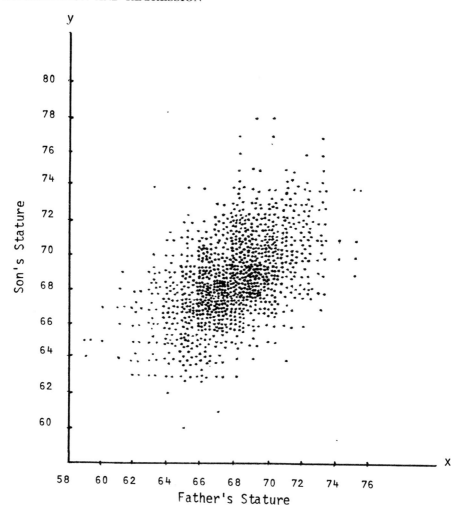

**Fig. 1.** Scatter diagram for (x) stature of father and (y) stature of son: 1 or 2 sons only of each father. Measurements in inches. [Constructed from data given in Ref. 66. Reproduced with the permission of the *Biometrika* trustees.]

For two random variates $X$ and $Y$, the form of the bivariate normal distribution is given by the formula

$$f(x, y) = \frac{\exp\left\{-\dfrac{1}{2(1 - \rho^2)}\left[\left(\dfrac{x - \mu_x}{\sigma_x}\right)^2 - 2\rho\left(\dfrac{x - \mu_x}{\sigma_x}\right)\left(\dfrac{y - \mu_y}{\sigma_y}\right) + \left(\dfrac{y - \mu_y}{\sigma_y}\right)^2\right]\right\}}{2\pi\sigma_x\sigma_y\sqrt{1 - \rho^2}}$$

where the parameters of the distribution are the means $\mu_x$ and $\mu_y$, the variances $\sigma_x^2$ and $\sigma_y^2$, and the correlation coefficient $\rho$ of the random variates $X$ and $Y$. Although the values of $x$, $y$, $\mu_x$, and $\mu_y$ may be any real numbers, the values of

Correlation table for stature of father and stature of son (1 or 2 sons only of each father; measurements in inches):

| Stature of Son (y) | 58.5–59.5 | 59.5–60.5 | 60.5–61.5 | 61.5–62.5 | 62.5–63.5 | 63.5–64.5 | 64.5–65.5 | 65.5–66.5 | 66.5–67.5 | 67.5–68.5 | 68.5–69.5 | 69.5–70.5 | 70.5–71.5 | 71.5–72.5 | 72.5–73.5 | 73.5–74.5 | 74.5–75.5 | Total |
|---|---|---|---|---|---|---|---|---|---|---|---|---|---|---|---|---|---|---|
| 78.5–79.5 | — | — | — | — | — | — | — | — | — | — | — | — | — | .25 | .25 | — | — | .5 |
| 77.5–78.5 | — | — | — | — | — | — | — | — | — | — | 1 | 1 | — | .25 | .75 | — | — | 3 |
| 76.5–77.5 | — | — | — | — | — | — | — | — | — | 1.25 | — | 1 | — | — | 1.5 | — | — | 4 |
| 75.5–76.5 | — | — | — | — | — | — | — | — | — | 1.25 | — | — | .5 | 1 | 1 | — | — | 4 |
| 74.5–75.5 | — | — | — | — | — | — | — | — | — | 1 | .25 | — | 2.5 | .75 | 1.75 | .5 | — | 8.5 |
| 73.5–74.5 | — | — | — | — | — | — | — | — | 2.5 | 5.25 | .25 | 2.5 | 6.5 | 3.25 | 3.25 | — | 2 | 29 |
| 72.5–73.5 | — | — | — | — | — | — | — | 1.5 | 7 | 7.5 | 2 | 6 | 7.5 | 6.25 | 3.25 | .5 | .5 | 42 |
| 71.5–72.5 | — | — | — | — | — | — | 1.5 | .75 | 10.75 | 7.75 | 2.25 | 11.25 | 10 | 8.5 | 2.75 | .5 | — | 63 |
| 70.5–71.5 | — | — | — | — | — | .25 | .75 | 1.25 | 11.75 | 19 | 6.5 | 20.75 | 10.75 | 8 | 5 | 1 | — | 108 |
| 69.5–70.5 | — | — | — | — | .5 | 3.25 | — | 8.75 | 16 | 19.5 | 10.75 | 19.5 | 14.5 | 6.25 | 3.5 | 1.5 | 1 | 128 |
| 68.5–69.5 | — | — | — | — | .5 | 2.5 | 5.75 | 18.75 | 31.5 | 24 | 14.75 | 21.5 | 10 | 3.5 | 2.25 | — | — | 149.5 |
| 67.5–68.5 | — | — | — | — | 1 | 5 | 12.75 | 18.25 | 25.75 | 23.5 | 22.5 | 13.25 | 8.5 | 9.5 | 2.25 | — | 1 | 173.5 |
| 66.5–67.5 | — | — | — | — | 5.25 | 10 | 10.25 | 24.25 | 17.5 | 19.5 | 29 | 13.75 | 3.25 | .5 | 1 | — | 1 | 148 |
| 65.5–66.5 | — | — | 1 | 2 | 7.5 | 13.75 | 19.75 | 26.5 | 7.5 | 16 | 12.5 | 2 | 2.5 | 1 | — | — | — | 89.5 |
| 64.5–65.5 | — | 1 | 1.5 | 4.75 | 3.5 | 9.5 | 10 | 16.75 | 3 | 5.5 | 5.25 | 2.5 | 1.25 | — | — | — | — | 61.5 |
| 63.5–64.5 | 2 | .5 | 2 | 2.25 | 5.25 | 9.5 | 13.5 | 10.75 | 2.75 | 1.25 | 3.5 | .75 | .25 | — | — | — | — | 38.5 |
| 62.5–63.5 | 1 | 1 | 1 | 3.75 | 3.25 | 4.25 | 8 | 9.25 | .5 | 1.25 | 1.5 | .25 | — | — | — | — | — | 20.5 |
| 61.5–62.5 | — | .25 | 1.5 | 2.25 | 3 | 2 | 4 | 5 | 1 | .5 | — | — | — | — | — | — | — | 3.5 |
| 60.5–61.5 | — | .25 | .25 | — | 2.25 | 1 | .25 | .25 | — | — | — | — | — | — | — | — | — | 1.5 |
| 59.5–60.5 | — | — | .25 | — | .5 | .5 | 1 | — | — | — | — | — | — | — | — | — | — | 2 |
| **Total** | 3 | 3.5 | 8 | 17 | 33.5 | 61.5 | 95.5 | 142 | 137.5 | 154 | 141.5 | 116 | 78 | 49 | 28.5 | 4 | 5.5 | 1078 |

(x) Stature of Father

**Fig. 2.** Correlation table for stature of father and stature of son: 1 or 2 sons only of each father. Measurements in inches. [66, reproduced with the permission of the *Biometrika* trustees.]

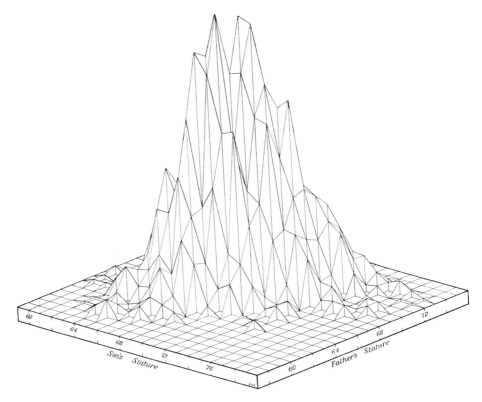

**Fig. 3.** Frequency surface for Pearson and Lee's data in Fig. 2, stature of father and stature of son. [105, reprinted with the permission of the authors and publisher.]

the standard deviations $\sigma_x$ and $\sigma_y$ are only positive, and $\rho$ is restricted to the open interval $(-1, 1)$; $-1 < \rho < 1$.

Restricting the value of $f(x, y)$ to a constant for a normal correlation surface, we can calculate the value of the quantity

$$\left(\frac{x - \mu_x}{\sigma_x}\right)^2 - 2\rho\left(\frac{x - \mu_x}{\sigma_x}\right)\left(\frac{y - \mu_y}{\sigma_y}\right) + \left(\frac{y - \mu_y}{\sigma_y}\right)^2 = C$$

given a constant value of $C$ which since $\rho^2 < 1$ is the equation for an ellipse known as an isodensity contour for the bivariate normal distribution. The contour is the outline of the cross section of the normal correlation surface made by a plane parallel to the $(x, y)$ plane intersecting the surface. Using various values for the constant, a family of concentric ellipses of different sizes with the same center and orientation are generated since $C$ merely determines the height at which a plane intersects the surface. The shape of the concentric contours for any normal correlation surface is determined by the values of $\rho$, $\sigma_x^2$, and $\sigma_y^2$. The parameters $\mu_x$ and $\mu_y$ merely determine the centroid of the distribution.

For $\sigma_x{}^2 = \sigma_y{}^2$ and $\rho = 0$, the equation for the isodensity contours becomes $(x - \mu_x)^2 + (y - \mu_y)^2 = $ constant, the equation of a circle with center at the point $(\mu_x, \mu_y)$. If $\sigma_x{}^2 \neq \sigma_y{}^2$, the equation becomes

$$\left(\frac{x - \mu_x}{\sigma_x}\right)^2 + \left(\frac{y - \mu_y}{\sigma_y}\right)^2 = \text{constant}$$

which defines ellipses with principal axes parallel to the $x$ and $y$ axes. In addition, if $\rho = 0$, the bivariate normal distribution can be expressed as a product of marginal univariate normal distributions $f(x)$ and $f(y)$ of the random variates $X$ and $Y$. The marginal distribution of $X$ is obtained by using the formula

$$f(x) = \int_{-\infty}^{\infty} f(x, y) \, dy$$

which for $f(x, y)$ defined by a normal correlation surface is the univariate normal distribution

$$f(x) = \frac{\exp\left\{-\frac{1}{2}\left(\frac{x - \mu_x}{\sigma_x}\right)^2\right\}}{\sigma_x\sqrt{2\pi}}$$

The marginal distribution of $X$ is most easily conceptualized as the projection of the points defined by $f(x, y)$ onto the plane determined by the $(x, z)$ axis in Fig. 4. The corresponding result for $Y$ follows by symmetry. When the joint

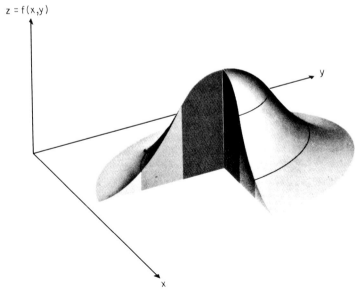

**Fig. 4.** A theoretical bivariate normal correlation surface. [93, reproduced with the permission of the author and publisher.]

distribution of two random variates can be expressed as a product of distributions of the individual variates, the random variates are said to be statistically independent. Hence for random variates defined by a bivariate normal distribution, if $\rho = 0$

$$f(x, y) = \qquad f(x) \qquad \cdot \qquad f(y)$$

$$= \frac{\exp\left\{-\frac{1}{2}\left(\frac{x - \mu_x}{\sigma_x}\right)^2\right\}}{\sigma_x \sqrt{2\pi}} \cdot \frac{\exp\left\{-\frac{1}{2}\left(\frac{y - \mu_y}{\sigma_y}\right)^2\right\}}{\sigma_y \sqrt{2\pi}}$$

so that $X$ and $Y$ are independent. However, if $\rho \neq 0$, then $f(x, y) \neq f(x) \cdot f(y)$ and $X$ and $Y$ are dependent. This would indicate that, at least for random variates with a bivariate normal distribution, $\rho$ measures the degree of the dependency between $X$ and $Y$.

For $\sigma_x^2 = \sigma_y^2$ and $\rho \neq 0$ the concentric ellipses become elongated as $\rho$ becomes more positive or more negative. If $\rho > 0$, the major axis of the ellipses intersects the $x$-axis at a 45° angle; if $\rho < 0$, the minor axis of the ellipses

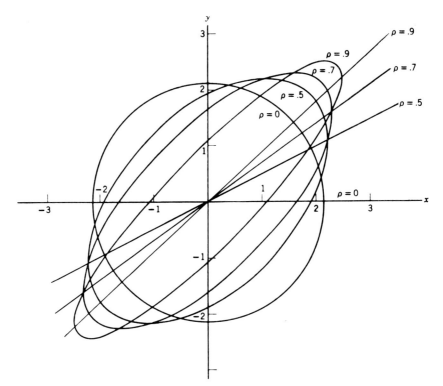

**Fig. 5.** Isodensity contours for a bivariate normal distribution ($\mu_r = \mu_y = 0$ and $\sigma_r = \sigma_y = 1$) and several values of $\rho$. [33, reprinted with the permission of the author and publisher.]

intersects the $x$-axis at a 45° angle. If $\sigma_x^2 \neq \sigma_y^2$, the angle made with the $x$-axis and the major axis if $\rho > 0$ or the minor axis if $\rho < 0$ is

$$\theta = \tfrac{1}{2} \tan^{-1} \left( \frac{2\rho\sigma_x\sigma_y}{\sigma_x^2 - \sigma_y^2} \right)$$

For $\sigma_x^2 = \sigma_y^2$ and $\mu_x = \mu_y = 0$, Fig. 5 illustrates the shape and orientation of some ellipses for a given value of $C$ and different values of $\rho$. Observe how the shape of the ellipses becomes more cigar-shaped as the dependency between the variates increases as indicated by $\rho$.

The dependency between $X$ and $Y$ as illustrated in Fig. 5 and for the data in Fig. 1 is of a special type. Investigating the conditional distribution for two random variates following a normal correlation surface defined by

$$f(y \mid x) = \frac{f(x, y)}{f(x)}$$

for $Y$ given $X = x$ and

$$f(x \mid y) = \frac{f(x, y)}{f(x)}$$

for $X$ given $Y = y$, it is easily shown (see, for example, Ref. 42) that the conditional distribution of $Y$ given $X = x$ is normally distributed with mean

$$\mu_{y \cdot x} = \mu_y + \frac{\rho\sigma_y}{\sigma_x} (x - \mu_x)$$

and variance $\sigma_{y \cdot x}^2 = \sigma_y^2(1 - \rho^2)$. Allowing $x$ to vary, the line expressed by

$$y = \mu_y + \frac{\rho\sigma_y}{\sigma_x} (x - \mu_x)$$

$$= \left[ \mu_y - \left( \frac{\rho\sigma_y}{\sigma_x} \right)\mu_x \right] + \left( \frac{\rho\sigma_y}{\sigma_x} \right)x$$

$$= \alpha_{y \cdot x} + \beta_{y \cdot x}x$$

with slope $\beta_{y \cdot x} = \rho\sigma_y/\sigma_x$ and intercept $\alpha_{y \cdot x} = \mu_y - (\rho\sigma_y/\sigma_x)\mu_x$ is the equation for the locus of the conditional means and is called the regression line of $Y$ on $X$. The regression line for $X$ on $Y$ follows by symmetry and is given by

$$x = \mu_x + \frac{\rho\sigma_x}{\sigma_y} (y - \mu_y)$$

Hence, if $X$ and $Y$ follow a bivariate normal distribution, the regression lines of $Y$ on $X$ and of $X$ on $Y$ are linear. Since $\rho$ appears in the slope of the regression line, $\rho$ may be interpreted as a measure of the linear dependency between the two random variates $X$ and $Y$. A positive correlation indicates that as one variate increases, the other also increases. A negative correlation means that as one variate decreases, the other decreases. If $\rho = 0$, we say that the two variates are uncorrelated and that there is no linear association between them. The correlation coefficient $\rho$ measures a linear relationship between the variates. When $\rho = 1$, the angle $\theta$ between the two regression lines,

$$\theta = \tan^{-1}\left[\left(\frac{\sigma_x\sigma_y}{\sigma_x^2 + \sigma_y^2}\right)\frac{1 - \rho^2}{\rho}\right]$$

is zero so that the two regression lines are identical. When $\rho = 0$, $X$ and $Y$ are uncorrelated and the regression lines are at right angles to each other. Since

$$\frac{\sigma_{y\cdot x}^2}{\sigma_y^2} = 1 - \rho^2 = \frac{\sigma_{x\cdot y}^2}{\sigma_x^2}$$

we see that when $\rho = 1$, the conditional variance equals zero, and when $\rho = 0$, the conditional variance is equal to the unconditional variance. Hence $\rho^2 = \beta_{y\cdot x}\beta_{x\cdot y}$ may be interpreted as the fraction of the variance of $Y$ accounted for by the regression on $X$, and conversely.

The regression equations given above are the basis for Galton's statement that the second generation of children's heights tend to regress toward the mean. Looking at the conditional mean of $Y$ given $X$,

$$\mu_{y\cdot x} = \mu_y + \frac{\rho\sigma_y}{\sigma_x}(x - \mu_x)$$

and allowing $\mu_x = \mu_y$ and $\sigma_x = \sigma_y$, which means that the population of fathers and sons is stable from generation to generation for Pearson and Lee's data, we see that

$$\mu_{y\cdot x} = \mu_x + \rho(x - \mu_x)$$
$$= x - (1 - \rho)(x - \mu_x)$$

If $0 < \rho < 1$ and $x > \mu_x$ so that $x - \mu_x > 0$, then

$$\mu_{y\cdot x} < x$$

so that the average value of a son's height $y$ given a particular value $x > \mu_x$ is less than the father's height. Thus, on the average, sons of tall fathers are not as tall as their father.

Investigating the relationship between heights of parents and heights of children, Galton was trying to establish a cause–effect relationship between the measures. However, investigating the reverse relationship using the regression line of $X$ on $Y$ we observe that, on the average, fathers of tall sons are not as tall as their sons. This is known as the regression fallacy in the statistical literature. There is, of course, no fallacy since a child's height does not affect the height of his parents.

To use the theoretical regression lines of $Y$ on $X$ and of $X$ on $Y$ for prediction, the parameters of the bivariate normal distribution need to be estimated from the data. For a random sample of $n$ pairs of observations from a bivariate normal distribution, the maximum likelihood (ML) estimators of the parameters are

$$\hat{\mu}_x = \frac{\sum x_i}{n} = \bar{x}, \qquad \hat{\sigma}_x^2 = \frac{\sum (x_i - \bar{x})^2}{n}, \qquad \hat{\rho} = \frac{\hat{\sigma}_{xy}}{\hat{\sigma}_x \hat{\sigma}_y} = \frac{\sum (x_i - \bar{x})(y_i - \bar{y})}{n \hat{\sigma}_x \hat{\sigma}_y}$$

$$\hat{\mu}_y = \frac{\sum y_i}{n} = \bar{y}, \qquad \hat{\sigma}_y^2 = \frac{\sum (y_i - \bar{y})^2}{n}$$

if all parameters of the distribution are unknown (see, for example, Ref. 42).

The formula for $\hat{\rho}$, denoted by $r$ by Pearson [59] following Galton [28], was derived by Pearson using the moments of the bivariate normal distribution and is called Pearson's product-moment correlation coefficient. The computational formula for $r$ is

$$\hat{\rho} = r = \frac{n \sum x_i y_i - (\sum x_i)(\sum y_i)}{\sqrt{[n \sum x_i^2 - (\sum x_i)^2][n \sum y_i^2 - (\sum y_i)^2]}}$$

for ungrouped bivariate data. For the data in Fig. 1, $r = +0.51$.

Although Pearson derived his formula for estimating the correlation coefficient using the moments of a bivariate normal distribution, no assumptions about the joint distribution of $X$ and $Y$ are necessary for the computation of Pearson's coefficient since its derivation only depends on the existence of the moments of any bivariate distribution. However, the interpretation given $r$ computed for models which are not bivariate normal requires special consideration [13]. Researchers who use correlation and regression as initiated by Galton often misuse the technique. The fact that two variables tend to increase or decrease together does not necessarily imply that one directly affects the other. Other factors may be influencing the relationship. Furthermore, the interpretation of $r$ is dependent upon the extent to which $X$ and $Y$ follow a bivariate normal distribution.

Substituting the ML estimators for the parameters of the bivariate normal distribution into the theoretical regression lines, the estimated regression equations used for predicting $y$ from $x$ and $x$ from $y$, respectively, are given by

$$\hat{y} = \bar{y} + \frac{\hat{\rho} \hat{\sigma}_y}{\hat{\sigma}_x} (x - \bar{x}) = \hat{\alpha}_{y \cdot x} + \hat{\beta}_{y \cdot x} x$$

and

$$\hat{x} = \bar{x} + \frac{\hat{\rho} \hat{\sigma}_x}{\hat{\sigma}_y} (y - \bar{y}) = \hat{\alpha}_{x \cdot y} + \hat{\beta}_{x \cdot y} y$$

Computational formula for the coefficients follow:

$$\hat{\alpha}_{y \cdot x} = \bar{y} - \hat{\beta}_{y \cdot x} \bar{x}, \qquad \hat{\alpha}_{x \cdot y} = \bar{x} - \hat{\beta}_{x \cdot y} \bar{y}$$

$$\hat{\beta}_{y \cdot x} = \frac{n \sum x_i y_i - (\sum x_i)(\sum y_i)}{n \sum x_i^2 - (\sum x_i)^2}, \qquad \hat{\beta}_{x \cdot y} = \frac{n \sum x_i y_i (\sum x_i)(\sum y_i)}{n \sum y_i^2 - (\sum y_i)^2}$$

The estimated regression lines for the data in Fig. 1 are graphed in Fig. 6.

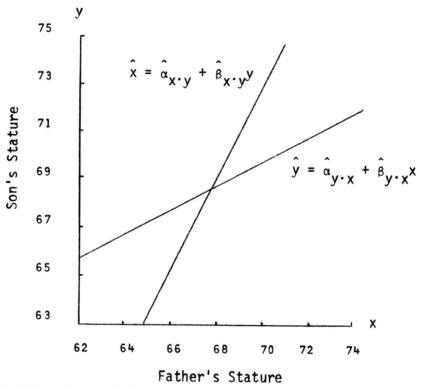

**Fig. 6.** Estimated regression lines for Pearson and Lee's data in Fig. 2.

Given the estimated regression lines of $Y$ on $X$ and of $X$ on $Y$, we may test that the population coefficients $\beta_{y \cdot x}$, $\beta_{x \cdot y}$ are zero and calculate confidence intervals for the coefficients. Since $\rho = \beta_{y \cdot x}\sigma_y/\sigma_x$ and $\rho = \beta_{x \cdot y}\sigma_x/\sigma_y$, testing $\beta_{y \cdot x} = 0$ or $\beta_{x \cdot y} = 0$ is equivalent to testing $\rho = 0$ since $\sigma_y$ and $\sigma_x$ are positive. Assuming $X$ and $Y$ are jointly bivariate normally distributed, Fisher [22] showed that

$$t = \sqrt{\frac{(n-2)r^2}{1-r^2}}$$

has a Student's $t$-distribution [91] with $n - 2$ degrees of freedom when $\rho = 0$. The statistic $t$ may be used to test the hypothesis that $\rho = 0$. Confidence intervals for $\rho$ may be constructed using charts prepared by David [16]. To test the hypothesis that $\rho$ is equal to a value $\rho_0 \neq 0$, Fisher's $z$-transformation must be employed [23].

Letting $\hat{\sigma}_{y \cdot x}^2$ denote the ML estimator of the variance of the conditional normal distribution of $Y$ on $X$,

$$\hat{\sigma}_{y \cdot x}^2 = \frac{\sum (y_i - \hat{\mu}_{y \cdot x})}{n}$$

$$= \frac{\sum (y_i - \hat{\alpha}_{y \cdot x} - \hat{\beta}_{y \cdot x}x_i)^2}{n}$$

which is a biased estimator of $\sigma_{y \cdot x}^2$ and

$$s_{y \cdot x}^2 = \frac{n \hat{\sigma}_{y \cdot x}^2}{n-2}$$

the unbiased estimator, it is easily shown that

$$t = \sqrt{\frac{(n-2)r^2}{1-r^2}} = \frac{(\hat{\beta}_{y \cdot x} - \beta_{y \cdot x})\sqrt{\sum (x_i - \bar{x})^2}}{s_{y \cdot x}}$$

is distributed as Student's $t$-distribution with $n-2$ degrees of freedom if $\beta_{y \cdot x} = 0$. Hence, testing $\rho = 0$ is identical to testing that a regression coefficient is equal to zero. A $100(1 - \alpha)\%$ two-sided confidence interval for $\beta_{y \cdot x}$ is given by

$$\hat{\beta}_{y \cdot x} \pm t^{\alpha/2}(n-2)\frac{s_{y \cdot x}}{\sqrt{\sum (x_i - \bar{x})^2}}$$

where $t^{\alpha/2}(n-2)$ denotes the upper $\alpha/2$ percentage point of Student's $t$-distribution with $n-2$ degrees of freedom. A similar result for testing $\beta_{x \cdot y} = 0$ follows by symmetry.


## INTERPRETING CORRELATION COEFFICIENTS

The population correlation coefficient $\rho$ and the sample estimator $r$, which is a biased estimator of $\rho$ [58], have been discussed for a bivariate normal distribution. For this situation, $\rho = 0$ implies $X$ and $Y$ are independent and $\rho^2$ is used as a measure of the strength of the linear dependency between $X$ and $Y$. In general, the correlation coefficient is defined as the ratio of the covariance between two random variates divided by the product of the square root of the variances:

$$\rho = \frac{\sigma_{xy}}{\sqrt{\sigma_x^2}\sqrt{\sigma_y^2}} = \frac{\sigma_{xy}}{\sigma_x \sigma_y}$$

where $\sigma_{xy}$ is used to denote the covariation or covariance between the random variates $X$ and $Y$. For random variates with an arbitrary joint bivariate distribution, if $\rho = 0$, $X$ and $Y$ are uncorrelated but not necessarily independent. For this reason, using $\rho$ or, more importantly, $r$ computed from a sample as a measure of independence causes some difficulty when $X$ and $Y$ are not bivariate normally distributed. Furthermore, $r^2$ is only a measure of the strength of the linear relationship between $X$ and $Y$. There may be a perfect curvilinear relationship between $X$ and $Y$ with $r^2 = 0$; in these situations, $r^2$ is not a helpful descriptive measure of the relationship. Instead, the correlation ratio is employed. The correlation ratio, which is not symmetric in $X$ and $Y$, is defined by

$$\eta_{y \cdot x}^2 = 1 - \sigma_{y \cdot x}^2/\sigma_y^2$$

$$\eta_{x \cdot y}^2 = 1 - \sigma_{x \cdot y}^2/\sigma_x^2$$

Pearson [61–63, 65]. $\eta^2$ is equal to $\rho^2$ if $X$ and $Y$ follow a bivariate normal distribution or if the relationship between $X$ and $Y$ is a strict linear functional relationship. In general,

$$0 \leq \rho^2 \leq \eta^2_{y \cdot x} \leq 1$$

$$0 \leq \rho^2 \leq \eta^2_{x \cdot y} \leq 1$$

It is possible to have $\eta^2_{y \cdot x} = \rho^2 < \eta^2_{x \cdot y}$. This would indicate that the regression of $Y$ on $X$ is linear and that the relationship between $X$ and $Y$ is curvilinear. A biased estimator of $\eta^2_{y \cdot x}$ for a sample of $n$ observations ($y_{ij}$, $x_i$) is given by

$$\eta^2_{y \cdot x} = \frac{\sum n_i \bar{y}_i^2 - n\bar{y}}{\sum \sum y_{ij}^2 - n\bar{y}}$$

where $\bar{y}$ is the grand mean of $Y$ and $\bar{y}_i$ is the mean of the $n_i$ observations in the $i$th class interval for $X$. The sample estimator of the correlation ratio and the correlation coefficient satisfy the relationship that

$$0 \leq r^2 \leq \hat{\eta}^2 \leq 1$$

so that $\hat{\eta}^2$ and not $r^2$ is a better measure of the strength of the relationship between two random variates.

Although Pearson's formula for $r$ may be used to compute the sample correlation coefficient for any kind of data, interpretation of $r$ requires careful consideration of the data collected. Carroll [13] discusses in detail how the interpretation of $r$ depends upon whether the data collected can be approximated by a bivariate normal distribution, upon whether the marginal distributions are of the same shape, upon whether the variates are measured with error, and upon whether the random variates can assume several values. As collected data depart from a bivariate normal probability model, interpretation of $r$ becomes less meaningful. If $X$ is highly positively skewed and $Y$ is highly negatively skewed, the maximum and minimum values of $r$ cannot be attained. Even if we can assume a bivariate normal model, if $X$ and $Y$ are measured with error, the correlation coefficient is corrected for attenuation [86a]. This is particularly important in mental test theory [51].

The correlation between a dichotomous variate and a continuous variate is called a point biserial correlation and denoted by $r_{\mathrm{pb}}$. If the continuous variate is also dichotomous, the correlation coefficient is termed a phi coefficient and is represented by $\phi$. Although Pearson's formula is employed to compute $r_{\mathrm{pb}}$ and $\phi$, neither is an estimate of $\rho$ in a bivariate normal population. Furthermore, interpretation of either coefficient presents special problems [13, 51]. To estimate $\rho$ from dichotomous data, we must assume that the underlying distribution of $X$ and $Y$ is bivariate normal. The estimator of $\rho$ in this case is called the tetrachoric correlation coefficient and is represented by $r_{\mathrm{tet}}$. The tetrachoric correlation coefficient is not calculated using Pearson's formula. The formula used to compute $r_{\mathrm{tet}}$ is a complicated expression involving the frequencies of a $2 \times 2$ contingency table. A computer program to calculate $r_{\mathrm{tet}}$ has been developed by Kirk [43]. Unlike $\phi$, the limits of $r_{\mathrm{tet}}$ are between $-1$ to $+1$. In addition, interpretation of $r_{\mathrm{tet}}$ is identical to $r$ because of the underlying bivariate normality assumption of the variates. If we can assume an underlying bivariate normal model, the correlation coefficient for estimating the correlation between a dichotomous variate and a continuous variate is called a biserial correlation coefficient and is represented by $r_{\text{bis}}$. Although $r_{\text{bis}}$ is not calculated using Pearson's formula and may be larger than 1, it is used to estimate $\rho$. The theory associated with the biserial and tetrachoric correlation coefficients was set forth by Karl Pearson. Distribution theory, recent developments, and the importance of such coefficients in mental test theory are discussed in Kendall and Stuart [42] and Lord and Novick [51].

Another correlation coefficient associated with Pearson's formula is Spearman's rank-correlation coefficient $r_s$ computed from ranks [86]. If we can assume that the underlying distribution of $X$ and $Y$ is bivariate normal and if $r_s$ is calculated from a very large sample, then $r_s$ can be treated as an estimate of $\rho$. Other measures of relationship or association which do not depend on Pearson's rationale are Kendall's tau, Kendall's coefficient of concordance, Yule's $Q$, intraclass correlation, Pearson's coefficient of contingency, and Goodman and Kruskal's gamma among others. References and discussion of these measures are included in Kendall and Stuart [42] and Anderson, Das Gupta, and Styan [6].

## REGRESSION MODELS AND PREDICTION

Even though the interpretation of a sample correlation coefficient depends upon the extent to which two variates can be approximated by a bivariate normal model, correlation coefficients are useful in determining the existence of linear relationships between variates. However, successful use of a correlation coefficient requires being familiar with the mathematical properties of the statistic and having a considerable amount of knowledge with the substantive field of application. Having found a real relationship between two variates, the primary basis for correlation is usually prediction. Although the bivariate normal regression model as developed by Galton, known also as the normal linear regression model or simply as the correlation model, may be used for prediction, in many applications the model is often unrealistic since many prediction problems involve variates where knowledge of the joint distribution does not exist or where one of the variates have a nonnormal distribution. In practice, many prediction studies involve observing a random variate $Y$ at selected fixed observed values of the random variate $X = x$ chosen in advance. For this data collection procedure $X$ and $Y$ need not be bivariate normally distributed, but we must assume that the relationship between $Y$ and $X$ is linear in $X$ and that the conditional distribution of $Y$ given $X = x$ is normal with common variance $\sigma^2$ for any given $x$,

$$f(y \mid x) = \frac{1}{\sigma\sqrt{2\pi}} \exp\left\{-\frac{1}{2}\left(\frac{y - \alpha - \beta x}{\sigma}\right)^2\right\}$$

to obtain results identical to the normal linear regression model. Equivalently, the preceding assumptions imply that the relationship between the random variate $Y$ and the value of the random variate $X$ is

$$Y_i = \alpha + \beta x_i + \epsilon_i$$

where the $\epsilon_i$ are independent unobserved random variates normally distributed with mean 0 and common variance $\sigma^2$. In either case, the regression model is referred to as the conditional linear regression model. An example of how data are collected for this model for son's heights given father's heights is displayed in Fig. 7. Here the random variate $X$ is treated as a mathematical variable rather than a random variate when the data are collected. Although $r$ may be calculated for data as given in Fig. 7, the interpretation of $r^2$ as a measure of the linear relationship between $X$ and $Y$ must be used with considerable caution since its value now depends upon the choice of the values of $X$. Since $X$ is fixed in the conditional linear regression model and not random as in the normal linear regression model, we may predict $Y$ from $X$ but not $X$ from $Y$.

A model which is similar to the normal linear regression is the stochastic linear regression model. For this model it is not necessary to assume that $X$ and $Y$ are bivariate normally distributed. Instead of collecting data for fixed values of $X$, data are collected in random pairs as in the normal linear regression model.

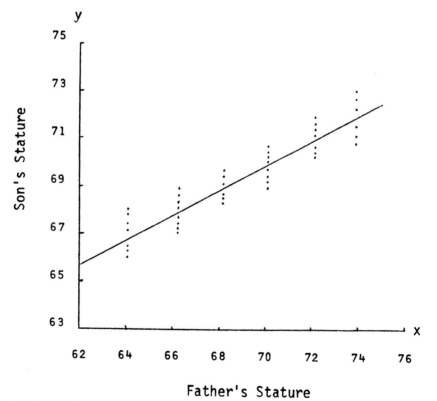

**Fig. 7.** Data collection procedure for a simple conditional regression model.

The linear model representation for $Y$ and $X$ is

$$Y_i = \alpha + \beta X_i + \epsilon_i$$

with $\epsilon_i$ defined as above and independent of $X_i$. Provided the distribution of $X$ does not depend on the regression coefficients or $\sigma^2$; estimates for $\alpha$, $\beta$, and $\sigma^2$ are the same as those given for the conditional regression model. However, if $X$ and $\epsilon$ are not independent, this is not the case. Procedures for the analysis of such models are discussed by Goldberger [31].

To predict $Y$ from $X$ using the conditional linear regression model, estimators of $\alpha$, $\beta$, and $\sigma^2$ are needed. Although these may be easily obtained using the maximum likelihood procedure [32], the estimators for $\alpha$ and $\beta$ are usually determined using the method of least squares [30]. That is, values $\hat{\alpha}$ and $\hat{\beta}$ for $\alpha$ and $\beta$ are determined which minimize the error sum of squares

$$S = \sum (y_i - \alpha - \beta x_i)^2$$

Using this technique, the least squares (LS) estimators for $\alpha$ and $\beta$ are identical to the ML estimators, and by modifying the ML estimator of $\sigma^2$ the unbiased estimator for $\sigma^2$ defined by $s_{y \cdot x}^2$ and given previously is obtained. Furthermore, the estimates of the regression coefficients are identical to those obtained using the normal linear regression model. This was shown by Yule in 1897 but never really accepted by Pearson [61].

Discussion of the conditional linear regression model has been restricted to linear relationships between $Y$ and $X$. More importantly, the conditional regression model allows us to fit curvilinear models of the form

$$Y = \alpha + \beta_1 x + \beta_2 x^2 + \cdots + \beta_k x^k + \epsilon = f(x) + \epsilon$$

called polynomial models to collected data [61]. For this situation we assume that the joint distribution of $X$ and $Y$ can be represented as

$$f(x, y) = \frac{h(x) \exp \{-[y - f(x)]^2/2\sigma^2\}}{\sigma\sqrt{2\pi}}$$

where $h(x)$ does not depend on the regression coefficients or $\sigma^2$. This implies that the conditional distribution of $Y$ given $X = x$ is normal with mean $f(x)$ and variance $\sigma^2$. To estimate the regression coefficients for this more general formulation we may find either maximum likelihood or least squares estimates of the coefficients since they are identical. We may also determine confidence intervals for the regression coefficients and test hypotheses. To measure the strength of the relationship between $X$ and $Y$, an estimate of the correlation ratio is employed.

Removing the restriction of bivariate normality of $X$ and $Y$ from the normal linear regression model, we have the stochastic regression model. Provided the conditional distribution of $Y$ given $X$ satisfies the assumptions given previously, it may be shown that in addition to identical estimated regression coefficients for the stochastic and conditional regression models, tests of hypotheses and confidence intervals for regression coefficients are identical for both models (see, for example, Refs. 31 and 32).

A model which is formally identical with the conditional linear regression model is the functional linear regression model. For this model we assume that there is a strict linear functional relationship between the mathematical variables $y$ and $x$ of the form $y = \alpha + \beta x$. If $x$ is observed without error, this means that $y$ is unobservable. Instead of observing $y$, suppose we are able to observe $Y_i = y_i + \epsilon_i$ where the $\epsilon_i$ are independent unobservable random errors with mean 0 and variance $\sigma^2$. The relationship between the random variate $Y$ and the mathematical variable $x$ becomes

$$Y_i = \alpha + \beta x_i + \epsilon_i$$

which is identical to the conditional linear regression model.

If the mathematical variable in the functional linear regression model is unobservable so that $X_i = x_i + \delta_i$, where $X_i$ is an observable random variate, the $\delta_i$ are independent normally distributed unobserved random variates with mean 0 and variance $\sigma_\delta^2$ and independent of the $\epsilon_i$, we have what is termed in the statistical literature the error in variables regression model. In this situation the model equations are written as

$$X_i = x_i + \delta_i$$

$$Y_i = y_i + \epsilon_i = \alpha + \beta x_i + \epsilon_i$$

where $\alpha$, $\beta$, the $x_i$, the $\delta_i$, and the $\epsilon_i$ are unknown. For this model the unknown parameters are $x$, $\alpha$, and $\beta$, and the error variances $\sigma_\delta^2$ and $\sigma_\epsilon^2$. This model was first discussed by Lindley [49], extends Pearson's and Gauss' ideas on regression, and has been considered in the literature by Kendall [39, 40], Madansky [52], Graybill [32], Kendall and Stuart [42], Spent [87], and Johnson [38], among others.

If the linear functional relationship between the mathematical variables given above is replaced by random variates when both random variates are subject to error so that the model equations become

$$X_i' = X_i + \delta_i$$

$$Y_i' = Y_i + \epsilon_i = \alpha + \beta X_i + \epsilon_i$$

we have what is called the error in variates model or the structural linear regression model. Using this model we usually assume that the observable variates $X_i'$, $Y_i'$ are identically jointly bivariate normally distributed or equivalently that $\delta_i$ and $\epsilon_i$ are independent and identically distributed for all $i$ and independent of $X$ and $Y$, and normally distributed with mean 0 and variances $\sigma_\delta^2$ and $\sigma_\epsilon^2$. We then have for the normal variates $X'$ and $Y'$ that

$$\mu_{x'} = \mu_x = \mu$$

$$\mu_{y'} = \mu_y = \alpha + \beta\mu$$

$$\sigma_{x'}^2 = \sigma_x^2 + \sigma_\delta^2$$

$$\sigma_{y'}^2 = \sigma_y^2 + \sigma_\epsilon^2 = \beta^2\sigma_x^2 + \sigma_\epsilon^2$$

$$\sigma_{x'y'} = \sigma_{xy} = \beta\sigma_x^2$$

The unknown parameters for this model are $\alpha$, $\beta$, the variance $\sigma_x^2$ of $X$, the error variances $\sigma_\delta^2$ and $\sigma_\epsilon^2$, and the mean $\mu$. Since the maximum likelihood equations are fewer in number than the number of unknown parameters in the model, there is no satisfactory ML solution to the estimation problem when all parameters are unknown. This means that additional assumptions must be added to the model. For example, if $\sigma_\delta^2$ is known, the estimator for $\beta$ is

$$\hat{\beta} = \frac{\hat{\sigma}_{xy}}{\hat{\sigma}_x^2 - \sigma_\delta^2}$$

where $\hat{\sigma}_x^2$ and $\hat{\sigma}_{xy}$ are maximum likelihood estimators. If $\sigma_\delta^2 = 0$ so that $X$ is observed without error, we see that the ML estimator for $\beta$ in the structural linear regression model is identical to the ML estimators of $\beta_{y \cdot x}$ using the stochastic linear regression model. Furthermore notice that $\hat{\beta}$ does not involve $\hat{\sigma}_\epsilon^2$ so that errors in $Y$ do not affect the estimation of $\beta$ for the regression of $Y'$ on $X'$. The structural regression model is a generalization of Galton's original conceptions of correlation and regression where now the variates are not error-free. Further discussion of the structural regression model is given by Kendall [39, 40], Kendall and Stuart [42], and Richardson and Wu [76]. Jöreskog [37] and Lawley and Maxwell [46] discuss the model using the basic model of factor analysis. A computer program for estimating structural relationships has been developed by Karl G. Jöreskog and Marielle van Thillo in an unpublished paper distributed by the Educational Testing Service; however, better algorithms for estimating structural relationships need further investigation.

Galton's discovery of correlation and regression involving two variates was conceptualized using the bivariate normal probability model and although the interpretation of a sample correlation coefficient between two random variates depends upon the extent to which the joint frequency distribution of the observations can be approximated by a bivariate normal distribution, there are several types of regression models which may be used for prediction involving two attributes which do not require bivariate normality. The most frequently used regression models in many applications are the conditional and functional regression models; however, choice of the most appropriate model depends to a considerable extent on the substantive field. In the social sciences like economics, education, and psychology, the stochastic, structural, and error in variables regression models are often most appropriate because of imprecise measurement instruments and the manner in which data are collected. An excellent introduction to the mathematical foundations of various regression models is included in Graybill [32] and Spent [88]. An elementary approach to correlation theory is obtained in books by Baggaley [8] and Ezekiel [21].

## MULTIVARIATE CORRELATION AND REGRESSION

Although Galton has to be credited with the formulation of bivariate normal correlation and regression theory, Pearson [59, 60] initiated the development of multivariate normal correlation and regression theory. However, Edgeworth [20] was the first person to derive the multivariate normal correlation surface, and Yule [103, 104] integrated Pearson's classical formulation with Gauss' theory of least squares.

Extending the bivariate normal surface to a $p$-variate normal surface, Pearson showed that the multivariate normal distribution for a $p$-dimensional random vector variate $\mathbf{U}$ is

$$f(\mathbf{u}) = (2\pi)^{-p/2} \mid \mathbf{\Sigma} \mid^{-1/2} \exp\left[-\tfrac{1}{2}(\mathbf{u} - \boldsymbol{\mu})'\mathbf{\Sigma}^{-1}(\mathbf{u} - \boldsymbol{\mu})\right]$$

where $\mathbf{\Sigma}$ is the symmetric positive definite variance-covariance matrix and $\boldsymbol{\mu}$ is a mean vector [3]. For $p = 2$, the distribution is seen to reduce to the bivariate normal distribution. The matrix $\mathbf{\Sigma}$ is represented by

$$\mathbf{\Sigma} = \begin{pmatrix} \sigma_{11} & \sigma_{12} & \cdots & \sigma_{1p} \\ \sigma_{21} & \sigma_{22} & \cdots & \sigma_{2p} \\ \vdots & \vdots & \vdots\vdots\vdots & \vdots \\ \sigma_{p1} & \sigma_{p2} & \cdots & \sigma_{pp} \end{pmatrix}$$

where $\sigma_{ii}$ is the variance of the $i$th variate of $\mathbf{U}$ and often denoted by $\sigma_i^2$ and $\sigma_{ij} = \sigma_{ji}$ is the covariance between the $i$th and $j$th variates. The correlation coefficient between $U_i$ and $U_j$ is defined as

$$\rho_{ij} = \frac{\sigma_{ij}}{\sqrt{\sigma_{ii}}\sqrt{\sigma_{jj}}} = \frac{\sigma_{ij}}{\sigma_i\sigma_j}$$

where $-1 < \rho_{ij} < 1$. For $p = 2$

$$\mathbf{\Sigma} = \begin{pmatrix} \sigma_{11} & \sigma_{12} \\ \sigma_{21} & \sigma_{22} \end{pmatrix} = \begin{pmatrix} \sigma_1^2 & \rho\sigma_1\sigma_2 \\ \rho\sigma_1\sigma_2 & \sigma_2^2 \end{pmatrix}$$

as expected.

To determine the regression function of any subset $s$ of the $p$ variates on the remaining $q = p - s$ variates, the $p$-variate vector $\mathbf{U}$ is partitioned into two subsets of variates. To easily see the correspondence between the multivariate and bivariate solutions, we associate with the first $s$ variates of $\mathbf{U}$ the vector variate $\mathbf{Y}$ and with the remaining variates the vector $\mathbf{X}$ so that $\mathbf{U}' = (\mathbf{Y}', \mathbf{X}')$. Partitioning the mean vector $\boldsymbol{\mu}$ and the variance-covariance matrix $\mathbf{\Sigma}$ correspondingly so that

$$\boldsymbol{\mu} = \begin{pmatrix} \boldsymbol{\mu}_y \\ \boldsymbol{\mu}_x \end{pmatrix} \quad \text{and} \quad \mathbf{\Sigma} = \begin{pmatrix} \mathbf{\Sigma}_{11} & \mathbf{\Sigma}_{12} \\ \mathbf{\Sigma}_{21} & \mathbf{\Sigma}_{22} \end{pmatrix}$$

where the submatrices $\mathbf{\Sigma}_{11}$, $\mathbf{\Sigma}_{12}$, $\mathbf{\Sigma}_{21}$, and $\mathbf{\Sigma}_{22}$ have dimensions $s \times s$, $s \times q$, $q \times s$, and $q \times q$, the conditional distribution of $\mathbf{Y}$ given $\mathbf{X} = \mathbf{x}$ and of $\mathbf{X}$ given $\mathbf{Y} = \mathbf{y}$ are easily determined [3].

The conditional distribution of $\mathbf{Y}$ given $\mathbf{X} = \mathbf{x}$ is multivariate normal with mean vector

$$\boldsymbol{\mu}_{y\cdot x} = \boldsymbol{\mu}_y + \mathbf{\Sigma}_{12}\mathbf{\Sigma}_{22}^{-1}(\mathbf{x} - \boldsymbol{\mu}_x)$$

and variance-covariance matrix

$$\Sigma_{y \cdot x} = \Sigma_{11} - \Sigma_{12}\Sigma_{22}^{-1}\Sigma_{21}$$

called the matrix of partial variances and covariances. The elements of $\Sigma_{y \cdot x}$ are represented by $\sigma_{ij \cdot s+1, \ldots, p}$. The locus of conditional means

$$\mathbf{y} = \boldsymbol{\mu}_y + \Sigma_{12}\Sigma_{22}^{-1}(\mathbf{x} - \boldsymbol{\mu}_x)$$

is the multivariate regression function of $\mathbf{Y}$ on $\mathbf{X}$ and the matrix $\Sigma_{12}\Sigma_{22}^{-1}$ is the matrix of regression coefficients. Following Yule, the elements of $\mathbf{B} = \Sigma_{12}\Sigma_{22}^{-1}$ are often denoted as $\beta_{ij \cdot (s+1), \ldots, (j-1), (j+1), \ldots, p}$. For $s = 1$ and $q = 1$, the theoretical regression function reduces to

$$y = \mu_y - \sigma_{12}\sigma_{22}^{-1}(x - \mu_x)$$

which is identical to the bivariate solution since $\beta_{y \cdot x} = \rho\sigma_y/\sigma_x = \sigma_{12}\sigma_{22}^{-1}$.

## MULTIPLE CORRELATION AND REGRESSION

A very important special case of the multivariate regression function is obtained by setting $s = 1$ and $q = p - 1$. Partitioning $\Sigma$ as follows,

$$\Sigma = \begin{pmatrix} \sigma_1^2 & \boldsymbol{\sigma}_{21}' \\ \boldsymbol{\sigma}_{21} & \Sigma_{22} \end{pmatrix}$$

the regression function becomes

$$\begin{aligned} y &= \mu_y + \boldsymbol{\sigma}_{12}'\Sigma_{22}^{-1}(\mathbf{x} - \boldsymbol{\mu}_x) \\ &= (\mu_y - \boldsymbol{\beta}'\boldsymbol{\mu}_x) + \boldsymbol{\beta}'\mathbf{x} \\ &= \alpha + \beta_1 x_1 + \beta_2 x_2 + \cdots + \beta_q x_q \end{aligned}$$

and is called the multiple or univariate linear regression function; the parameters of the model are the intercept $\alpha = \mu_y - \boldsymbol{\beta}'\boldsymbol{\mu}_x$ and the elements $\beta_1, \beta_2, \ldots, \beta_q$ of $\boldsymbol{\beta}' = \boldsymbol{\sigma}_{12}'\Sigma_{22}^{-1}$. The conditional variance of $Y$ given $\mathbf{X}$ is written as

$$\begin{aligned} \sigma_{y \cdot x} &= \sigma_1^2 - \boldsymbol{\sigma}_{12}'\Sigma_{22}^{-1}\boldsymbol{\sigma}_{21} \\ &= \sigma_1^2\left(1 - \frac{\boldsymbol{\sigma}_{12}'\Sigma_{22}^{-1}\boldsymbol{\sigma}_{21}}{\sigma_1^2}\right) \\ &= \sigma_1^2(1 - \rho_{1 \cdot 2, \ldots, p}^2) \end{aligned}$$

following the bivariate case. The quantity

$$\rho_{y \cdot x} = \rho_{1 \cdot 2, \ldots, p} = \frac{\sqrt{\boldsymbol{\sigma}_{12}'\Sigma_{22}^{-1}\boldsymbol{\sigma}_{21}}}{\sigma_1}$$

is called the multiple correlation coefficient of $Y$ with the $p - 1$ variates in $\mathbf{X}$ and is equal to the maximum correlation between $Y$ and linear functions of $\mathbf{X}$ [60].

Allowing $(Y, X_1, X_2, \ldots, X_q)$ to have any multivariate distribution, the correlation ratio

$$\eta_{y \cdot \mathbf{x}} = 1 - \frac{\sigma_{y \cdot \mathbf{x}}^2}{\sigma_1}$$

is equal to the maximum correlation between $Y$ and any curvilinear function of $\mathbf{X}$ (see, for example, Ref. 74). As in the bivariate case,

$$0 \le \rho_{y \cdot \mathbf{x}}^2 \le \eta_{y \cdot \mathbf{x}}^2 \le 1$$

where $\rho_{y \cdot \mathbf{x}}^2$ is a measure of the linear dependency between $Y$ and $X_1, X_2, \ldots, X_q$.

Sampling $n$ observations from a multivariate normal population with parameters $\boldsymbol{\mu}$ and $\boldsymbol{\Sigma}$, the sample biased ML estimator of $\boldsymbol{\Sigma}$ is represented by

$$\hat{\boldsymbol{\Sigma}} = \begin{pmatrix} \hat{\sigma}_1 & \hat{\boldsymbol{\sigma}}'_{21} \\ \hat{\boldsymbol{\sigma}}_{21} & \hat{\boldsymbol{\Sigma}}_{22} \end{pmatrix}$$

and the ML estimator of the multiple correlation coefficient of the first variate with the remaining $p - 1$ variates is

$$R_{1 \cdot 2, \ldots, p} = \sqrt{\frac{\hat{\boldsymbol{\sigma}}'_{12} \hat{\boldsymbol{\Sigma}}_{22}^{-1} \hat{\boldsymbol{\sigma}}_{12}}{\hat{\sigma}_1^{\,2}}}$$

The ML estimator of the parameter vector $\boldsymbol{\beta}$ and the intercept $\alpha$ are

$$\hat{\boldsymbol{\beta}} = \hat{\boldsymbol{\Sigma}}_{22}^{-1} \hat{\boldsymbol{\sigma}}_{21} \qquad \text{and} \qquad \hat{\alpha} = \bar{y} - \hat{\boldsymbol{\beta}}' \bar{\mathbf{x}}$$

Alternatively, replacing the ML estimator of $\boldsymbol{\Sigma}$ by the unbiased estimator

$$\mathbf{S} = \frac{n}{n-1} \hat{\boldsymbol{\Sigma}} = \begin{pmatrix} s_1 & \mathbf{s}'_{12} \\ \mathbf{s}_{21} & \mathbf{S}_{22} \end{pmatrix}$$

$\boldsymbol{\beta}$ is estimated by $\hat{\boldsymbol{\beta}} = \mathbf{S}_{22}^{-1} \mathbf{s}_{21}$ which is identical with the ML estimator.

If $Y$ is independent of $X_1, X_2, \ldots, X_q$, $\boldsymbol{\sigma}_{21} = \mathbf{0}$ and the population multiple correlation coefficient is equal to zero. To test the equivalent hypotheses $\boldsymbol{\sigma}_{21} = \mathbf{0}$, $\boldsymbol{\beta} = \mathbf{0}$, and $\rho_{1 \cdot 2, \ldots, p} = 0$, Fisher showed that if $\rho_{1 \cdot 2, \ldots, p} = 0$

$$F = \frac{N - p}{p - 1} \frac{R_{1 \cdot 2, \ldots, p}^2}{1 - R_{1 \cdot 2, \ldots, p}^2}$$

is distributed as Fisher's $F$-distribution with $p - 1$ and $N - p$ degrees of freedom. Although Fisher determined the distribution of $R^2$, Wishart [98] determined its moments and Olkin and Pratt [58] provided an unbiased estimator of $R^2$.

## MULTIPLE REGRESSION MODELS

If the observed data $p$-vector $\boldsymbol{\mu}'_i = (y_i, x_{i1}, x_{i2}, \ldots, x_{iq})$ is obtained from a multivariate normal distribution or any known joint distribution, the form of the regression function is found by determining the mean of the conditional distribution; the estimated regression function may be used for prediction by estimating the model parameters usually by using the ML procedure. When the joint distribution is unknown, the exact form of the relationship between $Y$ and the elements in $\mathbf{X}$ is unknown. In these situations the form of the relationship between $Y$ and $\mathbf{X}$ is often expressed using a linear model. Given $n$ sets of observed data $(y_i, x_{i1}, x_{i2}, \ldots, x_{iq})$, where $q = p - 1$ and $i = 1, \ldots, n$, the model for the multiple regression equation has the form

$$y_i = \alpha + \beta_1 x_{1i} + \beta_2 x_{i2} + \cdots + \beta_q x_{iq} + \epsilon_i$$

where the regression coefficients $\alpha, \beta_1, \beta_2, \ldots, \beta_q$ are unknown parameters and the $\epsilon_i$ are random variation. Setting $\mathbf{y}' = (y_1, y_2, \ldots, y_n)$, $\boldsymbol{\epsilon}' = (\epsilon_1, \epsilon_2, \ldots, \epsilon_n)$, $\boldsymbol{\gamma}' = (\alpha, \beta_1, \beta_2, \ldots, \beta_q) = (\alpha, \boldsymbol{\beta}')$ and the matrix of regressors

$$\underset{(n \times p)}{\mathbf{X}} = \begin{pmatrix} 1 & x_{11} & x_{12} & \cdots & x_{1q} \\ 1 & x_{21} & x_{22} & \cdots & x_{2q} \\ \vdots & \vdots & \vdots & \vdots\vdots\vdots & \vdots \\ 1 & x_{n1} & x_{n2} & \cdots & x_{nq} \end{pmatrix}$$

the multiple regression equation is written as

$$\underset{(n \times 1)}{\mathbf{y}} = \underset{(n \times p)}{\mathbf{X}} \quad \underset{(p \times 1)}{\boldsymbol{\gamma}} + \underset{(n \times 1)}{\boldsymbol{\epsilon}}$$

and is called the (univariate) linear model. Given the relationship among $\mathbf{y}$, $\mathbf{X}$, and $\boldsymbol{\epsilon}$, the problem associated with the linear model is the estimation of the unknown nonrandom parameter vector $\boldsymbol{\gamma}$, known as the theory of least squares, using the data in $\mathbf{y}$ and $\mathbf{X}$.

Fundamental to the linear model, $\mathbf{y} = \mathbf{X}\boldsymbol{\gamma} + \boldsymbol{\epsilon}$, is the random unobservable error vector $\boldsymbol{\epsilon}$. The components $\epsilon_i$ of $\boldsymbol{\epsilon}$ might represent random variation of two important kinds, equation error and measurement error. In either case, it is always assumed that the mean of $\boldsymbol{\epsilon}$ is $\mathbf{0}$. For purposes of inference it is usually assumed that $\boldsymbol{\epsilon}$ follows a multivariate normal distribution. The variance-covariance matrix $\boldsymbol{\Sigma}$ of the error vector also needs to be specified for a linear model. Although the errors may be correlated with arbitrary unknown structure $\boldsymbol{\Sigma}$, it is commonly assumed that we have sphericity of errors so that $\boldsymbol{\Sigma} = \sigma^2 \mathbf{I}$, where only $\sigma^2$ is unknown. Sphericity implies that the errors are uncorrelated and homoscedastic, all having equal but unknown variances.

With the assumptions on the error vector $\boldsymbol{\epsilon}$ specified, it is now possible, using the linear model, to classify regression models into some standard categories [32, 68].

The most useful and widely used regression model for prediction problems is the conditional regression model. For this model the random variate $Y$ and the $q$ variates $X_1, X_2, \ldots, X_q$ are assumed to have some joint distribution such that the mean of the conditional distribution of $Y$ given $\mathbf{X}$ is of the form $\mathbf{X}\boldsymbol{\gamma}$, where $\boldsymbol{\gamma}$ is a vector of unknown nonrandom parameters. The data for the random variate $Y$ are collected in $n$ repeated samples for fixed known values of the regressors in the design matrix $\mathbf{X}$ measured without error. Furthermore, the values of $Y$ in the regression model are observed without error.

A model closely associated and sometimes confused with the conditional regression model is the stochastic regression model. For this model the matrix $\mathbf{X}$ is random or stochastic rather than fixed. Data for this model are collected at random for the random tuples $(Y, X_1, X_2, \ldots, X_q)$ observed without error. Provided $\mathbf{X}$ and $\epsilon$ are independent and the distribution of $\mathbf{X}$ does not depend upon $\gamma$ and $\Sigma$, inferences about $\gamma$ and $\Sigma$ are identical with the conditional regression model. In practice, $\mathbf{X}$ and $\epsilon$ are often fully dependent and an alternative to least squares estimation needs to be used to estimate $\gamma$; these include two-stage least squares for single equation problems and three-stage least squares, linearized maximum likelihood, and Wold's generalized independent systems procedure for several equation systems. These methods are described in Christ [15] and Theil [94]. An important area of statistics where $\mathbf{X}$ and $\epsilon$ are not independent is in time series analysis (see, for example, Refs. 5 and 100).

Another model which is similar to the conditional regression model is the functional regression model. For this model the matrix $\mathbf{X}$ contains fixed known mathematical variables measured without error so that only $Y$ is random. Assuming a functional relationship between the mathematical variables $\mathbf{y}^*$ and $\mathbf{X}$ so that $\mathbf{y}^* = \mathbf{X}\gamma$, $\mathbf{y}^*$ is unobservable since $\gamma$ is unknown and nonrandom. However, instead of observing $\mathbf{y}^*$, suppose we observe the random variate $\mathbf{Y} = \mathbf{y}^* + \epsilon = \mathbf{X}\gamma + \epsilon$, where $\epsilon$ is measurement error; replacing the random variate $\mathbf{Y}$ with the observation vector $\mathbf{y}$, we see that the functional regression model fits the linear model formulation. A very important class of models which is a special case of the functional regression model are experimental design models. For experimental design models the values for the elements of $\mathbf{X}$ are restricted to 0 and 1. Such models are discussed in the general area of statistics known as the analysis of variance which was developed by Fisher [25]. A modern treatment of experimental design models is included in Scheffé [79], Graybill [32], and Searle [81], among others.

Estimation of $\gamma$ and $\sigma^2$ under sphericity of errors with no distributional assumption on $\epsilon$, known as the classical theory of least squares for functional and conditional regression models, was first discussed by Gauss [30] and later by Markoff [53]. To obtain the least squares estimator of $\gamma$, the sum of squares for error

$$S = (\mathbf{y} - \mathbf{X}\gamma)'(\mathbf{y} - \mathbf{X}\gamma)$$

is minimized. Differentiating with respect to $\gamma$ and setting the result equal to $\mathbf{0}$ yields the normal equations

$$(\mathbf{X}'\mathbf{X})\hat{\gamma} = \mathbf{X}'\mathbf{y}$$

Provided $\mathbf{X}'\mathbf{X}$ is nonsingular, the unique LS estimator of $\gamma$ is

$$\hat{\gamma} = (\mathbf{X}'\mathbf{X})^{-1}\mathbf{X}'\mathbf{y}$$

$$= \begin{pmatrix} \hat{\alpha} \\ \hat{\beta} \end{pmatrix}$$

where $\hat{\boldsymbol{\beta}} = \mathbf{S}_{22}^{-1}\mathbf{s}_{21}$. If $\boldsymbol{\epsilon}$ is normally distributed, the LS and ML estimator of $\boldsymbol{\gamma}$ are identical. In either case the LS estimator is the best linear unbiased estimator (BLUE) of $\boldsymbol{\gamma}$. Although Yule bridged the gap between the work of Gauss and Pearson, it was Markoff who established some of the important properties of LS estimators, and it was Aitken [1] who generalized the Gauss-Markoff theory of least squares by allowing a general variance-covariance matrix of the form $\boldsymbol{\Sigma} = \sigma^2\boldsymbol{\Omega}$ for $\boldsymbol{\epsilon}$ with unknown $\sigma^2$ and known positive definite matrix $\boldsymbol{\Omega}$. This allowed the errors $\epsilon_i$ to be correlated and heteroscedastic. However, it was Rao [69, 75] who provided a unified theory of least squares by allowing $\mathbf{X}$ to be singular, so that there was multicolinearity in the data, and $\boldsymbol{\Omega}$ possibly singular.

If the random variates in the stochastic regression model are not directly observable, we have the error in variates model or structural regression model. For these models we usually always assume that the errors are independent and normally distributed for mathematical simplicity [42]. If in the functional regression model the mathematical variables are not directly observable, we have the error in variables model which is sometimes called regression analysis with both variables subject to error. For either of these models the classical and generalized theory of least squares estimation is not applicable.

In all of the preceding models we have assumed that $\boldsymbol{\gamma}$ was unknown and nonrandom. Regression models with random $\boldsymbol{\gamma}$ are reviewed by Swamy [92] and are called random coefficient regression models. In analysis of variance these models are termed random effects models. A unified theory for least squares estimation for some of these models is given by Rao [70–72].

The preceding classification of univariate regression models is not exhaustive, there are numerous regression models encountered in practice which do not fit into any of the above-mentioned categories, the most important class of models being nonlinear regression models. The regression equation

$$y = \alpha + \beta_1 x_1 + \beta_2 x_2 + \cdots + \beta_q x_q + \epsilon$$

is linear in the elements of $\boldsymbol{\gamma}$. Any equation which cannot be put in the above form is called a nonlinear model; that is, nonlinear in the parameters, not in the variables. A discussion of the problems of estimation and computation associated with such models is reviewed by Draper and Smith [18].

Given one dependent variate $Y$ and a set of regressors $\mathbf{X}$, there are numerous types of regression models which may be used to predict $Y$ from $\mathbf{X}$ depending upon the specified relationships among $\mathbf{y}$, $\mathbf{X}$, $\boldsymbol{\gamma}$, and $\boldsymbol{\epsilon}$. Having selected the appropriate model class, there are other considerations besides estimation and testing that one must be aware of when fitting equations to data for prediction. These include checking that the assumptions of the model are satisfied, selecting the most appropriate regression equation, studying the estimated residuals $\hat{\boldsymbol{\epsilon}}$, and possibly using various types of transformations on the collected data to obtain the best prediction equation. These and other concerns of data analysis are dealt with by Wood and Daniel [101].

Another important consideration of regression analysis is writing and selecting a computer program to analyze data since calculation of estimates and summary statistics for large data sets is not feasible using a desk calculator. Although the most important aspect of any statistical package is precision [50, 101], which may be obtained through appropriately designed algorithms, other considerations in statistical computing include flexibility of input, documentation of output, and the ability of the package to quickly and easily do a variety of different analyses as they occur to the user.

In designing or evaluating a program for statistical computing, some effort should be made to see that the package allows for numerous forms of input in a variety of formats, includes a variety of data transformation options, includes general plotting flexibility, has built in facilities to recovery and save intermediate results and data, has procedures for checking data flow and accuracy of results, and includes adequate documentation of output for any user population. In addition, if the package is to be transported to run on many different machine configurations, it must be as machine-independent as possible. A comprehensive list of numerous regression statistical programs is contained in an article by Chambers [14].

## MULTIVARIATE CORRELATION COEFFICIENTS

Having discussed the development of some standard regression models for one criterion variate $Y$ and several regressors, we return to Pearson's original formulation of multivariate normal regression analysis to survey several types of correlation coefficients for normal variates.

Following his development of the simple correlation coefficient, Pearson derived the formula for the partial correlation coefficient. Given $p$-variates $U_1$, $U_2, \ldots, U_p$ which follow a multivariate normal distribution, the partial correlation between any two variates $U_i$ and $U_j$ in $\mathbf{Y}' = (U_1, U_2, \ldots, U_s)$ given $\mathbf{X}' = (U_{s+1}, \ldots, U_p)$ is

$$\rho_{ij \cdot s+1,\ldots,p} = \frac{\sigma_{ij \cdot s+1,\ldots,p}}{\sqrt{\sigma_{ii \cdot s+1,\ldots,p}}\sqrt{\sigma_{jj \cdot s+1,\ldots,p}}}$$

where $\sigma_{ij \cdot s+1,\ldots,p}$ is the $i.j$th element of the partial variance-covariance matrix $\Sigma_{\mathbf{y} \cdot \mathbf{x}}$. For $p = 3$ and $s = 2$, it is easily shown that

$$\rho_{12 \cdot 3} = \frac{\rho_{12} - \rho_{13}\rho_{23}}{\sqrt{1 - \rho_{23}^2}\sqrt{1 - \rho_{13}^2}}$$

which can be interpreted as the simple correlation between $U_1$ and $U_2$ for any one of the several values of $U_2$. A general recursion formula for computing partial correlations involving more than three variates is given by Anderson [3].

Estimating the partial correlation coefficient for a sample of $n$ observations from a multivariate normal distribution, the ML estimator of $\rho_{ij \cdot s+1,\ldots,p}$ is

$$\hat{\rho}_{ij \cdot s+1,\ldots,p} = \frac{\hat{\sigma}_{ij \cdot s+1,\ldots,p}}{\sqrt{\hat{\sigma}_{ii \cdot s+1,\ldots,p}}\sqrt{\hat{\sigma}_{jj \cdot s+1,\ldots,p}}}$$

where $\hat{\sigma}_{ij \cdot s+1,\ldots,p}$ is the $i,j$th element of $\hat{\Sigma}_{\mathbf{y} \cdot \mathbf{x}}$. Tests of hypotheses and confidence intervals for partial correlation coefficients were derived by Fisher [26].

Following Pearson, partial correlations under normality are no more than correlation coefficients in conditional distributions. Holding several variates constant in a multivariate normal distribution allows one to investigate relationships between two variates $U_i$ and $U_j$ by controlling for other variates which seem to be directly influencing $U_i$ and $U_j$.

Considering three variates $U_1$, $U_2$, and $U_3$, suppose that the relationship between $U_1$ and $U_3$ is linear, $U_1 = \alpha + \beta U_3$, that the relationship between $U_2$ and $U_3$ is linear, $U_2 = \alpha' + \beta' U_3$, and that the "cause" of the variation between $U_1$ and $U_2$ is influenced by the common variate $U_3$. Setting $\epsilon_1 = U_1 - \alpha - \beta U_3$ and $\epsilon_2 = U_2 - \alpha' - \beta' U_3$, the partial correlation between $\epsilon_1$ and $\epsilon_2$ is

$$\rho = \frac{\sigma_{\epsilon_1 \epsilon_2}}{\sigma_{\epsilon_1} \sigma_{\epsilon_2}} = \frac{\rho_{12} - \rho_{13}\rho_{23}}{\sqrt{1 - \rho_{23}^2}\sqrt{1 - \rho_{13}^2}}$$

which is identical to $\rho_{12 \cdot 3}$. Hence, assuming a linear relationship between $U_1$ and $U_3$, and between $U_2$ and $U_3$, the partial correlation coefficient is the simple correlation between the residuals $\epsilon_1$ and $\epsilon_2$. Furthermore, provided we have the causal relationship given by the causal system

for $U_1$, $U_2$, and $U_3$, we may interpret the partial correlation coefficient as a measure of the linear dependence between $U_1$ and $U_2$ controlling for $U_3$. If $U_3$ does not influence the variation in $U_1$ and $U_2$ as described above, the interpretation of partial correlations is unclear. The fact that estimates of partial correlation coefficients can be obtained from a linear regression model led Yule to refer to the partial correlation as the correlation between $U_1$ and $U_2$ "eliminating" the linear dependence of $U_1$ and $U_2$ on $U_3$, and this in turn provides us with a natural procedure for judging the contribution of the variate $U_3$ to a regression equation containing only $U_2$ to predict $U_1$. These procedures are discussed in general by Ezekiel [21] and Rao [74], among others, where general expressions for partial correlations are derived from multiple correlations.

Provided $U_3$ influences both $U_1$ and $U_2$, interpretation of the partial correlation coefficient is meaningful. Alternatively, suppose $U_3$ influences $U_2$ but not $U_1$, and that $U_2$ influences $U_1$:

$$U_3 \rightarrow U_2 \rightarrow U_1$$

Then a measure of the correlation between $U_1$ and $U_2$ is best obtained if the influence of $U_3$ on $U_2$ is controlled for by investigating the correlation between $U_1$ and $U_2$ partialling out the variate $U_3$ from only $U_2$. Such a correlation coefficient, called a part correlation coefficient, was developed by M. Ezekiel and B. B. Smith in 1926 [21], and is represented by

$$\rho_{1(2\cdot3)} = \frac{\rho_{12} - \rho_{13}\rho_{23}}{\sqrt{1 - \rho_{23}^2}}$$

for three variates. To derive $\rho_{1(2\cdot3)}$ following Yule, we assume a linear relationship between $U_2$ and $U_3$ and set $\epsilon_2 = U_2 - \alpha' - \beta'U_3$. The simple correlation between $U_1$ and $\epsilon_2$ is

$$\rho_{1(2\cdot3)} = \frac{\sigma_{u_1\epsilon_2}}{\sigma_{u_1}\sigma_{\epsilon_2}} = \frac{\rho_{12}\sigma_1\sigma_2 - \beta'\rho_{13}\sigma_1\sigma_3}{\sigma_2\sqrt{1 - \rho_{23}^2}\sigma_1}$$

$$= \frac{\rho_{12}\sigma_1\sigma_2 - \rho_{23}\rho_{13}\sigma_1\sigma_2}{\sigma_1\sigma_2\sqrt{1 - \rho_{23}^2}}$$

$$= \frac{\rho_{12} - \rho_{12}\rho_{23}}{\sqrt{1 - \rho_{23}^2}}$$

as claimed.

Following Fisher [26], to test the hypothesis that a partial correlation coefficient is equal to zero under normality, the $t$ statistic for testing that a simple correlation coefficient is equal to zero is modified by subtracting one degree of freedom from the sample size $n$ for every regressor removed. Thus, to test that the first-order partial correlation coefficient, $\rho_{12\cdot3}$, equals zero, the test statistic is

$$t = \sqrt{\frac{(n-3)\hat{\rho}_{12\cdot3}^2}{1 - \hat{\rho}_{12\cdot3}^2}}$$

which is distributed as Student's $t$ with $n-3$ degrees of freedom if $\rho_{12\cdot3} = 0$. Unfortunately, one may not merely substitute part correlations for partial correlations in the above formula to test that a part correlation is equal to zero. The test statistic for testing that a first-order part correlation is equal to zero is

$$t = \sqrt{\frac{(n-3)\hat{\rho}_{1(2\cdot3)}^2}{1 - \hat{\rho}_{12\cdot3}^2}}$$

which is distributed as Student's $t$ with $n-3$ degrees of freedom when $\rho_{1(2\cdot3)} = 0$. Since $\rho_{1(2\cdot3)}^2 \leq \rho_{23\cdot3}^2$, substituting $\hat{\rho}_{1(2\cdot3)}^2$ for $\hat{\rho}_{12\cdot3}^2$ in the $t$ statistic for testing $\rho_{1(2\cdot3)} = 0$ would only yield an approximate test procedure.

In addition to part and partial correlation coefficients, other simple correlations are also important to understanding linear relationships among variates; for example, suppose $U_3$ and $U_4$ are highly correlated and that the relationship among four variates is

$$U_3 \to U_2 \to U_4 \to U_1$$

To determine the correlation between $U_1$ and $U_2$ the linear influence of $U_3$ on $U_2$

and of $U_4$ on $U_1$ is controlled by using the bi-partial correlation coefficient

$$\rho_{(1\cdot4)(2\cdot3)} = \frac{\rho_{12} - \rho_{14}\rho_{24} - \rho_{13}\rho_{23} + \rho_{14}\rho_{43}\rho_{23}}{\sqrt{1 - \rho_{14}^2}\sqrt{1 - \rho_{23}^2}}$$

Alternatively, if the relationship among the variates is given by the system

$$\begin{array}{c} U_3 \rightarrow U_1 \\ \times \\ U_4 \rightarrow U_2 \end{array}$$

the partial correlation

$$\rho_{12\cdot34} = \frac{\rho_{12\cdot3} - \rho_{14\cdot3}\rho_{24\cdot3}}{\sqrt{1 - \rho_{14\cdot3}^2}\sqrt{1 - \rho_{24\cdot3}^2}}$$

would be of interest.

Extending Pearson's notation of multiple correlation, the maximum correlation between $Y$ and linear functions of several regressor variates, Hotelling [35] developed what are known as canonical correlations to express the maximum correlation between linear functions of two sets of variates $\mathbf{Y}' = (Y_1, Y_2, \ldots, Y_s)$ and $\mathbf{X}' = (X_1, X_2, \ldots, X_q)$. Assuming $\mathbf{U}' = (\mathbf{Y}', \mathbf{X}')$ is distributed multivariate normal with variance-covariance matrix

$$\mathbf{\Sigma} = \begin{pmatrix} \mathbf{\Sigma}_{11} & \mathbf{\Sigma}_{12} \\ \mathbf{\Sigma}_{21} & \mathbf{\Sigma}_{22} \end{pmatrix}$$

the square root of the nonzero eigenvalues $\rho_1 \geq \rho_2 \geq \cdots$ of the determinantal equation

$$| \mathbf{\Sigma}_{12}\mathbf{\Sigma}_{22}^{-1}\mathbf{\Sigma}_{21} - \rho^2\mathbf{\Sigma}_{11} | = 0$$

are the canonical correlations between the linear functions

$$\mathbf{a}_1'\mathbf{Y}, \mathbf{a}_2'\mathbf{Y}, \ldots, \mathbf{a}_s'\mathbf{Y} \quad \text{and} \quad \mathbf{b}_1'\mathbf{X}, \mathbf{b}_2'\mathbf{X}, \ldots, \mathbf{b}_q'\mathbf{X}$$

called canonical variates. For only one variate in the set $\mathbf{Y}$, the canonical correlation between $Y$ and $\mathbf{X}$ is equal to the multiple correlation coefficient. To estimate canonical correlations from a multivariate data set, sample variance-covariance or sample correlation matrices are used in place of the population variance-covariance matrices. For applications of canonical correlations, see Dempster [17], Morrison [55], and Press [68].

Generalizing partial correlations to the multivariate situation, the random vector $\mathbf{U}$ is partitioned as $\mathbf{U}' = (\mathbf{X}', \mathbf{Y}', \mathbf{Z}')$ and the variance-covariance matrix

$$\mathbf{\Sigma} = \begin{pmatrix} \mathbf{\Sigma}_{11} & \mathbf{\Sigma}_{12} & \mathbf{\Sigma}_{13} \\ \mathbf{\Sigma}_{21} & \mathbf{\Sigma}_{22} & \mathbf{\Sigma}_{23} \\ \mathbf{\Sigma}_{31} & \mathbf{\Sigma}_{32} & \mathbf{\Sigma}_{33} \end{pmatrix}$$

is associated with $\mathbf{U}$. Following Anderson [3], the variance-covariance matrix of the conditional distribution of $\mathbf{Y}$ and $\mathbf{X}$ given $\mathbf{Z}$ under normality is

$$\boldsymbol{\Sigma}_{.3} = \begin{pmatrix} \boldsymbol{\Sigma}_{11} - \boldsymbol{\Sigma}_{13}\boldsymbol{\Sigma}_{33}^{-1}\boldsymbol{\Sigma}_{31} & \boldsymbol{\Sigma}_{12} - \boldsymbol{\Sigma}_{13}\boldsymbol{\Sigma}_{33}^{-1}\boldsymbol{\Sigma}_{31} \\ \boldsymbol{\Sigma}_{21} - \boldsymbol{\Sigma}_{23}\boldsymbol{\Sigma}_{33}^{-1}\boldsymbol{\Sigma}_{32} & \boldsymbol{\Sigma}_{22} - \boldsymbol{\Sigma}_{23}\boldsymbol{\Sigma}_{33}^{-1}\boldsymbol{\Sigma}_{32} \end{pmatrix}$$

$$= \begin{pmatrix} \boldsymbol{\Sigma}_{11\cdot3} & \boldsymbol{\Sigma}_{12\cdot3} \\ \boldsymbol{\Sigma}_{21\cdot3} & \boldsymbol{\Sigma}_{22\cdot3} \end{pmatrix}$$

Solving the determinantal equation

$$| \boldsymbol{\Sigma}_{12\cdot3}\boldsymbol{\Sigma}_{22\cdot3}^{-1}\boldsymbol{\Sigma}_{21\cdot3} - \rho^2\boldsymbol{\Sigma}_{11\cdot3} | = 0$$

the square root of the nonzero eigenvalues of the equation are called partial canonical correlations. If $\boldsymbol{\Sigma}_{11}$ is a scalar in the determinantal equation, the partial canonical correlation is called a multiple partial correlation which is very useful in univariate regression analysis [74].

Extending the notion of part correlations to part canonical correlations, the matrix

$$\boldsymbol{\Sigma}_{1(2\cdot3)} = \begin{pmatrix} \boldsymbol{\Sigma}_{11} & \boldsymbol{\Sigma}_{12\cdot3} \\ \boldsymbol{\Sigma}_{21\cdot3} & \boldsymbol{\Sigma}_{22\cdot3} \end{pmatrix}$$

is formed; the square root of the eigenvalues of the determinantal equation

$$| \boldsymbol{\Sigma}_{12\cdot3}\boldsymbol{\Sigma}_{22\cdot3}^{-1}\boldsymbol{\Sigma}_{21\cdot3} - \rho^2\boldsymbol{\Sigma}_{11} | = 0$$

are called part canonical correlations. Test procedures, generalizations of bi-partial canonical correlations, and applications of canonical correlations in education and psychology are discussed further by Timm [95].

## MULTIVARIATE REGRESSION MODELS

Associated with canonical correlation analysis between the sets of variates $\mathbf{Y}$ and $\mathbf{X}$ in the multivariate random vector $\mathbf{U}' = (\mathbf{Y}', \mathbf{X}')$ is the multivariate linear regression function for predicting simultaneously all variates in $\mathbf{Y}$ from $\mathbf{X}$ or $\mathbf{X}$ from $\mathbf{Y}$. Associating with each variate in $\mathbf{Y}$, the linear model

$$\underset{(n\times1)}{\mathbf{y}_j} = \underset{(n\times p)}{\mathbf{X}} \underset{(p\times1)}{\boldsymbol{\gamma}_j} + \underset{(n\times1)}{\boldsymbol{\epsilon}_j} \qquad j = 1, \ldots, s$$

we may write the (multivariate) linear model for all variates simultaneous as

$$\underset{(n\times s)}{\mathbf{Y}} = \underset{(n\times p)}{\mathbf{X}} \underset{(p\times s)}{\boldsymbol{\Gamma}} + \underset{(n\times s)}{\mathbf{E}_0}$$

where $\mathbf{Y}$ is a data matrix of observations, $\mathbf{X}$ is a matrix of regressors, $\boldsymbol{\Gamma}$ is a matrix of parameters, and $\mathbf{E}_0$ is a matrix of random errors. Depending on the relationship among $\mathbf{Y}$, $\mathbf{X}$, $\mathbf{E}_0$, and $\boldsymbol{\Gamma}$, we may classify multivariate regression models according to the broad categories, conditional regression models, functional regression models, stochastic regression models, error in variables models, error in variates models, random coefficient models, and nonlinear multivariate regression models as was the case for univariate regression models. In addition, for multivariate models the matrix of regressors does not have to be the same for every variate in the matrix $Y$; this leads to a class of models known as multiple design multivariate models [89, 90]. Although all types of multivariate regression models have not yet been considered in the statistical literature, a monograph devoted to several of the central issues of these designs has been written by Roy, Gnanadesikan, and Srivastava [78]. Press [68] also discusses several multivariate regression models. In addition, Potthoff and Roy [67], Milliken and Graybill [54], and Kleinbaum [44] consider extensions of linear models. However, it was Hotelling [34], Wilks [97], Bartlett [9], and Roy [77], among others, who led the way for establishing the fundamental theory for multivariate data analysis. A complete bibliography of multivariate statistical analysis up to 1966 has been compiled by Anderson, Das Gupta, and Styan [6]. Important recent contributions are summarized by Rao [73].

Topics closely associated with correlation and regression include: factor analysis developed by Spearman [85] and discussed by Anderson and Rubin [7], Lawley and Maxwell [45], and Mulaik [56]; path analysis developed by Wright [102] and discussed by Wold [99], Duncan [19], and Blalock [10]; covariance structure analysis studied by Bock and Bargmann [11] and Anderson [4] and extended by Jöreskog [36]; multidimensional scaling developed by Shepard [82, 83] and surveyed in a two-volume treatise by Shepard et al. [84]; latent structure analysis developed by Lazarsfeld [47] and discussed by Lazarsfeld and Henry [48]; cluster analysis, discussed by Anderberg [2], discriminant analysis, spectral analysis and bioassay, among others.

## CORRELATION REGRESSION AND COMPUTERS

Although most of the theory of correlation and regression was established over 50 years ago, it has only been fully utilized with the extensive development of computer technology and numerical analysis. Problems associated with programming and developing efficient algorithms for statistical computing and Monte Carlo studies are essential to the further development of multivariate correlation and regression methodology. Many problems associated with statistical computing are discussed in Carnahan et al. [12].

To implement the many regression models and correlation techniques to data sets acquired in practice requires a large library of special purpose statistical programs. Although Chambers [14] and Press [68] provide a selected list of computer programs for many correlation and regression analysis procedures, an exhaustive list of routines written for IBM computers are available through the SHARE Library, COSMIC, University of Georgia, Athens, Georgia 30601. Programs written for CDC computers are available through the VIM Library, Software Distribution Department, Control Data Corporation, 3145 Porter Drive, Palo Alto, California. Other sources of statistical programs include the National Program Library and Central Program Inventory Service for the Social Sciences, 4430 Social Science Building, 1180 Observatory Drive, University of Wisconsin, Madison, Wisconsin 53706; Computer Information and Documents,

Bell Laboratories, 600 Mountain Avenue, Murray Hill, New Jersey 07974; Division of Psychological Studies, Educational Testing Service, Princeton, New Jersey 08540; and many major universities and industry.

The best available computer routine for the analysis of univariate linear regression models is the Linear Least-Squares Curve Fitting Program written by R. A. Brehmer, P. E. Piechocki, W. B. Traver, F. M. Jacobsen, F. M. Oliva, R. J. Toman, and F. S. Wood of the American Oil Company, Whiting, Indiana, and is available through the SHARE Library (Number 360 D-13.6.008) and the VIM Library (Number G2-CAL-LINWOOD) [101].

One of the best correlational analysis programs is the Statistical Package for the Social Sciences (SPSS) originally developed by Dale Bent and Norman Nie at Stanford University [57]. The program is distributed by the NORC Librarian, University of Chicago, 6030 South Ellis Avenue, Chicago, Illinois 60637.

# REFERENCES

1. Aitken, A. C., On least squares and linear combination of observations, *Proc. R. Soc. Edinburgh, A* **55,** 42–48 (1935).
2. Anderberg, M. R., *Cluster Analysis for Applications,* Academic, New York, 1973.
3. Anderson, T. W., *An Introduction to Multivariate Statistical Analysis,* Wiley, New York, 1958.
4. Anderson, T. W., Statistical inference for covariance matrices with linear structure, in *Multivariate Analysis II* (P. R. Krishnaiah, ed.), Academic, New York, 1969.
5. Anderson, T. W., *The Statistical Analysis of Time Series,* Wiley, New York, 1971.
6. Anderson, T. W., S. Das Gupta, and G. P. H. Styan, *A Bibliography of Multivariate Statistical Analysis,* Wiley, New York, 1972.
7. Anderson, T. W., and H. Rubin, Statistical inference in factor analysis, in *Proceedings of the Third Berkeley Symposium in Mathematical Statistics and Probability,* Vol. 5, 1956, pp. 111–150.
8. Baggaley, A. R., *Intermediate Correlation Methods,* Wiley, New York, 1964.
9. Bartlett, M. S., The vector representation of a sample, *Proc. Cambridge Philos. Soc.* **30,** 327–340 (1934).
10. Blalock, H. M., Jr., *Causal Models in the Social Sciences,* Aldine-Atherton, Chicago, 1971.
11. Bock, R. D., and R. E. Bargmann, Analysis of covariance structures, *Psychometrika* **31,** 507–534 (1966).
12. Carnahan, B., H. A. Luther, and J. O. Wilkes, *Applied Numerical Methods,* Wiley, New York, 1969.
13. Carroll, J. B., The nature of data, or how to choose a correlation coefficient, *Psychometrika* **26,** 347–372 (1961).
14. Chambers, J. M., Some general aspects of statistical computing, *Appl. Stat. J. R. Stat. Soc., Ser. C* **17,** 124–132 (1968).
15. Christ, C. F., *Econometric Models and Methods,* Wiley, New York, 1966.
16. David, F. N., *Tables of the Correlation Coefficient,* Cambridge University Press, London, 1938.

17. Dempster, A. P., *Elements of Continuous Multivariate Analysis*, Addison-Wesley, Reading, Massachusetts, 1969.

18. Draper, N. R., and H. Smith, *Applied Regression Analysis*, Wiley, New York, 1966.

19. Duncan, O. D., Path analysis: Sociological examples, *Am. J. Sociology* **72**, 1–16 (1966).

20. Edgeworth, F. Y., Correlated averages, *Philos. Mag., Ser. 5* **34**, 190–204 (1892).

21. Ezekiel, M., *Methods of Correlation Analysis*, 2nd ed., Wiley, New York, 1941.

22. Fisher, R. A., The frequency distribution of the values of the correlation coefficient in samples from an indefinitely large population, *Biometrika* **10**, 507–521 (1915).

23. Fisher, R. A., On the "probable error" of a coefficient of correlation deduced from a small sample, *Metron* **1**, 3–32 (1921).

24. Fisher, R. A., The goodness of fit of regression formula and the distribution of regression coefficients, *J. R. Stat. Soc.* **85**, 597–612 (1922).

25. Fisher, R. A., On a distribution yielding the error functions of several well known statistics, in *Proceedings of the International Congress of Mathematics, Toronto*, Vol. 2, 1924, pp. 805–813.

26. Fisher, R. A., The distribution of the partial correlation coefficient, *Metron* **3**, 329–332 (1924).

27. Galton, F., Family likeness in stature. *Proc. R. Soc. London* **40**, 42–72 (1886).

28. Galton, F., Co-relations and their measurement, chiefly from anthropometric data, *Proc. R. Soc. London* **45**, 135–145 (1888).

29. Galton, F., *Natural Inheritance*. Macmillan, London, 1889.

30. Gauss, C. F., *Theoria Motus Corporum Coelestium in Sectionibus Conicis Solem Ambientium*, Hamburg, 1809 (English translation by C. H. Davis, 1857).

31. Goldberger, A., *Econometric Theory*, Wiley, New York, 1964.

32. Graybill, F. A., *An Introduction to Linear Statistical Models*, McGraw-Hill, New York, 1961.

33. Hoel, P. G., *Introduction to Mathematical Statistics*, 4th ed., Wiley, New York, 1971.

34. Hotelling, H., The generalization of Student's ratio, *Ann. Math. Stat.* **2**, 360–378 (1931).

35. Hotelling, H., Relations between two sets of variates, *Biometrika* **28**, 321–377 (1936).

36. Jöreskog, K., A general method for analysis of covariance structures, *Biometrika* **57**, 239–251 (1970).

37. Jöreskog, K., A general method for estimating a linear structural equation system, in *Structural Equation Models in the Social Sciences* (A. S. Goldberger and O. D. Duncan, eds.), Seminar Press, New York, 1973.

38. Johnson, J., *Econometric Methods*, 2nd ed., McGraw-Hill, New York, 1972.

39. Kendall, M. G., Regression, structure and functional relationship I, *Biometrika* **38**, 11–35 (1951).

40. Kendall, M. G., Regression, structure and functional relationship II, *Biometrika* **39**, 96–108 (1952).

41. Kendall, M. G., Ronald Aylmer Fisher, 1890–1962, *Biometrika* **50**, 1–15 (1963).

42. Kendall, M. G., and A. Stuart, *The Advanced Theory of Statistics*, Vol. 2, Hafner, New York, 1961.

43. Kirk, D. B., On the numerical approximation of the bivariate normal (tetrachoric) correlation coefficient, *Psychometrika* **38**, 259–268 (1973).

44. Kleinbaum, D. G., Testing linear hypotheses in generalized multivariate linear models, *Commun. Stat.* **1**, 433–457 (1973).

45. Lawley, D. N., and A. E. Maxwell, *Factor Analysis as a Statistical Method,* 2nd ed., American Elsevier, New York, 1971.

46. Lawley, D. N., and A. E. Maxwell, Regression and factor analysis, *Biometrika* **60**, 331–338 (1973).

47. Lazarsfeld, P. F., The logical and mathematical foundation of latent structure analysis, in *Measurement and Prediction* (S. A. Stouffer et al., eds.), Princeton University Press, Princeton, New Jersey, 1950.

48. Lazarsfeld, P. F., and N. W. Henry, *Latent Structure Analysis,* Houghton Mifflin, Boston, 1968.

49. Lindley, D. V., Regression lines and linear functional relationship, *J. R. Stat. Soc., Suppl.* **9**, 218–244 (1947).

50. Longley, J. W., An appraisal of least squares programs for the electronic computer from the point of view of the user, *J. Am. Stat. Assoc.* **62**, 819–841 (1967).

51. Lord, F., and M. Novick, *Statistical Theories of Mental Test Scores,* Addison-Wesley, Reading, Massachusetts, 1968.

52. Madansky, A., The fitting of straight lines when both variables are subject to error, *J. Am. Stat. Assoc.* **54**, 173–205 (1959).

53. Markoff, A. A., *Wahrscheinlichkeitsrechnung,* Tebner, Leipzig, 1900.

54. Milliken, G. A., and F. A. Graybill, Extensions of the general linear hypothesis model, *J. Am. Stat. Assoc.* **65**, 797–807 (1970).

55. Morrison, D. F., *Multivariate Statistical Methods,* McGraw-Hill, New York, 1967.

56. Mulaik, S. A., *The Foundations of Factor Analysis,* McGraw-Hill, New York, 1972.

57. Nie, N. H., D. H. Bent, and C. H. Hull, *Statistical Package for the Social Sciences,* McGraw-Hill, New York, 1970.

58. Olkin, I., and W. Pratt, Unbiased estimation of certain correlation coefficients, *Ann. Math. Stat.* **29**, 201–211 (1958).

59. Pearson, K., Mathematical contributions to the theory of evolution III. Regression, heredity and panmixia, *Philos. Trans. R. Soc. London, Ser. A* **187**, 253–318 (1896).

60. Pearson, K., Mathematical contributions to the theory of evolution V. On the reconstruction of the stature of prehistoric races, *Philos. Trans. R. Soc. London, Ser. A* **192**, 169–244 (1898).

61. Pearson, K., Mathematical contributions to the theory of evolution. XIV. On the general theory of skew correlation and non-linear regression, *Drapers' Company Research Memoirs, Biometric Series, II,* Dulau and Company, London, 1905.

62. Pearson, K., On a correction to be made to the correlation ratio $\eta$, *Biometrika* **8**, 254–256 (1911).

63. Pearson, K., On the partial correlation ratio, *Proc. R. Soc. London, Ser. A* **91**, 492–498 (1915).

64. Pearson, K., Notes on the history of correlation, *Biometrika* **13**, 25–45 (1920).

65. Pearson, K., On the correction necessary for the correlation ratio, *Biometrika* **14**, 412–417 (1922–1923).

66. Pearson, K., and A. Lee, On the laws of inheritance in man. I. Inheritance of physical characteristics, *Biometrika* **2**, 46–462 (1903).

67. Potthoff, R. F., and S. N. Roy, A generalized multivariate analysis of variance

model useful especially for growth curve problems, *Biometrika* **51**, 313–326 (1964).

68. Press, S. J., *Applied Multivariate Analysis,* Holt, Rinehart and Winston, New York, 1972.

69. Rao, C. R., On the linear combination of observations and the general theory of least squares, *Sankhyá* **7**, 237–256 (1946).

70. Rao, C. R., Estimation of variance and covariance components—MINQUE theory, *J. Multivar. Anal.* **1**, 257–275 (1971).

71. Rao, C. R., Minimum variance quadratic unbiased estimation of variance components, *J. Multivar. Anal.* **1**, 445–456 (1971).

72. Rao, C. R., Estimation of variance and covariance components in linear models, *J. Am. Stat. Assoc.* **67**, 112–115 (1972).

73. Rao, C. R., Recent trends of research work in multivariate analysis, *Biometrics* **28**, 3–22 (1972).

74. Rao, C. R., *Linear Statistical Inference and Its Applications,* 2nd ed., Wiley, New York, 1973.

75. Rao, C. R., Unified theory of least squares, *Commun. Stat.* **1**, 1–8 (1973).

76. Richardson, D. H., and D. Wu, Least squares and grouping method estimators in the errors in variables model, *J. Am. Stat. Assoc.* **65**, 724–749 (1970).

77. Roy, S. N., *Some Aspects of Multivariate Analysis,* Wiley, New York, 1957.

78. Roy, S. N., R. Gnanadesikan, and J. N. Srivastava, *Analysis and Design of Certain Quantitative Multiresponse Experiments,* Pergamon, New York, 1971.

79. Scheffé, H., *Analysis of Variance,* Wiley, New York, 1959.

80. Seal, H., Studies in the history of probability and statistics XV. The historical development of the Gauss linear model, *Biometrika* **54**, 1–24 (1967).

81. Searle, S. R., *Linear Models,* Wiley, New York, 1972.

82. Shepard, R. N., The analysis of proximities: Multidimensional scaling with an unknown distance function I, *Psychometrika* **27**, 125–140 (1962).

83. Shepard, R. N., The analysis of proximities: Multidimensional scaling with an unknown distance function II, *Psychometrika* **27**, 219–246 (1962).

84. Shepard, R. N., A. K. Romney, and S. B. Nerlove, *Multidimensional Scaling,* Vols. 1 and 2, Seminar Press, New York, 1972.

85. Spearman, C., General intelligence objectively determined and measured, *Am. J. Psychol.* **15**, 201–293 (1904).

86. Spearman, C., The proof of measurement of association between two things, *Am. J. Psychol.* **15**, 72–101 (1904).

86a. Spearman, C., Correlation calculated from faulty data, *Br. J. Psychol.* **3**, 271–295 (1910).

87. Spent, P., A generalized least-squares approach to linear functional relationships, *J. R. Stat. Soc., Ser. B*, 278–297 (1966).

88. Spent, P., *Models in Regression and Related Topics,* Methuen, London, 1969.

89. Srivastava, J. N., Some generalizations of multivariate analysis of variance, in *Multivariate Analysis* (P. R. Kirshnaiah, ed.), Academic, New York, 1966.

90. Srivastava, J. N., On the extension of the Gauss-Markoff theorem to complex multivariate linear models, *Ann. Inst. Stat. Math.* **19**, 417–437 (1967).

91. Student, The probable error of a mean, *Biometrika* **6**, 1–25 (1908).

92. Swamy, P. A. V. B., *Statistical Inference in Random Coefficient Regression Models,* Springer, New York, 1971.

93. Tatsuoka, M. M., *Multivariate Analysis: Techniques for Educational and Psychological Research,* Wiley, New York, 1971.

94. Theil, H., *Principles of Econometrics,* Wiley, New York, 1970.

95. Timm, N. H., *Multivariate Analysis with Applications in Education and Psychology,* Brooks-Cole, Belmont, 1975.

96. Walker, H. M., *Studies in the History of Statistical Methods,* Williams and Wilkins, Baltimore, 1929.

97. Wilks, S. S., Certain generalizations in the analysis of variance, *Biometrika* **24,** 471–494 (1932).

98. Wishart, J., The mean and second moment coefficient of the multiple correlation coefficient in samples from a normal population, *Biometrika* **22,** 353–361 (1931).

99. Wold, H., *Econometric Model Building. Essays on the Causal Chain Approach,* North-Holland, Amsterdam, 1964.

100. Wold, H., *Bibliography of Time Series and Stochastic Processes,* Oliver and Boyd, Edinburgh, 1965.

101. Wood, F., and C. Daniel, *Fitting Equations to Data,* Wiley, New York, 1971.

102. Wright, S., On the nature of size factors, *Genetics* **3,** 367–374 (1918).

103. Yule, G. U., On the theory of correlation, *J. R. Stat. Soc.* **60,** 812–854 (1897).

104. Yule, G. U., On the theory of correlation for any number of variables, treated by a new system of notation, *Proc. R. Soc. London, Ser. A* **79,** 182–193 (1907).

105. Yule, G. U., and M. G. Kendall, *An Introduction to the Theory of Statistics,* 4th ed., 5th printing, Griffin, London, 1973.

*Neil H. Timm*

# COURTS

## HISTORY

### General

The legal profession is traditionally *one* of the most conservative, if not *the* most conservative of the elements in any culture. Substantive changes to laws and legal procedures are difficult enough: the changes to court procedures in either civil or criminal jurisdictions are even more complicated.

It is not difficult to understand, then, that acceptance of technology as a means to easing some of the problems encountered in the system is slow. Perhaps the first widespread use of computers by the law profession was, as in many other professions or businesses, in the bookkeeping and accounting phases of maintaining an office and its staff. As the "computer" assisted the lawyers in keeping their accounts up to date, they, perhaps, began to see the potential of rapid data calculations and routine printouts developed from the memory core. In this way the evolution of the computer into a vital professional tool has occurred.

The natural reluctance of people to embrace enthusiastically a new procedure or tool supposedly designed to assist them is, of course, based on the potential threat to the individual of that new procedure or tool. No one can predict what will happen to the normally delicate balances painstakingly developed among elements, groups, and individuals in any system which might well be thrown awry and cause hardships upon implementation of some change. This is a natural reaction. With the inherent deeply conservative attitudes of the law profession, the direct confrontation by the computer with legal problems and their solution was impossible. The first intentional use of the computer by the legal profession in a legal format was in the late 1950s in analyzing legislation.

At the University of Pittsburgh's Health Law Center, the director and staff were asked to assist a Pennsylvania legislator to make a phrasing change to the statutes. The change desired was from "retarded child" or ". . . children" to "exceptional child" or ". . . children." The phrasing "retarded child" or ". . . children" occurs across the entire scope of the statutes: statute areas on shoes, schools, and safety are examples of where the term was already used. Thus each statute from the time of the state's entry into the Union had to be read if the phrasing was to be changed.

The standard means for accomplishing such changes in the past had been to contract for a number of law students who would read all the legislation and record the areas where change was necessary. Control of the results of their reading was a great problem and errors were frequent. The Health Law Center began the task in the standard manner. One of the staff members, having had some computer experience, recognized that a computer would make no mistakes once the statutes were in memory.

Thus their final solution was to accumulate all the statutes in full text for computer use; and by programming for the phrase "retarded child" all the areas using that phrase were immediately available to the legislators. This task was completed and is now recognized as a legal profession milestone in the use of technology.

Upon its inception and completion, the legislators realized that a data base and thus a legislative drafting and modification tool was now available to them on the basis of this one problem. Based on this recognition, a meeting of lawyers took place in 1959 at Lake Arrowhead, California whose purpose was to examine and prepare for the computer's influence on the law. Discussions took place as to the appropriateness of computer usage in the law and whether or not the use of full text was necessary. The full text system compared to symbolic representation (or shorthand) means a substantial cost differential; however, any standardized language becomes highly restrictive to the legislative prerogatives.

A second conference took place at Lake Arrowhead in 1961 and aided in further stimulating the experimentation in use of computers by the legal profession begun by the earlier conference. Attendees now included symbolic logicians and experts in computers who received, perhaps, more recognition at this second conference.

Experimentation by various state and national groups progressed on a national basis across a wide scope of contributors. Among these were several different approaches which had diverse theories on the problem solution, and included:

1. The Southwest Legal Foundation in Dallas, Texas. A root-word system was the fundamental concept interfacing with the full text. This technique attempts to overcome some of the synonym problems found in a pure full text system where case use is the objective and graded word meanings have little use.

2. At the University of Oklahoma, a points-of-law system was developed wherein an in-depth index using Boolean logic formed the data base assembly mechanism. This system, refined and updated, has become the primary counterpoint to the full text data base. Proponents of the points-of-law contend that the "sense" of the legal thinking in a court case is more vital than the words used. Thus the point being made, as compared to the large amount of synonymous verbiage, is important. Legislators have the opposite problem where the words used can be selected carefully, and thus a full text system has the advantage.

3. The Internal Revenue Service implemented a system known as R.I.R.A. (Reports and Information Retrieval Activity) in the early 1960s which is a computer-maintained index with microfilm lookup of legal, factual, and procedural positions of the I.R.S.

4. There were several relatively small experiments using computer technology which are important in the sense that these added to the momentum of the profession's slowly increasing interest in technology. Projects such as the police departments' cooperation in cross-referencing of suspects, stolen property, etc. further exposed lawyers to the use of computers (New York City, Chicago, and other Police Departments are specific examples). In addition, Project LEX under the Department of Justice is useful to note in that the system was primarily an indexing system using the computer card-sorting format for retrieval of information.

5. At the Yale Law School, Professor Layman Allen began experimenting with the computer as an analytical tool instead of merely as a data retrieval or accumulation tool. Allen was perhaps the first lawyer to publicly propose the use of computers beyond the mere data base concept.

6. In California, Reed Lawlor experimented with the forecasting or predictive aspects of the computer's data base. The predictions centered about the decisions of judges, and quite naturally this became a controversial use of the computer. No one, and particularly judges whose decisions are so public, likes to feel that considerations other than those specified in an opinion enter the decision-making capability. Nevertheless, there is empirical evidence that decisions of the court can be predicted by "mapping" all positive and negative aspects of each element of the court's activities.

7. Still in the early 1960s, a joint effort by the American Bar Foundation and IBM evaluated the various indexing systems for cases and legislation then

being experimented with in the nation. Finding all existing systems wanting in one way or another, IBM developed a new approach. The concept centered about the information retrieval from the full text of legal matters, but in addition weighted and ranked aspects of language, syntax, and phrasings within the opinions as written by the legal minds involved. The system met varying degrees of success [1] and was never fully evaluated.

8. Several organizations, developed during the 1960s, built upon their computer skills to provide legal services to states or courts. Included in these are: the Aspen Corporation, an outgrowth of the University of Pittsburgh's Health Law Center; and the OBAR Corporation, which was most prominent for its very large data base.

9. Finally, significant computer usage is evident in the federal courts as well as state and local levels. The Federal Judicial Center is the research and development arm of the federal court system and is administered under the United States Supreme Court in Washington, D.C. Analysts at the center developed COURTRAN, a name given to a computer software system which provides information support services for court management and for analysis and evaluation of court procedures and processes. Major features of COURTRAN are a language for handling court transactions, modular programming, an expandable file structure, and modifiable external dictionaries and tables for information elements. There are presently four versions of COURTRAN: criminal operational, criminal research, civil operational, and civil research. The system was designed to be operated in federal courts by court personnel to serve local case management information needs and to provide a means of transferring local court data into a national statistics system. Plans call for implementation of both civil and criminal operational versions of COURTRAN in a number of the larger federal district courts and for extensive use of both research versions in the Federal Judicial Center. Information products of the COURTRAN system include periodic administrative reports, such as indices and inventories of pending and closed cases, case status reports for each judge and each court, monitoring reports for use in managing scheduled events, and monthly judicial statistics reports used by the Administrative Office of the United States Courts in compiling national statistics [2]. In addition, there are several special reports which are used by research specialists in modeling the stochastic processes of case flows in the courts.

There have been two commercial systems developed for research by private practitioners. The LEXIS system by Mead Data Central is an adaptation of the OBAR project and is an on-line, real time, full text system. Westlaw is an adaptation of the QUICLAW project developed at Queens University and uses the on-line, full text searching method for searching headnotes.

In its LITE project (Legal Information Through Electronics) the United

States Air Force adopted the University of Pittsburgh's system for purposes of searching legislation, comptroller general opinions, and other documents relevant to their research needs.

## Major Milestones

With all of these experiments by the legal profession in the use of the computer, there was still no significant use of the computer by the courts except in very peripheral support functions. Slowly, as the mystique of the computer dissipated and the analysis of courts became of extreme interest to the public in general, lawyers saw the computer as a tool in assisting them to understand the problems in the courts.

The mass of data, however, threatened inundation of the judicial study centers which sprang up around the nation. The study of statistics became the means to court systems analysis, and the use of computers became an almost obvious innovation, not only for static problems but eventually for the more dynamic as well.

The first recorded use of computers by a court for direct impact on a case decision was in a tax case before the Fifth Circuit Court in early 1966.[1] This milestone case was presided over by Judge John Robert Brown, who in deciding the case wrote a concurring opinion. In arriving at the decision, Judge Brown received approval from the United States attorney to search, via the R.I.R.A. system, for materials determining the interface of state and/or federal laws on the case at hand. The determination that federal law did not impact on this case was important and the task of so proving was immense as Judge Brown so stated:

> The task of searching tens of thousands of cases pending within the Internal Revenue Service and parallel court structures presenting an almost infinite number of legal decisions would have been both impracticable and impossible but for the machine. The machine, suspect as it is for the supposed lack of judgmental capacity essential to adjudication, bears out again the hopes and predications now bearing fruit in a variety of ways that it serves a useful, indeed perhaps an indispensable, function in the judicial process as the world, and the people in the world, face the increasing complexities of an expanding social and economic structure.
>
> John Robert Brown
> Judge
> 5th Circuit Court of Appeals

Perhaps the next most significant impetus for use of computers by courts was an indirect one. In the mid-1960s, as the federal government became intensely interested in the proliferation of crime, the President's Commission on Law

---

[1] *First National Bank of Birmingham* v. *United States*, 358 F.2d 625.

Enforcement and Administration of Justice completed its study in 1966 and published its report in early 1967 as *The Challenge of Crime in a Free Society* [3]. The importance of this commission is that a Task Force on Science and Technology was organized as a subcommittee to the commission. For the first time the federal government actively sponsored the use of a computer in a sophisicated manner to analyze a court system. Through Monte Carlo techniques and the use of a standard simulation language, the Institute for Defense Analysis was able to simulate the activities of a criminal justice system. Results indicated no significant problems in using similar computer analysis techniques in civil court analysis.

However, the Institute for Defense Analysis encountered critical problems in time and funds allotted them for their task. The success they experienced is perhaps best manifested by the research funds since provided by the National Institute for Law Enforcement and Criminal Justice. This arm of the Law Enforcement Assistance Administration (LEAA) has become one of the focal points for research in law. LEAA was established by the Omnibus Crime Control and Safe Streets Act of 1968, Public Law 90–351, and administered by the Department of Justice.

Following the establishment of this research arm, several projects were funded which resulted in at least exposing if not completely solving the extreme complexity of the criminal justice system in quantitative terms. Quantification of the problems becomes necessary in order to apply modern management and systems analysis techniques. Two separate counties or court jurisdictions may have apparently completely separate systems established using legal terms and processing steps which do not appear to be synonymous, yet are governed by the same state statutes and rules of procedure. Appearances may be extremely deceiving, however, and a mere comparison of court annual reports is not sufficient to reflect comparability. The need for advanced methods became patently obvious with the Crime Commission's Task Force on Science and Technology where voluminous data became unmanageable using previously routine analysis techniques.

The computer as the only vehicle capable of assimilating and manipulating large amounts of data across a broad scope of parameters became an essential tool. The Institute for Defense Analysis demonstrated this, and the analytical facet of the computer as compared to the function of information retrieval received final recognition.

**Advanced Data Retrieval**

In the late 1960s several large and complex judicial jurisdictions began to formulate computer-oriented functions. Among these, the New York State Information and Identification System was successfully established as a state-wide information sharing system. In 1968 the LEAA gave substantial impetus to the coordination of states' information systems through funding of Project SEARCH (System for Electronic Analysis and Retrieval of Criminal Histories).

This program is continuing to coordinate the large and complex data requirements for the nation.

The National Bureau of Standards developed several studies using the computer to run statistical comparisons of criminal court data. Thus statistics became another necessary tool to the analyst. Although this tool had been recognized as necessary, the extent and complexity of the statistical base had been largely overlooked in the search for "hard" data.

Various criminal courts in the nation received LEAA grants to study their complex court functions, and the computer became the assumed vehicle assembling the data. The RAND studies done in New York City on the Criminal Courts of Manhattan are examples of this work.

In the civil courts, this same impetus toward analysis has not developed. The reason for the criminal justice use of the computer and thereby the funding support provided by the Justice Department through its LEAA subordinate is no doubt based mainly on the public's outcry concerning the increase in crime.

**Administrative Data Needs**

Data inputs were limited up to this time to criminal histories, facts, decisions made, etc., which were then, on analysis approval, subjected to statistical tests (see below). The initial modeling work done by the Institute for Defense Analysis in the mid-1960s using Monte Carlo techniques was not pursued to a great extent for several years due to the primary concern with information gathering and retrieval functions requiring large computer memory facilities.

Slowly, however, high level analysts recognized that the computer had many advantages to offer the court system manager and not just the statistician or analyst. The control function of any manager is vitally dependent on proper, timely, and truly representative information derived from large amounts of data. As the manager receives this information (as now distinct from data), the allocation of resources among facilities, staff, and equipment is made simpler in the decision- making process. Demands for new buildings, additional judges, or administrative support staff or equipment needs could be better evaluated if the computer could be provided work measurement data, economic costs and projections, forecasts of population mobility, industrial expansion possibilities, and so forth. Seemingly all of the societal elements affecting the public's need for the legal profession might be computerized to assist the court managers in allocating the increasingly restricted primary resource—money.

As management control lost its novelty as a term in the legal profession, the police and lawyers in the courts speculated upon and began investigations on the use of computers to aid in the administrative control and supervision of caseloads. Thus theorizing on areas such as continuance granting, court calendaring, probable-cause hearing routines, and plea bargaining format now became subject to quantitative analysis and, at the extreme, even simulation. Many legal scholars have written at length about these problems, developing theoretical cause and effect relationships and establishing procedures for improving the legal or time aspects problem. These theories then become subject to validation.

These two frames of reference, legal functions and time required to process, have been the criteria normally used to critique the system. The computer has been seen as having a direct impact on the time aspect: data transmittal would be facilitated by computers as compared to the delivery of paperwork by mail or messenger delivery, and the administrative tracking and supervision of caseloads is simplified by computer monitoring of data input.

However, the computer's impact on legal functions such as modifications to existing laws and protection of the rights of the accused or the state is much more indirect. Interpretation by lawyers of the computerized information provided by the daily routine of the court is probably the primary computer use in this function. Examples of the results gained by this procedure involve changes to the grand jury system in the District of Columbia as suggested by the Institute for Defense Analysis [4] study in 1967, and changes to the plea bargaining procedures and elimination of motions for continuance prior to arraignment as suggested by the LEADICS [5] study in 1972. These modifications to court procedures were a result of lawyer groups interpreting data and suggesting means to improving the legal aspects of the procedures.

As the control aspect of the criminal justice oriented computer has emerged, judges, court staffs, and administrators have recognized the value of the computer as a tool in the improvement of court activities management. In this way the reduction of delay and the refinement of legal interpretations are direct results of technological assistance.


## STATISTICAL ANALYSIS REQUIRED OF COURT DATA

### General

Only with extensive knowledge can rational decisions be reached concerning the operation of a complex system. In many situations this information is in the form of "hard data" or statistics. These data are measures of various variables or parameters which characterize the system components. For example, the number of arrests is one measure of police activity. Since court systems change with time, differ from location to location, and operate on a demand basis in response to a varied human populace, justice system's operations are essentially irregular, random, or stochastic. No two court trials are ever identical. Consequently, a study of courts, civil and criminal, must involve the use of statistics and statistical analysis.

Another form of randomness can occur in any study of this nature—that of observational errors. Records are not always error-free, not all are similarly organized, and occasionally some are not even available. Because system operation is inherently stochastic, because of observational error, and because some systems are exceptionally complex, methods of statistical inference form an important component of a court system study. The basic goal of a statistical inference is to discover obscured underlying patterns and relationships among the variables which characterize the system. For example, it may not be evident to the people working in the court system, such as judges and prosecutors, that the assignment of bond is prejudicial toward some class of the accused, for example, women. It is within the province of methods of statistical inference to display a relationship among variables such as sex and amount of bond. On the other hand, a relationship or system characteristic may be known to exist or merely suspected. Here the use of statistical inference is to provide evidentiary support for a preconceived notion. In general, the goals of statistical methods are not only to uncover systematic variations of system operation but to also attach some measure of significance or confidence to the inference.

In almost every application of statistical analysis from the simple computation of averages to dynamic modeling of stochastic processes, the digital computer is indispensable. The following sections outline the particular applications of computer technology and statistical analysis to the study of court systems.

**Data Sampling**

Applications of statistical analysis have been enhanced in many fields of study, including court systems, because of the availability of computers. The obvious advantage of computer usage is the ability to perform many calculations, using multitudes of data. For many reasons (economy, availability, efficiency) however, it is generally better to collect as little data as possible, but to choose it wisely. This is one of the first areas where a researcher in court systems encounters the theory of statistics, specifically that of sampling theory [6].

Statistical sampling techniques are useful in at least two fundamental problem areas of studying court systems. These are in the selection of sample sizes and in the elimination of biased data. The most common criterion for establishing the size of a sample (how many courts should be included?, how many cases?, what time interval should be covered, etc.) is that the number of items or units sampled should be a minimum while still retaining sufficient levels of reliability or confidence. In this way the sample statistics accurately represent the system being studied. In order to determine effectively a sample size, it is necessary to acquire or assume some *a priori* knowledge of the statistical nature of the units under study. In most situations, previous, similar studies in other jurisdictions or some general knowledge of the same jurisdiction is sufficient. For example, suppose it is desired to determine the length of time a certain court system takes to reach a disposition following the date of arrest in cases involving armed robbery. It is extremely useful in this situation to know that this court system (or any similar court system) disposes of 90% of all types of cases within 1 year following arrest. The assumption can then be made that the average number of days from arrest to disposition for armed robbery cases in this jurisdiction is less than 365 days. Furthermore, the range (smallest value to largest value) of the sample will be near 365 days.

Statistical sampling is largely a means of reducing the amount of time for data gathering and analysis to manageable levels. With the use of computers, particularly where all court records are automatically computerized, random, partial sampling is minimally necessary since the entire population of data is available on the computer. Comprehensive computerization of court records is only beginning [7], however. Furthermore, some court activity is never recorded (on computers or otherwise) such as the amount of time an individual judge or attorney spends in a given court room, so some sampling will always be necessary.

Bias in the collection of statistical data can arise by inadvertently gathering all or a large portion of the data under common conditions of system operation. For example, in determining the fraction of arrests made in a given police jurisdiction for indecent exposure, a researcher might examine all arrest records for a 1-month period. If the monthly period chosen is January and the jurisdiction is in a colder climate, the results may be significantly different than if the month chosen was July. This is a seasonal bias. However, perhaps a ''warm-weather sample'' is actually preferable. In this instance, a randomly chosen sample of four of the weeks from a 13-week period during June, July, and August is better. An example of a particular sampling scheme in a study of the amount of time judges spend in court in Chicago is given in Ref. 8; other examples are given in Ref. 9.

The number of items needed for a reliable sample depends heavily on the statistical distribution of the variables being sampled. If the distribution is broad, a large number of samples is necessary. In sampling, some typical variables associated with crime and court systems such as time durations (number of days from arrest to dispositon, days from trial to sentence) and the amount of bond, it has been found that the distributions can be very broad [5]. It is not unusual to find that variance is equal to or greater in magnitude than the mean. The implication of this is that sample sizes must be large, making it imperative to use computers for data handling and analysis.

**Data Summarization and Presentation**

There exist many techniques for conveying statistical information. These can be grouped into three categories depending on the level of the complexity of the statistical analysis: in all cases the computer is extremely useful. These three are the presentation of:

1. Raw data
2. Statistical summaries such as means, variances, and correlation coefficents
3. Conclusions from statistical inference techniques

In many cases it is desirable or essential to present tables of data collected in a court study. If the data are stored on magnetic tape or punched cards, the computer can easily be used to select and categorize. Direct reproduction of computer output lists for publication is labor-saving and convenient. At this level there is almost no "statistical analysis."

At the next level of statistical sophistication, averages, medians, variances, standard errors, ranges, coefficients of variation, correlation coefficients, etc. are taken from the data. All of these are obtained by relatively simple numerical computations. They give an indication of the general nature or trend of large amounts or portions of data. Again, automatic computation of these quantities by the digital computer is extemely convenient. Furthermore, sample distributions can be summarized in the form of histograms, or, using curve-fitting techniques, the actual statistical distributions can be graphed. The latter can be done either in the form of cumulative distribution functions [4] or as probability density functions or both [10]. In the last reference, graphical displays generated by computer printout are used directly.

The third level of data presentation is a communication of the results of studies using methods of statistical inference rather than a presentation of data summaries. Here the value of the computer lies primarily in performing the calculations associated with the corresponding statistical method. These are discussed more fully in the next section.

## Statistical Analysis

The following paragraphs illustrate some of the particular questions answered by statistical analysis. They also briefly explain some of the more common techniques.

Following data collection, the researcher of a court system has at his disposition large amounts of data usually stored on a magnetic tape or on punched cards. These data are usually organized in a selected frame of reference according to units such as individual cases, courts, and crime. The variables associated with each unit might be type of crime, defendant characteristics, legal representation (retained or appointed lawyer), type of court (magistrate, superior, supreme), significant dates in the legal process, and so forth to achieve a complete profile of the case or other frame of reference.

The researcher, in a well-planned study, has specific questions to answer and uses the data to support or deny certain hypotheses. The data are used to determine the existence of interrelationships among variables. For example, it might be found that cases handled by public defenders are less likely to involve plea bargaining and, more often than not, involve a client not released on bail. Not only are relationships between variables identified but many statistical methods determine a measure of the degree of the interrelationship. Furthermore, a level of confidence is associated by the method to the conclusions drawn. One thing statistical methods cannot do is identify cause and effect.

## Specific Statistical Concepts

### Hypothesis Test

A hypothesis test is a direct comparison of some quantity, usually the average, between two categories of data. For example, the conviction rate for those accused of homicide in one jurisdiction can be hypothesized to be the same as that for another jurisdiction. Based upon the data, this hypothesis is either rejected or accepted at a given level of significance. Usually, the data are assumed to have a normal distribution for this test but this assumption may need testing.

### Goodness-of-Fit Testing

In many court studies it is either desirable or necessary to determine if the data closely follow a classical probability distribution. Some typical distributions are the normal, exponential, $\chi^2$, and Poisson.

Although several procedures are available for testing how closely a sample distribution agrees with a specified theoretical distribution, the $\chi^2$ test [11] is most commonly used for that purpose. This test is usually not reliable for samples containing fewer than 40 observations; however, the Kolmogorov-Smirnov test [12] and the Cramer-von Mises test [13] are both suitable for small samples in testing for agreement with the normal distribution.

The Kolmogorov-Smirnov test [12] requires the assumption that the population mean and variance are known and that the probability distribution under test is continuous, although these assumptions can sometimes be relaxed.

Although the techniques for goodness-of-fit testing are conceptually quite straightforward, the sheer volume of work involved with examining typical court systems data is most forbidding. Phillips [15] has developed a completely computerized procedure for goodness-of-fit testing. The researcher can select from the $\chi^2$, Kolmogorov-Smirnov, Cramer-von Mises, or moments tests, and compare sample distributions with any one of ten probability distributions, including the Poisson, exponential, normal, gamma, Weibull, lognormal, uniform, triangular, $\chi^2$, and Erlang distributions. All instructions for using the program are set forth in Ref. 15. The application of this program should greatly simplify and hasten work by court researchers in the area of goodness-of-fit testing.

### Correlation and Regression

Regression and correlation are potentially two of the most useful statistical tools for court systems researchers. Regression can be employed to describe the relationship between some court performance parameter, $y$, and some decision variable, $x$. Correlation is then used to measure the adequacy of this description.

For example, Katkin [16] employed regression and correlation to examine the relationship between trial time, $y$, and the number of witnesses, $x$, for six different felonies.

The simplest regression form is the linear model given by

$$y = b_0 + b_1 x$$

To develop such a relationship requires at least two data points $(x_i, y_i)$, but usually several points are taken. The "least-squares" method [17] is then used to determine the regression coefficient $b_0$ and $b_1$. These coefficients, which describe the "best line" through the data, can be tested for significance.

An easier method for assessing the adequacy of the linear regression model is to evaluate the sample correlation coefficient, $r$. This coefficient is dimensionless and carries the same sign as the regression coefficient, $b_1$, above. Values of $r$ near the extremes $-1$ or $+1$ indicate strong correlation between the varibles $x$ and $y$ for the sample, while values near zero signify little correlation. The coefficient $r$ can be tested for statistical significance using a $t$ test for normal populations.

It is often necessary to examine the dependency of a performance parameter, $y$, on several decision variables simultaneously. In the Katkin example [16], it might become important to test the relationship between trial time, $y$, and the number of "professional" witnesses, $x_1$, the number of "eyewitnesses," $x_2$, and the number of defendants, $x_3$. The multilinear regression model for this situation is then:

$$y = b_0 + b_1 x_1 + b_2 x_2 + b_3 x_3$$

Even more sophisticated court systems research could conceivably involve the estimation of nonlinear regression models. Draper and Smith [17] provide an excellent treatment of these.

The role of the computer in regression and correlation analysis ranges from that of a convenience, as in simple linear regression with few data points, to a necessity with complex models involving many data points. Certainly, the availability of computers should encourage the extensive utilization of regression and correlation in court studies.

### Contingency Tables—Independence of Factors

A statistical technique that is very useful for court systems analysis is that of the "contingency table." This technique is typically applied to hypothesis testing of the independence of two or more different factors affecting a population of items or cases. For each factor a given item (case) falls into a specific classification. Suppose that a researcher wants to test the hypothesis that the outcome of a felony case is independent of the nature of the charge. The several classifications of the "outcome" factor are, perhaps, Dismissal, Plea of Guilty, Verdict of Guilty, and Verdict of Not Guilty. The classifications of the "charge" factor might be Murder, Rape, Assault, Burglary, etc. A given case will fall within a specific cell in the contingency table: for example, the outcome Verdict of Guilty for the charge Burglary.

The test assumes a null hypothesis that the factors or variables are mutually independent. The results of the test indicate whether or not the data support acceptance or rejection of the hypothesis for a given level of significance.

## Factor Analysis

In situations involving many variables it often happens that some variables naturally group together or associate. These variable groups can sometimes be distinguished as separate "factors" which collectively influence the system. For example, it is reasonable to expect that variables associated with the police and bail-setting procedures would influence pretrial activity. Variables associated with the jury, trial judge, and sentencing procedures are more likely to influence posttrial activity.

Two fundamental techniques categorized as Factor Analysis have been developed to study variable groupings, one known as the Method of Principal Components and the other known as Factor Analysis [18]. The former gives rise to factors which are mathematically unique. Moreover, a computer program is available to carry out Factor Analysis by the Method of Principal Components. [19].

The LEADICS project [5] utilized Factor Analysis by the Principal Components Method to study criminal case processing in two urban counties in Indiana. The volume of data, involving over 2000 cases, necessitated considerable use of the digital computer. The results of the Factor Analysis study are given in Ref. 20.

## Analysis of Variance

Another statistical technique which could have significant importance in court systems studies is that called Analysis of Variance [21]. This technique is often employed as a means of detecting differences among the means of several populations in the presence of experimental "error." Consider the example wherein a court systems researcher wants to determine if there is a significant difference in the duration of case processing between cases in which counsel is retained and those in which counsel is appointed. This experiment would treat a single factor, that is, the method by which counsel is acquired, and two qualitative levels within that factor. The experiment would proceed by randomly selecting a sample of $n_1$ cases which are identical in every conceivable aspect that could affect case processing time and in which counsel is retained by the defendant(s). Another random sample of $n_2$ cases would be selected which are similarly identical, but in which counsel is appointed. The case duration in each category is recorded. The Analysis of Variance procedure is then invoked to separate the "within-category" variation from the total variation, the remaining variation being attributable to the difference between retained and appointed counsel. An hypothesis test is employed: the null hypothesis stating that there is no difference between the two mechanisms for acquiring counsel.

There are procedures for examining the effects of multiple factors as well as qualitative or quantitative levels within factors. One limitation of this technique is its requirement for "homoscedasticity of variance"; that is, the variances for the several samples must be equal. Given this condition, the technique is very useful.


## MODELS

### General

The term "model" is often used in the applied sciences without careful attention to its meaning. Intuitively, most technical specialists regard a model as any construction which helps in understanding the behavior of a subject. Unfortunately, in this usage, the term is probably a misnomer, for model has as its well-identified lingual meaning that upon which something else is patterned. From the vantage point of language, therefore, a court system model is that to which every exemplary court system should aspire instead of that which resembles court system behavior. A better term is facsimile, which clearly connotes the idea of being a copy. Nonetheless, the term model is firmly entrenched and will be used here in the sense of the technical specialist.

A court system model is any representation of the workings of a court. In this general sense, even a newspaper editorial on courts would serve as a model, though qualitative, thereof. Physical scientists have carried the concept of model making almost to its quantitative limits. They can do so because of the fact that devices which are solely physical, faithfully repeat their activities whenever the surrounding circumstances remain unchanged. Between these two extremes lies a wealth of model-making possibilities, parameterized by the degree to which quantitative methods are employed. It is in this middle ground where the specialist models a court system, and so it is evident that different researchers will impose various levels of quantitative structures on their court model in accordance with their assessment of the court as a working entity. Thus a unique court model is not to be expected, although one model may have advantages over another model with regard to a particular insight. The early value of a court model is determined primarily by its correspondence to fixed public records; the ultimate test of a court model is its ability to give genuine service in resolving the issues at hand.

The first step in modeling a court system is to make an exhaustive and careful study of the way in which the court system works. In contrast to the painstaking and precise observations often possible in the physical sciences, learning the intricacies of a court system is to a large extent possible only through qualitative assessments built up by interviewing court personnel. This process usually culminates in a pictorial diagram of some type, as for example the flow chart described below. The fine edge to which a court system model may eventually come is, of course, largely determined by the detail which goes into flow-chart construction. Selection of such detail is to a large extent straightforward; thus, for example, there is no need to study management operations within a prosecutor's office if there is no intent to make any recommendations thereon. Even courts in jurisdictions of small population are involved in a process beginning with accusation and ending with disposition; simplistic treatments of court systems often overlook myriad nontrivial steps, and thus court system flow charts are complex at best and extremely large-scale at worst.

The second step in modeling a court system is to determine a feature, or features, of it in such a way that questions which have prompted the study may be well described. Though important features, such as constitutional safeguards or individual rights, may be paramount, it is often necessary to reflect these features indirectly in terms of a parameter such as time. From this point of view an efficient court system could perhaps be regarded as one which moves defendants rapidly enough to protect the public interest but slowly enough to protect the rights of the accused. Though economics certainly plays a role, and though thousands of court questions can be examined in reasonably simple court models, it is now evident that time is going to be a very influential parameter in detailed court system models.

As a third step, data must be collected in order to provide information on each operation shown in the flow chart with respect to features chosen for emphasis. Unlike the case of the physical sciences, the court system is typical of many social systems with the property that any data gathered are exactly that in the public records. Experiments to uncover data not in the public record will generally be impossible for constitutional, legal, economic, and even ethical and political reasons. Examination of the public record associated with the various operations in a court system tends to support the choice of time as a principal parameter for the court model, for one of the most common entries in the record is the sequence of dates on which various steps in the process were made. It is the limitation fixed upon data collection by virtue of it all being confined to the public record which finally tends to act as a natural selector on court system models. (See below.)

Once flow charts, features, and data have been determined, the last ingredient necessary to compose a court system model is to establish a suitable logic within which these items may display their interrelations. In the last analysis this logic tends to be the electrical logic of a modern digital computer. Nonetheless, the digital computer grinds so exceedingly fine that there is room for considerable latitude in the choice of a larger, more encompassing logic. The choice of a system of logic depends for the most part upon how a given specialist chooses to reflect the simple fact that, no matter how refined the flow chart, no matter how simple the features, no matter how complete the public record, there is no certitude concerning what will happen tomorrow in the court. In applied science this difficulty is frequently called the "sensitivity" of a court system model to parameter uncertainty. The available logics for coping with uncertainty are relatively few in number; moreover, they all tend to be confounded somewhat by the aforementioned intermediate quantitative behavior of court systems. Placing

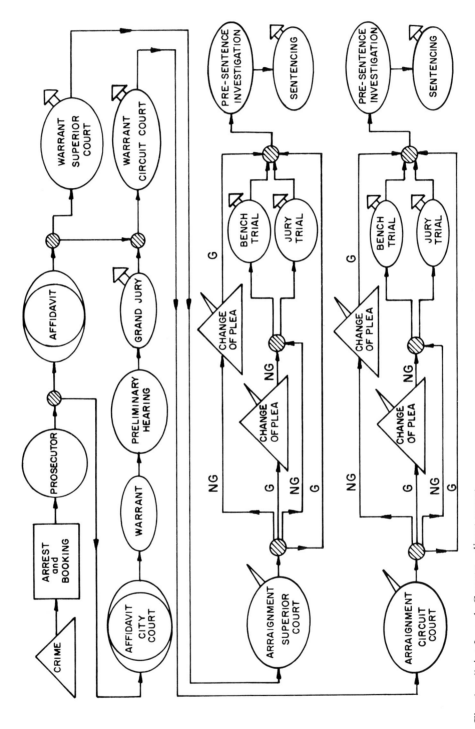

**Fig. 1.** Saint Joseph County—direct arrest.

a logic is therefore a challenging task, and two approaches representative of the state of the art are described herein.

## Specific Court System Models

The aggregate of court system flow chart, court system features such as time, the public records of law enforcement agencies such as prosecutors and courts, together with a logic to knit the whole together, is what is hereinafter called a court system model.

Consider now an illustration of a specific flow chart, as shown in Fig. 1. This is the sequence of steps which may be followed by an accused who is arrested in the commission of a criminal offense in St. Joseph County, Indiana. Each flow-chart operation is explained symbolically in Table 1. Though specific in nature, as all examples are, Fig. 1 is somewhat representative of many other court jurisdictions as well. If time is accepted for illustrative purposes as a feature of primary interest, then a cursory examination of Fig. 1 shows that, for purposes of time studies, a number of modifications would be most helpful. Such modifications may, of course, be regarded as the expected preliminary integration of flow-chart and feature selection with a view toward final court system model construction.

Figure 2 is a network diagram or revised flow chart for the court system of

**TABLE 1**
Network Diagram Nomenclature

| | |
|---|---|
| A-B$^a$ | Arrest-booking |
| Aff | Affidavit |
| Arr | Arraignment |
| BT | Bench trial |
| Cap | Capias |
| CP | Change of plea |
| Cr$^a$ | Crime |
| GJ | Grand jury |
| IA | Initial appearance |
| JT | Jury trial |
| MC | Master commissioner |
| PSI | Pre-sentence investigation |
| S | Sentence |
| T | Trial |
| War | Warrant |
| ○ | Node |
| ◯ | Probability block |
| ▢ | Function block |
| ▶ | Exit from system |

$^a$ E.g., Cr/A-B means lag from Crime to Arrest-booking.

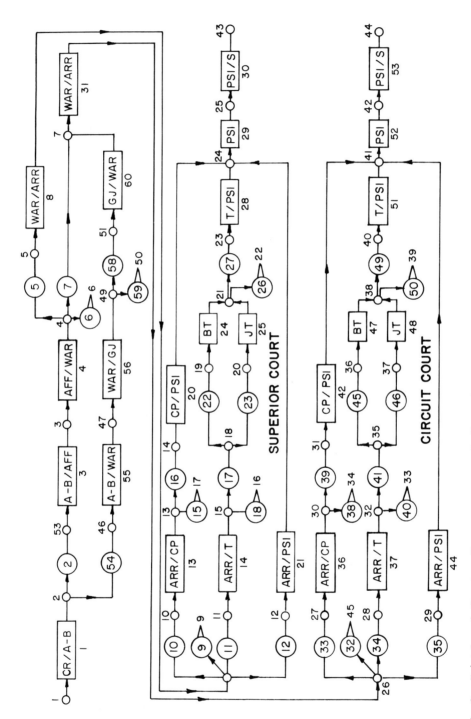

**Fig. 2.** Saint Joseph County—direct arrest (network diagram).

Fig. 1 and for the principal feature, time. Circles with integers outside designate events in the court system, such as trial or sentencing. Rectangular boxes refer to time intervals between events. Circles with integers inside should be understood as rectangular boxes with zero time intervals. These latter entities, called probability blocks in Fig. 2, merely measure the chance that a given court case will pass that way. Accused persons may exit from the system as solid arrow symbols.

As is apparent from Fig. 2, questions of choosing a logical framework for a criminal court system model are influenced essentially by two factors. The first factor concerns the choice of representation of a single rectangular block: the second factor concerns the choice of representation of the connections among blocks. Insofar as the latter issue is concerned, the main problems with connections arise when there is a closed path or loop of them. The search for overall relationships in the court model is notably complicated by such phenomena. An example showing how this could happen in a court system is easily brought forth by considering the chance that an accused is arrested again immediately upon leaving the court; another example is recidivism. Generally speaking, logics for relating flow charts, features, and data do not differ appreciably in their basic method of addressing connections. However, there may be indirect influences on the connection issue because of different methods possible for choosing a single block representation. Fig. 3 indicates such a single block. From the standpoint of giving a reasonable reflection of what has been done with regard to describing single blocks in the criminal justice system model, it is sufficient to divide all of the approaches into two categories. Colloquially, these two categories have come to be called Monte Carlo techniques and analytical techniques.

The adjective "Monte Carlo" is normally applied to those methods which cope with the uncertainty problem by regarding each block as a random variable before inferring any statistical results. There are presently a large number of Monte Carlo-type computer languages available for use in studying court systems. Examples are GPSS, GERTS, and SIMSCRIPT.

Monte Carlo approaches are very flexible in addressing court system questions. In effect, this flexibility leads to the possibility, at least in concept, of giving an "atomic"-type description of a court. A particularly interesting feature of the Monte Carlo method in court systems is its ability to give information about queues occurring at entries to principal functions and thus to provide help in determing whether government should supply more capital for courtrooms or more salaries for additional court officers. Tools as flexible as many of these Monte Carlo-based languages require, of course, that the user have his own capability to specify the minute detail necessary to integrate a court system model on the computer. Thus they may be most suitable for jurisdictions having a staff with hard technical expertise. Moreover, the possibility of the user interacting with the model is thereby somewhat decreased, at least insofar as legal personnel are concerned.

There is no shortage of examples using Monte Carlo technology to study court systems. Morin [22] has made such a model in which the effects of adding judges

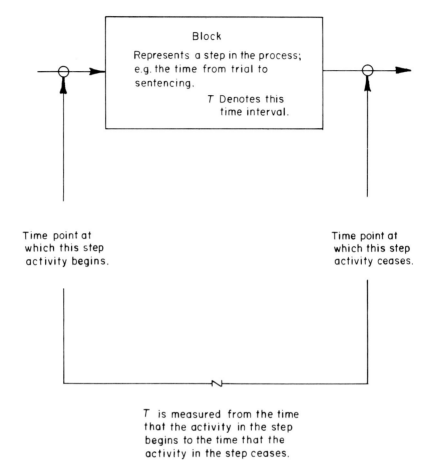

Fig. 3.   Single block representation.

to the Criminal Division of the Circuit Court of Milwaukee County, Wisconsin were examined. Lutz and Metcalf [23] applied GERTS in a study of judicial time required for alcohol-related cases associated with motor vehicles in the Municipal Court of Record in Oklahoma City. Hogg, DeVor, and Handwerker [24] have applied such a model to data for Champaign County, Illinois.

In an overall court system operation, Biles [25] used GERTS to study the time delay mechanisms in typical Indiana criminal courts. More recently [26] he has tried the same technique to study delays in several federal court systems dealing with both civil and criminal cases separately. A classic study of the entire court system was done by Taylor et al. [4] in the District of Columbia. Using GPSS, special emphasis was placed on total time to disposition, time intervals between major events, and potential delay areas. Simulations attempted to simulate the real system and hypothesize organizational changes. Many recommendations were made to the President's Crime Commission.

The Monte Carlo approaches, by virtue of their fine detail possibilities, gain great versatility at the cost of requiring considerable technical expertise. In contrast, analytical approaches seek to place more mathematical relationships on the model; analytical models are, therefore, generally less flexible than their Monte Carlo counterparts. However, the added mathematical logic present in analytical court models often permits more specific conclusions and more pointed observations. A single block in an analytical court model is usually described by a mathematical function constructed from the data associated with that block. Unlike the functions used in Monte Carlo models, though, the analytical model functions are not repeatedly sampled as random variables but are added and cascaded as entities in their own right during model operations. Historically, the application of analytical techniques in large-scale system models, of which the criminal court is an example, has been limited primarily because of the rapidly growing complexity of cascaded functions and because of the connection loop problem described in preceding paragraphs. On the other hand, analytical techniques offer, precisely because they have additional mathematics structure, considerably enhanced possibilities for understanding what the courts have done, what they are now doing—the so-called state of a court system—and what they may do in the foreseeable future.

From the mathematical viewpoint the function cascade difficulty can be ameliorated by applying the concept of a quotient. Intuitively, the mathematical quotient idea applied to, say, the trial-to-sentencing interval in a court system consists in "dividing" the total information about the interval into important information and lesser information. The line of demarcation can be placed wherever the user wishes, with the obvious understanding that the greater the information deemed important, the greater the computer requirements and the greater the computer operating costs. In principle, all available information can be regarded as important, at the greatest possible cost. Many court administrators do make decisions, however, on the basis of less than total information. To be useful in modeling a court system, a quotient must be compatible with large-scale systems. Further, it is very helpful if the quotient reduces the loop connection problem.

An example of such an analytical model of the criminal court system is given by the LEADICS study [5] conducted by engineers and lawyers on the St. Joseph County, Indiana criminal court system of Fig. 1. In this application the function constructed for each single block was a staircase function which rises one step each time a data point is encountered. Such a staircase function having, as is always true in the public record, a finite number of steps, it is uniquely related to the moments of the data. The mathematical quotient can be accomplished on the data moments, with the user keeping as many as he feels are significant. Illustrating the assertion that analytical models have a capability to provide certain specific conclusions not readily available in Monte Carlo runs, this model has a decided propensity to identify accumulation points of delay in the criminal court system. Such a notion corresponds rather closely to the idea of modes of behavior in the physical sciences. Moreover, the LEADICS quotient operation makes every criminal court model with connection loops mathematically equivalent to one without connection loops. It is perhaps of interest to observe that studies in these "court-system sciences" suggest that the classical statistical moment constructions, which have been displaced in the hard sciences by maximum likelihood estimation, may turn out to be well suited for such social system studies as those in the criminal court.

It should be observed that both Monte Carlo and analytical court models depend heavily for their utility on the assumption that each single block operates in a way that is essentially independent of the other blocks. Present tests indicate that this is indeed the case, and the balancing forces concept of government seems to assure the continued validity of the assumption. This is fortunate, for there seems to be little chance in this generation of a model logic to be effective in a highly coordinated court system.

## Simulation

By simulation of a court system is meant the use of a computer to exercise the model for purposes of emulating, verifying, interpolating, and extrapolating the behavior of the actual system under study. Using definitions already discussed, certain of the entities called facilities make up the static structure of the model, whereas dynamic entities called transactions "flow" through the system as a function of time. The computer provides the capability for storing the model and its associated data base and for producing a printed output of selected data generated by exercising the model over a specified period of time. A computer language is the vehicle used in communicating the model to the computer and in controlling the simulation.

In the simulation of a court system model such as Fig. 1, the Superior Court, the Circuit Court, and the Grand Jury are static entities or facilities, and the time intervals required for processing cases are attributes. The cases themselves are the dynamic entities or transactions which flow through the court system. Each case can have a number of attributes including the names of the defendants, the type of the crime, and date of arrest. Within a period of several minutes the computer can simulate the activity of the court system over a period of months or years. By modifying the structure and data base of the model and studying the results of the computer simulation, the investigator can develop a model which is optimal with respect to defined performance criteria.

Selection of a computer language for simulation of a court system is affected by the nature of the system under study, the complexity of the model, and the characteristics of the desired output data. A detailed account of the history and general properties of computer languages is given in Ref. 27 along with short examples of simulations using DYNAMO, GPSS, SIMSCRIPT, SOL, MILITRAN, SIMULA, and OPS. Reitman [28] devotes an entire text to the computer simulation of discrete systems.

Simulation languages may be divided into two classes: continuous and discrete. Those of the continuous class, such as CSMP, MIMIC, and DYNAMO, are used to simulate systems in which the variables are continuous functions of time. The languages of the discrete class, including all of those mentioned in the preceding paragraph, are used to simulate systems in which events occur at discrete instants in time. Only the discrete class has been used to any extent in the simulation of legal systems.

Simulation languages can be further classified as either event-oriented or block-oriented. Event-oriented languages, such as SIMSCRIPT and GASP, require the programmer to write a computer subprogram for each type of event which may occur in the simulation. This approach allows great flexibility at the cost of longer program development time. The block-oriented languages, such as GPSS, GERTS, and LEADICS, are programmed by specifying the topological interconnections of functional blocks and their associated parameters. These languages facilitate programming and interactive computation at the expense of flexibility.

Another dichotomy contrasts simulation languages by their mode of execution by the computer, i.e., interactive or batch-processed. An interactive language is designed so that execution is controlled by the user from a video or typewriter terminal. It allows the operator to change the model configuration and parameters, and to observe immediately the corresponding model output. A batch-processed language allows no intervention by the user once the program has been initiated. It does allow, however, for production of copious output data on a high-speed line printer. All of the languages discussed are available for batch-processing. In addition, interactive versions of GPSS [29] and LEADICS are currently in use.

**Basic Approach**

As referenced above, there are two basic approaches for generating solutions in a simulation: Analytical and Monte Carlo. In the Analytical method, all desired outputs are generated during a single run of the system being simulated during a specified time interval. All of the continuous simulation languages use the Analytical method by solving the mathematical equations associated with the model.

In contrast, the Monte Carlo approach, used in most of the discrete languages, accumulates statistical data by exercising the model through several hundred runs in order to produce a single output table. In this technique, random number generators are used in accordance with specified probability distributions to originate transactions in the model and to regulate their flow through the system. On the basis of relative frequency of occurrences, the computer program can calculate the percent utilization and average service time of facilities, average transition times for transactions, average length of queues, average waiting time in queues, etc. The program can also report the maximum and minimum length of queues and histograms of selected variables.

READY
BLOCK DIAGRAM ANALYSIS PROGRAM FOR POLYNOMIAL TRANSFER FUNCTIONS
MAXIMUM NUMBER OF BLOCKS OR NODES = 150
MAXIMUM NUMBER OF PARAMETERS PER BLOCK = 10
MAXIMUM TOTAL NUMBER OF PARAMETERS = 1000
OPTIONS
 0**TRANSFER FUNCTION
 1**TRANSFER PERMANENT FILE TO TEMPORARY FILE
 2**PRINT CONFIGURATION AND PARAMETER DATA
 3**CHANGE CONFIGURATION DATA
 4**CHANGE PARAMETER DATA
 5**CHANGE SCALE DATA
 6**TRANSFER TEMPORARY FILE TO PERMANENT FILE
 7**READ DATA FROM CARDS
TYPE OPTION NO.
1
PERMANENT FILE TRANSFERRED TO TEMPORARY FILE
TYPE OPTION NO.
2
TYPE FIRST AND LAST BLOCK NOS.
50  53

CONFIGURATION DATA

| BLOCK NUMBER | INPUT NODE | OUTPUT NODE |
|---|---|---|
| 50 | 38 | 39 |
| 51 | 40 | 41 |
| 52 | 41 | 42 |
| 53 | 42 | 44 |

PARAMETER DATA

| BLOCK NO. | PARAM | PARAMETERS, CONSTANT TERM FIRST | | | | |
|---|---|---|---|---|---|---|
| 50 | 1 | 0.416700E+00 | | | | |
| 51 | 1 | 0.100000E+01 | | | | |
| 52 | 10 | 0.100000E+01 | −0.184667E+02 | 0.206540E+03 | −0.458264E+04 | 0.662288E+05 |
| | | −0.859983E+00 | 0.987407E+07 | −0.100398E+09 | 0.911182E+00 | −0.745144E+10 |
| 53 | 10 | 0.100000E+01 | −0.195867E+02 | 0.142725E+04 | −0.137172E+06 | 0.110677E+08 |
| | | −0.737687E+09 | 0.417030E+11 | −0.204589E+13 | 0.886254E+14 | −0.343556E+16 |

TYPE OPTION NO.
TYPE INPUT AND OUTPUT NODE NOS.
2  36
TRANSFER POLYNOMIAL FROM NODE 2 TO NODE 36
PATH 1 CONTAINS BLOCKS 2  3  4  7  31  34  37  41  45
PATH 2 CONTAINS BLOCKS 54  55  56  58  60  31  34  37  41  45
TOTAL TRANSFER POLYNOMIAL, WITH CONSTANT TERM FIRST, IS
    0.201236E−02   −0.618567E+00   0.129788E+03   −0.235494E+05   0.405090E+07
    −0.677032E+09   0.109196E+12   −0.169083E+14   0.249862E+16   −0.350551E+18
TYPE TITLE (UP TO 80 CHARACTERS)
8 august 1973 test run 1
DENSITY PLOT? 1=YES,  2=NO
2
CUMULATIVE PLOT?  1=YES,  2=NO

**Fig. 4a.**  Example of an interactive simulation (LEADICS [5]). Extracted from a computer printout.

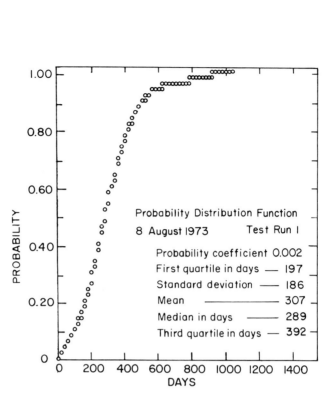

**Fig. 4b.** Probability distribution function.


## Examples

In order to demonstrate both of these approaches, two specific examples of the application of block-oriented simulation languages for this study of time delays in criminal courts are given here: the first uses the interactive version of LEADICS [5], the second uses GERTS [25].

The LEADICS example, shown in Figs. 4a and 4b, demonstrates interactive exercising of the St. Joseph County Court system model of Fig. 1. All of the configuration data and the parameter data corresponding to the network diagram of Fig. 2 are stored in the computer with catalog name FILE3. The LEADICS interactive program is stored with catalog name NDLAW. The user types NDLAW FILE3 to initiate the working session, and the computer responds as shown by listing the available options and by prompting the selection of an option. The operator can construct an entirely new model in a temporary file and exercise that model, or he can retrieve the model from the permanent file and exercise it with or without modifications. In this example a listing of a portion of the data from FILE3 is requested, and the unmodified model is exercised to find time delay information between nodes 2 and 36, that is, between arrest-booking and bench trial in Circuit Court. The computed data is displayed graphically by a cumulative probability function, and is summarized in terms of the mean, standard deviation, quartiles, and probability coefficient. The numerical data indicates that two out of a thousand cases (probability coefficient) would arrive

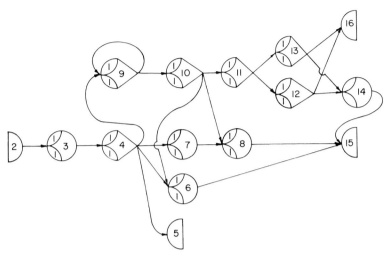

**Fig. 5.** GERTS-III model of the time delays in a criminal justice system.

TABLE 2

Node Descriptions; e.g., Criminal Justice Problem

| Node | Event description |
|------|-------------------|
| 2 | Criminal act; node 2 is the source node |
| 3 | Arrest and booking |
| 4 | Arraignment |
| 5 | Case dismissed at arraignment; sink node |
| 6 | Pre-sentencing investigation initiated and date of sentencing scheduled based on a plea of guilty as charged |
| 7 | Defendant pleads guilty to a lesser charge |
| 8 | Same as 6 for defendant who pleads guilty to a lesser charge |
| 9 | Pre-trial motion for a defendant who has pleaded not-guilty to the original charge |
| 10 | Final decision for change-of-plea for a defendant who has pleaded not-guilty to the original charge |
| 11 | Defendant elects trial by jury or bench trial |
| 12 | Conclusion of bench trial |
| 13 | Conclusion of trial by jury |
| 14 | Pre-sentencing investigation initiated and date of sentencing scheduled for person found guilty in trial |
| 15 | Sentencing completed for person guilty as charged; sink node |
| 16 | Case dismissed from person found not-guilty in trial; sink node |

at bench trial in Circuit Court after an average elapsed time of 307 days (mean), and that 25, 50, and 75% of these cases would have completed this transition in 197, 289, and 392 days, respectively (quartiles).

The second example [25], shown in Fig. 5, is an application of a batch-operated, Monte Carlo language GERTS-III to the simulation of time delays in a fictitious court system. The court is modeled by the network diagram of Fig. 5, where the numbered nodes represent corresponding events as tabulated in Table 2, and the interconnecting branches denote activities as listed in Table 3. The statistical results from running 5000 simulated cases through this system are tabulated in Table 4. The data show, for instance, that 7.18% of the cases (359/5000) reach the conclusion of a bench-trial (node 2) in a mean time of 371 days, with minimum and maximum times of 33 and 1227 days, respectively. This

**TABLE 3**
Activity Descriptions; e.g., Criminal Justice Problem

| Activity number | Start node | End node | Distribution type | Activity description |
|---|---|---|---|---|
| 1 | 2 | 3 | Exponential | Pre-arrest investigation |
| 2 | 3 | 4 | Exponential | Pre-arraignment investigation |
| 3 | 4 | 5 | Constant | Case dismissal |
| 4 | 4 | 6 | Exponential | Activity leading to plea of guilty as charged |
| 5 | 4 | 7 | Exponential | Activity leading to plea of guilty of a lesser charge |
| 6 | 4 | 9 | Exponential | Activity leading to pre-trial motions for defendant pleading not-guilty |
| 7 | 9 | 10 | Exponential | Activity leading to final decision on plea |
| 8 | 9 | 9 | Exponential | Another pre-trial motion |
| 9 | 10 | 6 | Exponential | Same as activity 4 |
| 10 | 10 | 8 | Exponential | Same as 5 |
| 11 | 10 | 11 | Exponential | Activity leading to selection of trial method |
| 12 | 11 | 13 | Exponential | Activity leading to trial by jury |
| 13 | 11 | 12 | Exponential | Activity leading to bench trial |
| 14 | 12 | 16 | Constant | Verdict of not-guilty |
| 15 | 12 | 14 | Exponential | Activity leading up to pre-sentence investigation |
| 16 | 13 | 16 | Constant | Same as 14 |
| 17 | 13 | 14 | Exponential | Same as 15 |
| 18 | 14 | 15 | Exponential | Pre-sentence investigation |
| 19 | 8 | 15 | Exponential | Same as 18 |
| 20 | 7 | 8 | Exponential | Same as 15 |
| 21 | 6 | 15 | Exponential | Same as 18 |

**TABLE 4**
GERT Simulation Example[a]

| Node | Probability | Mean | Standard deviation | Number of observations | Min | Max | Node type |
|---|---|---|---|---|---|---|---|
| 5 | 0.1030 | 55.8314 | 39.0777 | 515 | 2.2712 | 247.8532 | F |
| 15 | 0.8170 | 227.5358 | 188.7725 | 4085 | 7.0400 | 1466.4517 | F |
| 16 | 0.0800 | 357.1028 | 221.9979 | 400 | 33.2050 | 1153.8481 | F |
| 14 | 0.1594 | 379.3220 | 219.5564 | 797 | 61.7204 | 1465.2947 | F |
| 13 | 0.1676 | 339.6292 | 215.8571 | 838 | 34.2747 | 1402.1372 | F |
| 12 | 0.0718 | 371.9331 | 225.4666 | 359 | 33.2050 | 1227.3831 | F |
| 11 | 0.2394 | 341.2625 | 219.1144 | 1197 | 29.3181 | 1402.0813 | F |
| 10 | 0.3956 | 130.1507 | 66.2519 | 1978 | 8.9889 | 582.5098 | F |
| 9 | 0.3956 | 86.6684 | 51.6433 | 1978 | 1.3462 | 421.2109 | F |
| 8 | 0.2946 | 267.9875 | 192.2332 | 1423 | 27.4226 | 1204.1936 | F |
| 7 | 0.2088 | 269.4048 | 206.6633 | 1044 | 8.4858 | 1146.8127 | F |
| 6 | 0.3730 | 109.8849 | 67.1848 | 1865 | 1.9066 | 557.6580 | F |
| 4 | 1.0000 | 55.9304 | 40.8573 | 5000 | 0.1457 | 302.8931 | F |
| 3 | 1.0000 | 19.9622 | 20.2124 | 5000 | 0.0058 | 203.9314 | F |

[a] Final results for 5000 simulations.

program also generates histograms, not shown here, which give a more detailed account of the statistics at each node.

### Simulation Languages

GPSS and SIMSCRIPT are the most widely used discrete simulation languages. SIMSCRIPT II.5 [30] is a general high-level programming language with features found in PL/I and ALGOL as well as the simulation capabilities. GASP-II [31] is a FORTRAN-based discrete event simulation language, and GASP-IV is an extension of this including the capacity for simulating continuous systems. GERTS is a block-oriented stochastic network modeling program based upon GASP. QGERTS is an extension of GERTS to include queueing capabilities. All of these languages should be considered as possible candidates in the development of simulations for legal systems and all of them are, of course, computer oriented.

## THE FUTURE

As the National Crime Information Center has been a prelude to the data banks for criminal histories being developed by each state, so the computer usage by courts today is merely a prelude to its use tomorrow. Specific uses for the computer are: calendaring of court dockets; "tracking" of all cases—misdemeanor, felony, or traffic violations—so that control of the court activities can be managed properly; correlating of multiple charges so that the quality of justice is improved; performance evaluation of lawyers, police, judges, and prosecutors through monitoring of motions for continuance, change of venue, or other activities; and the very important reduction in multiple record keeping which is all too often highly repetitive. The analysis of court data is just beginning as of the early 1970s, and computer simulation of courts will very likely increase until basic problems have been researched.

There are problems. How much of the individual criminal's history should be made available to the court (judge and jury) and at which stages of the trial? When does the computer's data bank infringe on individual rights? How "secure" can the data bank be made so that unauthorized entry to obtain information or modify the data is minimized? These and other questions have yet to be answered by the courts as they begin to use this tool of the technician interfacing with a complex societal function.

## REFERENCES

1. American Bar Foundation/IBM Report, Published in 1969.
2. J. L. Ebersole and J. A. Hall, COURTRAN: *A Modular Management Information and Research System for Courts,* presented at the International Symposium on Criminal Justice Information and Statistics Systems, 1972.

3.  *The Challenge of Crime in a Free Society*, A Report by the President's Commission on Law Enforcement and Administration of Justice, U.S. Government Printing Office, Washington, D.C., 1967.

4.  *Task Force Report: Science and Technology*, President's Crime Commission Report, Washingtion, D.C., 1967.

5.  Daschbach et al., *Systems Study in Court Delay:* LEADICS, Report to the National Institute for Law Enforcement, University of Notre Dame, Grant No. NI-70-078, January 1972.

6.  W. G. Cochran, *Sampling Techniques*, Wiley, New York, 1953.

7.  *Designing Statewide Criminal Justice Statistics System—The Demonstration of a Prototype*, Technical Report No. 3, Project SEARCH, California Crime Technological Research Foundation, Sacramento, California 95814, 1970.

8.  R. Simon and P. R. Oster, Judges on bench 2 3/4 hours a day, *Chicago Sun-Times*, January 20, 1974.

9.  E. Nilsson et al., *Studying Criminal Court Processes: Some Tools and Techniques*, NBS Report 10 528, June 1970.

10. M. K. Sain, E. W. Henry, and J. J. Uhran, An algebraic method for simulating legal systems, *Simulation* (1973).

11. W. G. Cochran, The $\chi^2$ test of goodness of fit, *Ann. Math. Stat.* **23** (1952).

12. F. J. Massey, The Kolmogorov-Smirnov test for goodness of fit, *J. Am. Stat. Assoc.* **4** (1951).

13. D. A. Darling, The Kolmogorov-Smirnov, Cramer-von Mises test, *Ann. Math. Stat.* **28** (1957).

14. E. S. Pearson and H. O. Hartley, *Biometrika Tables for Statisticians*, Vol. 1, Cambridge University Press, New York, 1929.

15. D. T. Phillips, *Applied Goodness of Fit Testing*, Monograph No. 1, Operations Research Division, American Institute of Industrial Engineers, Atlanta, Georgia, 1972.

16. R. Katkin, *Courtroom Scheduling*, presented at 43rd National Meeting, Operations Research Society of America, Milwaukee, 1973.

17. N. R. Draper, and H. Smith, *Applied Regression Analysis*, Wiley, New York, 1966.

18. H. H. Harman, *Modern Factor Analysis*, University of Chicago Press, Chicago, 1967.

19. *System/360 Scientific Subroutine Package, Programmer's Manual*, International Business Machines.

20. R. M. Brach and D. R. Sharpe, *Statistical Analysis of Type of Counsel and Plea Bargaining in Criminal Court Systems*, Proceedings of the 3rd Annual Pittsburgh Systems Simulation Conference, University of Pittsburgh, 1972.

21. H. Scheffé *The Analysis of Variance*, Wiley, New York, 1959.

22. T. L. Morin, Optimization models and the administration of justice, in *Proceedings of the Sixth International Conference on Systems Sciences*, University of Hawaii, Honolulu, 1973.

23. R. P. Lutz and J. G. Metcalf, *Application of* GERT *to a Municipal Court System*, presented at 44th National Meeting, Operations Research Society of America, 1973.

24. G. L. Hogg, R. E. DeVor, and M. Handwerker, *Analysis of Criminal Justice Systems via Stochastic Network Simulation*, presented at 44th National Meeting, Operations Research Society of America, 1973.

25. W. E. Biles, *A Simulation Study of Delay Mechanisms in Criminal Courts*,

presented at 41st National Meeting, Operations Research Society of America, 1972.

26. W. E. Biles, *Systems Analysis Applied to Justice in Federal District Courts,* RANN Research Grant No. GI38979, 1973–75.

27. J. E. Sammet, *Programming Languages: History and Fundamentals,* Prentice-Hall, Englewood Cliffs, New Jersey, 1969.

28. J. Reitman, *Computer Simulation Application,* Wiley, New York, 1971.

29. GPSS/NORDEN *Simulation Language,* National CSS, Stamford, Connecticut, 1971.

30. Kiviat, Villanneva, and Markowitz, SIMSCRIPT *II.5 Programming Language,* Consolidated Analysis Centers, Los Angeles, California, 1973.

31. A. A. B. Pritsker and P. J. Kiviat, GASP II, *A* FORTRAN-*Based Simulation Language,* Prentice-Hall, Englewood Cliffs, New Jersey, 1969.

## BIBLIOGRAPHY

Brice, B., Data processing for law office management, *Jurimetrics J.* **9,** 202–206 (June 1969).

Clark, S. H., *Criminal and Juvenile Courts in Mechlenburg County, North Carolina: Measurement and Analysis of Performance,* Mecklenburg Criminal Justice Pilot Project, University of North Carolina, Chapel Hill, July 1972.

Elmaleh, J. S., Project Clam—Computer application to legal methodology, *Jurimetrics J.* **9,** 23–30 (1968–1969).

Freed, R. N., Computer law searching: Problems for the layman, *Datamation* (October 1967), at 38–41.

Katz, L., L. Lutwin, and R. Bainberger, *Justice is the Crime: Pretrial Delay in Felony Case,* Case Western Reserve University Press, Cleveland, 1972.

Locke, J. W., *et al., Compilation and Use of Criminal Court Data in Relation to Pre-Trial Release of Defendents: Pilot Study,* NBS Technical Note 535, August 1970.

Peterson, N. D., Notes on computers and legal research, *Pract. Lawyer* (November 1967), at 47, 48, 57–70.

Steighner, Pennsylvania legislative data processing center, *Public Automation, Output* (July 1968).

Trigg, C. D., Computers in state legislatures, *Public Automation, Output* (June 1968).

U.S. Department of Health, Education and Welfare, *Records Computers and the Rights of Citizens,* Report of the Secretary's Advisory Committee on Automated Personal Data Systems, July 1973.

Walsh, B., *Data Base—The Concept, The Commitment,* Paper presented to the Data Base Management Evaluation Panel-CAUSE, New Orleans, Louisiana, December 1973.

*James M. Daschbach*

*William E. Biles*

*Raymond M. Brach*

*Eugene W. Henry*

*David T. Link*

*Michael K. Sain*

*John J. Uhran, Jr.*

# CRIME

## INTRODUCTION

Crime is a natural accompaniment to the use of computers in view of the increasing application of computer technology to sensitive functions in a society where crime continually flourishes. The crimes associated with computers are common crimes: fraud, theft, vandalism, larceny, extortion, embezzlement, and industrial espionage. The environments, methods, kinds of losses, and the occupations of the perpetrators associated with computer-related crimes make such crimes new in terms of deterrents, detection, prevention, control, and recovery of the objects of the crimes. So as to eliminate consideration of the traditional forms of crime, it is more useful, therefore, to consider the general problem of computer abuse. To do so makes discussion of the problem more straightforward, since it avoids any need for defining crime, a subject of great complexity and much debate.

The general definition of computer abuse is derived from the initial attempt at definition in a study of computer abuse published at Stanford Research Institute in 1973 and funded in part by the National Science Foundation.[1]

Highly publicized incidents of computer abuse over the past few years, including fraud, embezzlement, thefts, vandalism, and terrorism, clearly indicate a social problem in the use of computers. This has also been suggested by legislative responses, such as the Privacy Act of 1974 (Public Law 93–579), controlling the use of computers. The extent of computer involvement in unlawful, antisocial, and unethical acts is not known with any useful degree of precision. A series of small research projects has been conducted to assess this problem empirically. Documents reporting incidents involving computers have been collected by the author on an informal basis since 1965. Research was started at the Stanford Research Institute (SRI) in 1970. The purpose of the research has been to document the existence of a problem, investigate the nature of that problem, perform an assessment, and apply the results in an empirical manner to the planning and development of computer security. This research has been performed to aid development of safe use of computer technology and effective evaluation of improved safeguards.

Considerable resources have been invested in the development of computer security, but until now work has been primarily based on a theoretically conceived and perceived problem. No other empirical research has been performed on computer abuse. However, Brandt Allen at the University of Virginia has collected and reported on financial fraud and embezzlement cases

[1] Any opinions, findings, conclusions, or recommendations expressed in this paper are those of the author and do not necessarily reflect the views of the National Science Foundation.

[1]. John R. Schultz of the U.S. General Accounting Office, Division of Financial and General Management Studies, is completing a study on computer fraud in the federal government. Three trade books have been written on computer crime that treat the issue in a popular, nontechnical manner [2, 4, 6]. Another trade book documents the Equity Funding Corporation of America fraud that partially involved computers [10]. A trade book on computer abuse, including a number of detailed case studies, was published in June 1976 [7].

The goal of this project is to develop both practical perspectives of the problem and empirical approaches for control and prevention of computer abuse. This is being done by developing a data base of information on reported cases of losses involving intentional abusive acts associated with computers. The data base is being used to develop a typology of the problem and a taxonomy of threats to define and analyze the problem, to support hypotheses and conjectures developed from studying actual experience, and to apply this new knowledge to deterrents, accountability, prevention, control, detection, recovery, and prosecution. The goal is to provide methods to make computer technology reasonably safe from abuse without needing to limit applications of the technology because of a lack of adequate safeguards. This article describes the technological and operational aspects of computer abuse. Another part of the project, presented in other writings, is concerned with juridical aspects.

The value of the research results is limited by the extent to which the data base of reported cases represents all cases. Conclusions must be based on the universe of the sample rather than the total universe of experience. Applying the conclusions to cases beyond those represented by the sample is subject to statistical uncertainty.

## COMPUTER ABUSE

Computer abuse is a term that covers a broad range of incidents. In this project the primary criterion for selecting incidents has been their function as a source of knowledge that can be used in attempts to eliminate computer-related intentionally caused losses. Computer abuse is any intentional act in which one or more victims suffered, or could have suffered, a loss, and one or more perpetrators made, or could have made, gain. The incident must be associated with computer technology or its use. A spectrum of acts covers the most severe case in which a perpetrator is convicted of a felony to the most innocuous case in which a perpetrator might be chastised by a superior or his peers. This range includes criminal acts, acts that result in civil suits, acts that result in termination of employment or contracts, and acts that result in business or personal disputes.

Incidents of white-collar crime, vandalism, and malicious mischief are included, as well as a few cases in which computers have been used as instruments in planning violent crime such as robbery. Also, a few cases involved international espionage that might not be called white-collar crime. Crime is not a well-defined term in criminology. Types of crimes and their names vary among legal jurisdictions, and white-collar crime has been defined in various ways. For the purposes of this exposition on computer abuse, a definition of white-collar crime taken from the science of criminalistics will suffice:

> Any endeavor or practice involving the stifling of free enterprise or the promoting of unfair competition; a breach of trust against an individual or an institution; a violation of occupational conduct; or the jeopardizing of consumers and clientele [3].

One or more of the following four roles of computers apply to computer abuse:

1. A computer can be the *object* of an act. In four cases, computers have allegedly been shot with guns. The computer as an object exists in 28% of the sample cases of computer abuse, although in many of the cases other roles might have existed.
2. The computer can be the basis for a unique *environment* in which an act occurs, or be the source for unique forms of assets. For example, computer programs, unique products of computer technology, represent entirely new types of assets subject to loss. About 61% of the sample cases involved computers in this role, although many may have the following two roles (3 and 4) present as well.
3. A computer can be the *instrument* of an act. For example, in one reported case a computer was used by an embezzler to simulate the operations of his company to plan and regulate his embezzlement. Only 3% of the sample included this type of role exclusively.
4. A computer can be used as a *symbol* to intimidate or deceive. A dating bureau falsely advertised that it used a computer to match the characteristics of potential dating partners. Only 9% of the sample cases included this role exclusively.

This definition is purposely broad because leeway is needed in these early stages of the research. New types of acts may be discovered that are not anticipated, especially with the rapid advancement of the technology. For example, electronic funds transfer systems and violations of the Privacy Act of 1974 will most likely generate new kinds of frauds and other violations of law. As another example, most organizations using computers view most computer programs developed for their own use and crucial to their business as being safe from theft. Nobody else could profitably use the same program. However, denying the use of these programs by the victim as a means of extortion has been overlooked. The computer-abuse study resulted in the discovery of this problem. In one verified case a programmer completed a set of programs and confiscated all copies of them, including the documentation, in an attempt to extort $100,000 from his employer for their safe return.

Early in this research, we found that terms such as "computer crime" and "antisocial use of computers" were too restrictive and constrained by the difficult sociological problems associated with crime and antisocial behavior. The purposes of the research might otherwise be diverted to purely social or legal issues, thus limiting the effort to address the problem in a multidisciplinary fashion in computer technology, sociology, and law.

Arguments have been made that such cases as the Equity Funding Insurance fraud [5] should not be included in computer abuse, since that fraud was a major crime committed by top management, and computers were not the focus of the planning and perpetration of the fraud. However, computers facilitated the large volume of fraudulent acts in producing and maintaining 64,000 fake insurance policies, and computers played a role in aiding the deception of the external auditors. A significant amount of knowledge is being gained from studying this case that contributes to safer ways of using computers. Therefore, it is included in the data base but excluded from loss totals. Any case is added to the file if knowledge can be gained from study of it to make computers safer to use.

## DATA-BASE TYPOLOGY

The data base of computer abuse consists of documents describing 381 cases that occurred from 1958 through October 1975. The collected documentation for each case ranges from a short paragraph in a newspaper article to several thousands of pages of documents, including newspaper and magazine articles; victim, perpetrator, and prosecutor interview notes; police and auditor investigation reports; and legal documents including arrest warrants, search warrants, charges, depositions, convictions, opinions, and court transcripts. The data were gathered from scanning news media, using a news clipping service, copying from legal and private files, and engaging in conversations and interviews with case participants. Approximately 20 cases have been investigated in depth by field interviews of victims, perpetrators, witnesses, investigators, and prosecutors. Authorizations to interview prisoners in state and federal penal institutions were obtained, and three perpetrators were interviewed while incarcerated.

Field investigations were concentrated in the New York City, San Francisco Bay, and Los Angeles regions. Several brief investigations were made in European cities. Cases were chosen for field investigation where the opportunity to gather detailed information seemed most promising to investigators and the information to be gained had the greatest potential for application to the safe use of computer technology and insights on applicable legal issues.

Seventy-one cases were reported in the form of returned questionnaires filled out by recipients of a report, *Computer Abuse* [8], documenting the first year of the research. Information gathered in several cases is private because victims and perpetrators agreed to provide the information only if they would not be indentified. Other content of the data base is in the public domain and available for inspection.

The data base is believed to represent a nearly exhaustive collection of all computer abuse that has been reported in the public media since 1965. Table 1 shows the distribution of 375 cases by source to October 15, 1975. The large number reported in *Computerworld* is because of this trade newspaper's practice of searching for cases, primarily from newspapers through clipping services. A

**TABLE 1**
Sources of 375 Cases to October 15, 1975

| Source | Number of cases |
|---|---|
| Questionnaires | 71 |
| *Computerworld* trade newspaper | 71 |
| Newspapers, newsletters | 76 |
| Private sources (letters, conversations) | 62 |
| Magazines, journals | 43 |
| Books | 22 |
| Speeches | 13 |
| Law enforcement agencies | 13 |
| Unpublished documents | 4 |
| Total | 375 |

number of cases found in newspapers and newsletters were subsequently reported in *Computerworld* but are attributed to newspapers and newsletters as the first source in which they were found.

It is conjectural as to what proportion of the total known cases this sample represents. Several Certified Public Accountants have indicated that they know of many confidential cases among their clients that have never been revealed to police agencies or the public and not included in the computer-abuse data base. Most universities and colleges have cases perpetrated by students, but only 70 were included in the computer-abuse data base. Many more cases can be found and included if resources to find them become available. Also, many more cases could be found by seeking case histories of white-collar crime where related data could have been stored or produced in computers. This type of case is discussed below. For now, the computer-abuse data base must be treated only as a sample of known cases where the computer has played a significant role. Business disputes over computer products and services where the types of products and services would make no substantial difference to the issues of the dispute are not included in the study. Possible biases of the sample are identified below.

Verifying the known cases and improving the accuracy of reported case information is a continuing activity. Verification is measured in five confidence levels. A case is verified at Level 1 if legal or law enforcement agency documentation exists and is sufficient to identify the method of procedure and role of computer technology in the case; at Level 2 if a description of the act has been obtained by a computer-abuse project staff member, directly from at least one reliable case participant or other reliable person if that person has supplied names of case participants; and Level 3 if a reliable public or trade media report exists that identifies the victim, and named investigating officials were quoted describing an accomplished act or stating official disposition of the case. Cases are not verified but counted at Level 1 if a reliable public or trade media report of a case identifies the victim; or at Level 2 if a reliable public or trade media report describes a plausible case but without naming a victim. About 77% of the cases are verified, and distribution by level of verification is as follows:

*Verified Cases*

| | |
|---|---|
| Level 1 | 40 |
| Level 2 | 150 |
| Level 3 | 105 |
| Total | 295 |

*Not Verified*

| | |
|---|---|
| Level 1 | 35 |
| Level 2 | 51 |
| Total | 86 |

Numbers of verified cases and all cases by year are shown in Fig. 1.

Two instances have occurred where verified cases were subsequently found to be fictional, or at least not to contain sufficient basis in fact. Several unverified reported cases in the file are suspected of being without basis of fact but they remain in the file as real cases until proven otherwise. A number of cases were removed from the data base after discovery that they either did not occur, or occurred in ways that did not meet the requirements of the data-base definition. The data base is suspected of being biased in some ways. This is discussed in the presentation of the statistics below.

The incidence of reported cases of computer abuse in Fig. 1 appears to show an exponential growth through 1973 but the growth rate may be inaccurate because of a sample bias caused by changing news reporting practices of publicized cases, changing amounts of resources available to search for and to record cases, changing willingness of victims to publicly reveal their experiences, or an increasing population of computers in environments where white-collar crime and malicious mischief is so commonplace that it is seldom reported. There might also be a "skyjack" syndrome effect causing an actual increased incidence where publicity of attractive and exciting types of crime encourages more of the same. This was evident in a series of computer-abuse incidents where blank deposit slips printed with perpetrators' MICR account codes were left on counters in banks resulting in crediting the perpetrators' accounts with deposits of other customers who used the blanks when computer processing was based on the MICR code alone. Many applicable cases may be overlooked because the involvement of a computer was not perceived and recorded.

The apparent downturn of incidence of computer abuse in 1974 and 1975, as shown in Fig. 1, is caused by a time lag between occurrence and reporting of cases. Cases continue to be discovered that occurred in the 1960s and early 1970s. The dotted lines in Fig. 1 indicate a probable range of slopes that the curve may assume in the future, based on previous estimates made when fewer cases were known.

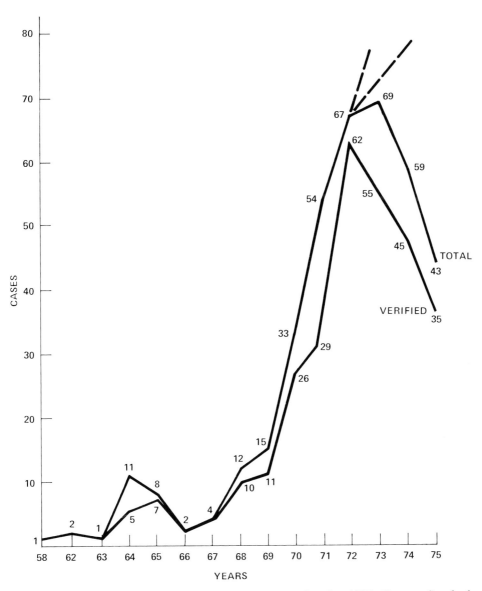

**Fig. 1.** Incidence of reported computer abuse cases to October 1975. (Source: Stanford Research Institute.)

The possible minimal seriousness of the problem of reported computer abuse might be seen by considering cases relative to the number of computers in use. Assuming there were 100,000 computers in 1965 and 200,000 computers in 1975 (worldwide) indicates one reported case per 10,000 computers in 1965 and possibly five cases per 10,000 computers in 1975 (assuming 100 cases will ultimately be reported for 1975). A rate of one case per year for each 2000

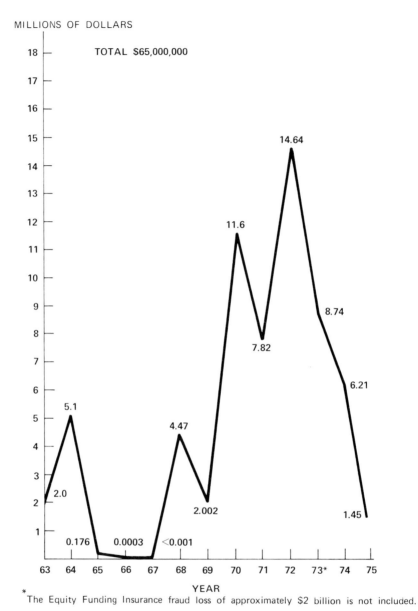

MILLIONS OF DOLLARS

**Fig. 2.** Losses in 144 reported cases of computer abuse to September 1975. (Source: Stanford Research Institute.)

computers seems unreasonably low, possibly indicating that only a small number of known cases are reported, or only a small number of computers are in risk environments.

Resources devoted to searching for and recording cases have been uniformly applied since 1970 to the present. However, a widening public awareness of the project has increased the number of unsolicited contributions of information about cases and has increased the number of cases privately reported. At the very least, the existence of the problem is demonstrated by the data presented in Fig. 1 with a documented lower bound of incidence that is contributing to the knowledge about the obviously growing problem.

Monetary losses are shown in Fig. 2 for 144 cases where such losses were discernible. The Equity Funding Insurance fraud in 1973 is not included in the loss data presented because the estimated $2 billion loss, including stockholder losses (or $200 million direct losses identified in litigation) in this case is so large that it distorts and drowns out the depiction of other data. However, the case demonstrates the potential for great losses.

Civil suit settlements are not included in the loss data because the few known cases involve settlements that include more than direct, reported losses.

It is clear from Fig. 2 that losses have averaged about $5 million per year over the past 11 years and about $10 million over the past 4 years (not counting the Equity Funding Insurance fraud). This is insignificant compared to estimates of losses from white-collar crime of all types. The U.S. Chamber of Commerce estimated current annual white-collar crime losses to be not less than $40 billion [11]. This estimate includes $100 million from computer-related crime (only 1/400th of all white-collar crime). Fraud and embezzlement incidence and losses in all United States financial institutions that are federally regulated or insured reported by the FBI[2] (commercial banks, mutual savings banks, savings and loan associations, and credit unions) compared to reported computer-abuse incidence and losses are shown in Figs. 3 and 4. According to these sources, known computer-abuse losses appear to be almost inconsequential.

The Institute for the Future published a report for the Skandia Insurance Company entitled, *On the Nature of Economic Losses Arising from Computer-Based Systems in the Next Fifteen Years* [9]. Loss estimates likely to arise by 1985 were made by 34 specialists who considered 20 computer applications, presumably worldwide. Yearly expected losses are as follows:

|  | Millions of Dollars |
|---|---|
| Central systems problems | 770 |
| Maintenance and use problems | 1380 |
| External problems (computer abuse) | 160 |

The same study also includes estimates of 200,000 computers worldwide and 20,000 minicomputers in the United States in 1975, and 450,000 computers worldwide and 40,000 minicomputers in the United States in 1985. If the number of computers doubles between 1975 and 1985, as estimated in this study, and computer abuse grows proportionally, the U.S. Chamber of Commerce estimate of $100 million annual loss currently being experienced is roughly consistent

[2] The great increase in incidence and losses shown in the FBI data between 1969 and 1972 has not been explained by the FBI. However, it may be the result of including a new violation, False Applications by Loan Applicants, in the statistics.

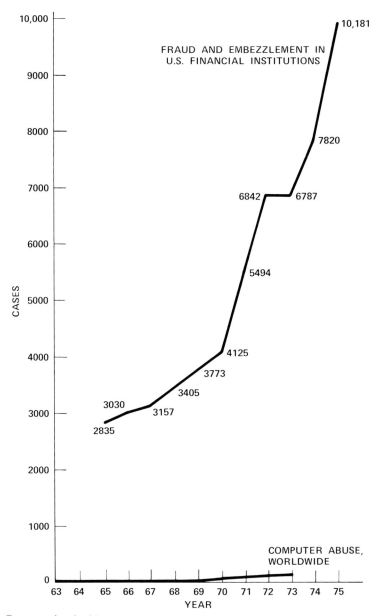

**Fig. 3.** Comparative incidence of worldwide computer abuse vs United States financial institutional fraud and embezzlement. (Sources: FBI and Stanford Research Institute.)

with the expected losses estimated for 1985 ($160 million). However, the study does not speculate on unforeseen changes in the nature of white-collar crime or degrees of protection afforded in new computer products or their use. The discouraging rise in bank fraud and embezzlement as reported by the FBI could indicate far higher computer-related losses in the future than these predictions

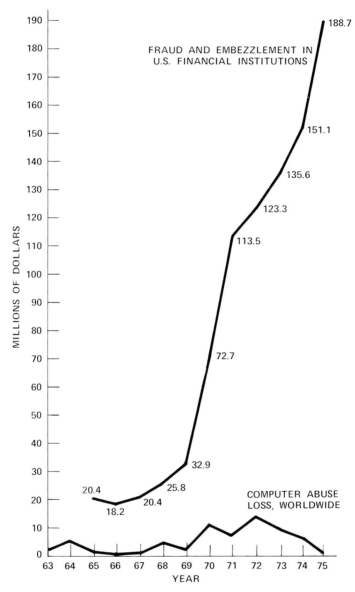

**Fig. 4.** Comparative losses of worldwide computer abuse vs United States financial institution fraud and embezzlement. (Sources: FBI and Stanford Research Institute.)

indicate as computers take over in the processing environments where this type of crime flourishes. The effect of growth of electronic funds transfer systems could also change the nature of bank fraud and embezzlement in unforeseen ways, making prediction of losses difficult.

Losses per incident of computer abuse provide further insight. The average loss per case of all bank fraud and embezzlement reported by the FBI was about

$7,000 in the late 1960s and increased to $19,000 per case in the 1970s. In another study from the computer abuse file of 42 computer-related bank frauds and embezzlements in the period 1962 to 1975, the average loss per case is $430,000 (total $18 million, range $200 to $6.8 million). The average loss over all reported computer abuse cases (not including the Equity Funding Insurance case) where dollar losses are stated (144 cases) is $450,000 per case.

Larger losses in computer-related cases could be explained in several ways. There might be bias in the sample, because cases with larger losses might be reported in the public media more than those with smaller losses. White-collar crime losses may be larger when they involve computers because the assets are more concentrated. Once a system is compromised, it is as easy to steal large amounts as small amounts (the automation of theft), and the danger of detection and greater efforts needed forces the perpetrators to look for a larger return on their investment in crime.

The ranges of losses over 90 cases are shown in Fig. 5. The incidence is skewed to smaller amounts, but several cases have resulted in large losses in the millions of dollars.

Losses can also be intangible. These are important in considering the seriousness of computer abuse and crime in general:

Cost of prosecution.
Loss of confidence in computers and computer users.
Loss of professional prestige and trust in computer technologists.
Loss of the perpetrator's value to society.
Loss of furture technology use.
Loss of services during recovery.
Loss of personal and organizational privacy.
Loss of personal well-being, love, respect, and friendship.
Encouragement of dishonest and socially harmful acts.

Possible gains from exposure of computer abuse are:

Entertainment and media sales resulting from reporting computer abuse.
Increased wariness of and safeguarding from computer abuse by potential victims.
Deterrence value of exposing perpetrators' failures and losses.
Success of perpetrators in solving their problems that motivated their acts.

Several cases investigated in depth have demonstrated the great suffering, misery, and loss of privacy often accompanying white-collar crime. In one case secret and illicit sexual liaisons were revealed, resulting in a death by suicide and a death complicated by alcoholism. In addition, a suspected attempt to frame an innocent participant caused him a serious mental breakdown. Embarrassing incidents in private lives are exposed in newspapers, in court testimony, and to law enforcement investigators. In another case a firm that suffered a program theft claims that lost customer trust resulting from harmful publicity caused

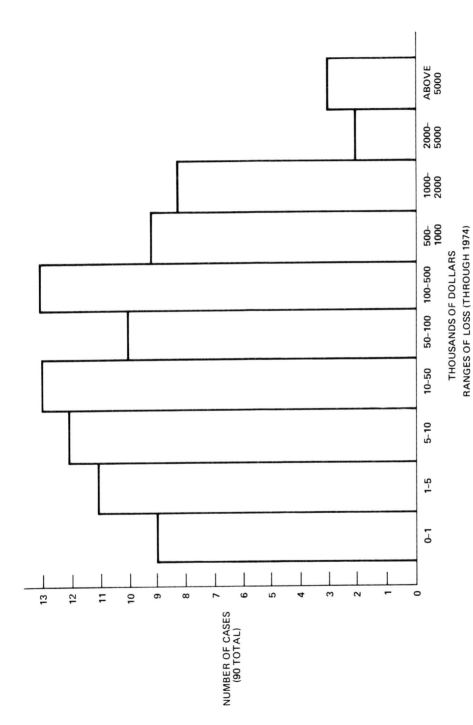

**Fig. 5.** Distribution of losses for 90 cases. (Source: Stanford Research Institute.)

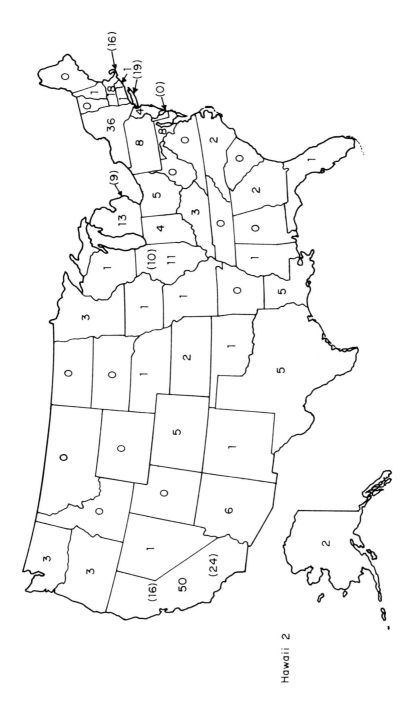

**Fig. 6.** Geographic distribution by states of reported United States computer abuse to October 1974 by the number of cases. Parentheses indicate distributions by city. (Source: Stanford Research Institute.)

greater economic loss than the theft. Research on losses and gains from computer abuse is an area for interdisciplinary attention of computer scientists and sociologists, and is not pursued further here.

There was concern that geographical bias might be present in the sample. Figure 6 shows the geographical distribution of cases, indicating a generally good correlation with population centers that likewise represent concentrations of computers. A particularly heavy concentration in California could demonstrate a small bias caused by location of the research project in the San Francisco region. Specific correlation with computer populations by states in Table 2 is low, but small numbers of cases in several states may account for this.

Distribution of cases in other countries is shown in Table 3. In Table 4 distribution of locations of cases among the more advanced computer-using countries tabulated by computer population shows two significant biases. The unexpected large number of cases in the United Kingdom is explained, in part, by more contacts among people of the United States and the United Kingdom who are interested in the subject. The English language media makes the search for published cases easier and, therefore, more complete.

The second discontinuity is the small number of cases in Japan coupled with the additional fact that all five Japanese cases occurred in 1974–1975. Discussions with several Japanese banking electronic data processing (EDP) professionals indicate that Japan has had practically no white-collar crime. This is attributed to social values including paternalistic, life-long relationships between employees and employers. However, this is changing; employee mobility is increasing and along with it, white-collar crime.

**TABLE 2**

Distribution of Computers (1970) and Computer-Abuse Cases (1958–1974) by State in the United States[a]

|  | | Computers (%) | | Cases (%) | Order by cases |
|---|---|---|---|---|---|
| California | | 10.8 | | 23.8 | 1 |
| New York | | 10.5 | | 17.1 | 2 |
| Illinois | | 6.6 | | 5.2 | 5 |
| Pennsylvania | | 6.1 | | 3.8 | 6 |
| Ohio | | 5.6 | | 2.4 | 8 |
| Texas | | 5.5 | | 2.4 | 9 |
| New Jersey | | 4.5 | | 1.9 | 10 |
| Massachusetts | | 4.4 | | 8.6 | 3 |
| Michigan | | 3.6 | | 6.2 | 4 |
| Washington, D.C. | | 1.2 | | 3.8 | 7 |
| Total | 33,985 | 100.0 | 210 | 100.0 | |

[a] Sources: *Computer Manpower Outlook Bulletin* #1826, U.S. Department of Labor Statistics, 1974. Stanford Research Institute.

## TABLE 3
Computer Abuse Throughout the World[a]

| Canada | 3 | Sweden | 3 | Korea | 1 |
|---|---|---|---|---|---|
| United States | 311 | Norway | 1 | Japan | 5 |
| Brazil | 1 | Denmark | 1 | Australia | 2 |
| | | Germany | 13 | | |
| | | East Germany | 1 | | |
| | | Belgium | 1 | | |
| | | United Kingdom | 20 | | |
| | | France | 8 | | |
| | | Yugoslavia | 1 | | |
| | | South Africa | 2 | | |
| Total: | 374 | | | | |

[a] Source: Stanford Research Institute.

There seems to be no difference in types of computer abuse among countries. Computers, computer operations, and computer applications are similar throughout the world—leaving little possibility for variations in computer-abuse methods and concentrating what differences there are in the areas of motives and social values.

A distribution of cases by type of business of the victims in Fig. 7 presents no surprises and represents the good quality of the sample. Expectation of incidence is high among financially oriented victims, such as banking and government, where there is significant monetary liquidity; this is supported by the data. The large number of reported banking cases is also high because of the legal requirements of banks to report fraud and embezzlement. The large number of cases in education results partly from the willingness to report cases

## TABLE 4
Distribution of Computers (1969) and Computer-Abuse Cases (1958–1975) by Country[a]

| | Computers | Cases | Order by cases |
|---|---|---|---|
| Germany | 6400 | 13 | 2 |
| France | 4803 | 8 | 3 |
| Japan | 4577 | 5 | 4 |
| United Kingdom | 4321 | 17 | 1 |
| Canada | 2037 | 3 | 5 |

[a] Sources: *World Markets for Electronic Data Processing Equipment*, AFIPS, 1971. Stanford Research Institute.

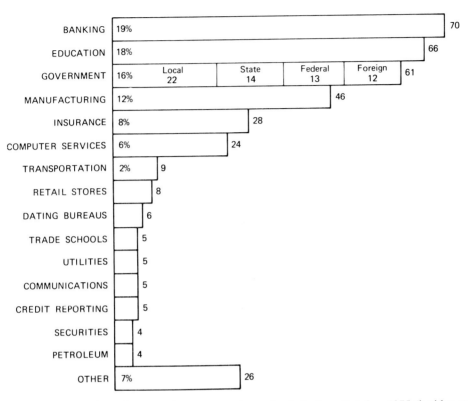

**Fig. 7.** Distribution of reported computer abuse, by industry, October 1975 (incidence and percentage of 375 cases).

publicly and the inability to control public exposure. Also, students represent a large population of potential perpetrators because of their access to computers.

There seems to be little correlation of case incidence to type of business based on the number of computers or of EDP personnel in those types of businesses as indicated in Table 5. This shows that reported computer-abuse incidence correlates with type of business and degree of asset liquidity and possibly with types of applications rather than with the amount of computing in these industries. However, the different practices of reporting computer abuse among types of businesses may introduce a strong bias in the results. For example, as stated previously, the banking industry (financial) is required by law to report fraud and embezzlement, and government agencies and educational institutions probably do not have the desire nor as much opportunity to hide computer abuse, compared to retail, wholesale, and services industries.

Computer abuse has also been identified by types of losses shown in Table 6 in the following four categories:

1. Loss from vandalism. This consists of destruction or damage of equipment, programs, data, facilities, or supplies. Losses are measured in estimates or

**TABLE 5**

Comparison of Computer-Abuse Incidence and Degree of Computer Use by Industry[a]

|  | Employment | | Computers | | Computer abuse | | Computer abuse ranking |
|---|---|---|---|---|---|---|---|
| Manufacturing | 260,000 | 34% | 12,600 | 37% | 50 | 13% | 3 |
| Services | 188,500 | 25% | 7,448 | 22% | 35 | 9% | 4 |
| Finance | 107,500 | 14% | 5,073 | 15% | 102 | 27% | 1 |
| Government | 62,630 | 8% | 4,401 | 13% | 61 | 16% | 2 |
| Wholesale | 95,000 | 12% | 2,388 | 7% | 8 | 2% | 6 |
| Transportation/utilities | 51,600 | 7% | 2,090 | 6% | 19 | 5% | 5 |

[a] Sources: *Computer Manpower Outlook Bulletin* #1826, U.S. Department of Labor Statistics, 1974. Stanford Research Institute.

actual costs of repair, replacement, and interruption or termination of computer services. Intentional acts causing such losses are called vandalism, sabotage, or malicious mischief. The acts originate in about equal numbers between external sources (people not employed in computing facilities such as those involved in riots) or internal sources (employees in positions of trust within computing facilities, most often motivated by

**TABLE 6**

Reported Cases of Computer Abuse by Year and Type of Loss

| Year | Vandalism | Information or property fraud, theft | Financial fraud or theft | Unauthorized use or sale of services | Total |
|---|---|---|---|---|---|
| 1958 |  |  | 1 |  | 1 |
| 1962 | 2 |  |  |  | 2 |
| 1963 | 1 |  |  |  | 1 |
| 1964 | 1 | 2 | 3 |  | 6 |
| 1965 |  | 1 | 4 | 3 | 8 |
| 1966 | 1 |  | 1 |  | 2 |
| 1967 | 2 |  |  | 2 | 4 |
| 1968 | 2 | 3 | 7 | 1 | 13 |
| 1969 | 4 | 6 | 3 | 2 | 15 |
| 1970 | 8 | 5 | 10 | 10 | 33 |
| 1971 | 6 | 19 | 23 | 6 | 54 |
| 1972 | 15 | 18 | 16 | 17 | 66 |
| 1973 | 11 | 20 | 26 | 11 | 68 |
| 1974 | 7 | 15 | 25 | 12 | 59 |
| 1975 | 6 | 7 | 26 | 4 | 43 |
| Total | 66 | 96 | 145 | 68 | 375 |

disgruntlement). When collusion involving both internal and external people is found, the case is identified as internal vandalism.

2. Loss from information or property fraud or theft. The perpetrator's gain may be financial but require the additional step of converting the results of the act to financial gain, if that is his purpose. An example is copying and selling computerized mailing lists.
3. Loss from financial fraud or theft. This results from the modification, disclosure, or denial of use of data that are or represent financial assets stored in computer systems or stored in forms meant for processing in computer systems. In this type the loss is directly financial rather than requiring conversion as in Type 2.
4. Loss from unauthorized use or sale of services. Many computer-abuse cases involve the theft of services, such as those provided by commercial time-sharing companies. Others involve EDP employees engaged in personal business ventures performing EDP services for their own customers, unknown to their employer. Several cases have also occurred where non-EDP employees obtain EDP services for unauthorized personal gain.

The four types are generically different in terms of direct losses, and the evidence that a loss has occurred is often in different forms. However, many cases of computer abuse include combinations of the four types of losses. Precedence ordering by type solved this problem. Thus a case of unauthorized use of a computer to manipulate both financial and nonfinancial data followed by destruction of the computer would be a case of Type 1 vandalism. If the computer had not been destroyed, it would have been a Type 2 data fraud. If the computer had not been destroyed and nonfinancial data had not been objects of the acts, it would have been a Type 3 financial fraud or theft. Finally, if none of the foregoing had occurred, it would have been an unauthorized use.

Evidence of acts can also be indentified in these four classifications. Damaged or destroyed equipment, facilities, programs and data, or supplies can be visually or functionally identified after the act or when use is attempted. There is no experience of more subtle forms of damage, such as causing computer logic circuit failures over a period of time, resulting in undetected but irreversible processing errors. Information theft is often difficult to detect because computer-stored data are not directly visible, and copies of the data can so easily be made without disturbing the data and without leaving a trail of records of access or copying. Financial fraud or theft detection is heavily dependent upon programmed controls and journaling within computer systems. However, in many cases the controls and journaling are usually subverted by the perpetrator. These cases are more often detected by irregularities in the negotiable instruments, printed financial records, or in handling records after removing them from the EDP environment. In such cases, detection requires close cooperation of the EDP organization and external organizations and individuals. Evidence of unauthorized use of services requires observation and analysis of service usage records. Again, as in financial fraud, the perpetrator usually destroys or changes the records (making the act a Type 2 case), poses as a legitimate service user, or makes the theft obvious but avoids being indentified by other means not related to his computer usage.

Financial fraud or theft is rapidly becoming the highest proportion of cases, as seen in Table 6. Vandalism incidence seems to grow at a slower rate and to vary according to the popularity of political violence and acts against "the establishment." Popularity of the use of commercial computer services, including time-sharing, affects rates of unauthorized use or sale of services.

## CONCLUSIONS

Computer abuse is a recent phenomenon unanticipated by most computer users, computer service suppliers, and computer manufacturers. Computers have been designed and used assuming benign, not hostile, environments. Computer abuse as crime is still categorized as fraud, embezzlement, theft, larceny, extortion, espionage, sabotage, and malicious mischief. However, beyond naming the crime, automation has significantly changed its nature. The occupations of perpetrators, the environments of acts, the modi operandi, and forms of assets attacked are all new, making the problem a new challenge to society.

Evidence indicates an emerging problem of computer abuse that could assume the proportions of current levels of white-collar crime. However, relative to white-collar crime incidence and losses today, the known problem seems minimal. The true size of the problem is not known, but the lower bound of incidence and loss based on the 381 reported, known cases demonstrates its existence and indicates significant growth. This is made more serious by the growing reliance on computers, proliferation of computer use into sensitive business and other societal functions, increasing storage of negotiable assets in computer systems, and concomitant increasing positions of trust required in the relatively new EDP occupations.

The nature of the problem so far revealed leads us to believe that computer abuse is of low incidence but results in large loss per incident. Computer abuse focuses on negotiable assets stored in computer media, on computer-stored data convertible to unauthorized gain, on vandalism, and on unauthorized use of services. It is perpetrated by the limited number of people who have computer-related skills, knowledge, access, and resources. Computer abuse is a universal and uniform threat wherever computers are used.

Much more can be said when more complete data are known for 1974, 1975, and the next few years.

## REFERENCES

1. Allen, B., Embezzler's guide to the computer, *Harvard Bus. Rev.* 79–89 (July-August 1975).
2. Farr, R., *The Electronic Criminals*, McGraw-Hill, New York, 1975.

3.  Kevan, Q., *et al.*, The role of criminalistics in white-collar crimes. *J. Crim. Law, Criminol. Police Sci.* **62**(3), 437–449 (1971).
4.  Leibholz, S., and L. Wilson, *Users' Guide to Computer Crime*, Chilton, New York, 1974.
5.  Loeffler, R. M., *Report of the Trustee of Equity Funding Corporation of America*, October 31, 1974.
6.  McKnight, G., *Computer Crime*, Joseph, London, 1974.
7.  Parker, D. B., *Crime by Computer*, Scribner, New York, 1976.
8.  Parker, D. B., S. Nycum, and S. Oura, *Computer Abuse*, Stanford Research Institute, Menlo Park, California, 1973 (NTIS #PB 231–320/AS).
9.  Salancik, G. R., T. J. Gordon, and N. Adams, *On the Nature of Economic Losses Arising from Computer-Based Systems in the Next Fifteen Years*. Institute for the Future, Menlo Park, California, 1972.
10. Sobel, R., and R. Dallos, *The Impossible Dream, The Equity Funding Story: The Fraud of the Century*, Putnam, New York, 1975.
11. U.S. Chamber of Commerce, *A Handbook on White Collar Crime*, Washington, D.C., 1974.

*Donn B. Parker*

# CRITICAL PATH METHODS

## HISTORY AND DEVELOPMENT OF CRITICAL PATH METHODS

Critical path methods are the basis of a special class of management information systems developed primarily for project management, that is, planning, scheduling, and controlling the work to carry out a specific project(s).

Projects may, on the one hand, involve routine procedures that are performed repetitively, such as the monthly closing of accounting books. In this case, critical path methods are useful for *detailed* analysis and optimization of the operating plan. Usually, however, these methods are applied to one-time efforts; notably construction work of all kinds; maintenance operations in factories, airplanes, etc.; moving, modifying, or setting up a new factory or facility of some sort; producing a play, movie, advertising, or political campaign; setting up the control of consultancy assignments; or even performing surgical operations such as kidney transplants. From these examples it is clear that critical path methods are applicable to projects which encompass an extremely wide range of resource requirements and duration times.

In project management, although similar work may have been done previously, it is not usually being repeated in the identical manner on a production basis. Consequently, in order to accomplish the project tasks efficiently, the project manager must plan and schedule largely on the basis of his experience with similar projects, applying his judgment to the particular conditions of the project at hand. During the course of the project he must continually replan and reschedule because of unexpected progress, delays, or technical conditions.

## History of the Early Development of Critical Path Methods

Until the late 1950s there was no generally accepted formal procedure to aid in the management of projects. Each manager had his own scheme which often involved the use of bar charts originally developed by Henry Gantt around 1900. Although the bar chart is still a useful tool in production management, it is inadequate as a means of describing the complex interrelationships among project activities associated with contemporary project management.

The basis for a more formal and general approach toward a discipline of project management occurred around 1957–1958. At this time several techniques were developed concurrently, but independently. The technique called Critical Path Method (CPM) was developed in connection with a very large project undertaken at Du Pont Corporation by Kelley and Walker [3]. The objective here was to determine the optimum (minimum total cost) duration for a project whose activity durations were primarily deterministic variables.

A similar development occurred in Great Britain where the problems of overhauling an electricity generating plant were being studied [4]. The principal feature of their technique was the determination of what they called the "longest irreducible sequence of events."

A somewhat different approach to the problem, called Project Evaluation and Review Technique (PERT), was developed in conjunction with the Polaris weapons system by Malcolm and others [5]. The objective here was to develop an improved method of planning, scheduling, and controlling an extremely large, complicated development program in which many of the activities being conducted were at or beyond the state of the art, and hence the actual activity duration times were primarily random variables with considerable variance.

Although the above developments were conducted independently, they are essentially all based upon the important concept of a *network* representation of the project plan. These ideas are illustrated for a hypothetical project in Fig. 1. At the top of this figure a typical bar chart plan is given which shows the project is broken down into five activities. The arrow heads indicate that "time now" is the end of the third week, activity D is on schedule, B is behind schedule, A is ahead of schedule, and activities C and E have not yet started.

The deficiencies of the bar chart are that not enough detail is given, and more importantly, the interrelationships of the project activities are not shown explicitly. These difficulties are alleviated by the use of the project network shown in the middle of Fig. 1 and the time-scaled network at the bottom of Fig. 1.

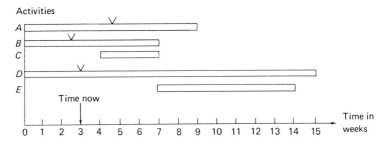

(a) Gantt bar chart

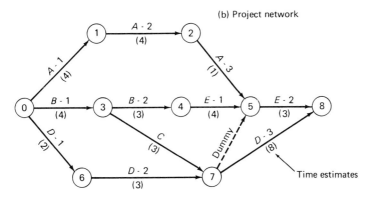

(b) Project network

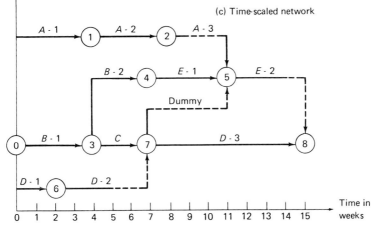

(c) Time-scaled network

**Fig. 1.** Comparison of bar chart, project network, and time-scaled network. (From *Project Management with CPM and PERT*, J. J. Moder and C. R. Phillips, © 1970 by Litton Educational Publishing, Inc. Reprinted by permission of Van Nostrand Reinhold Co.)

Before taking up the logic of networking, it will be useful to preview the scope of critical path methods as the basis of a dynamic network-based planning, scheduling, and control procedure, as shown in Fig. 2.

Step 1, which is the representation of the basic project plan in the form of a network, will be treated in the next section. Steps 2 and 3 will then be considered to estimate the duration of the project plan and determine its critical path. Considered next are the techniques which comprise Step 4; they are designed to modify the initial project plan to satisfy time and resource constraints placed on the project. Finally, the control phase of project management, Step 6, will be considered.

## THE LOGIC OF NETWORKS AS MODELS FOR PROJECT PLANS

The first step in drawing a project network is to list all jobs (activities) that have to be performed to complete the project, and to put these jobs in proper technological sequence in the form of a network or arrow diagram. Each job is indicated by an arrow, with nodes, called events, placed at each end of the arrows. Events represent points in time and are said to occur when all activities leading into the event are completed. In Fig. 3, for example, when the two activities "select operators" and "prepare training material" are completed, the event numbered 10 is said to occur. It should be pointed out that the two predecessor activities of Event 10 need not be completed at the same time; however, when they are both completed, Event 10 occurs, and only then may the activity "train operators" begin. Similarly, when this activity is completed, Event 15 occurs, and the successor activities "test process A" and "test process B" each *may* then begin. It is important to note that the ordering of these activities is based on the "technology" of the resources being utilized.

Activities require the expenditure of time and resources to complete; eight time units and three instructors in the above example. The length of the arrow is not important, but its direction relative to other activities and events indicates the *technological constraints* on the order in which the activities making up the project may be performed.

There is also a need for what is called a *dummy* activity, which requires neither time nor resources to complete. Activity 7-5 in the middle of Fig. 1 is an example of such an activity. Its sole purpose is to show precedence relationships, i.e., that activities C and D-2 must (technologically) precede activity E-2.

The project network is then constructed by starting with the initial project event which has no predecessor activities and occurs at the start of the project. From this event, activities are added to the network using the basic logic described above. This process is continued until all activities have been included in the network, the last of which merge into the project end event which has no successor activities. In carrying out this task the novice must be extremely careful to avoid the common error of ordering the activities arbitrarily according to some preconceived idea of the sequence that the activities will probably take when the project is carried out. If this error is made, the subsequent scheduling

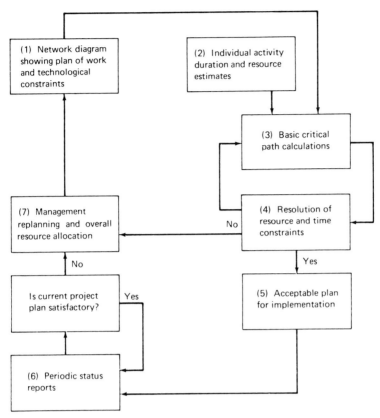

**Fig. 2.** Dynamic network-based planning, scheduling, and control procedure. (From *Project Management with CPM and PERT,* J. J. Moder and C. R. Phillips, © 1970 by Litton Educational Publishing, Inc. Reprinted by permission of Van Nostrand Reinhold Co.)

and control procedures will be unworkable. However, if the network is faithfully drawn according to technological constraints, it will be a unique project model which only changes when fundamental changes in the plan are made. It will also present maximum flexibility in subsequent scheduling of the activities to satisfy resource constraints.

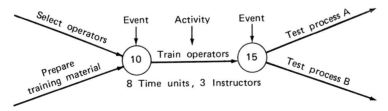

**Fig. 3.** Network or arrow diagram.

The preparation of the project network presents an excellent opportunity to try out, or simulate on paper, various ways of carrying out the project, thus avoiding costly and time-consuming mistakes which might be made "in the field" during the actual conduct of the project. At the conclusion of the planning operation, the final network presents a permanent record giving a clear expression of the way in which the project is to be carried out so that all parties involved in the project can see their involvement and responsibilities.

*The Time Element.* After the planning or networking, the *average duration* of each job is estimated, based upon the job specifications and a consideration of the resources to be employed in carrying out the job. The best estimates will usually be obtained from the person(s) who will supervise the work or who has had such experience.

These time estimates are placed beside the appropriate arrows. If we were then to sum the durations of the jobs along all possible paths from the beginning to the end of the project, the longest one is called the critical path, and its length is the expected duration of the project. Any delay in the start or completion of the jobs along this path will delay completion of the whole project. The rest of the jobs are "floaters" which have a limited amount of leeway (slack) for completion without affecting the target date for the completion of the project.

These concepts are illustrated at the bottom of Fig. 1 where the network activities have been plotted to scale on a time axis. This diagram shows the critical path quite clearly. It consists of activities B-1, C, and D-3, and has an overall duration of 15 weeks. The slack along the other network paths is shown by the dashed portion of the network arrows. For example, the path D-1 and D-2 has 2 weeks of slack, that is, 7 weeks are available to carry out these two jobs which are expected to require only 5 weeks to complete.

The above time-scaled network can be considered as a graphical solution to what is called the *basic scheduling computations.* This is not an operational procedure; it was used here primarily for illustrative purposes.

The objective of the scheduling computations is to determine the critical path(s) and its duration, and to determine the amount of slack on the remaining paths. It turns out that this can best be accomplished by computing the earliest start and finish, and latest start and finish times for each project activity.

## BASIC SCHEDULING COMPUTATIONS

A programmable algorithm for the basic scheduling computations is given by Eqs. (1) through (7) below, in terms of the following nomenclature.

$D_{ij}$      estimate of the mean duration time for activity $(i\text{-}j)$
$E_i$      earliest occurrence time for event $i$
$L_i$      latest allowable occurrence time for event $i$
$ES_{ij}$      earliest start time for activity $(i\text{-}j)$
$EF_{ij}$      earliest finish time for activity $(i\text{-}j)$

$LS_{ij}$     latest allowable start time for activity $(i\text{-}j)$
$LF_{ij}$     latest allowable finish time for activity $(i\text{-}j)$
$S_{ij}$      total slack (or float) time for activity $(i\text{-}j)$
$FS_{ij}$     free slack (or float) time for activity $(i\text{-}j)$
$T_s$       schedule time for the completion of a project or the occurrence of certain key events in a project

### Earliest and Latest Event Times

Assume that the events were numbered (or renumbered by a simple algorithm) so that the initial event is 1, the terminal event is $t$, and all other events $(i\text{-}j)$ are numbered so that $i < j$. Now let $E_1 = 0$ by assumption, then

$$E_j = \max_i (E_i + D_{ij}), \qquad 2 \leq j \leq t \tag{1}$$

$E_t$ = (expected) project duration, and
$L_t = E_t$ or $T_s$, the scheduled project completion time. Then,

$$L_i = \min_j (L_j - D_{ij}), \qquad 1 \leq i \leq t - 1 \tag{2}$$

### Earliest and Latest Activity Start and Finish Times and Slack

$$ES_{ij} = E_i, \qquad\qquad \text{all } ij \tag{3}$$

$$EF_{ij} = E_i + D_{ij}, \qquad \text{all } ij \tag{4}$$

$$LF_{ij} = L_j, \qquad\qquad \text{all } ij \tag{5}$$

$$LS_{ij} = L_j - D_{ij}, \qquad \text{all } ij \tag{6}$$

$$S_{ij} = L_j - EF_{ij}, \qquad \text{all } ij \tag{7}$$

The above equations embody two basic sets of calculations. First, the *forward pass calculations* are carried out to determine the earliest occurrence time for each event $j$ $(E_j)$, and the earliest start and finish times for each activity $i\text{-}j$ $(ES_{ij}$ and $EF_{ij})$. These calculations are based on the assumption that each activity is conducted as early as possible, i.e., they are started as soon as their predecessor event occurs. Since these calculations are initiated by equating the initial project event to time zero $(E_1 \equiv 0)$, the earliest time computed for the project terminal event $(E_t)$ gives the expected project duration.

The second set of calculations, called the *backward pass calculations*, are carried out to determine the latest (allowable) occurrence times for each event $i$ $(L_i)$, and the latest (allowable) start and finish times for each activity $i\text{-}j$ $(LS_{ij}$ and $LF_{ij})$. These calculations begin with the project end event by equating its latest allowable occurrence time to the scheduled project duration, if one is specified $(L_t \equiv T_s)$, or by arbitrarily equating it to $E_t$ $(L_t \equiv E_t)$ if no duration is specified. This is referred to as the "zero-slack" convention. These calculations then

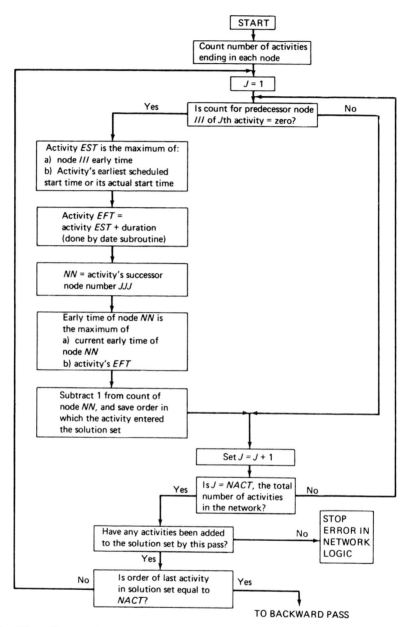

**Fig. 4.** Flow diagram for the basic scheduling computations. (From *Project Management with CPM and PERT*, J. J. Moder and C. R. Phillips, © 1970 by Litton Educational Publishing, Inc. Reprinted by permission of Van Nostrand Reinhold Co.)

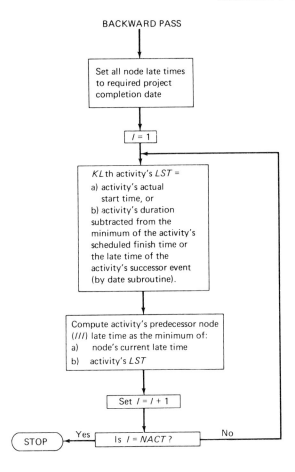

**Fig. 4.** (con't)

proceed by working backwards through the network, always assuming that each activity is conducted as late as possible.

A flow diagram to carry out these computations is given in Fig. 4. This diagram incorporates a number of additional features not yet treated, such as the ability to specify an arbitrary schedule for the start time of any activity, the use of actual start times when a project that is underway is being updated, and the transformation of elapsed working days to calendar dates, based on specified project start and end dates, and holidays to be observed.

Also included is a procedure to halt the computation if an error in network logic is detected. This is absolutely essential because a frequent error in drawing large networks is the inadvertent introduction of a closed loop, which is, of course, inadmissable according to the basic network logic. (Assigning the same number to two events will also produce a loop.) The presence of a loop will result in an infinite cycle in the Fig. 4 flow diagram. While early programs halted this situation by introducing a maximum run time, it is now accomplished by some variation of the check step used in Fig. 4, which also includes a loop identifying error message.

### Role of Hand Computation Procedure

The misuse of computers is not uncommon in the application of critical path methods. This occurs notably in making the above scheduling computations during the initial development of an acceptable project plan; an operation previously described as Steps 3 and 4 in Fig. 2. At this stage it is important that the momentum of a project planning session must not be broken by the requirement for a computer run, and furthermore, it is more economical to perform these computations once by hand, regardless of the size of the network.

For this purpose a set of special networking symbols is useful to avoid making arithmetic errors. The key to these symbols is given in Fig. 5, and their self-explanatory application is given in Fig. 6, where the network employed is essentially the same as that used in Fig. 1. The utilization of the network in this form is discussed below.

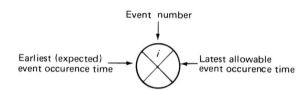

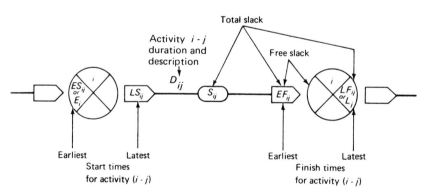

**Fig. 5.** Key to use and interpretation of space symbols. (From *Project Management with CPM and PERT*, J. J. Moder and C. R. Phillips, © 1970 by Litton Educational Publishing, Inc. Reprinted by permission of Van Nostrand Reinhold Co.)

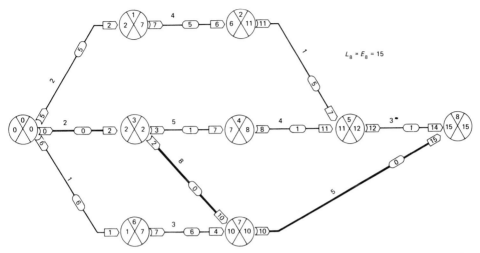

**Fig. 6.** Illustrative network employing the special activity and event symbols, showing completed computations. (From *Project Management with CPM and PERT*, J. J. Moder and C. R. Phillips, © 1970 by Litton Educational Publishing, Inc. Reprinted by permission of Van Nostrand Reinhold Co.)

## The Critical Path and Slack Paths

Among the many types of slack defined in the literature, two are of most value and are discussed here; they are called total activity slack, or simply total slack, and activity-free slack, or simply free slack. They are also referred to as total float and free float, with the same definitions.

### Total Activity Slack

*Definition*: Total activity slack is equal to the difference between the earliest and latest allowable start or finish times for the activity in question. Thus, for activity $(i\text{–}j)$, the total slack is given by

$$S_{ij} = LS_{ij} - ES_{ij} \qquad \text{or} \qquad LF_{ij} - EF_{ij}$$

### Activity-Free Slack

Merge point activities, which are the last activities on slack paths, have what is called activity-free slack.

*Definition*: Activity-free slack is equal to the earliest occurrence time of the activity's successor event, minus the earliest finish time of the activity in question. Thus, for activity $(i\text{-}j)$, the free slack is given by

$$FS_{ij} = E_j - EF_{ij} \quad \text{or} \quad ES_{jk} - EF_{ij}$$

## Critical Path Identification

*Definition*: The critical path is the path with the least total slack.

We will point out later that whenever scheduled times are permitted on intermediate network events, the critical path will not always be the longest path through the network. However, the above definition of the critical path always applys.

If the "zero-slack" convention of letting $L_t = E_t$ for the terminal network event is followed, then the critical path will have zero slack. This situation is illustrated in Fig. 6, where $L_8 = E_8 = 15$. However, if the latest allowable time for the terminal event is set by $T_s$, an arbitrary scheduled duration time for the completion of the project, then the slack on the critical path will be positive, zero, or negative, depending on whether $T_s > E_t$, $T_s = E_t$, or $T_s < E_t$, respectively. The last situation indicates, of course, that the completion of the project is expected to be late, that is, completion after the scheduled time, $T_s$. This is generally an unsatisfactory situation, and replanning (Steps 3 and 4 in Fig. 2) would be required.

To carry out this replanning, it is quite helpful to be able to determine the critical path and its duration with a minimum of hand computation. This can be accomplished from the forward pass computations alone. Referring to Fig. 6, start with the end event, 8, which must be on the critical path. Now trace backwards through the network along the path(s) with $EF_{ij} = E_j$. In this case we proceed to event 7 because $EF_{78} = E_8 = 15$, while $EF_{58} = 14 \neq E_8$. In like manner we proceed backwards to event 3 and then to the initial event zero. Thus, the critical path is 0-3-7-8, with a duration of 15 time units, determined from the forward pass computations alone.

If the backward pass computations are also completed, then total slack and free slack can also be computed. For example, path 0-1-2-5 has a total slack of 5. This is the amount of time by which the actual completion time of this path can be delayed without causing the duration of the overall project to exceed its scheduled completion time. When the critical path has zero slack, as in this example, then the total slack is equal to the amount of time that the activity completion time can be delayed without affecting the earliest start time of any activity or the earliest occurrence time of any event *on the critical path*. For example, activity 0-1 has a total slack of 5 and a free slack of 0. If its completion time is delayed up to 5 time units, it will affect the early start times of the remaining activities on this slack path; however, it will not affect any event on the critical path (event 8 in this case). On the other hand, activity 2-5 has a total slack of 5 and a free slack of 4. Its completion can be delayed up to 5 time units without affecting the critical path (event 8), and it can be delayed up to 4 (free slack) without affecting *any* other event or activity in the network.

## Multiple Initial and Terminal Events, and Scheduled Dates

In certain projects there may be several key events, called milestones, which must occur on or before an arbitrary scheduled date. To handle these situations, the following conventions are usually adopted.

*Conventions:*  A scheduled time, $T_s$, for an initial project event (one without predecessor activities) is interpreted as its earliest expected time, i.e., $T_s \equiv E$ for initial project events. A scheduled time, $T_s$, for an intermediate (or terminal) project event is interpreted as its latest allowable occurrence time, i.e., $T_s \equiv L$.

To illustrate the effect of a scheduled time for an intermediate network event, suppose that $T_s = 10$ for event 5 in Fig. 6. In this case, with $L_5 = T_s = 10$, the critical path would become 0-3-4-5, since it would have the least slack of $-1$ time units. The longest path through the network would, of course, continue to be 0-3-7-8.

Another network complication is the occurrence of multiple initial and/or terminal events. For example, suppose there are several projects, each with their own networks, that are competing for a common set of resources. Since a number of algorithms require single initial and terminal events, a procedure is needed to combine these projects into one network with a single initial and terminal event. This can be accomplished by the use of dummy activities with specified duration times.

For example, consider two projects, A and B, where A is scheduled to start at the beginning of the year ($T_s = 0$), while B is to start 2 weeks later ($T_s = 2$). Also, A and B are scheduled to be completed at the end of weeks 40 and 35, respectively. They can be tied into a single network preserving the specified schedules, as shown in Fig. 7.

## TIME-COST TRADE-OFF PROCEDURES

The determination of the critical path and its duration was described above. This constitutes Step 3 in Fig. 2. Moving on to Step 4, if the earliest occurrence time for the network terminal event exceeds the schedules project duration, then some modification of the network may be required to achieve an acceptable plan.

These modifications might take the form of a major change in the network structure. For example, changing the assumption that one set of concrete forms is available to the availability of two sets may result in a considerable change in the network and reduction in the project duration.

A different procedure that is frequently employed to handle this problem is referred to as time-cost trade-off. Referring to Fig. 6, we might ask the question, how can we most economically reduce the duration of this project from its current level of 15 time units, say weeks, to 14 weeks. To accomplish this, the critical path, i.e., 0-3, 3-7, 7-8, must be reduced by 1 week. The decision in this

|         | Scheduled | |
|---------|-----------|-----|
| Project | Start     | End |
| A       | 0         | 40  |
| B       | 2         | 35  |

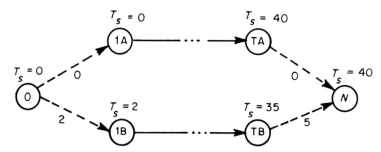

**Fig. 7.** Combination of projects A and B into a single network, preserving scheduled dates.

case would be to buy a week of time on that activity(s) where it is available at the lowest additional cost. If this turns out to be activity 3-7 or 7-8, then the resulting project will have two critical paths, each of 14 weeks duration, i.e., 0-3,3-4,4-5, 5-8, and 0-3, 3-7, 7-8. Thus further reductions in this project duration will be more complicated because both paths must now be considered. One must also constantly consider buying back time previously bought on certain activities. This problem very rapidly reaches the point where a computer is required to obtain on optimal solution.

**The Critical Path Method (CPM)**

The CPM procedure, developed by Kelley and Walker [3] to handle this problem, arises when we ask for the project schedule that just balances the value of time saved against the incremental cost of saving it. This point is shown in Fig. 8 where the total cost curve reaches a minimum. This total cost is made up of the indirect costs, determined by the accounting department considering normal overhead costs and the "value" of the time saved, plus the minimum direct costs, determined by the CPM procedure. This is, in fact, one of the major contributions of the CPM procedure—the determination of the relationship of the *minimum* direct costs and the project duration, together with the corresponding activity scheduled times.

The CPM computational algorithm is based on an assumed linear cost vs time

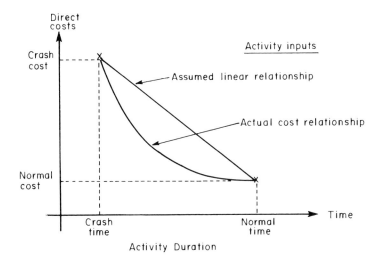

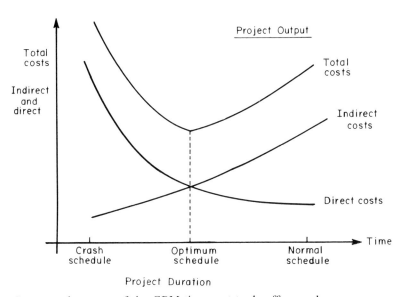

**Fig. 8.** Inputs and outputs of the CPM time-cost trade-off procedure.

relationship for each activity as shown at the top of Fig. 8. It should be added that as long as this relationship is convex, a series of straight lines can be used to approximate this function as closely as desired. With this input, this problem can be formulated as a linear programming problem to minimize the total project direct costs, subject to constraints dictated by the activity time-cost curves, and the network logic. The dual of this formulation can be interpreted as a network flow problem which can be solved with very modest computer capacity compared with that required to solve this problem using the Simplex method.

Although this is an elegant algorithm, it is rarely applied, primarily because of the unrealistic basic assumption of the unlimited availability of resources. Nevertheless, it is an important concept that is frequently applied in the simple manner illustrated at the beginning of this section. The important consideration of limited resources is treated in the next section.

## SCHEDULING ACTIVITIES TO SATISFY TIME AND RESOURCE CONSTRAINTS

To illustrate how Fig. 6 can be used to solve resource allocation problems, suppose that activities 1-2, 3-4, and 5-8 require the continuous use of a special piece of equipment during their performance. Can this requirement be met without causing a delay in the completion of this project?

With the aid of Fig. 6, it is very easy to see that the answer to this question is yes, if the following schedule is used. The reasoning proceeds as follows. First, activities 1-2 and 3-4 must preceed 5-8, so the first question is which of these two activities should be scheduled first. Reference to Fig. 6 indicates that both have an early start time of 2, and since the slacks are 5 and 1 for activities 1-2 and 3-4, respectively, the activity ordering of 1-2, 3-4, and 5-8 follows.

One can, of course, ask more involved questions dealing with the leveling of the demand for various personnel skills. From a computer standpoint, these questions are the most important ones involved in the use of critical path methods.

### A Heuristic Resource Scheduling Procedure

Resource allocation problems in general can be categorized as the determination of the scheduled times for project activities which:

1. Level the resource requirements in time, subject to a constraint on the project duration; or
2. Minimize the project duration subject to constraints on the availabilities of resources; or
3. Minimize the total cost of the resources and the penalties due to project delay—the long-range planning problem.

A naive scheduling procedure to solve the first and second problems is shown in Fig. 9. This procedure has been applied to the network shown in Fig. 6, with requirements for two different resources, A and B, as shown in Fig. 10. The results recorded there are based on the restriction that no more than 8 units of A and 6 units of B will be scheduled on any one day. From this figure we note that these resource restrictions have resulted in an increase in the project duration from 15 to 18 days. Our objective is, of course, to minimize this increase.

The combinatorial nature of the above problem has prevented it from yielding to the solution techniques of mathematical programming. While the problem can be formulated using integer programming, only networks of up to approximately 50 activities can be solved. One such procedure, using bounded enumeration, is given by Davis [1].

Because of this lack of success with optimization procedures, major attention has been devoted to developing heuristic procedures which produce "good" feasible solutions. The procedure given in Fig. 9 is a typical scheduling heuristic; it can be shown that its application in Fig. 10 gives an optimal solution, but this will not always be the case. The heuristics or rules used in obtaining such solutions are essentially schemes for assigning activity priorities in making the activity sequencing decisions required for resolution of resource conflicts.

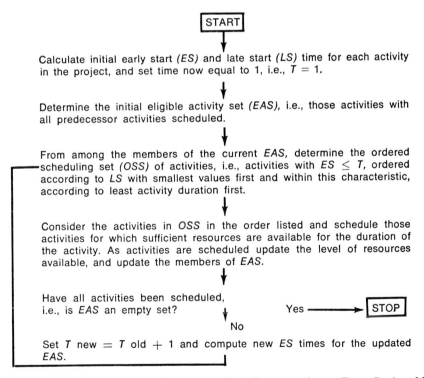

Fig. 9. A basic multiproject, multiresource scheduling procedure. (From *Project Management with CPM and PERT,* J. J. Moder and C. R. Phillips, © 1970 by Litton Educational Publishing, Inc. Reprinted by permission of Van Nostrand Reinhold Co.)

| Activity | A | B | D | ES | S | LS | 1 | 2 | 3 | 4 | 5 | 6 | 7 | 8 | 9 | 10 | 11 | 12 | 13 | 14 | 15 | 16 | 17 | 18 |
|---|---|---|---|---|---|---|---|---|---|---|---|---|---|---|---|---|---|---|---|---|---|---|---|---|
| | *Resource Req.* | | | | | | | | | | | | | | | | | | | | | | | |
| 0–1 | 3 | — | 2 | 1 | 5 | 6 | | | x 3A | x 3A | | | | | | | | | | | | | | |
| 1–2 | — | 2 | 4 | 3 | 5 | 8 | | | | | | | | x 2B | x 2B | x 2B | x 2B | | | | | | | |
| 0–3 | 6 | — | 2 | 1 | 0 | 1 | x 6A | x 6A | | | | | | | | | | | | | | | | |
| 3–4 | — | 2 | 5 | 3 | 1 | 4 | | | x 2B | x 2B | x 2B | x 2B | x 2B | | | | | | | | | | | |
| 2–5 | 4 | — | 1 | 7 | 5 | 12 | | | | | | | | | | | | | | x 4A | | | | |
| 4–5 | 2 | — | 4 | 8 | 1 | 9 | | | | | | | | x 2A | x 2A | x 2A | x 2A | | | | | | | |
| 0–6 | 3 | — | 1 | 1 | 6 | 7 | | | | x 3A | | | | | | | | | | | | | | |
| 3–7 | 4 | 4 | 8 | 3 | 0 | 3 | | | 4A 4B | 4A 4B | 4A 4B | 4A 4B | 4A 4B | 4A 4B | 4A 4B | 4A 4B | | | | | | | | |
| 6–7 | 5 | — | 3 | 2 | 6 | 8 | | | | | | | | | | | x 5A | x 5A | x 5A | | | | | |
| 5–8 | — | 5 | 3 | 12 | 1 | 13 | | | | | | | | | | | | | | | x 5B | x 5B | x 5B | |
| 7–8 | 2 | — | 5 | 11 | 0 | 11 | | | | | | | | | | | | | | x 2A | x 2A | x 2A | x 2A | x 2A |

Level of resource A unassigned (periods 1–18, struck progression shown):

| 1 | 2 | 3 | 4 | 5 | 6 | 7 | 8 | 9 | 10 | 11 | 12 | 13 | 14 | 15 | 16 | 17 | 18 |
|---|---|---|---|---|---|---|---|---|---|---|---|---|---|---|---|---|---|
| 6̸ 2 | 6̸ 2 | 6̸ 4̸ 1 | 6̸ 4̸ 1 | 6̸ 4̸ 1 | 6̸ 4 | 6̸ 4 | 6̸ 4̸ 2 | 6̸ 4̸ 2 | 6̸ 4̸ 2 | 6̸ 1 | 6̸ 3 | 6̸ 3 | 6̸ 4̸ 2 | 6̸ 6 | 6̸ 6 | 6̸ 6 | 6̸ 6 |

Level of resource A assigned (y-axis grid lines 6, 4, 2):

```
6                                             x
      x   x   x                   x           x
4 x x x x x           x   x   x   x           x
  x x x x x           x   x   x   x   x   x   x
2 x x x x x x x x x x x x x x
  x x x x x x x x x x x x x x x x x x
   1 2 3 4 5 6 7 8 9 10 11 12 13 14 15 16 17 18
```

Level of resource B unassigned (periods 1–18, struck progression shown):

| 1 | 2 | 3 | 4 | 5 | 6 | 7 | 8 | 9 | 10 | 11 | 12 | 13 | 14 | 15 | 16 | 17 | 18 |
|---|---|---|---|---|---|---|---|---|---|---|---|---|---|---|---|---|---|
| 6 | 6 | 6̸ 2̸ 0 | 6̸ 2̸ 0 | 6̸ 2̸ 0 | 6̸ 2̸ 0 | 6̸ 2̸ 0 | 6̸ 2̸ 0 | 6̸ 2̸ 0 | 6̸ 2̸ 0 | 6̸ 4 | 6 | 6 | 6 | 6̸ 1 | 6̸ 1 | 6̸ 1 | 6 |

Level of resource B assigned (y-axis grid lines 6, 4, 2):

```
6     x x x x x x
      x x x x x x x x         x x x
4     x x x x x x x x         x x x
      x x x x x x x x         x x x
2     x x x x x x x x x       x x x
      x x x x x x x x x
   1 2 3 4 5 6 7 8 9 10 11 12 13 14 15 16 17 18
```

**Fig. 10.** Application of basic multiproject, multiresource scheduling procedure to the network given in Fig. 6. (From *Project Management with CPM and PERT*, J. J. Moder and C. R. Phillips, © 1970 by Litton Educational Publishing, Inc. Reprinted by permission of Van Nostrand Reinhold Co.)

## Evaluation of Several Scheduling Heuristics

Two categories of heuristics that have been found most effective are those incorporating some measure of time, such as activity slack or duration, and those incorporating some measure of resource usage. Davis [1] has made an extensive comparison of eight heuristics on some 83 network problems for which the optimal solutions were obtained using his bounded enumeration procedure. The rules tested included:

1. *Minimum Late Start Time* (LST)—order by increasing LST.
2. *Minimum Late Finish Time* (LFT)—order by increasing LFT.

3. *Resource Scheduling Method*—order by increasing $d_{ij}$, where $d_{ij}$ = increase in project duration resulting when activity $j$ follows $i$; = $\max[0; (E_i - L_j)]$, where $E_i$ and $L_j$ denote the early finish time of activity $i$ and the late start time of activity $j$, respectively. The above activity comparison is made on a pairwise basis among all activities in the eligible activity set.

4. *Shortest Imminent Operation*—order by increasing activity duration.

5. *Greatest Resource Demand*—order by decreasing total resource demand.

6. *Greatest Resource Utilization*—priority is given to that combination of activities which results in maximum resource utilization in each scheduling interval; a rule which requires the use of zero–one integer programming to implement.

7. *Most Jobs Possible*—similar to Rule 6, except the number of active jobs is maximized.

8. *Select Jobs Randomly*—order the eligible activities by a random process.

The first four rules above were studied because they are very popular in the open literature on scheduling. The next three rules were included because they have been reported to be used in some of the many computer programs available for project scheduling on a commercial basis. The detailed workings of these programs have been kept secret. The last rule was included as a benchmark of human performance–presumably an experienced scheduler can out-perform this rule.

The primary evaluation made in this study was based on the average percentage increase in project duration over the optimal schedule. On this basis the first three rules, having percentages of 5.6, 6.7, and 6.8, respectively, were considerably better than Rule 8, based on random selection, which had a percentage of 11.4. Also, Rules 5, 6, and 7, having percentages of 13.1, 13.1 and 16.0, respectively, gave poorer schedules than Rule 8.

While average performance is a reasonable guide in selecting scheduling rules, it should be pointed out that it is the nature of heuristics that no one rule will always give the best schedule. For this reason, one can argue that if the problem warrants a near optimal schedule, then several different heuristics should be applied. It also suggests that an important research area is to relate heuristic rule performance with simple parameters that describe the network and its resource constraints.

**A Realistic Scheduling Procedure**

Although the scheduling procedure given in Fig. 9 is oversimplified for most practical applications, it has three important properties. First, it can handle any number of resources. Second, it can handle any number of projects as long as their scheduled start and finish times are given, using the procedure shown in Fig. 7. Finally, the procedure can be used as the basis for a more generally applicable scheduling procedure, such as that developed by Wiest [9].

The flow diagram for Wiest's procedure is shown in Fig. 11. Some of its features include:

1. Variable crew sizes are permissible.
2. Splitting or interrupting an activity is permissible.
3. Assignment of unused resources is incorporated.

The application of Wiest's procedure to solve Problem 2 cited in the section entitled A Heuristic Resource Scheduling Procedure is obvious. It can also be used to solve the long-range planning problem, 3 above, by evaluating the total cost of alternative levels of available resources and the penalties associated with delays in the completion of certain projects, as indicated by the upper right-hand corner of Fig. 11.

These procedures can also be used to solve the first problem cited in the section entitled A Heuristic Resource Scheduling Procedure, that is, the resource leveling problem with a constrained project duration. They proceed by first applying the above procedure with unlimited resources, and then progressively cutting back the availabilities of each resource until a feasible solution can no longer be found. The effect of this will be to level the resource requirement in time.

## STOCHASTIC CONSIDERATIONS IN NETWORKING

There are two stochastic aspects of critical path methods that are of some importance. The first involves those projects in which special milestone events occur, such as the end of test or evaluation activities. The special nature of these events is that they may have several *possible* successor activities, but only one will be selected and the others will be ignored. This situation is referred to as probabilistic branching. For example, in a space vehicle project, an evaluation activity may result in the choice of a solid or a liquid fuel engine, but not both. Also, as a result of a "failure" in some test, such projects may require recycling to an earlier network event, forming a closed loop. Neither of these situations is permissible according to the network logic assumed above.

The occurrence of these situations can be handled by drawing the network in general rather than specific terms. For example, the network plan for the above situation would be drawn up without reference to whether the engine was liquid or solid fuel. Also, the loop situation would be handled by omitting the loop, and including its time effect in other network activities. Where more refined planning is required, a special simulation language called GERT (Graphical Evaluation and Review Technique) has been developed by Pritsker [8] which permits the above situations to be built into the network. Since GERT will be covered elsewhere in this *Encyclopedia*, it will not be treated further here.

The second stochastic aspect of critical path methods deals with the fact that the actual duration of a project activity is usually a (hypothetical) random variable rather than a deterministic constant. Up to now, the effects of the

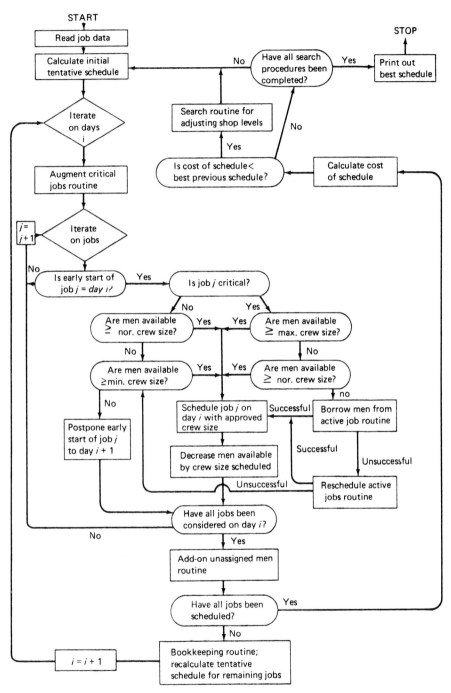

**Fig. 11.** Flow diagram for SPAR-1 scheduling program for allocating resources. (From *Project Management with CPM and PERT*, J. J. Moder and C. R. Phillips, © 1970 by Litton Educational Publishing, Inc. Reprinted by permission of Van Nostrand Reinhold Co.)

variance in activity performance times on the procedures we have discussed have either been assumed to be negligible or have been neglected. The initial consideration of this problem led to the development of PERT, as cited in the opening section.

## The PERT Statistical Approach to Project Management

One of the chief concerns in the development of PERT was meeting the schedules placed on key milestone events, where considerable uncertainty in actual activity performance times existed. Because of this emphasis on events, which is a long-standing United States government practice in controlling projects by monitoring milestones, the activity labels were placed inside the event symbols. This convention, however, has no effect on the network logic described above, and thus represents a minor difference from the networking procedures described in the section entitled The Logic of Networks as Models for Project Plans. A major difference in procedures arises, however, from the efforts to estimate, from the project plan, the probability that the milestone schedules would be met.

The approach to this problem, which is frequently taken in developments of this type, was to collect input information on the basic elements of the system, and from it synthesize their effects on system performance. In this case the input information consisted of a measure of the uncertainty in activity duration times, and from this the uncertainty in meeting schedules was computed.

## PERT Three Time Estimates

In the PERT approach, the actual activity performance time, $t$, is assumed to have a hypothetical probability distribution with mean, $t_e$, and variance, $\sigma_t^2$. It is referred to as hypothetical because its parameters must be estimated before any actual observations are made. When the activity is finally completed, the actual time can be regarded as the first (and last) sample from this hypothetical distribution. Estimates of $t_e$ and $\sigma_t^2$ must therefore be based on someones judgment, which in turn is based on a ''sampling'' of prior work experience.

The PERT activity input data is in the form of three time estimates, called $a$, $m$, and $b$. They denote the optimistic, most likely, and pessimistic estimates of $t$, respectively. Statistically, these are the zero percentile, the mode, and the 100 percentile of the hypothetical probability distribution.

A rule of thumb in statistics is that the standard deviation can be estimated roughly as $\frac{1}{6}$ of the range of the distribution. This follows from the fact that at least 89% of any distribution lies within three standard deviations from the mean, and for the Normal distribution this percentage is 99.7+%. Thus the estimate of the variance is given by

$$\text{variance of } t \equiv \sigma_t^2 = [(b - a)/6]^2 \qquad (8)$$

While the above formula is a part of the original PERT procedure, the author prefers to define $a$ and $b$ as the 5 and 95 percentiles, which in turn calls for replacing the divisor 6 in Eq (8) by 3.2 (see Ref. 6, p. 285).

To derive an estimate of the mean requires an assumption about the shape of the probability distribution of $t$. In the development of PERT, it was assumed that a plausible (and mathematically convenient) distribution for $t$ is the Beta distribution whose standard deviation was $\frac{1}{6}$ of its range. For this distribution, Eq. (9) gives a linear approximation to the true (cubic) relationship between the mean, $t_e$, and the mode, $m$:

$$\text{mean of } t \equiv t_e = (a + 4m + b)/6 \tag{9}$$

## PERT Probability Calculation

At this point the scheduling computations described in the section entitled Basic Scheduling Computations can be carried out using only the mean values computed from Eq. (9) for each activity. The PERT procedure then considers the activities on the critical path(s) through the network, and ignores all others. Assuming the actual activity performance times for these activities to be *independent random variables* with means, $t_{ei}$, and variances, $\sigma_{ti}^2$, the statistical properties of the "project" duration follows directly from the Central Limit Theorem. Assuming the critical path consists of $N$ activities, and denoting the sum of their actual durations by $T$, this can be written as follows:

$$T = \sum_{i=1}^{N} t_i$$

$$\text{mean of } T \equiv T_e = \sum_{i=1}^{N} t_{ei} \tag{10}$$

$$\text{variance of } T \equiv \sigma_T^2 = \sum_{i=1}^{N} \sigma_{ti}^2 \tag{11}$$

shape of distribution of $T$: Normal

$$\text{probability of meeting schedule } T_s = P\{T \le T_s\} = P\left\{Z \le \frac{T_s - T_e}{\sigma_T}\right\} \tag{12}$$

where $Z$ has a Normal distribution with zero mean and unit variance, so that the last probability is read from the standard table of the cumulative normal distribution.

The basic assumption that the $t_i$'s above are independent random variables must be emphasized. Since a project manager will normally expedite a project when it falls behind schedule, the independence is violated. Hence the interpretation of the probability given by Eq. (12) is *the probability that the project will meet the schedule without having to be expedited*. This, or course, is very useful for planning purposes since it is computed at the outset of the project. If the calculated probability is low, say $<0.75$, then the project manager can anticipate the need to expedite the project and can exercise convenient or inexpensive options early in the project.

**Effects of Errors Introduced by the PERT Assumptions**

Much has been written about this subject, but very little of it is of importance in the applications. Two of the PERT assumptions will be considered here. First, the assumption that the random variable, $t$, has a Beta distribution has no practical significance when one considers the level of accuracy of the three time estimates.

The second assumption is more important; that is, basing the probability computation on the critical path and ignoring all others. It is possible for a subcritical path, with a relatively high variance, to have a lower probability of meeting a schedule than the "longer" critical path. A more bothersome point is that the effect of this assumption at every network merge event is to introduce a negative bias in the estimated earliest expected time for the event. While these effects can assume practical significance, it is surprising to the author how accurate the PERT estimates are in most cases.

There are ways of estimating when the above assumption will cause a significant error (see Ref. 6, p. 304). This reference also discusses analytical procedures to remove the merge event bias; however, they are not considered to be practical for routine application. The most appropriate solution, where the refinement is called for, is to use simulation. The GERT language cited earlier is very easy to use for this purpose. The output of the simulation includes, among other things, the probability that each activity will be on the actual critical path through the network. This notion replaces the idea of a fixed critical path and slack on the remaining paths.

**Applications of PERT**

PERT is much like the CPM time-cost trade-off algorithm in that it is seldom used. However, the reasons are different. It is the author's opinion that most project managers either have not learned to use PERT probabilities effectively, or they have no confidence in them. This is unfortunate because there are legitimate situations where PERT probabilities can be a useful tool, and there are also some basic advantages in the three time estimate system.

Several studies have shown that when the variance of $t$ is high, the mean activity duration time can be estimated more accurately using the three time estimate PERT procedure, than the one time estimate system which is now used quite widely (see Ref. 6, p. 286). Also, a project manager's attention should be drawn to the high variance activities as potential problem areas in the conduct of the project.

## NETWORK TIME AND COST CONTROL PROCEDURES

Having completed the presentation of planning and scheduling techniques, the attention now turns to project control as depicted by Step 6 in the dynamic project management procedure outlined in Fig. 2. To periodically assess how well the plan is working, actual progress information regarding time and cost performance of activities is entered into the system, and the network is updated.

### Network Time Updating

Updating a network to reflect current status is similar to the problem introduced in the section entitled Multiple Initial and Terminal Events, and Scheduled Dates, in that a project underway is equivalent to a project with multiple start events. After a project has begun, varying portions of each path from the initial project event to the end event will have been completed. By establishing the status on each of these paths from progress information, the routine forward pass scheduling computations can then be made. No change in the backward pass computation procedure is necessary, since progress on a project does not affect the network terminal event(s), unless the scheduled completion date is revised.

Additional updating information is required if changes in the project plan are made which require revisions in the network or in the activity duration time estimates. Also, if an activity has not started, but its predecessor event has occurred since the last network update, then a scheduled start time or some "built-in" assumption about its start time must be entered into the system.

One additional convention is needed for network updating in the case where scheduled dates are associated with intermediate network events.

*Convention:* The latest allowable time for an intermediate network event on which a schedule time, $T_s$, is imposed, is taken as the earlier (smaller) of the scheduled time, $T_s$, and the latest allowable time, $L$, computed in the backward pass.

An update may indicate that the critical path has shifted, or more important, that the slack on the critical path has become negative. In this case, replanning will be in order to bring the project back onto schedule.

### Network Cost Control

Network cost control considers means of controlling the dollar expenditure as the project progresses in time and accomplishment. While network-based expenditure status reports may take many forms, they are primarily directed at the following basic questions.

1. What are the actual project costs to date?

2. How do the actual costs to date compare with planned costs to date?
3. What are the project accomplishments to date?
4. How do the actual costs of specific accomplishments compare with the planned costs of these accomplishments?
5. By how much may the project be expected to overrun or underrun the total planned cost?
6. How do the above questions apply to various subdivisions and levels of interest within the project?

The major problem in the development of systems to answer these questions is the conflict between traditional functionally orientated accounting and a system based upon network activities. One solution to this problem is the use of groups of activities, called "work packages," in the coding of cost accounts. For example, in the construction industry a work package is often taken as a separate bid item. This, however, still does not solve all of the problems of allocating overhead and sharing various joint costs.

The use of network activities as an accounting base lend themselves to major increases in the amount of detail available to and required of the manager. This is both the promise and the inherent hazard of such systems, and it is one of the primary tasks of the system designer to achieve the level of detail that provides the greatest return on the investment in the system.

Network cost control employs an "enumerative cost model" in which activity costs are assumed to occur linearly in time. Thus, if the project budget is apportioned among the activities, cumulative cost vs time curves can be computed based on the earliest and latest allowable activity times. These two curves will bound the curve based upon the scheduled times for each activity. The latter is then taken as the plan against which progress is measured.

**Illustrative Time and Cost Control System**

An illustrative computer update of a very basic time and cost control system is presented in Fig. 12. The first group of 10 activities have already started, so their EARLY START DATE column gives actual start dates. The next two columns are blank for these activities, and for those with 100 under PERCENT ELAPSED, the actual finish date is given in the LATE END DATE column. The VALUE COMPLETED is merely the product of the two columns to its left.

The third and fourth columns of this report, called RES and ID, permit the activities to be coded in two ways so that separate detailed output reports can be prepared for each RESource and/ or ID type, as well as summary cost reports. The latter are shown at the bottom of Fig. 12.

Each of the major computer firms, plus a number of other corporations, have developed computer packages that vary in complexity from the above system, which is a very basic one, to extremely elaborate systems. The latter may

| I NODE | J NODE | RES | ID | ACTIVITY DESCRIPTION | EARLY ST. DATE | TOTAL SLACK **** | LATE ST. DATE | DURA-TION | LATE END DATE | PERCENT ELAPSED | TOTAL $ VALUE | $ VALUE COMPLETE |
|---|---|---|---|---|---|---|---|---|---|---|---|---|
| 5 | 6 | 4 | 2 | ORDER HUB COMPONENTS | 11/15/68 | | | 3 | 11/20/68 | 33.3 | -0 | -0 |
| 19 | 21 | 4 | 2 | RECEIVE GEAR BOX | 11/14/68 | | | 45C | 12/30/68 | 4.4 | 1250 | 55 |
| 1 | 2 | 1 | 1 | PREPARE FOUNDATION | 11/14/68 | | | 5 | 11/21/68 | 40.0 | 625 | 249 |
| 18 | 19 | 4 | 2 | ORDER GEAR BOX | 11/13/68 | | | 1 | 11/14/68 | 100.0 | 50 | 50 |
| 17 | 21 | 4 | 2 | RECEIVE HYDRAULICS | 11/13/68 | | | 45C | 12/30/68 | 6.7 | 1750 | 116 |
| 1 | 11 | 1 | 1 | BRAKE DRAWINGS | 11/12/68 | | | 15 | 12/ 4/68 | 26.7 | 1875 | 499 |
| 16 | 17 | 4 | 2 | HYDRAULIC COMPONENTS | 11/11/68 | | | 1 | 11/12/68 | 100.0 | 25 | 25 |
| 1 | 18 | 1 | 1 | GEAR BOX SPECS. | 11/ 6/68 | | | 5 | 11/13/68 | 100.0 | 625 | 625 |
| 1 | 16 | 1 | 1 | HYDRAULIC DETAILS | 11/ 1/68 | | | 5 | 11/11/68 | 100.0 | 625 | 625 |
| 1 | 5 | 1 | 1 | DRUM DRAWINGS | 10/30/68 | | | 10 | 11/14/68 | 100.0 | 1250 | 1250 |
| 13 | 20 | 2 | 1 | FABRICATE BRAKE | 12/20/68 | 12 | 1/10/69 | 5 | 1/17/69 | | 1500 | |
| 20 | 21 | 2 | 1 | INSTALL BRAKE/KNIFE | 12/31/68 | 12 | 1/17/69 | 2 | 1/21/69 | | 300 | |
| 21 | 23 | 3 | 1 | SUBPLATE/GEARS/HYDRS | 1/ 3/69 | 12 | 1/21/69 | 5 | 1/28/69 | | 750 | |
| 21 | 22 | 2 | 1 | SUBPLATE/GEARS/HYDRS | 1/ 3/69 | 12 | 1/21/69 | 5 | 1/28/69 | | 1500 | |
| 23 | 22 | | | DUMMY | 1/10/69 | 12 | 1/28/69 | 0C | 1/28/69 | | -0 | |
| 22 | 24 | 3 | 1 | TEST ASSEMBLY | 1/10/69 | 12 | 1/28/69 | 2 | 1/30/69 | | 600 | |
| 24 | 25 | 3 | 1 | INSTALL IN SHIP | 1/14/69 | 12 | 1/30/69 | 1 | 1/31/69 | | 150 | |
| 11 | 12 | 4 | 2 | ORDER BRAKE MATL'S | 12/ 4/68 | 13 | 12/23/68 | 2 | 12/27/68 | | 50 | |
| 12 | 13 | 4 | 2 | REC BRAKE MATERIALS | 12/ 6/68 | 13 | 12/27/68 | 14C | 1/10/69 | | 450 | |
| 7 | 8 | 2 | 1 | FABRICATE DRUM | 12/ 4/68 | 14 | 12/26/68 | 10 | 1/10/69 | | 3000 | |
| 8 | 20 | 2 | 1 | INSTALL HUB/DRUM | 12/18/68 | 14 | 1/10/69 | 5 | 1/17/69 | | 2250 | |
| 6 | 7 | 4 | 2 | REC. HUB COMPONENTS | 11/20/68 | 15 | 12/12/68 | 14C | 12/26/68 | | 500 | |
| 4 | 8 | 2 | 1 | FABRICATE FOUNDATION | 11/29/68 | 17 | 12/26/68 | 10 | 1/10/69 | | 3000 | |
| 2 | 4 | 4 | 2 | FOUNDATION WORKLIST | 11/21/68 | 18 | 12/18/68 | 4 | 12/26/68 | | 500 | |
| 2 | 3 | 4 | 2 | ORDER FOUND. MAT'S | 11/21/68 | 19 | 12/19/68 | 1 | 12/20/68 | | 50 | |
| 3 | 4 | 4 | 2 | REC. FOUND. MAT'S | 11/22/68 | 19 | 12/20/68 | 6C | 12/26/68 | | 1000 | |
| 5 | 7 | 1 | 1 | DRUM WORKLIST | 11/18/68 | 20 | 12/17/68 | 5 | 12/26/68 | | 300 | |
| 1 | 9 | 1 | 1 | KNIFE DRAWINGS | 11/18/68 | 20 | 12/17/68 | 12 | 1/ 7/69 | | 1500 | |
| 9 | 10 | 4 | 2 | KNIFE WORKLIST | 12/ 5/68 | 20 | 1/ 7/69 | 3 | 1/10/69 | | 200 | |
| 10 | 20 | 2 | 1 | FABRICATE KNIFE | 12/10/68 | 20 | 1/10/69 | 5 | 1/17/69 | | 1250 | |
| 11 | 13 | 4 | 2 | BRAKE WORKLIST | 12/ 4/68 | 22 | 1/ 8/69 | 2 | 1/10/69 | | 250 | |
| 1 | 14 | 1 | 1 | SUBPLATE SPECS. | 11/18/68 | 24 | 12/23/68 | 2 | 12/27/68 | | 250 | |
| 14 | 15 | 4 | 2 | ORDER SUBPLATE | 11/20/68 | 24 | 12/27/68 | 2 | 12/31/68 | | 50 | |
| 15 | 21 | 4 | 2 | RECEIVE SUBPLATE | 11/22/68 | 24 | 12/31/68 | 21C | 1/21/69 | | 250 | |
| | | | | ***TOTAL*** | | | | | | | 27725 | 3494 |

| I NODE | J NODE | RES ** | ID | ACTIVITY DESCRIPTION | EARLY ST. DATE | TOTAL SLACK | LATE ST. DATE | DURA-TION | LATE END DATE | PERCENT ELAPSED | TOTAL $ VALUE | $ VALUE COMPLETE |
|---|---|---|---|---|---|---|---|---|---|---|---|---|
| 1 | 5 | 1 | 1 | DRUM DRAWINGS | 10/30/68 | | | 10 | 11/14/68 | 100.0 | 1250 | 1250 |
| 1 | 16 | 1 | 1 | HYDRAULIC DETAILS | 11/ 1/68 | | | 5 | 11/11/68 | 100.0 | 625 | 625 |
| 1 | 18 | 1 | 1 | GEAR BOX SPECS. | 11/ 6/68 | | | 5 | 11/13/68 | 100.0 | 625 | 625 |
| 1 | 11 | 1 | 1 | BRAKE DRAWINGS | 11/12/68 | | | 15 | 12/ 4/68 | 26.7 | 1875 | 499 |
| 1 | 2 | 1 | 1 | PREPARE FOUNDATION | 11/14/68 | | | 5 | 11/21/68 | 40.0 | 625 | 249 |
| 5 | 7 | 1 | 1 | DRUM WORKLIST | 11/18/68 | 20 | 12/17/68 | 5 | 12/26/68 | | 300 | |
| 1 | 9 | 1 | 1 | KNIFE DRAWINGS | 11/18/68 | 20 | 12/17/68 | 12 | 1/ 7/69 | | 1500 | |
| 1 | 14 | 1 | 1 | SUBPLATE SPECS. | 11/18/68 | 24 | 12/23/68 | 2 | 12/27/68 | | 250 | |
| | | | | ***TOTAL*** | | | | | | | 7050 | 3248 |

| RES | TOTAL $ VALUE | $ VALUE COMPLETE | RES | TOTAL $ VALUE | $ VALUE COMPLETE |
|---|---|---|---|---|---|
| 1 | 7050 | 3248 | 2 | 12800 | 0 |
| 3 | 1500 | 0 | 4 | 6375 | 246 |

| ID | TOTAL $ VALUE | $ VALUE COMPLETE | ID | TOTAL $ VALUE | $ VALUE COMPLETE |
|---|---|---|---|---|---|
| 1 | 21350 | 3248 | 2 | 6375 | 246 |

**Fig. 12.** Computer output on an update run. (From *Project Management with CPM and PERT*, J. J. Moder and C. R. Phillips, © 1970 by Litton Educational Publishing, Inc. Reprinted by permission of Van Nostrand Reinhold Co.)

include:

1. Separate progress report outputs for three or more levels of indenture in the organization, e.g., a program manager report, subproject manager reports, and finally task manager reports under each subproject.
2. Elaborate computer printed graphical type outputs of resource requirements vs time; actual and planned expenditures vs time; bar chart type outputs showing activity early start, late finish, and scheduled times; etc.
3. Data base reports for cost estimating, labor standards, etc.
4. All too infrequently they include a resource leveling subroutine.

   Although it is technically possible to only elect those options of a program that are desired, most users find that these elaborate packages are quite difficult to implement in this way.

## OTHER NETWORKING SCHEMES

   The activity-on-arrow networking logic presented in the section entitled The Logic of Networks as Models for Project Plans was the system utilized in the development of PERT and CPM, and is today the one most widely used. However, it is not the easiest for the novice to learn. For this reason, another scheme, called activity-on-node, will undoubtedly continue to gain popularity and should someday become the standard method.

### The Activity-on-Node Networking Scheme

   The activity-on-node system is merely the reversal of the other, that is, the nodes represent the activities and the arrows become the connectors to denote the precedence relationships.

   This system is illustrated in Fig. 13 where the simple task of framing a three-story structure and applying siding is condidered. In Fig. 13(a) the activity-on-arrow network indicates the strictly sequential project plan will require 6 weeks to complete. To reduce the project duration, we can let these two activities proceed basically in parallel. By letting the framing proceed alone during the first week, and applying the siding alone on the last, the project duration is reduced to 4 weeks. This network, given in Fig. 13(b), requires a total of seven activities, one of which is a dummy. It is the latter which presents a problem to the novice, and it is this problem that is eliminated by the use of the activity-on-node scheme, which is drawn in Fig. 13(c).

   Neither of these networking schemes, however, can cope with the problem of rapidly escalating numbers of activities when two or more jobs follow each other with a lag, such as occurred in Figs. 13(b) and 13(c). Since this situation occurs quite frequently, particularly in construction work, the following networking scheme is gaining considerable attention.

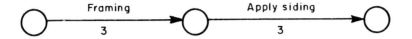

(a) Sequential plan with activity—on—arrow

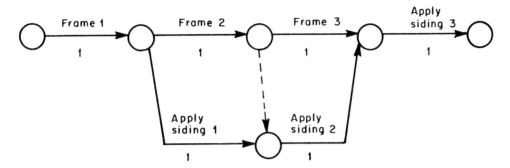

(b) Parallel plan with activity—on—arrow

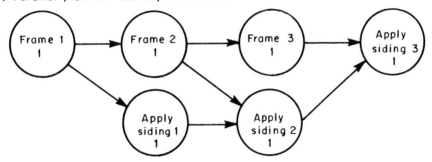

(c) Parallel plan with activity—on—node

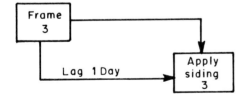

(d) Parallel plan with precedence diagramming

**Fig. 13.** Comparison of alternative networking schemes.

## Precedence Diagramming

An extension of the original activity-on-node concept called "precedence diagramming" appeared around 1964 in the User's Manual for an IBM 1440 computer program (see Ref. 2). The modifications introduced by this scheme consist of several additional ways of displaying the dependency relationships between activities. Instead of strictly discrete dependencies, the precedence rules permit more liberal specification of lags and delays among both activity start and finish constraints.

As an example, the project plan shown in Figs. 13(b) and 13(c) is repeated in Fig. 13(d) using precedence diagramming. Only two nodes and two arrows are required, indicating that this can be a considerably more efficient scheme for networking this type of project activity. Another advantage for cost control purposes is that each of the two major activities, framing and apply siding, are shown as single activities.

A limited number of computer programs are available to handle the networking schemes described in this and the preceding section. As the use of these schemes increases, the availability of computer programs should increase.

## THE COMPUTER AND CRITICAL PATH METHODS

Critical path methods represent a modern tool to aid the project manager. As such, the computer represents an adjunct which may or may not be useful to him. For example, suppose a surgeon uses critical path methods in planning his surgical operations. His networks would probably be of modest size, they would be developed for each patient and presumably never updated, and no sophisticated questions are asked. In this case the computer is really unnecessary, even though the technique may be extremely useful. However, if the surgeon was interested in research, he could pose some sophisticated questions which would change this answer.

In general, when sophisticated resource allocation, project control, or database development questions are asked, or when the project network must be updated a number of times during the life of a project, then the computer becomes a useful adjunct. What then should the computer be asked to do?

Given below is a list of 15 features of computer programs used in critical path methods, along with comments by the author for their incorporation in general purpose programs.

1. *Basic Scheduling Computations*. Required of all programs; however, computer CPU time can vary appreciably depending on the algorithm that is used.
2. *Network (Time) Updating*. Required of all programs; attention should be given to flexibility and ease of use and interpretation.
3. *Network Cost Analysis and Control*. Optional, but strongly recommended for general purpose programs.
4. *Time-Cost Trade-Off Algorithm*. Not recommended because of low demand for this feature.
5. *Resource Allocation* (techniques described in the section entitled Scheduling Activities to Satisfy Time and Resource Constraints). Optional but strongly

recommended because of the large potential pay-off in many project management situations.

6. *Three-Time Estimate System* (ability to accept three-time estimates, in place of one, to estimate the mean activity duration time). Optional; recommended because of its potential value and ease of implementation.

7. *PERT Probability*. Optional; weak recommendation; feature not as important as Item 6.

8. *Network Condensation* (ability to automatically restructure the network preserving only an arbitrary set of milestone events). Optional; recommended for applications to very large-scale projects.

9. *Output Sorts* (ability to list the project activities that have been sorted on one or more keys, e.g., by increasing slack and then by early start time would group the critical path activities first in the output). Required of all programs.

10. *Scheduled Dates* (ability to specify arbitrary scheduled dates for activity start times or event times). Optional but strongly recommended.

11. *Calendar Dates in Output*. Optional; strongly recommended.

12. *Multiple Initial and Terminal Events*. Optional; a nice feature, but the user can avoid the need for it.

13. *Random Event Numbering* (as distinguished from the requirement that $i < j$ for all activities $i$-$j$). Required of all good programs; this is relatively easy to incorporate, and it removes a significant burden from the user.

14. *Network Error Detection* (ability to detect and specify network loops in error messages). Required of all good programs.

15. *Graphical Type Outputs* (output in the form of bar charts, histograms, or curves relating cost, resource requirement, etc. as a function of time). Optional; recommended for systems where reports for ''upper'' management are prepared as well as reports for lower levels of indenture.

A selected survey of computer programs for project planning and control was prepared by Paulson [7]. This survey, which includes both interactive and batch-type programs, indicates which of the 15 features listed above are included in the program. Further discussion of this subject will also be found in Ref. 6 and in the publications of the Project Management Institute.

The development of computer programs incorporating the features recommended above, and based on good algorithms, should open many new doors for the application of critical path methods in the future. These management information systems are expected to incorporate the cathode-ray tube, and other hardware, as input–output devices more and more, as we approach the total management information system. This will include the ability to produce bar-chart-type network displays at several levels of detail, which in turn will permit management to creatively interrogate the computer and carry out rather sophisticated analysis on a real time basis. This appears to hold real promise to the solution of many communication problems of functionally organized businesses that are heavily engaged in project-type activities.

## REFERENCES

1. Davis, E. W., and J. H. Patterson, A comparison of heuristic and optimum solutions in resource constrained project scheduling, *Manage. Sci.* (1974).
2. IBM, *Project Management System, Application Description Manual* (H20-0210), IBM, 1968.
3. Kelley, J. E., Critical path planning and scheduling: Mathematical basis, *Oper. Res.* **9**(3), 296–320 (1961). J. Kelley and M. Walker, Critical-path planning and scheduling in *Proceedings of the Eastern Joint Computer Conference,* 1959.
4. Lockyer, K. G., *An Introduction to Critical Path Analysis,* 3rd ed., Pitman, London, 1969, p. 3.
5. Malcolm, D. G., J. H. Roseboom, C. E. Clark, and W. Fazar, Applications of a technique for R and D program evaluation (PERT), *Oper. Res.* **7**(5), 646–669 (1959).
6. Moder, J. J., and C. R. Phillips, *Project Management with CPM and PERT,* 2nd ed., Van Nostrand Reinhold, New York, 1970.
7. Paulson, B. C., *Man–Computer Concepts for Project Management,* The Stanford Construction Institute's Technical Report No. 148, Palo Alto, California, August 1971 (see Appendix B).
8. Pritsker, A. B., and R. R. Burgess, *The GERT Simulation Programs*, Department of Industrial Engineering, Virginia Polytechnic Institute, 1970. (See also the section on GERT in this encyclopedia.)
9. Wiest, J. D., A heuristic model for scheduling large projects with limited resources, *Manage. Sci.* **13**(6), B359–B377 (February 1967).

*Joseph J. Moder*

# CRYPTANALYSIS

## WHAT IS CRYPTANALYSIS?

There are many situations in which a person needs to communicate, but also needs to be discreet. These occur often in everyday life, and it may be that only in extreme cases does one have to resort to ciphers. One such extreme might be a conspiracy; the conspirators must be able to tell each other what they are doing or intend to do, but not let this information get to the opposition or to the police. The rumrunners of 1930 used encipherment to set up rendezvous for delivering spirits. The Coast Guard was charged with balking them, and was in turn forced into using ciphers.

Diplomats often find it necessary to keep negotiations secret. Experience shows that it is impossible to arrange trades with an interested audience, despite President Wilson's ambition for "Open agreements openly arrived at." Labor negotiators have the same problem, but usually solve it by meeting personally. When Secretary of State Seward wanted to warn the French that the United States was ready to go to war if necessary over the installation of Maximilian as Emperor of Mexico, it was essential that this ultimatum not be made public. If it had been public, then the French government might not have been able to back down as it did do, and Seward might have had to keep up his belligerent attitude.

As an example of how serious the effect of such analysis can be, take the case of the so-called Zimmermann note. President Wilson cited it in his request of Congress for a declaration of war. This was a message sent in code by Zimmermann, the Foreign Minister of Germany, to his ambassador in Washington for forwarding to the German minister in Mexico, discussing the inducements that they could offer to Mexico to make war on the United States if the United States declared war on Germany. President Wilson had a copy of the clear text from the British, who had inferred its meaning. The President had released it to the Press, so that the Congress knew what he meant. Of course, at that time the route by which the President had acquired the text was known to only a very few; the British were anxious that the Germans should not realize the weakness of their codes, and went to great lengths to obscure the source of the information. This is an illuminating example of the importance of secrecy. Kahn pp. 282–297 [1,] has a vivid account.

Military forces use ciphers extensively. The commander needs to know the situation, and the enemy must be kept ignorant. Position reports by navy units are a good example. The commander cannot use the unit unless he knows where and in what condition it is, and this very information is just what the enemy needs in order to counter it.

Cryptanalysis is the art of reading ciphers without the key. By contrast, the science of designing ciphers is called cryptography. The cryptographer needs to know all that he can about cryptanalysis in order to guard against it. Sometimes the inferences that can be made by cryptanalysis are astounding and dramatic; at other times they can be frustratingly vacuous.

## IS IT TRUE THAT ANY CIPHER CAN BE BROKEN, OR IS THERE AN UNBREAKABLE CIPHER?

In "The Gold Bug" Poe asserts that any cipher can be broken. In his autobiography, *A Mathematician's Apology,* G. H. Hardy says that the existence of an unbreakable cipher is obvious. Who is right? In order to judge, it must first be understood just what was meant. As I take it, these two authors were thinking of a single message enciphered by a method used only once, and the result presented as a challenge from one of them to the other. But how long is the message? And what does it say, and in what language? These are pertinent points. If the message is one letter long, a "y" for yes and an "n" for no, then Hardy is right. But if it is the Charter of the United Nations, then one cannot be so sure, both because of the greater length with which the analyst can work and because the plain text is already available to him (although he may be unaware of this). The statements of Poe and Hardy have meaning only when the characteristics of the text to be transmitted are known.

In a practical situation, as for example a cryptographer who is designing a cipher for diplomatic use, the type of message, the method of forwarding, the amount of risk which is acceptable in view of the costs, and other factors—such as who will be doing the enciphering, how skilled is he—are considered. Messages from the ambassador to the chief of state will be formal, explicit, and urgent. Messages from the chief clerk to a consul will be *pro forma* (using abreviations) and long, such as lists of travelers to be expected and how to treat them, authorizations for expenditures, and directives. Messages by mail will have less exposure to analysis than those sent by radio. Traffic from a consul may reasonably be risked more than that from the ambassador. If the system is to be used by the ambassador himself, it can be anticipated that more mistakes will be made than if it is to be implemented by a well-trained clerk. Costs are an everpresent consideration. Many of the old books recommend elaborate ways of concealing the very presence of the critical message, but this is by current methods very expensive, since it multiplies the length by three or more. When traffic went by mail, this length mattered little.

In order to limit stresses on his system, the crytopgrapher may end up putting restrictions on its use. He may say that no signal longer than a thousand words will be sent in it, or that no information will be put into it which is also sent by another way, or that the total information sent in it will not exceed a million words. Usually the design will have in it some parameters which can be changed. Often there is a setting for a period of time, and a particularization for the message itself. Typically, it is forbidden to use the message key again in the same key period.

The cryptographer will schedule key changes depending on the traffic load and on the delays encountered with communications. If the period is made too short, then the cipher clerk will be repeatedly confronted with late messages for which he will have to revert to the old key. On some cipher machines this is a tedious and error-prone chore; on the Hagelin device described below it involves the setting of 185 toggles. The greatest danger is that he will reset to the old key, read the delayed message, and then set up the current key with an error—like the one illustrated below perhaps—and then send out an erroneous and maybe commissive transmission. One can guard against this by giving him two machines, one for incoming and one for outgoing traffic. The machine for incoming may be repeatedly reset, but any error in doing this will be readily detected and corrected without penalty, while that for outgoing is used only for the one purpose and set once permanently each period.

In all of this we see that the type and amount of communication is the paramount consideration in designing the cipher. No matter how sophisticated the system is, it still can be overloaded. One effect of an overload is to cause the reuse of parameters. For example, if the setting for a message is a letter of the alphabet, then the twenty-seventh communication of the period necessarily implies a duplication. Another effect is to give more opportunity for mistakes. Even though the setting for a message may be five letters, allowing for over four hundred thousand settings in a period—enough for any use—still reuses will mount as traffic gets heavy. Retransmissions mount up too; for the importance of these see below.

The title of this section is a meaningless question. A similar but more realistic question is: Given the body of information that has already been transmitted through this cipher system, is it now readable? In other words, is it time for a change?

When the engineers of the Bell Telephone System had developed the teletype machine, which is a typewriter run over a telegraph line together with the capability to retain and reproduce information by means of a paper tape, then they were in a position to make a cipher machine. Gilbert Vernam did just that in 1917, using the paper tape to hold the key which was combined with plain text typed on the keyboard to give cipher text which was sent over the telegraph line. At the far end of the line an exact copy of the key was also held on punched paper tape and combined with the cipher text to form plain text, which was typed by the teletype.

Vernam's invention had two elements of significant novelty. One was that his device enciphered and transmitted simultaneously, the first "on-line" system. Another was that he provided for no reuse of the key tape, so that his key was "one time." When the Vernam device was demonstrated to Major Mauborgne of the Army, the problem of supplying and accounting for (and especially accounting for, since after use every copy of the key must be destroyed) enough key tape for one-time use seemed too great, and he asked for reconsideration. The Bell group then suggested using two key tapes, allowing reuse of the two separately and independantly. Two loops of tape of lengths 999 and 1000 were then tried, but, as used by Vernam and subject to a somewhat artificial test, proved to give inadequate protection, so that Mauborgne returned to the one-time tape concept, despite its massive production and distribution problems.

Enthusiasts claim that a one-time key gives an unbreakable system. Their reasoning is based on two unstated assumptions. One is that there is more key than traffic. The other is that the key has been made in an unsystematic fashion.

Neither of these can be expected to hold without exception. How can one, in advance when the key is being made, know what the traffic load will be? How can one make large volumes of key without using a system?

Once upon a time there was appointed a Very Distinguished Man to the post of Preeminent Ambassador. Knowing something about the problems of secret communications, he consulted the records and found that never in the past had there been more than a thousand messages from one ambassador in a month. Therefore he insisted that he be supplied each month without fail with enough one-time key for three thousand telegrams.

But the man who had to supply the key was not distinguished; his resources were not adequate to his task even before the unusually heavy demand of the V.D.M. At first he tried to make the key by doodling on the keyboard, but then he found that he was falling into patterns. Later it occurred to him that he could take the punched tape put out by his first efforts and feed it in again to get another. Although the output was a copy, he reasoned that it was not so, because the beginnings were different. Later he devised means of copying the tape with changes, such as reading it backwards, or upside down, or other ways. Who would know? Not the Foreign Minister; he never looked at these things. Not the V.D.M.; he did not look closely at the key. Not the coding secretary; it looked random to him.

It is not possible to supply large amounts of key without a system to generate it, and a key that has been generated by a system is systematic. Thus Assumption 2 cannot be fulfilled, not over an unlimited span. Even Assumption 1 can be satisfied only within a certain probability, for the amount of traffic cannot be controlled by the coding secretary, nor by the ambassador, be he ever so distinguished, nor even by the Foreign Minister; it depends on international affairs, threats of war, economic moves, and other surprises in the news.

## SHOULD THE CRYPTOGRAPHER DESIGN A SINGLE LARGE SYSTEM OR MANY SMALL ONES?

Besides having to supply unsystematic key in quantities greater than the anticipated traffic, the cryptographer must adapt his system to the structure of the communications system on which it is carried. The military have their own communications, and their ciphers are carried thereby. Thus routing, priorities, and protocol on error correction and repeats are prescribed. Diplomats, on the contrary, usually use commercial facilities, and routing, priorities, and protocol are what they can contract for. One of the complications of the Zimmermann note was that the war had interrupted the normal German route to Mexico, so that the note had to be sent via Washington where it had to be decoded and then reencoded. Had the communications been slightly different, the note might not have been read by the British. If Zimmermann had organized his codes differently, the note would not have needed reencoding.

Should the chief of state write to all of his ambassadors in the same system, or should each have his own cipher? If the latter, he will have compartmentation against disaster, but each circular sent to all diplomats will necessarily go out in many versions, an invitation to analysis.

There are many solutions and compromises with this quandary. The military tend to like systems in which each unit can talk to each other, for they never know in advance what coordination will be required. Many ambassadors insist on having their own private systems, possibly because they feel that they cannot conduct their affairs with someone looking over their shoulders. Business men and agents in general go for private systems, perhaps because they have little need for broadcasting, or because compartmentation appeals to them.

By the use of many systems, each with only a small number of correspondents, the cryptographer can keep the volume of any one system low, but the total volume will thereby be increased by duplications between systems. By providing a single general purpose cipher for all users, he can keep the total volume down, and, more important, minimize the dangerous reenciphering from one system to another. But in an omnibus system the plain text is (potentially, at least) available in many places, so that the chance that it will escape is increased. And if it does escape, and if as a result the keys are deduced, then everybody in the system is exposed, together with all of their correspondence since the system was put into effect.

There is no avoiding the choice. One must take the one risk or the other.

## WHICH METHOD OF ENCIPHERMENT SHOULD THE CRYPTOGRAPHER USE?

Whatever method of encipherment is used, basically it will be to substitute one unit of communications for another. This can be done with a table in which the representative is looked up. The unit may be one letter, in which case the method is called "substitution," or it can be a syllable or a word or a phrase, in which case the method is called a "code," or at the smallest it could be a binary digit in the coding of the letters.

If the operation is not to be done with a table, then it must be done by means of an algorithm. One algorithm which has occurred often is that of using the original units but to rearrange or "transpose" them. The message CALL AT TWELVE TONIGHT could be written first as

```
C  A  L  L  A
T  T  W  E  L
V  E  T  O  N
I  G  H  T  X
```

and then as L W T H C T V I L E O T A L N X A T E G.

An objection to any serious use of this method is that a mistake on one letter may jeopardize the whole message; if a letter is omitted in transmission, then all the subsequent letters are out of place, and the message may be incomprehensible. A cryptanalyst might very well be able to reconstruct the error and the message, but the legitimate recipient, with other urgent matters on his mind, is unlikely to be able to do so with certainty. For longer texts there is more calculation involved in deciphering, there is more chance that the cipher was mutilated en route, and the effect of an omission is more disrupting. For these reasons transpositions are not much used.

Furthermore, the process of transposing is difficult to mechanize. The entire text is operated on as a whole, rather than letter by letter as in other systems. In the present state of affairs this is less attractive. A computer can do it, of course, but our man in Havana may not have a computer.

It is convenient to work with letters as the units to be enciphered. One way is to write an alphabet, and on the next line below that another, scrambled.

```
A B C D E F G H I J K L M N O P Q R S T U V W X Y Z
C O M P E N S A T I B D F G H J K L Q R U V W X Y Z
```

Then one can replace each letter in the plain text in its turn by its equivalent from this table. The upper line is given here as a normal alphabet, although it need not be. The upper line can be permuted into any sequence one likes; if each letter has its lower equivalent permuted with it, then it still has the same effect. The only advantage in having an unusual sequence in the upper line is that a complex sequence may be remembered better as a combination of two simple sequences; in some applications it is necessary to memorize the cipher.

If the second line is also a normal alphabet, slid to the left and around the end, then this is the simplest of all simple substitutions, attributed to Julius Caesar. Another popular and simple version is to have the bottom line be the reverse of the alphabet above. In this way the operation of deciphering is just the same as that of enciphering; if A goes to Y, then Y goes to A.

Even simpler, mechanically, would be to put in the place of the commutator a barrel, with contacts on its two ends and scrambled wires inside (see Fig. 1). This idea has been patented four times, by Scherbius, Koch, Hebern, and Damm. Each position of the barrel gives a substitution, and all the positions together give a table. But the table is not a Vigenère square. Mathematically the rows are related by being transforms of one another under the permutation defined by the wiring on the end plates. The table when written out is called a Friedman square, for it was William F. Friedman who pointed out that the square had the end plate sequence running down its diagonals. Again, by having a varying key of enough sophistication, one can get good security.

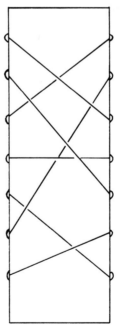

**Fig. 1.** Rotor. Each face of this thick disk has on it 26 contacts, one for each key of a typewriter. The two faces are wired together, contact to contact, with a scramble. A rotation of $\frac{1}{26}$ revolution will change the effect of the scramble. Rotors can be used in series to make a more effective encipherment.

Another way to get security without elaborating the key too much is to make a succession of barrels, each of which can be positioned erratically. The motion of the rotors must be such that a large number of settings are gone through before repeating. A number of cipher machines have been based on the wired rotor, the most famous being the Enigma, a German machine sold commercially before World War II.

The Enigma had some wiring at the end of the stack of rotors which sent the electric current back through the maze, (see Fig. 2). This had two effects; it made the decipherment the same operation as encipherment, so that no special provision had to be made for deciphering, and it prevented a letter ever representing itself. If you saw a letter R in the cipher you could be sure that the related plain letter was not an R. Many cipher systems have this property, Playfair being another. Other cipher machines have an encipher–decipher switch, which has the effect of turning the maze around; this is not so on the Enigma.

The Japanese used some cipher devices which were like rotor machines except that they used telephone stepping relays instead of a barrel. That is, their barrels could assume any one of twenty-five positions (the telephone companies make ten position and twenty-five position, but not twenty-six position switches), and at each would give a scramble. But the twenty-five scrambles were not related as they would be with a rotor, but were completely independent. This is an advantage in security in that the cryptanalyst is given a bigger job to recover all of them, and a drag in that the manufacturer also has a bigger job and more chances to make mistakes. Stepping switches are less rugged than rotors.

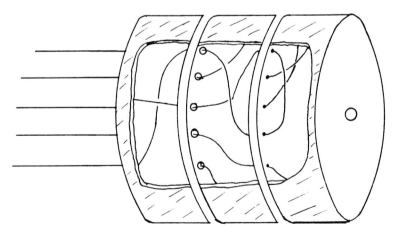

**Fig. 2.** Enigma. The figure shows three rotors, capped on the right by a reflector. A circuit is shown: one of the 26 contacts on the left is connected by means of the keyboard to a source of voltage, which voltage appears at exactly one of the remaining 25 grounded contacts, where it can be sensed and displayed or recorded. The rotation of one or more components will then present a new scramble.

Still another cipher device, the last machine to be described here, is the so-called Bazeries cylinder (see Fig. 3). Bazeries was a French cryptologist who recommended this device around 1891, but it was known much earlier, to Thomas Jefferson among others. One way of making it is as a succession of disks, say 25 of them, mounted on a spindle. No two of the disks are alike, so that their order on the spindle is a key. Around the edge of each disk is an alphabet, no two alike. If the disks are twisted relative to each other until a text is lined up, such as I O N L Y R E G R E T H A V I N G B U T O N E L I F E, then any other parallel line will be cipher text. If we agreed to always use the fourth line under, then we would have a multiple substitution with period 25, as each twenty-fifth letter would be enciphered by the same alphabet. This would be a reasonable usage, but an even better one is simply attained. Notice that if in our excitement one of us had used the fifth instead of the fourth line, the other in reading it might not even perceive the error, for in looking for plain he might not count the lines. Why then insist on a preset number? Take the lines at random. With this usage the period is no longer 25, for with different numbers of lines the substitutions are different. This cipher can be very effective. It requires no electricity, and the disks can even be simulated with paper. Of course, it does not make a copy of the text, either plain or cipher, and there is the possibility of confusion in searching for plain text.

If we want to use a unit other than the letter for substitution, a good system is the Playfair. In this cipher we substitute pairs of letters for pairs. We do this by means of a five by five array, as for example

$$
\begin{array}{ccccc}
W & H & E & A & T \\
M & P & Q & R & O \\
L & Y & Z & S & N \\
K & X & V & U & B \\
I & G & F & D & C \\
\end{array}
$$

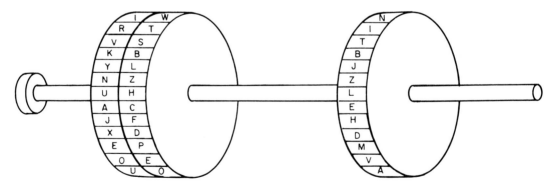

**Fig. 3.** Bazeries cylinder. The 25 solid aluminum disks are mounted in some order on the spindle. On each disk is a scrambled alphabet. The order of the disks on the spindle is critical; it must be right. To encipher, one rotates each disk in turn until the message can be read on one line. Another line is then the cipher.

Each pair will define a rectangle on which the pair are opposite vertices. For example, take the pair ER. In the square it appears

E A
Q R

The substitute is then the other vertices of the rectangle, read up or down in the same direction as the original. ER is replaced by AQ, and RE by QA. The pair NE becomes ZT. But if the two letters are on the same line, the rule collapses. In that case take the image of each to be the next on its right, going around the end if necessary. If the two are in the same column, then take the next below. Thus TE becomes WA, and US goes to DU. If the pair is a doublet, such as LL, either insert a null letter, say X, or drop one of the offending pair; no doublets are allowed. Thus ALL might be sent as AL, cipher WS, or ALXL, cipher WSKY. This cipher, which was invented by Sir Charles Wheatstone, of Wheatstone bridge fame, is very simple and surprisingly effective.

Among these and many other methods the cryptographer has a wide choice. He is even free to combine them in new and unusual ways. But whatever his choice, he will have to stick by it in later times, even if it proves vulnerable, because the replacement of a cipher system requires the coordination of many remote people under trying security restrictions.

## WHEN DOES THE CRYPTANALYST GET A BREAK?

The analyst in attacking a cipher system must diagnose the method and then recover elements of keys. He should first study thoroughly the body of traffic, learning its characteristics and looking for symptoms of the method. There are a number of situations which, if they should be present, favor the analyst. Some are of only minor advantage, so that the analyst must be patient and accumulate enough of them.

Consider the following example. One day a message of 17 groups is passed. The next day another of 17 groups appears from the same originator. Perhaps they have the same underlying plain test? Comparison of the beginnings shows

T H H M S   A C D H C   F U I F N R I S C P     from one and
T M H M N   A C I H H   A P I K N M D S H P     from the other

Between the two, exactly half of the letters coincide. This pattern persists throughout; in the 85 positions there are 42 coincidences. Probably a mistake was made in the first version, then corrected in the second. The coincidences occur in a pattern of 19 positions, and is repeated four times; the little excerpt above had the complete pattern. Looking closely, one sees that when the letters do not coincide, then they differ by five in the standard alphabet, H to M, S to N, D to I, and so forth. The enciphering procedure must have a component which changes at every step, and repeats after 19 steps. When active it causes the cipher to be five letters greater. Looking even more closely at the text we see that where they disagree it is sometimes the first that is more advanced and sometimes the second. A little study will disclose the pattern of the underlying 19-component; its position differs by three in the two versions of the cipher. This suggests strongly that the cipher system is based on one of the Hagelin machines, the C38, which has a 19-wheel among its six wheels.

To return to the example above, since we now know that the system is based on the Hagelin machine and is therefore vulnerable to depth, we will search for depth, and if we find 30 groups or more, and if we can read it, then we may be able to read all the traffic of the period.

There is another favorable case which in its mechanics resembles depth, and that is the case of sending the same message twice on different keys. To fix the ideas, suppose this has happened on a Vernam system. Then, as with depth, if one can guess some key for one, then the key for the other will appear, and if one can recognize key, then he can read the single message. The trouble is that one cannot expect, in most systems, to be able to recognize key. In their efforts to get very long keys, some people have used whole books (as was illustrated in "Schweik the Good Soldier") as key, called "running key" or "book cipher." With such key the coherence of the book would enable one to recognize it as key, and the message could be read.

But even when the key is featureless, the analyst should not despair. Suppose the following situation. A Foreign Office which uses Playfair sends a message to each of its representatives abroad, one in each of the United Nations. The messages are not all the same length, so they are certainly not all the same, but there is reason to believe that they are all on the same subject, and that they may all have the same beginning. If we write the 76 (we missed some) texts, one above the other on a long sheet of paper, and remember that in Playfair each plain letter is always replaced by a different letter, then we can look down each column and the one letter that is not there will be the common plain text. If in some columns there is more than one missing letter then the coherence of the natural language—whatever it is—will enable us to select the right one from the two or three alternatives.

An important case is that where the analyst has both the plain and cipher texts together. This can happen if texts are subsequently released, as Ellsberg did with the "Pentagon Papers," or as Tyler Kent did with 1500 documents from the American Embassy in London when Joseph P. Kennedy was Ambassador.

Such material does not tell the analyst directly what the method is, but it is rich material for him to work with. His first task is to get the plains paired off with and lined up properly with the ciphers. There may be discrepancies, if the plains have been edited for instance; these must be reedited to fit the ciphers. A normal way to proceed is to form a working hypothesis and then test it. If an hypothesis fits well enough so that all of the parameters can be recovered, that is good enough. It may be false, but if it works, then it is usable. More often it fails because parameters cannot be found to adapt it to the case in hand. In the face of such a failure, one must revise the hypothesis and start again.

There is a great deal of information in a page of matched plain and cipher. By the very nature of ciphers it is not possible to give a recipe for reducing this information to the algorithm of encipherment, but a few such pages can give away any system, after sufficient computation.

## HOW CAN COMPUTERS BE USED IN CRYPTANALYSIS?

Computers can be used in three ways; to simulate cipher machines which either do not exist yet or do not exist here, to do clerical work such as indexing the available traffic, and to make trial decipherments.

To take up the last of these three first, suppose that it is known that a message was enciphered on an Enigma machine, and the rotors and the order in which they go into the machine are known, but the starting alignment is not known. A computer can be programmed to decipher the first ten letters assuming each possible start in turn; there are only about eighteen thousand such starts. But the analyst would have to be desperate to try what has just been described, for to look among eighteen thousand lines to see which one was English is an impossible job. Better to program a preliminary selection, with the analyst examining a few hundred of the best. The program will have to do its selection purely on the basis of statistics, such as a preponderance of E's or the rarity of X's, Q's, J's, and Z's. More than ten letters will be needed, maybe fifteen words. A more refined test but more expensive would be to compare the putative plain with a dictionary of words and frequent letter combinations. If those which pass this test are printed out, together with the parameters of the key by which they are derived, then the analyst can make his inspection. However good they look, at most one of them can be right. If the statistical test allows more than fifty to pass, then it can still be a difficult test for the analyst.

One reason for simulating a cipher machine which does not exist is to exercise the machine and see what kind of cipher text it would give or what kind of performance. This would be of use to the cryptographer, who habitually studies any new cipher system at great length before releasing it for use. He might simulate the encipherment of texts which were usually favorable for analysis and then study the cipher texts to see how probable breaking would be. He might even employ analysts to try to break them; if they succeeded or if they came too near doing so, he would then revise the system. In this way he can avoid unpleasant surprises later in the development or deployment.

The analyst also has use for simulation. After studying the accumulated traffic he may arrive at an hypothesis about the unknown cipher. He will then concentrate on his hypothesis. By means of simulation he will attempt to duplicate the characteristics of the traffic. Such experience will help him to modify his hypothesis realistically.

If the analyst is lucky and finally understands the system, then he is in the enviable but awkward position of being surrounded by volumes of communications which helped him to infer the keys, but which now stand between him and completion of his task. The translation of so many ciphers to intelligence may be a gargantuan job; it certainly will be if he has nothing but pencil and paper to do it with. A computer can, of course, do it quickly and neatly.

Another clerical application for the computer is in a cryptanalytic attack on a code. Suppose for definiteness of ideas that the code is made up of four digit groups. It may be that 7689 means "verify," 4449 means "message number" (the following group to be read as a number), and 5271 means "period." Then the excerpt 7689 4449 0133 5271 means "verify msg. #133 stop." But the analyst does not know this to start. He examines a large number of dispatches to find that 5271 never occurs at a beginning, and very often occurs at an end. He finds that 4449 always appears before groups of the style 0023, which might be message numbers, and 7689 often appears before 4449. On the basis of this he guesses at a few meanings, and then goes over the entire corpus of traffic again in the light of these inferences. If he knows anything about msg. #133, he may be able to fill in other groups. Given enough traffic, enough collateral information, and enough time, then he can read the code. A computer can save him enormous amounts of time, for only it can accept his inferences, fill them in, and start on the next iteration with a small turn-around time. The computer, properly programmed, can even call his attention to interesting and productive phenomena, such as three and four group repeats. Without the use of a computer, this procedure is terribly cumbersome.

Another technique usable on the computer is for reading depths on a Vigenère or similar system. In a depth of two, knowing a word in one will give—with suitable calculation—the corresponding text of the other. For example, if CORRECTION is in one, then the other may show NDSTODETER. (The Vernam systems normally include all the control functions of the teletype system: space, carriage return, line feed, and case shifts. Other systems economize by omitting these, some even doing without the space between words, as here.) Notice that the two E's and two T's make it plausible that this is plain text, but the proposition is by no means compelling. If we try the probable word CORRECTION in several hundred places, we will get several looking as good as the above by chance. (NDSTODETER is part of "seconds to determine.") Most would look much worse; here are two incorrect taken at random, XFAMYCBUKM and TRGYKSYLIN. To illustrate again the difficulty of recognition, dragging the word STATEMENT reveals AULNINEPR at the right place (Part of Paulnine program).

Dragging probable words is a lot of work, and a computer can be very valuable. The recognition is difficult and is best done by eye and by secondary testing, unless the probable word is very long—a probable phrase. By secondary testing I mean trying to extend the texts to right or left of the "break."

A computer can also be used to manage the mass of telegrams. It can help find instances of messages of the same length originated at nearly the same time, which may be resends or corrections. It can note cases of repeated first groups, or better yet, cases where the first groups are not the same but are nearly so. It can find pairs of messages which have small parts of them the same. It can look for words, for sometimes what purports to be cipher is inadvertently plain text. Any plain is intelligence, of course, but plain found under the semblence of cipher may be the plain of the preceding or following cipher; somebody sent both plain and cipher. What a find!

There are other ways the computer can do clerical work for the analyst. One of these is to count statistics of the telegrams he is working over. A few statistical calculations often show that the analyst is misled by his intuition, and that any pile of twenty million letters could be expected by the laws of chance to have what was found.

The inference of the meaning of enciphered messages is a matter of considerable sophistication and offers opportunities to use computers in clever ways. The subject has never-ending variation because it is essentially a game; each advance of the analyst can be countered by the cryptographer by using a different twist. The prize goes to him who is most persistent, most industrious, and most ingenious.


## REFERENCE

1.  D. Kahn, *The Code Breakers,* Macmillan, 1967. Comprehensive.


## SELECTED BIBLIOGRAPHY

Candela, R., *The Military Cipher of Commandant Bazeries,* New York, 1938. An essay in decrypting.
Eyraud, C., *Precis de Cryptographie Moderne,* Editions Raoul Tari, Paris, 1953. Modern.
Gaines, H. F., *Cryptanalysis,* Dover, 1956. Elementary but thorough.
Givierge, M., *Cours de Cryptographie,* Berger-Levrault, Paris, 1932. Outstanding but dated.
Sacco, L., *Manuale di Crittografia,* Rome, 1947. Thorough.
Sinkov, A., *Elementary Cryptanalysis; A Mathematical Approach,* Random House, New York, 1968. A textbook.

*Howard Campaigne*


# CRYSTALLOGRAPHY


## INTRODUCTION

### History and Scope

Until a few decades ago, crystallography was confined to the study of crystal optics and descriptive work on their outer form and habit for the purpose of identifying and classifying minerals. In 1912 Max von Laue discovered that X-rays were diffracted by the atoms (the electrons in the atoms) in a crystal. This significant observation confirmed the existence of structural order within crystals, a fact that previously had only been inferred from their regular outer shapes. In 1913, W. H. Bragg and his son W. L. Bragg determined for the first time the internal structure of some well-known crystals such as NaCl, KCl, ZnS, $CaF_2$, and $FeS_2$. This early work started the development of many of the mathematical procedures and experimental techniques that are used very effectively by contemporary crystallographers in their study of the internal structures of complex compounds. Today, crystallography is considered to be a basic scientific tool capable of supplying researchers with data and information unobtainable by other techniques. This information is derived after extensive mathematical and numerical analysis of the diffraction pattern which is produced when a crystal is bombarded by X-rays, or sometimes by neutron or electron rays. The results usually include details about the relative positions of atoms in a molecule, the modes and amplitudes of their thermal vibration, the types and lengths of bonds between atoms, the valency angles between such bonds, the symmetries between the molecules (or groups of atoms) within the crystal, and the orientation of the molecules relative to the crystal faces and edges. Such detailed information has been widely utilized by chemists, biochemists, biologists, pharmacologists, metallurgists, and mineralogists. An example of the molecular structure of an alkaloid as determined from an X-ray analysis is illustrated in Fig. 1 [2].

## Unit Cell

A crystal can be visualized as consisting of unit blocks (parallelelepipeda) which are stacked side by side in a three-dimensional array. These blocks, known as the *unit cells*, are identical in shape, dimensions, and contents. Each unit cell may contain only one molecule or a few *equivalent* molecules (or atomic groups) which are related to each other through some *symmetry operation* such as translation, rotation about an axis, reflection across a plane, or inversion through a center of symmetry, or a combination of some of these operations. The unit cell is identified by three *axial lengths* (cell edges) $a$, $b$, $c$ which are not necessarily equal, and three *interaxial angles* $\alpha$, $\beta$, $\gamma$ which are not necessarily 90°. For simplicity in calculation, the *atomic coordinates* $(x, y, z)$ are quoted relative to the unit-cell axes which do not necessarily form a Cartesian set.

## Miller Indices

When a small *single crystal* is rotated in an X-ray beam, the resulting *diffraction pattern* is a series of discrete beams which register as spots on a photographic film. Each spot is the result of diffraction of the X-ray beam by a set of equidistant parallel planes within the crystal volume. The diffraction occurs at the instant when the set of planes is in a position satisfying *Bragg's law* of diffraction

$$\lambda = 2d \sin \theta$$

where $\lambda$ is the wavelength of the incident beam, $d$ is the interplanar spacing of the diffracting planes, and $\theta$ is the angle between the incident beam and the set of planes (*glancing angle*). For indexing of the diffraction spots, the *Miller indices hkl* are used to identify the set of planes producing the diffracted beam. The three indices are integer numbers that define the direction of the set of parallel planes relative to the unit-cell axes. Because the incident and diffracted

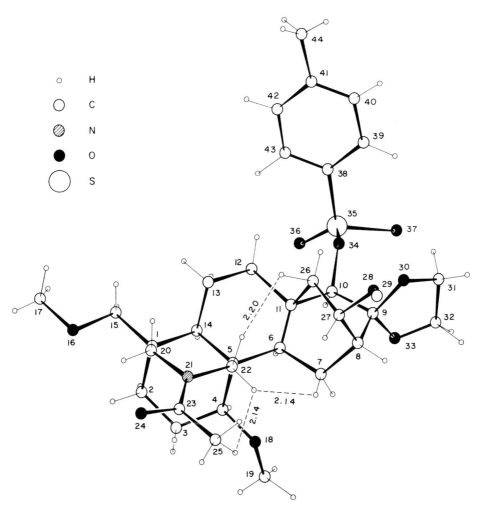

**Fig. 1.** Molecular structure of the alkaloid $C_{33}H_{47}NO_9S$ as determined from an X-ray analysis [2]. The shortest H..H contacts are shown in dotted lines, with the distances in Ångstrom units (1 Å = $10^{-8}$ cm).

beams obey the same laws as for reflection of light by a mirror, the diffraction spots are often referred to as the *reflections* (*hkl*). The geometry of the diffraction pattern is directly related to the unit-cell parameters ($a$, $b$, $c$, $\alpha$, $\beta$, $\gamma$).

## Intensity Data

In general, the reflections (*hkl*) have different *intensities* denoted by $I(hkl)$. To a first approximation, *Friedel's law* holds for all reflections, namely,

$$I(hkl) = I(\bar{h}\bar{k}\bar{l}) \qquad (\bar{h} = -h, \text{ etc.})$$

In addition, because of the symmetries between equivalent molecules in the unit cell, additional relationships may hold between the intensities of reflections, and certain classes of reflections may be systematically extinct. Such equivalences and systematic absences in the diffraction pattern define the existing symmetries among the equivalent molecules of the unit cell.

The intensities are measured in one of two ways: (1) the diffraction pattern is recorded on a series of *photographic* films from which the intensities can be measured by visual comparison with an intensity scale or by an automatic film scanner, or (2) the crystal is mounted on a *diffractometer* and is oriented so that one of the diffracted beams enters through the window of a *scintillation counter* which records the intensity, and the process is then repeated for each of the other reflections. The raw intensity data are then recorded in digital form on punch cards or magnetic tape for processing and structure determination.

## Structure Factors

The quantities used in structure determination are not the raw intensities $I(hkl)$ but the *structure factors* $F(hkl)$, where

$$F(hkl) = K \left[ \frac{1}{Lp} \frac{1}{T} I(hkl) \right]^{1/2} \qquad (1)$$

where $K$ is a scale factor, $1/Lp$ is the correction for the Lorentz and polarization effects, and $1/T$ is the correction for the absorption of the X-rays by the crystal. The structure factors are generally complex quantities of the form

$$F(hkl) = |F(hkl)| \exp[i\alpha(hkl)] \qquad (2)$$

$$= A(hkl) + iB(hkl)$$

where $\alpha$ is the phase angle, and $A$ and $B$ are the real and imaginary components of $F$. Only the structure factor amplitudes $|F(hkl)|$ can be derived from the experimental data, while the $\alpha(hkl)$ cannot be measured experimentally. Estimating these phases has been one of the main problems in X-ray diffraction, and various procedures for solving the problem have been developed through the years. The complexity of the problem increases with the number of nonequivalent atoms in the unit cell, and the problem is not yet fully solved.

## Electron Density

In X-ray diffraction the atoms are identified by the positions of electron density maxima within the unit cell. Therefore, one of the main steps in crystal structure analysis is to evaluate the *electron-density distribution* $\rho$ at the points $(X, Y, Z)$ of a fine three-dimensional grid superposed on the unit cell, by computing the Fourier series

$$\rho(XYZ) = \frac{1}{V} \sum_h \sum_k \sum_l | F(hkl) | \cos [2\pi(hX + kY + lZ) - \alpha(hkl)] \qquad (3)$$

where $V$ is the unit-cell volume, and the sums are for all available values of *hkl* in the range $-\infty$ to $+\infty$. Thus the phase angles $\alpha(hkl)$ have to be *estimated* in order to compute expression (3). The resulting map is usually referred to as the *Fourier map*. By contouring the different sections of the map, the atoms can be identified and their positions can be read from the map.

## Evaluation of the Structural Model

Once a trial structure has been found, the crystallographer (or the computer) has to check its validity and estimate its accuracy. First, he has to ascertain that the model makes chemical sense, which implies that it must contain the expected number and types of atoms, that the atoms have the correct valencies and form bonds of acceptable lengths, and that the atoms of neighboring molecules are at distances consistent with acceptable van der Waals contacts. Second, he has to check that the calculated structure amplitudes $| F_c(hkl) |$ for the assumed model agree fairly well with the observed structure amplitudes $| F_o(hkl) |$. The general structure factor expression is

$$F(hkl) = \sum_{i=1}^{N} f_i \exp [(- B_i \sin^2 \theta)/\lambda^2] \exp [2\pi i(hx_i + ky_i + lz_i)] \qquad (4)$$

but it is evaluated in steps as follows:

$$A(hkl) = \sum_{i=1}^{N} f_i \exp [(- B_i \sin^2 \theta)/\lambda^2] \cos [2\pi(hx_i + ky_i + lz_i)]$$

$$B(hkl) = \sum_{i=1}^{N} f_i \exp [(- B_i \sin^2 \theta)/\lambda^2] \sin [2\pi(hx_i + ky_i + lz_i)]$$

$$F(hkl) = [A^2(hkl) + B^2(hkl)]^{1/2} \qquad (5)$$

$$\alpha(hkl) = \tan^{-1} [B(hkl)/A(hkl)]$$

where $N$ is the number of atoms in the unit cell, $f_i$ is the *scattering factor* of atom $i$ [this is a function of $(\sin \theta)/\lambda$ which depends on the atom type], $B_i$ is the *temperature factor* (to correct for atomic thermal vibration, assumed here to be isotropic), and $(x, y, z)_i$ are the *fractional coordinates* $(x_i = X_i/a)$.

The *discrepancy R* between the observed and calculated structure amplitudes is evaluated by the expression

$$R = \sum || F_o | - | F_c ||/\sum | F_o | \tag{6}$$

where the sums are over all the measured reflections. Today, crystallographers also evaluate the *weighted discrepancy*

$$R_w = \left[ \sum w(| F_o | - | F_c |)^2/\sum w(| F_o |)^2 \right]^{1/2} \tag{7}$$

where $w$ are the weights assigned to the individual observed structure amplitudes $(w = 1/\sigma^2 | F_o |)$. Both $R$ and $R_w$ should be fairly small (0.03 to 0.07) for a well-refined structural model.

## Space Groups

The amount of computing required in crystal structure analysis can be reduced considerably by taking into account the symmetries within the unit cell. As an example, if a structure has a center of symmetry, each atom at $(x, y, z)$ would have an equivalent atom at $(-x, -y, -z)$; hence the structure factor expressions can be reduced to

$$F(hkl) = A(hkl) = 2 \sum_{i=1}^{N/2} f_i \exp [(-B_i \sin^2 \theta)/\lambda^2] \cos 2\pi(hx_i + ky_i + lz_i)$$

$$B(hkl) = 0 \tag{8}$$

$$\alpha(hkl) = 0 \quad \text{or} \quad \pi$$

Thus, for all centrosymmetric structures, $A(hkl)$ can be evaluated from only one-half the atoms in the unit cell, and $\alpha(hkl)$ is taken as 0 if $A$ is positive, or $\pi$ if $A$ is negative. Further simplifications can be obtained if all the other symmetries are taken into account. Altogether there are 230 combinations of the symmetries, referred to as the 230 *space groups*. The corresponding simplified structure factor and electron-density expressions are listed in Vol. 1 of the *International Tables of X-ray Crystallography* [50].

## EARLY COMPUTING PROCEDURES

### Main Calculations

The main time-consuming calculations are those involving the Fourier series in expressions (3) and (5). The number of terms in each series is usually quite large, and each expression must be evaluated thousands of times, depending on the size of the structure. The lack of computing facilities in the early days forced crystallographers to seek simplifications and devise computing aids to minimize the chore of computing. Some of these techniques are described briefly in the following paragraphs.

## Analysis in Projections

The analysis with three-dimensional data is straightforward, but involves a large amount of computing. In the early days the studies were carried out in two-dimensional projections, and their results were then combined to produce the approximate three-dimensional structure. The expressions for two-dimensional work are much simpler and involve only about one-tenth of the data needed for three-dimensional work. However, there are two main drawbacks to this procedure, namely, the results are less accurate than three-dimensional analyses, and the atomic electron densities can overlap, thus making it difficult to identify the exact positions of the atoms.

## Beevers-Lipson Strips

Even for the two-dimensional work, the computing task is quite considerable if done without the aid of a computer. Beevers and Lipson [10] presented a scheme for calculating two-dimensional Fourier series by first expanding the trigonometric part into the product form, and performing the calculation in two stages of single summations. Thus

$$\sum_h \sum_k A(hk0) \cos 2\pi(hX + kY) = \sum_k \left[ \sum_h A(hk0) \cos 2\pi hX \right] \cos 2\pi kY$$
$$- \sum_k \left[ \sum_h A(hk0) \sin 2\pi hX \right] \sin 2\pi kY$$

To simplify computation of the single Fourier summations, they took the grid intervals as integer multiples of 1/60th of the cell edges, and produced a set of about 4000 card strips. Each strip contained the products $A \cos 2\pi hX$ or $A \sin 2\pi hX$ for one value of $A$ ($=1, 2, \ldots, 99$) and one value of $h$ ($=0, 1, 2, \ldots, 20$), for the range of $X = 0, 1/60, 2/60, \ldots, 15/60$. For $X$ values beyond $\frac{1}{4}$ of the cell edge, the antisymmetry of $\cos \varphi$ about $\varphi = 90°$, and the symmetry of $\sin \varphi$ about the same point were used. The single summations were evaluated by simply selecting the appropriate strips and *summing* the entries on the different strips for a given value of $X$, and repeating similarly for the other values of $X$. The sums from the first stage single Fourier summation were then used as amplitudes for the second stage. Thus the Fourier map could be calculated with the aid of the strips and an adding machine. This procedure was widely used for many years until the introduction of the Hollerith tabulating machines. Later on, other strips of higher accuracy were developed by Robertson and by Beevers, and for a brief description of these and of other early computing aids refer to the article by Niggli [70].

## Mechanical Devices

Several mechanical devices were designed to speed up the calculation of Fourier syntheses, but most of them were one of a kind. Robertson [74] designed a one-dimensional digital device, RUFUS, that combined high accuracy with low cost, as described by Robertson [75]. A mechanical analog device consisting mostly of Meccano parts (the *Fourier electron-density balance*) was designed by Vand [86] to calculate two-dimensional Fourier syntheses. Hoppe and Pannke [45] built the *Fourier synthesizer* whose accuracy was superior to most electric analog computers.

## Electric Analog Computers

The most effective special-purpose analog computer ever built for crystallographic calculations was a large machine called X-RAC, which was designed by Pepinsky for the computation of two- or three-dimensional Fourier syntheses, with visual presentation of accurate contour maps. It produced a two-dimensional contour map in 1 sec, once the Fourier coefficients were inserted into the machine. Associated with X-RAC was the X-FAC system for computation of two-dimensional structure factors. The machines were assembled in Alabama in 1947 and 1948, then transferred in 1949 to the Groth Institute of the Pennsylvania State University, where they operated almost continuously for about 12 years. Detailed descriptions of these machines were given in the articles by Pepinsky [72].

Other electric analog computers were designed by Hagg and Laurent [34]; by Shimizu, Elsey, and McLachlan [81]; and by Azaroff [8]. These machines performed one- or two-dimensional Fourier summations by adding alternating potentials whose amplitudes and signs were set manually on a series of potentiometers and switches.

## Optical Analog Devices

The use of optical methods in place of calculations was first suggested by W. L. Bragg. The optical analog devices that were designed were particularly suitable for two-dimensional work; their limited accuracy was somewhat compensated for by high speed and convenience. They were based on the idea of superposing the sinusoidal light–dark band patterns of masks with the different masks representing the terms of a double Fourier series. The most convenient device was the *photosummator* designed by von Eller [31]. An optical analog device designed specially for calculating Fourier transforms in two-dimensions was the *optical diffractometer* by Hughes and Taylor [48]. This instrument was commercially available, together with a pantograph punch for preparing masks representing two-dimensional trial structures. Placement of the mask in the path of a parallel beam of light produced the diffraction pattern of the trial structure on a photographic film which could then be compared to the crystal's X-ray pattern. Applications of this instrument have been described by Hanson, Lipson, and Taylor [37].

## Hollerith Procedures

For several years prior to the wide use of electronic general-purpose digital computers, Hollerith equipment built by both the International Business Machines Corporation (IBM) and the British Tabulating Machines (BTM) was available to crystallographers. Using the card sorter, the reproducing punch (comparing reproducer), the multiplying punch, and the tabulator, the calculations were done more accurately and at a much faster rate than before. Some of the procedures applied were direct applications of the principles of the Beevers-Lipson strips, while others included table look-up of cosines and sines from prepunched master decks by *sorting* and *intersperse gang-punching* (using the sorter and comparing reproducer). Multiplications were performed either with the aid of the multiplying punch or the tabulator. On the BTM rolling-total tabulators, multiplication was not readily available as one of the mathematical operations, and had to be performed through panel wiring to cause one counter to roll into another a number of times, thereby adding the contents of the first counter to the second. Thus, by sorting the multipliers in ascending order, and rolling the multiplicands from one counter to the other, multiplication by factors of 1 to 9 could be achieved. Multiplication by factors of 10, 100, etc. was accomplished by preparing additional cards with the multiplicand fields shifted to the left by one or more columns. Combination of these two procedures could then produce the Fourier sums required. Several descriptions of these procedures have been published; see Cox, Gross, and Jeffrey [17] and references therein.

## PRESENT COMPUTING PROCEDURES

### Introduction

The main calculations of today's crystal structure analysis are summarized in the block diagram shown in Fig. 2. Computing for the very large (protein) crystal structures is somewhat different and is described separately. Programs for executing these calculations are available in both FORTRAN and ALGOL, and in machine codes for some minicomputers. Most of the programs are written in a *generalized* form so that they can be applied to any crystal structure in any space group, but at the same time they are organized to take as much advantage as possible of the simplifications resulting from the symmetries in the different space groups. Unlike computing in engineering and other scientific fields, crystallographic programs have wider applications and much longer life, and this has made it worthwhile to properly plan and document crystallographic programs so that they can operate efficiently and be of wide use. It has been preferable since the 1960s to plan a set of homogeneous programs which use and produce data files in standard formats, so that the programs can be called in succession without human intervention. Such sets are known as *crystallographic computing systems* as, for example, the XRAY system by Stewart, Kruger,

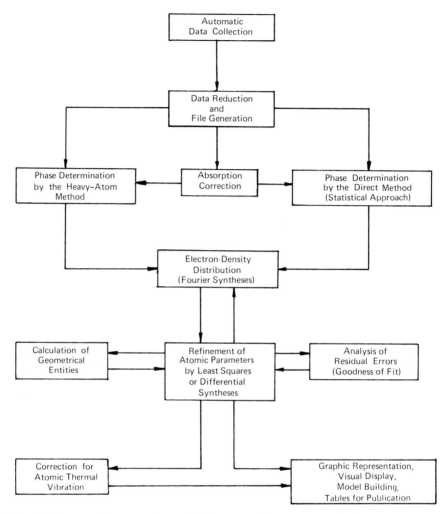

**Fig. 2.** Main computing procedures in X-ray crystal structure analysis.

Ammon, Dickenson, and Hall [85] at the University of Maryland; the NRC system by Ahmed, Hall, Pippy, and Huber [5] at the National Research Council of Canada; UNICS by Sakurai in Japan, and CRYSNET at the Brookhaven National Laboratory.

Some individual programs have been widely accepted for their efficiency and thoroughness and have been incorporated without too many alterations in the different systems. The best known programs in this class are: ORFLS by Busing, Martin, and Levy (Oak Ridge National Laboratory [13]) for least-squares refinement, ORTEP by Johnson (Oak Ridge National Laboratory [52]) for plotting of molecular structures and ellipsoids of thermal vibration, and MULTAN by Main, Woolfson, and Germain (Universities of York and

Louvain [63]) for phase determination by the direct method. Most of the crystallographic systems and programs are available with proper documentation for distribution to other crystallographers. Details of the main calculations, outlined in Fig. 2, are described in the following sections.

**Automatic Data Collection**

For each crystal structure, 1000 to 6000 intensities have to be measured. The modern diffractometers on which these measurements are made consist of: (1) a stable X-ray generator, (2) a four-circle goniostat for orienting the different ($hkl$) planes and for positioning their diffracted beams one at a time, and (3) an on-line minicomputer. In most cases the necessary software is supplied by the manufacturer.

The data collection program usually starts with rough values of the unit-cell parameters and the angular settings of three noncoplanar ($hkl$) vectors, where each vector represents the normal to the corresponding ($hkl$) diffracting planes, as well as the X-ray wavelength. During a preliminary step, the program performs the following operations:

Calculates the approximate crystal orientation matrix from the given information.
Calculates the approximate angular settings of all ($hkl$) vectors.
Measures quickly the peak heights of the ($hkl$) intensities.
Selects a dozen of the strongest reflections at high $2\theta$, and proceeds to center each reflection into the counter through small adjustments of the goniostat and counter settings.
Using the refined angular settings, it calculates the refined unit-cell parameters and crystal orientation matrix by a least-squares procedure.

With these refined parameters and matrix, the program calculates the exact angular settings of each reflection, *scans* the reflection to measure its integrated intensity, and measures the background intensity before and after the scan range. During this operation the program instructs the diffractometer to measure the intensities of selected standard reflections at regular time intervals to guard against variations in the X-ray output, any changes in the crystal due to X-ray bombardment, and any crystal movement. All measurements are recorded on magnetic tape or paper tape for further processing.

**Data Reduction and File Generation**

In this step the program subtracts the background from the gross intensities, corrects them for the Lorentz and polarization errors, sorts them in any desired order, and generates the *standard lists* that will be needed by all the other programs of the system. The information in these lists is used several times by the programs of the system, and is therefore computed and stored to avoid repetitive calculations.

## Absorption Correction

For accurate crystal structure analysis, it is necessary to correct the measured intensities for known sources of error. Absorption of the X-ray beam by the crystal can be a serious source of error for crystals which contain heavy atoms. The calculation of absorption correction is quite simple if the crystal is nearly spherical or cylindrical, but is complex for other crystal forms. Busing and Levy [12] described a general method for applying the absorption correction to four-circle diffractometer data, and this method has been programmed by different authors and used widely by crystallographers. This procedure uses the $m$-point Gaussian integration formula where the crystal volume is approximated by $m_1 \times m_2 \times m_3$ points (see Margeneau and Murphy [64] or Hartree [40]). A more complex analytical method that includes no approximations has also been described and programmed by Alcock [6]. For details, see the articles in *Crystallographic Computing* [22].

Absorption by the crystal results in reducing the X-ray intensity $I_0$ by the transmission factor $T$ to the measured value $I_m$ so that

$$I_m = I_0 T \tag{9}$$

The transmission factor through a crystal with no reentrant angles can be calculated from the *m-point Gaussian integration formula*

$$T = \frac{1}{v} \sum_{i=1}^{m_1} \sum_{j=1}^{m_2} \sum_{k=1}^{m_3} (B - A)[D(x_i) - C(x_i)] \tag{10}$$

$$\times [F(x_i, y_j) - E(x_i, y_j)] R_i R_j R_k \exp(-\mu r_{ijk})$$

where $v$ is the crystal volume; $\mu$ is the linear absorption coefficient that depends on the atom types; $r_{ijk}$ is the path length of the primary ($r_p$) and diffracted ($r_d$) beams through the crystal to and from a point $(x_i, y_j, z_k)$ as shown in Fig. 3; and $m_1$, $m_2$, $m_3$ are the subdivisions of integration in the $x$, $y$, $z$ directions. $A$ and $B$ are the limits of the crystal in the $x$ direction; $C$ and $D$ are the limits along $y$ at $x = x_i$; $E$ and $F$ are limits along $z$ at $x = x_i$ and $y = y_j$. The coordinates of the representative Gaussian points are

$$
\begin{aligned}
x_i &= A + (B - A)u_i, & i &= 1, \ldots, m_1 \\
y_j &= C(x_i) + [D(x_i) - C(x_i)]u_j, & j &= 1, \ldots, m_2 \\
z_k &= D(x_i, y_j) + [F(x_i, y_j) - E(x_i, y_j)]u_k, & k &= 1, \ldots, m_3
\end{aligned}
$$

$R$ and $u$ are the Gaussian integration constants [62].

To illustrate the amount of computation required, expression (10) is evaluated once for each reflection, and this involves calculation of the path lengths $r_p$ and $r_d$ (Fig. 3) to each of the integration elements $(x_i, y_j, z_k)$ within the crystal volume. In order to calculate $r_p$ and $r_d$ the program has to derive the directions

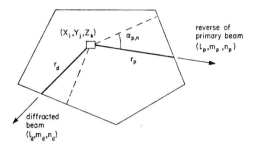

**Fig. 3.** Path lengths of the primary and secondary X-ray beams through the crystal to and from an element of the volume.

of the beams and their intersections with the crystal faces. In preparation for this calculation, the crystal must be measured accurately under a high magnification microscope, and its faces and edges must be defined for the program.

**The Heavy Atom Method**

As described earlier, the structure factors are complex quantities whose phases $\alpha(hkl)$ cannot be measured experimentally. However, the phases can be estimated either by the heavy atom method or by the direct method. To apply the heavy atom method, when the molecule consists only of light atoms (C, N, O, H) the chemist must insert one or more heavy atoms such as Cl, Br, or I into the compound before crystallization, and the analysis is then carried out on the heavy atom derivative. This procedure involves the basic assumption that the shape and conformation of the molecule under study do not change by insertion of the heavy atom.

When the unit cell contains *a few* heavy atoms, their positions can be determined from a study of the *Patterson function* [71] which has the form

$$P(UVW) = \frac{1}{V} \sum_h \sum_k \sum_l |F(hkl)|^2 \cos 2\pi(hu + kv + lw) \qquad (11)$$

This function is *independent* of the phase angles and can be computed with the same program that calculates the Fourier maps. The peaks in the Patterson map represent the *vector set* among the atoms of the unit cell, with the highest peaks representing the vectors between the heavy atoms. Thus if the cell has heavy atoms at the positions $r_1$, $r_2$, $r_3$, and $r_4$, the Patterson map would have high peaks at the positions $\pm(r_1 - r_2, r_1 - r_3, r_1 - r_4, r_2 - r_3, r_2 - r_4, r_3 - r_4)$ and a very large peak at the origin representing the four self-atom vectors. From the vector set it is possible to deduce the positions of the heavy atoms, especially if the atoms in the cell are related by some crystallographic symmetry.

The structure factor phases can then be calculated from expression (5) assuming, for a first approximation, that the structure consists only of the derived heavy atoms. With these estimated phases the electron-density distribution can then be calculated from expression (3), and the resulting map usually produces the approximate structure. This method of structure determination has a very good record of success, but the presence of heavy atoms in the structure usually reduces the overall accuracy of the analysis.

## The Direct Method

### Introduction

The direct method of phase determination is the most effective procedure for solving structures that do not contain heavy atoms. This is mainly a probabilistic approach to the phase problem, and its *strength* is based on the fact that the number of observations far exceeds the number of unknown parameters by a factor of about 4 to 10 or more. Through this procedure, one tries to find a solution that "best" fits the highly redundant experimental data. The *principle* of the method is based on the *nonnegativity criterion*, namely that the electron density must be nonnegative throughout the unit cell. This property was utilized by Karle and Hauptman [56] to obtain the main formulas for phase determination, which consisted of a set of inequalities valid for all space groups. This set was shown to include the useful set of inequalities (for phase determination) which had been derived earlier by Harker and Kasper [39] on the basis of the Schwarz and Cauchy inequalities. In studying the probabilistic aspects of the inequalities, Hauptman and Karle [43] introduced the joint probability distribution theory which led to the derivation of the formulas labeled *sigma-1, sigma-2, sigma-3*, etc. The results of this study and its application to phase determination were published by Hauptman and Karle [44] as Monograph No. 3 of the American Crystallographic Association.

### Main Formulas

In applying this method, the structure factors $F_\mathbf{h}$ are replaced by the *normalized structure factors* $E_\mathbf{h}$, where

$$|E_\mathbf{h}| = |F_\mathbf{h}| \Big/ \left[\left(\epsilon_\mathbf{h} \sum_{j=1}^{N} f_{j\mathbf{h}}^2\right)\right]^{1/2} \tag{12}$$

$\mathbf{h} \equiv (h, k, l)$, $\epsilon_\mathbf{h}$ is a factor to account for symmetry reinforcement of $|F_\mathbf{h}|$, and $N$ is the number of atoms in the unit cell.

As summarized by I. L. Karle [54], the most useful relationships between phases and magnitudes as applied for practical solution of crystal structures are the following:

*For centrosymmetric structures*, where all phases are either 0 or $\pi$, or equivalently the signs of the structure factors are either $+$ or $-$, the sigma-2 formula applies,

$$s(E_\mathbf{h}) \approx s(E_\mathbf{k}E_{\mathbf{h}-\mathbf{k}}) \tag{13}$$

or for several contributions,

$$s(E_\mathbf{h}) \approx s\left(\sum_\mathbf{k} E_\mathbf{k} E_{\mathbf{h}-\mathbf{k}}\right) \tag{14}$$

where the symbol $s$ means "the sign of," and the vectors $\mathbf{h}$, $\mathbf{k}$, and $\mathbf{h} - \mathbf{k}$ refer to different reflections. Thus, knowing the signs of $E_\mathbf{k}$ and $E_{\mathbf{h}-\mathbf{k}}$, it is possible from relation (13) to determine the sign of $E_\mathbf{h}$. As the signs of more reflections get to be known, relation (14) can be used to combine the individual indications for the signs of new $E_\mathbf{h}$'s. In order to insure that the sign has been correctly determined, the *probability* $P_+(E_\mathbf{h})$ that the sign of $E_\mathbf{h}$ is positive, has to be evaluated by the expression

$$P_+(E_\mathbf{h}) = \tfrac{1}{2} + \tfrac{1}{2}\tanh\left(\sigma_2^{-3/2}\sigma_3 \,|\, E_\mathbf{h} \,|\, \sum_\mathbf{k} E_\mathbf{k} E_{\mathbf{h}-\mathbf{k}}\right) \tag{15}$$

where $\sigma_n = \Sigma_{j=1}^N Z_j^n$, $Z$ is the atomic number. Thus the larger the $|E_\mathbf{k}|$ and $|E_{\mathbf{h}-\mathbf{k}}|$ amplitudes, the higher will be the probability of a correct sign assignment.

*For noncentrosymmetric space groups*, where the phase of a structure factor $\varphi_\mathbf{h}$ can assume values from $-\pi$ to $+\pi$, the following phase relationships are most useful [56, 58]:

$$\varphi_\mathbf{h} \approx \langle \varphi_\mathbf{k} + \varphi_{\mathbf{h}-\mathbf{k}} \rangle_{\mathbf{k}_r} \tag{16}$$

where $\langle \ \rangle_{\mathbf{k}_r}$ means average value over the set of data $\mathbf{k}_r$ which is restricted to the largest $|E_\mathbf{k}|$ magnitudes; and the *tangent* formula: [57]

$$\tan\varphi_\mathbf{h} = \frac{\sum_\mathbf{k} E_\mathbf{k} E_{\mathbf{h}-\mathbf{k}} \sin(\varphi_\mathbf{k} + \varphi_{\mathbf{h}-\mathbf{k}})}{\sum_\mathbf{k} E_\mathbf{k} E_{\mathbf{h}-\mathbf{k}} \cos(\varphi_\mathbf{k} + \varphi_{\mathbf{h}-\mathbf{k}})} \tag{17}$$

The *variance* associated with the determination of $\varphi_\mathbf{h}$ can be derived from the probability formula of Cochran [14] and is given by Karle and Karle [58]:

$$v = \frac{\pi^2}{3} + [I_0(\alpha)]^{-1} \sum_{n=1}^\infty \frac{I_{2n}(\alpha)}{n^2} - 4[I_0(\alpha)]^{-1} \sum_{n=0}^\infty \frac{I_{2n+1}(\alpha)}{(2n+1)^2} \tag{18}$$

where

$$\alpha = \left\{\left[\sum_\mathbf{k} 2\sigma_3\sigma_2^{-3/2} \,|\, E_\mathbf{h} E_\mathbf{k} E_{\mathbf{h}-\mathbf{k}} \,|\, \cos(\varphi_\mathbf{h} + \varphi_{\mathbf{h}-\mathbf{k}})\right]^2 \right.$$
$$\left. + \left[\sum_\mathbf{k} 2\sigma_3\sigma_2^{-3/2} \,|\, E_\mathbf{h} E_\mathbf{k} E_{\mathbf{h}-\mathbf{k}}) \sin(\varphi_\mathbf{h} + \varphi_{\mathbf{h}-\mathbf{k}})\right]^2 \right\}^{1/2} \tag{19}$$

The $I_n$ are Bessel functions of imaginary argument. Thus, in noncentrosymmetric structures, the large $|E|$ amplitudes lead to small variances (errors) for the estimated phase angles.

## Computer Application

From the outset there have been quite different philosophies to the computer application of these procedures, some of which are described in the two volumes *Crystallographic Computing* [22] and *Crystallographic Computing Techniques* [23]. The present state of the art is such that fairly complex light-atom structures can now be solved in a relatively straightforward manner. The computer application of these procedures may be divided into five main steps [4]:

1. Calculation of normalized structure factors $|E_\mathbf{h}|$.
2. Generation of sigma-2 triples (i.e., triples of reflections $\mathbf{h}, \mathbf{k}, \mathbf{h} - \mathbf{k}$).
3. Selection of the initial phase set.
4. Phase determination by symbolic addition.
5. Phase extension and refinement by the tangent formula.

These steps are described briefly in the following account.

### Calculation of Normalized Structure Factors

The measured structure factors are usually on some arbitrary scale which has to be estimated, together with the overall thermal vibration of the atoms, in a preliminary step. These parameters are obtained from a linear plot of

$$\log_e \left\langle \sum_\mathbf{h} m_\mathbf{h} \epsilon_\mathbf{h} \sum_{j=1}^{N} f_{j\mathbf{h}}^2 \right\rangle \Big/ \left\langle \sum_\mathbf{h} m_\mathbf{h} \mid F_\mathbf{h} \mid^2 \right\rangle \text{ versus } (\sin^2 \theta)/\lambda^2$$

where $m_\mathbf{h}$ is a multiplicity factor. The observed structure factors are then adjusted, using the derived parameters, to the absolute scale and zero temperature. The adjusted structure amplitudes are substituted in Eq. (12) to derive $|E_\mathbf{h}|$ for all reflections in the data set. At the end, the program calculates the average values $\langle |E_\mathbf{h}| \rangle, \langle |E_\mathbf{h}^2| \rangle, \langle |E_\mathbf{h}^2 - 1| \rangle$, and the percent of reflections with $|E| > 3$, $|E| > 2, |E| > 1$. These averages and percentages provide some vital information about the internal symmetry of the structure, mainly whether the structure is centrosymmetric or noncentrosymmetric.

### Generation of Sigma-2 Triples

In essence, this step is a repetition of the following search operation: for a given $\mathbf{h}_1$ and $\mathbf{h}_2$ in the data set, is there a third reflection $\mathbf{h}_3$ that satisfies the sigma-2 condition? Each $\mathbf{h}$ represents the three Miller indices (*hkl*). This search must include all symmetry equivalents of $\mathbf{h}_2$ and $\mathbf{h}_3$, and is one of the lengthiest single operations in this procedure. Programs performing this search must be efficiently planned to save computer time by utilizing the order of the data, by employing efficient algorithms for sorting and searching, by restricting the search to the strong $|E|$ amplitudes that are likely to produce reliable single sigma-2 relationships, and by avoiding redundancies in the triples. Also, time can be saved if the $h$, $k$, $l$ indices are packed into one word, presorting the packed indices in ascending order and according to parity, thus limiting the search for $\mathbf{h}_3$ to only one of the possible eight parity groups of $hkl$.

## Selection of Initial Phase Set

To apply relationships (14)–(17), it is necessary to start with some known or assumed phases of a few reflections with high $|E|$ amplitudes. Since the success of these methods can depend on the selection of the starting reflections, it is necessary to program this step carefully and allow for human interaction if need be. The main criterion is that the starting reflections should interact rapidly in *reliable* sigma-2 relationships to provide new phase estimates, and this is enhanced if the reflections have high $|E|$ amplitudes, a large number of sigma-2 interactions, and represent a variety of parity groups. This set usually includes the reflections needed to define the unit-cell origin and the molecule's enantiomorph (its handedness), and a few others with assumed phase values. The assumed phases may be either numeric or symbolic, depending on the program procedure.

## Phase Determination by Symbolic Addition

The use of symbolic phases with sigma-2 relationships was first introduced by Karle and Karle [55]. In this procedure the origin- and enantiomorph-defining reflections are given numeric phase values (0, $\pm\pi/2$, or $\pi$) as appropriate, and the other reflections of the starting set are assigned symbols $A$, $B$, $C$, . . . to represent their unknown phases. The sigma-2 relationships are then applied to generate the phases of the other reflections of the data set in terms of the assumed numeric and symbolic phases of the initial set. During this process, some reflections will have multiple indications for their phases. By accumulating all the multiple indications and correlating them, it is usually possible to deduce the numeric values of the assumed symbols.

For centrosymmetric structures the assumed symbols are taken to represent the signs + or − of the structure factors. Thus, if reflections $\mathbf{k}$ and $\mathbf{h} - \mathbf{k}$ have symbolic signs $A$ and $B$, then the sign of reflection $\mathbf{h}$ is deduced from expression (12) as the symbol product $AB$. In general, the determined signs can be +, −, $\pm$ a symbol, or $\pm$ a product of two or more symbols. Different programs handle the representation of symbols and their multiplication in different ways. The symbolic addition program by Hall and Ahmed reserves separate counters for each type of sign representation, for each of the reflections, and uses those counters to accumulate the probability sums of the sign indications for further correlation. The multiplication of symbols is handled by table look-up in a numerically coded multiplication table. In Dewar's program MAGIC [25], the symbolic sign of each reflection is represented by one word, with each bit position representing one symbol, and the bit is set to 1 if the symbol is present or 0 if it is absent. The multiplication of symbolic phases is performed by a

Boolean operation, as shown in the following example:

| | Value | A | B | C | D | E | F | G | H | I | J |
|---|---|---|---|---|---|---|---|---|---|---|---|
| | | Coded representation | | | | | | | | | |
| Phase of **k** | *ABD* | 1 | 1 | 0 | 1 | 0 | 0 | 0 | 0 | 0 | 0 |
| Phase of **h** − **k** | *ADFG* | 1 | 0 | 0 | 1 | 0 | 1 | 1 | 0 | 0 | 0 |
| Phase of **h** | *BFG* | 0 | 1 | 0 | 0 | 0 | 1 | 1 | 0 | 0 | 0 |

One difficulty with this coding is that it requires manipulation of bits which is rather difficult with some versions of FORTRAN.

In general, the symbolic addition procedure is used for centrosymmetric structures and only in the preliminary stages of noncentrosymmetric structures where formula (16) is applied. However, a program that applies the more accurate tangent formula (17) using symbolic phases has been written by Grainger [33].

*The Tangent Procedure*

In this method the phases are estimated from formula (17), and their variances or simply the corresponding $\alpha$ values are calculated from expressions (18) and (19). The list of sigma-2 triples is scanned, and when a triple is found to have two reflections with known phases, its contributions are added to the tangent sums of the third reflection. The sums are consequently used to estimate the phase values, and the whole process is repeated until the phases converge to a self-consistent set. The tangent procedure is therefore iterative and simultaneously estimates unknown phases and refines the known phases.

The computer application of this procedure is quite varied. In the program MULTAN by Main, Woolfson, and Germain [63] *weights* are included in the tangent sums to emphasize the contribution of the more reliable phases. Where no weights are used, it is usually necessary to apply certain *acceptance criteria* of the estimated phases, based on their expected reliability, so that the poorly determined phases will not influence the others. Another common approach is to constrain the tangent extension and refinement process within series of *thresholds* based on the $|E|$ amplitudes, to ensure that the more reliable triples are used in the initial phase estimates. In this way the phases of the highest $|E|$ amplitudes are refined to a self-consistent set before the threshold is lowered in two or three stages.

It is important with these procedures to be able to assess the reliability of the determined phase set. A number of parameters have been introduced for this purpose, namely, the measure of success, reliability index, and figure of merit. No single parameter appears to fully satisfy the intended purpose, but the parameters generally serve as indicators of phase correctness. For a summary of these parameters, see Ahmed and Hall [4].

## The Multisolution Procedure

This method relies on the power and speed of present computers. The idea was first introduced by Germain and Woolfson [32] and has been incorporated in the program MULTAN (Multiple-tangent-formula method) by Main, Woolfson, and Germain [63]. In this approach the origin- and enantiomorph-defining reflections are given appropriate numeric phases, and the remaining reflections in the initial set are given *numeric trial values* (0 and $\pi$), ($\pi/2$ and $3\pi/2$), or ($\pi/4$, $3\pi/4$, $5\pi/4$, and $7\pi/4$) depending on the reflection type and the restrictions imposed on its phase by the space group symmetries. The weighted tangent formula is then applied for *each combination* of the initial phase values to deduce the unknown phases of the other reflections. This results in one set of phases for each of the combinations, and it is necessary then to grade the phase sets to predict which of them are likely to produce the correct structure. Finally, the $E$-maps, which are equivalent to the electron-density maps, are calculated for each of the promising phase sets.

The program MULTAN has been developed into a comprehensive system that starts with the measured intensities and proceeds automatically to the computation and scan of $E$-maps, and finally produces a list of the bond lengths and a plot of the molecular structure. For details, see Woolfson [87].

## The Cosine Seminvariants

The aforementioned techniques apply the cosine seminvariant relationship

$$\cos (\varphi_{h_1} + \varphi_{h_2} + \varphi_{h_3}) = +1 \qquad (20)$$

for $h_1 + h_2 + h_3 = 0$. Although Eq. (20) is correct for most triples, it does not actually hold for all triples, especially in structures with considerable overlap of vectors in the Patterson function. Therefore, for the successful development of phases it is sometimes necessary to identify the triples which do not satisfy that relationship and exclude them from the phasing process. An even better approach is to evaluate the expected value of each cosine seminvariant and use those values in estimating the phases. Most of the development work on these lines has been done by Hauptman, as described in his book [42] and in his article [41]. Calculation of the cosine seminvariants is carried out by an iterative process that requires a substantial amount of computation. Programs for executing this procedure are available from Hauptman's laboratory in Buffalo, and have been applied successfully for solving structures of 40 to 50 nonhydrogen atoms in the asymmetric unit cell.

## Fourier Series

### Introduction

Lengthy Fourier series have to be calculated at various stages in the course of a crystal structure analysis. Each series has to be evaluated at the points of a three-dimensional grid superposed on the unit cell or its asymmetric part. A given Fourier series may contain 1,000 to 10,000 terms, and the grid may consist of 10,000 to 100,000 points. An efficient *Fourier program* is therefore essential to any crystallographic computing system. The program is usually designed in a "general" format so that it can be applied to structures in any space group and for all the types of maps that are normally encountered. The general expression for the Fourier-type calculation is

$$G(XYZ) = C \sum_h \sum_k \sum_l A(hkl) \cos 2\pi(hX + kY + lZ)$$

$$+ B(hkl) \sin 2\pi(hX + kY + lZ) \quad (21)$$

where $G$ is the function to be evaluated, $C$ is a constant, $A$ and $B$ are the real and imaginary parts of the amplitudes, and the summations are over all accessible values of $h$, $k$, $l$ from $-\infty$ to $+\infty$.

The Fourier program is usually called to calculate the following types of maps:

*Patterson map*, where $A(hkl) = |F(hkl)|^2$, $B(hkl) = 0$.
*Electron density map*, where $A(hkl) = |F_o| \cos \alpha(hkl)$ and $B(hkl) = |F_o| \sin \alpha(hkl)$, and $o$ means observed amplitude.
*E-map*, where the $|F_o|$ amplitudes are replaced by the $|E|$ values. This is equivalent to the electron-density map and is calculated after phase determination by the direct method, see Fig. 4.
*Difference map*, where the amplitudes are the real and imaginary parts of $\|F_o| - |F_c\|$, where $o$ means observed and $c$ means calculated. This map gives the electron-density distribution after the known atoms of the structure are subtracted. It is used mainly to locate the H atoms in the structure, as shown in Fig. 5. It is also computed at the end of the refinement to verify the model and observe the bonding electrons between atoms.

### Computation Procedure

The Fourier-type calculations are usually carried out with the trigonometric functions in the expanded triple product form, after collecting the like terms together. Thus

$$G(XYZ) = C \sum_h \sum_k \sum_l R_i(hkl) \, \text{trg} \, (2\pi \mid h \mid X) \, \text{trg} \, (2\pi \mid k \mid Y) \, \text{trg} \, (2\pi \mid l \mid Z)$$

$$+ \text{similar terms for different } R_i \text{ and different trigonometric functions}$$

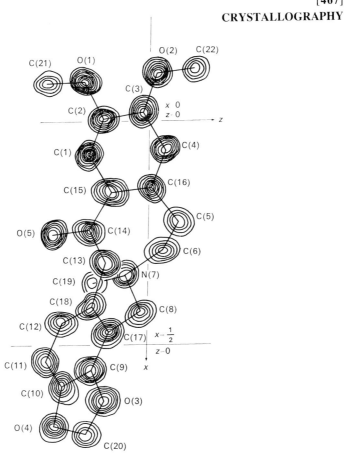

**Fig. 4.** Composite drawing of the *E*-map of the cryptopine molecule showing its nonhydrogen atoms [36].

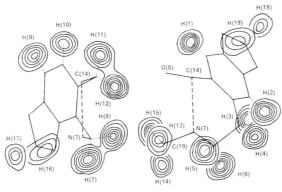

**Fig. 5.** Composite drawing of the difference map of the protopine molecule, showing the locations of the H atoms [35]. For clarity, the molecule is divided at the dotted line.

where $\quad R(hkl) = m[\pm {}^A_B(hkl) \pm {}^A_B(\bar{h}kl) \pm {}^A_B(h\bar{k}l) \pm {}^A_B(hk\bar{l})]$
$\quad\quad\quad$ trg = cos or sin

The calculation involves the following main steps [1]:

Sorting the data on $|h|$, $|k|$, $|l|$.
Calculation and storage of the $R_i$ amplitudes.
Evaluation of the Fourier summations in three separate stages.
Output of the results.

The sorting sequence is usually dependent on the preferred layout of the Fourier map, which is decided by the order of the three stage summations. Assuming $|h|$ varies least frequently, $|k|$ is the intermediate varying index, and $|l|$ varies most frequently, the summations are performed in the following order:

$\quad$ I. $\quad C_i = \sum_{|l|} R_i \text{ trg } 2\pi |l| Z$, for constant values of $|h|$ and $|k|$.

$\quad$ II. $\quad D_i = \sum_{|k|} C_i \text{ trg } 2\pi |k| Y$, for constant values of $|h|$.

$\quad$ III. $\quad G(XYZ) = C \sum_i \sum_{|h|} D_i \text{ trg } 2\pi |h| X$.

Stage I is computed for one value of $Z$ at a time, Stage II for all values of $Y$ at every change in $|k|$, and Stage III for all values of $X$ at every change in $|h|$. Thus the sums are computed simultaneously for all grid points in one section, and the order of the data is utilized to the best advantage.

$\quad$ Some programs limit the summations to the range 0 to 0.25 for $X$, $Y$, $Z$ as for the Beevers-Lipson strips, keeping the sums of Stage III separate, then combining the results in different ways for the complete range of coordinates 0 to 1.0. Details of this procedure have been described by Cruickshank, Pilling, Bujosa, Lovell, and Truter [21]; and Sly and Shoemaker [83]. The latest Fourier programs apply the Cooley-Tukey algorithm for *fast Fourier transforms* [15] and show improvement in speed over the earlier procedures. For details, see Immirzi [49].

## *Peak Search*

$\quad$ In order to study Fourier maps, the normal practice is to print the results in sections, contour them manually, and find the locations of the peaks. With the direct methods it is quite often necessary to compute several $E$-maps for different estimated phase sets before the correct structure can be located. Several programs have been written to perform the peak search automatically. A brief description of such a program has been given by Stewart [84]. Basically, the program sweeps through the output from the Fourier, locating in each section all the peaks above a certain cutoff, and if in the process it finds that there are too many peaks (low cutoff), it discards the very lowest peaks and saves the others. It then proceeds to the next section until any given peak begins to decrease in height. At that point the program performs a parabolic interpolation to locate the maximum, and saves those maxima. Toward the end it calculates all symmetrically equivalent peaks and selects a unique asymmetric set of these peaks, then sorts them in descending order of their magnitudes.


## Refinement of Atomic Parameters

### Introduction

Because of the high ratio of X-ray measurements to unknown parameters, it is usually possible to derive accurate atomic parameters. These are best derived through numerical iterative procedures, such as the least-squares [47] or the differential synthesis method [11]. About 50% of the total computing time in crystal structure analysis is spent on the refinement of atomic parameters.

### Least-squares

Through this procedure the atomic parameters are adjusted to obtain the best fit between the observed and calculated structure amplitudes, $|F_o|$ and $|F_c|$, for all reflections. The function most commonly minimized is

$$R_1 = \sum_{hkl} w(|F_o| - |F_c|)^2$$

where the sum is over the set of nonequivalent reflections, and $w$ are weights equal to the inverse of the variances of $|F_o|$. Some programs, however, minimize the function

$$R_2 = \sum_{hkl} w(|F_o|^2 - |F_c|^2)^2$$

The main parameters that are refined through this procedure are:

The scale $K$ of the observed structure amplitudes.
The atomic fractional coordinates $(x, y, z)_i$.
The atomic thermal parameters: $U_i$ if the vibration is assumed isotropic, or $(U_{11}, U_{22}, U_{33}, U_{23}, U_{13}, U_{12})_i$ if the motion is anisotropic.
The occupancy $n_i$ of the atomic sites (only if full occupancy of a given site is in doubt).

Sometimes the least-squares refinement is extended to include extinction parameters [16, 61] and group parameters for planar groups of atoms [30].
A general description of the least-squares procedures as applied in crystallographic work has been given by Rollett [76], and the details of the corresponding normal equations have been described by Cruickshank [20]. Assuming there are $n$ parameters $(p_1, \ldots, p_n)$ entering in the calculation of $|F_c|$, and that those

parameters are to be refined by minimizing $R_1$, it is necessary to set up $n$ normal equations of the type

$$\sum_i c_{ij}\epsilon_i = d_j \qquad (j = 1, \ldots, n) \tag{22}$$

where $\epsilon_i$ are the shifts to be applied to the parameters $p_i$,

$$c_{ij} = \sum_{hkl} w \frac{\partial |F_c|}{\partial p_i} \frac{\partial |F_c|}{\partial p_j}$$

$$d_j = \sum_{hkl} w(|F_o| - |F_c|) \frac{\partial |F_c|}{\partial p_j}$$

The $n \times n$ normal matrix on the left-hand side of Eq. (22) is symmetric, and only the $n(n - 1)/2$ elements on or above the leading diagonal need be stored. Handling the full matrix for an intermediate structure with 30 atoms and about 300 parameters would require large core storage. Steps to overcome this difficulty have been adopted by taking into account the fact that the off-diagonal elements in the normal matrix are usually small relative to the principal diagonal elements. As a compromise, the atoms can be treated as independent of each other, so that the full matrix is replaced by blocks of 9×9 or 10×10, each representing the parameters of one atom. Both the *full matrix* and the *block-diagonal* procedures are commonly used in structure analysis.

After the shifts have been derived, their *estimated standard deviations* are calculated from the expression

$$\sigma(p_i) = \left[ (a^{-1})_{ii} \sum_{hkl} w(|F_o| - |F_c|)^2/(m - n) \right]^{1/2}$$

where $(a^{-1})_{ii}$ is a diagonal element in the inverse matrix, $m$ is the number of reflections included, and $n$ is the number of variable parameters.

### Differential Syntheses

Cruickshank [18] has shown that refinement of atomic parameters by differential syntheses is equivalent to least-squares refinement with unit weights for all reflections. The two procedures, however, are conceptually quite different. The aim of the differential synthesis method is to locate exactly the positions of maximum electron-density distribution, $\rho$, where

$$\frac{\partial \rho}{\partial x} = \frac{\partial \rho}{\partial y} = \frac{\partial \rho}{\partial z} = 0 \tag{23}$$

Thus, starting with approximate peak positions in Ångstrom units, one has to calculate the shifts $(\epsilon_x, \epsilon_y, \epsilon_z)$ so that Eqs. (23) are satisfied at $(x + \epsilon_x, y + \epsilon_y, z + \epsilon_z)$. Using Taylor's expansion and omitting the second-order terms, Eqs. (23) are reduced to three linear equations of the form

$$\epsilon_x \frac{\partial^2 \rho}{\partial x^2} + \epsilon_y \frac{\partial^2 \rho}{\partial x \partial y} + \epsilon_z \frac{\partial^2 \rho}{\partial x \partial z} = - \frac{\partial \rho}{\partial x} \quad \text{etc.} \tag{24}$$

where the derivatives in Eq. (24) are to be evaluated at the assumed $(x, y, z)$ positions. The positional shifts are then calculated by solving the three linear equations of each atom. Their estimated standard deviations are calculated by the expression

$$\sigma(x) = \frac{2\pi(\Sigma h^2 m \mid F_o - F_c \mid^2)^{1/2}}{aV \mid \partial^2\rho/\partial x^2 \mid}$$

Since the electron densities $\rho$ in expression (24) involve the calculation of Fourier series, the shifts should be corrected for the effect of finite summation. This is achieved by doing the calculations once with $F_o$ and once with $F_c$, and taking the difference (obs − calc) as the corrected shift.

## Geometrical Entities

At various stages throughout the refinement, several geometrical entities are calculated and examined. These include the following.

### Bond Lengths

Each molecule is held together by a series of bonds between pairs of atoms. They are identified for the program as the intramolecular distances which are within a specified limit. The bond lengths and their estimated standard deviations are calculated from the atomic parameters and unit cell dimensions.

### Intermolecular Distances

These are defined as the distances between atoms of neighboring molecules. To perform this calculation, the program must derive the atomic coordinates for all the equivalent molecules in the unit cell and in the neighboring cells, and scan all the distances between the atoms of the original molecule and all its neighbors. Short intermolecular distances can identify hydrogen bonds or signify an incorrect structure.

### Valency Angles

These are the angles between pairs of bonds that have one atom in common.

### Mean Plane

It is often important to examine whether a group of atoms is planar or not. The mean plane through the atoms is calculated by a least-squares procedure, minimizing the perpendicular distances of the atoms from the plane. Their planarity is then assessed by means of the chi-square test.

### Torsion (Conformation) Angles

For the bonded atoms A—B—C—D, the torsion angle of the middle bond B—C is defined as the dihedral angle between the planes $ABC$ and $BCD$. These angles must be expressed in the range $-180$ to $+180°$, and their signs must be properly decided according to established conventions.

## Residual Errors

Before termination of a structure refinement, it is important to check that there are no outstanding anomalies in the data or proposed structure. The $R$ and $R_w$ indices defined in Eqs. (6) and (7) are measures of the overall agreement between the observed and calculated structure amplitudes. Calculation of a difference Fourier map at the end of the refinement, with all the known atoms subtracted, can sometimes show evidence of additional atoms in the structure from the solvent, or indicate minor disorder where molecules in a few unit cells are not exactly in the same positions or orientations as in the other cells. The analysis of $|F_o - F_c|$ for ranges of $|F_o|$ or $\sin^2 \theta$ may also shed some light on the systematic errors in the data.

## Analysis of Thermal Motion

### Introduction

Crystal structure analyses yield the *mean* atomic positions and the atomic thermal parameters. The mean positions represent averages over time and crystal volume, and any bond lengths based on these parameters do not give the true instantaneous interatomic distances. Omission of the relative motion of pairs of atoms usually leads to an *apparent shrinkage* in the interatomic distances. Therefore, correction of the bond lengths and valency angles for the thermal motion must be included in any accurate crystal structure analysis. However, for structures with high thermal motion, it is preferable to collect the data at a very low temperature. For a comprehensive account of this topic, see the articles by Johnson in *Crystallographic Computing* [53].

### Thermal Motion of a Rigid Body

The single most important model for interpreting the thermal motion of molecules in crystals is the *rigid-body model*. The method for determining the mean-square amplitudes for rigid-body motion from anisotropic thermal parameters was first developed by Cruickshank [19] and is known to be valid only for special cases. The general method for determining rigid-body motion in the quadratic approximation was developed by Schomaker and Trueblood [80] and has been programmed by them and by other authors.

The first general treatment of rigid-body motion is obtained by using first-order instantaneous displacement parameters in translation **t** and rotation $\boldsymbol{\lambda}$. In this approximation the displacement **u** of an atom from its equilibrium rest position **r** is (in matrix notation)

$$\mathbf{u} = \mathbf{t} + \boldsymbol{\lambda} \times \mathbf{r} = \mathbf{t} + \mathbf{A}\boldsymbol{\lambda}$$

where

$$\mathbf{A} \equiv \begin{bmatrix} 0 & r_3 & -r_2 \\ -r_3 & 0 & r_1 \\ r_2 & -r_1 & 0 \end{bmatrix}$$

The fundamental equation relating the mean-square rigid-body motion to the mean-square displacements of atoms has the form

$$U_{ij} = \sum_{k,l=1}^{6} E_{ik}E_{jl}C_{kl} \qquad (i,j = 1, 2, 3)$$

where $C_{kl}$ are the components of the rigid-body motion tensor to be determined. However, many molecules have large amplitude modes of internal vibration such as torsional oscillation about a single covalent bond. In such cases, *coupled rigid-bodies* can sometimes be used to allow for this internal motion.

### Mean Separation of Two Atoms

The interatomic distances between the *mean* positions of atoms A and B (in cartesian coordinates) is

$$d_0 = [(x_B - x_A)^2 + (y_B - y_A)^2 + (z_B - z_A)^2]^{1/2}$$

At any instant the atoms are displaced from their mean positions by $\Delta x_B$, $\Delta y_B$, $\Delta z_B$, $\Delta x_A$, $\Delta y_A$, $\Delta z_A$. If the $z$ axis is selected along the $AB$ vector, then the instantaneous interatomic vector may be written as

$$d \approx d_0 + \Delta z + (\Delta x^2 + \Delta y^2)/2d_0 - (\Delta x^2 \Delta z + \Delta y^2 \Delta z)/2d_0^2$$

where $\Delta x \equiv \Delta x_B - \Delta x_A$ is the relative displacement along $x$, and similarly for $y$ and $z$. In the *quadratic* approximation, the mean interatomic distance is

$$d_q \equiv \langle d \rangle \approx d_0 + (\langle \Delta x^2 \rangle + \langle \Delta y^2 \rangle)/2d_0$$

where $\langle \ \rangle$ indicate time and lattice averaging. The term $(\langle \Delta x^2 \rangle + \langle \Delta y^2 \rangle)/2$ is simply the average mean-square relative displacement in the $xy$ plane (normal to $AB$). Unfortunately, this term cannot be determined from the diffraction data, and only its upper and lower limits can be calculated, depending on the mathematical model used.

## Graphic Representation

Computer graphics of molecules and unit-cell contents, in both mono and stereo, have become quite popular mainly because of the sophisticated software available for this purpose. The most renowned of these programs is ORTEP (Oak Ridge Thermal Ellipsoid Plot Program) by Johnson [52], and its operation has been described briefly by Johnson [53]. A sample drawing by ORTEP of the unit-cell contents of (±)β-promedol alcohol is shown in Fig. 6 [24].

The illustrations produced by ORTEP are principally of the ball-and-stick type. The graphic representation of an atom can be a circle, a sphere, or a thermal ellipsoid that represents the relative amplitudes and directions of thermal vibration. From a given list of atomic parameters the program selects the atoms to be plotted according to the user's coded instructions, and identifies where bonds should be drawn between pairs of atoms. Bonds are drawn tapered to give the perspective view, and labels for atom symbols, and for bond lengths, can be plotted. For stereoscopic drawings, the labels and captions can be plotted in perspective in planes defined by the user. One of the outstanding advantages of computer graphics is that the precision obtainable through machine plotting

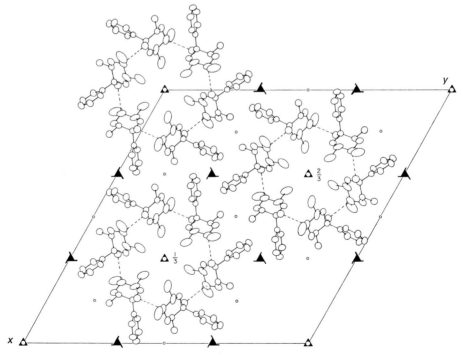

**Fig. 6.** A projection of the unit-cell contents of (±)β-promedol alcohol as produced by the ORTEP program. Each six molecules are connected by hydrogen bonds, as shown by the dotted lines, to form a hexameric ring [24].

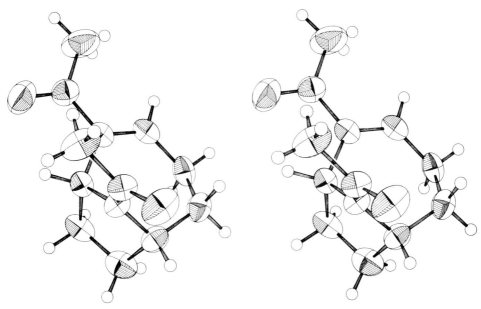

**Fig. 7.** A pair of stereoscopic drawings of a toxin molecule, as produced by the ORTEP program. The ellipsoids represent the modes of thermal vibration of the atoms [46].

makes feasible the routine production of detailed illustrations. An example of the stereoscopic pair of a toxin molecule [46] is presented in Fig. 7.

## Visual Display

The application of interactive displays in crystallography has been relatively small because of the limited availability of equipment. The majority of applications have been for model building and for macromolecular crystallography. Details of the applications and procedures have been described by Sakurai [78], Nagano [69], and Morimoto and Meyer [68] in *Crystallographic Computing Techniques*.

With this technique a protein model, consisting of thousands of atoms, is constructed inside a computer, then the full molecule, parts of it, or just the skeleton can be viewed on a screen from any desired angle. The technique is also useful in the application of prediction procedures of macromolecules, and for fitting a molecular model to an electron-density map. Realistic three-dimensional views of a complex figure are obtained by elimination of hidden lines, by changing the sizes due to perspective view, and/or by variation of brightness. The facility of rotating the figure about an axis can also help the sense of stereo. If a color cathode-ray tube is available, two-color images viewed through filtered glasses give a true stereoscopic view [66].

## Model Building

Various model kits are available for construction of small molecular models without the aid of a computer. For macromolecules, the traditional method of model building from prefabricated wire components in conjunction with an electron-density map is usually performed using a Richards' optical comparator [73]. A description of computerized model building techniques has been given by Diamond [28].

There is usually little problem in making the model of a macromolecule if its chemical sequence is known, but the task is much more difficult if the sequence is unavailable. The correct model is constructed to be stereochemically acceptable and to correspond to the available electron-density distribution. Active work is being carried out to perform this operation with the aid of interactive computing and a visual display. A well-developed and effective procedure is that described by Diamond [26], where a trial model is constructed with wire components, and its coordinates are input to a program that makes the necessary adjustments to improve the fit between model and electron-density distribution. This program can also produce coordinates for missing or unmeasured atoms in the model. The method works well if *guide coordinates* (of $C^\alpha$, $C^\gamma$, and O atoms) are given for each of the protein residues. The procedure recognizes that bond lengths do not change from their expected values, while conformation angles can change. The atomic coordinates are adjusted to produce the best fit to the input guide points.

## Structure Factor Tables

A depository of the observed and calculated structure factor tables has been set up by the International Union of Crystallography for all structural papers published in *Acta Crystallographica*. These tables are produced by the computer in a specific compressed format suitable for storage on microfiche. This storage system has proved to be quite worthwhile in cutting down the volume and costs of publication.

# MACROMOLECULAR STRUCTURES

## Introduction

The study of macromolecules involves some quite different procedures from those already described. A typical macromolecule, such as a protein or enzyme, contains $100\times$ the number of atoms of smaller structures, its crystals are less stable in terms of elapsed time and X-ray exposure time, and its atoms usually have a much higher apparent thermal motion. The net result is a much lower ratio of observations to unknown parameters, and this makes it impractical to apply the very successful direct methods of phase determination, and reduces the ultimate accuracy of the X-ray analysis. The phase problem for these compounds is handled by the following procedures: (1) isomorphous replacement, (2) anomalous scattering, and/or (3) use of noncrystallographic symmetry.

The common procedure in the study of proteins is to prepare suitable crystals of the *native protein* and of one or more heavy atom *isomorphous derivatives*, which means that the crystals have similar unit cell dimensions and belong to the same space group as those of the native protein. The X-ray intensity data are then collected (by photographic or diffractometer techniques) for the native protein and for each of its isomorphous derivatives. Their corresponding structure amplitudes $|F_P|$, $|F_{PH1}|$, $|F_{PH2}|$, etc. are then derived as described earlier, where $P$ stands for protein and $PH$ for protein plus heavy atoms (i.e., isomorphous derivative).

### Data Reduction

During this step the data are corrected for all known sources of error, and *analyzed* for consistency and reliability. The sources of error which are particular for protein data are:

1. Radiation damage which results in a continuous drop of the diffracted intensities, and has to be estimated by measuring an adequate sample of the reflections at regular intervals of time.
2. Because of the crystal deterioration in the X-ray beam, it is necessary to use more than one crystal for the data set, and it is then necessary to estimate the scales of the crystals used and apply those scales to the appropriate data.
3. Since protein crystals have to be in continuous contact with some of the mother liquor throughout the experiment, the absorption in this case is caused by the crystal, the mother liquor, and the enclosing glass capillary.

### Heavy Atom Positions

The first step is to determine the relative scale and temperature factor of $|F_P|$ and $|F_{PH}|$ from a linear "relative Wilson plot" of log $(\langle|F_{PH}^2|\rangle/\langle|F_P^2|\rangle)$ against $\sin^2\theta$. A Patterson map is then calculated for each isomorphous derivative with the $(|F_{PH}| - |F_P|)^2$ amplitudes (after normalizing the two data sets). The peaks in this map represent only the vectors among the heavy atoms, from which the positional parameters of the atoms can be deduced. The coordinates, occupancies, and temperature factors of the heavy atoms are then refined by successive cycles of least-squares and difference maps. For detailed description of the refinement of the heavy atoms, see Dodson [29]. With the refined parameters, the $|F_H|$ and their phase angles $\alpha_H$ are calculated.

### Multiple Isomorphous Replacement

In this step, one has to determine the phase angles $\alpha_P$ from the known values of $|F_P|$, $|F_{PH}|$, $|F_H|$, and $\alpha_H$ by applying the vector relationship $\mathbf{F}_{PH} = \mathbf{F}_P +$

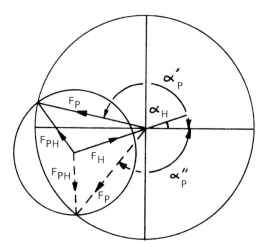

**Fig. 8.** The Harker construction [38] for evaluating the protein phases $\alpha_P$. Given $|F_P|$, $|F_H|$, $|F_{PH}|$, and $\alpha_H$, there are two possible solutions $\alpha_P'$ and $\alpha_P''$. The circles have radii $|F_P|$ and $|F_{PH}|$, and their centers are offset by the vector $\mathbf{F}_H$.

$\mathbf{F}_H$. As demonstrated by the Harker construction [38] shown in Fig. 8, the relationship leads to two possible solutions for each $\alpha_P$. In order to resolve the ambiguity, it is necessary to repeat the procedure with a *second isomorphous derivative* and combine the two sets of results. Under ideal conditions there will be one value $\alpha_P$ common to the two pairs of solution. In practice, however, experimental errors and the lack of exact isomorphism can affect the unique solution of the phase problem. This would necessitate the use of more than two derivatives to obtain a satisfactory solution. For further details of this procedure, see Kartha [59, 60] and Matthews [65].

### Anomalous Scattering

The main advantage of this procedure is that it provides an effective way of determining the protein phases from a single isomorphous derivative. The principle of the method is based on the fact that the atomic scattering factors are complex numbers, which for heavy atoms and suitable X-ray radiations have small but significant imaginary components. Consequently, the $|F(\mathbf{h})|$ and $|F(\bar{\mathbf{h}})|$ are not equal in noncentrosymmetric structures, contrary to Friedel's law. In the isomorphous derivatives the differences in these structure amplitudes are usually measurable and are referred to as the Bijvoet or *anomalous scattering differences*. Although the differences have small amplitudes, they can be deduced fairly accurately since $|F(\mathbf{h})|$ and $|F(\bar{\mathbf{h}})|$ are measured from the same crystal and within a few minutes from each other.

From the known heavy atom parameters it is straightforward to calculate $|F_H(\mathbf{h})|$, $|F_H(\bar{\mathbf{h}})|$, $\alpha_H(\mathbf{h})$, and $\alpha_H(\bar{\mathbf{h}})$, and the vector $\mathbf{F}_H(\mathbf{h}) - \mathbf{F}_H(\bar{\mathbf{h}})$. These values are then combined vectorially with $|F_{PH}(\mathbf{h})|$ and $|F_{PH}(\mathbf{\bar{h}})|$ to produce two possible solutions for each $\alpha_{PH}(\mathbf{h})$. Having two values of $\alpha_P(\mathbf{h})$ from the isomorphous replacement procedure and two values $\alpha_{PH}(\mathbf{h})$ from the anomalous dispersion procedure, it is possible to select the correct value of $\alpha_P(\mathbf{h})$. For details, see the articles mentioned in the preceding section.

## Structure Determination

The electron-density map of the *native* protein is calculated using the observed $|F_P|$ and the calculated $\alpha_P$, and is studied in conjunction with known chemical information about the molecule. Protein molecules consist mainly of standard subunits (or atomic groups) linked together to form a continuous chain with a number of bends, helices, and/or loops. The dimensions and shapes of the subunits are well-known from X-ray structural work on smaller molecules. In studying the electron-density map, one tries to identify the subunits from their shape and dimensions, and it is usually of considerable help if the sequence of the subunits in the chain is known from biochemical studies of the protein. In practice it is usually necessary to perform this study with the aid of models or an interactive visual display. The necessary software to fit the model to the electron-density distribution has been described earlier.

## Structure Refinement

For the refinement of protein structures at the atomic level, it is necessary to have high resolution data, 2.5 Å or better. The main refinement procedures [51] are the following.

1. By use of the $(F_o - F_c)$ difference syntheses which are sensitive and display errors in atomic parameters. The atomic shifts are calculated from the formula

$$\Delta x_{ij} = -(\partial\rho/\partial x_i)_j / (\partial^2\rho/\partial x^2)_j \qquad (i = 1, 2, 3; j = 1, \ldots, N)$$

2. By the $(2F_o - F_c)$ Fourier syntheses which represent a superposition of an $F_o$ and an $(F_o - F_c)$ maps, and are particularly useful for locating atoms that were missed from the model.
3. By differential syntheses.
4. By least squares as described earlier, or in a modified form to fit the model parameters to the $F_P$ electron-density map [27]. In the Diamond procedure [27] the number of parameters to be refined is about half the number of atomic positional parameters.

Such refinements are computationally expensive and time-consuming, and are carried out only where significant improvement of the model is needed. The development of effective and more economical refinement techniques is under active study, as described by Sayre [79].

## Use of Noncrystallographic Symmetry

In recent years several procedures have been developed to make use of known information about the internal (noncrystallographic) symmetry within the asymmetric unit cell. Such symmetry can occur in subunit proteins, enzyme systems, small viruses, and in structures with two similar molecules in the asymmetric unit. The subunits are assumed to be rigid (except for side chains) and to relate to each other by three rotational and three translational degrees of freedom, and the object of the procedures is to derive these parameters by systematic searches of the Patterson function. This is carried out in two stages, a rotational search and then a translational search. Descriptions of these procedures are available in two books: *The Molecular Replacement Method* [67] and *Crystallographic Computing Techniques* [23].

The basic concept is one of comparing Patterson functions in different orientations to match the identical vector sets of variously oriented subunits. Rossmann and Blow [77] introduced the rotation function

$$R(\theta_1 , \theta_2 , \theta_3 ) = \int_U P_2(x_2) \, P_1(x_1) \, dx_1$$

which compares the two Patterson functions $P_1$ and $P_2$ within the volume $U$ for a given set of rotation angles $(\theta_1 , \theta_2 , \theta_3)$ in the Eulerian space. The resulting three-dimensional map gives peaks at the angular values that relate the two functions. The translational problem is more complex, and its satisfactory solution requires additional information such as the known structure of a similar molecule.

## MISCELLANEOUS CRYSTALLOGRAPHIC COMPUTING

### The ACA Software Survey

A survey conducted in 1973–1974 by the Computing Committee of the American Crystallographic Association showed that about 90% of the computing time used by crytallographers is for X-ray single crystal work which has already been described. The remaining 10% of the time is spent on X-ray powder work (4%), neutron and electron diffraction (3%), small-angle scattering (2%), and neutron powder (1%). In the X-ray single crystal work, half the time is spent on structure refinement, 22% on structure solution, 13% on preliminary data processing, and the rest on publication preparation and data retrieval. Most of the crystallographic computing, 83%, is done in the batch mode, while only 6% is carried out via TTY terminals and 11% on dedicated in-house computers.

### X-Ray Powder Diffraction

This is a very useful technique, used mainly for identification of unknown compounds from their X-ray powder diffraction patterns. The pattern in this case consists of a series of diffraction lines of different spacings and intensities, and the identification is carried out by matching the strongest few lines with one of the patterns in a standard *powder diffraction file* of known compounds. The file is maintained and updated annually by the Joint Committee on Powder Diffraction Standards, and is available as microfiche, as a data base on magnetic tape and 2dTS (diffraction data tele-search), computer time-sharing, as well as on printed data cards and in book form. The total file contains over 26,000 numeric diffraction patterns of crystalline material. The computer software for searching the file is also available.

## Exchange of Programs

Most of the crystallographic computer programs are quite complex, but they have long life and can be applied without change to any crystal structure. Consequently, only a small percentage of crystallographers develop programs, while the majority relies on available programs from other centers. To enhance this exchange of programs, the Computing Commission of the International Union of Crystallography has compiled and published three editions of the *World List of Crystallographic Computer Programs* [9, 82]. Each program is described briefly in two or three sentences, and the authors undertake the distribution and updating of their own programs. Also, to enable crystallographers to check the programs, the commission has prepared a set of *Standard Tests for Crystallographic Computer Programs* [3]. Every few years the commission holds an international summer school on crystallographic computing to acquaint crystallographers with the latest developments in the field. The proceedings of these schools are then published for wider distribution.

## Data Storage and Retrieval

The fast computers, the sophisticated crystallographic software, and the automated equipment for data collection have combined over the past 10 years to drastically increase the output of crystallographers. In 1955 the number of organic structure analyses was less than 500, by 1965 this figure had risen to 2,500, and by early 1975 had exceeded 12,000 [7]. To assist in the retrieval and proper utilization of this valuable information, the Cambridge Centre (U.K.) has established three computer files of information concerning these structures, together with extensive file-handling software. The files contain classified bibliographic, numeric data, and chemical connectivity (bond lengths and angles) records since 1935. The information is available in machine-readable form and in the book reference series *Molecular Structures and Dimensions*. It is now possible to utilize the bibliographic and numeric data files for a wide range of research projects.

# REFERENCES

1. Ahmed, F. R., Fourier techniques, in *Crystallographic Computing,* Munksgaard, Copenhagen; 1970, pp. 355–359.
2. Ahmed, F. R., Crystal structure of $C_{33}H_{47}NO_9S$, an advanced intermediate in the synthesis of talatisamine, *Acta Crystallogr., Sect. B* **30,** 2558–2564 (1974).
3. Ahmed, F. R., D. W. J. Cruickshank, A. C. Larson, and J. M. Stewart, Standard tests for crystallographic computer programs. I. Calculations commonly used in crystal structure analysis. *Acta Crystallogr., Sect. A* **28,** 365–393 (1972).
4. Ahmed, F. R., and S. R. Hall, Computer application of the symbolic addition and tangent procedures, in *Crystallographic Computing Techniques,* Munksgaard, Copenhagen, 1976, pp. 71–84.
5. Ahmed, F. R., S. R. Hall, M. E. Pippy, and C. P. Huber, NRC system of crystallographic programs for the IBM 360 systems, *J. Appl. Crystallogr.* **6,** 309–346 (1973).
6. Alcock, N. W., The analytical method for absorption correction, in *Crystallographic Computing,* Munksgaard, Copenhagen, 1970, pp. 271–278.
7. Allen, F. H., O. Kennard, W. D. S. Motherwell, and D. G. Watson, The Cambridge Crystallographic Data Centre: Computer files and file-searching techniques, *Acta Crystallogr., Sect. A* **31,** S3, 278 (1975).
8. Azaroff, L. V., A one-dimensional Fourier analogue computer, *Rev. Sci. Instrum.* **25,** 471–477 (1954).
9. Bassi, G. C., IUCR world list of crystallographic computer programs, 3rd ed., *J. Appl. Crystallogr.* **4,** 309–346 (1973).
10. Beevers, C. A., and H. Lipson, An improved numerical method of two-dimensional Fourier synthesis for crystals, *Proc. Phys. Soc., London* **48,** 772–780 (1936).
11. Booth, A. D., A differential Fourier method for refining atomic parameters in crystal structure analysis, *Trans. Faraday Soc.* **42,** 444–448 (1946).
12. Busing, W. R., and H. A. Levy, High speed computation of the absorption correction for single crystal diffraction measurements, *Acta Crystallogr.* **10,** 180–182 (1957).
13. Busing, W. R., K. O. Martin, and H. A. Levy, *ORFLS,* Oak Ridge National Laboratory Report ORNL-TM-305, 1962.
14. Cochran, W., Relations between the phases of structure factors, *Acta Crystallogr.* **8,** 473–478 (1955).
15. Cooley, J. W., and J. W. Tukey, Algorithm for the machine calculation of complex Fourier series, *Math. Comput.* **19,** 297–301 (1965).
16. Coppens, P., The evaluation of absorption and extinction in single-crystal structure analysis, in *Crystallographic Computing,* Munksgaard, Copenhagen, 1970, pp. 255–270.
17. Cox, E. G., L. Gross, and G. A. Jeffrey, A Hollerith technique for computing three-dimensional differential Fourier syntheses in X-ray crystal structure analysis, *Acta Crystallogr.* **2,** 351–355 (1949).
18. Cruickshank, D. W. J., On the relation between Fourier and least-squares methods of structure determination, *Acta Crystallogr.* **5,** 511–518 (1952).
19. Cruickshank, D. W. J., The analysis of the anisotropic thermal motion of molecules in crystals, *Acta Crystallogr.* **9,** 754–756 (1956).
20. Cruickshank, D. W. J., Least-squares refinement of atomic parameters, in *Crystallographic Computing,* Munksgaard, Copenhagen, 1970, pp. 187–200.
21. Cruickshank, D. W. J., D. E. Pilling, A. Bujosa, F. M. Lovell, and M. R. Truter,

Crystallographic calculations on the Ferranti Pegasus and Mark 1 computers, in *Computing Methods and the Phase Problem in X-ray Crystal Analysis,* Pergamon, Oxford, 1961, pp. 32–78.

22. *Crystallographic Computing* (F. R. Ahmed, S. R. Hall, and C. P. Huber, eds.), Munksgaard, Copenhagen, 1970.

23. *Crystallographic Computing Techniques* (F. R. Ahmed, K. Huml, and B. Sedláček, eds.), Munksgaard, Copenhagen, 1976.

24. De Camp, W. H., and F. R. Ahmed, Structural studies of synthetic analgetics. III. The crystal and molecular structure of the rhombohedral form of (±)-β-promedol alcohol, *Acta Crystallogr., Sect. B* **28,** 3484–3488 (1972).

25. Dewar, R. B. K., Use of Computers in X-ray Phase Problem, Thesis, University of Chicago, 1968.

26. Diamond, R., A mathematical model building procedure for proteins, *Acta Crystallogr.* **21,** 253–266 (1966).

27. Diamond, R., A real space refinement procedure for proteins, *Acta Crystallogr., Sect. A* **27,** 436–452 (1971).

28. Diamond, R., Model building techniques for macromolecules, in *Crystallographic Computing Techniques,* Munksgaard, Copenhagen, 1976, pp. 336–343.

29. Dodson, E., A comparison of different heavy atom refinement procedures, in *Crystallographic Computing Techniques,* Munksgaard, Copenhagen, 1976, pp. 259–268.

30. Doedens, R. J., Group least-squares refinement, in *Crystallographic Computing,* Munksgaard, Copenhagen, 1970, pp. 198–200.

31. Eller, G. von, *Bull. Soc. Fr. Mineral. Cristallogr.* **78,** 157 (1955).

32. Germain, G., and M. M. Woolfson, On the application of phase relationships to complex structures, *Acta Crystallogr., Sect. B* **24,** 91–96 (1968).

33. Grainger, C. T., The solution of non-centrosymmetric structures by symbolic tangent refinement, *Acta Crystallogr., Sect. A* **29,** 382–388 (1973).

34. Hagg, G., and T. Laurent, A machine for the summation of Fourier series, *J. Sci. Instrum.* **23,** 155–158 (1946).

35. Hall, S. R., and F. R. Ahmed, The crystal structure of protopine, $C_{20}H_{19}O_5N$, *Acta Crystallogr., Sect. B* **24,** 337–346 (1968).

36. Hall, S. R., and F. R. Ahmed, The crystal structure of cryptopine, $C_{21}H_{23}O_5N$, *Acta Crystallogr., Sect. B* **24,** 346–355 (1968).

37. Hanson, A. W., H. Lipson, and C. A. Taylor, The application of the principles of physical optics to crystal-structure determination, *Proc. R. Soc. London, Ser. A* **218,** 371–384 (1953).

38. Harker, D., The determination of the phases of the structure factors of non-centrosymmetric crystals by the method of double isomorphous replacement, *Acta Crystallogr.* **9,** 1–9 (1956).

39. Harker, D., and J. Kasper, Phases of Fourier coefficients directly from crystal diffraction data, *Acta Crystallogr.* **1,** 70–75 (1948).

40. Hartree, D. R., *Numerical Analysis,* Clarendon, Oxford, 1955.

41. Hauptman, H., The calculation of structure invariants, in *Crystallographic Computing,* Munksgaard, Copenhagen, 1970, pp. 41–51.

42. Hauptman, H., *Crystal Structure Determination—The Role of the Cosine Seminvariants,* Plenum, New York, 1972.

43. Hauptman, H., and J. Karle, The probability distribution of the magnitude of a structure factor, *Acta Crystallogr.* **6,** 136–141 (1953).

44. Hauptman, H., and J. Karle, *Solution of the Phase Problem. I. The Centrosymme-*

*tric Crystals* (American Crystallographic Association Monograph No. 3), Edwards, Ann Arbor, Michigan, 1953.

45. Hoppe, W., and K. Pannke, Eine Mechanische Analogierechenmaschine für die ein- und Mehrdimensionale Fouriersynthese und analyse, *Z. Kristallogr.* **107**, 451–463 (1956).

46. Huber, C. P., The crystal structure and absolute configuration of 2,9-diacetyl-9-azabicyclo[4,2,1]non-2,3-ene, *Acta Crystallogr., Sect. B* **28**, 2577–2582 (1972).

47. Hughes, E. W., The crystal structure of melamine, *J. Am. Chem. Soc.* **63**, 1737–1752 (1941).

48. Hughes, E. W., and C. A. Taylor, Apparatus used in the development of optical-diffraction methods for the solution of problems in X-ray analysis, *J. Sci. Instrum.* **30**, 105–110 (1953).

49. Immirzi, A., Fast Fourier transform in crystallography, in *Crystallographic Computing Techniques,* Munksgaard, Copenhagen, 1976, pp. 399–412.

50. *International Tables for X-ray Crystallography,* Vol. 1, 2nd ed., Kynoch, Birmingham, 1952.

51. Jensen, L. H., Protein model refinement by Fourier and least-squares methods, in *Crystallographic Computing Techniques,* Munksgaard, Copenhagen, 1976, pp. 307–316.

52. Johnson, C. K., *ORTEP: A* FORTRAN *Thermal Ellipsoid Plot Program for Crystal Structure Illustrations,* Oak Ridge National Laboratory Report ORNL 3794, 1965.

53. Johnson, C. K., An introduction to thermal motion analysis; The effect of thermal motion on interatomic distances, in *Crystallographic Computing,* Munksgaard, Copenhagen, 1970, pp. 207–226.

54. Karle, I. L., Practical aspects of direct phase determination, in *Crystallographic Computing Techniques,* Munksgaard, Copenhagen, 1976, pp. 27–70.

55. Karle, I. L., and J. Karle, An application of a new phase determination procedure to the structure of cyclo(hexaglycyl) hemihydrate, *Acta Crystallogr.* **16**, 969–975 (1963).

56. Karle, J., and H. Hauptman, The phases and magnitudes of the structure factors, *Acta Crystallogr.* **3**, 181–187 (1950).

57. Karle, J., and H. Hauptman, A theory of phase determination for the four types of non-centrosymmetric space groups $1P222$, $2P222$, $3P_12$, $3P_22$, *Acta Crystallogr.* **9**, 635–651 (1956).

58. Karle, J., and I. L. Karle, The symbolic addition procedure for phase determination for centrosymmetric and non-centrosymmetric crystals, *Acta Crystallogr.* **21**, 849–859 (1966).

59. Kartha, G., Use of isomorphous series and anomalous scattering data in structure determination of large molecules, in *Crystallographic Computing,* Munksgaard, Copenhagen, 1970, pp. 132–145.

60. Kartha, G., Protein phase evaluation: Multiple isomorphous series and anomalous scattering methods, in *Crystallographic Computing Techniques,* Munksgaard, Copenhagen, 1976, pp. 269–281.

61. Larson, A. C., The inclusion of secondary extinction in least-squares refinement of crystal structures, in *Crystallographic Computing,* Munksgaard, Copenhagen, 1970, pp. 291–294.

62. Lowan, A. N., N. Davids, and A. Levenson, Tables of the zeros of the Legendre polynomials of order 1–16 and the weight coefficients for Gauss' mechanical quadrature formula, *Bull. Am. Math. Soc.* **48**, 739–743 (1942).

63. Main, P., M. M. Woolfson, and G. Germain, *MULTAN: A Computer Program for*

*the Automatic Solution of Crystal Structures,* Universities of York and Louvain, 1971.

64. Margeneau, H., and G. M. Murphy, *The Mathematics and Physics of Chemistry,* Van Nostrand, New York, 1943.

65. Matthews, B. W., Determination and refinement of phases for proteins, in *Crystallographic Computing,* Munksgaard, Copenhagen, 1970, pp. 146–159.

66. Meyer, E. F., Jr., Three-dimensional graphical models of molecules and a time-slicing computer. *J. Appl. Crystallogr.* **3,** 392–395 (1970).

67. *The Molecular Replacement Method* (M. Rossmann, ed.), Gordon and Breach, New York, 1972.

68. Morimoto, C. N., and E. F. Meyer, Jr., Information retrieval, computer graphics and remote computing, in *Crystallographic Computing Techniques,* Munksgaard, Copenhagen, 1976, pp. 488–496.

69. Nagano, K., How to simulate protein folding with interactive computer graphics, in *Crystallographic Computing Techniques,* Munksgaard, Copenhagen, 1976, pp. 344–352.

70. Niggli, A., Small-scale computers in X-ray crystallography, in *Computing Methods and the Phase Problem in X-ray Crystal Analysis,* Pergamon, Oxford, 1961, pp. 12–20.

71. Patterson, A. L., A Fourier series method for the determination of the components of interatomic distances in crystals, *Phys. Rev.* **46,** 372–376 (1934).

72. Pepinsky, R., *Computing Methods and the Phase Problem in X-ray Crystal Analysis,* Pennsylvania State College Congress, University Park, Pennsylvania, 1950.

73. Richards, F. M., The matching of physical models to three-dimensional electron-density maps: A simple optical device. *J. Mol. Biol.* **37,** 225–230 (1968).

74. Robertson, J. M., A fast digital computer for Fourier operations. *Acta Crystallogr.* **7,** 817–822 (1954).

75. Robertson, J. M., A digital mechanical computer for Fourier operations, in *Computing Methods and the Phase Problem in X-ray Crystal Analysis,* Pergamon, Oxford, 1961, pp. 21–24.

76. Rollett, J. S., Least-squares procedures in crystal structure analysis, in *Crystallographic Computing,* Munksgaard, Copenhagen, 1970, pp. 167–181.

77. Rossmann, M., and D. M. Blow, The direction of sub-units within the crystallographic asymmetric unit, *Acta Crystallogr.* **15,** 24–31 (1962).

78. Sakurai, T., Role of interactive displays in crystallography, in *Crystallographic Computing Techniques,* Munksgaard, Copenhagen, 1976, pp. 478–480.

79. Sayre, D., Recent developments in the technique of lease-squares phase refinement based on the squaring-method equations; overview of other direct methods available for the phasing of protein crystal diffraction data, in *Crystallographic Computing Techniques,* Munksgaard, Copenhagen, 1976, pp. 322–327.

80. Schomaker, V., and K. N. Trueblood, On the rigid-body motion of molecules in crystals, *Acta Crystallogr., Sect. B* **24,** 63–76 (1968).

81. Shimizu, H. P., J. Elsey, and D. McLachlan, A machine for synthesizing two-dimensional Fourier series in the determination of crystal structures, *Rev. Sci. Instrum.* **21,** 779–783 (1950).

82. Shoemaker, D. P., *IUCR World List of Crystallographic Computer Programs,* 1st ed., V.R.B., Groningen, 1962; 2nd ed., Bronder-Offset, Rotterdam, 1966.

83. Sly, W. G., and D. P. Shoemaker, MIFR: A two- and three-dimensional Fourier summation program for the IBM 704, in *Computing Methods and the Phase*

*Problem in X-ray Crystal Analysis,* Pergamon, Oxford, 1961, pp. 129–139.

84. Stewart, J. M., Description of a peak picking program, in *Crystallographic Computing Techniques,* Munksgaard, Copenhagen, 1976, p. 193.

85. Stewart, J. M., G. J. Kruger, H. L. Ammon, C. H. Dickenson, and S. R. Hall, *Crystal Structure Calculations System XRAY,* University of Maryland Computer Science, Technical Report 192 (1972).

86. Vand, V., A Fourier electron-density balance, *J. Sci. Instrum.* **29,** 118–121 (1952).

87. Woolfson, M. M., Doing without symbols—MULTAN, in *Crystallographic Computing Techniques,* Munksgaard, Copenhagen, 1976, pp. 85–96.

*Farid R. Ahmed*

# CURRICULUM COMMITTEE ON COMPUTER SCIENCE

## INTRODUCTION

The Curriculum Committee on Computer Science ($C^3S$) of the Association for Computing Machinery (ACM) was initially formed in 1962 as a subcommittee of the Education Committee of ACM. It was established as an independent standing committee of ACM in 1964 and has continued to work, as such, since that time. The following pages will outline the activities of $C^3S$. The reports of the committee will be only briefly discussed since these reports are available from ACM.

Two major reports have been issued by $C^3S$; the first in 1965 [9] and the second in 1968 [10]. This leads to a natural organization for this report. First the activities of the committee prior to the 1965 report will be considered, then the 1965 report will be presented, followed by a discussion of the 1968 report of $C^3S$. Finally the activities of the committee following the publication of the 1968 recommendations will be considered.

## ACTIVITIES PRIOR TO THE 1965 RECOMMENDATIONS

During the first few years of its existence $C^3S$ functioned informally by sponsoring a number of panel discussions and other sessions at national computer meetings.

The most significant of these panel sessions was held at the 1963 ACM

Annual Conference in Denver. The papers of this session by Perlis [24], Arden [2], Forsythe [14], Korfhage [18], Gorn [15], and Muller [23] appeared in a special report on curriculum in computer science in the April 1964 issue of the *Communications of the ACM*. To these papers were added papers by Keenan [17] attempting a definition of computer science and a paper by Atchison and Hamblen [4] indicating the current state of computer science education.

In Keenan's [17] definition of computer science, he identifies four basic topics of interest to the computer scientist:

1. Organization and interaction of equipment constituting an information processing system.
2. Development of software systems with which to control and communicate with equipment.
3. Derivation and study of procedures and basic theories for the specification of processes.
4. Application of systems, software, procedures, and theories of computer science to other disciplines.

He then goes on to give examples of the kind of work that goes on under each of these topics.

Within this broad definition of the field, Keenan turns to the question of education in computer science. Here he identifies five areas of concern in computer science education:

1. General education—to insure that the public is properly aware of computers and what they can do.
2. Training of programmers.
3. Orientation of scientists.
4. Education of computer specialists.
5. Development of computer scientists.

Keenan then notes that each of these areas carries its own problems of emphasis and standards, and relates the material in the set of papers to these levels of education:

> The courses described in this issue neither encompass the full domain of material available in computer science, nor signify the end product of the present curriculum evaluation. The descriptions give but a snapshot of current thought on desirable material and methods of presentation in selected areas. Some of the courses (Perlis, Arden) are appropriate as introductions for computer specialists or for the orientation of students of other sciences; others (Muller, Korfhage, and Forsythe) described courses for computer specialists—i.e., undergraduate computer scientists—which may also merit consideration as electives for other discipline; Gorn describes material largely of his own development which is placed at the graduate level in computer science.

Perlis [24] describes a one semester first course in programming. The course, which covered (1) structure of algorithms, (2) structure of languages, (3) structure of machines, (4) structure of programs, and (5) structure of data, did not concentrate on the details of a language or a machine, leaving the mastery of this material to problems and exercises. Perlis then goes on to outline a curriculum for an option in computation in an undergraduate mathematics major. Effectively this option adds to a traditional mathematics major the programming course described, and courses in Boolean Algebra and Switching, Constructive Logic, and Advanced Theory of Computation.

Arden [2] presents a course designed as an introduction to computing for engineering and science students. Recognizing that such students will only have an opportunity to take one course in computing, this course attempts to select significant topics from computer systems, numerical analysis, and programming. As with Perlis's course, a great deal of emphasis is placed on exercises which supply many of the details not covered in the classroom.

Forsythe [14] presents a curriculum in Numerical Analysis consisting of a one-quarter freshman–sophomore course, a three-quarter senior course, and a three-quarter graduate course. Here, too, the importance of programming exercises is stressed.

Korfhage [18] recognizes the special place of logic in the education of a computer scientist and proposes a sequence of four courses in the area: Introduction to Logic and Algorithms, Logical Design, Mathematical Logic, and Computability and Algorithms.

Muller [23] also addresses the problems of introducing logic into the educational program of the computer scientist, but he does it in terms of a sequence in logical design and switching theory.

Gorn [15], with little discussion, outlines a graduate course in mechanical languages.

Atchison and Hamblen [4], in the concluding article of the sequence, consider existing programs in computer science. A survey they conducted in 1963 identified 28 such programs with another 18 anticipated. It was noted that the programs arose from, or were housed in, mathematics, engineering (usually electrical but occasionally industrial), or business administration, with mathematics departments the most common:

> At this point in time, most existing computer programs have come from the first of these, namely mathematics. Most of these programs still have a very strong orientation toward mathematics. Many of them are, in fact, little different from a degree program in numerical analysis where the computer has been used in problem solution. Others have developed to a point where they have a strong emphasis in advanced programming and the development of computer languages. Some are laying down a broader base by including in their preparation of computer oriented personnel such things as logic, Boolean algebra, theory of automata and artificial intelligence. Others have a very strong emphasis on the statistical side.
>
> There are people who contend that after all computer science is nothing

but a portion of applied mathematics. There is certainly no question but what the rigorous thought-processes that are required in mathematics are likewise required in the computer field. This is not to say, however, that an excellent mathematician will be a good computer man or conversely. It should be remarked that there are mathematics departments which already have or are planning to incorporate some computer training in their calculus sequence. The view is frequently expressed that some day computer science will crystallize out of mathematics, as has statistics.

## THE 1965 RECOMMENDATIONS

C³S became an independent committee of the ACM in 1964 and began an active effort to formulate detailed recommendations in computer science. The first result of this work was "An Undergraduate Program in Computer Science, Preliminary Recommendations" [9] published in the September 1965 issue of the *Communications of the ACM*. The 1965 recommendations were drawn up by a committee consisting of:

William F. Atchison, Chairman
S. D. Conte
John W. Hamblen
Thomas A. Keenan
William B. Kehl
Silvio O. Navarro
Werner C. Rheinboldt
Earl J. Schweppe
David M. Young, Jr.

The 1965 report was the product of approximately 3 years of work, and at the time of its publication anticipated that the report would primarily be a basis from which more detailed and comprehensive recommendations could be developed. A great deal of effort was made in the 1965 work to justify the existence of computer science as a field of study:

> Although much change has been accomplished within existing programs, such as mathematics and electrical engineering, there is a sizable area of work which does not naturally fit into any existing field. Thus it is now generally recognized that this field, most often called computer science, has become a distinct field of study. This development is reported by the Committee on Uses of Computers of the National Academy of Science, by several individual authors and in a report of the Committee on the Undergraduate Program in Mathematics (CUPM) . . . . [9].

The hope of the committee in this report was that the report would be a coordinating force for the many efforts already going on in university education in computer science.

It was recognized that there was a definite demand for computer work in various academic programs. This, however, was not the primary purpose of this report:

> The Committee has chosen to direct its attention first to students whose primary interest is in computer science. The Committee solicits comments and criticisms of the present report with the view of both strengthening the current recommendations and illuminating the relation between computer science and other fields of study [9].

The curriculum was intended to meet the usual requirements of undergraduate programs; entrance to graduate programs in computer science, direct entry into the profession, or entrance to graduate study in other fields. Thus the program consisted of a small number of required courses:

1. Introduction to Algorithmic Processes
2. Computer Organization and Programming
3. Numerical Calculus
4. Information Structures
5. Algorithmic Languages and Compilers

A series of "highly recommended electives":

6. Logic Design and Switching Theory
7. Numerical Analysis I
8. Numerical Analysis II
9. Computer and Programming Systems

and finally a list of "other electives":

10. Combinatorics and Graph Theory
11. Mathematical Optimization Techniques
13. Constructive Logic
14. Introduction to Automata Theory
15. Formal Languages
16. Heuristic Programming

Mathematics and other related courses were also mentioned within the context of "required," "highly recommended electives," and "other electives."

Considerable attention was given in the report to a definition of computer science and its justification as a discipline.

> Computer science is concerned with information in much the same sense that physics is concerned with energy; it is devoted to the representation,

storage, manipulation and presentation of information in an environment permitting automatic information systems. As physics uses energy transforming devices, computer science uses information transforming devices. Some forms of information have been more thoroughly studied and are better understood than others; nevertheless, all forms of information— numeric, alphabetic, pictorial, verbal, tactile, olefactory, results of experimental measurements, etc.—are of interest in computer science.

Mathematics, too, is concerned with information and its structure and this tends to confuse those not well versed in both mathematics and computer science. The mathematician is interested in discovering the syntactic relation between elements based on a set of axioms which may have no physical reality. The computer scientist is interested in discovering the pragmatic means by which information can be transformed to model and analyze the information transformation in the real world. The pragmatic aspects of this interest lead to inquiring into effective ways to represent information, effective algorithms to transform information, effective languages with which to express algorithms, effective means to monitor the process and to display the transformed information, and effective ways to accomplish these at reasonable cost [9].

In the description of courses, there were hard decisions to be made as to whether a course was assigned to computer science or was assigned as a supporting course from another discipline. The decision was made on the basis of the relevancy of the material in question to the entire computer science program.

Several courses recommended were considered to serve a service need as well as the computer science program. Course 1 (Introduction to Algorithmic Processes) would be appropriate for science and engineering students. A selection of courses could be chosen to meet the requirements for the CUPM major in mathematics with emphasis in computing. Course 6 (Logic Design and Switching Theory) is appropriate for engineering students. Course 10 (Combinatorics and Graph Theory) and the courses in numerical calculus and numerical analysis (courses 3, 7, and 8) are of value to a number of science-related fields.

The committee concluded the formal portion of the report with their anticipation of future work, and their feeling of the limitations of this report:

The work of C³S is in its early stages. Readers of this report are encouraged to communicate their ideas, experiences and criticisms to the committee. Not only will the present recommendations need periodic review but many suggestions concerning future computer-oriented curricula are sought. Study of the computer science needs of students in the non-physical sciences is appropriate. It has been suggested that the educational needs of those who will plan and design the computing and communication equipment of the future should be given special consideration. More specific thought will be given to the education of those wishing to prepare themselves for work in information retrieval, management science, the life sciences, and the behavioral sciences. Finally, the present recommendations do not deal with graduate computer science. A committee to study graduate curricula is in the process of formation [9].

## THE 1968 RECOMMENDATIONS

In the 2 years following the publication of the 1965 recommendations, the work of the committee was devoted to revising the recommendations on undergraduate programs and developing recommendations for graduate programs. This work was reported in "Curriculum '68: Recommendations for Academic Programs in Computer Science" [10], appearing in the March 1968 issue of the *Communications of the ACM*.

Conte [8] in comparing the 1965 and 1968 reports notes the following:

> . . .as compared with the 1965 report, the 1968 report accomplishes the following:
>
> 1. Revised some of the 1965 recommendations, sharpened some of the course outlines and added some new courses.
> 2. Attempted to produce some order out of the diverse aspects of computer science by introducing a classification scheme.
> 3. Make some recommendations on graduate programs in computer science especially at the MS level.

In the period following the publication of the 1965 report the National Science Foundation funded the project allowing for more frequent meetings, and Thomas E. Hull, Edward J. McCluskey, and William Viavant joined the committee.

The Curriculum Committee viewed "Curriculum '68" as a major refinement and extension of the 1965 work:

> Of the sixteen courses proposed in the earlier recommendations, eleven have survived in spirit if not in detail. Two of the other five have been split into two courses each; and the remaining three have been omitted since they belong more properly to other disciplines closely related to computer science. In addition seven new courses have been proposed of which course B3 on "discrete structures" and course I3 on "computer organization" are particularly notable [10].

The major sections of the report are classification of computer science, description of courses, undergraduate programs, master's degree programs, doctoral programs, service courses, minors and continuing education, and implementation. This is followed by more detailed course outlines and bibliographies. It must be observed that the recommendations are limited in scope and objective and this is clearly stated at the outset:

> . . .the recommendations are not directed to the training of computer operators, coders, and other service personnel. Training for such positions as well as for many programming positions can probably be supplied best by applied technology programs, vocational institutes, or junior colleges. It is also likely that the majority of application programmers in such areas as business data processing, scientific research, and engineering analysis will continue to be specialists educated in the related subject matter areas, although such students can undoubtedly profit by taking a number of computer science courses [10].

"Curriculum '68" does not contain the lengthy justification of the field found in the 1965 report, but rather defines computer science in terms of three major subject areas:

Subject Areas of Computer Science
I.   Information Structures and Processes
    1. Data Structures
    2. Programming Languages
    3. Models of Computation
II.  Information Processing Systems
    1. Computer Design and Organization
    2. Translators and Interpreters
    3. Computer and Operating Systems
    4. Special Purpose Systems
III. Methodologies
    1. Numerical Mathematics
    2. Data Processing and File Management
    3. Symbol Manipulation
    4. Text Processing
    5. Computer Graphics
    6. Simulation
    7. Information Retrieval
    8. Artificial Intelligence
    9. Process Control
    10. Instructional Systems

It is further noted that there are a number of related areas essential to a balanced program in computer science, and additional sections of the classification system are included for the areas of mathematical science and physical and engineering sciences.

To meet the educational needs of computer science, 22 courses are specified, divided into basic (freshman–sophomore level), intermediate, and advanced

# CURRICULUM COMMITTEE ON COMPUTER SCIENCE

(junior–senior or beginning graduate level):

The Courses of "Curriculum '68" [10]
Basic Courses
   B1.   Introduction to Computing
   B2.   Computers and Programming
   B3.   Introduction to Discrete Structures
   B4.   Numerical Calculus
Intermediate Courses
   I1.   Data Structures
   I2.   Programming Languages
   I3.   Computer Organization
   I4.   Systems Programming
   I5.   Compiler Construction
   I6.   Switching Theory
   I7.   Sequential Machines
   I8.   Numerical Analysis I
   I9.   Numerical Analysis II
Advanced Courses
   A1.   Formal Languages and Syntactic Analysis
   A2.   Advanced Computer Organization
   A3.   Analog and Hybrid Computing
   A4.   System Simulation
   A5.   Information Organization and Retrieval
   A6.   Computer Graphics
   A7.   Theory of Computability
   A8.   Large-Scale Information Processing Systems
   A9.   Artificial Intelligence and Heuristic Programming

The special place of mathematics is recognized with reference specifically given to the report of the Committee on the Undergraduate Program in Mathematics (CUPM), *A General Curriculum in Mathematics for Colleges* [6]. A parallel structure in mathematics within the structure of prerequisites for computer science is given in the report.

A detailed prerequisite structure is given; however, it is noted that other structures are possible, and that the given structure will likely change as the field advances.

Within the structure, of particular interest, is the collection of courses that is considered the core. This includes the computer science courses: B1—Introduction to Computing, B2—Computers and Programming, B3—Introduction to Discrete Structures, B4—Numerical Calculus, I1—Data Structures, I2—Programming Languages, I3—Computer Organization, and I4—Systems Programming. Included also in the core are the mathematics courses; Introductory Calculus, Mathematical Analysis I, Linear Algebra, and Probability.

With the core as a base, an undergraduate program was specified which was to integrate the basic concepts of computer science with professional techniques.

In terms of computer science courses for the program, in addition to the core courses, at least two of I5—Compiler Construction, I6—Switching Theory, I7—Sequential Machines, I8—Numerical Analysis I, and I9—Numerical Analysis II were considered necessary. Mathematics courses for the undergraduate program in addition to the core courses were at least two of Mathematical Analysis II, Advanced Multivariate Calculus, Algebraic Structures, and Probability and Statistics.

Students were encouraged to take technical electives in computer science and related fields, and reference was made to inclusion of some form of "true-to-life" programming work in the course of study.

It is of some note that the committee observed that professionals were divided as to whether or not undergraduate programs should be started at the time of the writing of the report, and although recommending in favor of such programs, a warning was sounded against allowing the glamour of the field to lead to the premature establishment of programs and thus lowering of the standards.

The master's degree program was considered, and as constructed required a bachelor's degree in computer science, or at least a major portion of it, as a prerequisite. The master's program itself is described in somewhat more general terms than the undergraduate program:

> The master's degree program in computer science should consist of at least nine courses. Normally at least two courses, each in a different subject area, should be taken from each of the following subject divisions of computer science:
>
> I. Information Structures and Processes
> II. Information Processing Systems
> III. Methodologies
>
> Sufficient other courses in computer science or related areas should be taken to bring the student to the forefront in some area of computer science [10].

The program was then to have degrees of both breadth and depth; the breadth from the requirement for at least two courses in each of the three major subject divisions of computer science, and the depth from the selection of courses to bring the student to the state of the art of some area of computer science. The special place of mathematics was noted here as in the undergraduate program with recommendation that the student who does not have a "strong" mathematical background take additional mathematics courses or computer science courses with a high mathematical content. Examples were given of possible programs in a variety of specializations.

The doctoral program is not specified in any way in the report. The committee did consider ways in which guidelines could be developed, and acknowledged that many of the problems of the doctoral program were addressed at the Stony Brook Conference [13]. Additionally, a series of articles on problems of doctoral programs was anticipated to appear in the *Communications of the ACM* shortly after the report.

Additional topics covered in the report included minor programs and service courses. In these cases it was felt that the courses specified, possibly with some modification, could serve these needs. Continuing education was mentioned, but no firm recommendations for courses were given. Finally, problems associated with the organization of departments and facility requirements were considered.

## ACTIVITIES SINCE THE 1968 RECOMMENDATIONS

$C^3S$ did not regard its mission as complete with the publication of the 1968 report. Conte [8] makes reference to anticipated future activities:

> Because computer science is still in a rapidly changing state and because we feel that curriculum is an evolving process, the committee feels that a continuing body should be established to constantly examine the development of programs in the country. In addition to a continued examination of curricular matters there are a number of aspects of computer science education which our committee did not have time to explore.

Among the new problems to be addressed were programs for smaller colleges, junior colleges, and technical schools; the relationship of computer science to other disciplines including both those things computer science might offer other departments in the university, and what the computer science student would need from other departments; program implementation problems and related costs; the development of graduate programs; and course content development. In addition it was anticipated that the curriculum committee would sponsor a program of visitation and consultation to further assist in the development of computer science programs.

These objectives have been met to varying degrees with the exception of programs for junior and community colleges and technical schools. It was generally found that the problems of these institutions were quite different from those of the 4 year schools, and in 1972 ACM formed a separate committee on computer science in 2-year institutions. Initial work in this area is reported by Connelly [7]. In 1974 this committee was made a subcommittee of $C^3S$, and in the summer of 1975 a 3-day workshop was held to consider curricula recommendations in the area. A report is anticipated in 1976.

Though not a direct activity of $C^3S$, several members of the committee joined with other professionals in 1968 to form the ACM Special Interest Group on Computer Science Education (SIGCSE). Since its founding, SIGCSE, through its newsletter the *SIGCSE Bulletin* and its technical meetings, has made a most significant contribution to computer science education. The history and activity of SIGCSE is reported by Aiken [1].

In terms of sponsored activities of C³S, the first involved was the doctoral program. Reference to this work is made in the report itself:

> In 1966 Professor Thomas Hull was asked by ACM to examine the questions of doctoral programs in computer science. After discussions with members of this committee and with many other interested persons, Professor Hull decided to solicit a series of articles on the research and teaching area which might be involved in doctoral programs. Each article is to be written by an expert in the particular subject area, such as programming languages, systems programming, computer organization, numerical mathematics, automata theory, large systems, and artificial intelligence. Each article is to attempt to consider all aspects of the subject area which might be helpful to those considering a graduate program, including as many of the following topics as possible:
>
> a. Definition of the subject area, possibly in terms of an annotated bibliography.
> b. Prerequisite for work in the area at the doctoral level.
> c. Outlines of appropriate graduate courses in the area.
> d. Examples of questions for qualifying examinations in the area.
> e. Indication of suitable thesis topics and promising directions for research in the area.
> f. The extent to which the subject area ought to be required of all doctoral students in computer science [10].

This effort resulted in four articles being published in the *Communications of the ACM:* "Automata, Formal Languages, Abstract Switching, and Computability in a Ph.D. Computer Science Program," McNaughton [20]; "Computational Linguistics in a Ph.D. Computer Science Program," Kuno and Oettinger [19]; "The Role of Programming in a Ph.D. Computer Science Program," Arden [3]; and "Information Science in a Ph.D. Computer Science Program," Salton [26].

C³S, or individuals serving on the committee, has been involved in programs for smaller colleges and universities, consulting activities on curriculum and related matters, and further work on the master's program. Much of the work of discussing programs and course content problems has properly fallen to SIGCSE.

In 1970 a subcommittee of C³S was formed to address problems of smaller colleges [25]:

> A sub-committee of the ACM Curriculum Committee has been established with the goal of studying the problem of Computer Science instruction in four-year undergraduate colleges, and recommending a course of action designed to alleviate the matriculation problem described above. This proposal seeks funds for the work of the sub-committee and for an

experimental summer program designed to introduce faculty members from small colleges to the structure and content of a group of courses.

In its initial activities the subcommittee gathered and reported information on the nature of programs in computer science in small colleges [11].

With support of the National Science Foundation, an institute was held at Purdue University in the summer of 1971 in which four fundamental courses — discrete structures, programming languages, operating systems, and data structures—were presented to 53 individuals from small colleges. The courses were taught as normally done, except that they were compressed into a 4-week per course time frame. It was anticipated that the attendees would take the material presented to them and offer it at their home institutions, thus forming a strong core for a computer science program.

Difficulties in finding funds for continuation of such programs led the subcommittee to authorize a report to recommend appropriate programs in computer science for small schools. This appeared in 1973 [5].

> This report gives recommendations for the content, implementation, and operation of a program of computer science courses specifically directed to small colleges. In no way does this material represent a major program in computer science. It does describe a program for those schools with limited resources, but with an interest, enthusiasm and desire for some course offerings in computer science. Those institutions interested in computer science and with resources necessary for a major program in this field should refer to the existing reports of ACM's Committee on Curriculum in Computer Science (C³S), and other curriculum studies. Institutions which desire to complement computer science offerings with a set of courses in computational mathematics should consider the report of the Committee on the Undergraduate Program in Mathematics.

The report emphasizes a program that would be within the reach of institutions with limited resources, includes an extensive library list, comments on staff and equipment requirements, and considers how the courses can be designed to meet a variety of objectives for an institution which cannot afford both a series for computer science students, and a series for departments using computer science:

> Four courses are described and suggestions made for additional study and courses for students interested in further work. No names have been given to the four courses, but they roughly correspond to the areas of algorithms and programming (course 1), application of computers and their impact on society (course 2), machine and systems organization (course 3), and file and data organization (course 4). Though these courses in a real sense represent a coherent program they are structured so as to allow a

student with limited objectives and limited time to pick and choose those parts most relevant to his needs [5].

C³S has also continued to be concerned with graduate programs in computer science, and a subcommittee reported, in 1973, on a program of study leading to a master's degree in computer science [21, 22]. This program, which modifies the master's recommendations of "Curriculum '68," based on experience, requires nine three-semester-hour courses, at least five of which are graduate. A thesis is optional. A high level of competence in at least one programming language is required as well as proficiency in a fundamental core of knowledge common to all subfields of computer science. This should be covered in the material taught in four to six courses (upper division or graduate) and includes formal linguistics, programming languages, computer architecture, and systems programming. A major should be completed in one of the established fields of computer science which includes theory, programming languages, systems, architecture and design, and artificial intelligence, the major in some sense being designed to meet the student's ultimate objectives. In addition it was strongly recommended that a minor be included through a coherent sequence of courses in some application area.

It was also observed that C³S upon completion of work on "Curriculum '68" planned to develop a program of visitation and consultation. In 1968–1969 this was handled through the ACM Visiting Scientist Program which gave way in the latter part of 1969 to the ACM College Consulting Service, supported by a grant from the National Science Foundation. In the period 1969–1973 nearly one hundred institutions were visited by computer professionals to offer various comments and suggestions on computer science curriculum, computer uses in education, and facilities. The material encompassing the reports on these visits has been collected and published [16].

The activities described above indicate most of the formal and published material of the C³S subsequent to the publication of "Curriculum '68." In addition to this the committee has met regularly to discuss current issues in computer science education, and to supply input for additional work through the ACM Education Board. Included in these activities is a study leading to recommendations for certification of computer science teachers for secondary schools, and a study of the area of computers and society and computer literacy courses and materials.

Throughout the period following the publication of "Curriculum '68," discussions involving need for revisions and updatings have continued. This effort resulted in a concentrated 3-day working session of the committee in the summer of 1974. Resulting from this meeting was a sense of direction for the preparation of subsequent reports which would be developed by the committee. The first two such reports, dealing with curriculum development since 1968 and a revised series of recommendations for the first 2 years of the undergraduate program, are to be published in 1976. A report of the working meeting was given at the

1975 IFIP World Conference on Computers in Education [12]. A list of activities resulting from the 1974 meeting appears as an Appendix to this article.


## FUTURE WORK AND PROBLEMS

In addition to the report on curriculum for the first 2 years of an undergraduate program mentioned above, there are reports on intermediate courses and on advanced courses under preparation. After these three levels of reporting are complete, the current plan is to compile, adjust, and update these and other reports in order to produce and publish a new complete curriculum package.

There are a number of problems in the curriculum area which still have not had adequate treatment. One is the appropriate relations between the new computer science departments and other fields such as mathematics, electrical engineering, information system management, and data processing. The boundary zones between computer science and each of these need to be addressed more definitely. Also, more needs to be said about the current discussion on software engineering versus computer science as analogous to chemical engineering versus chemistry.

Service courses in computer science departments for other departments are not yet on a firm footing. Efforts in this direction should be directed toward minimizing the proliferation of computer science courses in other departments as has been the case with statistics courses. With the pressures currently on educational programs to be more responsive to the needs of the real world and not just to the need to propagate themselves, it is highly important that computer science develop courses useful to other sectors of the educational community. As a particular example of this, the need to develop courses for the training of secondary school teachers of computer science is becoming more and more urgent. This urgency is brought on by the very rapid increase in the number of and use of computers at the secondary level. This teaching must be done well to help insure the proper use and place of computers in society. Needless to say, this also points up the need for appropriate courses on the role of computers in society.

Last, but certainly not least, is the problem of continuing education. This is particularly acute in the rapidly moving field of computer science itself. It is very difficult for both the teachers and the practitioners out in the field to keep abreast of the latest developments. Explicit steps must be taken to solve this problem and not just let it solve itself by default. It also is very evident that the computer scientist is in a unique position with powerful computers as his main tool to contribute to the problem of continuing education as a whole. More explicitly, the recent advancements in the use of computer networks, computer-aided, and computer-managed instruction can be powerful tools in continuing education if properly used.

$C^3S$, in conjunction with the other educational committees and groups in ACM, is addressing these questions. Where possible, reports will be issued giving recommendations in these areas, and monitoring of programs and updating and revising guidelines will be a continuing activity of the committee.

## APPENDIX

### Activities Resulting from the Summer 1974 VIMS Meeting

*Publications*

September 1974 *SIGCSE Bulletin,* Vol. 6, No. 3:

Service course position paper, G. E. Stokes, pp. 18–20.
Initial report: The revision of 'Curriculum '68,' G. L. Engel, pp. 79–80.
Numerical analysis position, J. M. Ortega, pp. 86–87.
Software and Curriculum '68, B. L. Bateman, pp. 88–89.
Recommendations for an operating systems course, P. Denning, p. 90.
Computer science education in business schools, D. Chand, pp. 91–97.
The community colleges and Curriculum '68, J. C. Little, pp. 98–102.
Some thoughts on the role of hardware in computer science education, M. Faiman, pp. 103–105.
Position statement, mathematical computer science courses, D. Loveland, pp. 106–108.
Statistics for computer scientists, J. W. Hamblen et al., pp. 109–111.

December 1974 *SIGCSE Bulletin,* Vol. 6, No. 4:

The Heart of computer science, N. E. Gibbs, D. W. Loveland and J. M. Ortega, pp. 13–14.

*Proceedings of the IFIP Second World Conference on Computers in Education,* American Elsevier, New York, 1975

The revisions of Curriculum '68: Background and initial development, G. L. Engel and B. H. Barnes, pp. 263–272.

*Meeting Presentations*

Technical Program, ACM Annual Conference 1974, Panel Discussion titled *Report on Curriculum '68.*
Second IFIP Conference on Computers in Education, Presentation in session on *Informatics in Universities,* and participation on panel on *Trends in University Informatics Curriculum Development.*

## CURRICULUM COMMITTEE ON COMPUTER SCIENCE

*Committee Activity*

Draft report covering background material and the first two years was prepared for discussion at the 1974 ACM Annual Conference. With guidelines for revisions of the report given at that meeting, the report was revised, again circulated, and discussed at the committee meeting at the 1975 N.C.C. This report is undergoing final revision based on input received at and since the 1975 N.C.C. and will be presented for approval by the committee at the 1975 ACM Annual Conference. Work relating to the intermediate level courses and other matters has been assigned and is scheduled for discussion at the 1975 ACM Annual Conference.

## REFERENCES

1. Aiken, R. M., Purposes, goals, and activities of SIGCSE, in *Proceedings of the World Conference on Computer Education 1970.* Science Associates/International, New York, 1970, II/153–II/156.
2. Arden, B. W., On introducing digital computing, *Commun. ACM* **7**(4), 212–214 (1964).
3. Arden, B. W., The role of programming in a Ph.D. computer science program, *Commun. ACM* **12**(1), 31–37 (1969).
4. Atchison, W. F. and J. W. Hamblen, Status of computer science curricula in colleges and universities, *Commun. ACM* **7**(4), 225–227 (1964).
5. Austing, R. H., and G. L. Engel, A computer science course program for small colleges, *Commun. ACM* **16**(3), 139–147 (1973).
6. Committee on the Undergraduate Program in Mathematics (CUPM), *A General Curriculum in Mathematics for Colleges.* CUPM, Berkeley, California, 1965.
7. Connolly, F. W., A community/junior college view of Curriculum '68, *SIGCSE Bull.* **5**(1), 68–69 (February 1973).
8. Conte, S. History and activities of the ACM Curriculum Committee, in *Proceedings of the Park City Conference on Computers in Undergraduate Education* W. Viavant, ed., University of Utah, Salt Lake City, 1969, pp. 38–50.
9. Curriculum Committee on Computer Science (C³S), An undergraduate program in computer science, preliminary recommendations, *Commun. ACM* **8**(9), 543–552 (1965).
10. Curriculum Committee on Computer Science (C³S), Curriculum '68, recommendations for academic programs in computer science, *Commun. ACM* **11**(3), 151–197 (1968).
11. Engel, G. L., Computer science instruction in small colleges—An initial report, *SIGCSE Bull.* **3**(2), 8–18 (June 1971).
12. Engel, G. L., and B. H. Barnes, The revisions of curriculum '68: Background and initial development, in *Proceedings of the Second World Conference on Computers in Education.* American Elsevier, New York, 1975, pp. 263–272.
13. Finerman, A., *University Education in Computing Science,* Academic, New York, 1968.
14. Forsythe, G. E., An undergraduate curriculum in numerical analysis, *Commun. ACM* **7**(4), 214–215 (1964).

15.  Gorn, S. Mechanical languages: A course specification, *Commun. ACM* **7**(4), 219–222 (1964).

16.  Hamblen, J. W., G. L. Engel, V. H. Swoyer, and L. Oliver, Administrative and instructional computing in minority institutions, in *Proceedings of the AEDS 13th Annual Convention,* Association for Educational Data Systems, Washington, D.C., 1975, pp. 121–131.

17.  Keenan, T. A., Computers and education, *Commun. ACM* **7**(4), 205–209 (1964).

18.  Korfhage, R. R., Logic for the computer sciences, *Commun. ACM* **7**(4), 216–218 (1964).

19.  Kuno, S. and A. G. Oettinger, Computational linguistics in a Ph.D. computer science program, *Commun. ACM* **11**(12), 831–836 (1968).

20.  McNaughton, R., Automata, formal languages, abstract switching and Computability in a Ph.D. Computer Science Program, *Commun. ACM* **11**(11), 738–740, 746 (1968).

21.  Melkanoff, M. A., An M.S. program in computer science, *SIGCSE Bull.* **5**(1) 77–82 (February 1973).

22.  Melkanoff, M. A., B. H. Barnes and G. L. Engel, The Master's Degree program in computer science, in *Proceedings of the AFIPS 1973 NCC,* AFIPS Press, Montvale, New Jersey, 1973, p. 563.

23.  Muller, D. E., The place of logical design and switching theory in the computer curriculum, *Commun. ACM* **7**(4), 222–225 (1964).

24.  Perlis, A. J., Programming of digital computers, *Commun. ACM* **7**(4), 210–214 (1964).

25.  Rechard, O. W., ACM Curriculum Committee proposal, *SIGCSE Bull.* **2**(2), 28–30 (June–July 1970).

26.  Salton, G., Information science in a Ph.D. computer science program, *Commun. ACM* **12**(2), 111–117 (1969).

*Gerald L. Engel*
*William F. Atchison*